THE
MELLONS

THE
MELLONS

*The Chronicle of America's
Richest Family*

David E. Koskoff

THOMAS Y. CROWELL COMPANY

Established 1834

NEW YORK

For

POPPA

Grateful acknowledgment is made for permission to reprint excerpts from *Duveen* by S. N. Behrman. Copyright 1951, 1952 by S. N. Behrman. Reprinted by permission of Random House, Inc. Excerpt from *Age of the Moguls* by Stewart H. Holbrook. Copyright 1953 by Stewart H. Holbrook. Reprinted by permission of Doubleday & Company, Inc.

FIRST EDITION

Designed by Stephanie Krasnow

Library of Congress Cataloging in Publication Data

Koskoff, David E., 1939–
  The Mellons: the chronicle of America's richest family.
  Bibliography: p.
  Includes index.
  1. Mellon family. I. Title.
HC102.5.M38K67 1978   338'.092'2[B]   77–25947
ISBN 0–690–01190–3

78 79 80 81 82 10 9 8 7 6 5 4 3 2 1

Contents

Cassis Tutissima Virtus

—Motto on the Mellon family Coat of Arms:
"Virtue Is the Safest Defense," or, as
updated by Judge Thomas Mellon,
"Honesty Is the Best Policy"

BOOK I

The Founder of the Fortune

Now when nearing the end of my
journey and reviewing my past life, I
find no instance where I had set my
mind earnestly on an object that I did
not succeed in devising ways and
means to accomplish it.

—JUDGE THOMAS MELLON
Thomas Mellon and His Times

O ne fine day in 1958 Karl Mellon picked up the telephone and called the trust department at Pittsburgh's Mellon Bank. "This is Karl Mellon, and today is my twenty-first birthday. I understand that us Mellons are supposed to come into a lot of money when we're twenty-one." The voice on the other end of the phone had been warned about Karl. "Well . . . ah . . . er . . . a little money," the trust officer replied. "By my reckoning, $1.2 million, and I'm coming over!" Karl yelled at the banker as he slammed down the receiver. Minutes later Karl stormed into the bank, plunked a suitcase on the counter before the cashier, and directed the man behind the glass: "Fill 'er up!"

This book is about Karl and his family: how they came to be the richest family in America, what they have done with their money, what their money has done to them, and how it and they have affected their surroundings and been affected by their surroundings.

Karl didn't get his suitcase full of money; instead, he settled for the transfer to his checking account of a substantial sum. But the money was there, lots of money, and there is more of it now than there was in 1958.

Today the Mellon wealth must be reckoned at something in excess of $5 billion. $5,000,000,000. The Rockefellers long ago slipped from the ranks of the very richest. When *Fortune* last updated its roster of America's richest in 1968, three Mellons were included among the richest eight. By that time there were no Rockefellers anywhere near the top of the list. Du Ponts and Fords must be grouped with the Rockefellers among the mere super-rich. Only the new-monied people, the families of oil men J. Paul Getty and H. L. Hunt, shipping magnate Daniel Ludwig, and the heirs of Howard Hughes (whoever they may be), begin to approach the Mellons in terms of wealth. The Getty family probably comes closest, but the Getty empire is most often valued at a trifling $2 billion.

Mellon wealth controls Gulf Oil Corporation, tenth largest industrial corporation in the world. Gulf's assets far exceed in value the combined gross national products of all of the countries of Central America. Its annual revenues are greater than those of any single one of the United States. The Mellons are the principal stockholders of Alcoa, the world's largest manufacturer of an increasingly vital metal. They dominate Mellon Bank, the "key" bank in Western Pennsylvania, a financial institution whose control of a varying $8 to $10 billion in trust funds puts it in a position to control dozens of other major American corporations. The Mellons are controlling or major stockholders in a number of other "Fortune 500" businesses.

Despite their wealth and the power that springs from their wealth, the Mellons are about the least known of the country's richest people. They like it that way. Probably most Americans would ascribe no special significance to their name. It is well known in Allegheny County, Pennsylvania, however, where people still say "Nothing moves in Pittsburgh without the Mellons." Art fanciers may know the name as that of the founder of the National Gallery of Art in Washington, whose descendants continue to be the gallery's mainstays. Grant seekers know their name; their combined charitable foundations control over a billion dollars in potential grants, which they disburse in support of such varied activities as bolstering the ballet as an art form or introducing military training in high schools. Readers in their seventies may recall the name of Andrew William Mellon, "the greatest Secretary of the Treasury since Alexander Hamilton" from the days when he was "the man under whom three Presidents served" in the 1920s. Slightly younger readers may recall A. W. as "the man who caused the Great Depression," or as "the millionaire who was caught cheating on his taxes."(All such recollections are incorrect.)

This book covers a long time, from the birth of Judge Thomas Mellon on a marginal potato farm in North Ireland in 1813, during the administration of the American President James Madison, through subsequent periods of great and lesser world leadership, countless wars, and innumerable inventions that altered the contours of Judge Mellon's world unrecognizably. During that period Judge Mellon and his progeny have produced a total of 168 descendants. Depending on how one wants to count the generations, this book spans as few as three generations—the Judge's grandson Paul Mellon is alive and very well indeed in Virginia—or as many as six generations, for the Judge has many great-great-great grandsons and daughters scattered about the country, all, one hopes, thriving. This book does not purport to be a compendium of all of their biographies, or the genealogy of the family; rather, it is a history of one family in its surroundings over time.

The young lawyer's father would not remain another day in Pittsburgh; he was tied, emotionally, to the farm, and to it he must return. What justification could the lawyer then have for continuing to maintain a house of his own? There could never be justification for such extravagance; he would have to move back to a boardinghouse or to a hotel, a discouraging prospect. There was only one alternative: marriage. Why not? He had daydreamed of the time when he would be able to live with a family of his own, and rather liked to think of himself as a family man. The aggressive young barrister had already accumulated some $12,000—a vast sum in 1843 —by trading in other people's debts. He was of a mature enough age, thirty years, to be able to make the important selection, as he later wrote, with a mind "clear of the fog" arising from what he called "the *veally* condition of the emotions at an earlier date," when he might have been "led astray in my selection by premature emotional excitement or falling in love."* He set out in search of a wife.

Decisions of such sort had to be made on objective bases. He looked for a woman like his own grandmother: "one of those devoted wives and mothers who are happy in self-sacrifice when promoting the happiness of husband and children; kind, intelligent, and unceasing in attention to her family duties." Good health was most important in the prospective bride, so he quickly eliminated Sarah Liggett—"I feared hereditary consumption. Her brother William, my friend and college mate, had died of it, and her own appearance indicated a tendency that way." Accomplishments did not much matter, and beauty was only "an excellent but dangerous substitute for either money or other good qualities in a lady," not a first consideration.

Sarah Jane Negley was not beautiful. But she appeared to have other good qualities. Her late father, Jacob Negley, had been the overlord of Negleystown, the hamlet that is now the East Liberty section of Pittsburgh, in the early part of the century. He had been wiped out shortly before his death by changes in the economic climate that reflected no ill on himself or his heirs. Fortunately, Negley's friend U.S. senator James Ross had preserved the best of Negley's properties for Negley's heirs, and by 1843 they were again one of the finest families in Allegheny County.

Sarah Jane herself was a leader of the younger ladies of such upper crust as then existed in the Pittsburgh area. Thomas Mellon's friend Dr. Richard Beatty had been interested in her himself but had rejected her, finding that "she was rather too independent for him, had no elasticity in her composition, and did not seem to appreciate gentlemen's attentions." That intrigued Thomas Mellon, and he determined to look more closely. He was so busy

*Unless otherwise noted, quotations from Thomas Mellon come from his autobiography, *Thomas Mellon and His Times,* privately printed in 1885 "for his family and descendants exclusively."

nurturing his practice that he only hoped that the inquiry would not take too much time away from professional pursuits.

The courtship of the coquettish Sarah Jane was formal and, to the impatient young man, maddening. Month after month,

> she evinced the dexterity of a special pleader in evading all approaches to any discussion of the real business I had in hand. I was not there to take lessons in flora culture or botany, or to learn the history of birds, fishes or butterflies. I did not want to spend evening after evening in admiring pictures in her album, or in having items read to me from her scrap book. But to her credit I must say that she never inflicted any music upon me, as she professed no special efficiency in that accomplishment.

She persisted in parrying his every effort to turn the conversation to "some tender sentiment." Finally he could wait no longer:

> At the very next interview, in the dusk of evening when the clear moonlight was streaming through the curtains, we happened to be left alone for a minute or so—an unusual circumstance. Feeling that now was the time I drew my chair up closer to her than I had ever ventured before and remarked that I supposed she was aware I had not been paying attention to her so long without an object, and that I had some time ago made up my own mind and now wished to know hers, as I was satisfied if she was, to risk the future together. She neither spoke nor gave any sign. I drew her to me and took a kiss unresisted and said that would do, I was satisfied; and left her abruptly, feeling unnerved for conversation.

Thomas Mellon reflected that night on his first view, as an urchin aged ten, of the Negleys' great meadow and mansion, and how he had "imagined how proud and happy must be the family which possessed them." The couple were married soon after, or as Thomas Mellon put it, "the transaction was consummated." He was confident that love would blossom after marriage, and so it did for sixty-five years. When he was himself an old man, their son James Ross Mellon recalled his parents "in their last days, sitting one at each side of the fireplace in the evenings like two doves." At the time, though, Thomas wrote,

> There was no love making and little or no love beforehand so far as I was concerned: nothing but a good opinion of worthy qualities, and esteem and respect. When I proposed if I had been rejected I would have left neither sad nor depressed, nor greatly disappointed, only annoyed at loss of time.

It should not be surprising that such a man had become a significant financial success at such an early age, or even that he was to become the founder of Pittsburgh's leading family. His earlier life makes the story more remarkable.

Thomas Mellon was born February 3, 1813, in humble surroundings on a twenty-three-acre farm in County Tyrone, North Ireland. In his memoirs, *Thomas Mellon and His Times,* he devotes a hundred-odd pages to detailing his ancestral background, but the short of it all was, he wrote, that in his direct line "I find that they have all been of the common industrial class." They were, however, of respectable Presbyterian Scotch-Irish background, a matter in which he took no little pride, and if, as he wrote, they were "notable only for good habits and paying their debts," that was at least much more than could be said for the barbarous Celts of Southern Ireland, from whom Thomas Mellon took great pains to disassociate himself.

Life was not easy on a small plot, and little by little the Scotch-Irish emigrated to larger farms and broader horizons in the United States. In the early 1800s they made western Pennsylvania their new world. Thomas Mellon's uncles moved there; then his grandparents; and finally, when Thomas Mellon was five years old, his father, Andrew Mellon, moved the last branch of the family to Westmoreland County, Pennsylvania, and to the aptly named town of Poverty Point. There, Andrew Mellon maintained his good habits, paid his debts, and tried to instill the values of the soil in his young son, Thomas. Through hard work and thrift he managed to hold his new farm through the depression of 1819 and, later, to increase his holdings with additions of nearby acreage. It was a hard but honorable life, and Andrew Mellon looked forward to seeing his son emulate it. The son, though, was increasingly, and to some extent secretively, intellectual. His brief terms at "pay school" lighted his curiosity. As he followed the team behind the plow he read incessantly, often with another book tucked in the crown of his hat: Pope and Goldsmith, Burns, Shakespeare, and finally the work whose influence changed the course of his life:

> It was about my fourteenth year . . . that I happened upon a dilapidated copy of the autobiography of Dr. Franklin. It delighted me with a wider view of life and inspired me with new ambition—turned my thoughts into new channels. I had not before imagined any other course of life superior to farming, but the reading of Franklin's life led me to question this view. For so poor and friendless a boy to be able to become a merchant or a professional man had before seemed an impossibility; but here was Franklin, poorer than myself, who by industry, thrift and frugality had become learned and wise, and elevated to wealth and fame. The maxims of "Poor Richard" exactly suited my

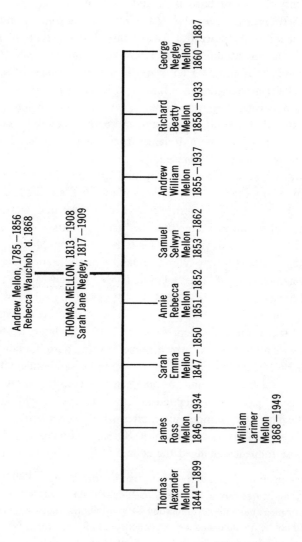

Andrew Mellon, 1785–1856
Rebecca Wauchob, d. 1868

THOMAS MELLON, 1813–1908
Sarah Jane Negley, 1817–1909

Thomas
Alexander
Mellon
1844–1899

James
Ross
Mellon
1846–1934

William
Larimer
Mellon
1868–1949

Sarah
Emma
Mellon
1847–1850

Annie
Rebecca
Mellon
1851–1852

Samuel
Selwyn
Mellon
1853–1862

Andrew
William
Mellon
1855–1937

Richard
Beatty
Mellon
1858–1933

George
Negley
Mellon
1860–1887

sentiments. I read the book again and again, and wondered if I might not do something in the same line by similar means.

It was four years earlier that Thomas Mellon, the farmer's boy, had taken his long walk from the countryside to the city, Pittsburgh, and had enjoyed his first view of the grandeur of Negleystown. Negleystown and the great mansion had seemed impossible of attainment for a boy of such lowly origins. Benjamin Franklin told the lad that it was not impossible at all. Thereafter Thomas Mellon was a new person, with new ambitions. It became apparent to him for the first time that the values of the farm could be challenged, and therefore he began to challenge them, at first quietly. He thought of the professional life, wealth, literature. He took his mother into his confidence and found her sympathetic, but he feared his father's reaction:

> He looked upon farming as the best, safest, most worthy and independent of all the occupations of men; and anyone who forsook it for something else was regarded as led astray by folly and nonsense. . . . For me to abandon the honest and noble pursuits of an independent farmer, and become a doctor or teacher or miserably dependent preacher; or what was in his eyes worst of all, to enter the tricky, dishonest profession of the law, was a proposition which seemed to him too preposterous to contemplate. I knew that nothing could induce him to acquiesce in such a course. Hence I was backward in breaking the matter to him; and when I did my worst fears were realized.

A term at boarding school highlighted for Thomas Mellon the differences between competing worlds, farm and town, and sharpened the choices for him. His farm neighbors were largely Pennsylvania Dutch, and in two respects

> they did not altogether come up to the Scotch-Irish standard of morality—sexual intercourse and religious observances, and on account of this my parents did not approve of close social intimacy with them. Although not as a general rule immoral or licentious, the sentiments of many of them regarding sexual intercourse were rather loose, and organized religious worship could hardly be said to exist.

Culturally they were "for the most part rude and coarse, though clever and good natured, and wholly uncultivated. With them my literary aspirations found no sympathy." At school in the county seat, Greensburg, he saw a more sophisticated world. An important man's well-fitted parlor "was quite dazzling to my inexperienced eyes, and strongly impressed me with the advantages of wealth," but it was not wealth alone that impressed him:

With them a higher estimate was placed upon refinement than wealth, and they constituted a sort of aristocracy. Our county towns then contained many of this class, dignified and stately in their manners, exclusive in their companionship, high toned in regard to honor and morality! As a rule they were educated and well informed people; mostly belonging to the professions, but not at all dependent on wealth for prestige.

After his brief exposure to the better life, he returned to the farm, but knew that he could not stay. The battle of wills and worlds continued, sometimes openly and sometimes quietly, until, when he was seventeen, the important decision had to be made when his father proposed to buy another farm, one that the father could not manage unless his son were to commit his life to working it. The father expected that the purchase "would extinguish my foolish hankerings," and "anchor me permanently to farming as a pursuit." At length the son consented, and the father together with the seller set off for Greensburg to finalize the sale and purchase. The son stayed behind and from a hill looked down at the property shortly to be acquired,

> the farm that I was to own when I became of age and it was paid for; and on which, if I should marry, I was to spend my lifetime making an honest, frugal living by hard labor, but little more. . . . All my air castles and bright fancies of acquiring knowledge and wealth or distinction were wrecked and ruined, and to be abandoned forever. Must this be? I suddenly realized the tremendous importance of the moment. The utter collapse of all my fond young hopes thus suddenly precipitated nearly crazed me. . . . I put on my coat, ran down past the house, flung the axe over the fence into the yard, and without stopping made the best possible time on foot for the town. . . . It was ten rather long miles over a hilly, rough and muddy road, in March. I noticed little by the way, for time was precious. The papers might be signed before I got there.

As buyer and seller stood on a Greensburg corner discussing which lawyer to visit to make the papers, the exhausted and panting youth caught them and blurted out that "I had come to stop it, and it must be stopped so far as I was concerned." The seller accepted the news graciously, the father less so, and Thomas Mellon began his new life with the encouragement of his mother and such little support as she could lend. His father would give none.

Thomas Mellon was undecided as to precisely what he wanted to do with his life, but he knew that he did not want a life on the farm, and he was satisfied that a college education would be helpful on whatever exit route he chose. He turned to his studies with greater attention, first at the Tranquil Retreat Academy, for college preparation, and then at Western University, predecessor to the University of Pittsburgh. The college president, a Dr. Bruce, "was one of a class of men rarely met with: modest and retiring of manner, shunning notoriety, and averse to anything having the appearance of ostentation"—a characterization that would later typify comments about the young man's own most-famous son, Andrew W. Mellon.

Thomas Mellon was one of the most impoverished of students, but he earned a little money teaching school while continuing to help his father in the fields at home. His schooling was continually being interrupted by the need for his help on the farm: "Not infrequently in the summertime I would walk home from the city, eleven miles, between sundown and midnight, to be ready for work in the harvest field the next day." Finally he graduated. The college graduation ceremonies were unimpressive; indeed, the whole college experience had been unimpressive:

> Had I not gotten such an education, I have no doubt I would always have greatly overrated my loss. It is well for every young man to see for himself how much less there is in it than he expected to find. . . . he who has gone through a college course and has to elbow his way up afterward among those who have not had that advantage, but are self-taught, will more clearly realize the fact that he has gained no monopoly of knowledge by it; and also that he has spent much valuable time in acquiring certain kinds of knowledge which he will very soon lose again for want of any use or necessity for them.

When Thomas Mellon left college he was still unsure of what path he would take. Though decidedly liberal in their religious thinking, he and his parents were sincerely religious, and Thomas seriously considered the ministry. He found that

> Two insuperable objections existed to the ministry: I could not give up the hope of bettering my condition by the acquisition of wealth, nor could I submit to become a pliant tool of any church organization, or be subject to the unreasonable prejudices and whims of those who rule in congregations.

He had some reservations about the law, particularly arising out of his belief that it required eloquence—a quality that he did not respect and thought he lacked himself. "I was not aware then that the money-making part of the business lay in the background, and not in the line of speech-making." He does not tell us what finally prompted him to choose the law, but after a spell as a fill-in Latin professor at Western University, he entered the Pittsburgh office of Judge Charles Shaler as a law student. For support he took a job in the office of the prothonotary, the clerk of the court, and though Judge Shaler generally neglected his students, between his exposure to Shaler and his work in the clerk's office, Thomas Mellon acquired his trade. After a year and a half he appeared, nervous and anxious, for examination for admission to the bar before a panel of distinguished men—"all able and critical lawyers and rather jealous of each other's pretensions." The examiners' questions were charged with the personal animosities between them, but he responded to their questions diplomatically, and "in due course" received his certificate of admission to the bar.

The year 1839 was a good time to become a lawyer in Pittsburgh. The nation was in the early stages of its great industrialization; natural factors made it inevitable that Pittsburgh, population 21,000, would play a major role in it. Only in Pittsburgh did two important factors coincide: the city was at the confluence of two major rivers, so that traditional means of inexpensive transportation were available; and coal, the motive power for the industrialization of America, was abundant in the hills all around Pittsburgh.

Little by little men of Scotch-Irish extraction, harsh in their self-denials, and trading on mutual trust between themselves, came to dominate the city. The young lawyer, handsome in a manly way with his strong, sharp features, was tall and lean-built, sinewy from his hard work on the farm. He brought with him from the farm, and from his Scotch-Irish Presbyterian background, "those root principles of right and duty, tenacity of purpose, patient industry and perseverance in well doing which have accompanied me through life," to which he added an inexhaustible curiosity and a penchant for minute detail, all of which would go to give him an important role in the city and its development.

Thomas Mellon's first office was plain, sparsely and cheaply furnished, but he soon drew a respectable clientele. Briefly he retained his position in the prothonotary's office, and he later ascribed the foundation of his success to the acquaintances he had made there. He also found small but good business opportunities at the prothonotary's, and "invested from time to time in little speculations in the purchase of small judgement, mechanics liens and like securities wherever the holders were anxious to realize without the delay of awaiting their maturity." As a lawyer, he was well prepared, diligent, thorough, and efficient, all to the end of doing an outstanding job for his client, building a practice, and making money. Years later he wrote this frank appraisal of his own motives and those of his brothers at the bar:

> There may be a phenomenal lawyer who would practice law for the love of it,
> but in my forty years about the bar I did not meet with him and have set him

down to be a mythical character like the wandering jew . . . professional life is not followed for the love of it; and from the outset I had husbanded my means with a view to independence and ultimate retirement from it.

In no time he was bustling about the courts, appearing with regularity before Judge Benjamin Patton, a man of "poor health and moderate ability [who] continued to worry through the business of the court for many years," and before Judge Robert C. Grier, later of the United States Supreme Court, "a learned and able judge . . . arbitrary however in his rulings and proceedings, as able judges generally are." Thomas Mellon's only shortcoming, as he tells it, was in the fixing of his fees:

I never overrated the value of my services—in fact I rather underrated them; and in looking back over my professional career, if there is any one thing more than another in which I feel that I was to blame, it is for having done too much service for too little money.

Notwithstanding his reasonableness about such matters, by the end of his first year in practice he had already accumulated $1500 through his efforts and investments and, mostly, through his frugality. "My nature and early training protected me from the folly of earning money and throwing it away," he writes. He saved, scrimped, did without, and took his satisfactions from watching his net worth grow, a penny at a time. Life became even better when Thomas Mellon persuaded his father, by then in his late fifties, to lease the farm to tenants and come to the "city" with Thomas's mother and unmarried sisters to establish residence with him. The practice grew busier and busier, and though the father quickly saw that he could no more abide city life than his son could abide farm life, the law business was so good that the money compensated for the family disappointments. By the time of his marriage, Thomas Mellon's worth had increased to $12,000. After it, there was "nothing left to distract my attention from business. I could feel that I was fairly settled and could work with a will without further interruption; and I did so with gratifying results."

Thomas's father returned to his farm, where he worked out the rest of his days. His health began to fail early in 1856, according to his son from "over-work at a period of life when the system was unable to recuperate the vital energy thus wasted." He died that year at the age of seventy-one. After the father's death Thomas's mother, Rebecca Wauchob Mellon, remained at the homestead for a few years, but as she grew older she joined a daughter and son-in-law, Eliza and George Bowman, on their farm outside of McKeesport, just a little southeast of Pittsburgh. As her end approached, her children gathered about her, and, according to Thomas Mellon, "when

the end came, with seeming unconsciousness she quietly dropped into her
final sleep in my arms, on the 9th day of May, 1868, at the age of seventy-
nine years."

Thomas Mellon and Sarah Jane Negley were married on August 22,
1843. In the seventeen years that followed, Thomas Mellon's hair thinned
and grayed. His eight children were born: first Thomas Alexander, born in
1844 ten months after the wedding, then James Ross in 1846, Sarah Emma
the following year, Annie Rebecca in 1851, Samuel Selwyn in 1853, William
Andrew (but known as Andrew William) in 1855, Richard Beatty in 1858,
and finally George Negley Mellon, born when his father was forty-seven in
1860. There was some sadness in those years, such as was occasioned by
the brief life and long death of his third-born, Sarah Emma:

> During her short existence the poor child suffered the pains of death perhaps
> more than a hundred times . . . she was every now and then shaken with a
> paroxysm of excruciating pain, mostly ending in a swoon from which she
> would gradually recover in a weakened condition. . . . Finally on the Sunday
> evening of her death her painful swoon occurred for the last time. It did not
> seem more severe than the others which she had so often survived. . . . I held
> her in my arms, waiting to see her recover consciousness as usual; but no
> recovery came and at length the painful truth was forced upon us that she was
> gone. . . . She had suffered many deaths but now was at rest. Such are among
> the pains and penalties of parentage. It increases the measure of our sorrows
> as well as our enjoyments. Wherever happiness dwells, pain is a near neighbor.

Annie Rebecca, born the following year, filled the gap only briefly and died
herself in childhood.

Greater in number and intensity were the gratifications arising from
Thomas Mellon's own successes in life: Thomas Mellon grew rich. His
practice grew, but his greater wealth grew from his investments. His money
was always working for him: in commercial paper at 10 to 15 per cent, in
mortgages, other people's judgments and claims, and anything that looked
to be sound. Little by little the land records became cluttered with the name
of Thomas Mellon, as owner or as mortgage holder; then the courthouse
records began to carry his name increasingly, as plaintiff in claims arising
from the debts due him, or as foreclosing party on a defaulted mortgage.
He could be considerate, even patient, with a debtor who worked hard and
lived frugally, as he himself did, but he would not be sentimental over that
great mass of mankind destined for failure. He later lamented the lesson of
experience: "that the more I did for incompetent men, the greater their ill
will when I had to refuse them further favors." Sarah Jane's mother was

one of his great teachers. She prodded her son-in-law to bring legal pressures for her over a debt due her from her own son; though she bore the son no ill will, she insisted that their business dealings be formal and unaffected by their familial relationship. Thomas Mellon learned from her, and the courthouse indexes bear the names of long-destroyed files with tantalizing captions: *Thomas Mellon v. John Mellon; Felix Negley v. Thomas Mellon.*

After Pittsburgh was devastated by the "Great Fire of 1845," opportunities were especially plentiful in the real estate market, and Thomas Mellon began buying, selling, and building, including construction of "some eighteen small dwellings which brought me an income of about 10 per cent on the investment, until I sold them at a profit afterwards in 1860." It was easier to make money in real estate in that pre–Civil War era, he wrote in 1885, because "taxes were not so exorbitant then." These eighteen workingmen's dwellings built by Thomas Mellon in 1846 appear to be the first investments in the history of the Mellon family fortune that relied for success upon satisfying the needs of the laboring class. Thereafter much of the fortune was rolled up by meeting those needs.

In 1850 Thomas Mellon, a wealthy man in early middle age, began construction of a house—a large imposing home far out North Negley Avenue, set on a generous plot given by Sarah Jane's mother, and surrounded by farmland for miles around. The house and outbuildings were well equipped; the grounds were studded with "fine orchards of the choicest fruits." Nonetheless, the home was, as he later described it,

> modest in style, without any ostentation in architectural adornments: planned for comfort and convenience, but harmonious to the eye and in conformity with the fundamental principles of good taste. Apart from the egregious folly of wasting large amounts of money on costly buildings of pretentious appearance in a country where the style and surroundings of buildings change so frequently . . . I have always thought it unwise and in bad taste to make an ostentatious display of wealth in this way. It requires ability to accumulate wealth, but a still higher degree of ability to use it so as not to show the spirit of shoddyocracy common among those grown suddenly rich.

Thomas Mellon lived in the house from 1851 until his death in 1908, and though his sons built more splendid mansions close by, the founder's home remained the mother house for generations of Mellons thereafter.

The practice of law grew, but the demands of managing his own investments and affairs grew at the same time. Lawyering had fulfilled its purpose for Thomas Mellon; its attractions waned, and then it began to chafe. He attempted to cope with his practice by taking partners, only to learn that "There is no benefit in law partnerships. The confidential relation of attorney and client is of a personal character, and the attorney who has sufficient ability to attract clients can accomplish as much by competent clerks as by partners." Thomas Mellon was ready to take an escape route from a practice in which he had lost interest, and from partners whom he found burdensome, when a delegation of distinguished men approached him to urge him to become a candidate for election to the bench.

In the election of 1859 whoever received the Republican nomination for the judgeship was assured of election; getting sufficient delegates to win the nomination was all that counted. Two vigorous candidates, James Kuhn and Edwin Stowe, were already running hard street-corner campaigns when Thomas Mellon announced. His was a different campaign style: "I did not go out at all or appear in public, leaving electioneering in that line to my friends, confining my own exertions to writing notes to such of my intimate friends and acquaintances as I could rely on to exert themselves in my favor." His later account of the pre-convention machinations is colorful and timeless; witness his account of his capture of the delegates from Penn Township. Penn Township was regarded as solid Kuhn territory, and Mellon's advisers counseled him not to challenge Kuhn for its delegates; his chances for success there were remote, and if he challenged Kuhn in Penn, he would risk losing the Penn delegates if Kuhn should later withdraw from the three-man race. The decision had been made to let Kuhn have the Penn delegates by default when a knock came at Mellon's door:

> David Collins, a popular man and warm friend of mine in that township, called to see me to know why no exertions were being made in my behalf; and when I informed him the reasons he took in the situation, but a mischievous twinkle of his eye showed he had something in his mind. He did not divulge what it was, but acquiesced in our plan; said it was just right; that to make a fight in his township for delegates if unsuccessful would be injurious. Accordingly, when he returned home and reported what my friends had told him of their intention of making no exertion for delegates in his township it relieved the minds of Mr. Kuhn's friends of all apprehension, so they made less exertion. But on the evening of the primary, when the election was proceeding quietly and but an occasional voter appearing at intervals and casting his vote for the Kuhn delegates, the only ones in the field, a procession of hay wagons appeared in the distance carrying thirty to forty voters who when they arrived voted solidly for David Collins and another of my friends as delegates in my behalf; and they were elected by a large majority.

When the patriarch of an important Wilkinsburg family favored the Stowe candidacy, Mellon enlisted the older man's ne'er-do-well son on his own behalf, knowing "that character and standing went for nothing and often the greater rowdy was the more efficient local politician . . . and sure enough, to the surprise of my opponents, two of the best delegates in the convention were sent in for me from Wilkins."

Mellon won the nomination, after which the election was routine, and in December 1859 Thomas Mellon became Judge Mellon of the Court of Common Pleas for Allegheny County. The excitement in his own life that year no doubt obscured for him the significance of an odd procedure conducted in nearby Titusville, Pennsylvania. That year a railroad conductor, "Colonel" E. L. Drake, drilled the world's first oil well, a matter that would have greater significance in the Mellon family history than even Thomas Mellon's elevation to the bench.

Judge Mellon joined a senior member on the bench, Judge William B. McClure, whom Mellon described as

> a high toned gentleman of the old school, pure and honorable, and of fine literary attainments, and reasonable ability in the law; but was subject to a slight mental obliquity regarding criminals in general and homicides in particular. He was determined to let no guilty party escape; but his prejudice against the class was so great as not always to discriminate between the guilty and the innocent.

Judge Mellon became the "soft" judge on the criminal docket, soft only by comparison, as his own penological views were unfinicky:

> It is an unpleasant and painful duty for the judge to pronounce sentence of death in such cases—a duty which devolved on me on several occasions in regard to both males and females during my term; but where it is the result of their own wicked doings, and the protection of society requires it, there need be no regrets. In fact, on the part of the unthinking multitude there is entirely too much sympathy and consideration for criminals, and too much time wasted and expense incurred by the public on their behalf. . . . It is only the mean spirited and cowardly, for the most part, who occupy the time and attention of our courts through long trials under trumped up pleas of insanity and other excuses, and invoke public sympathy to screen them from their just desserts.

He was heartened by what he detected to be "a growing tendency to self-destruction on the part of criminals, and it is a course not to be discouraged." In both criminal and civil matters, the Judge lost his once-high regard for the jury system. He devoted many pages of his memoirs to its deficiencies, principally revolving around his belief in the incompetence of the common man to reach proper decisions, and to his high regard for Judge James P. Sterrett, who so reviewed the evidence for the jury "that the stupidist juror could not be mistaken as to how to find."

Judge Mellon's court kept long hours, longer than was customary at the time, but after a few years the Judge himself began to pay less careful attention to the proceedings, often considering his personal affairs or writing letters to sons away from home while routine business was conducted before him. In 1921 attorney Josiah Cohen recalled the Judge on the bench for the Western Pennsylvania Historical Society:

> I remember the first petition that I presented in the Court of Common Pleas at a time when his honor, Judge Mellon, was sitting on the bench. He was engaged in writing, as he usually was. He lifted his eyes and said, "What did you say that petition is for?" I said, "For a charter, Your Honor, a charter for a Jewish burial ground." "A place to bury Jews?" he said. "Yes, Sir," I replied. "With pleasure, with pleasure," responded the Judge as he signed the petition.

Thomas Mellon admits in his memoirs that "Infancy beyond the natural affection that it excites, was never very attractive to me." What he found attractive were the inquiring minds of "miniature men and women," as he was inclined to think of children. Busy as he had always been, Thomas Mellon spent what time he could spare or make in "the study of the opening minds and characters of my two little boys," Thomas Alexander and James Ross. Much of the time his children attended private schools, and

> seldom the public school. The chief objection to the latter was the associations there met with—too many of that misgoverned or neglected class of children, outcasts as it were from the parental and moral influences of a happy home, whose parents govern them in a manner calculated to produce defiance and disregard. Frequently coarse and low by nature, this class of schoolboy rejoices in vulgarity, disobedience and contempt for study. Such associates are injurious to those of gentle and higher nature.

He was little more impressed with private schools, which he thought to be subject to the same objection. They had a further defect: "The principal of the private school depends on the patronage of parents and guardians, and this again depends too much on the good will of the pupils themselves [and so] . . . wholesome exercise of authority is apt to be withheld to the child's disadvantage." Mellon felt most comfortable when his children were attending *his* school, in the schoolhouse that he built on his property. There he employed a private teacher for his children, occasionally "admitting a few other pupils of proper character in order to lessen the expense. Here the branches taught and methods of teaching were under my control." The branches taught were the basics; the method was thoroughness.

The judiciary allowed Thomas Mellon greater time to know and to mold his sons more intensely, more carefully. By the late 1850s Samuel Selwyn, a hauntingly beautiful child born in 1853, was his delight, but the more responsible duties were with his older sons, Thomas and James, who were "approaching to manhood—the time when all boys are in greatest danger." Andrew William and Richard Beatty, still infants, could wait.

Thomas Mellon as patriarch emerges most clearly from *Letters,* a book of highly opinionated but thoroughly charming correspondence from a domineering father to his seemingly obedient son James, which the family published in 1935. The most interesting letters date from a period when James was sixteen to eighteen years old; they reflect the father's efforts to deal with his son's "approach to manhood." The letters' closings would indicate a stiffness between father and son when the Judge signs as "Your father, Thos. Mellon"; the son as "Your son, James R. Mellon," or sometimes as "J. R. Mellon," and only infrequently as "Your affectionate son, James R. Mellon." In any case, the formality of surface relations was only that: a formality on the surface. In an 1862 Christmas letter to Thomas and James the Judge asked his sons for "a Christmas gift which I would prize more than all things":

> *your confidence*—to trust all your secrets to me; to keep nothing back; to confide in me all your troubles and desires and all your hopes, fears and plans; to consult freely with me about everything without fear or backwardness; making me your most intimate friend—never deceiving; always relying on me for sympathy and advice for what you do wrong as well as for what you do right.

If the sons were to do that, the father might be able "to save you from temptations and perhaps deliver you sometimes from evil." It is apparent from the correspondence with James that he at least confided some of his wrongs as well as his rights. In an early letter, written when he was about sixteen, James wrote his father of this escapade:

> There is a preacher's son here [at Jefferson College, where James was briefly a student] and he is a great fellow and we go nearly every evening about three or four miles in the country and get apples and peaches as many as we want. the [sic] other day we went to get some pears off a pear tree near the road and did not think the man cared much about them for they were so small but he was not at home I guess and Wagoner the boy that was with me began to club

> them down and I picked up and here we looked we saw the man running down
> the hill and we started and he chased us about a quarter of a mile and we
> wanted to keep out of his road so we ran with all our might right into a peach
> orchard because that was the only way to get away and so when we got into
> the peach orchard and looked back we did not see him and so we got as many
> as we could eat and did not trouble him again.

The dour Judge could not have approved of the prank. Years later the Judge
wrote that one of the greatest sources of his happiness was "the free inter-
change of thought and implicit trust and confidence between me and my
children in their youth."

The degree of openness between father and sons enabled the father to
guide the development of his sons to an unusual degree. His principal effort
was in developing "moral" sons, and his letters to James most often dwell
upon the virtues of conventional nineteenth-century morality, and especially on the need to resist those sinful handmaidens sensuality and idleness.
As for sensuality, the Judge's letters are clear if not explicit, as witness this
letter to James, just past his eighteenth birthday, about to accept a job away
from home:

> The only serious objection I have about your staying away so long and so far
> from home is the danger of company and habits at your age and inexperience.
> . . . My advice is that if you think well of it yourself and think you can resist
> temptations of all kinds and not forget yourself, you have my consent. . . . You
> have no idea now, but you will have in after life, of the vast importance in all
> respects to a man's happiness and prosperity to have a pure, moral character
> free from vice and bad habits of all kinds and to be truthful, honest and
> honorable in all respects.

The son made a spirited response to the effect that there had been "a great
deal of advice in your letter which I do not need," but the father was not
to be dissuaded from his paternal responsibilities and in his next letter spoke
openly about women:

> I have never warned you enough against female company keeping. I know
> nothing which so unfits a young man for manly serious studies and business
> and it is worse than useless. No man but a fool will think of marrying till he
> is over twenty-five years of age and in proper situation to keep a family and
> for any other use in the way of company, female society is injurious. . . . It
> is all proper to treat female company when necessarily thrown into it with
> proper manly politeness, but what character is more odious to males or females
> than a *ladies' man*. Both sexes despise him and no wonder.

Constrained to get it all off his chest, the Judge went on:

> Another bad habit which I suppose you have shunned since making a fool of
> yourself and being talked about for it while at Canonsburg is writing letters
> to girls. This is even worse than keeping company with them occasionally
> because it is more serious and is a great injury to the girl. Who wants a wife
> that has been writing love letters to every fellow and all such letters are love
> letters, disguise them as you will.

Male company, or at least fun male company—the company of what the
Judge described as "foolish men of good intentions but wrong notions"—
was no better. Such men were "frequently the most agreeable companions
and always the most dangerous," because they threatened to open the doors
to character-wrecking sensuality. It was therefore necessary that his sons

> Make no friends, that is companions of theatre-going, party-going, or young
> men who talk of the pleasure of company and the like; not that such things
> are so bad in themselves as the influences and connections and temptations
> they bring about. Remember you are yet very inexperienced and remember
> particularly Burns' advice to a young man. I think you committed it to mem-
> ory.

This is almost certainly a reference to Robert Burns's "Epistle to a Young
Friend," one of the Judge's favorite poems by his favorite poet, in which
the Scottish moralist gives shrewd advice while exhorting his reader to walk
the straight and narrow from a feeling of personal honor. The poem consists
of ten eight-line stanzas of thick archaic Scottish dialect, very difficult to
read, let alone memorize. When the Judge wrote his son, "I think you
committed it to memory," this author suspects one of the Judge's rare lapses
into wishful thinking.

Writing letters to men was a much lesser offense than corresponding with
maidens:

> It is very well for you to write a letter sometimes (not often, however) to your
> near friends, but don't spend your time writing foolish letters to young people
> who are mere acquaintances. Too frequent writing of foolish letters to mere
> acquaintances is indicative of softness.

Fortunately, there was at least *one* person with whom James might
honorably correspond. The father told James, "I will write you about once
a week, but you may write twice a week or oftener, being careful of your
spelling and composition so as to improve you."

Closely related to the sin of sensuality was the sin of idleness, and in letter
after letter the Judge repeats his warnings about it: "what I most dread is

your not having occupation of some kind"; "Being unemployed is a serious
evil"; "You will feel so much better when you have plenty to do and be so
much less inclined to form useless connections." How one filled up his time
was also important. The Judge counseled his son to "Read no light or
frivolous works like novel reading and light literature—it unhinges the
mind entirely for manly employment." Physical exercise was a good way
to occupy one's time, though the Judge wasn't keen on gymnastics: "It is
all humbug. . . . Edw Graham slid down a pole at school the other day and
nearly knocked his face off in some gymnastic lesson." Still, gymnastics was
better than idleness, and "if you have nothing else to do you had better be
doing so than be idle."

The recipient of all of this advice, J. R., as James Ross Mellon came to
refer to himself,* was a much freer spirit than the Judge. He married at the
age of twenty-one, and late in life confessed to a prohibition audience an
early incident of drunkenness when he had been at Jefferson College. In all
likelihood, away from home he lived a somewhat more pleasant life than
his letters to the Judge might indicate. He knew how to play his father's
biases. In an early letter from Jefferson College, on the heels of one of the
Judge's hectoring be-good admonitions, he wrote that he was attending
prayers daily; in a later letter he wrote the Judge that he had spent the
previous night reading *Principles of Bookkeeping;* in another he explained
that he had declined a job on the railroad because "the company of men
which I would be among would not benefit me any."

Aside from matters of conventional morality, the Judge attempted to
instill the habit of serious thought in his sons. A chatty letter from his
eighteen-year-old son in Milwaukee brought this fierce response from the
no-nonsense patriarch:

> Now in regard to this letter of yours and other commonplace generalities about
> the weather, strawberries and the like. These are of no interest whatever.
> Nothing of that kind could interest, except it were something very uncommon.
> What is it to me whether it rains or shines at Milwaukee? What interests me
> is yourself and whatever concerns yourself. What I like to read is your thoughts
> of your heart, your hopes and fears, wishes and desires, opinions and sugges-
> tions. There is nothing like a young man thinking for himself.

*The Judge's sons and oldest grandsons regularly identified themselves by their first two
initials and last name, a practice that others picked up in time, and that the author will often
follow. In order of age, T. A. refers to Thomas Alexander Mellon; J. R. is James Ross Mellon;
A. W., Andrew William Mellon; R. B., Richard Beatty Mellon; and W. L. is J. R.'s oldest
son, William Larimer Mellon.

Most often the matter of thinking related to business. Even in childhood the Judge began instilling in his sons a strong pecuniary interest. Every little task a child performed was rewarded with a coin; conversely, his grandson William Larimer Mellon (W. L.) later wrote, "I can't remember ever getting any money without at least going through the form of earning it."

The Judge saw his sons as miniature businessmen, and molded them in that direction from their earliest days. While his own success had been founded on lawyering, he in no way encouraged his sons to follow that path. When James wrote of entering a lawyer's office as a clerk, the Judge responded that about six months in that pursuit was all that it warranted. Success in the law business, the Judge explained in his memoirs, required

> first class business talents; but if pecuniary success is the object first class business talent can mostly be utilized to better advantage in other pursuits: especially is this the case if the party has any capital of his own to operate with. . . . Attention to other people's business is a waste of time when we have profitable business of our own to attend to.

On balance he saw more talent and ability in the businessmen that he knew than in the lawyers. He was also not interested in apprenticing any of his sons in a bank—at least not in any banks other than his own. He wrote James that the

> bank clerk who sticks to it for some years is never fit for much else. He just knows how to count and judge of money or keeps the books and nothing else. He never exercises his judgement in making bargains—buying notes or securities or the like as a general businessman or president or manager of a bank.

It was to business at large that he encouraged his sons. Success in business required an inquiring mind and a penchant for detail. He wrote James on how to learn:

> . . . associate with businessmen in different departments and pump them. You recollect Girard's course in that respect. He squeezed all the information out of every man he met like he would a sponge and did it without their suspecting he had any design in it. By appearing communicative and talking about the business and asking questions you can get any man to give information. This information is not about what they are making particularly, for in this they are apt to lie, but as regards the details of the business—the prices—the freights —the risks—the expenses—the amount sales—or amount consumed, etc., etc. Thus the coal business is important to be known, where the coal comes from, what it costs at the mines, the freight, cost of handling, quantity consumed at the gas works and where obtained and by what route, etc. Learn the modus operandi of the coal business and merchandising and iron business or other

important branches of manufacturing. It may be useful to us hereafter. . . .
Remember a young man can never have too much useful information and
everything relating to active life is useful nowadays.

Proper attitude toward important connections was also important for
success in business. He wrote James at Jefferson College,

Judge Sterrett will be out at Jefferson as he is one of the trustees. Don't hesitate
to call on him . . . and whilst he is there go up to him and speak to him on
every occasion that you meet him. Show that you regard him as your particular
friend by your conduct towards him. Young men lose a great deal of advantage
by too much backwardness in this respect. There is all the difference in the
world between impudence and boldness and proper friendly attentions to
superiors and persons older than yourself.

A proper impression required, though, that a young man's contacts not
"form an indifferent opinion of him. They must see that he is always ready
and willing to oblige, and prefers his business at all times to pleasure, and
is anxious to get on in the world."

Increasingly the correspondence between father and son is cluttered with
numbers, most of them preceded by dollar signs. The father encouraged his
son to use lighter writing paper so as to save postage; the son echoed his
father's thrift:

I find it as cheap, or rather twice as cheap, to wear paper collars as I have to
pay five cents to get a collar washed, and I can get paper collars for one and
a half cents apiece. To buy them by quantity, I get twenty for thirty cents. I
wear two a week, costing me three cents a week where it would cost ten cents
to wear cloth collars.

There was an occasional lucky coup; James wrote his father on one occasion, "I got my trunk checked free this morning without buying a ticket."

By the time that James was eighteen, his letters were discussing intricate
business propositions and details in a manner impressive for one of his age,
and in another year it is apparent from the correspondence that his father
and he trusted each other's business judgment.

The Civil War created great opportunities for moneymaking through
commodities speculation. James wrote his father that "This war is a source
of wealth to speculators; they are continually growing richer and do not
care when the war closes. The longer it lasts the better for them and so it
goes." He was anxious to get into it himself, and in letter after letter to both
his father and his older brother, T. A., nineteen, he speaks ecstatically about
the vast profits to be made in tobacco speculations. He realized that his

attitude was not a patriotic one, but as he saw things, corruption among President Lincoln's highest officials set the standard: "The only way a person can do is get as much out of the government as he can and that seems to be the best policy now among the cabinet et al. The more a person can get, the better." The father attempted to be a restraining influence on the boy's enthusiasm, but he was thrilled that his son was thinking the right way. He wrote back his congratulations on the letter: "These views please me all the better perhaps because they accord in a great measure with my own. There is no doubt that in a general shipwreck the best way to save one's self is to keep afloat." He then wrote his son a lengthy lecture on how to make money in wartime, concluding in a merry Scot way that "If a dollar is but a dollar when the war is over, the more we have of them, as you say, the better for us."

James himself was not unpatriotic. He wrote his father for consent to join the Union Army. His father's concept of patriotism, however, did not require enlisting in any army. The Judge remembered, with approval, how his own Uncle Thomas had evaded the British draft in his exit from North Ireland by dressing as a woman; his own instinct was that soldiering was no pursuit for any of his kin. In his memoirs he wrote his matured and tempered view on the subject:

> There may be occasions justifying war and making it the duty of every citizen to engage in it, but in the present state of civilization such occasions can seldom occur; and there is always a disproportionately large class of men fitted by nature for a service which requires so little brain work as that of the common soldier, and who are more valuable to their country and themselves as soldiers at such a time than in any other capacity. It is a mistake to suppose it the duty of every man to enlist when his country needs soldiers. . . . If a man is wise, and can perform the duties of private life with credit to himself and improve his condition at home, he will avoid the folly of soldiering . . . a man whose life is of much value to himself or his family should stay at home.

He permitted his oldest son, Thomas, to make a two-week enlistment with a Pittsburgh company because Thomas "was taken with the war fever to such a degree that had it not been for my influence over him he would have enlisted in the service generally. Sometimes it is wiser to indulge rather than entirely deny such impulses of youth; otherwise they may go to the extreme of disregarding parental control altogether." The Judge was confident that a brief enlistment would sour Thomas on military life, and so it did.

When James wrote requesting consent for a hundred-day enlistment with

the Wisconsin troops, the Judge reacted with fury and disgust. He fired back
a brief telegram: "Don't do it. I have written"—which he followed up with
a total of five letters on the subject of enlisting. From the first:

> It makes me sad to see this piece of folly. . . . I had hoped my boy was going
> to make a smart, intelligent businessman and was not such a goose as to be
> seduced from his duty by the declamations of buncomed speeches. . . . As to
> the twenty-five dollars a month [salary to be paid the soldiers] what signifies
> that? It is nothing to me. I am able and willing to pay all your expenses till
> you find some legitimate business that suits you and there are thousands of
> poor, worthless fellows fit for soldiering, but fit for nothing else, whose duty
> is to go. . . . But perhaps there is no use in advising. Perhaps it is a parent's
> lot to be disappointed in their hopes and expectations about their children.

The second: "It is only the greenhorns that enlist without wrong induce-
ments of very high bounties and having nothing to do elsewhere. . . . I think
it will be best for you to come home." The third: "Those who are able to
pay for substitutes do so and no discredit attaches to it. . . . I feel that now
as your health is restored, you ought to be more with me and have some
manly, regular employment of your own. I want to have you with me." The
fourth: "You say 'I need not be afraid of your ever enlisting without my
consent.' These words have the true ring of a manly good heart." The fifth:
"In time you will come to understand and believe that a man may be
patriotic without risking his own life or sacrificing his health. There are
plenty of other lives less valuable or others ready to serve for the love of
serving."

Sarah Jane also wrote a lengthy hand-wringing letter of like purport:

> I had thought you were a boy of stronger mind and better sense or I never
> would have allowed you to go from home. You are a poor, misguided boy and
> that you will find both to you and your parents' sorrow. . . . My dear son,
> abandon the idea and come home as soon as you can. . . . Come home, come
> home. Wait not for anything. I can't write any more but the same over and
> over again. Come home!

It should be apparent from the quoted portions of the correspondence
that the Judge was a determined, sometimes brutally domineering father.
As one might expect, the manuscript letters themselves, now at the Western
Pennsylvania Historical Society in Pittsburgh, show the Judge with a forceful, firm hand, his script easily decipherable a century later. The son's letters
are now faded nearly to imperceptibility. Surprisingly, though, the hand in
James's later letters grows stronger. He did not enlist, but neither did he
give in to his parents' hysterical demands that he come home. When he

returned to Pittsburgh three months later it was in accord with his own schedule.

Much of the fierceness in the Judge's child-rearing technique went out of him with the death of his favorite, Samuel Selwyn, in 1862 at the age of nine. Twenty-three years later he wrote that "Time has brought me consolation in all other deaths but this: for Selwyn I cannot be comforted." Selwyn became ill with diphtheria; eight days later he was dead. In his diary, the Judge recorded a

> DAY OF SORROW. At half past ten o'clock this evening one of our loved ones, Selwyn, passed away in the morning of life. It is hard, but it may be, after all, the merciful hand of a kind providence, to shield him from the heat and burden of midday, and the penalties of age. But, Oh God, thy will be done. The parting is hard, very hard.

When he later thought of Selwyn, he was haunted by his own actions and attitudes: "The recollection of every little unkindness I subjected him to affects me with remorse. When I review in memory his short life in sickness or in health, I discover nothing to justify the slightest harshness of treatment." Thoughts like those, he wrote, "softened me so much toward those who remained that a harsh word or action to any of them went against the grain."

His view as to the importance of his own role as a father had also changed over the years, relieving him of the burden of sternness:

> Like most parents we at first placed undue importance on personal training. I had a high opinion of the strict exercise of parental authority. I had heard so much about the necessity of coercion and chastisement in the proper training of children, when necessary for their future good, and my desire was so strong to bring them up in the right way, that at the outset I was in danger of overdoing the business in that line.

There was no point to severity, because, he concluded, "The foundation for good or evil is laid in the child's nature."

Selwyn's younger brothers were the principal beneficiaries of the changes in the Judge and his attitudes.

The Judge did not neglect his own business affairs while on the bench, but at first they took a back seat to his judicial duties. Partly it was the preoccupations of his new duties; partly it was that the economy was sluggish from the late 1850s until the Civil War began. Thomas Mellon had always believed coal to be the touchstone of wealth, and by the early 1860s much of his significant accumulation of assets was in coal lands and coal enterprises. His name continued to appear in the commercial journals as the foreclosing party at land sales, but with less regularity.

Pittsburgh has always thrived on war, and the Civil War completed its transformation from a major backwoods outpost into a major industrial center. The war had its bad sides for Thomas Mellon. He outlines some of his worries in his memoirs:

> . . . before military operations progressed very far I found I had enough of interests at stake in money and property to afford me much anxiety for their safety. Forced levies of money and taxation for war purposes were heavy, and no telling whether they might become heavier, or how long they might continue. The waste and extravagance indulged in by the state and local authorities in military affairs was amazing. Besides this our homes and property were at one time in actual danger of destruction by the rebels.

A coal company in which he was the chief investor and owner had some $30,000 worth of coal "disappear" for two years behind the southern lines without word as to its whereabouts. Ultimately it surfaced, to be sold for $40,000 to the Union Army, but then Union officers solicited a bribe as the price for speedy payment of the bill. Judge Thomas Mellon would be no part of any bribe. He went direct to Washington over the matter:

> It was in the time of the greatest excitement and heat of the war, when Washington itself was threatened; and the War Department at Washington was crowded every day with officers on urgent and important business. But I relied on my intimacy with Stanton, the Secretary of War, for a hearing: we had long practiced at the same bar here before I went on the bench.

Ultimately he had to bring suit for the debt due.

At the same time, the war brought good to Thomas Mellon, and to his family. When Sarah Jane's brother, General James S. Negley, was called to the war, T. A., the eldest son, then about eighteen, borrowed $3000 from his father, bought out the general's extensive nursery farm, and over the course of two years repaid his father the loan and the 12 per cent per year interest that his father demanded on it, and liquidated the stock at a profit of several thousand dollars for himself.

By 1864 both T. A. and J. R., the second son, were in coal businesses financed by their father, always on "the usual terms," as their father put it in his memoirs, with a clear understanding that the rent and interest were to be promptly paid. It was important, he wrote, that his young sons experience "the difficulties and responsibilities of business." Only when they had made themselves successes did the Judge soften in his dealings with his sons. The Judge also advanced his sons money for acreage, which they divided into tiny homesites and sold off at profits that their proud father described as "enormous."

In time T. A., joined by J. R. as a partner, owned a substantial lumber and coal yard, and the brothers became the principal backers of the East End Bank, a small bank in the East Liberty section of Pittsburgh. The Mellon boys subdivided acreage into homesites sold at a profit; sold their buyers lumber with which to construct their humble dwellings at a profit; financed the transactions through their bank, profitably; and then sold the coal with which to heat the houses, again at a profit. By the mid-1860s the Mellon boys, T. A. and J. R., were pioneering in the vertical integration of the enterprises that would make their younger brothers, Andrew William (A. W.) and Richard Beatty (R. B.), two of America's richest men. Before they were twenty-one, the Judge writes, T. A. and J. R. had accumulated a combined net worth of some $100,000. He was much gratified at their success.

As for himself, the Judge was anxious. His coal operations did well enough for him, as did a foundry and machine shop that he established in nearby Braddock, Pennsylvania. He also interested himself in various banking ventures, and briefly lent his name as first president of the People's Savings Bank in 1866. But he saw many more opportunities to make money pass him by only because of his inability to make the time to properly evaluate them. War conditions made it easy to grow rich, richer, if only one could maximize the many opportunities; he grew impatient seeing his own sons and many lesser men profiting from the times more than himself.

Perhaps he thought of his young friend the greenhorn Andrew Carnegie, more than twenty years his junior, who had been secretary to a railroad executive when Thomas Mellon had become Judge Mellon, but who had used the decade that Mellon had sat on the bench to greater advantage than the Judge had, transforming himself into a wealthy and important man in the iron world. Harvey O'Connor, the first chronicler of the family history, wrote in his 1933 best seller *Mellon's Millions* that "every fiber of Judge Mellon's being quivered when he saw other men burying their hands in the golden stream of profits while he sat on the bench listening to people's troubles." When his ten-year term of office expired in 1869, Judge Mellon declined to stand for re-election. The explanation he gave in his memoirs was twofold: "General business became so active that such opportunities for making money had never before existed in all my former experience. . . . in holding [judicial office] I was making too great a pecuniary sacrifice, and my salary afforded no adequate compensation for the loss sustained by declining passing opportunities for making money." There was more to it, though, than personal greed; there was also the progenitor's sense—familial greed. While T. A. and J. R. were by then well established, the Judge had remaining sons, "bright boys . . . the idols of my heart, merging on manhood, and with fine business capacities, whom I was eager to launch on this flood tide of business prosperity, and to pilot them in the channel for some part of their way." At the time of his retirement from the bench, Andrew William, the oldest of those remaining sons, was fourteen years old.

Thomas Mellon largely missed the great moneymaking opportunities of the 1860s, but the future beyond was also bright, as he stepped into private life in 1870. The nation was continuing in the industrial expansion spurred by the Civil War. There were still many dollars to be made in the roaring decades ahead, and the former Judge Mellon, a young man at fifty-eight and destined to live an alert ninety-five years, was going to make more than his fair share of them. That year he founded his private banking house, T. Mellon & Sons, today the nation's thirteenth largest bank as the Mellon National Bank. In Cleveland, Ohio, not far from Pittsburgh, another man also took a significant step. The war had made the fledgling oil refiner John D. Rockefeller into a major force. In 1870 he reorganized his firm, Rockefeller, Andrews & Flagler, into a new entity, for which he found a catchy name, the Standard Oil Company.

On January 1, 1870, a new sign went up on a modest building at 145 Smithfield Street: T. MELLON & SONS. At first the principal "son" of T. Mellon & Sons was J. R., whom the Judge borrowed when necessary from James's innumerable partnerships with the Judge's older son T. A. By 1870 J. R. was a substantial young man of twenty-five. At sixteen he had attended Jefferson College for about six months as an "irregular" student, but he became sickly, and in the belief of the day he was sent for restoration to enjoy the recuperative benefits of life in the northern climes. He set out for St. Paul, Minnesota, but got held up by bad weather, so he stopped instead at Milwaukee, where he ultimately accepted a position as clerk in the office of prominent Milwaukee attorneys. Whether or not attributable to the chillier latitudes, his health was restored by the time he was eighteen. Rather than have James return directly to Pittsburgh, the Judge sent him first to Leavenworth, Kansas, to check on the Judge's numerous real estate investments there, and on the man who managed them. The father had an ulterior motive in giving such a seemingly important assignment to such a young man: doing so would help to develop the son's self-confidence. In Leavenworth, James met and became entranced with Rachel, young daughter of the Judge's good friend General William Larimer, one of the founders of Denver, Colorado. Whatever virtues Rachel might have had have been lost to history, and today all that can be said with certainty is that they did not include physical beauty. After his return to Pittsburgh, J. R. quickly prospered in his various enterprises. Through correspondence, his involvement with Rachel became serious.

The Judge was alarmed because of the couple's tender years, but he was hesitant as to how to deal with the situation:

> I felt that he would respect my commands even to the laceration of his own feelings; and on that account I must deal tenderly. He was of ardent and impulsive disposition, and to prevail on him to break it off might do violence to his nature, and he might not make so good a choice again. . . . In every other respect than the age of both parties, the union would be a suitable one.

Instead, the Judge asked that the couple wait a year, after which he would withdraw all objections. A year later, in 1867, they were wed; and the following year they presented the Judge with his first grandchild, William Larimer Mellon (W. L.).

Judge Mellon rented his offices at 145 Smithfield Street. He did not like to rent. Business quickly justified him in indulging his natural inclinations, so the following year he bought the lot at 512–14 Smithfield Street, which, together with substantial additions of land, today accommodates the main office of the Mellon Bank. On it the Judge built a typical post–Civil War office building, four stories high, with a "modern" iron front appropriate to the iron city, and it stood as a city landmark for forty years. The doorway was surmounted with an iron statue, almost life-size, of Benjamin Franklin. By the time that T. Mellon & Sons moved in to occupy the first floor of the grand new building, J. R. had been freed to devote all his energies to his own burgeoning enterprises; he was supplanted as principal "son" of T. Mellon & Sons by his younger brother, Andrew William Mellon.

A. W. Mellon was born on March 24, 1855, the fourth son of the prosperous lawyer, and spent a family-centered childhood, dependent for almost all of his contacts upon his brothers and his family's retainers, notably a woman later recalled by W. L. as "old Mrs. Cox":

> The picture I find easiest to evoke is that of a thin old woman taking her repose close to the warm bricks of the stove. Her chin and nose came close together for lack of teeth; so, as she sucked at her short-stemmed clay pipe, nose and chin and pipe seemed to form a trinity of features.*

*Except as otherwise noted, the many quotes that the author attributes to W. L. come from *Judge Mellon's Sons,* privately printed in 1948 as the work of William Larimer Mellon "with Boyden Sparkes, collaborator." W. L. provided Sparkes with the factual data in innumerable

Sarah Jane was occupied with the kinds of things that occupied socially prominent ladies of the day, and Mrs. Cox ran the household. According to W. L.,

> Every man in the family during his boyhood had come under the sway of her dual power which was equally capable of delighting him with goodies or of whipping him within an inch of his life. I know that she thrashed me and my father before me.

At first A. W. was educated by "Taylor," who had tutored his older brothers in the Judge's little schoolhouse, but the death of Selwyn in 1862 terrified the Judge with fears for the health of his remaining children in plague-ridden Pittsburgh, so A. W. was sent to live with relatives in a "healthier" town some five miles distant. The Judge's schoolhouse was closed forever. When A. W. returned home at about nine years old, he was enrolled in a Pittsburgh school. Every day the Judge and his son commuted "downtown" from their home far out in the East Liberty section, the Judge to his courthouse and the son to his school. If freed from school, A. W. might go into town with his father anyway and hide under the bench, listening to the proceedings, his presence unknown to anyone but the presiding officer. A closeness developed between them, closer no doubt than existed between the Judge and any of his other children. According to W. L., "the Judge talked to his son not as to a little boy but as to one with a mature intellect and thereby challenged the youngster to think as a man."

Like any good son of the Judge, A. W. was earning money from an early age. As a small boy he cut and tied the hay produced on the Judge's estate and sold it from the roadside to passing travelers for their horses. J. R. wrote in an 1864 letter to his father that "Andy," then nine, "has a load of potatoes and apples for marketing tomorrow," also fruit of the father's farmlands. Later the Judge established his son at a newsstand, thinking that it would be a good bookkeeping experience for the child. There was never much time for play.

At thirteen, not an unusual age for the time, A. W. entered the Western University of Pennsylvania. The Judge was dubious about the value of college—his sons T. A. and R. B. and grandson W. L. had none at all. His view, summarized in W. L.'s *Judge Mellon's Sons,* was that "Colleges were developing into institutions where rich men's sons more often than not were spoiled." "Many a time," W. L. recalled, "I heard him predict that boys

---

long interviews, but all of the words were Sparkes's, as was much of the philosophizing, a matter which left W. L., then eighty, rather uncomfortable about the final product.

who were going away from our neighborhood to college would return only
to amount to nothing." Only A. W. attended college for any length of time,
and that in his home town, under his father's watchful eye. There were no
dormitories, and A. W. lived in the Judge's home with his parents, his
younger brother Richard Beatty (R. B.), the Judge's last-born child George
Negley, older brother J. R., the bride Rachel, and the baby W. L. He was
midway in his college studies when the bank was opened, and thereafter he
was there more and more, watching, learning. Among his main duties was
"security." T. Mellon & Sons' great safe was not only locked in the usual
manner, but was doubly secured by a heavy cable twisted around it and
joined by a padlock. It took two men to unwind the cable, and the Judge
directed that A. W. was to be one of the two.

There was never much of a boyhood. In the late 1920s, A. W.'s first
biographer, Philip H. Love, attempted to round up classmates' remembrances of the then Secretary of the Treasury, and found little more than
recollections of his appearance: "slight and handsome, with a round, fair
face and light hair. He was quietly cordial." Classmates also remembered
him as bright.

A. W. had a slight stammer in his speech and was always uncomfortable
about public speaking; in order to graduate from the university and receive
his diploma, he had to make a brief address at commencement. What cared
Judge Thomas Mellon for diplomas? While the Judge acknowledged that
he had derived some benefit from his college studies, the diploma itself was
another matter, and in his memoirs the Judge wrote that "from the circumstance of having a diploma I never derived any benefit whatever. In the
professions and business management certificates of either ability or learning are valueless. In the battle of real life an exacting public will only
estimate the ability and qualifications they see in actual practical use."
A. W., seventeen, withdrew from the university shortly before graduation.
For the next forty-eight years he was a full-time businessman. Full time:
twenty-four hours a day. Walt Whitman might have had him in mind when
he lamented "the melancholy prudence of the abandonment of such a great
being as man is, to the toss and pallor of years of moneymaking."

Just as the Judge had sent J. R. on business to Leavenworth at the age
of eighteen, so he had A. W. traveling on business for him at an early age.
At seventeen A. W. was sent to Philadelphia to oversee the operation of a
theater on which the Judge held a defaulted mortgage. Later the same year
he went to Baltimore to purchase some eighty well-located acres for the
Judge on what later became the Baltimore–Washington Turnpike. Then,
perhaps also with an eye to developing the young man's self-confidence, he

set A. W. up in his own business, a lots-and-lumber operation similar to that of T.' A. and J. R. He gave A. W. as an aide and partner young R. B., age fourteen, who left school at the time never to return. For an operations site, the Judge selected Mansfield, now Carnegie, Pennsylvania, about as far to the west of downtown Pittsburgh as the East Liberty yard of T. A. and J. R. was east of it, so that the Mellon operations would not be competing. There the Judge purchased an acceptable piece of ground for a lumber yard and several nearby tracts suitable for division into building lots. He then turned his adolescent sons loose. They supervised the building of their offices and storage sheds, and were soon fully stocked and fitted out for business. They surveyed and laid out their real estate subdivisions and did their own conveyancing. They kept up their payments to the Judge. After eighteen months of modest success, the business climate turned sour.

In the years following the Civil War the nation experienced an overexpansion of business and of credit with a significant movement of capital from productive ventures to pure speculation. The bust was inevitable. Its onset was signaled by the failure in 1873 of the respected New York financier Jay Cooke and his pet corporation, the Northern Pacific Railroad. The stock market reacted immediately with a disastrous plunge, and then there was a calm before the "depression of 1873" hit every aspect of the American economy. Momentarily, real estate values held their own, and in the lull A. W. succeeded in unloading considerable undeveloped acreage that the brothers had recently acquired. At a propitious moment the entire stock of A. W.'s principal lumber competitor in Mansfield was wiped out by fire; the generous young brothers permitted their competitor to buy out their stock, together with their contracts for future delivery. The lumber yard was leased out, and the unsold lots were held until times brightened years later. The boys were out of business with a small profit, better than a loss, before the depression of 1873 hit their line of business. Thereafter, A. W. went into the bank on a full-time basis while R. B. spent several years on ad hoc assignments for the Judge.

The Judge himself had more anxious moments during the depression. Years later in his memoirs he analyzed the causes for the depression in a manner similar to that set forth above, and accepted by historians, but at the time he was caught, as he puts it, "off guard":

> At an early age I had seen the disasters produced by the great collapse of 1819, which followed the war of 1812; and expected a similar collapse after the late

war, but had forgotten the fact that the collapse of 1819 was delayed so long after the war of 1812; and, in the present instance, the time of prosperity was so remarkably prolonged that I began to doubt my apprehensions, and to think it possible that some special virtue in our new greenback currency and national banking system had averted a collapse altogether.

At first the Judge was slow to appreciate the implications of Cooke's failure.

On the 16th of September, 1873, while seated at my desk, Mr. Whitney, our notary public, on his customary call at three o'clock, looked in and inquired if I had heard the news of Jay Cooke's failure. I replied, no. He said it had occurred that morning, and there was a good deal of excitement over it in New York and Philadelphia. This news did not disturb me, indeed it scarce attracted my attention as we had no business relations with Cooke or his railroad projects; and I supposed it would blow over without any serious effect, as it had done after similar failures of others.

The stock market crash concerned him little more. He wasn't into stocks, and no doubt considered the stock market manipulations of New York's robber barons immoral. He probably shared the typical western Pennsylvania reaction summarized by George Harvey in his biography of Mellon associate Henry Clay Frick that the crash was

A mere "Wall Street panic," presumably involving only gamblers in money, stocks and bonds, [which] was no concern of those actively engaged in legitimate industry and wholly engrossed in their own affairs. They had no interest in the cut-throat games of kid-gloved and silk-stockinged parasites who, producing nothing themselves, fought over the fruits of the toilsome enterprises of honest men and were regarded as natural enemies. What mattered it if ruin should overtake the rascals? Good enough for them! The upset might teach them a lesson. It would be all over in a month anyway.

The Judge's own investments had been conservative, so the collapse "cost us no embarrassment in regard to private debts or liabilities." But the money crunch that followed Cooke's failure and the stock market crash very quickly put T. Mellon & Sons and T. A. and J. R.'s East End Bank in an embarrassing situation. Confident of the times, the Judge had paralleled most wise bankers and had invested the depositors' money in long-term mortgages so as to earn the higher rates of interest that they carried. Just days before Cooke's failure, he had put much of the bank's cash reserves into "gilt-edged" Pennsylvania Railroad bonds so that "our cash on hand was reduced greatly below our custom or the point of prudence." Banks across the country began to fail, and as depositors began streaming into the Mellon banks seeking withdrawals, there was only $60,000 to cover

ten times as much in depositors' money. Most of the bank's many investments were sound but not liquid, and were therefore useless in such a
situation. The Judge's sons' efforts to call in past-due obligations were a
stopgap, but only a brief one: no one had any cash.

At length the Judge was faced with

> a bitter pill for me however to acknowledge present inability to pay every
> demand upon me. Neither myself nor any of my ancestors so far as I knew had
> ever been in that condition before. . . . The end was approaching and already
> in sight. The extremely disagreeable announcement must be made, which I
> knew would cause a very great sensation, as we were supposed safe if there was
> safety in a bank anywhere. After all our exertions, the cash balance for both
> banks fell to nearly twelve thousand dollars, and as our suspension was not to
> be a failure involving loss to anyone, I considered it better to keep this much
> on hand, to meet any necessitous cases of depositors likely to suffer want of
> their funds; and at the close of banking hours on the 15th day of October, 1873,
> I directed the officers to stop payment the next day to all except special cases,
> but not to close the doors of either bank: I thought it more satisfactory to
> customers to keep them open, and continue the officers in their places to
> explain the situation to those interested and this did have a good effect in
> preventing alarm; we had no run nor excitement at either place; and I have
> ever since felt gratified at the generous consideration with which we were
> treated. Whilst we met many anxious faces, there was not an unkind word or
> disagreeable reflection made by anyone. . . . We were never closed at either
> bank, and never entirely stopped payment to those in actual need, and in less
> than a month from the time we suspended we were prepared to pay all checks
> as presented.

The Judge, however, was distraught enough over the experience to consider abandoning the banking business altogether. He finally decided that
the staff he required for his own affairs, and the facilities that he owned,
could best be utilized by continuing T. Mellon & Sons; but at his direction
the East End Bank paid off its depositors and stockholders and terminated
its existence.

The depression of 1873 brought genuine hardship to the common man,
which was not unappreciated by the Mellon family. W. L. later recalled the
soup kitchen that the family provided at T. A. and J. R.'s lumber yard, the
huge caldrons of soup, the bread, and "those who came to get it . . . really
hungry people—whole families of them." The Judge makes no mention of
such hardships in his memoirs. What he learned from the depression was
more coldly scientific:

. . . property of all kinds remained, but it was set afloat in search of its true owners, who could only be discovered through the tedious process of judicial sales in the bankrupt and other courts. . . . Nothing but a process of general liquidation could determine what any man owned or was worth. The stock had to be boiled down to evaporate the water from it. Real and fictitious wealth had become so mixed up that the refining process of bankruptcy and sheriff's sales became necessary to separate the dross from the true metal. And when in this way the real owners of property and wealth were ascertained, they were found to be only the few who had paid as they went, or confined their business and speculative operations to what was clearly within their power to hold.

A. W., in 1930, would remember his father's conclusion.

There was, of course, unpleasantness in the depression even for the Mellons; in addition to the Judge's personal embarrassment, the family suffered some discomfort in the balance sheet. Many of the purchasers of lots sold and financed by the Mellons defaulted on their payments, and when the Mellons took back the lots at foreclosure sales, the debts due them on the real estate exceeded what they could be sold for in those bleak days. But the Mellons could wait for better times, and so they did, until they were able to sell again at respectable figures years later. Their financial setback amounted to little more than temporary, if unhappy, bookkeeping adjustments.

The expansion of credit in the years immediately following the Civil War had prompted a geometric growth in the number of banks in America, which dwindled to the same extent in the depression of 1873. Those banks like T. Mellon & Sons that survived '73 could look forward to the greatest industrial development in history, and the opportunities to finance that development.

With the abundance of coal in the mountains surrounding Pittsburgh, and its advantageous location at the confluence of two major rivers, it made economic sense to bring iron ore to Pittsburgh for fabrication rather than to bring the coal and transportation resources to the ore regions. Pittsburgh became the steel city and, so, the heart of the industrial revolution in America. Pittsburgh's population grew to meet the manpower needs of its growing industries, and with the population growth came a proportionate increase in the demand for housing, building materials, and financing in the Pittsburgh area. The Mellons were prepared to meet those demands. During this period the Mellons developed more than fifty tracts of land into subdivisions for small houses for the labor force that served Andrew Carnegie's huge furnaces, George Westinghouse's labs and factories, the glass and paint works, and later the aluminum mills that combined would give the city its important role in American history.

During this period of development in America, Pittsburgh, and banking, Thomas Mellon yielded more and more to his son, the slight, quiet A. W. The Judge quickly entrusted him with authority to approve loans, knowing —hoping—that A. W. would make some of those errors with the Judge's money that make for learning experiences. When A. W. made a substantial loan to a man that the Judge regarded as a poor risk, the Judge made no comment to his son but privately confided to others, "I think I would like Andrew to lose that loan. It would teach him a lesson." The loan proved good and the Judge grew comfortable with his strong right arm.

In 1874 he gave A. W. the respectable salary of seventy-five dollars a month, together with a one-fifth interest in the bank, signaling the father's recognition of the son's importance to the enterprise, and perhaps his own ultimate plan for distribution of the bank equally among his five surviving sons. However, he continued to appear at the bank daily, and from its offices he supervised his own involved business affairs and investments, which seemingly extended to every corner of the world of moneymaking. His real estate investments were scattered across the United States. He owned coal mines and businesses, foundries, what he described in a letter to J. R. as "a small car shop" (whatever that might have meant in the 1800s), street railways and a cable car line to scale one of greater Pittsburgh's many extreme heights, and all manner of utilities.

Even in advanced age the Judge understood every one of these investments intimately. "When it came to investments," W. L. wrote, "that jaw of his did not relax any more than the doors of a locked iron safe until his mind had explored every possibility of losing some of his money." Judge Mellon, together with Jay Cooke, eight years younger than himself, and J. Pierpont Morgan, twenty-four years his junior, was an early American example of the finance capitalist: a man who invests money in an enterprise not for a return at a fixed percentage of interest but for a stake in the business itself.

In most of these investments the Judge involved one or more of his sons. In one of them, the Ligonier Valley Railroad, he involved all of his immediate family and most of his descendants remained involved for almost fifty years after his death.

Today a network of highways traverses the small town of Ligonier, some fifty miles east of Pittsburgh, and the valley around it. Automobiles cover the region with ease, thereby obscuring the natural isolation of the valley. In the 1800s the steep slopes of the topographical rim surrounding Ligonier all but cut it off from the outside world. For years the leading citizens of Ligonier dreamed of a railroad line to link the valley with the town of Latrobe, on the other side of the heights, where an existing Pennsylvania Railroad line would connect Ligonier with the world beyond. A corporation was organized to build the railroad and laid out a roadbed before going bankrupt; a few stockholders interested in keeping the dream alive purchased its assets at the bankruptcy sale. In 1877 these gentlemen approached Judge Mellon with a proposition. If he would lend his skills and risk his money in building the railroad, they would give him a mortgage for the amount of his expenses plus 80 per cent of the stock and a $10,000 bonus for his profit. The Judge realized that these inducements would be worthless unless the railroad were to show a profit, but he was willing to investigate. He sent his sons to Ligonier to scout out the possibilities and posted a man —nine-year-old W. L.—to make a traffic count on the rough "highway" out of the valley. Their reports, and perhaps a desire to find some occupation for R. B., encouraged him to proceed. He entered a contract with the stockholders and then threw his entire family into the project. T. A. handled the local population and did most of the surveying; J. R. was quartermaster for the job; A. W., least involved, was corporate secretary; and R. B. actually supervised the construction. Even Sarah Jane had a role in the project; she was in charge of refurbishing the secondhand coach that the Mellons bought for their railroad.

At a time when the Pennsylvania Railroad was paying ninety cents a day for laborers, the Mellons paid a dollar, thereby insuring their pick of the labor market. They encouraged the work force by use of the carrot and stick rather than with the harsh words and exhortations used by more experienced railroad foremen. Every morning T. A. drove his wagon past the track layers with a keg of beer prominently in view, which he stored a respectable distance down the roadbed so that the men could see the bonus that would await them if they laid enough track that day. Shirkers were dismissed. Sixty days after commencement of the project, W. L. later recalled, the first train rolled into Ligonier:

> . . . one passenger coach and our only freight car, hauled by our lone engine . . . we were all aboard, scattered all the way from the engine cab to the rear platform. My grandfather, as the backer of the enterprise, had a place of honor aboard the train, and Grandmother sat beside him. Uncle Tom, the president, naturally was a conspicuous passenger. But the great man aboard that day was Dick Mellon. He wore a leather-visored cap and across the front was embroidered in heavy gold thread a one-word badge: "Conductor." Dick ran the train!

The Ligonier Valley Railroad enabled development of the valley's vast coal and quarry resources and of its rich recreational potential. The little railroad, affectionately known as the "Doodlebug," also played a part in the childhood of every person to grow up in the valley for seventy-five years.

The Mellons grew to love the valley. The Judge bought up huge tracts within it. J. R., R. B., and R. B.'s children and grandchildren all built their favorite retreats there on their own vast estates. The Mellons and their businesses have been the dominant influence in the lives of many "company" towns, but of them all the Mellons continue to take an active interest only in Ligonier; it is the only Mellon company town that has avoided decay.

Over the years the Ligonier Valley Railroad became the pet business of the Mellon family. R. B. remained its operating manager for several years after it opened, managing and working in every aspect of the business—even loading the baggage. In his time off from school, W. L. served as ticket agent, until he outgrew the function at seventeen and was replaced by T. A.'s son, Edward Purcell Mellon, a boy of about twelve. Fifty years later the railroad's management was little changed. T. A. had died and been succeeded as president by J. R.; T. A. Jr. was vice president; R. B. was secretary; and his son, R. K. (Richard King Mellon), was treasurer. All of the directors were Mellons.

With time, the automobile and the highway system were developed; the valley's coal and stone were mined and quarried away. The railroad's profitability became marginal and then nonexistent, but the Mellons continued to operate the Ligonier Valley Railroad as a nostalgic experience until in 1952 the Doodlebug puffed its last.

Today the railroad's station, incomprehensibly described as "handsome" in *Ligonier: The Town and the Valley,* serves as area headquarters for the Pennsylvania Game Commission; its engine house is a Catholic church and parochial school; its ticket office is an apartment house. A snip of land adjacent to the station and once part of its grounds bears an identification tablet: MELLON PARK. It was donated to the town by R. K. in memory of his father, R. B., in 1958, Ligonier's bicentennial year, and though Mellon Park is too small and too poorly situated to be of much use as a park, the gift of it was only one of the family's many nice gestures to Ligonier—the town and the valley.

The retired Judge Mellon also found time for public affairs. Though his Republican credentials were well in order, he was a man motivated principally by personal standards as opposed to party loyalties. He was unimpressed with President Abraham Lincoln, or, more accurately, with the irregularities of Lincoln's administration. The administration of President U. S. Grant, with its blatant corruptions, thoroughly repelled and disgusted him with what he terms in his memoirs "Grantism." Upon the expiration of Grant's first term in 1872 Thomas Mellon abandoned the President—the "regular" Republican candidate—when Grant tried for re-election. The judge favored Horace Greeley—the "Liberal Republican" candidate, who was also backed by the Democratic Party—and Greeley's reform views, most significant of them being Greeley's call for an end to "Reconstruction" in the south. Shortly after he retired from the bench, Judge Mellon toured portions of the defeated south and personally

> attended one or two meetings of that august assembly, the legislature of Louisiana; and it was suggestive to see a presumably dignified body comprised of stolid, stupid, rude and awkward field negroes, lolling on the seats or crunching peanuts, except when the white leaders would by sign or signal arouse them to what was going on at the point where their votes were wanted: These white members among them standing in with the governor and other carpetbag parasites in promoting all manner of corrupt schemes to rob the property owners and taxpayers.

He could appreciate Greeley's Reconstruction arguments, and he also approved of Greeley's demand for civil service reform and his support of the high protective tariff. That last was good for Pittsburgh. The Judge admired Greeley, editor of New York's *Tribune,* not only as a political philosopher but also as a writer. In the course of the 1872 presidential campaign, the Judge wrote that he made

> a dozen or so of speeches [for Greeley] at public gatherings. I felt a satisfaction in thus unburdening my mind on existing evils, and always had an attentive audience, although fun and anecdote and clap-trap declamation calculated to create a laugh are more acceptable to the majority in crowds who attend such meetings, than sound reasoning. In this city and county we had quite encouraging prospects; but after all the office-holding federal power was too much for us.

Grant carried all but six southern states; had Greeley been the winner, it is entirely possible that Judge Mellon might have assumed an important federal position.

Judge Mellon had previously run for public office in the election of 1859 that elevated him to the bench, but he regarded his involvement in Greeley's campaign as "my first campaign in party politics." It was not a happy experience for him: "The manifest advantage of false and impudent assertions, trickery and deception over truth and merit in the support of men and measures satisfied me that it was not in my line, and so thoroughly disgusted me that I have taken no active part in politics since."

By 1881 the memory of the bad odors and foul tastes of the Grant-Greeley campaign must have faded, because that year the Judge accepted the nomination of East End Republicans for a seat on Pittsburgh's City Council. The Judge does not discuss the campaign in his memoirs, but from contemporary press reports, his party's mayoralty candidate, W. S. Humphries, sounds to have been what the Judge would have called a "blatherskite." The Judge failed to make a scheduled campaign appearance with Humphries and could not have been too disappointed when Major Robert W. Lyons, an upright citizen albeit a Democrat, won an upset victory over Humphries. The Republicans, though, took control of the City Council, and among the successful candidates was the sixty-eight-year-old Thomas Mellon.

By orientation and temperament no one was less suited to run for elective office in a bustling politically active working-class town than the elitist Judge. From some Olympian perch in 1864 he wrote J. R.,

> You see mankind is truly "an unco squad."* . . . See how people are led by the nose in religion and party politics, the more ignorance of course, the more ease with which they are led and the more tenacity with which they follow their leaders, but life is too short for the better educated to become fully enlightened and hence all are miserably ignorant, lead and are led, adopt and carry out absurd opinions.

The success of the Mormon Church in the nineteenth century he saw as proof positive of "what a miserable, foolish animal is ignorant humanity."

Today many of the Judge's razor-thin views might be seen as more amusing than alarming or offensive, unless one is a Mormon or an Irish Catholic. The Judge had a strong bias against Roman Catholics and especially Jesuits with their "worldly shrewdness," and despite his colorful delivery, his views on what he variously describes as "Celtic Irish," "Catholic Irish," or "South Irish" might reasonably be regarded as vicious. Pages heaping abuse on Irish Catholics—some written with apparent scientific detachment—are scattered throughout his memoirs.

There were, of course, "good" Irish:

---

*"Ye'll find mankind an unco squad,/And muckle they may grieve ye . . ." From Robert Burns's "Epistle to a Young Friend." "Unco" meant "strange" in the Scotland of Burns's day; "muckle" translates to "much."

I have known many good, honest, industrious and humane people among them, of both sexes; but these are the exceptions to the general rule, and as usual in all such cases, they are overborne by numbers and helpless to oppose the folly and wickedness of their countrymen.

He had no doubt that Catholic Ireland was incapable of self-government and favored a scattering of the Celts across the globe, and assimilation of them into other cultures. Otherwise he saw little hope for South Ireland: "Irish character and affairs do not seem to grow better. It was bad enough in Bishop Berkeley's time." In his later days he told W. L., "I have come to the conclusion that the only way to settle the Irish question would be to sink the island."

Judge Mellon had some sympathy for the mass-production worker:

The employees and their families in the larger manufacturing and mining establishments are often designated each by his number, and live in numbered tenements, and are all subjected to the same routine, and treated alike; too much like the soldiers of an army or the inmates of a prison. The opportunity to work up and out and better their conditions is rendered so remote as to appear to them hopeless.

In theory, the Judge could have lived with "responsible" unionism, but when push came to shove, he was strongly out of sympathy. He personally believed that organized labor's effort to get a bigger slice of the pie for the workingman ran counter to natural justice, that the country's wealth "is distributed between capital and labor fairly and under the natural economic laws, each getting his due proportion." The violence of labor disputes particularly repelled him, and he knew where to put the blame: "In all strikes and labor troubles, outrages committed by individuals or sub-combinations are promptly disavowed by the main body. It is their policy to do so, although in sympathy with the wrong-doers."

The Judge's East End constituency included few Catholics, fewer laborers, and no Mormons at all. They elected him to three consecutive two-year terms before he declined renomination in 1887. For six years his constant concern was keeping taxes down; all his other interests—curbing expansion of public services and extravagance in government spending; opposing public bond issues—were functions of keeping taxes down. Taxes seemed to go up and up. They dizzied and demoralized him, and actually made Thomas Mellon sick, emotionally distraught. In an 1864 letter—seventeen years before his service on the City Council—he had written J. R. that he felt very gloomy and melancholy this evening and look forward to the probability of the time coming around when my home will not be in Allegheny County. Tax after tax is levied, and one batch of bonds issued after another for illegitimate purposes to such an extent that our property must be confiscated in the end.

In his memoirs he variously describes bond issues and what he regarded as extravagances in government spending as "public robbery," the "trade of public plunderers," and as "spoliation, pure and simple." It was the work of "a wrong principle to allow irresponsible politicians, mostly without any property interests of their own, to mortgage at will the private property of the citizens," and the inevitable result of having an electorate which, for the most part, was "too lazy to have anything to tax but ready enough to hold public meetings and pass resolutions to tax people that own property." It made one question the democratic premise:

> Those who have nothing to pay with and are indifferent have the numerical majority of votes and elect their own class to office; and however this may be, experience, which ought to but does not teach fools, proves conclusively that universal suffrage does not as a rule place honest, prudent and competent men in power.

He viewed public spending, and especially issuance of public bonds, as a form of class warfare, in which "tax eaters of all classes prey upon the taxpayers." It was worse than communism, which he saw as

> honest and respectable compared with this system of depredation. Communism would openly and avowedly take property and the fruits of labor from their owners and distribute them equally to all. There is some show of equity in this. But this thing of contracting debts [through municipal bond issues] for other people to pay, and converting the proceeds so often to the subsistence of those who contract them, is communism in the livery of law.

He personally favored repudiation by the municipality of the debts covered by ill-advised bond issues, and most of them he would have regarded as ill-advised. There would be no dishonor in such a course—"there is no more injustice or dishonesty in their repudiation than would be in the repudiation of a forged note or check"—but he acknowledged the probable futility of attempted repudiation, due to the "ingenuity of judges [who] can find some plausible pretext for holding them valid and enforcing their payment."

Thomas Mellon knew that things would get worse, not better, and by the time he entered the City Council they had. Councilman Mellon fought the trend—not simply for himself, as one of Pittsburgh's biggest taxpayers, but for the little man:

> The industrial classes are the real sufferers—they are the taxpayers. . . . One of the insuperable principles of economic law, or science of political economy as it is called, is that the user of property or consumer of commodities must necessarily pay the full cost of construction or production, besides a profit to the owner or producer. Hence every one except the thief and pauper pays indirectly his full share of all tax burdens.

At his very first council meeting he introduced a resolution calling for retrenchment in public expenditures, and two others designed to save money in the operation of the city waterworks and in the city attorney's office. Thereafter he opposed expenditures for almost everything: a proposal for an up-to-date communications system for the police department, electric lighting for public buildings. He alone voted against acceptance of his good friend Andrew Carnegie's offer of a grand public library because of the expense to the taxpayers of maintaining the institution. He offered to contribute $2000 to a private fund to run the library, but thought that municipal support of it would simply be another "injustice to tenants and small property owners who are the actual taxpayers in the end." He was even ambivalent about public education:

> There is no more reason for compelling one man to pay, not only for the education of his own children, but for the education also of other men's children, than to compel him to feed and clothe other men's children: unless he receives value for it in the greater security to his person and property.

As he saw it, the price of free public education was being paid, but the "greater security to person and property" were not being received. The free public schools might develop intellectual faculties but they were ignoring what he called the "moral faculties" and worst of all they were not teaching "political economy," i.e., the importance to everyone of keeping taxes low, the virtues of the capitalistic system, and the sacredness of private property. Sure, more people learned the three R's, but his own experience had been that "the adroitest thieves and crooks were always among the best educated inmates of the jail," and on the balance, he preferred the good old days when

> they were all pay schools. Free schools with their advantages to ambitious local politicians, and affording a wider but thinner spread of knowledge with the disadvantages of heavier expense to parents and taxpayers, were not yet introduced.

A bond issue even for a courthouse offended him, even if it was a courthouse designed by the celebrated architect Henry Hobson Richardson. In
the Judge's view, the grand courtrooms envisioned by Richardson were
precisely what wasn't needed; he argued that rooms "about forty feet square
would . . . best serve the purposes of justice. The general public have no
necessary occasion to be there." Richardson's masterpiece would only attract "loafers and hangers-on." He felt so strongly about the matter that
when his vote against the bond issue fell with the minority, he personally
litigated the matter all the way to the Pennsylvania Supreme Court, unsuccessfully, producing another $2000 in expenses for the "tenants and small
property owners" to pay through their taxes, to cover the city's costs in
opposing the Judge's suit.

Corruption in government, whether by bribery or in its less blatant forms,
was repugnant both to the Judge's sense of thrift and to his solid moral
upbringing. In the Pittsburgh of the period it often involved municipal
franchises for utilities or streetcar lines. Time and again, invariably without
success, the Judge opposed franchise giveaways that promised substantial
profits to well-placed speculators who would simply sell for money what
their connections had obtained for them for free. Streetcar lines proliferated
without rhyme or reason, other than to create something someone could
sell, sometimes with an adverse effect on congestion and traffic. The Judge
was opposed. One such proposal he labeled the biggest steal that had been
perpetrated upon the city "since the notorious water works contracts." He
proposed a resolution to establish a committee to investigate corruption in
the granting of municipal franchises, and though the resolution carried, the
investigating committee soon discovered that it lacked the power to compel
testimony, whereupon it disbanded.

But for his appropriately low opinion of the state of public morality at
the outset, Judge Mellon would have been disillusioned by his six years on
the City Council. He seems to have stood almost alone as a rapacious city
government indulged itself and its friends in typical Tweed-era shenanigans.
Pittsburgh at the time was dominated by Christopher Magee and William
Flinn, a pair of Republican bosses who gave their names to the city's
Magee-Flinn era. Magee's brother Fred was the pair's attorney and regularly appeared before the council on behalf of this or that pillager. In pique
the Judge courageously rebelled:

> We all know that when Mr. Magee comes in here and indicates his desires, he
> generally gets what he wants. Anything he wants must succeed, it always
> succeeds. This is a coincidence, a phenomenal fact that always does occur. Did

you ever see, did any man ever see an ordinance that he advocated that did not go through? Any man who has the faintest political aspirations in city, state or nation always votes as Mr. Magee desires.

It made no difference.

The six years were an unhappy experience for the Judge, who avoids any discussion of them in his memoirs other than a brief conclusion that "no more unsatisfactory position could be held by one of my disposition. I have for over forty years been combating municipal abuses without any appreciable effect. The drift has been steadily towards folly and extravagance, and those who oppose it are usually in the minority." The soundness over time of his historical analysis must be a matter of value judgment. His assertion that those who oppose the "folly and extravagance" are usually in the minority is documentably correct in the case of Pittsburgh, 1881–87; almost invariably Councilman Mellon's votes were cast with the minority.

More and more in his business ventures Judge Mellon relied upon and delegated work to A. W. As early as 1875, when A. W. was twenty, he was given his father's limited power of attorney; two years later his name was first entered in the clerk of the court's indexes as plaintiff in an eviction; in 1880 a document was recorded giving A. W. comprehensive right to sign for and act for his father in all matters. Two years later, after the Judge had begun his service on the council, he was sixty-eight years old, and signaled his own essential "retirement" from business by execution of this significant document:

> Pittsburgh, January 5, 1882
>
> Proposition to son Andrew for services past and future.
>
> He to have the entire net profits of the bank from January 1, 1881, including my salary, the books to be readjusted accordingly, from 1st January instant. He to have entire net profits of bank and pay me an annual salary of two thousand dollars as its attorney and fifteen hundred per annum rent for the banking room; and I to allow him forty-five hundred per annum for attending to my private affairs and estate—selling lots, collecting rents, etc., as done heretofore.
>
> This arrangement to last till superseded by another or annulled by either party.
>
> Thomas Mellon

In *Judge Mellon's Sons,* W. L. writes that by this document Thomas Mellon "gave" T. Mellon & Sons to A. W.; and A. W. himself, perhaps partly in reliance upon private conversations between himself and his father, would later point to the note as the document by which he owned the business then known as the Mellon National Bank. On its face, though, the note was not an absolute gift of anything; it was an employment contract, and a revocable one at that. The meticulous and methodical Judge was to live another twenty-six years, but in that most important matter of who "owned" the banking business, he left strings untied, and if after 1882 he gave any further thought to the subject, he left no record of it. Long before the Judge's death his son, equally meticulous and methodical, was running the bank like his own, even to the point of conveying out interests in it, but apparently it never occurred to him either to have his father put the documents in appropriate order. Half a century later hard questions would be asked about rights and titles, and there would be unpleasantness among the descendants of Thomas Mellon.

At the time, though, the Judge accomplished what he had had in mind when he freed himself from his business burdens to immerse himself in other joys and sorrows. His service on the council was probably one of the sorrows, as surely was his concern for his son George.

George Negley Mellon, last born of the Judge's children, was sixteen years younger than his oldest brother, T. A., and only eight years older than his oldest nephew, W. L. He started out like any other son of Thomas Mellon, at the age of twenty superintending construction of some fifteen to twenty buildings for his father. Then in 1881 his health began to fail. He was still alive when the Judge published this account of George's early problems:

> He was not aware of the serious nature of the ailment, and disregarded it at first; and none of us supposed it to be more than the effect of a bad cold which would pass off in time. . . . If we had known the serious nature of his trouble then and had applied the proper treatment, and he had left off work for a time, his health might have been thoroughly restored in two or three months without any dangerous consequences. But neither he nor anyone else was aware that bronchitis had set in and progressed to such an extent that the upper part of his right lung had become slightly affected.

It looked like "consumption"—tuberculosis. Both father and son spent months reading everything they could find about the disease and consulting the most prestigious doctors. Finally, in the fall and winter of 1881–82, George, accompanied by his parents, went to the wholesome climate of Aiken, South Carolina, for treatment by the former chief medical officer of the Confederate Army. The Judge's regular letters home to his sons in Pittsburgh were morose:

My sorrow is great for our poor George, although I do not want him to know it. I have very poor encouragement from the doctors for his recovery. . . . It is easy for an old person to die when he has gone through and knows how little happiness compared with its troubles life affords, but it is hard for the young to die with the world and its hopes and prospects all before them untried.

George became totally preoccupied with his situation; the Judge wrote that George was constantly studying or talking about his condition. To the father he seemed "catching at everything like a drowning man catching at straws to save him." Together, father and son demoralized each other:

I believe I am the worst companion he could have. I sympathize so much with him, he can read my innermost thoughts. Every downward move of his depresses me so much it has a still further depressing effect on him. . . . It is unfortunate that he sees too clearly his condition. It is that of a man in health condemned to die, with but slight hopes of reprieve. . . . He watches the slightest change of symptom either way, and is elated or depressed accordingly. He thinks and talks about nothing else. . . . I can't admit the thought of parting with him.

Miraculously, George was granted a reprieve. His health improved to such an extent that the Judge began to dream that he might have a reasonably productive life and gainful employment in some healthier environment than Pittsburgh. Richard Beatty Mellon and George went north in search of the ideal place. They rejected Winnipeg (1972 population 548,573) as a town with no future, and instead settled in Bismarck in the booming Dakota Territory (1970 population, 34,703). (R. B. would later delight in recounting their bad judgment in the selection of Bismarck.) For the next four years R. B. was to share George's exile as his almost constant companion.

Bismarck showed promise, never realized, of being a second Chicago, and together the brothers opened a Mellon Brothers Bank there in a narrow one-story western-looking frame building. They operated a town-sized ranch on the lonely treeless prairie outside of town. In the summers they were joined by their nephew, W. L., whose later account of their lives in Dakota captures much of the flavor and mystique of the wild west of the period.

In his memoirs, published in 1885, the Judge included this capsule biography of George:

In 1880 he gave high promise of energy, industry, and first class business capacity. Although but a boy he showed the ability of a man of experience; and his ambition for active employment was so strong that when his health failed and we took him to the South, in the winter of 1881, on meeting with other invalids like himself, some of whom had spent three successive winters there, he declared that if such was to be his fate he would rather die at once than spend so much time in tedious idleness. He has become inured to it, however. The past is the fourth winter he has spent in the South. His business at Bismarck is thus so much interrupted as to destroy the continuity of regular pursuit, and what the ultimate effect will be yet remains to be seen. I still retain the hope that robust health and vigor will restore his desire and capacity for regular employment. But however that may be, or should his health not be so fully restored, I rely upon his good common sense to restrain him at all times within the bounds of his income.

Thereafter things turned bad for the Dakotas and worse for George. Adverse economic changes in 1886–87 brought a bust to the wild west, and spelled the end of the Mellon Brothers Bank, which lingered only until after George's death. After six years of survival, the family had come to believe that George had won the battle with tuberculosis, and so he had. But on a rugged wilderness journey from Bismarck to Denver he contracted spinal meningitis, and was dead of it in a matter of days. The Pittsburgh *Commercial Gazette* carried no obituary but only this routine inclusion in their deaths column: "Mellon—at Denver, Col., April 15, 1887, George N. Mellon, in the 27th year of his age. Funeral services at his paternal home, Negley Ave., East End, at 3 o'clock Wednesday afternoon. Interment private."

Such joy as there was for the Judge came not only from the successes of his healthy sons, but also from his work in writing his rich and varied memoirs, *Thomas Mellon and His Times,* from which most of the quotations in this book that are attributed to the Judge were taken. Over the course of his life the Judge wrote snatches of autobiography, many of which found their way into the memoir, but the bulk of it was written in 1884 and 1885, when the Judge was in his early seventies. W. L. later recalled the Judge at work on the book: the old man

> had preempted a storeroom in the back of the bank. In this sparsely furnished office day after day he concentrated on his message. His eyesight had failed him so nearly to the point of blindness that the letters formed by his pencil were vastly disproportionate. Nevertheless he so greatly felt the need to say what was inside of him that he finally accepted what at first he had denounced as an extravagance. Thereafter he had the help of a new, and in that time a remarkable "convenience," a stenographer. The sight of her confidently recording my grandfather's stream of words made such an impression on me as a youth that even now I seem to see her plainly, a small woman, not young at all and always encased in a duster.

Thomas Mellon and His Times is poorly organized, repetitious, and often rambling. It needed a skillful editor, and years after its publication found one in the Judge's great-grandson, Matthew T. Mellon, Ph.D., who privately printed an abridged but not expurgated edition in 1970. Despite its organizational defects, though, it is so well worded that the Judge's every digression and the ornamentation of his artful parentheticals make it a charming book even when illustrating the Judge's reactionary views. On the balance, it is outstanding literature, which today seems an unusual product from a businessman of narrow social outlook.

The book begins with a lengthy section, no doubt largely inaccurate, on the ancient history of the family, followed by many more pages, presumably correct, of biblical-style recitation of the Judge's more recent ancestors. He then traces his own life, more or less chronologically, including some excellently done vignettes on the times, such as his fascinating account of immigrant farm life in the Jacksonian era. There is wry humor (President Garfield "gets credit for a degree of piety, honesty and wisdom, surprising to his personal friends") and there is tenderness, sometimes combined with humor, as in his description of "the sweet, soft sadness of calf-love," and of his horror when, years later, he successfully sought out the recipient of his early affections. The book is ornamented with plenty of homespun advice to youth, translated from the original farm-folk patois into crisp banker's verbiage, only occasionally marred by nineteenth-century rich men's homilies ("If poverty is a cruel master you will find it also a great coward and utterly unable to withstand courage, industry and economy").

Included are critiques of the great men of literature: Shakespeare ("The fine sentiments of Shakespeare seemed to cost too much sifting among the quarrels of kings and vulgar intrigues of their flunkies, and the obsolete manners of a rude age"), and especially Burns, his favorite. He discusses contemporary philosophy at length and particularly what he calls the "New Philosophy" of Darwin, Spencer, and Huxley. He was especially impressed with Spencer, darling of the American "Social Darwinists," whom he quotes and recommends. He provides a long history and analysis, still useful, of socialist movements in Europe and America through time, up to and past Marx, and indicates a sophisticated understanding of the cleavages within the left. Somewhat less sophisticated was a little ditty about socialists that he included:

> What is a Socialist?
> One who hath yearnings
> For equal division of
> Unequal earnings.

Idler or bungler, or both
He is willing
To fork out his penny and
Pocket your shilling.

By 1885 the Judge was deeply pessimistic about the future of American government, and especially the capitalist system (". . . but I am aware of the effect of years to cast a sombre shade on men's view and opinions, and therefore would hope that these fears may be unfounded"). The book is cluttered with considerable conservative hand wringing. But it was not the left that worried Thomas Mellon so much as it was Magee and Flinn and their counterparts dominating governmental units throughout the country: "Our present danger is not from blatant social theorists, but from the ignorant hoodlum and political demagogue, void of theory or principal of any kind."

Other references throughout the book to Hume, Berkeley, Adam Smith, Ricardo, and J. S. Mill, and discussion of their thoughts, make clear that the Judge was expansively read, unemotionally analytical, and a fine thinker on a broad scale. To his sons he passed on his keen business acumen and his incessant acquisitiveness, but he failed—and from his letters to J. R. it seems he made no effort—to transmit to them his ceaseless and boundless intellectual curiosity on matters other than moneymaking. Not until the "rebellion" of subsequent generations would the family have other genuine intellectuals.

Thomas Mellon emerges from *Thomas Mellon and His Times* as irascible, rigidly strait-laced from birth and stuffy, often outrageous, thoroughly reactionary (except on matters of religion), and self-righteous (he discusses four suits brought against him in a section headed "Vexatious Litigation"). At the same time he is erudite, a poignant and charming raconteur, and an immensely likable old man. In the preface to his own autobiography, the Judge's friend Andrew Carnegie referred to the pleasure and satisfaction he had derived from *Thomas Mellon and His Times.* Carnegie wrote that "The book contains one essential feature of value—it reveals the man."

The title page announces that the book was written "for his family and descendants exclusively," and the preface tells us that the book contains "nothing which it concerns the public to know, and much which if writing for it I would have omitted." The Judge's particular hope for it was that a copy might someday "happen to fall into the hands of some poor little boy among my descendants in the distant future," and that it might "impress on him the truth of that important rule of life which demands labor, conflict, perseverance and self-denial to produce a character and accomplish purposes worth striving for. And it may tend to assure him that such a course carries with it more real satisfaction and pleasure than a life of ease and self-indulgence."

Ninety-one years after its publication, this author questioned eight of the Judge's descendants between the ages of nineteen and forty, none impoverished, and some living lives of ease if not self-indulgence. Most (but not all) claimed to have read "parts" of the book, and only two claimed to have read the whole of it. However, a respectable publisher that specializes in reprinting books deemed to be of particular historical value, has reprinted the full original volume for sale to the general public, and today it is, presumably, inspiring "poor little boys" from a wider circle than originally intended by the Judge.

When it was finally completed in August 1885, the Judge had Wm. G. Johnston & Co., Printers and Stationers, print it up, impressively bound, with *T. Mellon and His Times* gold-stamped on the spine. "Thomas" was shortened to T. so that "Mellon" could appear in larger letters than would otherwise have been possible. The publication was an act of extravagance to which the Judge was unaccustomed but one to which he was entitled. Once the book was finished, he took such justified delight in it that he let his vanity overcome his original purpose and the volume's intended privacy. He circulated it widely among his group of friends and business associates —the leaders of Pittsburgh. With its exposition of the Judge's sometimes incendiary views and its revelation of rather personal details about the lives of his sons as well as himself, the very private A. W. could only have been horrified, and according to O'Connor's *Mellon's Millions,* A. W. made some effort to round up and suppress the copies that his proud father had passed out.

Thereafter Judge Mellon continued to come regularly to the bank, as of old. He would sweep in almost every morning, past the large iron stove in the center of the main room and the double row of clerks on their high stools working in the enormous ledgers perilously perched on the high slanted tables, and would go to his desk. There was scarcely a hello. W. L. explained that "It is true that he spelled work with a capital W, but that was not the reason he came and went without greetings. Rather it was because his mind was busy incessantly." Now it was occupied with lesser demands; he would busy himself with his personal affairs: writing further voluminous autobiographical memoranda, few of which have been made public, or visiting with ingratiating young favor seekers who would listen, or feign listening, to the Judge's helpful lectures on the advantages and challenges of poverty.

One can picture the Judge as he must have appeared to his young callers. He describes himself at seventy-two as five feet nine inches tall, 160 pounds, dark eyes and dark complexion, "and thick hair once jet black though now white, but not as bald as my photograph would indicate." His face was old and lined, but clearly once quite handsome, and from the photographs his strong chin appears to have become markedly protruding in a Lincolnesque way in his old age. His expression was stern and a little forbidding. O'Connor, who grew up in Pittsburgh and whose life there overlapped the Judge's by about a decade, reports that those who knew the Judge only casually had remarked that the face "had never been seen to relax into a smile; indeed, the lines appeared so hard that a smile would have cracked the face to bits." Though the sack business suit was by then the custom, the Judge was wearing the older style of dress—a black long-skirted frock coat of the type he had worn when he was on the bench, and which he thereafter wore to the end of his days. His shirt and its separate collar were starched stiff and glossy, but the collar never quite met as it was supposed to, so one could see his Adam's apple rise and fall during his discourse:

> Poverty may be a misfortune to the weaklings who are without courage or ability to overcome it, but it is a blessing to young men of ordinary force of character: it protects them from excesses, withholds unwise pleasures and indulgences, teaches the value of time and of wealth, and the necessity of well doing to better their condition. It brings out their latent energies in a manner to train them thoroughly for the active duties of life. If I had been raised in the lap of wealth my nature would have led me to greater indulgence in ease and luxury. I would have lived higher, spent more money, indulged more in company and recreation, would in short have taken it easier. But I do not believe I would have realized as much true happiness by such increased indulgences as I did without them. . . . It requires a higher nature than the average youth possesses to resist the temptations of wealth and ease. It is not impossible, but the instances are exceptional.

Of those who heard him out, the lucky ones were rewarded with a copy of Benjamin Franklin's *Autobiography.*

Retirement, and a life such as that, however, was never for a man of the Judge's temperament. His sons had by then become rich men in their own right; "the Mellon boys" had replaced him as influences on the Pittsburgh scene, which is how he would have had it. Still, it left the Judge in an odd position for one so addicted to the active life. In his 1885 memoirs he had lamented that all, or nearly all, of my contemporaries who knew me intimately in active life, and would be interested in me or in what I might write or say, are gone; and nearly all of my friends and associates whom I would feel an interest in communicating with are gone also. To the general public which surrounds me now, I am as a stranger in a strange land.

He would either have to die or make a new life for himself, and though he was fully prepared for death, it stubbornly refused to call him. His hands were tied.

In 1890 he and Sarah Jane conveyed everything they owned to A. W. in trust for their four surviving sons. At the time there were no inheritance taxes to motivate their gift, and the Judge was surely familiar with King Lear's experience, but he had no doubt as to the fairness of his offspring, already wealthy themselves, and he had greater confidence in A. W.'s abilities and judgment than he had in his own.

As a younger man of seventy-two, he had written in his memoirs of

so many of my business contemporaries having acquired wealth in the prime of life, and letting it slip through their fingers in old age. Without prudent children or others to guard it, it is a natural consequence that a man's wealth will begin to waste away with his mental and physical energies.

Ever objective, he well knew that the same might happen to his own fortune, and he was worried about the effect of age on his own judgment and what he might do or cause A. W. to do at his insistence. True, he had already freed himself of management by his memorandum of 1882, but mere title weighed heavily upon him. In a later writing he noted, "I had attained [wealth] and had abandoned the labors and special attention necessary for the acquisition and accumulation but found I was not entirely free." So he gave it all away—according to W. L.'s later reckoning, property worth some $4 million at the time.

At last free, seventy-seven years old, nearly blind and perhaps just a bit forgetful but otherwise alert, and with a net worth of zero, he left Sarah Jane, his wife of forty-seven years; T. A.; J. R.; A. W.; R. B.; and his nine grandchildren, W. L., S. N., S. M., R. M., T. A. Jr., E. P., T. M. II, M. C., and little S. L.—and moved to Kansas City!

Kansas City, Missouri, 1890, was Pittsburgh of years before—a new young city ready for the Judge to conquer. He was soon investing in real estate and planning transportation facilities that might be feasible for the community and might earn the Judge a fresh fortune. William A. Mellon, son of the Judge's brother Samuel, was then running a small Kansas City newspaper, the *Leader,* and when the "boodlers," as the Judge called them, on the City Council turned a deaf ear to the Judge's petition for a franchise, he struck back with editorials that he drafted for the *Leader;* and according to W. L., the Judge's crusade led to investigation and indictment of several councilmen. From time to time various family members were sent out to see that the Judge was all right, but for the most part he spent five years alone in Kansas City, making a new life and a new circle for himself.

Besides its promise for the future, there was another attraction—possibly an even stronger one—that drew him to Kansas City: a celebrated medium there reputedly made the departed not only speak but also appear. In the late 1800s many respectable thinkers were investigating communication with the dead; it was the great day for "spiritualism," and a genuine interest in it was not necessarily inconsistent with Thomas Mellon's thoroughly rationalistic outlook. The Judge wanted very much to believe in the possibility that he might establish contact with the other world, and especially with his departed Selwyn. Why was that impossible? He wrote in his memoirs that "An inexplicable circumstance" at the time of Selwyn's death "was that Thomas, without any knowledge of [Selwyn's] illness whatever, had an irresistible impression that a terrible calamity was happening at home, and obtained leave of absence to solve the mystery, a day too late to see him alive." Whether or not that "irresistible impression" had been transmitted by Selwyn, T. A. had received a supernatural communication at the time of Selwyn's death. That being the fact, why was it not possible that other messages, clearer messages, might not also be transmitted? Though his sons were skeptical of spiritualism to the point of embarrassment over the Judge's interest, he attended séances in Pittsburgh, sometimes with W. L. in tow, and finally he went to the great Kansas City séance. A. W. accompanied him and either A. W. or the Judge was probably the source for W. L.'s later report of it:

> They were in a parlor gathering. When they had seated themselves in a circle, they had been asked to cross their arms in front of them and in that position to "close" the circle by grasping the hands of their neighbors. They were warned of dire consequences if the chain should be broken. This imposed on the timid a disposition to clutch almost fiercely so that any bolder ones present were really being restrained by the fearful. The medium went into a trance. From beyond some heavy portieres suddenly came cries, as from a child: "Father! Father!"
>
> The Judge for a time was sure he recognized the voice of his little dead son, Selwyn. Then, abruptly in a ghastly illuminated area between the portieres a little boy appeared, holding the handles of a toy wheelbarrow. The clothing

worn by the apparition was in the style of that worn by little Selwyn in the pictures of him in our family albums.

W. L. does not tell us what next occurred, but it seems likely that the medium overplayed the hand, because the Judge soon after concluded that spiritualism was a fraud. He would have to wait for his reunion with Selwyn.

The Judge took a rationalistic approach to religion, scoffed at the Bible as history and even as a good source for moral guidance, thought the "power of faith" to be but superstition, and disapproved of churchly types. Still he believed in a Supreme Being, and in one respect he remained tied to traditional religious supports—he retained a conventional concept of the afterlife. In an 1895 letter, at the age of eighty-two, he wrote his children that he had "very strong hope and assurance that I shall be with you all as much afterwards as before until we all meet again face to face, and I expect also to enjoy happy communion with all my children and other loved ones who have gone before me."

In his memoirs Thomas Mellon analogized that "A long life is like an ear of corn with the grains shriveled at both ends. The few years at the end of an old man's life are of as little account to him or others as the few years of childhood at its beginning." It was an old man who returned to Pittsburgh in 1895. He would live another thirteen years, and his later letters still demonstrate a crisp, able mind without a sign of loss. Matthew Mellon insists that the Judge was clear to the end, though his great-grandfather would stop his conversation mid-sentence, with his mouth open, to collect himself before completing his thought. Clear or not, the Judge's productivity was spent, and productivity was the standard by which Thomas Mellon had always judged men. By his standard the grains had shriveled. His sons were by then active in such a dizzying array of businesses—oil, steel, banking enterprises of enormous complexity, street railways and other public utilities, manufacture of railway cars, and the milling of a bright new superlight metal with great potentials—that it was beyond his patience for him to try to follow it all, even if he would have wanted to intrude himself. Occupying the days wasn't always easy. An 1897 letter to James begins

> I thought I would write you this morning as it helps me to consume time.
> Times lies heavy on one's hands when we cease to need it, but after spending
> as long a lifetime as I have done, in its profitable use, then ceasing to make
> any valuable use of it at all, is too radical a change to be agreeable.

One way that he passed the time was to have the family youngsters read
to him. His sight had been weak for decades. His own sons had read aloud
to him, then his grandchildren, and in his very last years his first great-
grandchild, Matthew Mellon, spent Sunday mornings reading aloud to him.
The Judge thereby participated in the education of descendants down the
line, and rewarded each for his labors, and for the delight that he took in
them, with a coin.

Though he cautioned his children against pleasure travel as not worth
"the worry and expense," the Judge himself had traveled much and enjoyed
and been broadened by it immensely, as is apparent from the accounts in
his memoirs of his journeys in America, Ireland, and England. Now his
traveling was limited to an occasional trip back to his father's old farm, and
to the days of his childhood. He still had friends on the farm: "The rocks
and glens, the meadows and streams, and such of the buildings and other
landmarks as remain are still my friends and acquaintances, or seem to me
so when I visit them; and appear as if they remembered me and were glad
to welcome me."

In 1973 the Pittsburgh *Press* interviewed Edgar Marts, owner of the old
Mellon farmhouse, who had himself been born in it seventy-eight years
earlier. Marts recalled that when he had been a small boy the ancient Judge
and his middle-aged unmarried son A. W., had come to visit the homestead.
His mother had fed the distinguished visitors mush and milk, which, according to Marts, the Judge had praised. "I had a toy wagon," Marts
continued, "and before they drove away in their buggy, they asked me if
I could haul money. Then each of them tossed a silver dollar into it."

Mostly, though, the Judge sat at home. It was the same home he had built
half a century before, but through time there had been additions to it—first,
a "daughter-in-law" wing for the J. R. family to occupy, and then other
rooms added here and there. Running water and plumbing were installed,
then gas lighting, followed by electricity, which the Judge's seventeen-year-
old grandson, W. L., put in in 1885; and then came the telephone. In his
sitting room within the by then rambling house, the Judge passed much of
his old age rocking, rocking; forty years after the Judge's death W. L. could
still hear him creaking back and forth.

Nearby were his family. T. A. built his own elegant home next door, and
across the street J. R. constructed his huge formal mansion. The trio of
Mellon estates became known locally as the "Mellon patch," a term later
applied to their city itself. A. W. and R. B. both built their own showy
homes not far away. R. B.'s was the showier.

In 1897, at the age of thirty-nine, the Judge's son R. B. married Jennie

Taylor King, whose family lived on property that had once been General Alexander Negley's. The Pittsburgh *Commercial Gazette* reported that it was "The most brilliant wedding ever solemnized in the East Liberty Presbyterian Church . . . undoubtedly the most important in social circles since the marriage of Miss Margaret Darlington and Mr. Stephen Bennett of Boston four and a half years ago." At the reception were presents that the press described as "unusually handsome and probably more in number than any bride in Pittsburgh has ever received before. They represented everything costly and beautiful." To house them R. B., by 1897 a rich man, built a mansion to end all mansions, a cold and dark stone monster from the outside but with some pleasant touches. When it was ultimately demolished, the Philadelphia *Inquirer* cited its caretaker as authority that it contained eleven bathrooms, including a master bath lined with $10,000 worth of Italian marble and fitted with gold-plated fixtures. The caretaker said that there were "about sixty or sixty-five other rooms"—he wasn't exactly certain. There were three terraces, each with its own formal garden: respectively, French Renaissance, Italian, and Spanish. A stagelike landscape was created with a man-made sky, a brilliant moon and stars, and an artificial lake of mirrors, ornamented with life-sized illuminated statues. (There was nothing that Judge Mellon despised so much as ostentation, but just as the Judge reflected the values of the successful people of his day, so too was R. B. in step with his times.)

W. L., twenty-eight, was also married at about the same time, to May Taylor, whose father had become close to J. R. when the two had shared sunny winters together in Palatka, Florida. The wedding was held in Palatka, removed from the Pittsburgh social scene, but almost all of the family made the journey down to attend it in March of 1896. Though the Judge had to stay at home, Sarah Jane undertook the trip. In his book *Watermellons* Matthew Mellon tells a story, possibly apocryphal, of the arrival for the wedding in Florida of the Mellon contingent. As the trainload of Mellons disembarked, W. L. initialed them out for his intended—there was T. A., and A. W., and so forth. When ancient Sarah Jane stepped down, the bride-to-be asked W. L., "Who is that, B. C.?" W. L. also built a splendid mansion not far from the Mellon patch.

There were lovely weddings, and great Victorian mansions, but there were also funerals. In 1899, T. A., the Judge's oldest son, died at the age of fifty-four. Of all the Judge's sons, T. A. grew up in the most hectic period of his father's life, and perhaps received the least attention. It seems likely that J. R., rather than T. A., was the favored of the older generation of the Judge's offspring. In one of the published letters to J. R., the Judge compliments the younger brother on his penmanship: "I would give one hundred dollars if Thomas could equal it." One wonders whether he might have chided Thomas with his younger brother's success in this and perhaps in more significant endeavors. T. A., though, in many ways paralleled his father more closely than did any of his brothers. On the surface he inherited the Judge's love of horticulture, which in T. A. became an obsession. There were other ways in which he emulated his father. Witness his approach to teaching his sons the value of money: W. L. wrote that T. A. would sometimes ask his son Edward Purcell Mellon (E. P.)

> "What are you thinking about?" Then when he heard a boyish answer he would say: "Now, now, you should be thinking of the real things of life." One time Ed wanted a bicycle and told his father that it would cost about thirty-five dollars. Uncle Tom said: "Which would you rather have: the bicycle now, or when you are twenty-one the money accumulated from that thirty-five dollars invested at six per cent?"

Like the Judge's own sons, before they were out of short pants T. A.'s T. A. II and E. P. were established as partners in an ice business. Later, at the time of T. A.'s death, they were still partners, as the Judge's sons were always partners. T. A. had established T. A. II, twenty-six, and E. P., twenty-four, as heads of the Kensington Improvement Company and Water Works, in a suburb of Pittsburgh. Like T. A. himself and most of his brothers, neither of his sons wasted any time on any extensive academic education.

Such education as T. A. had was in the Judge's little schoolhouse and at the "East End Academy." Early in life he managed the Judge's car works at Braddock, Pennsylvania, and then he became the principal in a number of coal ventures. Ultimately the lumber and coal yard and the land development ventures that he engaged in with J. R. became his principal occupation.

In 1870 T. A. married Mary C. Caldwell, another Leavenworth, Kansas, lady. She had been a Pennsylvania girl originally, but after the death of her father, Captain James Caldwell, in the Mexican War, she was raised by her older brother, Alexander Caldwell, in Leavenworth. Alexander Caldwell, like General Larimer, was an authentic western capitalist type. He was with his father when the captain met his heroic end at the Battle of Chapultepec; then he moved to Kansas, where he became a successful banker before serving two years in the United States Senate. His little sister Mary became close to General Larimer's daughter Rachel. After J. R. and Rachel married, T. A. and Mary became close. Besides their two sons T. A. and Mary also had a daughter, who bore the same name as her mother, Mary Caldwell Mellon. At the time of her father's death she was fifteen, a student at a fashionable eastern boarding school in Pelham, New York. Later she would become the first of the few strong female descendants of Judge Thomas Mellon.

T. A. loved all aspects of wildlife. He was a noted hunter, and W. L. attributes his success at it to "such a knowledge of wild creatures and their habits as entitled him to be called a naturalist." He never tired of his nature studies. He also loved his fine hunting dogs, and spent hours upon hours caring for the firearms in his impressive gun collection, portions of which are still treasured by his grandson Edward P. Mellon II (Ned).

T. A. enjoyed his retreats from Pittsburgh even more than his life within it. He and J. R. maintained a farm for their families just outside of Greensburg, about thirty miles east of Pittsburgh, where they had captive deer and even a buffalo for the endless delight of the children. He was also the first to establish a winter home in Florida; his was at Summer Haven, today a tiny community just south of St. Augustine. In those days before construction of Florida's coastal highway, it was not even dotted on the map. There he built a small pagoda-shaped cottage right on the Atlantic Ocean. Later J. R.'s family would also join him there, and today Ned and Ned's son Thomas Alexander Mellon IV (Alec) live throughout the year at Summer Haven, not a tenth of a mile from T. A.'s first cottage. The pagoda is still standing, looking very uninviting to motorists whizzing past on U.S. Route 1A.

One way that T. A. differed from his father was in his personal habits, especially with regard to tobacco. The Judge never used tobacco in any form, and in his memoirs the Judge singled it out as an evil:

> The injury resulting from stimulants is manifest to every one, but that resulting from tobacco, though less manifest, is not less certain. I have just been to see an esteemed friend, Hon. Edgar Cowan, at his home in Greensburg, who has been suddenly compelled to abandon his worldly pursuits, and prepare for death by the lingering torture of cancer in the tongue, produced by smoking, as he is advised by the best medical authorities at home and abroad, and as he fully believes from his own experience. Similarly has ex-president Grant's life been shortened by the same habit.

If he was writing for T. A., he wrote without effect. T. A. was addicted to tobacco. As W. L. told it, he made something of a fetish over his cigars:

> There were special closets down there in Uncle Tom's cellar in which his stock of cigars was stored at just the right degree of humidity. It was a brand made

and sold only in Philadelphia and called Juan Fortuando: a five-cent cigar
made of light tobacco.

Uncle Tom bought them by the thousands. He aged them carefully; and it
seemed to give him a deep satisfaction to have a great hoard of his favorite
cigars on hand. He was a tremendous smoker. Always, it seemed to me, there
was a lighted cigar in his mouth. Probably that constant smoking caused the
cancer that developed in his mouth and throat.

In his last couple of years he was compelled like the Judge's esteemed friend
to "abandon his worldly pursuits" and suffer a steady, painful decline.
Perhaps for relief from the pain he began to drink a little more heavily than
befitted a son of the Judge, who strongly disapproved of excess in the use
of what he called "stimulating beverages," and who viewed the habitual
drinker contemptuously. In his last few months T. A. II wrote his brother
from Summer Haven that their father was in constant pain.

The Judge survived the death of T. A., and lived on to enjoy many more
years of family parties. There were get-togethers for Thanksgiving, Christmas, and New Year's, with the gatherings generally rotated among the
houses at the Mellon patch; but all such celebrations were insignificant
compared to that held for the annual birthday party on February 3—
coincidentally the birthday of both the Judge and Sarah Jane. The double
celebration drew relatives and friends from a wide area, and was held
annually for as far back as W. L. could later recall, until February 3, 1908.
That day, on his ninety-fifth birthday, Thomas Mellon died. No man was
ever readier for death. He wrote in his memoirs that in old age "we are made
to see or at least feel, with the wise man, that all is vanity. And so we are
prepared to step out without regret."

On the balance, it was a happy life, and it was surely a successful life.
Thomas Mellon was the authentic Alger hero: the country boy who came
to the city—not the city, the symbol of evil as it later became, but the city,
the nineteenth-century symbol of opportunity—where he made himself a
grand success through honesty, hard work, thrift, and clean habits. He was
satisfied. In his memoirs, written twenty-three years before his death, he was
gratified to be able to write "now when nearing the end of my journey and
reviewing my past life, I find no instance where I had set my mind earnestly
on an object that I did not succeed in devising ways and means to accomplish it." For the most part the object that he set his mind on was accumulating money. His approach, though, was profoundly conservative,
too much so to enable him to become one of the tremendously wealthy men
that the second half of the nineteenth century produced.

Fate must have intended a Pittsburgher to corner the oil-refining indus-try. In the years before and after the Civil War virtually all of the world's petroleum supply came from within fifty miles of Pittsburgh, and the city's transportation facilities were superior to those of competing locations. The industry was too speculative, though, and as the Judge wrote, he never speculated "without I saw a sure thing in it." Oil was no sure thing, and so he left that field to people like that unlikely young man in unlikely Cleveland, Ohio, John D. Rockefeller, who had nothing to lose. John D., the Judge, and Andrew Carnegie shared common philosophical outlooks on almost everything. For most of the quotes in this book attributed to the Judge, parallel language, or actions indicating parallel beliefs, can be found in the writings or lives of Carnegie or Rockefeller. But the Judge lacked the imagination or vision of the others, and especially he lacked Rockefeller's willingness to take the big risk, even though it was a carefully analyzed risk. The Judge never gambled, even when the odds were with him, and so of all the important men of the age of the moguls, he remained a relatively poor man.

The Judge's public visage was crusty, and he unapproachable. He pat-terned his public self after his early mentor, Judge Shaler:

> without a spark of pride or hauteur in his disposition, he would seem on the street to those unacquainted with him the embodiment of pride and self-sufficiency. In fact, there was an air of reserve and dignified superiority about all the lawyers of the old school in those days which has long since disappeared, and as I think, much to the injury of the profession.

Thomas Mellon was a lawyer of the old school. But he was also a dynamic, hearty man with a vital interest in living and learning, and though he sampled his joys and pleasures with moderation, he enjoyed them to the hilt. He was a strong, large-egoed man, expansive and extroverted, with a well-integrated and uncomplicated personality, seemingly without emotional problems of any kind. He was almost totally without a trace of the pretense or affectation that he abhorred in others, and found too often in the "shod-dyocracy" that he saw around him. Among his own, he did not lack the qualities of warmth or generosity.

Little has been said here of Sarah Jane, who followed her husband a year later; unfortunately there is almost no source material available on her. Such data as we have about her as a young lady comes from the Judge's account of their courtship, during which she was proper if not chilly. He reports that on their wedding trip they were on shipboard for a dangerous crisis and it was then, the Judge noted, that he "first noticed my wife's entire command of her feelings in the suppression of every sign of fear or alarm."

We get a later glimpse of Sarah Jane in middle age from a couple of her letters published by the family in 1935 in which she appears a somewhat doting mother. It is clear from her previously quoted letter on the subject of J. R.'s proposed enlistment in the Union Army that by that time she was no longer the iceberg of her youth, capable of "the suppression of every sign of fear or alarm." The awkward prose of her correspondence to J. R. seems especially unlearned when printed, as it was, sandwiched between the Judge's fine letter-essays.

For Sarah Jane as an old lady we can draw upon Matthew Mellon's remembrances of her; he recalled his great-grandmother as quiet, "over pleasant" but otherwise stiff, and always dressed up to the neck with things wrapped around her neck. She busied herself among her collections of photos of presidential log cabins and the like and scrapbooks filled with mottos and maxims. Sarah Jane died on January 19, 1909, at the age of ninety-one, unexpectedly and without suffering ill health. Her obituary in the Pittsburgh *Dispatch* noted her lifelong interest in her favorite charity, Pittsburgh's Home for Aged Protestant Couples.

BOOK II

The Rolling-Up of a Fortune

To catch dame Fortune's golden
  smile,
Assiduous wait upon her;
And gather gear by every wile
That's justified by honour

—ROBERT BURNS
"EPISTLE TO A YOUNG FRIEND"

W ith George gone and the Dakota boom turned to bust, there was nothing to hold Richard B. in Dakota territory. He closed up the Mellon Brothers Bank and returned home to Pittsburgh in 1887, unemployed at twenty-nine. His father, seventy-four, was for all practical purposes retired. His older brothers, Thomas A., forty-three, and James R., forty-one, were both married; T. A. with three children, J. R. with five, both independent of the paternal homestead and well established as partners in the lumber and development business in which they continued as partners, and in their own bank, City Deposit Trust, which they got into after memories of the 1873 panic had faded. Of his brothers, only A. W., thirty-two, still lived with the old folks at "401"—401 Negley Avenue, the Judge's mansion, to which R. B. returned.

No doubt external pressure was unnecessary; like any true son of the patriarch, A. W. made room for his brother not just at "401" but in the bank. He took R. B. in as his full partner. There was no written document setting forth the terms of the partnership that lasted for over thirty years, until 1918, when changes in tax laws, developments in the laws of partnership, and considerations of estate problems in the event of death dictated a formalization of their relationship. They were just partners on a word, and surely they made, simultaneously, one of the most unlikely and one of the most successful partnerships in history.

Differences in the brothers' appearances were not simply superficial but were reflective of the fuller picture. A. W. was an elegant man in every way, and most obviously in appearance. His face was cameolike, finely chiseled yet strong. His chilly blue eyes were sunk deeply into their setting; the nose was longish and a bit equine; his mustache was short-cropped, dignified, and always carefully trimmed. He had a firm, square chin. His porcelain ears looked to have been separately cast. His hair and mustache were a reddish brown, but one suspects that both were white long before they were supposed to be. It was an open face, free from any negative tinges such as John D. Rockefeller's sharklike smile. Of all the Judge's sons, he alone could fairly have been called handsome. (J. R. was not bad-looking, but T. A. and R. B. were.) His hands were long-fingered and graceful. He was short, lean, always neatly and conservatively dressed. He looked almost fragile.

A. W. was shy, painfully shy; the gifted writer Lucius Beebe, an intimate of a later generation of Mellons, called it a "measureless shyness." A lot of it was self-effacement and diffidence, which manifested itself in the apologetic tone so often in his voice. His small constrained signature is reflective of his humility and modesty as well as his tightness. He valued his money greatly, but he valued his privacy equally; and just as he did not like to bother anyone else, he preferred to be left alone himself. Few dealt with him directly; according to W. L., "there were many important employees of the bank who knew A. W. scarcely at all. If the latter had just been haunting the place, he could scarcely be less visible to most of them." The richer he got, the more he withdrew. W. L. said that he "really liked to talk with anyone in whose company he felt at ease," but there must have been very, very few of those. People who did speak with him found him formal, without much give to him but polite, even courtly, and instinctively courteous. He gave his full attention to whomever was on the other side of the desk. He himself did little of the talking, and when he spoke he spoke so softly that his listener often had to strain to hear his words. It was as if speaking required a tremendous exertion on his part to overcome that "measureless shyness," perhaps heightened by self-consciousness over his insignificant speech defect. A relative and an unconnected government associate both described him privately as "sweet." A. W. regarded his own thought processes as "slow," and in approaching a business proposition he was as profoundly conservative as the Judge himself.

It is difficult to understand how such a man could abide being in business with one such as Richard B. Mellon, a bear of a man, bearlike in disposition as well as in physiognomy. R. B. was always stocky, his face oval, the most obvious aspect of it being the same domineering ruddiness that marked J. P. Morgan's countenance. He was as hearty and full-blooded as his brother was delicate. He enjoyed having a good time, while A. W. never seemed to know what fun was. He was as witty as A. W. was formal. He was as gregarious as his brother was anthropophobic. He liked society and Society, and while A. W. retreated from people, R. B. immersed himself in them. He knew just about everyone, and at the bank he was accessible to just about everyone. Not even W. L. deigned to call A. W. "Andy," but hundreds claimed to be intimates of "Dick." Many of them were. On the other hand, R. B. lacked A. W.'s calm and even-tempered disposition. W. L. wrote that "Dick was often out of temper but never for long." His moments of distemper may have been brief but they were horrible. He might do something like humiliate a customer on the crowded banking floor. Once he served on a board with the brothers' most trusted underling, Howard Johnson. After R. B. had expressed his view, Johnson began, "I beg to differ with you, Mr. Mellon." R. B. was in one of his moods; he exploded with denigrating language about Johnson's status in life and then hurled an inkwell at his trembling employee.

R. B. tried to be the cultured person that A. W. was, but it didn't work. He had his Reynolds and his Gainsborough, but they were poor examples, and frequent visitors to the house never heard anyone play the prominently displayed organ. What R. B. preferred were the mementos of his life in the Dakota territory: the garish buffalo-horn hatrack that he proudly displayed in his entrance hall (to the horror of his wife, Jennie), his creditable collection of lithographs of notable Indian chiefs; a taxidermied *half* of a buffalo head. As cosmopolitan as A. W. became, R. B. remained a provincial who lived and died in Pittsburgh. This aspect of R. B. had its positive side. He was civic minded and was personally active in city planning efforts. It bothered him that so many men—Carnegie, Frick, Schwab—grew rich on Pittsburgh, only to abandon it once wealthy for "better" places.

In business R. B. was probably the more imaginative of the two, and he was certainly the more impetuous. A. W. approached things from Methuselah's vantage, while R. B. was more decisive. About the only thing that the two seemed to have in common was their incessant acquisitiveness.

If there was a forlorn quality to A. W. reminiscent of some character from an Edwin Arlington Robinson poem, R. B. was equally suggestive of Sinclair Lewis's most renowned protagonist—right down to the plaque that adorned his desk: "It can be done!"

From 1887 until R. B.'s death in 1933 these two were partners; until A. W. became Secretary of the Treasury in 1921, partners in almost everything, and thereafter partners in almost everything except the bank. When either one decided to buy a stock, he frequently ordered a like amount for the other. If either made a contribution, he might give a like amount from his brother's money in the other's name. They approached the world as one; both began to use the phrase "My brother and I . . ." with such regularity that it became a cliché in upper-crust Pittsburgh circles. Over the years their three locked leather wallets grew fatter and fatter. One contained securities standing in A. W.'s name; another of about the same thickness and value was R. B.'s; and a third contained securities which they held jointly, sometimes in both names, frequently in the name T. Mellon & Sons, and sometimes in the name of some nominee. A trusted employee, Henry A. Phillips, held the key to the locks and kept track of the inventories. Another employee, Walter Mitchell, who came to the bank in 1870 and remained there until he died sixty years later, presided over the blue ledger and the yellow ledger, one recording the brothers' purchases and sales of securities, and the other their transactions in real estate.

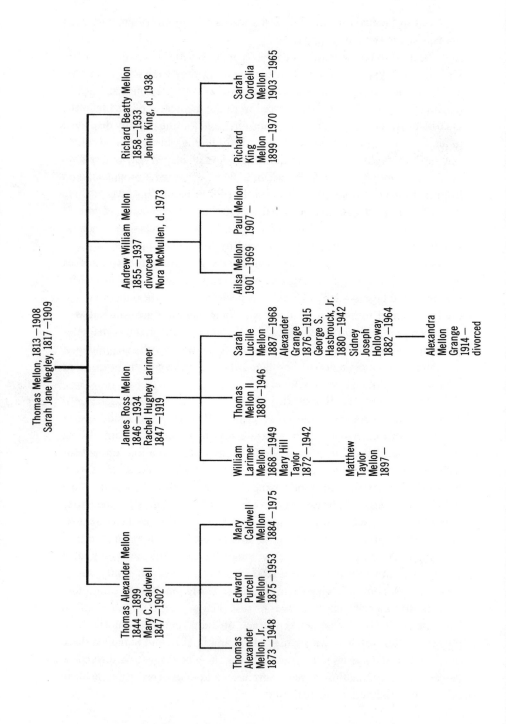

Thomas Mellon, 1813 –1908
Sarah Jane Negley, 1817 –1909

Thomas Alexander Mellon
1844 –1899
Mary C. Caldwell
1847 –1902

James Ross Mellon
1846 – 1934
Rachel Hughey Larimer
1847 –1919

Andrew William Mellon
1855 –1937
divorced
Nora McMullen, d. 1973

Richard Beatty Mellon
1858 –1933
Jennie King, d. 1938

Thomas
Alexander
Mellon, Jr.
1873 –1948

Edward
Purcell
Mellon
1875 –1953

Mary
Caldwell
Mellon
1884 – 1975

William
Larimer
Mellon
1868 –1949
Mary Hill
Taylor
1872 –1942

Thomas
Mellon II
1880 –1946

Sarah
Lucille
Mellon
1887 –1968
Alexander
Grange
1876 –1915
George S.
Hasbrouck, Jr.
1880 –1942
Sidney
Joseph
Holloway
1882 –1964

Ailsa Mellon
1901 –1969

Paul Mellon
1907 –

Richard
King
Mellon
1899 –1970

Sarah
Cordelia
Mellon
1903 –1965

Matthew
Taylor
Mellon
1897 –

Alexandra
Mellon
Grange
1914 –
divorced

At the bank their offices were adjacent, small, scantily furnished work-rooms, separated only by a swinging door of early-saloon design. Later they each ordered identical mahogany desks, marvelous desks equipped with disappearing shelves which, when drawn, transformed the desks into immense tables on which large plans or blueprints might be unrolled.

Lunch was together, usually at Pittsburgh's staid Duquesne Club—still the most respectable luncheon spa for the elite of Pittsburgh's business community, the membership still closed to females. In time they began to lunch daily with the same group of men, the most high-powered clique in the history of Pennsylvania: the Mellons; Judge James Reed, brilliant attorney for Carnegie Steel and the Pennsylvania Railroad; Henry Clay Frick; Philander C. Knox, later U.S. Attorney General and Secretary of State; John G. Leishman, erstwhile ambassador and erstwhile president of Carnegie Steel; later U.S. senator David A. Reed; and W. L., president of Gulf Oil. When there were guests, they were important guests. Even on Sundays the two brothers were together, working and analyzing on the day of rest, sometimes with a top executive from one of the businesses that they backed.

The success of the partnership was so great that today the riches of their combined heirs, their foundations, and their heirs' foundations exceeds the combined wealth of any other American family, including foundations. Mostly it was A. W.'s success. Family members agree with the judgment of history that he was the keener of the two intellectually, and the dominant member of the team. Still, R. B. had his important part in their success. He attracted most of the bank's routine business, which would have been driven away by A. W.'s unapproachability; and on the bigger matters his adventuresome spirit was a healthy antidote to his brother's overriding conservatism.

By the time that A. W. went to Washington in 1921, the outline of their enterprises had been filled in. Its major divisions at that time were Gulf, Alcoa, the Union Trust and Mellon National Bank (as it was by then known), Carborundum Company, Koppers, Standard Steel Car, Pittsburgh Coal, McClintic-Marshall Company, Mellon Securities, and Union Insurance. R. B. was left behind in Pittsburgh to oversee the able management of each. During R. B.'s stewardship the Mellon companies blossomed. It seems likely that either of them would have been able to turn their father's wealth into an impressive fortune. Together, they were stronger still.

Then there was Frick. The friendship of Henry Clay Frick and A. W. was as close as either of them was capable of closeness. Frick was about the only man to rise to the top of the Pittsburgh heap who wasn't a Scot. He was born in 1849, six years before A. W., to a farmer of Swiss descent. His mother, from "better" stock, was an Overholt from the wealthy Mennonite family already justly famed for their Old Overholt whiskey. Frick himself had limited formal education, terminated when he was sixteen, and thereafter he worked in various clerkly positions. In 1871 he was twenty-one years old and overpaid at $1000 a year as a bookkeeper in his grandfather's distillery, when he established Frick & Company with assorted relatives to build and operate "coke ovens" to refine the neighborhood's soft coal into the higher grade fuel required by new innovations in the steel industry. Frick & Company managed to accumulate 123 acres of coal lands and build a few modest ovens, but Frick had far bigger plans. The upstart's schemes were only presumptuous because of what might have seemed an inability to obtain financing. He called on Judge Thomas Mellon.

Judge Mellon's father had been friendly with Frick's maternal grandfather, Abraham Overholt, and the Judge himself had known Frick's mother from the time that she had been a little girl; but Thomas Mellon did not lend money on sentimentality. He lent money on security and on the quality of the promise. Frick asked $10,000 for six months at 10 per cent with which he might build fifty coke ovens; he offered Frick & Company's undeveloped acreage as security. He described the coking process and the increased importance of the higher grade fuel to the steel industry. Judge Mellon had more than a little feel for the subject. Much of his own money was in coal lands and he no doubt appreciated that a large-scale coking industry promised to increase the value of his own acreage. He was impressed by the young man's understanding of his subject and his wealth of detail.

Frick got the loan, and before his first fifty ovens were completed he came back for another $10,000 for an additional fifty. This time the Judge sent out an agent to evaluate what could be seen. The agent's report was not encouraging; he was displeased that Frick devoted time to other affairs such as sideline bookkeeping work and to his interest in "prints and sketches." The Judge was likewise unimpressed by an interest in "prints and sketches," but the fact that Frick held other remunerative employment struck him as a recommendation rather than a negative sign. For another opinion he sent another agent, this time his old coal-mining partner, James B. Corey. Corey reported, "Land's good, ovens well built; manager on job all day, keeps books evenings, may be a little too enthusiastic about pictures but not enough to hurt; knows business down to the ground; advise making the loan." Frick got the money; his hundred ovens were soon turning a profit; the loans were being repaid on schedule; and Frick himself was becoming a success by the time of the depression of 1873, which hit coal-related enterprises as hard as any.

As the price of coal and coke dropped, the value of coal lands dropped with it. Most coal producers halted production, but Frick decided it would cost him more to stop and later resume than it would cost him to weather the storm, selling without profit if necessary. So he did. In the next few years owners of coal lands saw their properties become unsalable at any price except to young Mr. Frick. Little by little he became the owner of the most desirable coal properties in the Connellsville Coal District, with its abundance of low-phosphorus coal ideal for coking. Finally his determination was rewarded. By the late 1870s the steel industry overcame the depression of '73; its demands for coke began to rise, and by then Henry Clay Frick controlled Connellsville coal. He could push the price of coke to its older levels and beyond, and he did. It moved from ninety cents up to five dollars a ton; and Henry Clay Frick, aged thirty, became a millionaire. By that time he had become friendly with the Judge's son.

Frick had been doing business with T. Mellon & Sons for several years before the Judge and Frick stopped at the son's desk for a brief introduction in 1876. Soon after, A. W., twenty-two, accepted an invitation to join Frick, twenty-eight, for a weekend at Frick's place outside of Pittsburgh. Thereafter the younger man was frequently with Frick. In 1880 Frick celebrated his new millionaire's status by taking a European tour; A. W. went along with him and saw a new world. Among other things A. W. brought back from Europe was a memory that was to replay itself in his mind throughout his life. He later recalled for Lucius Beebe "listening when I awoke in the morning to the clopping of horses' hooves on the wooden blocks which paved the street under my window at Brown's [Hotel]. It seemed to me they were the everlasting voice of London, those horses' hooves." Thereafter A. W. and Frick would return to Europe many times together, almost always stopping in London, and A. W.'s love for England and things English grew. A. W. also brought back his first painting, for which this conservative man paid $1000—a huge sum at the time. His father's contemporaries were aghast. Over the years A. W.'s love for paintings grew too.

Frick's successes proceeded geometrically and revolved principally around his off-again, on-again relations with Andrew Carnegie and the Carnegie steel interests. In 1882 the Frick coke and Carnegie steel interests began merging, and in 1889 Frick became chairman of the board of Carnegie Steel. Frick was in charge at the time of the Homestead Strike against one of Carnegie's huge plants in 1892, a key incident in the history of American labor relations. Carnegie, reputedly "soft" on labor, was loved by the lowliest of his employees; either by coincidence or design, he was out of the country at the time of the strike. Whichever, the other major stockholders of Carnegie Steel were pleased by his momentary exile. One of them,

Henry Phipps, later explained that "We were of the opinion that the welfare of the company required that he should not be in this country at this time. We knew of his extreme disposition to always grant the demands of labor, and all rejoiced when we were permitted to manage the affair in our own way." Carnegie's absence left Frick, the heavy, in control. Frick was not soft on labor, nor was he loved. New Deal senator Joseph F. Guffey later described Frick as "without question the most cold-blooded man I have ever known—absolutely without trace of any sympathy for the working man. Loss of life meant nothing to Frick." While personal differences may have prompted Guffey to overstatement, it is clear that Frick was without that tinge of sentiment or sentimentalism, whichever it was, that gave Carnegie his touch of warmth. The specter of Frick made labor equally resolute. "It wasn't a question of dollars," one of the rank and file later told Carnegie. "The boys would have let *you* kick them, but they wouldn't let that other man stroke their hair."

Frick imported strikebreakers, and labor reacted with violence; Frick's Pinkertons met the violence with volleys of bullets and eventually won. In the course, Frick himself was shot and wounded by the anarchist Alexander Berkman, now a folk hero to the far left, largely because of his romantic association with Emma Goldman. Frick proved that no matter what else, he was courageous. "Don't kill him!" he shouted at his bodyguards as they tussled with the anarchist, ". . . but raise his head and let me see his face." Judge Mellon wrote Carnegie his approbation of Frick's conduct of the battle against what he called "labor parasites"; later his son's corporations would emulate Frick's labor policies.

Frick's greatest triumph, in the literature if not in fact, was the part he played in engineering the creation of United States Steel by J. P. Morgan, who in 1901 bought out Carnegie Steel for too much money as the key component of Morgan's great new United States Steel Corporation. Frick's own fortune grew astronomically by the Morgan syndicate's purchase.

Frick was as different from A. W. as R. B. was, and then some. On the surface Frick was a dandy in his dress and affectations, paralleling A. W.'s elegance; and A. W. sometimes approached Frick's financial brilliance, but R. B. was much closer to Frick's personal style. To R. B.'s robustness, Frick added a creative earthiness. Among his famous lines, Frick is supposed to have said of President Theodore Roosevelt, "We bought the bastard, but he didn't stay bought." After a final bitter falling out with Carnegie, Carnegie mellowed in old age and sent an intermediary to Frick in hopes of arranging a reconciliation before Carnegie's death. Frick, so the books tell us, gave the emissary a cruel rebuff: "Tell Mr. Carnegie I'll see him in hell."* Talk of that sort was so totally foreign to a person of A. W.'s sensibilities that it is hard to understand how A. W. could be friendly with such a man, but one of the quirks of his personality was the delight he took in having associates of more flamboyant nature than himself.

Over the years the involvement between the Mellons and Frick grew complex; they were partners in innumerable businesses, including each other's family businesses. The Mellons bought a one-third interest in the Overholt distillery for $25,000 in 1887 (which they sold in 1915 for $675,-000); Frick became a stockholder in the Mellon National Bank, successor to T. Mellon & Sons, and its allied institution, the Union Trust Company; and he sat on their boards of directors together with his associate Henry Phipps. Frick's great fortune functioned through the Mellon banks, which gave the Mellons greater influence over Pittsburgh finance than they would otherwise have enjoyed. They worked together in numerous joint ventures, some of which are catalogued later in this book, many of which are now impossible to trace, but which, according to their mutual associate Colonel George Harvey, occupied much of A. W.'s time. Even after Frick's death in 1919, the Frick and Mellon interests remained intertwined. A. W. took a seat as trustee overseeing Frick's huge trust estate, while Frick's son, Childs Frick, a paleontologist of some note, took his father's place on the board of the Mellon National Bank, where he remained until after A. W.'s death almost twenty years later.

Besides the Judge, Frick was the other great teacher in A. W.'s life. He taught A. W. about art, how to buy it and perhaps to some extent to appreciate it; about politics, how to live in the same world and make peace with the Magees and the Flinns that the Judge had abhorred and denounced, for the mutual advantage of both the bosses and the businessmen; about business, how to think and work in bigger arenas than those of his mercantile-banker father. The Judge's devotion to the society of bygone days of smaller business and industrial units made him unwelcoming of the big industry that brought his sons greater wealth than he might ever have dreamed possible.

The bank served as the seat of the Mellon operations, though in time it became one of the less important of their enterprises in its own right. In the late 1800s goods were often sold with a three- or four-month grace period between date of delivery and due date for payment. The signed notations as to amounts due were sold at some discount to bankers, who would hold

---

*And no doubt he did.

them until maturity and then collect the full amount. While bankers also dealt in land mortgages, the bulk of a private banker's business at the time was in such unsecured commercial paper. T. Mellon & Sons did a big trade in these documents. In addition to their own and Frick's money, their depositors included none other than Carnegie himself, whose papers at the Library of Congress include deposit slips from the bank and its annual reports, indicating that Carnegie followed the progress of his friend's sons. Soon T. Mellon & Sons was the largest private bank between New York and Chicago.

T. Mellon & Sons did a somewhat limited form of banking business; to expand the range of their operations, the Mellons organized the Fidelity Title and Trust Company together with Frick and a few other investors in hopes of garnering some of the lucrative business of handling trust estates and related work. Fidelity quickly found that it had a lot of business that it would have to send over to rival trust companies in order to avoid "conflict of interest" situations prohibited by law if not by ethics, so it established its own "rival." In 1889 Fidelity gave birth to Union Transfer and Trust Company. As W. L. explains it, Fidelity's stockholders could then "keep for themselves the profits of business which under existing circumstances they were obliged to let go adrift." Union opened its offices in the Fidelity Building with A. W. as its nominal, unpaid president. Union's original purpose and its original name proved to be less than adequate. The volume of referral business from Fidelity proved to be insufficient to support a separate entity, while the word "Transfer" in Union's name attracted a healthy volume of inquiries about Union's imagined moving and warehousing services.

The name was soon shortened to Union Trust Company, and in 1894 A. W. urged that Union either fold up or expand its scope of operations in the hope of becoming a significant profit maker. He urged the latter. Most of Fidelity's other stockholders preferred neither, so A. W. and Frick bought them out. Of Union's original 5000 shares, A. W. emerged with almost half, or 2400, and Frick held another 1500 giving them some 80 per cent between them. The revived corporation brought in James S. McKean, Pittsburgh's former postmaster, to replace A. W. and serve as Union's full-time president, and to open street-floor locations for general banking business. Union retained its intimate relationship with the private firm of T. Mellon & Sons, but in the eyes of most uninitiated Pittsburghers, it quickly outshone the older bank. In 1899 Union moved into a main office described by Edward White in *A Century of Banking in Pittsburgh* (1903) as second to none in the United States for convenience, elegance and general security . . . one of the handsomest and most substantial structures of its kind in the country. It is richly furnished in the costliest of marbles and the rarest of woods and is fitted and furnished with every device of convenience and comfort that modern handicraft could suggest.

McKean died in 1900. At that time Henry Clay McEldowney was thirty-two and held a thoroughly respectable position for one of his age as assistant cashier of the Pittsburgh National Bank. McEldowney was of lowly origins; his father had been a house painter, and McEldowney had begun his banking career at the lowest rung: messenger. A. W. detected his real talent and suggested him to Frick as McKean's successor. Frick thought him too young until A. W. wired Frick from a vacation spa in Europe reminding Frick of Frick's own successes by the age of thirty-two. McEldowney was hired and remained for thirty-five years, becoming in time the nation's highest-paid bank officer and one of a small handful that made up the Mellons' inner coterie of associates and advisers. So close were his involvement and his public association with the Mellon family that by the time of publication of Edward White's *Century of Banking in Pittsburgh,* Henry Clay McEldowney had ceased to exist: Union's president had become H. C. McEldowney.

H. C.—with the resources of the Mellons and Frick and propitious times for Pittsburgh banking—guided Union to its important place in the history of banking and the history of the Mellon family fortune. In the period 1898 to 1902 the demand for financing in Pittsburgh increased so greatly that interest on deposits attracted considerable out-of-state money, much of it to Union. By the time of White's book in 1903, Union's capital surplus of $16 million exceeded that of the Bank of England or the combined capital surplus of all forty-one national banks in Boston. McEldowney led Union through the great period of expansion and absorption.

In 1902 Union took over the Citizens National Bank, and established its own subsidiary, the Union Savings Bank, with offices in the "Frick Building." Union Savings paid an impressive 4 per cent per year on deposits, more generous than was available anywhere else in the world, and attracted depositors from all over with its innovative "banking by mail" promotions. The following year Union Trust absorbed the Farmers Deposit National Bank and Farmer's subsidiaries, the Farmers Deposit Trust Company and Reliance Life Insurance Company. Later, in 1918, it bought out the majority interest in J. R.'s City Deposit Bank.

T. Mellon & Sons continued to function as a separate entity only until

1902. That year it joined the national banking system as a federally chartered bank with a new name, Mellon National Bank, and was immediately
bought up by Union Trust. The Mellons wanted to consolidate the organization of their banking interests and regarded Union as the more appropriate vehicle to be the "parent" corporation. Mellon National became an
almost wholly owned subsidiary of Union, which increased its capitalization to effectuate the acquisition. Union's shares were doubled to 10,000,
3000 of which were used to buy the "good will" of Mellon National Bank,
valued at $1 million. After reshuffling between themselves, A. W. and Frick
each came out with 2750 shares, and R. B. with another 1500. The Mellons
then dominated a much larger bank, which controlled the one originally
founded by their father as well as several others. In 1903 Union's Mellon
National Bank absorbed the Pittsburgh National Bank of Commerce; later,
in 1913, it took over the business of the Federal National Bank.

The branches of Union Trust, Union Savings, and Mellon National increased in number, and huge new buildings were constructed for their main
offices: the magnificent Union Trust Building at the corner of Fifth and
Grant Streets in downtown Pittsburgh, built in 1923 in late Flemish Gothic
style, followed by the Mellon National Bank Building nearby, a "Greek
temple" erected on the site of the Judge's iron-fronted bank, which opened
the next year. Both modifications of traditional architectural types, they are
nonetheless among the most aesthetically appealing of all the buildings
associated with the Mellons.

A number of satellite businesses developed alongside the Mellon banking
interests. In 1883 T. Mellon & Sons purchased the Union Insurance Company; Union Trust got into the underwriting and distributing of corporate
securities, eventually spinning off Mellon Securities to handle the business;
and in 1908 they acquired and began to operate a travel agency that with
time became wholly absorbed as a bureau of the Mellon National Bank.

With Union Trust and Union Savings as Pennsylvania banks, and Mellon
National a federally chartered corporation, the Mellons then had available
to them the best working advantages and benefits of both state and federal
banking systems. Combined, the Mellon banks could finance virtually any
enterprise or undertaking in America, and bankers and industrialists within
hundreds of miles turned to the Union-Mellon network as the bankers'
bank. Before his death Judge Mellon's sons had become the most influential
bankers between the coasts.

Banking made for profits from banking, but much more. It meant opportunities for the Mellons to invest their own money in enterprises promising

far greater return than a fixed rate of interest. Of those enterprises still retaining an important role in the Mellon family portfolio, the earliest of them to attract the Mellons was aluminum. They made their first loans to the new industry when A. W. was thirty-four, and R. B. thirty-one.

Aluminum is one of the most common elements that go to make up the earth's surface, but how economically to transform the planet's crust into shiny paper-thin flip-top beverage cans puzzled metallurgical engineers for more than a century after man first became aware of aluminum's independent existence in the eighteenth century. Early in the nineteenth century German scientists succeeded in isolating pure aluminum but at a cost that made aluminum the world's most expensive substance. It was saved for such symbolic uses as the glans of the Washington Monument. Finally in the 1880s several experimenters elaborating on earlier efforts discovered more or less simultaneously the "electrolytic" process for refining aluminum which promised to reduce its costs to such a level as would at last allow its practical use. Among those shouting eureka was Charles Martin Hall (always referred to as such, and with reverence, by employees of Aluminum Company of America), who made his discovery in what his biographer refers to as "the Immortal Woodshed." Inasmuch as Hall's Pittsburgh Reduction Company, later known as Aluminum Company of America, or more commonly as Alcoa, won the crucial patent litigation, he must be regarded (at least outside of Germany, France and Scandinavia) as the "inventor" of aluminum.

Hall was a young student at Oberlin College when his chemistry professor, F. F. Jewett, spoke words suborning of alchemy: "If anyone should invent a process by which aluminum could be made on a commercial scale, not only would he be a benefactor to the world but he would also be able to lay up for himself a great fortune." Hall was inspired. Turning to a classmate, he whispered, "I'm going for that metal." At the age of twenty-two he found it, thereby insuring his place as a benefactor to the world.

The lesser matter of the laying up of the fortune was a mite more difficult. No one wanted to finance an experimental plant that would be the acid test of the commercial feasibility of the Hall process. After several turn-downs, Hall ended up in Pittsburgh at the offices of the Pittsburgh Testing Laboratory of Captain Alfred Ephraim Hunt and his partner George Clapp, two pioneer metallurgists who had already won renown for innovations in the steel industry. According to the institutional history, Hunt and Clapp put their faith in the brilliant young inventor. Not only that, they also put up money. They organized a group of five friends to invest a total of $20,000 to form the Pittsburgh Reduction Company and build a small factory. Hall devoted all of his waking hours to the business, at $100 a week, and was becoming haggard from overwork when Hunt brought in relief for him by adding to the factory's minuscule staff Arthur Vining Davis (Ar. Vi. Da., as in Arvida, the name Davis later used for his own corporation and foundation), young son of a Hunt family friend and fresh out of Amherst College. Thereafter, Hall and Davis split the day, each working twelve-hour shifts supervising the production of ingots, supplanted by Captain Hunt, who gave the better part of his remaining few years to the young industry's white-collar needs. Hunt died a relatively young man of forty-four in 1899, but his son, Roy Hunt, and Roy's sons, Alfred and Tod (Torrence) inherited the captain's continuing interest in the Pittsburgh Reduction Company and devoted their own lives to the firm. Captain Hunt's grandsons remain as officers of the company today.

By 1889 the Pittsburgh Reduction Company needed money—$4000 with which to honor an overdue loan. The company's promise was obvious, if uncertain, but its balance sheet was embarrassing; it had not yet shown a profit and its production was insignificant. None of the Pittsburgh Reduction crowd were familiar with the Mellons, but through a mutual associate an introduction was secured. According to the literature, including W. L.'s *Judge Mellon's Sons* (but skeptically viewed by this author), Hunt, Clapp, and Davis appeared at A. W.'s office and mystified him with a highly burnished lump of Hall's genius. In any event, A. W. also had faith. After he and R. B. inspected the company's tiny plant on Smallman Street, A. W. advised the officers that they needed considerably more money than just the pressing $4000. He advanced their immediate needs and extended a line of credit to insure working capital. Thereafter the Mellons and the Mellon banks were the bankers for an industry, though as late as 1903 the Mellon brothers continued to require the personal endorsement on Pittsburgh Reduction's loans of Hunt, Hall, or Davis.

Not long after his first contact with aluminum, A. W. made his first purchase of stock in Pittsburgh Reduction. On January 16, 1890, he acquired 60 of the corporation's 10,000 shares from those assigned to Hall himself, for $100 a share. While the company's balance sheet was still bleak, the likelihood that its promise would be realized had become a probability. In the years that followed, the Mellons increased their holdings. By May of 1894 they held 1235 shares, or 12.35 per cent; in 1917 they acquired 1438 shares held by wealthy Pittsburgh lumberman David L. Gillespie, thereby increasing their interest to 26.73 per cent; by 1920 their interests were about a third. Finally they rounded out their holdings in the mid-1920s to 35.22 per cent of the common and 35.22 per cent of the corporation's preferred stock.

The Mellon brothers' front role in Alcoa's business was minimal. A. W. first joined its board in 1891 and briefly served as corporate treasurer in 1892, while R. B. was Alcoa's nominal president for eleven years after Hunt's death until 1910; but throughout their office-holding period, they deferred to Davis as the active head of management. Hall remained active in the business until his premature death in 1914, but he devoted himself to technological aspects; Arthur Vining Davis was the great builder of Alcoa. A. W. later said, "I have depended entirely on Mr. Davis. You might say that he was practically the whole business." The Mellon brothers, however, were tremendously enthusiastic about aluminum. The Mellon National Bank installed 10,000 aluminum safety deposit boxes (though aluminum would not seem to be particularly desirable for such use and still remains "second" in that market); during A. W.'s tenure as Secretary of the Treasury, aluminum became an important component in government buildings; R. B. personally approached Nicholas Murray Butler to urge his use of aluminum furniture in a new New York Life Insurance building; in a rare lapse into ostentation, A. W. purchased one of the nation's two all-aluminum autos. R. B. drove the other. Moreover, the Mellons kept a close eye on important doings. They had learned one unhappy business lesson from *Thomas Mellon and His Times:* Don't trust to partners. They involved themselves in essentials to the point that A. W. personally accompanied Davis on inspections of potential hydroelectric power sources—an essential element in the aluminum industry—however remote and inaccessible a dam site might be. A. W. is credited with having inspired the integration of operations that marked all of the Mellon enterprises. For the most part Alcoa owned its own power sources, its own sources of bauxite, the richest aluminum-bearing ore, its own transportation facilities, its own rolling mills and fabricating plants, its own sales outlets. By the time that A. W. became Secretary of the Treasury, Alcoa's subsidiaries and affiliates numbered in the dozens, many with foreign names.

Just as the Mellons credited Davis with this accomplishment, Davis came to regard the Mellons, his chief stockholders, his chief bondholders, and his chief sounding boards, as the whole show. "This company really consists of A. W. Mellon and R. B. Mellon," he told the Federal Trade Commission in the 1920s. Whether Davis was right, or whether A. W. was right in describing Davis as "practically the whole business," together they were unquestionably correct. When the Mellons' 35.22 per cent was put together with the stock that Davis owned in his own right and that which he voted as trustee for Hall's estate, the Mellons and Davis owned more than half the stock, and all of the control, of the Aluminum Company of America.

By 1891 Alcoa's Smallman Street plant was hopelessly overburdened with orders. That year the Burrell Improvement Company, a real estate firm connected with T. Mellon & Sons, made an offer that couldn't be refused. Burrell was developing a new community, New Kensington, Pennsylvania, nineteen miles north of Pittsburgh. If Pittsburgh Reduction would relocate, becoming the nucleus of the Burrell development, it could have a four-acre site for free with a $10,000 bonus from Burrell to help in construction of a new plant. The Smallman Street installation was abandoned; within a year Pittsburgh Reduction had increased production at its new location by geometric proportions and New Kensington became the spiritual heart of an industry.

The company was no sooner settled than its further radical expansion was prompted by its victory in a critical patent suit. Charles Hall had been employed for a while at the pioneering Electric Smelting and Aluminum Company, owned by a Cowles family in Lockport, New York. After Hall's Pittsburgh Reduction Company entered production the two corporations engaged in vigorous competition for the market, and in claim and counterclaim in the courts over their respective patent rights. In 1893 a portly young federal judge, William Howard Taft, decided in Hall's favor and enjoined the Cowleses out of business. As O'Connor put it, the signature "Taft, J.," was worth $100 million to the Mellons. Competition between Cowles and Pittsburgh Reduction had reduced the price of aluminum to fifty cents a pound; it quickly shot up to eighty cents. More important, Alcoa's legal monopoly was insured for the life of Hall's patent. Pittsburgh Reduction had to build more plants to meet the demands prompted by industry's growing awareness of aluminum's limitless uses as well as by the demise of the Cowles factory. In 1894 Alcoa built at Niagara Falls, New York, its first installation designed to profit from cheap hydroelectric power. Later it built plants at Massena, New York, on the St. Lawrence River; in East St. Louis, Illinois; Badin, North Carolina; Alcoa, Tennessee; Garwood, New Jersey; Mobile, Alabama. In the 1920s it and its Canadian affiliate opened a huge installation together with a model city on the banks of the raging Saguenay River, far in the north woods of Quebec Province, at Arvida, Canada.

World War I was good to aluminum. Alcoa's capacity increased by 50 per cent between 1915 and 1917. The increase in the need for aluminum for the adolescent aircraft industry was only the most obvious of the expanded requirements generated by the war. Aluminum time fuses could be used for shrapnel instead of brass ones, and Alcoa sold millions of them to Russia. Aluminum was used for bullet heads, for radiators on machine guns, for high-powered explosives, for trench hats and for the ubiquitous mess kits carried into battle by, among others, Stewart H. Holbrook, who describes them in his *Age of the Moguls:*

> Each of us two million soldiers possessed one aluminum mess kit, one aluminum canteen and holder used for a cup, one aluminum bacon can and one aluminum condiment can.
>
> Now, the canteen and cup and the mess kit were light, serviceable and of use.
>
> The other two items, which belonged to a day when soldiers carried and cooked their own rations, were absolutely worthless. They were worse than that; they were added burden and they took up space. But we lugged these two useless things over much of Europe. They had to be displayed on our bunks for daily inspection. We cursed them daily. We cursed the men who thought them up. We cursed the men who made them.
>
> In time we came to use the bacon can to carry extra plug chewing tobacco. But the condiment can, a fearful thing of complicated design and several compartments, would hold nothing that soldiers had to carry. It was merely cute. The Mellons were of course not to blame for giving us obsolete equipment made from a new metal. The responsibility lay with some old cavalryman of the Army, still thinking of a muzzle-loading war when soldiers were their own cooks. Enormous profit, however, lay in supplying us with this needless stuff —impedimenta of the worst kind.

Increased demands meant increased prices. At the time of the outbreak of the war in 1914, aluminum was at an abnormal low of nineteen cents a pound; world demand increased its price for regular orders to thirty-five cents a pound by the time that the United States entered the fray. The Mellons were patriotic. Bernard Baruch, head of the government's War Industries Board, asked them for a price break and he got it. The price was fixed for government needs at thirty-two cents, three cents under the market price, but substantially less than what aluminum could be sold for on speculative orders to other than "regular" Alcoa customers. Baruch later wrote that "Mellon sent Alcoa's president, Arthur Davis, to me with instructions to do whatever I asked of him. As a result, Alcoa was virtually placed at the disposition of the government." When the war demands subsided, aluminum quickly dropped to twenty-two cents; Alcoa kept producing it, at a profit.

Until the 1940s, competition was no problem at all for Alcoa. The Hall patent insured Alcoa's legal monopoly until 1906, and a related patent controlled by the Cowleses was purchased by Alcoa and extended its technological monopoly until the expiration of the Cowles patent rights in 1909. At that time anyone at all was free to enter the aluminum business so long as he had bauxite, power sources, customers, and experienced personnel. By that time Alcoa owned or controlled the richest of America's bauxite resources and many of the most inviting power sources. Independent bauxite mines and electric utilities from whom Alcoa purchased were contractually obligated to refuse to sell for aluminum manufacture to anyone else. As demand for aluminum spiraled with the growth of the auto and aeronautics industries, Alcoa doubled and redoubled its plant capacities, a step ahead of the inevitable increases in demand and before others could enter the field, so that any newcomer would be greeted by Alcoa's abundant capacity, free from the bugs that must inevitably accompany any new operation, molded into a great organization and with a corner on resources, experience, trade connections and the elite of personnel.

With the odds so stacked in Alcoa's favor, no one could consider the idea of opening a competing plant without tremendous capital. In 1914 an experienced and well-connected French producer found members of the American finance fraternity unwilling to consider such an investment, either because of the odds or out of deference to the Brothers Mellon. When a couple of serious attempts to enter aluminum production were in the planning stages, Alcoa somehow ended up buying out the projects before they left the drawing boards.

In the early days competition with foreign suppliers was restrained by every manufacturer's local demands; later it was restrained by an unabashed cartel understanding, essentially dividing up the world into territories. America was Alcoa's. That understanding was voided by a stipulated anti-trust judgment against Alcoa in 1912, but thereafter the healthy protective tarriff survived, enabling Alcoa to keep a step ahead of foreign competitors. After 1912 the price of imported aluminum remained the only ceiling to what Alcoa might charge; the import duties plus transportation expenses allowed Alcoa a lot of leeway.

The net result was that nothing changed for Alcoa after its patents expired in 1909; it and its subsidiaries remained the sole American producers, and virtually the only American suppliers, of virgin aluminum—the strongest and most unassailable of America's monopolies—until World War II, when Reynolds Metals Company and Kaiser Aluminum and Chemical Corporation went into aluminum production with the essential assistance of the United States government.

Labor was a thornier but not insurmountable problem when it was confronted with dispatch and a respect for law. In 1900 Alcoa had its first strike when thirty-seven employees of the wire-drawing department at New Kensington affiliated with the American Federation of Labor and demanded union recognition. It was settled when the company quickly agreed to recognition and negotiated a contract. For several years things went evenly, until 1908, when four unions clamored for recognition at New Kensington. Alcoa took the occasion to come out for an "open shop" and survived the subsequent strike. In the years that followed, Alcoa's relations with labor went downhill. The heat of the furnaces, the maddening twelve-hour day, the marginal wage, the wretched company houses, transformed even the most appreciative south-central European peasant into a labor radical, while on the other side, the natural economic laws passed down by Judge Mellon provided long-lingering guidance for management. Not surprisingly, the early history of Alcoa's labor relations is marked with strike-breakers, National Guardsmen, bullets, and blood.

A. W. Mellon was outside the firing range. No one knew him; scarcely anyone knew *of* him. He liked it that way. Frick and John D. Rockefeller were known, or at least widely known *of;* they could be vilified. But one cannot vilify someone of whom one is unaware, and so the Mellons escaped. A. W. could be a contemplative man and he no doubt understood the hopelessness of the plight of Alcoa's employees. His father's social attitudes were born of an earlier industrial age of small producers, each competing, each with a few employees who were free to try for themselves. The Judge's social views had relevance to that age, and in it his views had appeal to natural justice. A. W.'s industrial environment was a much different one, in which only his father's social views survived. Still, nature was nature, business was business, and the world a hard one.

At about the time that Pittsburgh Reduction was beginning to show a profit, the Mellon brothers got into the next of those industries that were to loom large in the family portfolio: Carborundum. Their introduction to the substance was again by sample. The story, at least as it runs in the folklore of the Carborundum Company, goes like this:

One fine summer day in 1895, A. W. received an obscure but destined visitor, Edward G. Acheson. Acheson had spent ten years at Menlo Park, New Jersey, assisting Thomas A. Edison; later he had worked for another celebrated genius, George Westinghouse. He was as imaginative as his mentors, if less scientific and less successful in life's pursuits. At the time of his visit he was president of a small-town utility company, the Monongahela City Light Company, and of an even less impressive corporate entity called the Carborundum Company. As Acheson recounted his interests to the forty-year-old banker, he toyed with the financier's heavy glass paperweight. At the crucial moment he removed from his vest pocket a gem of a chunk of—Carborundum!—and slashed an incision into the paperweight. The demonstration produced, at least to the ears of Carborundum's president William H. Wendel, "the scratch heard 'round the world." A. W. was impressed. Where, he asked, had Acheson obtained such a huge and beautiful diamond? "I made it," was the answer.

Acheson's Carborundum, touted by the company as the first man-made abrasive, was similar to Hall's process for reducing aluminum in that it also depended upon common materials and vast quantities of electricity. In 1891 Acheson had electrified a pot of clay and powdered coke for reasons now lost to history. In any event, he later wrote that the experiment "did not fulfill my expectations." By chance, though, he "happened to notice a few bright specks on the end of an arc carbon. I placed one on the end of a lead pencil and drew it across a pane of glass. It scratched the glass like a diamond." Believing, incorrectly, that he had fused carbon and corundum, a natural abrasive commonly used at the time, he named his discovery "Carborundum." Carborundum had obvious utility as an abrasive if it could be produced at a lesser expense than natural abrasives of equal hardness. He sold his first homemade vial of it to a diamond cutter at a hefty price, but Carborundum had a much wider potential use. It could be used in every industry for grinding, cutting, or polishing. In September 1891 he incorporated the Carborundum Company—about the only enterprise associated with the Mellons that still bears its original corporate name—with a $150,000 investment provided by local Monongahela, Pennsylvania, investors.

Acheson had planned to sell Carborundum particles to manufacturers of abrasive equipment as a component of their finished products, but he was unable to interest the leading grinding-wheel producers, so his new company was soon busily engaged in making not only its own Carborundum but its own grinding wheels. The company's big problem was costs. In its small Monongahela plant Carborundum cost so much to produce that its resultant price made it unsalable for most purposes. Jewelers and dentists were about the only tradesmen whose needs warranted the price.

The harnessing of Niagara Falls in the mid-1890s opened up prospects that cheap power might reduce the cost of Carborundum to such a level that it could compete with better-established abrasives, and Acheson proposed to his board of directors that the company build a much larger plant at Niagara, close to the inexpensive power. The board was unwilling to take the big gamble, and when Acheson, who was a majority stockholder, insisted, Carborundum's directors, small-town men to a man, to a man resigned and walked out. Acheson restaffed the board and signed a contract with the Niagara Power Company for a huge amount of electricity, thereby becoming the utility's second largest customer. Niagara already had one big buyer in the burgeoning Pittsburgh Reduction Company.

Carborundum managed to get its substantial brick buildings erected on its new site before it ran out of money, unable to equip the plant. Acheson made what he calls in his memoirs "a great struggle" to secure financing sufficient to acquire and settle the necessary machinery, but he found no interest anywhere in the company's bonds. Perhaps it was a Niagara connection who told him of the far-sighted bankers in Pittsburgh. Anyway, he approached the Mellons and he got the money.

The Mellon role in the history of Carborundum is more typically that of the finance capitalist than was the case of their role in Alcoa's history. They purchased their stock in Alcoa, the same as the Hunt-Clapp associates, David Gillespie, or any other well-placed investor might have. In Carborundum they acquired it for the most part as "bonuses" for making interest-bearing loans to the business. The loans and the interest on the loans were repaid a hundred cents on the dollar; their more significant equity interest in the Carborundum Company came mostly for "free." Free, that is, except for the headaches of coping with the disorganization generated by the brilliant but overextended Acheson, and with personality peculiarities that revolved around the inventor's egocentricity (he titled his obscure autobiography *Pathfinder*). Hall viewed himself as an engineer and welcomed an able business manager like Davis; Acheson saw himself as a man for all seasons. From the start of their relationship, a collision between the pathfinder and his bankers was inevitable, and the conflict's surviving party predictable.

After the reverberations of the scratch in A. W.'s office subsided, the Mellons took $50,000 of Carborundum Company's bonds, receiving as a bonus their first interest in the corporation: stock with a par value of $12,500 on a total capitalization of $200,000, or a 6.25 per cent interest in the company's total ownership. In the next few years tremendous expansion of the plant and of the company's lines required more and more money, and each time that the Mellons made the needed loans, at interest, they received another bonus of a further stock interest in the corporation. The bonuses dwindled Acheson's majority interest to less than half while the Mellon interests increased, but together the Mellons and Acheson owned a continually increasing proportion of the corporation, so that the Mellons' irritating terms combined with Acheson's consistently bad business judgment whittled away the interests of the original minority stockholders and their successors. As Acheson tells it in *Pathfinder,* the bonuses for loans in the

first years of the company's dealings with the Pittsburgh bankers gave the
Mellons an interest of 46.58 per cent of the company's stock—in addition
to which the Mellons received 6 per cent on all of their loans. By purchases
from minority stockholders, they increased this "free" interest to a majority
holding, giving them control of the business. Thereafter Acheson was
rudely if justifiably pushed out of the Carborundum Company.

W. L. was at T. Mellon & Sons one morning in 1897 and heard R. B.
talking to Acheson in Niagara Falls on the phone "in such a tone of voice
as to make me wonder whether it was really necessary for him to use the
telephone to make himself heard up there." Orally R. B. insisted that
Acheson keep more up-to-date books and claimed that "the whole concern
is sadly in need of push and energy and unless an immediate improvement
is shown we shall have to put in someone to protect our interests." By letter
he amplified: "It is my opinion that all, both officers and employees of the
Carborundum Company, are a come-easy-go-easy set and should have a
lively shaking up and the lightweights skimmed off. I mean this in the
strongest terms." Attitude was only the most serious defect with corporate
management as R. B. saw it; otherwise, no one had any concept of delegation of authority, with the result that corporate officers were buried in
"routine duties so they had [no] time to do the really creative work of top
business executives." From the Mellon viewpoint, things got no better. The
following year A. W. wrote Acheson chiding him for failure to devote his
entire interests to the Carborundum Company and pointing to the corporation's lax management and its failure to show a profit. The situation was
such that by continuance of it "my brother and myself will have lost an
immense sum of money, while on your part you would have received in one
way or another a very considerable amount."

The Mellons were not ones to stand for that kind of injustice. At their
prodding, Carborundum took on a few new employees such as Frank W.
Haskell, a Mellon auditor; Frank J. Tone, who had been a Mellon man in
street railways (and whose son took the name of Franchot and became
something of a celebrity); and Frank Manley, a Mellon oil employee. According to W. L., the Mellon men tried to bolster rather than supplant
Acheson's administration of the company. If so, they were regrettably
unsuccessful. In 1901 Acheson was ousted as president and replaced by
Haskell. From that day forward, W. L. wrote, "the Carborundum Company began to grow in strength and its usefulness expanded wonderfully.
That usefulness to America and to civilization can scarcely be exaggerated."
Acheson, not surprisingly, saw things differently; in *Pathfinder* he recounts
the unhappy course of his dealings with bankers whom he identifies only
as "A" and "B."

Probably the largest single element of the Mellon family fortune since the 1920s has been its interest in the Guffey Petroleum Company, or Gulf Oil, as it has been known since 1907. Gulf was essentially the creation of a most underrated man, W. L. Mellon. His own father, J. R., made apologies for him to W. L.'s brilliant future father-in-law, Matthew Taylor ("Will is not one of these showy fellows, but you have to respect him. Will is sound and true") and W. L.'s son Matthew Taylor Mellon no doubt without intent to belittle his father, stresses the importance of A. W.'s role in his father's success. Frank Kent, the perceptive political commentator of the Baltimore *Sun* and close associate of the *Sun*'s better-known journalist, H. L. Mencken, characterized W. L. in 1926 as a

> fairly able middle-aged man with good business equipment but not much else. Without the Mellon connections he would probably have been a leading member of the Pittsburgh Rotary Club, or something like that. He is, of course, a man of his word . . . is pleasant personally but not particularly stimulating and with no distinguishing traits to lift him above the average.

Yet it was W. L. who built the greatest (meaning only the most substantial) of the Mellon enterprises.

W. L. was a hearty and active fellow. His Mellon background and inspiration made him a curious, imaginative, and acquisitive sort, willing to work hard, and would have insured him some success in life even if that Mellon background had not included the Mellon millions. With it, he was a big success.

The lack of appreciation for W. L.'s talents perhaps stems from his common ways. Of the "founding" Mellons, only the Judge and A. W. had any extensive formal education, but only in W. L. was the lack of it betrayed by a rather basic vocabulary and a reluctance to travel in well-spoken circles. The lovely wording of his *Judge Mellon's Sons* is attributable to W. L.'s collaborator, Boyden Sparkes; W. L. felt more at home trading in folksy aphorisms like "Absence of body is better than presence of mind," or "You can't have a successful oil company without oil." The only music that he ever expressed any fondness for was "Chicken Charlie," a banjo record. He too invested in art, but his most prized canvas, a portrait of Rembrandt, was almost certainly not the *self*-portrait that he thought it to be.

W. L.'s closest friend was probably Dave, whom he described in *Judge Mellon's Sons* as "the little grey-haired colored man who stays with me in Florida in the winter and at Squirrel Island in Ontario in the summer. . . . Dave has been with me so long I have forgotten when he came." Dave

had a last name—Floyd—but it is not revealed in *Judge Mellon's Sons.* To
the Mellons he was just Dave, first W. L.'s "boy," later W. L.'s "man." To
Matthew's recollections, "Dave always played the 'Uncle Tom' darky to us
but underneath it all he felt the white man's injustice to his race."

Fishing was W. L.'s great recreation and escape. Matthew wrote in
Watermellons that it gave his father "an appreciation of the vast lonely
stretches of the sea; for he found in them a protection against the time-
killing distractions of civilization." When he escaped to the sea, it was never
without Dave, and together they fished and fished. W. L.'s grandson Karl
recalls Grandpa and Dave as truly "kindred spirits, though only the very
young could see it." When W. L.'s will was probated, no one was surprised
to see that W. L. had provided a lifetime pension for Dave.

W. L. lived his first five years in the Judge's house, the next many years
across the street from it, and the two great influences on his youth were the
Judge and Uncle A. W., two strong men who obscured his own father,
J. R. All his life W. L. remained devoted to A. W., never acknowledging,
even to his own son, the slightest fault in his uncle and benefactor. Their
relationship was always formal, however. Though W. L. was only thirteen
years younger than A. W., he explained in *Judge Mellon's Sons* that "I
never quite bridged that short gap of years by calling Andrew William
Mellon 'Andy' . . . to me he was always 'A. W.' "

W. L.'s youth, like that of his uncles, was busied with moneymaking, at
first, as in their cases, by carrying the produce of the Judge's estate to
market: in late spring rhubarb; by mid-summer tomatoes; and as the fall
approached, sweet corn. "That money I spent as I got it; for a beanshooter
one time, a mouth organ another. But I never was given money in those
days. I had to earn it." Nothing delighted the Judge so much as "the sight
of me, the donkey and the produce-laden wagon, setting off for some market
I had found for myself, most likely down on Penn Avenue. But he had the
good sense to seem to ignore what I was doing." It was a somewhat easier
childhood, though, than the stern Judge's own sons had endured, and as he
outlined it in *Judge Mellon's Sons,* there was time for good fun and for the
pranks of an upper-class boyhood.

His education was at first in East Liberty public schools, "but my
mother's and grandfather's views about public schools coincided. She
thought I would grow more civilized if I went to a more polite school [so]
I had been getting my schooling from two elderly spinsters who ran what
was known as the Ford and Sackett School." Then he was sent to the
Pennsylvania Military Academy in Chester, Pennsylvania, from which,
Matthew Mellon wrote in *War Log: 1917–18,* W. L. "had the good sense

to run away after a short exposure." He also tried a Shortledge Academy at Media, Pennsylvania, but finally the conclusion could not be escaped: "It was useless to try to pour any more formal education into my hard head." W. L. was an active, somewhat mischievous and accident-prone adolescent; school administrators of today would no doubt have labeled him "hyperkinetic." The big problem, he wrote, was that "I was attached to my uncles' generation. School, it seemed to me, was dragging me farther and farther behind the important excitement which all of them were experiencing." With the Judge's blessings and encouragement his formal education terminated, a matter which W. L. sporadically regretted throughout later life. Thereafter he was employed in the gamut of early Mellon businesses. By the age of majority every Mellon boy had had an amazing variety and depth of experience, perhaps W. L. most of all: in the railroad, in the wild west, in electricity, lumber, speculative house building, and most important for W. L. and for the family, in oil.

Petroleum came at the right time for mankind. The birth of the business about coincided with the death of the whaling industry which had provided oil to light the world. Petroleum and its wonderful by-product, kerosene, came just in time to keep the lamps burning. When Colonel Drake sank his first well at Titusville in 1859, no one could have known that the principal demand for oil, lighting, would disappear in a matter of some twenty years with the harnessing of electricity, or that the former demand would be replaced by the infinitely greater demands generated by the development of the internal combustion engine.

Until the late 1800s "oil country" meant western Pennsylvania, where pure green oil sometimes oozed from the rocks and the stream beds. Many producing wells can still be visited in Butler County north of Pittsburgh, though now they drip only a small fraction of the fine quality petroleum that they yielded a century ago, all of which is saved for use in pharmaceuticals and high-grade lubricants. In Drake's day there was enough oil in western Pennsylvania to waste, and though an occasional fool might venture to suggest that even richer finds might be made in such unlikely places as Texas, sounder heads knew better. Pennsylvania was it. John D. Archbold, later Rockefeller's chief executive, offered to drink every drop of oil found west of the Mississippi.

For a while Drake's well spurted twenty-five barrels a day—a substantial quantity by the standards of the time—and drew the world's supply of gold-rush types to western Pennsylvania, where overnight they created cities of oil and booze, with telling names like Oil Creek, Petrolia, Oil City, Wellsville, many of which stand today as ghost-town mementos of Pennsylvania's oil boom. About the last of the fast-talking oil-lease fellers to get into the field was W. L. Mellon. By 1889 much, but far from all, of the seamy glamour of the early boom days had dissipated and the Standard Oil Company had secured its monopoly over the transmission and refining of crude oil; but for a little while longer money could still be made in Pennsylvania oil. The Mellons made the last of it.

W. L. was in the process of leaving a position with T. A. and J. R.'s lumber yard to become agent for A. W. and R. B.'s gas plant at Connellsville, when oil was struck at nearby Economy, Pennsylvania. Curiosity prompted W. L. to go out and take a look. By the time he got to the farm with the new well, the hillside was "carpeted with horses and rigs," and there was a big crowd around the well—"lease buyers who had swarmed to the scene as mysteriously as a special kind of fly gathers around a souring crock of fruit." In the center of the hubbub was "an incredible fountain spewing out of the earth in a great column that turned greenish-orange in color, where the sunlight shone through it, as it showered back to earth." W. L. never got to the Connellsville gas plant.

Among the crowd at Economy, W. L. spotted a familiar face, the field agent for A. W. and R. B.'s Bridgewater Gas Company, a man with some experience securing oil rights on his own account. The agent was in the scramble for rights at Economy. W. L. tagged along with him for a few days, learning his routine and as much of the trade as could be absorbed in a few days. After this brief "schooling," W. L. Mellon, oil man, set out for Hookstown in Beaver County, Pennsylvania, site of fresh excitement generated by the gush of a new 600-barrel-a-day well.

By 1889 cajoling farmers into granting oil rights, or "oil leases" as they are known in the business, had become a high art form designed to secure the property owner's signature on a standard and time-tested form. By the customary form, the oil man was given the right to prospect for oil on the farmer's property, or a designated portion of it, and generally committed himself to sink a well within one year. If any oil was found, the farmer got one-eighth as his share; if the endeavor was unsuccessful, the losses were all the oil man's. When a farmer's land was close by an already producing well, he might receive some additional bonus if he demanded it; if his land was virgin territory, he was lucky to get the contract at all. At Hookstown in the spring of 1889 W. L., twenty years old, secured his first lease and a seemingly desirable one at that, as it covered property adjacent to that of the new 600-barrel well. W. L. later reminisced about how "The boat bobs back and forth and perhaps I land a fish—perhaps even a big one. But no catch no matter how spectacular, can possibly bring me the pleasure that

I experienced when I landed the first oil lease." With money advanced by
A. W. and R. B. he hired a well driller and started drilling immediately.
Week after week he sat and watched the rig:

> During the first several weeks of our drilling I was a fairly calm and collected
> oil prospector. But as we went into the fourth week and began to get promising
> signs, I couldn't force myself to leave the premises in daylight; and later I
> stayed on the ground at night. Drilling went on night and day, in twelve hour
> tours, which in the oil field were called "towers." Then she came in! But it was
> no gusher; just a little well with a production of twenty to twenty-five barrels
> a day. That was such an anti-climax after my grandiose expectations that I was
> crestfallen when I reported to my uncles at the bank.

Other wells followed, profitable wells and big wells, drilled by W. L.
Mellon throughout western Pennsylvania, and later in adjacent sections of
Ohio and West Virginia. In no time a substantial stream of Mellon's crude
oil was flowing into Rockefeller's Standard Oil pipelines, for processing by
Rockefeller's Standard Oil refineries and sale to Standard Oil's customers.

There was money to be made in all aspects of the petroleum industry: in
the exploration for it, in the drilling for it, in the transmission of it through
pipelines or in tank cars over the railroads, in the refining of it, in the sale
of the finished product to wholesale or retail consumers. W. L. and his
partners, "the Mellon boys," were making money from the exploration and
the drilling for it but as to the price that they and other wildcatters received
for their crude, they were at the mercy of John D. Rockefeller, whose
Standard Oil Company was the only significant buyer for crude because it
controlled the pipelines and the refineries, the only avenues from crude to
consumer. Without Standard Oil, the wildcatter's crude would just pond up
at the base of the well. John D. wasn't that difficult to deal with. When a
significant oil field opened up, Standard would extend its pipeline to any
important well; it paid cash at the wellhead for crude, and a price which
seemed to bear some reasonable relationship to the day's supply and the
predictable pace of the demands of the ultimate consumer. To a great extent
John D. and Standard brought a measure of stability to an industry in which
radical price fluctuations had made and then irrationally devastated too
many fortunes. Producers could also comfort themselves in the knowledge
that Standard did not compete with them. It bought crude but did not
produce any significant quantities of crude itself, making its profits instead
from the transmission and refining of it and the sale of the refined product.

W. L. wrote that "A. W. frequently reminded me that the real way to
make a business out of petroleum was to develop it from end to end; to get

the raw material out of the ground, refine it, manufacture it, distribute it. He believed in that scheme of operation not alone for petroleum but for many other types of business." It was almost by accident, perhaps without realizing the implications of his crucial steps, that young W. L. embarked on pursuit of a particular business opportunity that would ultimately cause him to pursue A. W.'s vision of an integrated oil business, thereby challenging, on behalf of himself and on behalf of a significant portion of his uncles' fortunes, the great American monopoly of John D. Rockefeller.

Over the years Standard had had many competitors. The weaker ones it crushed; the stronger ones it bought out. One of the stronger ones was a firm known as Elkins & Widener, who purchased crude at the fields in western Pennsylvania and shipped it by tank car to Philadelphia, where they refined it and sold it for export to foreign buyers. In 1890 Standard bought them out, leaving Elkins & Widener's buyers no reliable supplier but Standard. A connection from Elkins & Widener tipped off W. L. that their biggest customer, Fenaille & Despeaux, a French refiner that purchased crude, preferred not to deal with Standard, so W. L. called on the Frenchmen's American representative and together they agreed to eliminate the middleman. The bulk of W. L.'s production continued to be siphoned into the Standard pipeline, but now he began selling direct to Fenaille & Despeaux. He shipped his crude by tank car over the railroad to New York, where it was loaded onto the buyer's small steamships. Then a Spanish buyer emerged and another French customer. Soon the Mellons owned a sizable fleet of tank cars, and their wells were coming in strong too. They had become a significant element in the export trade. It was inevitable that they would begin thinking of building their own pipeline or perhaps of entering the refining business.

Around 1891 W. L. "borrowed" a refinery at Badin, Pennsylvania, from an associate who would otherwise have had to shut it down at considerable expense—mostly for the experience of running one. Soon a network of small pipelines was bringing oil to him from as far away as West Virginia—both his own oil and that of other producers from whom he bought. At Badin it was processed and then shipped in the Mellons' tank cars, which grew to number two hundred, over the Pennsylvania Railroad's tracks to New York, where a still-growing number of foreign customers took all that W. L. could supply. The Mellons had now become a small but respectable enough competitor of the Standard Oil Company to warrant the giant's attention. The Standard operating procedure in such situations had already become well established: Crush the competition if in any way possible, and if impossible, then buy them out. Standard tried the one first, unsuccessfully, and then the other with a degree of success that was gratifying to the Mellons.

Standard Oil was so much the best customer of the Pennsylvania Railroad that the corporate entities seemed to function as one. The Mellons received notice from the Pennsylvania that it was raising shipping charges just enough to wipe out their margin of profit; they were almost certainly correct in seeing Standard's influence behind the railroad's memorandum. At the same time their own investment in the oil industry had become so substantial that they might have already passed the point of no return, and they surely knew from recent history that John D. Rockefeller appreciated a good fight and was willing to reward an able opponent.

A little inquiry found them their way out. If they could get their oil to the Reading Railroad hookup at Carlisle, Pennsylvania, halfway between Pittsburgh and the eastern border of Pennsylvania at the Delaware River, the Pennsylvania Railroad's little competitor would haul their tank cars to the Delaware at a favorable rate. W. L. scouted around for a site on the Delaware banks that could serve as a terminal for ocean-going vessels— someplace near that natural juncture of New Jersey, Delaware, and Pennsylvania. It had to be reasonably close to the Reading Railroad's terminus; it had to be big enough to justify the overall expense; and it had to be in Pennsylvania, the last being what W. L. described as a "common sense" requirement, "because we had friends all over Pennsylvania." He found and acquired two ideal adjacent properties which together could accommodate a great port and a great refinery as well, right on the Delaware River at the Pennsylvania-Delaware border. John D. Rockefeller, the world's richest man, was in for a battle with W. L. Mellon, aged twenty-three, and his wealthy young uncles. W. L. wrote that R. B.'s nostrils flared at the smell of the fight, but A. W. viewed it calmly. It was he who would call the plays for the Mellon forces.

W. L. bought his pipe, on credit, and was in the process of building a pipeline halfway across the broad state of Pennsylvania to Carlisle when there was a strange shake-up in the management of the Reading Railroad. Its president was fired and his successor promptly repudiated the railroad's contract with the Mellons, no doubt the result of John D.'s tremendous influence. It was too late for the Mellons to turn back though; they would run their pipeline across the entire state of Pennsylvania, 271 miles to their new base on the Delaware River.

In the Pennsylvania of that day anyone who wanted to build a pipeline had rights of "eminent domain." A prospective pipeline company had to pay damages for the right to cross a property owner's land, but the landowner could not refuse to allow the pipeline to traverse his property. The Mellons therefore did not have to worry about major problems in obtaining rights-of-way. They did have to worry about sabotage. W. L. wrote that

> The Pennsylvania Railroad in those days was something relatively new in the universe. It was enormous and powerful and jealous. . . . The men on its payrolls were wonderfully devoted to it, as faithful as watchdogs and sometimes no more discriminating. When we came along, some of those men were determined that this upstart pipeline company should never cross their tracks. So, when we would build our pipeline under tracks or through a culvert, and then breathe a sigh of relief, we would breathe it too soon, for the next day our pipe would be found torn up.
>
> It wasn't a sensational fight, and I don't know now that the Standard Oil was behind it, but I assume that some people in the Standard Oil and some people in the Pennsylvania Railroad were pretty jealous. I do know that at every point where the Pennsylvania lay across my path, there was a row. . . . Each time some of our pipe was torn up, we had a few employees of the Pennsylvania arrested. Then we relaid it and had, as a rule, no further trouble at that particular point. But for me, it was like slaying dragons to get that pipeline built.

Fortunately for W. L., the Standard Oil forces were simultaneously being diverted by another independent pipeline, the U.S. Pipeline, which was apparently regarded as the bigger threat, and which was met more ruthlessly, forcefully, and openly, allowing the Mellons to sneak through relatively unharassed. In November 1892 their battle was over; W. L. climbed to the top of a storage tank at the Delaware River and waited until the voice of an employee carried upward to him:

> "Here she comes!"
> A cavernous belching sounded in the tank. Then it came! The greenish oil jumped into view and held its shape as an arching girder, seeming to support the tank from its bottom, rather than to be an opaque fluid falling into it. My big job was done.

There were still "little" jobs: building the refinery and rounding up sufficient customers to justify the total investment. After the pipeline, those were small matters. By the beginning of 1893 the Mellons' Crescent Pipeline Company, Crescent Oil Company, Crescent Connecting Railroad Company, and their allied oil enterprises represented a fully integrated oil operation with 10 per cent of the American export market. By A. W.'s calculations, the package had cost them over $2.5 million.

The Mellons had earned the reward that initiative and hard work promise: Standard Oil bought them out. By the time that Crescent became a significant factor in world oil, the role of Pennsylvania crude was declining. The state was beginning to run dry and oil was being discovered farther and farther afield and in such quantities as to once again jeopardize oil's historically precarious price stability. Crescent was no sooner operating than Standard was undercutting its European markets by reducing its export price to levels at which the Mellons could not compete. Continuing in the business indefinitely would likely have required a disproportionate amount of the Mellons' money and of the Mellons' attention. It didn't make sense to stick it out any longer, not when Mr. Rockefeller was showing that he really was a reasonable man. He paid them $4.5 million. In 1893 Pennsylvania law prohibited the merger of competing pipelines; in August of that year contracts were quietly concluded between the components of the Crescent enterprises and agents for the Standard components. After the law was changed in 1895 it was announced that Standard had taken over Crescent.

The costs for sinking that first well at Hookstown, about $10,000, and all of the wells that followed and the tank cars, pipelines, docks, and refineries were paid out of a bank account at T. Mellon & Sons labeled "W. L. Mellon Special." A. W. and R. B. lent the W. L. Mellon Special account the seed money and thereafter made substantial other loans to it, but the earnings of W. L.'s oil enterprises (less a modest draw for W. L.) were funneled into the account, so that with time W. L. Mellon Special became able to participate itself in the funding of its ventures, thereby lessening to some extent the need for financial assistance from the Mellon brothers. The three men were partners in W. L.'s businesses for five years before they got around to putting their understanding as to their respective interests into writing:

> Memo of agreement under which the business and operations have been carried on between A. W. Mellon, R. B. Mellon and W. L. Mellon, associated together as "W. L. MELLON SPECIAL," comprising the W. L. Mellon oil producing properties, the Crescent Oil Company, Ltd., the Crescent Connecting R.R. Co., and the Bear Creek Refining Co., Limited.
>
> That A. W. Mellon's share of the whole is thirty-five per cent—; R. B. Mellon's thirty-five per cent—; and the share of W. L. Mellon thirty per cent—
>
> That all salaries from any of the companies or interests for services by either of us shall be turned into the account (W. L. Mellon Special) without regard to who shall have earned the same, and be treated as other earnings of the

association, excepting that W. L. Mellon shall receive from the association a
personal salary of Two Hundred Dollars per month from July 1st, 1893.

Pittsburgh, June 20, 1894

A. W. Mellon
R. B. Mellon
W. L. Mellon

W. L.'s 30 per cent interest in the Crescent-related ventures made him a
wealthy man in his own right by the age of twenty-five. Throughout later
life both he and his father, J. R., remained deeply grateful to A. W. and
R. B. for all that they had done for him, though in the nature of things it
might appear to some that the gratitude ought to have flowed in the other
direction.

W. L. and his wife, May, whom he had married in Florida in 1896, settled
down in Pittsburgh. Their marriage was soon blessed with children: Matthew Taylor Mellon, named for his maternal grandfather, born in 1897,
followed by Rachel in 1899 and Margaret (Peggy) in 1901. Like the Judge,
W. L. was incapable of inactivity and he kept busy in his uncles' varied
enterprises, particularly in their streetcar lines in Pittsburgh. He described
himself in *Judge Mellon's Sons* as the "outside man" for the bank.

The Mellons may have thought that they were out of oil, but they weren't.
W. L. had to delay his honeymoon in 1896 to go to Texas to inspect a new
find at Corsicana, the first of the Texas strikes, and though he discouraged
his uncles from getting into the Corsicana situation, their loans to oil men,
and especially to John Galey and his partner, James M. Guffey, in time
brought the family back into active management in oil, this time forever.

The history of Guffey, Galey, and Gulf is tied to Beaumont, Texas, today
a big town or a small city not far from the Louisiana border and not far
from the Gulf of Mexico. In the late 1800s it was a sleepy little town whose
principal industries were rice and lumbering in the Gulf Coast swamps. One
of those swamps, adjacent to a prominent hill, was noted for a curious
phenomenon. Little bubbles of air filtered up from someplace beneath its
bottom, bubbles of air which would ignite at the touch of a match. On wet
days the hill itself would blossom with the explosive bubbles. As a boy
Patillo Higgins was entranced by those bubbles. As a young man Higgins
had been the fiercest brawler west of the Sabine; even after he lost an arm
in a lumbering accident he was more than a match for most two-armed men.
After years away from his home town Pat Higgins returned to Beaumont,
an older, redeemed man. He had found God. He became a respectable

member of the community, taught Sunday school down at the Baptist church, and became modestly but solidly established as a real estate broker.

Only one aspect of his past still haunted Higgins: the bubbles. On his travels Pat Higgins had picked up that rule-of-thumb "folk" geology of the unschooled oil man; he read the swamp bubbles, and the hill, as spelling oil. He organized a few local investors and in 1893 began drilling for oil. After a couple of dry test holes, Higgins's backers lost their enthusiasm. Higgins tried to interest others and did: Captain Anthony Lucas, a Yugoslav mining engineer with a more formal grasp of geology. Lucas had served in the Austrian Navy before the gold bug bit him; then he came to America, assumed the title "Captain" (which he had never been), and set out for gold. By the time that he read Higgins's newspaper advertisement seeking a buyer, he was employed in the more prosaic salt industry, living a respectable life with his well-to-do American wife. Lucas went over to Beaumont, where he read the signs in the swamp and on the hill the same way that Higgins had read them. With a $10,000 deposit toward a $33,500 sales price, Lucas bought up almost all of Higgins's rights and those of Higgins's Gladys City Oil, Gas & Manufacturing Company. Higgins retained a portion of the hill for himself and, as part consideration, got a 10 per cent interest in Lucas's venture.

Lucas started drilling, down and down, 575 feet, before he ran out of money and everything that could be sold for money. By that time he was certain that he was on the right track, if only sufficient capital could be brought in to impel the drill deeper still. Dr. William B. Phillips, director of Texas's geological survey, examined what came up on Lucas's drill bit and agreed. Lucas approached Standard Oil for assistance, and his presentation was sufficiently impressive that they sent their most experienced field examiner, Calvin Payne, to inspect the site. Payne said no. The positive signs were misleading; the important signs were absent. At Dr. Phillips's suggestion, Lucas then turned to Guffey and Galey, about the two best-known oil speculators in the business, in faraway Pittsburgh. Money or access to capital had enabled Lucas to drive a hard bargain with Patillo Higgins; now money or access to capital enabled Guffey and Galey to drive a hard bargain with Anthony Lucas. He traded the rights and assets of Gladys City Oil for a one-eighth interest in a new syndicate, the J. M. Guffey Company; Guffey and Galey got seven-eighths for their access to capital.

John Galey's father and Judge Thomas Mellon had arrived in the new world on the same vessel; his brother Sam Galey was one of the few men that A. W. ever called by his first name, and whose references to "Andy" were not resented as presumptuous. Sam had partnered with W. L. on some of W. L.'s early oil ventures. John himself was also close to the Mellons; among his more successful wells had been two that he had named "Andrew" and "Mellon." W. L. regarded Galey as the greatest wildcatter, or speculative well driller, of all times, and though Galey may not have been the greatest he was certainly among the country's most far-reaching wildcatters. He drilled everywhere between the successful wells that he sank on the Pacific Coast, and the unsuccessful well that he sank within the city limits of Washington, D.C. As with most wildcatters, easy-come money had led Galey into easy-go improvidence; he was financially irresponsible, and between fortunes he was often in financial difficulties. Both W. L. and A. W. had considerable personal affection for John Galey, but A. W. wrote a banking correspondent in 1897, "With us, we do not loan John money because it is so difficult to collect that I always feel we can keep better friends by refusing in the first place."

Galey's longtime partner and the strong man of the two was Colonel James M. Guffey, a highly colorful man whose many eccentricities were highlighted by his outlandish garb and by what, among Pennsylvania's men of stature, could only have been taken as bizarre political activity. He was the state's representative on the Democratic National Committee. His showmanship made him a celebrity in the worlds of both oil and politics.

W. L. looked down on Guffey as a "promoter," rather than a genuine oil man like himself and Galey, and the ill will was reciprocated. Guffey resented W. L. as that bad influence that killed financing for so many of Guffey's projects down at T. Mellon & Sons. A. W., however, the most unobtrusive of men, had a weak spot for the flamboyant Guffey. Guffey was only a little better in handling his affairs than Galey, but at least he was a little better; to him, A. W. would consider making loans.

Galey, Guffey, and Lucas all appreciated that if the venture were to be inordinately profitable they would have to acquire the most desirable leases in advance of any strike, and that if Galey were to do the lease acquiring his presence would arouse suspicions and make for stiffer terms than if Lucas did the negotiating. It was decided that Lucas would be the "front" man, with his Pittsburgh connections kept in the background. Lucas went back to Beaumont to begin signing up leases while Guffey went down to T. Mellon & Sons to begin rounding up the necessary capital. The partnership envisioned using a new and more expensive kind of drilling equipment that would require a greater investment. Guffey struck pay dirt. The Mellons agreed to extend a line of credit of up to $300,000 for the project. It was a highly speculative venture, and whatever the terms of the loan might have been they should not have been soft. No doubt Guffey and Galey had to pledge their existing and future assets, and to W. L.'s later recollection, "A. W. and Dick probably were to get back their money and a profit by an agreement that gave them half of any oil until the loan was paid."

Galey picked a fresh spot to probe, and in October 1900 Lucas and his silent partners began drilling. They were over a thousand feet down when, on January 10, 1901, Spindletop, as the hill came to be known, proved the investment worthwhile with a gush that looked to be worth (though it wasn't) 100,000 barrels a day. The well, formally known as Lucas No. 1, is probably the most important oil well in the industry's history. It spelled the end of the Standard Oil monopoly; it was the first major well to be brought in by a professional engineer using modern engineering approaches; and it established the vital significance of two entities in the world oil picture: the state of Texas and an entity that was to become the Gulf Oil Company. Spindletop was also to spawn another of the "seven sisters" of world oil: the Texas Oil Company.

As fortunes in Spindletop's oil splashed down over the ground to be lost forever in runoff, it was immediately apparent that the J. M. Guffey Company had made a discovery of incalculable value, whose value as things stood could easily be calculated. It was worthless because the prospectors neither had, nor had access to, storage facilities, pipelines, or refineries, none of which existed in the state of Texas. Guffey and Galey had made and squandered millions from earlier strikes; refining Spindletop's crude into dollars would require the kind of money that they might have had if either had exercised self-restraint. Even if Guffey could have stomached dealing with the "octopus" that he despised, there was no point in the partners approaching the Standard Oil Company for the kind of help that Standard had rendered in the merchandising of Pennsylvania crude. Standard had had a bad brush with Texas anti-trust enforcement officials that soured John D. on Texas forever.

Lucas, joined by Galey in Beaumont, recruited every possible man to raise dikes around the well to hold the partnership's riches, then to extinguish the horrifying fire, either carelessly or intentionally set, which engulfed their valuable reservoir and their geyser in flames, consuming their fortunes. Finally, on the tenth day of waste, they managed to cap the gusher with a massive iron cover. Back in Pittsburgh, Guffey had an equally maddening task: impressing the Mellon brothers with the urgency of their need for money, fortunes of money, to turn Spindletop and the prospects opened by it into greater fortunes of money. Spindletop was drawing to an area a hundred miles around Beaumont the spiritual sons of the flock who had crowded Drake's first derrick at Titusville; opportunities were being lost. Meanwhile, the Mellons seemed to take forever in their deliberations.

Five months later, in May of 1901, the Mellons and Guffey worked things out. They organized a new corporation, the J. M. Guffey Petroleum Company, with 150,000 shares of stock, to undertake the financing of the development of Spindletop. A. W. and R. B. each bought 10,000 shares at thirty dollars a share, giving them a 13.33 per cent interest for $600,000. Judge James Reed; Boss Flinn, the city's Republican leader; J. D. Callery, a onetime Mellon competitor in an amicably settled battle for control of Pittsburgh's street railways; and three other Mellon associates each took 5000 shares. All totaled, the Mellon group put $1.5 million in the new corporation's treasury for 50,000 shares of stock representing a one-third interest in the company. W. L. and Frick, who shared W. L.'s disdain for Guffey, declined to participate. The J. M. Guffey Petroleum Company used the $1.5 million, plus 70,000 more shares of its stock, to buy out the prospecting J. M. Guffey Company. By that time Lucas and Galey had gotten the situation in Texas under control and the partnership's impressive assets included four producing wells on Spindletop's hill, a storage capacity of a million barrels of oil, four other wells under way, leases covering a million acres of land in Texas and adjacent portions of Louisiana, sixteen miles of pipeline from Spindletop to a prospective refinery site in Port Arthur, Texas, on the Gulf of Mexico, 375 acres of land, mostly at Port Arthur, a number of contracts with railroads, and a hundred tank cars.

Division of the sale price among the prospecting partners was not easy, but after A. W. personally intervened as mediator, Lucas accepted $400,000 of the partnership's cash proceeds and 1000 of its 70,000 shares for his interests. A suit which Higgins brought against Lucas for Higgins's 10 per cent interest in Lucas's project was settled privately. Guffey bought out Galey for $365,000 plus what Craig Thompson describes in the official Gulf history, *Since Spindletop,* as "a hatful of mining company stocks Guffey happened to have in his office safe." Even after paying off the Mellon brothers' advances and the partnership's other obligations, Guffey himself came out with a lot of cash and 69,000 shares or a 46 per cent interest in the new company, and he became its first president, with A. W. Mellon as treasurer.

The J. M. Guffey Petroleum Company then owned the assets of the former partnership and had 30,000 shares of its own stock to sell for development. At precisely that moment a fresh crop of buyers came along.

Andrew Carnegie had early established a progressive prototype profit-sharing plan at his steel works whereby the company periodically distributed stock in the business to its employees. Few of the employees took the shares that they received seriously until the sale of the Carnegie company to J. P. Morgan's U.S. Steel syndicate, when some thirty of Carnegie's employees, many of whom had performed only the humblest of tasks, discovered that overnight they had become millionaires—"Carnegie millionaires," as they became known in Pittsburgh. One bookkeeper came out of the sale to Morgan with $1,900,000. The remaining 30,000 shares of the J. M. Guffey Petroleum Company were quickly sold to Carnegie millionaires, among them Charles M. Schwab, later president of U.S. Steel and owner of a controlling interest in Bethlehem Steel. The Carnegie millionaires paid sixty-six dollars a share, more than doubling the value of the original investors' interests and putting just under $2 million into the company treasury. This money was augmented by a bond issue. T. Mellon & Sons bought $2.5 million of the company's bonds; and their allied bank, Old Colony Trust of Boston, took another $1.5 million. As an added incentive to the bankers to make the loan, Guffey himself personally guaranteed the payment of the notes and pledged some of his stock in the enterprise as collateral. His willingness to take a greater personal risk than the other stockholders would come back to haunt him.

The J. M. Guffey Petroleum Company now had working capital. It started work on its huge refinery at Port Arthur and bought some tanker ships.

One of management's early decisions was that the enterprise's refining and distributing aspects should be handled by a corporate entity separate from its production-of-crude arm, which might thereby deal more easily with outside suppliers of crude. As a name for the corporation that would do the refining, they decided that something linking the company with the locale might appeal to regional pride and give the "Yankee" business a more hospitable reception in Texas. Something like, perhaps, Texas Oil Refining Company sounded pretty good, and could lend itself to some catchy logo like "Texaco." When they found that that name had already been reserved by another significant syndicate, Guffey Company's general manager at Beaumont, J. C. McDonnell, reserved the name "Gulf Oil Refining Company," thinking that at least that name indicated their location on the Gulf of Mexico. The name took. But for a quirk of timing, Gulf today would be Texaco, and possibly Texaco, Gulf. Stock in Gulf was distributed to the stockholders of the J. M. Guffey Petroleum Company in proportion to their respective interests, and the corporations shared common officers.

The Guffey Company and Gulf were beset with problems. Their own tremendous output of crude and the successes of the wildcatters that their gushers attracted to the area increased the production of Texas crude so greatly that its price plummeted to a low of five cents a barrel. At that price it could not be profitably merchandised—even if it could be refined. And it defied refining. Pennsylvania crude was light-bodied, green, relatively free from sulphur, and paraffin-based. It smelled sweet and it was called "sweet." Texas produced heavy black sulphur-laden, asphalt-based gunk that was appropriately known as "sour." Guffey Company and Gulf made repeated expensive experiments to refine the stuff and seemed to be getting nowhere. As "crude," its uses and salability were severely limited. Then the worst came: Spindletop ran dry. W. L. wrote that he was working late at his desk at T. Mellon & Sons, wrapping up details to extricate the family from its street railway interests,

> when I heard footsteps and a cough. By the lightness of the step and the apologetic note of the cough, I knew without looking that my visitor was A. W. . . . When I looked up, he was standing in my doorway.
> "Will, those Texas wells have stopped flowing."
> I knew that the wells he referred to were the oil wells near Beaumont, Texas. Spindletop! . . . I well remember the things he said because each sentence was a cord further binding me to an unwelcome duty . . . when A. W. said: "Somebody ought to go down and look into this, somebody who knows oil," I knew that it was up to me even before he added: "Will, I think you're the one to go."

W. L., who still had no personal financial interest in the situation, went reluctantly to Beaumont in August of 1902 and remained with the Gulf Oil Company until he retired as chairman of the board forty-six years later. At that time he wrote, no doubt sincerely, "When I go to the office of Gulf Oil I am swept by a deep regret that I am not starting again with them. They speak a language I love and understand." The unsigned foreword to *Since Spindletop* attributes Gulf's greatness principally to him: "There was one man whose contributions were of such scope and constancy that the company came to reflect his character—to think and feel and act as he did. That man was William Larimer Mellon." While the foreword smells a mite of sycophancy (W. L.'s family were still Gulf's principal stockholders), it was probably true.

W. L. found Beaumont a depressing town. "It impressed me most by its mud. It was liquid mud in which its blocks of houses were an archipelago." Sulphur fumes from Guffey Company's Spindletop had eaten away most of the paint from the structures, giving the town "an appearance indescribably shabby." His view of the Guffey Company was equally bleak. Production of crude was not, in his view, the biggest problem. He correctly surmised that Spindletop's impotence could be remedied through pumping operations. Colonel Guffey was the real problem. He thought Guffey guilty of incredible and consistent mismanagement. He had passed up the right leases, bought the wrong leases, and squandered the corporation's assets with typical wildcatter's abandon. (As for the leases, Guffey largely agreed but blamed Lucas's bad judgment for the selection.) Righting the corporate wrongs, as W. L. related it to A. W., would take, among other things, the infusion of not less than $12 million. Among the other things that it would require was the removal of Colonel Guffey himself from active management.

"Something had to be done," W. L. wrote. What else could be done? What else had ever been done? A. W. and W. L. journeyed to New York, home of the great offices of the Standard Oil Company. They had made the trip before, with satisfactory results. At the famed but restrained Holland House Hotel, favorite of visiting industrialists, they closeted themselves with Standard's highest operating executives, Archbold and Henry H. Rogers. Would Standard buy out the Gulf and Guffey companies or at least come into Spindletop with them? The answer was firm: "We're out," said Rogers. "Standard won't touch this. After the way Mr. Rockefeller has been treated by the State of Texas, he'll never put another dime in Texas."* As W. L. told it, with the respectable authority of letters that he quoted, there was nothing that A. W. and R. B. wanted less than to get back into the oil business on other than a banker's basis, but at that point their alternatives were either to take an active role in management or to call their own $3.1 million investment in stocks and bonds and the $2.4 million that had been invested in stocks and bonds by their own circle a virtual total loss.

The way that W. L. told it, concern for their unfortunate associates impelled them to take the reins of Gulf. Guffey's 46 per cent interest was

*In his account, W. L. stressed what he described as a closeness between Guffey and the Standard people. "In times past one of the reasons I had shied away from Guffey was that he would cheerfully do me a bit of harm any time he could do the Standard Oil some good. That was the kind of bird he was, in my eyes." The implication of W. L.'s account, clear though not expressly stated, was that Standard declined to get into the Guffey Company–Gulf Oil situation because Archbold and Rogers saw the Mellon overtures as a move hostile to their ally Guffey. Most histories of the American oil industry accept as correct Guffey's portrayal of himself as an enemy of Standard. The conflict in evidence highlights a phenomenon common in political situations dominated by a single power. The "outs" (which in the case of oil historically meant everyone other than those openly affiliated with Standard Oil) invariably suspect that their fellow "outs" are secretly conniving with the "ins." Had Guffey known about the Mellons' visit with Archbold and Rogers, he would surely have drawn the same conclusion about the Mellons that W. L. had drawn about Guffey, and W. L.'s recitation makes clear that Guffey would have been right.

a very long way from 51 per cent; he knew that in any personal contest virtually all of the other 54 per cent would be voted by A. W. Mellon, so he voiced no objection when his board of directors voted him an unwanted assistant. They established the office of executive vice president and gave the new officer complete executive authority. The man who filled the position, W. L. Mellon, hadn't had amicable relations with the company's president since as long as anyone could remember. Guffey remained nominal president of the Guffey Petroleum Company–Gulf Refining until 1907, when, as he put it with his folksy charm, "They throwed me out."

After W. L.'s appointment Guffey's principal function, as the Mellons viewed things, was to get in the way. W. L. wrote that "the president of the Guffey Petroleum Company was not always realistic about his situation. Consequently, in my position as the executive vice president in charge of management, I was obliged at times to be quite arbitrary with him. It is very hard for me to be patient with incompetents." Much in W. L.'s history would bear out his son Matthew's insistence that W. L. was a kind, generous, and tolerant man; he seems, however, to have been willing to make at least one exception.

W. L.'s first concern was to recruit top-level management people and principally George H. Taber, a self-taught Standard Oil chemist and protégé of Henry Rogers. Even W. L. described Taber as crotchety and irritable, but at least Taber understood refining. He was set to work at figuring out how to cook Texas crude. Then came George Craig, a Pennsylvanian of great experience in the business, who was placed in charge of the business's pipelines. Other crucial people brought in by W. L. in the early days were Frank Leovy, who led the Gulf efforts to find new sources of crude, and Gale R. Nutty, master salesman. W. L. lacked A. W.'s finesse but he shared his uncle's ability to select able people.

Next came the matter of a contract that Guffey Company had entered into that threatened the very existence of Guffey Company and Gulf. In the early 1900s one of the last of the world's great sea traders was still going strong. Traditionally, the trader had dealt in seashells from which mother-of-pearl could be extracted and utilized by European craftsmen, and it took its name, Shell Transport and Trading Company, from its original line. By the time of Spindletop it was still buying and selling seashells, but it had branched out and was involved in a less placid sideline; it was the world's most significant dealer in Russian oil. Shell wanted to transport and trade in Spindletop's crude, and in June of 1901 Guffey Company contracted to sell Shell 4.5 million barrels a year at twenty-five cents a barrel for the next twenty years. Guffey Company had insured itself a ready buyer for about half of Spindletop's production, and at a profit, regardless of how many other big strikes might be made to depress the market! As the price of crude dropped to a nickel a barrel, Colonel Guffey's legendary reputation for shrewdness was once again borne out, and remained firmly established until, that is, Spindletop dried up and the price of crude soared to such heights that fulfilling the Shell contract would bust Guffey Company and Gulf. In his memoirs W. L. heaped blame on Colonel Guffey for having made the contract with Shell. British records would exonerate the Colonel. Shortly after Shell's negotiator for the contract had first arrived in Pittsburgh, he had wired back that the key man with whom he talked was none other than A. W. Mellon himself, a man "reported of the highest social and financial standing in Pittsburgh":

> As a banker his desire to be absolutely secured in any event I frequently found a stumbling block during the negotiations, but as his financial interest in the Guffey Co. was very large, and he protruded his personality and experience on all occasions, his friends were, to my regret, obliged to give very great weight to his views, and little or nothing was done without his approval.

If A. W. had gotten the company into the situation, he would take responsibility for getting it out. In a bold stroke he personally journeyed to England as the agent for Guffey Company–Gulf to discuss the lamentable situation with Marcus Samuel, strongman of Shell. Suit between the parties was clearly imminent, and Shell's attorneys could have instituted their action more advantageously in England than America; A. W.'s presence in England as agent for Guffey Company–Gulf invited a visit from the process server, bringing papers starting the suit. Shell, by common consent, could have forced Guffey-Gulf to continue fulfilling the contract to the point of bankruptcy, and even, perhaps, have picked up the balance of the Americans' assets in settlement of the balance of Shell's claims.

If ever the oil business knew a gentleman, it was Marcus Samuel. His admiring biographer, Robert Henriques, wrote that

> It is within the living memory of many people that Marcus was completely won by Andrew Mellon. . . . Mellon was a man of immense charm and attractive personality, of a most distinguished appearance and aristocratic bearing, somewhat incompatible with the tough and ruthless ethics of his business career. His manners were perfect and he spoke always very courteously and in a mild, gentle voice. Once more Marcus yielded to the pressure of charm.

The oil business may never have known any gentlemen. Perhaps Samuel was interested in the preservation of a strong American outfit that would thereafter be undyingly allied with him in his off-again, on-again feud with none other than the Standard Oil Company. In any event, Samuel let Guffey-Gulf out of its contract.

Gulf's biggest problem was in obtaining adequate sources of crude. Their whole project had been geared to handling and refining Spindletop's early vast output, and their network of operations could not profitably operate with significantly smaller quantities. They were pumping oil out of Spindletop, but it was yielding barely enough to keep the corporate head above waters, and even that gave ominous signs of giving out. Discoveries of Spindletop-size in the Indian Territory solved that problem. The Indian Territory oil (as it was known in the business long after anyone still recalled that Oklahoma was the "Indian Territory") had properties similar to Pennsylvania sweet: easier to refine and generally of a "better" grade than Texas sour. W. L. said that the new finds represented "Pennsylvania quality in Texas quantities." It was additionally inviting because it lent itself nicely for manufacture of "gasoline," a petroleum by-product already in substantial demand in France as the propellant for the *automobile* being developed and aggressively merchandised there. The Indian Territory was a long way from Gulf's Port Arthur refinery—twice the distance that W. L.'s Crescent Pipeline had run—but it looked to be easier terrain to pipe than Pennsylvania.

Getting into Indian Territory oil was going to take money, at least $4 or $5 million and probably more. It was tempting, indeed it was almost certainly necessary for the survival of the enterprise, but as W. L. told it, "It certainly was not tempting to invest 4 or 5 million dollars more in the Guffey Company. . . . Naturally, A. W. and Dick Mellon had no intention of pouring more money into the J. M. Guffey Petroleum Company unless there was a change of structure." W. L. didn't explain why his uncles' reluctance to proceed without "a change of structure" was "natural" but he did tell us that there was a change of structure. A new corporate entity, the Gulf Oil Company (the word "Refining" being absent from the new title), was organized to take over the J. M. Guffey Petroleum Company and the Gulf Oil Refining Company. Colonel Guffey would have no part of it, at least not of his own volition, and declined to trade his shares into the new company. But there were ways of dealing with that. W. L. wrote that

> Guffey owed the Mellon brothers a million dollars of principal and unpaid interest on money borrowed by the two Guffey companies. At the same time he owed much more money to other Pittsburgh banks. Against these new debts he had put up as collateral with A. W. and Dick 24,000 shares of his Guffey Petroleum Company stock.

Of those shares that Guffey hadn't already sold to support his improvident lifestyle, he had no doubt pledged many more to the other Pittsburgh bankers for his debts. His situation was such that he could be pressured, and he was. While most of the other stockholders simply traded in their Guffey and Gulf Refining stock for shares in the reorganized ventures, Guffey finally sold outright. (*Since Spindletop* points out that though Guffey had complained that "They throwed me out," "the record shows it was Guffey who did not choose to stay in.")

Securing a share of Indian Territory oil couldn't wait for formal reorganization of the Guffey-Gulf corporations. Standard Oil was already strengthening its early interests in Oklahoma; its quick action threatened to transform its foothold into a stranglehold on the crude that was essential to the preservation of the Mellon interests in Guffey-Gulf. The Mellons therefore organized other corporations to get into it, which might later be absorbed into the Gulf framework if absorption looked to be desirable, such as the H. Y. Arnold Company (H. Y. had been the manager of the Gulf Oil Refining Company until he decided that he preferred to live in Tulsa, Oklahoma) and the Gypsy Oil Company (Leovy named it after his boat, *The Gypsy*). At government auction Leovy acquired valuable rights for Gypsy Oil but at costs which totaled a staggering $3,888,000. It was only over the long haul that the purchase proved to be a wise investment, with ultimate total production of 6,945,077 barrels. According to *Since Spindletop,* Gypsy's purchases brought $14,000 to every member of the Osage Indian nation.

With Gypsy's new resources and a reorganized Gulf Oil Company, the venture was off the ground, and (as W. L. would have it) at last with sound management. ("I must say that both A. W. and Dick were in a happier frame of mind.") A. W. Mellon was Gulf Oil Company's first president, shortly to be succeeded by his nephew, W. L. Mellon. Ultimately the corporations that had been established to take advantage of the Indian Territory opportunities were absorbed by Gulf. The sources do not make clear the percentages by which the Mellon family increased their interests in the corporation at the time of its succession to the Guffey-Gulf Refining interests, or at the time of the absorption by Gulf of the corporations that had been founded to get into the Indian Territory oil; nor do they make clear the increased investments required of the Mellon family to effectuate these changes and developments. All that can be reported with certainty is that at the time that Gulf "went public" in 1943 forty-two Mellons, Mellon trusts, and Mellon foundations owned 70 per cent of Gulf. It remains the family's single most important asset.

After Guffey was "throwed out," things went from bad to worse for him, but through it all he tried to keep his dignity. Matthew Mellon recalled seeing Guffey

> one day when I was having lunch with father and A. W. at the Duquesne Club about 1915. He was dressed entirely in black and with his flowered waistcoat, drooping grey mustache and thin black ribbon bow tie, he struck me as someone who had just stepped off one of Mark Twain's riverboats. He walked by our table as if we didn't exist while father and Uncle Andy exchanged amused glances.

In *Judge Mellon's Sons,* W. L. claimed to have felt sorry for him:

> If only Colonel Guffey could have been persuaded by his own better judgement or the counsel of his friends to go along with the reorganization that was proposed, he would have lived all his days in comfort and died a well-to-do man. However, within nine years from the day that Spindletop came in, Colonel Guffey was in dire distress for money.

His affairs went into the hands of receivers. Years later he brought suit against the Gulf Oil Company.

Among the assets of the original J. M. Guffey partnership had been a lease known as the "Page lease," which the partnership had sold at a bargain price to a former Texas governor in the hopes of currying local political favor, with payment to have been over time on an installment basis. More than twenty years after the formation of the new corporation, Guffey, a broke and broken old man at eighty-six, brought suit against Gulf, successor to the J. M. Guffey Petroleum Company. He and his witness, J. C. McDowell, first general manager of the new corporation, testified that at the time of conveyance of the partnership's assets to the new corporation it had been clearly understood that the installment payments for the Page lease were to be Guffey's money and not that of the new corporation, but that when the installments came in, Guffey, president of the new corporation, had permitted them to be received into the corporation's treasury as a loan from himself, to help the new corporation in times of temporary cash bind. Guffey became involved in other things and forgot about the matter until 1920, when McDowell reminded him of it. He thereupon made demand for reimbursement from Gulf, was denied, and then brought suit over the matter.

A. W. and the other surviving original stockholders of Guffey Company testified that no reservation had been made as to the proceeds from the Page lease and that they had believed they were acquiring the right to the installment payments as well as the partnership's other assets. Guffey bristled at their testimony: "How can you beat perjury like that?" he muttered loud enough to be heard. "And it means so much to me and so little to them!" The jury awarded Guffey $348,000, but their decision was overturned by an appellate court, which directed that a new trial be held. On retrial, the judge directed the jury to find for Gulf. Guffey died not long after.* It is possible that neither side knowingly "lied" during the proceedings, that memories of the crucial discussions had faded badly in twenty years and then been restored to firmness in reliance on mental pictures that may well have been crisped by subconscious considerations.

John Galey, like his longtime partner, also died broke, he in 1912. Anthony Lucas fared somewhat better. He ended up in Washington, D.C., where he did consulting work for geological projects and busied himself in the work of scientific and technical societies until his death in 1921. Later the American Institute of Mining and Metallurgical Engineers established the Anthony E. Lucas Gold Medal, an award to recognize "distinguished achievement in improving the technique and practice of finding and producing petroleum." Patillo Higgins fared perhaps best of all the originals. He spent the rest of his life puttering around in oil prospecting and made a few minor hits, though he never became wealthy. Disappointed at the lack of Beaumont support for one of his ventures, the Higgins Standard Oil Company, he moved to Houston and then to San Antonio, where he died in 1955 at the age of ninety-two.

There were other enterprises, many other enterprises, most of which have either long been out of the family's portfolio or have ceased to play a major role in it: utility companies owned entirely or predominantly by the Mellons, important tracts of real estate in downtown Pittsburgh, large developments in the suburbs, and significant investments in a score of lesser businesses. By 1900 "River Coal," the Monongahela River Consolidated Coal & Coke Company controlled by the Mellons and Frick, dominated the coal fields south of Pittsburgh. River Coal, together with Pittsburgh Coal Company, which was dependent on the Mellon banks for financial stability, monopolized the coal resources of western Pennsylvania and adjacent portions of West Virginia—resources that together with the Frick mines powered the industrial heart of America.

*In the A. W. Mellon tax trial years later, A. W.'s coal holdings were explored in depth by the government. One of those coal lands owned jointly by A. W. and R. B. was carried on the books as "the J. M. Guffey coal lands."

Streetcars consumed much of the Mellons' time and especially W. L.'s attention. The importance of the streetcar in the development of America has been neglected; W. L. highlighted its role:

> The streetcars meant [that the laborers] could spread farther as they sought places to live. When their day's work was done, they could ride home and they could ride to work; and moreover, ride fast. Every decision we made [as to extending a Mellon streetcar line] was based on just one thing: How many people could we serve? Looking back we ought to see more clearly what an enormous change for the better was worked in people's lives by the coming of electric streetcars. That was rapid transportation. What has blinded us largely to its enormous value in the development of the American standard of living was the coming of the automobile rather sooner than anybody had dared expect.

The family's concern for municipal transportation stemmed back to the Judge's early investments in horse-drawn carriage lines between his East Liberty section of town and Oakland, a closer-in Pittsburgh community. Their interest was reinvigorated in the mid-1890s, when the Mellons entered the toll-bridge business with a new bridge linking two Carnegie company towns. It was a good sturdy bridge that might carry a streetcar. The bridge led them into the electric streetcar business, which led them into a new network of electric utilities, which led them into more streetcars. The electricity was generated by coal—Mellon coal. W. L., between his Crescent and his Gulf ventures, created a streetcar network that was truly "modern," with tracks worthy of the Pennsylvania Railroad and cars engineered by Pittsburgh's great inventor George Westinghouse especially for the area's steep hills and abrupt precipices. They were "luxury" cars and allowed a tired workingman a comfortable ride and even a taste of elegance. They were painted, as W. L. later described them, "as yellow as paint could make them." The Mellon lines extended farther and farther out, and as they were extended, the family's Monongahela Light and Power Company absorbed electric utility companies along their routes.

W. L. established Kennywood Park, an amusement park far out of town, where he offered swimming pools, dance floors, ferris wheels, pony rides, merry-go-rounds, roller coasters, and a free vaudeville show. There was no admission fee at Kennywood Park for anyone arriving by streetcar. The Mellon streetcar made the run. Years later W. L. recalled one fine summer night when he and his uncles went out to Kennywood Park, "in summer flannels and straw hats. . . . There, A. W. along with the rest of us, rode on all the rides and saw the vaudeville."

The Judge was alive and well during the Mellons' streetcar period but no longer followed business matters. It was just as well. He would have disapproved of his sons' easy relationship with ostensible competitors like Consolidated Traction, whose manager was Christopher Magee, the city's Republican boss. Nor would he have approved of A. W.'s offer to sell a "paper" railway line at a profit, or the technique followed to secure small-town franchises from local officials ("There were all kinds of influences making hidden currents in these turbulent little political areas around Pittsburgh," W. L. wrote). Early in the twentieth century the other two major streetcar operations in greater Pittsburgh merged as Pittsburgh Railways Company, and absorbed the Mellon lines late in 1901 for stock valued at $6 million plus a rental for the Mellons approaching half a million dollars a year. In 1910 the city had an outside expert appraise Pittsburgh Railways' operations. He concluded that the company was very much overcapitalized and its values inflated and unrealistic, to the detriment of fare-paying passengers and those who might have purchased their stock at excessive levels. The Judge would have been displeased, but by that time he was gone.

The family also had substantial investment in the steel industry, notably in Union Steel. The short life of Union is tied to the exciting story of the creation of United States Steel, a story of giants in battle: Carnegie, Morgan, Rockefeller, Frick, and Charles M. Schwab. Union is a subplot in the U.S. Steel story, with the Mellons as principal characters in that subplot.

Throughout its history Carnegie Steel was the nation's major steel producer. Until late in the 1890s it so dwarfed its nearest competitors as to make them insignificant. In 1898, however, Judge Elbert H. Gary, as agent for J. Pierpont Morgan, brought together a combination of smaller steel producers and some important steel fabricators, and a new corporation emerged: Federal Steel. Though Carnegie Steel still dominated the market, Federal was its first significant competitor, and with the Morgan interests and their money behind Federal it threatened to become a fierce one. Carnegie himself was then in his early sixties, wealthy beyond anyone's wildest dreams, eager to begin enjoying his wealth, and reluctant to get into fresh fights. He wanted out. Frick, the principal stockholder after Carnegie himself, had had years of friction with Carnegie and wanted an end to the relationship.

With Carnegie's encouragement, early in 1899 Frick negotiated an option by which William H. Moore and his brother, James H. Moore, Chicago's diversely interested tycoons, and their associates would buy out Carnegie's stock in Carnegie Steel Company at a price of $157,950,000. The Moore

syndicate paid an option price of $1,170,000 and had ninety days in which
to consummate the transaction or lose their deposit. The Mellons were not
in on the ground floor of the syndicate, and Frick's efforts to get the Moores
to sell the Mellons an interest in it were unsuccessful even though Frick
promised the Moores a 100 per cent profit on such portion of their investment as the Mellons might assume. A quirk of fate prevented consumma-
tion of the sale to the Moores. As the ninety days were running out, Roswell
P. Flower, an important figure on Wall Street and the Moores' New York
contact, died. His passing disordered the financial community, with the
result that the Moores were unable to arrange their financing in time to
close the deal.

Financial interests tied to Morgan were not about to back a transaction
that might threaten Morgan's Federal Steel interests, and if the Moores
approached the Mellons at all, the Mellons could not have forgotten the
rebuff that the Moores had given them so shortly before. The Moores and
Frick assumed that Carnegie would allow an extension of the option, but
by the time the ninety days had run, Carnegie had thought better of the deal.
He declined to have further discussion with the Moore syndicate and sent
their million-plus deposit off to one of his favorite charities. Frick himself
had had a substantial interest in the syndicate and its deposit; Carnegie had
encouraged Frick to take a personal financial interest in it. Under the
circumstances, the loss of the deposit money aggravated the long-standing
bad blood between the principal partners in Carnegie Steel.

The final open break between Carnegie and Frick came a few months
later, in the fall of 1899. Frick—the chairman of the board of Carnegie Steel
—had bought himself some land adjacent to a major Carnegie installation
for half a million dollars. Almost immediately he resold it to the corporation
for three times as much. Perhaps he viewed his conduct as righting the
wrong to which Carnegie had recently subjected him, but Carnegie could
not have viewed it in such a light. The next time that Carnegie was in
Pittsburgh there were hot words. The purchase of Frick's acreage was
canceled, and Frick was ousted from his position as chairman of the board.
Suit between the partners was instituted.

Frick's biographer, Colonel George Harvey, an intimate of A. W.'s,
writes that Union Steel was born of the blowup between the two Carnegie
partners. The timing would seem to bear him out. Immediately after Frick's
termination, Union Steel emerged. It had four equal partners: Frick, A. W.
Mellon, R. B. Mellon, and William H. Donner. Donner had entered steel
from the tin business and was to be the operating head of the business. Their
Union Improvement Company bought up a hypothesized city, "Columbia,"

Pennsylvania, consisting of 342 acres and a handful of insignificant houses on the Monongahela River south of Pittsburgh. Overnight they built Union Steel's wire and nail mill on the riverbank and a new town, Donora, Pennsylvania, to house and meet the needs of the huge work force that Union's enterprises would demand. By the time of Donora's first official census in August of 1902 it had a population of 5082.

Frick didn't need Carnegie; as things turned out, Carnegie needed Frick. As 1900 opened, his new competitor was not his major thorn; Federal Steel was his big problem. As fabricators affiliated with the Federal interests failed to renew their contracts with Carnegie Steel, Carnegie and his new head of operations, Schwab, declared war against Federal and its components by cutting prices and by preparing to enter competition in every product line with every Federal affiliate. Carnegie geared for expansion of his mills, product lines, and transportation facilities; his company's plans and actions were well publicized and designed to demoralize Morgan and his Federal crowd. They did. In the midst of his big battle with Morgan, Carnegie could not also make war on the less important Union Steel; indeed, he needed Union as a customer to pick up ingot output formerly sold to Federal fabricators, and Carnegie contracted to sell Union ingots for Union's use in manufacturing rods, nails, and wire.

After a year of this Morgan was ready to come to terms with Carnegie. Early in 1901 he agreed to take over the Carnegie Steel Company at a price of $492 million. There was no negotiating; that was Carnegie's price. His own share of the sale price came to over $300 million; Frick's was some $61,400,380 in U.S. Steel bonds and preferred and common stock.

In a matter of a couple of months Morgan had merged Federal, Carnegie Steel, Rockefeller's iron ore interests in the Minnesota Mesabi range, and related concerns into a monster corporation, U.S. Steel—"the steel trust," as it became known. They were unable to bring Union into their fold; the Mellons wanted too much. In the spring of 1901 Morgan's stock market manipulators created a market for U.S. Steel securities, in which Frick liquidated the holdings that had come to him as part of his share of Carnegie Steel's proceeds.

Andrew Carnegie's technique for bringing Morgan to terms was not new to A. W. Mellon; Mellon had taken the same approach in his Crescent battles with Standard Oil: threaten serious competition, show that you mean business, and the competition will come to terms with you. As soon as Carnegie's signature was dry on the buy-sell agreement with Morgan, Union Steel followed suit. It embarked on a radical expansion of production facilities, product lines, and transportation resources. It contracted a desirable agreement for acquisition of iron ore in the Mesabi region. In November 1902 Union absorbed Sharon Steel, run by Christopher Magee's partner in political shenanigans, Boss William Flinn, and its press releases spoke of further major expansion plans. By that time Union was already a fully integrated steel enterprise and it looked to be developing into the kind of threat to U.S. Steel that Federal had been to Carnegie. The most irritating aspect of the situation to the Morgan interests was that Union's early contract with Carnegie Steel, binding on U.S. Steel as successor to Carnegie, enabled Union to undersell U.S. Steel on items made from ingots purchased by Union from its bigger competitor. Union did not seem amenable to pressure of any kind.

To make matters worse for the giant, it was beset with important personnel problems. Schwab had emerged as first president of U.S. Steel, but Morgan put greater reliance on Judge Gary, whom he had installed as chairman of the board. Schwab was an earthy man; Gary, oppressively sanctimonious. The two could not get on. As their friction approached the point of breakdown, Morgan urged Frick, a nominal member of the U.S. Steel board of directors and one of the few board members with any real experience in the steel industry, to take a more active role in the corporation's management. Frick—of a sudden concerned about business ethics—explained that his conflicting interests in Union prevented him from doing so. The Union group used both carrot and stick in its ballet with the giant: the promise of Frick's greater involvement in U.S. Steel and the threat of renewed competition. U.S. Steel decided that it ought to buy out Union. For $30,860,501. The sale price was negotiated by A. W. Mellon for Union with U.S. Steel's representative Judge James Reed, A. W.'s longtime intimate and erstwhile personal attorney. Once again the Mellons had increased their fortunes essentially by making their enterprises nuisances to their competitors.

In later years the Mellon brothers made occasional forays into the steel industry, but with the sale of Union in 1902 they were essentially "out" of the steel business as such. Just as they had made integrated enterprises out of Alcoa, Crescent, Gulf, and their street railway interests, though, their Union interests led them into numerous related enterprises, three of which remained in their portfolios long after they liquidated Union itself. Earliest of these ventures was the New York Shipbuilding Company, whose shipyards on the shores of the Delaware River built all-metal ships, mostly from Union's steel. Frick and the Mellons held controlling interests. Shipbuilding went into a significant slump in the years between the Spanish-American War and the First World War, and New York Shipbuilding's stock gradually dropped from fifty to twenty while the Mellons increased their interests in it. With the outbreak of the war in 1914, A. W. was set upon by investors eager to buy out the Mellon interests or to absorb the corporation itself. The Mellons were unwilling to sell; A. W. explained to prospective purchasers that

> this maritime business is a kind of a little hobby with me. When I lie awake of nights I enjoy myself picturing these ships going to strange ports in Java and Africa and China. Would you deprive me of the pleasures of imagination?

By 1917 just about every ship had been built that was to be built until Adolf Hitler revitalized the shipbuilding industry, and A. W. had tired of his imaginary journeys to exotic destinations. At the perfect moment, New York Shipbuilding was sold to Robert Dollar of the Dollar Lines for $11,500,000.

The McClintic-Marshall Construction Company was born in 1900. Charles D. Marshall and Howard W. McClintic had been classmates in engineering at Lehigh University; after college they spent ten years at Pittsburgh's Shiffler Bridge Works. They had become minor partners at Shiffler when more senior members of the firm decided to sell the concern to American Bridge Works, soon to become a component of Morgan's U.S. Steel. At that point the two young men decided to go out on their own. Their particular field of expertise was structural steel—steel for building components. Seventeen years earlier William LeBaron Jenney had built a ten-story building in Chicago supported by a steel frame; by the time that the young men approached the Mellons for financing, the steel-skeletoned building was becoming common in the windy city but had not yet come into its full flower. As cities became more congested and land values increased, it was inevitable—obviously inevitable—that the skyscraper would become the dominant form of downtown building. A. W. Mellon understood that. McClintic and Marshall understood the buildings.

At about the time that McClintic and Marshall approached A. W. for help in financing what they envisioned as a small steel-fabricating business, the Mellons took over a structural steel plant at Pottstown, Pennsylvania. While the brothers considered McClintic and Marshall's plea, they asked the young engineers to evaluate their own new acquisition. Marshall's bleak analysis of the Mellons' investment impressed A. W. He then moved to the younger men's interest. As W. L. later recounted A. W.'s talk, the banker told the two engineers,

> The loan you have in mind is too small. This is often the case with borrowers. It seems to us that you ought to have at least $100,000 of working capital. My

brother and I will be glad to take a half interest in such a company as you want to form, and we will put in $50,000 if you provide the other $50,000. We want to put into the deal this Saylor plant at Pottstown, which now belongs to us, at its appraised value.

When McClintic and Marshall pleaded their inability to come up with anything approaching $50,000, A. W. pushed them. Why not borrow their share from Marshall's father? Why not place new mortgages on their homes? When the young men squirmed, A. W. asked hard questions: "Would your father not have faith in you?" Their unwillingness to refinance their homes forced A. W. to an unhappy conclusion: "Your reluctance makes it appear as if you do not have faith in yourselves or in this enterprise." The young men realized that they would have to demonstrate willingness to take financial risks themselves if they were to expect the Mellons to take the risks with them. At length they agreed. They would approach Marshall's father; they would refinance their homes. As W. L. told it,

> it was A. W. who then breathed a sigh of relief. He told them he appreciated and sympathized with their feelings, not only as to mortgaging their homes but as to approaching Mr. Marshall's father.
>
> "Neither of these steps will be necessary," said A. W. "My brother and I will lend you the additional money. You should be able to repay us out of profits of the business." . . . Invariably, A. W. and Dick were generous in trades of that character. Of course, both of them liked to make a good trade, but "good trading" to them never meant taking advantage of some man simply because he lacked money.
>
> In his trade with these young men, a part of A. W.'s pride lay in taking care of them, in seeing that their interest was big enough to make it impossible for them to be tempted away from what they were setting out to create.

A. W. and R. B. put in their Pottstown plant and their $100,000, $50,000 of which was a loan to the younger men, in exchange for which the brothers took a 60 per cent interest in the corporation with 40 per cent allowed to the corporation's front partners. Frick, offered a chance to participate, declined; the business was too risky. In the years that followed, the McClintic-Marshall Construction Company's steel and engineering expertise became the framework for the Waldorf-Astoria Hotel, the Graybar and R.C.A. buildings in New York, the George Washington Bridge, Grand Central Terminal, Chicago's Merchandise Mart, the Cathedral of Learning at the University of Pittsburgh, and the Golden Gate Bridge in San Francisco. The corporation lost $2 million on the locks that it made for the Panama Canal but reaped ten times as much in publicity value from the contract. Their plants grew to half a dozen—in California, Buffalo, Chicago, and Pennsylvania. McClintic and Marshall were indeed able to repay what they had borrowed for their cash investment long before McClintic-Marshall Construction Company was merged into Bethlehem Steel in 1931. In the intervening years the corporation paid out dividends to its four stockholders totaling $8 million.

The Mellons played an important management role in the early history of Carborundum Company. McClintic and Marshall, however, were left pretty much alone. Shortly before Marshall's death in 1945 he recalled that his visits with A. W. generally had boiled down to two questions that the banker would ask him: "How much do you want? And when?"

The last of the steel-related enterprises to attract the Mellons was Standard Steel Car, born in 1902 as an outgrowth of a battle for control of the leader in the steel railroad car business. The Shoens, K. T. and his nephew W. T., were pioneers in the business of making steel railroad cars. By the turn of the century their Pressed Steel Car Company dominated the field. Their success was largely due to Pressed Steel's brilliant engineer-designer John W. Hanson and to its masterful salesman James Buchanan Brady, who ornamented his balloon-shaped form with such an array of gemstones as to give birth to his nickname, "Diamond Jim." In the early part of the century the Shoens lost control of Pressed Steel Car (as W. L. would have it, through the indecencies perpetrated upon them by another Pittsburgh-area banker). They left Pressed Steel, taking with them the corporation's two most valuable assets, Hanson and Diamond Jim, to form Standard Steel Car. Their new company badly needed capital. The Mellons advanced a $200,000 loan and made a factory that they owned just outside the city limits of Butler, Pennsylvania, available to the new company, taking bonds for their cash and a 20 per cent interest in the corporation by way of compensation for their factory and "bonus." Part of the understanding was that the indispensable Diamond Jim would be permitted to pay for his stock interest in the company out of the commissions he would likely earn in the future. The Shoens were not able businessmen, and neither Hanson nor Brady claimed to be. Their basic circle was rounded out with Mellon designees who filled up the company's board and saw to its financial well-being. Over the years A. W. and R. B. were regularly and directly involved in Standard's business affairs.

With Hanson and Brady, Hanson's excellent relationship with E. H. Harriman and Harriman's railroad network, and Mellon supervision and financing, Standard Steel Car couldn't fail, and didn't. Like shipbuilding, the railroad car business is a feast-or-famine enterprise, with periods of big ups and big downs. In the down times the Mellons acquired more and more stock in Standard. Before they sold out, they had bought the Shoens' holdings and had picked up additional shares, giving A. W. and R. B. each a 40 per cent interest in Standard, with still more of its stock owned by W. L. Together the family held well in excess of 80 per cent of the stock of Standard Steel Car.

Standard established its principal plant outside Butler, almost forty miles north of Pittsburgh. Butler had enjoyed a historic past as center for much of the oil activity in the great days of Pennsylvania oil, but Standard Steel Car added a vigorous new dimension to the area. Standard's "Lyndora" community attracted thousands of East-European laborers, all housed in the company's "Red Row"—its endless rows of red-painted company houses. (Red was the least expensive paint color at the time.) The public-spirited corporation contributed land close by its plant for the establishment of a state police barracks.

World War I was good to Standard. Major war-related contracts with the French and United States governments led to establishment of two Standard plants in France, bringing their total to eight factories. Standard's plant at La Rochelle, France, manned largely by captured German soldiers, played an important part in the French defense efforts, though its contract with the American government was too late in coming to enable it to participate significantly in the American drive. It actually produced only one howitzer carriage for the United States forces prior to the armistice, but Standard honored its contract and after the peace delivered 200 useless carriages to the United States at $25,000 each. Irate congressmen later railed that Standard's contracts were "permeated with corruption."

When the war was over, Standard "readjusted" wage scales, prompting an unhappy strike at Butler in 1919, but the helpful state police unit nearby acted with honor, firmness, and dispatch in re-establishing law, order, and the rights of private property. Thereafter, backed-up demands of railroads in the United States, Europe, and South America could be quickly and profitably satisfied.

The Koppers Company was the last of the businesses that the Mellons entered that are still important in the family's holdings. It was created by the Mellons together with Harry W. Croft, Hamilton Stewart, and Henry B. Rust to capitalize on the coke ovens invented by Dr. Heinrich Koppers, a German inventor who discovered a coal distillation process that would recover the by-products of coal that had previously been lost up the chimney of the coke oven. The Koppers coal-to-coke oven added an entirely new dimension to the chemical industry, and it so revolutionized the coking process that at times the coke itself became the by-product, with the principal value in the gases that until Koppers's invention had been wasted as atmospheric pollutants. The Koppers process salvaged gas that could be used for domestic lighting, cooking, or heating, and tars that could be used in a wide range of esoteric applications far removed from a raw lump of black coal. The military uses of the products salvaged by the Koppers process were even more intriguing. Among other things, the Koppers oven recovered quantities of toluol, the basic ingredient for yesterday's super-weapon, TNT, and a host of other spectacular killers.

Koppers developed his new oven in Germany in the early part of the twentieth century. U.S. Steel brought him to the United States in 1908 to build a batch of his ovens for its use. For several years thereafter Dr. Koppers and an increasing staff built plants for the manufacture of coke ovens in the United States for U.S. Steel and other customers, but Koppers never got around to merchandising his process in a way designed to make the most of its American potential.

Around 1913 or early in 1914, Croft, Stewart, and Rust decided to maximize the dollar by-product of the Koppers process, and in 1914 they approached the Mellons for help in reorganizing Koppers's ventures. The promise of the Koppers oven had already been realized; all that the proposed enterprise had to do was to popularize and merchandise it in the United States. That was simply a matter of money and management, two things that were well within the sphere of the Mellon brothers' expertise. The brothers were never ones to be rushed, and after World War I broke out in Europe in the summer of 1914, Dr. Koppers became visibly anxious for a speedy resolution of the discussions over the fate of his American rights. He wisely realized that the dollar value of United States patent rights owned by a German on a military tool might be wiped out by a change in the American political climate, and he could see the change in the climate coming. A. W. noticed Dr. Koppers's anxiety and mentioned it to W. L. Finally the Koppers enterprises were reorganized early in 1915; for his patents and existing operations Dr. Koppers received a 20 per cent interest in a new corporation capitalized at $1.5 million and a contract for future "consulting services" for which he was to receive $10,000 a year. Of the remaining stock, A. W. and R. B. owned 37½ per cent and Stewart and Croft the balance of 42½ per cent. Dr. Koppers's pre-existing organization of sixty-seven men stationed in Illinois was moved to Pittsburgh, where the Mellons could keep a closer eye on their new enterprise. The Koppers men arrived in March 1915; their operations were immediately stimulated by sales of munitions to the European belligerents and then to the United States. After the war the Koppers Company continued to grow dramatically throughout the 1920s.

Like other Mellon businesses, Koppers became a many-armed enterprise. From building plants and ovens for others, it moved to processing coal and its derivatives on its own account, becoming a major coke supplier and chemical company in its own right. If it was going to process coal, the company might as well own coal fields, so it began to buy up coal acreage far afield from Pittsburgh. If Koppers Company gas was to be sold, it might as well be sold by Koppers Company, and throughout the 1920s it acquired gas utilities throughout the eastern United States.

Dr. Koppers's obvious anxiety in 1914 no doubt cost him a better initial deal than he might otherwise have had. In normal times his fears would better have been hidden, but as things turned out, none of it made any difference. After the United States entered the war in 1917 it created the office of Alien Property Custodian, filled by A. Mitchell Palmer, later to earn notoriety as Attorney General for perpetrating the country's first major Red Scare. As Alien Property Custodian his duty was to round up any American property owned by a German national that might be worth bothering about and "sequester" it in the name of the American people. The Koppers Company patriotically called to the attention of his office that a Dr. Heinrich Koppers of Essen, Germany, owned a substantial block of stock in their enterprise. The custodian did his duty and succeeded to Dr. Koppers's interest in the Koppers Company. Joseph F. Guffey, nephew of Gulf's Colonel James Guffey and later a United States senator, was placed on Koppers's board to represent the federal government's interests until such time as Dr. Koppers's stockholdings could be auctioned off late in 1917. At the auction the only bidder for the enemy's stock was Hamilton Stewart, bidding on behalf of himself, A. W., R. B., and Croft. They acquired the stock with a bid of $302,250, representing the original book value of Dr. Koppers's stock share plus small accrued dividends.

Not long after, Croft and Stewart sold out their interests to the Mellons and Rust, and for many years thereafter the sole ownership of the Koppers Company was vested in a small number of close Mellon intimates: themselves, Rust, McClintic, and Marshall. Koppers Company rounded out the important elements of the Mellon family portfolio.

Today A. W. Mellon is known as one of the most successful men of "the age of the moguls." As such, he is most untypical of the lot. His story has none of the "gangland" aura that surrounds the history of the Vanderbilt and railroad men's millions; he cannot be accused of the kind of ruthless crushing of competition of which Rockefeller was certainly "guilty." He was never into the rough and tumble barbarism (sometimes racketeering) of the stock market of his day, and he strongly disapproved of it. Such "unfairness" as one might care to find in his treatment of Gulf's Colonel Guffey, Carborundum's Acheson, or Koppers's Koppers would have to rest upon the assertions of the disappointed or on arguable value judgments. In any case, all three were big boys. Charles Martin Hall, Arthur Vining Davis, McClintic and Marshall, W. L. Mellon, and H. C. McEldowney all became fabulously wealthy men. Whether or not they received their "fair" share of the profits generated by the combination of their ingenuity, initiative, hard work, and determination with the Mellon money backing is again a matter of value judgment, but none of them ever gave the slightest sign that they thought they had been shortchanged by the bankers. Only by straining the genus can A. W. be lumped with the "robber barons."

A. W.'s closest parallel in the age of the moguls would surely be the less successful J. P. Morgan (the elder, the great Morgan, who died in 1913) because both were similarly employed: they were finance capitalists. They were not "captains of industry" in the sense that they built industries as did Carnegie, Rockefeller, and Henry Ford; they financed others who built industries, taking a share of the profits as their reward. Otherwise, Mellon and Morgan were as different as the cigars to which both were addicted. Morgan's fat black oversized Havanas were as overpowering as he was himself. A. W.'s cigars were small and elegant, understated. Morgan wanted power and he exercised it. Money may have been the bigger part of Morgan's power, but the tremendous force of his personality was also part of it. He is generally given personal credit for keeping the "panic of 1907" from turning into a major depression. The combined assets of the Mellons and of the gigantic corporations they controlled gave A. W. tremendous power, but he never attempted to marshal all that power for evil —or for good. He would never have presumed to challenge the gods in the manner that Morgan did in 1907. He was not interested in power, and for that matter he was not really interested in money. Money was just the by-product of the ways that the Judge had taught him to keep himself busy. If A. W. did not ponder them closely, he was at least aware of the existential questions, unlike Morgan or any of the other men with whom he is so often grouped.

A. W. had many traits that contributed to his success as a businessman. Before he invested in an industry, he studied every aspect of the business.

He had remarkable powers of concentration, a terrific sense of order, a fine memory, and an inquiring mind. David Finley, who later became his closest aide, wrote that A. W. had "a disconcerting way of saying 'Why?' " He paid attention to the answer. He would not be rushed into making a business decision, but once into a young enterprise, patience was his greatest virtue. In the business world (if not in other arenas) he had a fine sense of timing.

Perhaps most important, A. W. was an excellent judge of men. He knew how to select and to keep men. Many served his interests for years, in a variety of positions. Colonel Frank Drake, for example, first came to the Mellons as W. L.'s aide at Gulf, then he was A. W.'s private assistant at the Treasury Department, president of Standard Steel Car, then an officer of Pullman, Standard's successor, and finally he was president of Gulf. Many others were with the Mellons for virtually their entire productive careers, including Howard Johnson and Henry A. Phillips, the most important personal assistants to A. W. and R. B. in their business careers, the former of whom echoed A. W.'s personality and manner, the latter, R. B.'s. A. W.'s technique was to coordinate the efforts of his network of competent underlings.

Once into a business, he remembered the Judge's advice: Don't trust to partners. He followed the family's more important interests himself and the lesser ones through surrogates. In any case, he confined his involvement to decisions of major import, and to "bottom-line" review of the books, and stayed out of the day-to-day workings of all of the businesses. Getting into such matters would have distracted him from more important considerations. His aloofness from operational concerns also spared him from being tarred with unhappy brushes, and particularly with blame for the labor policies of his companies. He was not directly involved in the titanic struggle between labor and management in Pittsburgh, the birthplace of the C.I.O., and therefore he was never personally identifiable as the laborer's nemesis. Harvey O'Connor's attempt in *Mellon's Millions* (1933), the leading biography of A. W., to hold the principal responsible for the acts of his agents never quite made an impact; as everyone well knew, Mellon himself had never caused anything particularly mean to be done.

As much as any of the moguls, A. W. appreciated the trend to combination, and the economic impetus for it. Like the other moguls, he insisted that consolidation of competing units into fewer ones, bigger ones, was good for the citizen at large, not bad. Anyway, it was as inevitable as the laws of nature themselves. In a world of survival of the fittest, it was only appropriate that Alcoa utilize every possible device to maintain its monopoly status, that Gulf "cooperate" with its "competitors" for the good of all.

In the 1920s he applauded the fact that in the Coolidge era "the distrust of great corporations has largely passed away, as it has become more and more evident that organization on a large scale is necessary in a country as large as this." It showed that "America has succeeded in adjusting herself to the economic laws of the new industrial era." A. W. was more visionary than most of the moguls. Not only were most of his enterprises wholly integrated operations but his interests as a whole were integrated. New York Shipbuilding built Gulf tankers out of Union's steel, all financed and insured through Mellon companies. Alcoa's laborers lived in houses financed by Union Trust, built on Mellon lots out of Mellon lumber, heated by Mellon coal, lit by Mellon utilities, and they rode to work on Mellon streetcars. If they had any money left at the end of the week, it went into a Mellon bank. Few had any money left at the end of the week.

In his investment approach, A. W. was almost as conservative as the Judge himself. Andrew Carnegie said, "Pioneering don't pay," and A. W. did little pioneering. The family's investment in Alcoa is typical. The original venture capital came from Captain Alfred Hunt and those who relied upon Hunt; Alcoa was an adolescent enterprise of great and obvious promise when the Mellons took small interests in it. Their loans to the business were carefully secured not only by the corporation's pledge but by the personal pledge of its chief officers. The Mellons increased their investments in it only as the ultimate success of the venture became more and more apparent, and their interests in it did not really blossom until 1917, after the beginning of the corporation's tremendous World War I growth, when they bought out most of the very substantial interest of David Gillespie, a personal friend of Hunt's. It was Gillespie, not Mellon, who had been the courageous (foolhardy) investor who had utilized his capital creatively.

In Gulf, again, the original financial risks were taken by James Guffey and John Galey, not Mellon; they pledged their souls, as well as their assets, as security. Only when circumstances locked the Mellons into Gulf did they go in big. Only in the case of Howard McClintic and Charles Marshall did the Mellons use their money creatively; they invested in two men, a riskier proposition than investing in a patent or in a balance sheet. It was one of the smaller of their investments, and as things developed, it was one of their wiser ones.

What has been said above about A. W. as mogul indicates an extremely high degree of executive ability, truly impressive. Whether it adds up to "genius," financial or otherwise, is another question, on which reasonable men can reasonably differ. Charles J. V. Murphy, author of an excellent three-part *Fortune* series on the Mellons published in 1967 had no doubt:

> Andrew Mellon was possibly the most brilliant businessman whom our society has produced. J. P. Morgan, for example, was picturesque and splendid; but the details of business privately bored him. Men like Frick and Henry Ford were geniuses but in their special theatres. Andrew Mellon, by contrast, ranged the business spectrum. He was a banker who understood corporations and an investor who understood men.

This author is less certain. A. W.'s mind was acute; he was trained by his father to read behind a balance sheet and to detect small problems about the plans unfurled on his huge desk. But except when locked into a position, he followed the Judge's example and would not "speculate" "without I saw a sure thing in it." What he accomplished in the business world, measurably by numbers of astronomical size, required and demonstrated intelligence and judgment, much concentration, and some shrewdness. But as Frank Kent wrote, after all was said and done, A. W.'s career as mogul showed "financial dominance, not personal dominance." It did not demonstrate "genius." The size of the numbers is probably more appropriately attributable to being born at the right time to the right father, at the confluence of two important rivers, amid hills of coal. Modest, but not falsely modest, A. W. himself would have insisted that that was the case.

By the turn of the twentieth century A. W. Mellon was not an old man —forty-five—but old far beyond from that toss and pallor of years of moneymaking. He was also lonely; always lonely, but more so after R. B., W. L., and Frick began making separate lives in their marriages. A. W. himself showed no interest in marriage, at least not outwardly. Seemingly he refused to recover from an early disappointment, described by the Judge in his 1885 memoirs:

> Being of a social disposition, he at first went into society a good deal, and a mutual attachment sprang up between him and a young lady acquaintance. She was of good family, and in every way worthy of him; and the attachment between them ripened into a marriage engagement which was entirely satisfactory to both families, and would have been consummated in the spring of 1882, but her health began to fail, and as the disease developed, it proved to be of so serious a nature that by the advice of her physician marriage was deferred till the result would be known. She continued to decline slowly, however, until all hope was abandoned, and died in about a year afterwards. Since then he has gone but little into ladies' society, and become more and more absorbed in business pursuits.

W. L. wrote that in the last years of the nineteenth century "A. W. had been growing increasingly wistful," and most notably so "on those frequent evenings when he would come to my house to watch my children romping before they were put to bed." In 1899 A. W. and Frick were sailing to England on the *Germanic*. The outgoing Frick, always at ease in a social situation, became friendly with another passenger, Alexander McMullen, whose family made the famous beer, Guinness Stout. McMullen, his wife, and their daughter, Nora, were returning to their castle, Hertford Castle, after a visit in America. McMullen was interesting enough; his daughter, nineteen, fresh and gay, educated and beautiful, was entrancing. Frick introduced his friend, an older person than Nora, it was true, but refined, gracious, soft-spoken, truly handsome for a man of his age, yes and rich, very rich. After a brief courtship the couple became engaged. When A. W. told W. L. that he was going to be married, the uncle seemed "positively boyish."

A delegation of important Pittsburghers made the journey to England in September of 1900 for a week of parties and the wedding. In some ways the McMullens and the Mellons enjoyed parallel situations among their people. McMullen was the lord of the manor; he knew and loved his peasants and they him, while the groom too was overlord of thousands of employees scattered throughout his family's enterprises. The McMullens were clearly pleased about the groom and the match, and their villagers reflected their pleasure by decorating the whole town with buntings. The happy couple agreed to spend part of each year with those common people of Hertford-shire who had shared their happiness. After the wedding, W. L. wrote, "there were wrestling and boxing, bowls and other games and finally a tug of war in which the contestants were five of the Hertford villagers against the five strongest of the bride's seven brothers." By then the newlyweds had departed on their honeymoon. R. B. wrote his parents, "The last I saw of A. W. there were two of him." He was mistaken.

A. W. brought Nora to Pittsburgh and to an environment very different from that which she had known. She was no doubt haunted by thoughts of the difference between what she had left and that to which she had come, a comparison ably drawn by the couple's poetic son, Paul Mellon. Her new home

> was very dark and the halls were very dark and the walls were very dark and outside, Pittsburgh itself was very dark. [In England, though] I re-member huge dark trees and rolling parks . . . flotillas of white swans on the Thames . . . soldiers in scarlet and bright metal drums and bugles,

laughing ladies in white with gay parasols and men in impeccable white
flannels and striped blazers.

Her husband was not there much, and when he was home he was not free
but was closeted in his study at work. His absence for the wedding and the
wedding trip had left him far behind with work that required his attention
and then other work, work in his oil business, his steel and aluminum mills,
work related to his abrasives enterprise, his street railways, his banks;
always there was work, work at the office or work at home. Except, that
is, when he took the recreation to which he was entitled: poker. There were
occasional poker games with Frick, Knox, and the inventor George Westinghouse. His day was so busy. It was a matter of work, it was a matter of
recreation, and perhaps it was also a matter of escape from the demands
of a wife scarcely out of girlhood that could be met only with increasing
difficulty. He tried to be a good husband; he even named a town for her:
Donora, Don-Nora, which he and his associate William Donner had named
partly for Donner and partly for Nora. There was a nice gesture but an
empty one that did not substitute for human values. Such joy as there was
for Nora came from the children. They agreed that she would name any
girls and he would name any boys. Their daughter was born in 1901, and
Nora gave the baby an ancient Scottish name, Ailsa. Six years were to pass
before the birth of their son, named Paul by A. W. The father declined to
give the boy a middle name, because he did not want the child to become
known as P. T. or P. R. A. W. was tired of hearing initials.

Otherwise, Nora's society was constrained and limited. It was only natural that her closest friend was expected to be Jennie, Mrs. R. B. Mellon,
many years her senior, a good-hearted, simple soul, lower-class in her tastes
and affectations, whose flaming red hair, later replaced by her flaming red
wigs, told the story of an outgoing, slightly raucous personality unknown
in Hertfordshire. Jennie was the best of it. In *Watermellons,* Matthew
Mellon described the typical Mellon social life in the early part of the
century as being dominated by " 'teas' that had to be attended and 'calls'
that had to be made; long, dull Sunday dinners with aunts and uncles who
didn't have much to say to each other." To a vibrant young English girl
such rituals became unendurable.

Nora's own very moving account of the difficulties in her situation
focused upon more fundamental differences:

> I saw myself in the role of the mistress of the manor who lightens the burden
> of the peasant. I imagined myself as a link between the old and the new world.
> . . . I would go into my husband's American towns and plan and plant and
> win the love and affections of his people, and give them an heir that I would

bring up good and kind and generous, a master of his fortune, not its slave. All idle dreams . . .

My first great disillusion came when I learned that his people were not of his people at all. "They are foreigns, Huns and Slavs and such as that, and you can't do anything with them," I was told about the people whose affections I had dreamed of winning for my children.

It made me sick at heart to live in the center of so much I was told to despise. It was not only men. There were women and children too, all toilers in my husband's vineyard; but none of them given the laborer's recognition, toiling and working on the estate and adding to its wealth, but not recognized as part of it. The whole community spirit was as cold and hard as the steel it made, and chilled my heart to the core. . . .

Then my boy was born, as fine a baby as any mother ever was blessed with. But my joy was saddened by the dread of the thought that this baby was to grow up to stand all alone as the master, not of a loyal set of workmen, devoted tenants and affectionate servants, with an intelligent appreciation of the master's trials, but as the master of an unreasoning horde of wage slaves, with an instinctive hatred for the man in the manor who knows them less than they know him.

I took my baby boy to Hertfordshire. I wanted to nurse to life in him my own love for the green fields and the open sky. I wanted him away from the gray-smoke and dust-filled air of my husband's gold and grim estate. I wanted him to grow big and strong, prizing health more than wealth in himself and in others. I wanted him to grow up as master not as slave of his fortune: to use it not as a club to dominate with, but as a magic wand to spread health, happiness and prosperity with through his land among all those already dependent on the enterprise of the fortune my boy was to inherit.

I wanted my baby boy to inherit not a town of stony walls, but a town of human hearts, and if I could not prepare that town for him, I wanted to instill in him the inclination and ability to build it for himself when he came into his heritage.

Nights that I spent in my baby boy's bedroom, nursing these thoughts for his future, my husband, locked in his study, nursed his dollars, millions of dollars, maddening dollars, nursed larger and bigger at the cost of priceless sleep, irretrievable health and happiness. Always new plans, always bigger plans for new dollars, bigger dollars, robbed him and his family of the time he could have devoted far more profitably to a mere "Thank God we are living."

In that way, each attracted by the pole of his own magnet, he by the magnetic force of his money, I by my babies, we drifted apart.

Nora relished increasingly the visits of her English friends, and especially that of Alfred George Curphey, tall, well built, athletic, and fifteen years younger than her husband, an adventurer whose past was largely shrouded in mystery. Curphey was a man who inspired imaginations.

More and more Nora was away from Pittsburgh, but after the beginning of 1909 she was rarely alone. Curphey was usually with her, and invariably she had unseen companions—A. W.'s detectives—who silently accompanied the young couple from hotel to hotel to hotel, in Buffalo, Pittsburgh, London, New York, Paris.

A. W. could have appreciated the needs of a younger woman. He might have tolerated a quiet affair. But when it assumed such proportions, the situation had to be confronted.

At first it appeared that things could be worked out privately and amicably. In August of 1909, after nine years of marriage, the Mellons agreed to separate. After a respectable period apart, A. W. would divorce Nora on grounds of desertion. As part consideration, A. W. established a trust of $1,350,000 that would pay Nora $60,000 a year, a grand sum in 1909. She would have the children for seven and a half months each year, he for the balance.

After the first year A. W. became disturbed—possibly rightly so. Was Nora perhaps poisoning the children against their father, as so often happens in the case of separated or divorced parents? From Nora's above-quoted statement of their differences, it does not seem unlikely. In any case, the children were scheduled to leave from New York for England with their mother on the *Oceanic,* sailing on June 3, 1910. A. W. was prepared to honor the agreement, or so he thought, but as his vehicle approached the wharf, he determined that he would be strong; he would take the hard road; he would not give up the children! He ordered the driver to turn around. As the liner's last whistle blew, Nora, sensing what had happened, jumped ashore, leaving baggage and servants on shipboard. An hour later her servants were bound for England on the *Oceanic;* A. W., Paul, and Ailsa were on the train for Pittsburgh; and Nora was on the next train right behind them. Boldly she appeared at the A. W. Mellon house. No one would turn away the mistress, and there she ensconced herself, with her husband, her children, their servants, and the thirteen acoustical devices that A. W. soon installed throughout the house to pick up Nora's every word. A servant tipped off Nora, and for a while she amused herself with chatter designed to send A. W.'s spies on wild-goose chases. A press report sympathetic to Nora later claimed that one of the detectives, Bernard Devlin, a former Pittsburgh saloonkeeper, "went so crazy over the task that it was necessary to send him to an asylum." Ultimately Nora grew bored with playing games on A. W.'s spies and spent a day finding and destroying all but one of the black boxes. Her lawyer would later display the last "contemptible and despicable device" as convincing evidence of A. W.'s ruthlessness. A. W.'s tactical decision backfired.

The divorce suit was formally filed by A. W. on September 14, 1910, not on the grounds of desertion as had been discussed and agreed upon the previous year but on the grounds of Nora's adultery with Alfred George Curphey. Proof of the harsher grounds would eliminate the possibility that Nora might take any more of A. W.'s money, and would give him a chance to win full custody of the children. In addition to the usual battery from Judge Reed's office, A. W.'s team of counsel was supplemented by Rody P. Marshall, Pittsburgh's leading criminal lawyer; Marshall's perennial rival William A. Blakeley, the chief but part-time prosecutor; former Pennsylvania governor William A. Stone; and the firm of Watson & Freeman. It might seem that in any trial all of these lawyers would be falling over one another, that too many lawyers would spoil the brief. Most of them, though, were never expected to actively participate in A. W.'s case. The instinctive monopolist was proceeding on the principles of the industrial world: he monopolized Pittsburgh's best available talent so that outstanding local counsel would be unavailable for hire by Nora. Any out-of-towner, no matter how able, would be at some disadvantage because of unfamiliarity with the local terrain. Nora retained Philadelphia's best, Paul S. Ache.

For several months the case moved ploddingly along. Though Pittsburgh's journalists covered the hearings, not a word ended up in the newspapers. Stray busybodies who might come to the prothonotary's office to inspect the public's records would find no notations of any case such as *Mellon* v. *Mellon*. The prothonotary took it upon himself to maintain the court's set of the papers privately in his personal office, where they could be guarded from prying eyes, until Ache demanded that they be handled like the papers in any other case. Even thereafter reporters were continually given the run around by both clerks and judges in their demands for access to the file.

George Seldes, later to become one of America's most respected crusading journalists, attended the early hearings in the Mellon case. In *Tell the Truth and Run* (1953) Seldes wrote that

> the proceedings became almost entirely biological. Mellon family doctors and gynecologists were called to give expert testimony on sexual relations. The most intimate affairs of a man and a woman were [disclosed] by the Mellon lawyers, providing at times nuances of vulgarity.

Seldes did not elaborate further, but explained the situation as he now recalls it in a 1975 letter to the author: A. W. and Nora "were unfitted sexually—unfitted in the actual sense of the word. Their sexual organs were unfitting: his too large or hers too small . . . sexual intercourse was a horrible experience to both of them."* For one reason or another, the hearings were adjourned.

The most pressing matter in the early stage of the litigation was the question of custody of the children during the pendency of the suit. In most cases where both parties are living in the same house with the children the question of "custody *pendente lite*" never arises. The parties simply share custody. A. W., however, moved that he be granted custody, both permanently and during the pendency of the suit. Just before he did so, there was a curious confrontation at the Mellon mansion. As Nora later told it, she, the children, and her lady friend, a Mrs. Anna Beal Crawford, were in the sun parlor. Nora returned to the main hall for a moment and was surprised to find A. W. home, standing by a packed trunk. In the front of the house was a crew of what today would be described as "goons," among whom one "gentleman" stood out. The trunk was packed with the children's clothing and playthings. Their two nurses also appeared ready to depart. At that moment the nanny of one of Ailsa's playmates appeared at the house; Nora asked the governess to call Nora's attorney, and moments later the lawyer was there together with Mrs. Crawford's brother, who just happened to be arriving at that moment to pick up his sister. It turned out that the gentleman in the crowd was none other than Judge Reed. A. W. explained that he had come home because he had been concerned to hear that a number of "suspicious characters" had been milling about the house, but that he was now satisfied that he had responded to a "false alarm." He and Judge Reed left and the goon squad dissipated. Nora was satisfied that A. W. had been planning to "kidnap" the children. Thereafter, she maintained bodyguards.†

---

*It seems unbelievable that the problem could have been that A. W. was too big and unlikely that Nora was too small after the birth of their two children. It is possible that her vaginal canal was of unsatisfactory depth, a situation that would not have been affected by childbirth, but it seems much more likely that the problem was a form or degree of frigidity, at least with her husband, that manifested itself in remarkable involuntary resistance—a problem that today might be classed as a variety of vaginismus.

†It is possible that Nora lied in her account of the incident and that it was she who had intended to kidnap the children; that Mrs. Crawford's brother had not "coincidentally" arrived, but that he had arrived right on schedule to expedite the removal of the trunk, nurses, and children to some location within Nora's control; that A. W. had caught wind of the scheme and had arrived with Judge Reed and the goon squad just in time to prevent effectuation of Nora's scheme; and that Nora twisted the facts and later told them to the press for whatever reasons. The only other reasonable explanation for the series of incidents

When the matter of custody during the pendency of the suit came up for argument, the parties agreed that a governess, a Fräulein Bertha M. Meyer, should be appointed by the court to move into the mansion with the family and serve as legal guardian of the children instead of either or both of the parents. A couple of months later A. W. returned to court, complaining that because his absence from the home was so often required by his business affairs, Nora had greater opportunity to win the children's affection and to poison them against him. Over Ache's objection, the court ordered that the Fräulein move out of the Mellon mansion, taking the children with her, and that she establish a separate residence for herself and the children where access of each of the parents might be rationed equally—a highly unusual order and the only one issued in the Mellon divorce case that strikes this author as showing inordinate concern for the father. The Fräulein was to begin immediately searching for an appropriate residence.

As the case marked time the Pennsylvania legislature met and considered its many dull and technical pieces of proposed legislation, including one that hardly anyone was even aware of, the Scott divorce bill. Representative John R. K. Scott's bill would have altered the state's divorce law by eliminating the right to a jury trial in a divorce case, and allowing hearings of the evidence in private, either before a judge or before a "master," a non-judge who might travel around taking evidence. This significant change, which today would be regarded as progressive and positive by domestic relations judges and lawyers, was passed without discussion as a routine matter, 168 to 0, and was routinely signed by the governor. Though all efforts, no matter how minor, no matter how well endorsed, to alter Pennsylvania's divorce law in prior years had been hotly debated and had suffered ultimate death in committee, the Scott divorce law slipped through unnoticed. Ache realized the significance of the new law and discerned, no doubt correctly, that it had been quietly moved by Mellon's powerful associates in the legislature at the behest of Mellon or his lawyers. At the same time, the new law gave Ache the clue to the nature of his prey—that the weak spot in A. W.'s armor was his concern for his own privacy. Ache had to have realized that his case was not a strong one—even he must have thought it curious that Nora and Curphey should have rented an English residence together in the name "Mr. and Mrs. Curphey." But he would use

---

would be that A. W. had in fact intended to kidnap the children.

Judge Reed's firm is still Pittsburgh's leading businessmen's law firm, numbering among its clients Seward P. Mellon, whose own domestic relations seem to involve curious parallels to those of his granduncle. If Nora's suspicions were correct, then Judge Reed's ghost still haunts the firm.

what tools he had, and he had only one: the ability to demolish A. W.'s private world with publicity. A. W.'s brightest realistic hope could be to appear in the unflattering role of cuckold.

The Philadelphia *North American* then published the first hint to appear in any newspaper about the Mellon scandal. It was an editorial attacking the change in the divorce law, and though the editors named no names, they prophesied that

> there can be little doubt that an investigation will disclose, sooner or later, in whose interest this legislation has been quietly placed upon the statute book. Potent, indeed, must be the influence of the person powerful enough to have the divorce code of an entire commonwealth changed to facilitate the dissolution of a single marriage relation.

A couple days later the *North American* ventured its theory that the villain was probably from the western part of the state, a remarkable deduction, inasmuch as Scott was a Philadelphian. The next day they were able to disclose who dunnit. It was A. W. Mellon, described uncharitably:

> fifty-eight years old, small, gray haired and nervous. . . . The Mellons have no free library notions [unlike Carnegie, who gave millions to establish public libraries]. They have never been ashamed of dying rich . . . while other Pittsburgh millionaires have devoted the last chapters of their life to spreading the glitter of Pittsburgh gold around the world, the Mellons have stuck to their Pittsburgh lasts and kept on quietly and unassumingly making money and yet more money.

They reviewed the background of the case with similar impartiality ("Mrs. Mellon is wondering now how far the Mellon millions can reach and to what lengths they may go to crush her"). For weeks Ache and the journalists played up A. W.'s evil influence on the state legislature. They began with a statement from "Nora" (hopefully, not her product):

> Gold may crush me. Gold and politics may take my babies from me. But if they do, it will be because the manhood of Pennsylvania has sunken so low that it is willing to surrender the motherhood of the state to the pillage of gold and politics. . . . That's not American, and I don't believe it is Pennsylvanian.

Ache then kept the "issue" alive with spurious pleas to the King of England to intervene on Nora's behalf in the interests of securing justice for a British subject, thereby enabling two more releases on the subject: one when they asked the King, and another when the royal officers declined to become involved. The reporters rounded up hostile comments about the change in the law from both Catholic and Protestant clergymen, and from legislators who claimed to have been duped, together with a rather dispassionate but unfavorable critique of the law by a Mrs. Enoch Rauh, identified in the *North American* as "Pittsburgh's most prominent social worker, member of the Juvenile Court Association, president of the Council of Jewish Women of Pittsburgh; president of the Nathan Straus Milk and Ice Association and famous throughout the country as the leader and originator of esthetic sex hygiene as part of children's education." A. W.'s forces had made another tactical error.

Newspaper readers all along the eastern seaboard were at last able to follow what must have ranked as one of the most exciting divorce battles ever tried in the press. It was a one-sided battle. The press arrayed itself solidly behind the beautiful and sympathy-evoking wife and against the greedy miser so ably described in Nora's delicate polemic, quoted above, which was printed in full in the *North American.* The reportage, principally in the *North American* and only slightly less dramatically (and no less one-sidedly) in the New York *Times* and the Baltimore *Sun,* reads like a Hildy Johnson story from Ben Hecht's *Front Page.*

A. W., like the responsible client of any responsible lawyer, declined to try his case in the press. That worked against him too. A brazen reporter for the *North American* managed to steal his way into the banker's office, and even A. W.'s reasonable reactions to the journalist came out badly in print. In the paper's hostile account, the interview had taken place in Mellon's "gilded banking office," and the banker's "emaciated body shook like a window pane in a storm, but he kept his head as cool as ever, and his voice never once rose above its usual modulated softness." The reporter asked whether A. W. had engineered passage of the Scott divorce law. His answer ("he almost whispered, and looked away from his interviewer across the room") was

> Nonsense.
> Q: Do you know if the law was introduced at the request of one of your lawyers?
> A: I don't know anything about it, but why do you come here and ask me such impudent questions; what business of yours is it?
> Q: Will you say then that you do not intend to take advantage of this new law?
> A: No, I will not. I will say nothing about it.
> Q: But isn't that the way to deny your interest in this law?
> A: I don't know and I will not talk about it. What right have you to come here and ask me such questions about my private affairs? What business of yours is it, tell me that?

The next question, phrased with implicit morality that could only impress *North American* readers, was answered "But what about my family affairs?" The next was answered "But why do you come to me about all this?" And the final question was answered "I will state nothing." Any lawyer would think that his client should politely have expelled the visitor from the start, and failing that, that the client had done as best as could be hoped for in such a confrontation. The headline read "Pennsylvania's Richest Millionaire Shakes with Anger When Questioned." A. W. almost certainly had the evidence, but in the greater battle he couldn't win.

Pittsburgh readers, curiously, found little or nothing about the divorce of the century in their dailies. The author scanned the Pittsburgh *Dispatch,* then a heavyweight paper but with a taste for scandal and crime, for the period May 3 to May 20, 1911, when the Philadelphia *North American* carried its most explosive news. The Mellon name appeared in the *Dispatch* almost every day—always in advertisements for Union Trust or Mellon National Bank, in ads reminding readers that "It is pleasanter to carry your account where you are sure of good treatment." If the message was lost to the *Dispatch*'s readers, it was not lost to its publishers. George Seldes details in his *Freedom of the Press* (1935) and *Tell the Truth and Run* (1953) the network of debts that bound Pittsburgh's newspapers to the Mellon family. All the Pittsburgh newspapers assigned reporters to cover the Mellon divorce case (including Seldes, reporter for the *Leader*), but their stories were never printed. Instead, Seldes writes, the copy was filed for potentially more valuable use by publishers who might later require an extension on an overdue note, or a fresh advance, or a particularly generous advertisement for some "anniversary" issue. He cites the Mellon divorce case as an outstanding example of how the press of the period corrupted and was corrupted by powerful financial interests.

Out-of-town newspapers carried the stories, but their reporters found their work being sabotaged by the local Western Union dispatchers, who held up, "lost," or garbled their copy. When the outside newspapers arrived on the train at Pittsburgh, they were bought up by Mellon agents at the railroad station.

A. W.'s side quickly showed its intention to avail itself of the new law. He moved for the appointment of a "master," a non-judge, to go to Europe and take the testimony of his witnesses there. According to the New York *Times,* the probable master would be John F. Cox, speaker of the Pennsylvania House of Representatives, who would receive the position, the *Times* speculated, "as reward for forcing the bill through the legislature and

guarding so well the secrecy with which passage was effectuated." At a
hearing on A. W.'s motion, the presiding magistrates seemed favorably
disposed and commented that "Pittsburgh recently has had some unpleasant instances of publicity" in divorce cases. They were unimpressed with
the four affidavits presented by Nora's lawyers from parties who claimed
to have been offered bribes for giving false statements solicited by A. W.'s
investigators. The court would consider the matter.

While the judges considered it, other magistrates considered Nora's plea
to stop the removal of the children to the separate house that Fräulein
Meyer had at last found in nearby Sewickley, Pennsylvania. The house,
Nora argued, was inaccessible; its floors and walls were cracked and moist;
it was generally unsanitary; and the fogs in the area made it "an unhealthy
location for persons afflicted with catarrhal conditions or subjected to cold
like four-year-old Paul Mellon." Furthermore, the children didn't want to
go. As the *North American* reported it:

> "I don't care what the judge says, I won't go," declared Ailsa when her
> mother told her that she would have to leave home.
>
> "But you must, the court has ordered it," insisted Mrs. Mellon.
>
> "But I won't go," cried Ailsa, and threw her arms around her mother in full
> verification of Mellon's remarkable complaint that the children are growing
> too fond of their mother and not fond enough of him, a matter that he is
> endeavoring to have regulated by the court order to take the children away
> from their mother.

After fumbling through the Yellow Pages, a magistrate appointed an architect and plumber of his own selection to make an independent appraisal of
the Sewickley home.

While Pittsburgh's judiciary pondered these two important questions,
who should arrive in town but "Captain Alfred George Curphey, the Boer
War hero," as the *North American* identified him. Curphey was "as long
and handsome as his name," at least to the eye of their reporter. He was
accompanied by his friend and companion, Captain Thomas W. Kirkbridge, and had come to demand an explanation and an apology from the
man who would put a blot upon Curphey's good name:

> I shall certainly endeavor to make clear and absolutely distinct to this Mr.
> Mellon that he dares not cast reflection on the name and reputation of an
> Englishman. It shall be my pleasure also, if I am privileged to do so, to teach
> Mr. Mellon that, no matter who he is, he owes some respect to an English
> woman even though she is his wife. . . . If I did not have such a decided
> advantage over him I could find it in my heart to thrash him. Really for the

satisfaction of thrashing him I could find it in my heart to wish I was his size and weight.

The *North American*'s lead read "Won't Thrash Him but Would Like to If Millionaire Were His Equal," and it printed two fanciful silhouettes, one labeled "Mellon 5 feet 4 inches 135 pounds," the other identified as "Curphey 6 feet 190 pounds."

The next morning the Boer War hero presented himself at the offices of the Mellon National Bank. A. W. was out. Curphey told the press,

> I timed my call according to my information that Andrew W. Mellon is almost invariably to be found at the bank at this hour. His secretary, however, informed me that Mr. Mellon was not in. Whether that circumstance was fortunate or otherwise, I hardly know.
>
> In any case, I decided not to wait about for him indefinitely, but left a message with his secretary to the effect that I had come to Pittsburgh in order to bring myself within the jurisdiction of the Allegheny county courts, and immediately prepared to receive service of any papers from Mr. Mellon or his attorneys. In fact, I told them it would be necessary only to telephone to Mr. Ache in order to make an appointment, and I will attend at any time or place.

While Curphey was at it, he shared with the world his opinions on the subject of the Scott divorce law.

Though Curphey did not get to meet A. W., he did get to meet George Wagoner, onetime county detective, the chief investigative officer of the district attorney's office. Ache noticed Wagoner skulking about the entrance to the office building in which he had taken space, and he drew an entirely reasonable conclusion. He approached Wagoner. Again from the *North American:*

> "Are you waiting for Mr. Curphey?" asked Attorney Ache of Detective Wagoner.
>
> "Well, I have read about him and thought I would like to see what he looks like," answered the detective.
>
> "As a matter of fact, you are employed to shadow Mr. Curphey," said Attorney Ache. "I want to tell you that we are not going to put any obstacles whatever in your way. If you come up to my office now, I shall introduce you to Mr. Curphey."
>
> "All right, I will go [with] you," answered Wagoner, and a few minutes later he was introduced to Curphey and Captain Kirkbridge by Attorney Ache.
>
> "Mr. Curphey, Captain Kirkbridge, this is Detective Wagoner, who will be your shadow while you are in Pittsburgh," said Mr. Ache in introducing his clients.
>
> "You need not fear him: Mr. Wagoner is a very good fellow. Mr. Wagoner,

if you at any time have any papers to serve on these gentlemen, come right up
or telephone and they will be right on hand."

A. W.'s lawyers then made their first correct tactical decision. They
decided to call the bluff and that afternoon caused subpoenas to be served
on Curphey and on Kirkbridge, commanding them to give testimony before
a court reporter at Judge Reed's offices. At last, A. W.'s side would get to
take testimony from one of the participants under oath and an opportunity
to highlight for the courts the embarrassing aspects of Nora's situation!
Curphey and Kirkbridge, English gentlemen to the last, would die before
they would perjure themselves (at least in a situation in which they might
get caught at it). They would flee before they would tarnish a lady's reputation. So they fled, with A. W.'s detectives not far behind.

Several days later Curphey and Kirkbridge were sitting down for dinner
at the Ritz-Carlton in New York when they were arrested for "obstructing
justice" in having ignored the subpoenas and were held on bond for possible
extradition to Pennsylvania. The Englishmen's lawyers later argued persua-
sively that the Pennsylvania governor must have signed the request for
extradition even before the date of the hearing at which they had failed to
appear.

The morning after their arrest a New York *Times* reporter attended the
preliminary hearings at the New York court, when Curphey explained that
in England

> a subpoena granted by the authority and backed by the dignity of a governmen-
> tal court is returnable to a court. This paper was returnable before a firm of
> private lawyers—the lawyers for the other side. We could not believe it was
> genuine. We wished to know from our lawyer and were informed over long-
> distance telephone to come to New York at once for a consultation before
> putting ourselves on record before such an incomprehensible tribunal.

Their attorney protested the shabby way his clients had been treated, insisting that Captain Kirkbridge was an officer of the British Army and that
both were English gentlemen. A. W.'s attorney responded, "They may both
be Englishmen, and one of them may be an officer, but they are no gentlemen."

While Curphey's explanation as to why they had left was not unreasonable, his spirited resistance to extradition back to Pennsylvania, where he
would have been forced to testify, is difficult to reconcile with any conclusion other than that honest testimony from him would have clinched
A. W.'s case. He and Kirkbridge were released on bond in New York
pending determination of the extradition question, but before it was re-

solved they decided to forfeit their bond and sail for England.

Back in Pittsburgh, the magistrate's independent architect and plumber made their report: The Sewickley house selected by the Fräulein would be satisfactory. The court lost no time in issuing its order that on the following Monday the children were to be removed to Sewickley with the Fräulein and Nora was to vacate A. W.'s mansion. Among those who just happened to be present at the Forbes Avenue residence when A. W.'s representatives appeared to effectuate the order was the gentleman from the *North American.*

Mrs. Mellon today not only had torn from her her two sobbing and heart-broken children, but suffered besides the sight of her loyal friend, Mrs. Anna Beal Crawford, being assaulted by one of Mellon's negro servants. Finally, she herself was thrust out of her home by five strong-arm men in the hire of Andrew W. Mellon.

Added to this, Mellon's servants took from her, after she had parted with her two children, every belonging—food, clothing, linen, even her wedding presents.

"We are working for Mr. Mellon, not for you, and when he says we are to take these things away you just try to stop us," said the servants, and snapped their fingers at the sorely tried mother who had been their mistress.

The parting was especially hard for Ailsa, less so for Paul:

Ailsa the nine-year-old girl would not be consoled. She cried all morning and appealed with tears to all around her to let her stay with her mother. As the hour for parting, 1 P.M., drew nearer the children became more and more disconsolate. Within an hour the child appeared to grow older by many years, and her big brown eyes looked with the despair of a full-grown woman at a Pittsburgh newspaper man and a *North American* reporter who had come to see Judge Miller's unprecedented order carried out.

"Come, Ailsa, won't you take this doll along?" suggested Mrs. Crawford, Mrs. Mellon's friend.

"Oh, no, I want my mother! Please don't talk to me," answered the child, and threw her arms around her mother's neck, sobbing to break her heart.

"Ailsa, Ailsa, don't cry, dear; we will bring you back soon; this will be only for a short time," said Mrs. Mellon, and endeavored to stop the child's crying while the tears were flowing down her own cheeks.

"Come into the house, Ailsa, and get stockings on for the trip," called Fraulein Meyer, who in signing the last petition for the removal of the children from their mother served the purposes of Andrew W. Mellon.

"Yes, Ailsa, go to the fraulein and get stockings on," said Mrs. Mellon to the child, who was in sandals. But Ailsa stayed in the house only a minute, then she came bursting out again and threw herself sobbing into her mother's lap on the porch steps.

"Mamma, please, mamma, save me! Don't let them take me away! Don't, don't! I don't want to go to papa; he doesn't like us, mamma. Oh, won't you keep me here, mamma?" cried the semi-hysterical child.

Paul, the four-year-old boy, was meanwhile kept in happy ignorance by the story that he was going on an automobile trip, then "on the chu-chu cars" and then on the boat. "On the boat," to Paul, meant across the ocean to England, where everybody loves both him and his mamma, and where there were no ugly looking men sneaking around the house at all hours in the pay of Paul's father.

The prospects of going "on the boat" kept Paul happy, and he took a final spin on his little automobile just before he was lifted from the smaller to the bigger automobile that carried him away from his mother.

Playmates of Ailsa called to bid her goodby. They cried with her. Mrs. Mellon cried. Mrs. Crawford broke down and cried, and across the street people watching the pathetic scene cried with and over poor Ailsa, who clung to her mother's dress until Fraulein Meyer pulled her by the hand to the waiting automobile.

After that, all hell broke loose as A. W.'s employees physically removed Nora's contingent, in the course of which Mrs. Crawford, having left the mansion for a moment, "found both her arms grabbed by Bert Stuart, Mellon's negro servant," who declined to permit Mrs. Crawford to re-enter. From the *North American* account, it appears that Mr. Stuart was the gentleman of the crowd.

Nora was removed to the home of Mrs. Crawford, where she collapsed in the care of a Dr. Westervelt. The doctor was still present when the telephone rang. It was Ailsa. By that point even the *North American* editors must have been getting weary of the Victorian melodrama. Though they printed the full text of the conversation in their issue of June 14, 1911, they placed it on page three, and for present purposes, the above recitation should suffice to convey the general tenor of Ailsa's further plea.

At last, proceedings took a crucial turn for Nora. Ache's associate, Judge James Gay Gordon, prevailed upon the court to decline to apply the Scott law to the Mellon case, which had been instituted prior to the passage of Scott's amendments. Nora could have her jury trial! Ache realized that his hand would never be stronger. While A. W. dreaded the further publicity that a jury trial would entail, Nora's case was not strong. A. W. might win; Nora could lose custody and money. The time for negotiations had come; as a gesture of his own reasonableness it would help matters if Ache were to cease embarrassing A. W., at least pending the outcome of negotiations. The

Mellon case dropped out of print. The *North American* did not even report Nora's victory on the most important question of her right to the jury trial.

Finally it was agreed as a stipulated matter that the case could be heard in private before a "master" without any publicity whatsoever. The divorce would be granted to A. W. on the grounds of desertion rather than adultery. Custody was to be divided equally between the parties, six months to each, and Nora was to get some small addition to the monies previously given to her. No doubt there was also an understanding as to the amount of further assistance Nora would get in order to pay for attorneys' fees, though that was never reported. The master accepted the agreement of the parties and recommended its adoption by the court, and months later the master's report was accepted and ordered implemented. Again by agreement of the parties, A. W.'s lawyers were permitted "to withdraw from the records the papers filed in the above case for examination, excepting the final decree of divorce." They were withdrawn—physically removed from the court's file. The "examination" has indeed been prolonged; as of 1977 they had not yet been returned.

The *North American,* with dubiously warranted self-satisfaction, proclaimed it a "Victory for Mother Over Money Power"; the New York *Times* chalked it up as a triumph for A. W. Whichever was correct could only have been known by someone thoroughly acquainted with the evidence actually available to both sides—probably no one at all in 1910, and surely no one now alive. In one particular, however, the *North American* was unquestionably correct: it characterized the battle as having been one between "Millions of dollars and powerful political pull on the one side and publicity on the other." Perhaps the two pernicious influences had struck a draw. Only the war's losers can be identified with any degree of certainty: Ailsa Mellon and Paul Mellon.

The years were not kind to Nora Mellon. Her Irish beauty faded; she grew paunchy. Curphey dropped out of her picture. In 1923, when A. W. was Secretary of the Treasury, when Ailsa was the most sought after girl in Washington at twenty-one, and when Paul was an awkward sixteen, Nora herself was clearly middle-aged at forty-four. She proved that she had learned nothing from her marriage to a much older man, and she married a much younger man, Harvey Lee, thirty, an Englishman who sometimes ran an art and antiques shop on New York's Lexington Avenue. The Lees were divorced in Reno in 1928, and a couple of years later Nora began using the name "Mrs. Mellon" again. She explained, "During the few years I was married to Mr. Lee none of my friends got used to the name. They all continued to call me Mrs. Mellon. . . . My son is very anxious that I should take his name." Her life's experiences were over, though she lived on, mostly in England, Virginia, and in the fashionable Connecticut towns of Litchfield and Greenwich, until 1973, when she died at the age of ninety-four. In her last years at Greenwich Nora received some kind of recognition as a Mellon family curiosity. Dutiful visits to her were periodically made by her grandson Timothy, Paul's son, and from her great-grandchildren, the offspring of Ailsa's daughter, Audrey Bruce Currier; and occasional visits to her were made by Matthew Mellon's son Jay, a Yale undergraduate, and from other passing-through Mellons.

A. W. disappeared under a monolith of paperwork. There he was oblivious to such minor slights as the fact that when President Taft invited Pittsburgh's business leaders to the White House in 1912 the banker that received the invitation was R. B. Mellon. The trauma of the divorce understandably heightened his reserve and his shyness, and reasonably increased his apprehension of journalists. His acceptance of the position of Secretary of the Treasury after a mere nine years of recuperation is attestation to considerable resiliency.

The wound of that marriage, and of that divorce, lived on. After the pain to which the two had subjected each other without significant result, he and Nora worked out their difficulties amicably. The children drew them into constant contact, and as Paul Mellon entered adolescence and manhood he made persistent efforts to reconcile his parents. As early as 1913, a year after the divorce was finalized, the Baltimore *Sun* reported that the two would shortly remarry. Similar reports crept into the newspapers periodically throughout the remainder of A. W.'s life. They never did remarry, but by the early 1920s an affection had been reborn between them that survived until A. W.'s death.

The Boer War hero is surely the most interesting character in the great Pittsburgh scandal. Alfred George Curphey was a hoax, a fraud whose most regular occupation seems to have been "guest." He was also a very beautiful person, a poetic man, a philosopher, a lover who also loved. Throughout his life there was always an aura of scandal about him.

Curphey's background was very different from what Nora probably thought it to be. His parents were Protestant Irish, but not, as he claimed, from huge estates in Ireland. They were Liverpool Irish, his father, Samuel Curphey, a carpenter, his mother, Georgina Susan Pearce, the daughter of a shipwright. When Curphey was born in 1872, his father described himself on the birth certificate as "contractor and builder," but if so, it was not on any significant scale. There is no record of any Alfred George Curphey at either Oxford or Cambridge, and when Curphey himself married in 1893 he listed his occupation as "surveyor." His address as shown on the marriage certificate was at a boardinghouse. His wife, Grace Robertson, however, was a woman of impressive social standing as the daughter of Stewart Souter Robertson, chaplain to His Grace the Duke of Hamilton. She was an older girl, twenty-six, and perhaps to make her feel a little less uncomfortable about the matter, Curphey added five years to his own age and told the registrar that he too was twenty-six. Grace was probably Curphey's entrée to the English upper class. Throughout his later life he mixed in circles far above those of his origins. When and why he fell out with her is unknown. Her younger brother put a bullet through his skull at Caddenfoot Church, Selkirk, in 1903, and at that time Grace was identified in the public records as the wife of "Alfred Curphey," but presumably she and Curphey parted prior to his involvement with Nora.

Curphey could talk for hours on end with his endless stories of his last-minute rescue from death at the hands of the Mexican revolutionaries, his experiences in Czarist Russia, his youth on the vast estate in Ireland. C. Jose Beldam, a little girl in the 1930s, listened with awe to what she now describes as his "incredible tales. How much of what he told us was true, I can't say." But she can say that she loved "Curph," as she called him.

Many of the tales were false. The records at the National Army Museum Library in London do not list any "Captain Alfred George Curphey" and neither *The Times* of London nor the *Illustrated London News* for the period of the Boer War reports the heroism of any such person. On the other hand, some of his tales were unquestionably true. One of those that he told only to his closest intimates—and only to adults—was of the exciting divorce case in which he and his friend Kirkbride (it was Kirkbride, not Kirkbridge, but he really was a captain) had been involved in in America many, many years earlier.

Curphey's occupational history is unclear. He was often in financial difficulties. He borrowed money from his friends, and when that ran out he "borrowed" their jewelry, presumably to pawn. The jewelry was never returned. Ms. Beldam's brother says that Curphey was never regularly employed, that "he lived by his wits."

In his last year, the Beldams were Curphey's only "family" and his only social contact. George W. Beldam, inventor, cricketer and action photographer, disbursed a couple of fortunes in his lifetime through generosity to people like Curphey. Over the years of their friendship Curphey was always in debt to Beldam, and he made pretense of making partial repayment of his obligations by conveyance to the Beldam family of such things as "valuable heirlooms" (as he represented them to be) from the Romanoff family.

Beldam died in the fall of 1937. A few days later Curphey paid a courtesy call on his widow and stayed ten months, until he died himself in October of 1938. When his own end was approaching he told Mrs. Beldam that he would tell her what it was like to die, until he could speak no longer. This he did. Mrs. Beldam told her daughter, "He said to the end how beautiful it was—a lovely garden with music he couldn't describe." Then he lapsed into a coma and died. Ms. Beldam remembers her mother "wearing black gowns and being very sad and upset that Christmas of '38—she was, in fact, going to marry Mr. Curphey. She loved him very much."

Curphey told Mrs. Beldam to keep his ashes until she could do so no longer, and then to scatter them at some placid spot. She kept them for some twenty years in an oak box atop of which was a brass plate inscribed with his name, and then, on a windy gray day, she caused them to be let free on a moor at a point known as Three Legged Cross, not far from Wimborne, Dorsetshire. Mementos of Curphey survive: a monocle, a painted miniature, a Mexican sombrero.

By the time the United States entered the great European war in 1917, the sons of Judge Mellon were no longer young men; and though the family was still close-knit, each of the Judge's four sons had created a full set of branches on his own family tree. The Judge's oldest, Thomas Alexander Mellon, was by then long departed; his wife Mary Caldwell Mellon had followed him to the grave three years after. But their three children were well established with families of their own.

His oldest, Thomas Alexander Mellon Jr. was by then forty-four, active in his lumber and coal enterprises, and blessed with two little daughters, Elizabeth and Helen, and a sturdy son, Ned. T. A. Jr.'s brother, Edward Purcell Mellon, had had an odd turn. Of a sudden he had picked up and fled Pittsburgh, moved to Rome, and at a relatively advanced age had become an architect. Most untypical for a Mellon. E. P. had two daughters —Mary and Jane.

T. A.'s daughter, Mary, orphaned at the age of seventeen, had made a bad marriage to a difficult man named John H. Kampman, who had moved her to Texas. There they had had an odd son—classed as retarded, but that probably wasn't it—aged ten by 1917, and a daughter, Mary. She had extricated herself from Kampman simply by picking up and stealing away to Colorado. By Texas law of the day, she had "deserted" Kampman, and she paid dearly for it. Kampman ended up with a sizable chunk of her inheritance, but it was worth it, or so she always claimed. Now she had married again, to a lawyer named Samuel Alfred McClung, and if some of the family thought McClung little better a bargain than Kampman, at least Mary never seemed to know it.

The Judge's second son, James Ross Mellon, had never been the business-man that his younger brothers were. He lacked their singleness of purpose and they lacked his *joie de vivre.* Whether because of a timidity of nature or an unwillingness to ride the coattails of his kid brothers, J. R. passed up the chance to participate in young Mellon ventures like Alcoa and Gulf and stuck to his pedestrian if large-scale merchanting. His substantial profits were put into safe rather than dynamic investments, with the result that he never became more than a mere multimillionaire. He was, however, the smartest of the Mellons. Around 1905, at the age of about sixty, he essen-tially retired and devoted his remaining three decades to harmless self-indulgences.

J. R. lived in three homes, each with its special delights for him. His estate on North Negley Avenue, across from the Judge's and T. A.'s, contained one of his earliest extravagances: his father's birthplace. Well, almost. J. R. —eight years before the Judge himself returned to his first home—was the first of the family to make the pilgrimage to Camp Hill in North Ireland to see the house where the Judge had been born. He was accompanied by an artist, one Van Buskirk, who painted the scenes for the family back home. Later J. R. decided to go one better, and he had a replica of the humble cottage constructed in his back yard. Many people somehow got the impression that J. R. had had the original homestead dismantled and sent to Pittsburgh for resurrection. Perhaps J. R., who often exaggerated, was responsible for the impression.

"Rachelwood," J. R.'s mountaintop summer home north of Ligonier, was his big showplace, and a fascinating and educational amusement park for the children. Its 3500 acres were studded with souvenirs and reminders of J. R.'s travels throughout the world, including a Pacific Coast totem pole brought back from Alaska, a huge stone Buddha from the Orient, Moroc-can pavilions that housed a swimming pool, arcades of fancy statues that J. R. called "my $1.98 Versailles," and his Bavarian-castle mansion, de-signed for him by an Austrian architect ("My $1.98 Schloss"). The great European war put an end to one of J. R.'s plans that, according to his son, W. L.

really disturbed some of the family. He announced that, as a memorial to the vanished Indian inhabitants of his mountain ridge, he was going to engineer the biggest piece of sculpture in America. It would be a statue of an Indian and stand ninety feet tall somewhere in the vicinity of the house. The one blessing of the first World War of which we were aware was that it interfered with this plan. A certain kind of cement, as I recall it, normally manufactured in Europe, fortunately became unobtainable in the throes of war.

Rachelwood had a small pet cemetery enclosed by a low stone wall, each grave marked by a diminutive tombstone bearing an epitaph drafted by the bereaved. Matthew Mellon characterizes his grandfather's poetry on such occasions as "horrible little limericks," but let the reader be the judge:

> Here lies the body of our Little Jack.
> He was hit by an auto—a helluva crack,
> Smashed his tail and broke his back.

Country folk puzzled over a Stonehenge-like assemblage of whitewashed stones set on a hillside and visible for miles around that looked like

$$\Phi \ \Delta \ X$$

It was Theta Delta Chi, the fraternity that J. R. had joined during his brief stay at Jefferson College and to which he remained devoted throughout life. He was forever entertaining "brothers" that he had never known he had.

Rachelwood's greatest attraction was its miles and miles of woods where children could whoop it up with no one to say, "Quiet down." J. R. was an expansive man who loved children, not just his own children and grandchildren, but all children. When his wife's niece, also named Rachel Larimer, was orphaned at the age of four, the J. R.s took her in and raised her as their own, essentially as a sister to their children. His nephew's son Ned recalls his many good times with his granduncle, chasing butterflies together and hearing the old man's preposterous yarns. He describes J. R. as "a most lovable man," a description that he would not apply to his two more "successful" granduncles.

J. R. was an indulgent, affectionate father, and he outdid himself as a grandfather; little wonder that the grandchildren looked forward to their visits to Rachelwood. "Foxy Grandpa," as they appropriately called J. R., was an incurable practical joker, and some of his most elaborate jokes were designed with them in mind. Perhaps no one ever went to greater trouble to create a practical joke than did J. R. in set-

ting the stage for the arrival at Rachelwood of a fabulous bird, the
"Plymouth Roc." W. L. related that

> One year as our boys and girls were arriving for their long visit, halfway up
> the drive father, uttering a loud exclamation, abruptly stopped the horses. He
> asked if the others in the buck wagon had seen "it." Nobody had seen anything.
> But he said a flying bird, a gigantic bird, had just vanished behind the trees.
> So all the children climbed out of the wagon and followed their grandfather.
> Walking as he did, with exaggerated tiptoe steps, they went down an embank-
> ment and behind some trees where suddenly they came upon a nest of awful
> proportions. It measured yards across. It was made, not of twigs, but of
> saplings and larger tree trunks. The very thought of the talons that had
> constructed this nesting-place was enough to chill anybody's blood. True
> enough, the feathers with which the nest was upholstered were suspiciously
> like those of Plymouth Rock chickens, but father said that a Plymouth Rock,
> after all, was just a midget "roc." This nest belonged to such a "roc" as had
> flown away with Sinbad the Sailor on its back. He refused to let the children
> correct him as to the spelling. "Rock," he said, was just a misprint in the books.
>
>   The last shred of doubt evaporated when the children from a relatively safe
> vantage point could see over the great thatched mass of the nest into its heart.
> There were eggs in it, white as paint could make them and big as cannon balls,
> which they were. Of course, the children marvelled over this for days and never
> failed to be up in time for breakfast, always in the hope that this would be the
> day they would catch a sight of the roc coming down out of the sky to warm
> its eggs.

There were similar if less elaborate practical jokes scattered about Rachelwood, such as a gigantic flat stone that bore the inscription "Turn me over."
W. L. wrote that it required "some expense to fingernails and muscles" to
follow the cryptic direction; those who did found only another inscription
on the reverse: "Stung! Turn back. Fool the next one." W. L. said that his
father had been "tireless in creating such devices."

J. R. was a visionary practical joker; he was most inventive when creating
a shock for posterity. Into one of Rachelwood's stone walls he implanted
an anthropological skeleton that he had acquired in Florida because, he
explained (after extracting oaths of secrecy), "Maybe it will be a hundred
years from now, but someday this wall will be torn down and people will
exclaim, 'That old so and so Mellon! He buried a man alive!' "

Every fall J. R. would close up Rachelwood and board the train for
Palatka, Florida. He always enjoyed the train. Passage was free for him
wherever he might wander with that identification card that identified him
as the president of an American railroad—the Ligonier Valley Railroad—

and he took a childlike delight in riding the rails on the same terms as the chief executive of the New York Central.

Palatka was a sleepy town on the Saint Johns River, some twenty-five miles southwest of Saint Augustine. Matthew Mellon writes that at Palatka his grandfather "enjoyed being a big frog in a little pond." J. R. loved Palatka and Florida. Palatka later named a school in his honor, in recognition of his contributions to the community.

J. R. had a more leisurely life in Palatka, though the grandchildren visited him there as well. He never missed one of the weekly winter meetings of the Palatka Rotary Club and enjoyed telling people about the time that William Jennings Bryan had been the club's guest speaker and had put his arm around him and greeted him, "Well, brother Mellon, its high time we got to know each other." J. R., as Republican as his brother A. W., claimed to have disengaged himself from the Great Commoner.

J. R. could practical joke south as well as north. W. L. wrote that

> Most tourists were unfamiliar with Florida vegetation, so my father fixed various kinds of fruit to the wrong trees, using wires and thread. His trees alone of all those in Palatka were suddenly bright with oranges. But some of the oranges were "growing" on fig and pomegranate trees. He bought a lot of artificial flowers from a millinery shop and had paper roses blossoming on his bougainvillea vines, and other shrubs were "flowering" with imitation blooms not indigenous to Florida. The whole place became a riot of misplaced color and many a tourist had gaped credulously before a particular stranger had come along.
>
> This big, florid-faced man, with snowy beard and hair, instead of marveling at the fruit and flowers, glared at them. He stuck his cane through the tall iron fence and poked at the only blossom within reach until he knocked it loose from its wire moorings. Then he gave a snort of triumph. Whereupon my father began to laugh and emerged from his ambush to share the joke.

The gentleman with the cane became one of J. R.'s dear friends; he was Matthew Taylor, whose daughter May later married W. L.

Rachel was with J. R. through most of their lives. From W. L.'s *Judge Mellon's Sons* she emerges as a remarkably cultured and independent woman, an accomplished artist who passed a winter painting in Italy after the birth of her first child and spent her time at home principally painting in her studio or studying the stars at night from the astronomy tower that J. R. added atop the Negley Avenue house for her. Her grandson Matthew's recollections of her are seemingly inconsistent. Rachel's brief biography *William Penn: A Short Account of His Life and Views,* edited and privately printed by Matthew in 1972 in fulfillment of a fifty-year-old promise to his grandmother, is notable only for Matthew's unflattering preface in which he sketches "Grandma" as "short and stout and rather pompous . . . a person, who was often overwhelmed by her own deep feelings and emotions, few of which she could clearly express." As for the writing of *Penn,* he says that "Grandma" had

> employed as a "companion" a Miss Sara E. Barber of Lewistown, Pennsylvania, who had been a schoolteacher to revise some of the cryptic language she was wont to write. Therefore, just what this booklet owes to Miss Barber shall probably never be known. She fought a brave battle to tone down the grandiose style of her employer.

Matthew's preface does not mention any astronomy or painting, but rather Rachel's "positive passion for genealogy." As he recalls her today, it is as a woman "rather taken with herself."

If Matthew was less than enchanted with "Grandma," "Grandpa" was. After her passing in 1919, J. R. contributed the Larimer Memorial Library in her honor to the town of Palatka. The Palatka Library that preceded it had always been one of Rachel's favorite charities. At the time of her death a twenty-five-dollar check made payable to the Palatka Library was found in her sewing basket, apparently an intended contribution that she had not gotten around to mailing. J. R. also had constructed the Rachel Larimer Mellon Church in the Wilderness on his Rachelwood estate. He journeyed to Palestine to visit the supposed Tomb of Rachel, where he took precise measurements and he patterned his church after its ancient inspiration. Though he was frequently an officer, sometimes president, of the East Liberty Presbyterian Church, and was devoted to conventional Presbyterianism, he designed and installed an altar in the Church in the Wilderness that could be moved in such a manner as to make the building suitable for religious observances by Protestants, Catholics, or Jews, compatible with the traditions of either. Over the doorway he had inscribed a motto consistent with his ecumenism: "There is neither Jew nor Greek; there is neither bond nor free, there is neither male nor female: for ye are all one in Christ Jesus" [Galatians, 3:28]. Ligonier Valley commoners considered it a special treat to be married at J. R.'s Church in the Wilderness, and the signore went out of his way to make it available to any petitioner for such occasions, often at considerable inconvenience and expense to himself.

By wartime, J. R.'s children were all well established. We have heard enough, for the moment, of his eldest, W. L. J. R. had two other children that lived to adulthood. A daughter, Sarah Lucille, was educated at Miss

Porter's School, the first of several Mellon girls to attend the fashionable Farmington, Connecticut, "finishing" school. She thereafter attended Briarcliff College. She traveled widely with her parents until 1909, when the three were aboard the S. S. *Republic* when it sank in the Atlantic Ocean. As the "abandon ship" cry was sounded, Rachel rushed back to the cabin for a skirt, while J. R. paced the deck grumbling that the life preserver was the wrong size and that he could not find his socks. Finally Rachel found her skirt, J. R. found his socks (they were in his coat pocket), and all three were safely in the lifeboat, where Sarah Lucille, age twenty-two, found a husband—dashing Alexander Grange, thirty-two. After their marriage, she moved to Berwyn, Pennsylvania, a Main Line town outside of Philadelphia. There the Granges, both accomplished horsepeople, ran the Mellgran farm, a showplace of a horse farm, and lived an appropriate life until 1915, when Grange died at the age of thirty-eight. According to his obituary in the New York *Times,* the "prominent clubman" met an Edward Gorey end and expired "as a result of meningitis brought on by injuries suffered in cross-country riding with the Radnor Hunt last Saturday." He left Sarah Lucille with a three-month-old daughter, Alexandra Mellon Grange, but no financial worries. Sarah Lucille would survive two subsequent husbands, both of whom shared her undying passion for riding. She died in 1968 at the age of eighty at the Devon Manor Nursing Home. She was survived only by her daughter Alexandra, now in her very early sixties.

Every large family has its casualty; in the Mellon clan it would surely be Thomas Mellon II, J. R.'s younger son. Rachel had seen her eldest, W. L., snatched away from her by the more powerful influence of the Judge and A. W. She clasped Thomas Mellon II to her bosom and never let him loose. His photographs, both the one reproduced herein and those published with his obituary, convey that certain Lou Costello effeminacy of a mamma's boy. Even as a five-year-old his grandfather had described him in *Thomas Mellon and His Times* as "amusingly careful to be correct in what he says"; already his course as a goody-goody was clear.

Thomas Mellon II educated himself to the point of attendance at both Harvard Law School and Princeton Graduate School; he received a law degree (and later a graduate degree in medieval history) from the University of Pittsburgh. But W. L. writes that his little brother's "health was poor and this accounted for his early abandonment of the practice of law." He spent much of his life in prayer and collected ecclesiastical items such as "a page from the Gutenberg Bible" (as he believed it to be). Much of the rest of his time he spent designing stained-glass windows in the medieval style, many of which he commissioned to be executed, and presented as gifts to various Christian organizations. One of his more noteworthy benefactions was his gift of a copy of Dagnan-Bouveret's "Disciples at Emmaus," painted by Pittsburgh copyist Verona Kiralfy, to the Saint Barnabas House.

Thomas Mellon II was also devoted to the work of the Sons of the American Revolution (Rachel was a national vice president in the Daughters), and he was a sometime officer of the Western Pennsylvania Historical Society. The society's magazines of the 1920s onward document a constant stream of knickknacks and memorabilia with which he blessed the organization, for the most part things of sentimental value only: a complete set of photocopies of the title pages of the textbooks from which his grandfather the Judge had studied; a series of "suitably framed colored lithographs"; mementos of Admiral Dewey. In 1935 he published and circulated a historical pamphlet, *The Forsythe Log House,* a poorly written piece probably not even of local interest. He sent endless care packages of secondhand clothing and much-demanded copies of *Thomas Mellon and His Times* to deserving parties in Northern Ireland. Matthew Mellon remembers "Uncle Tom" as deeply religious, invariably immaculate—and otherwise not too charitably. Tom never married and, as Matthew puts it, "lived, grew up and died in the same room." In today's freer world, this gentle and apparently somewhat simple soul might have found a fuller life in an alternate arrangement, but he would probably have been too frightened of either hell or dirt to have given himself the chance. A tasteful eulogy to him by Charles Locke in the *Western Pennsylvania Historical Magazine* notes "an unostentatious life devoted to useful and honorable effort, a life marked by simplicity and earnestness and sincerity, and one which gives confidence that in the Divine Wisdom there has been fulfilled for him the beatitude of the pure in heart."

Richard Beatty Mellon shared his brother J. R.'s love for the area around the Ligonier Valley. Whenever possible, R. B. would escape from the dizzying burdens that he shared with A. W. in downtown Pittsburgh to his humble Ligonier retreat, about ten miles south of J. R.'s Rachelwood. There he would hunt and fish and ride with his son and love, Richard King Mellon, whose oddly appropriate middle name was taken from his mother, Jennie King. Few fathers and sons have ever enjoyed a "better" relationship (by conventional American standards) than R. B. and R. K. Their interests and temperaments were identical; there seemed to be no distance between them, no gap at all. When the father was not with his brother A. W., he was with his son, R. K. Their faces were dissimilar: R. K. was a handsome young man, while his father was markedly homely, but their body frames were the same. They could and sometimes did share wardrobes. In the decade beginning in 1917, father and son together built one of the most remarkable institutions in social America, Rolling Rock Farms and its country club.

In the early part of the century R. B. began buying acreage in the Ligonier Valley, and then more and more acreage until his private preserve, Rolling Rock Farms, totaled 18,000 acres. He would take his son and his friends to Rolling Rock for the best of outdoor life, housing them in a simple log cabin. According to W. L., R. B. "was most happy when he was having a party," and about 1916 he conceived the idea of building a little club in the middle of his estate where he could enjoy himself "in the company of the people he cared for most—his son and daughter, his wife, and literally all their friends." There, their friends might come to weekend without ever having to feel that they were directly imposing on their hosts. Rolling Rock Club was born. Construction of the clubhouse was begun in 1917 and took four years to complete. Over time it grew, with elaborate stables, well-stocked trout streams, a golf course, swimming pool, and finally skiing facilities.

R. B. not only paid for the clubhouse and the amenities, he established endowments to pay taxes and upkeep expenses. Until after his death there were no dues and no initiation fees. Membership in Rolling Rock Club was a little token of R. B.'s esteem for those so honored. Everyone was his guest. To minimize the king-and-courtier relationship, R. B. deeded the immediate area around the clubhouse to the Union Trust as trustee for the club, and leased to it many more acres of the farm. He insisted that he never be asked to serve as an officer of the club.*

Even before completion of the clubhouse, R. K. set out to develop the club and Rolling Rock Farms as a horseman's paradise. He went to England in 1921 to begin the important but difficult task of developing a suitable pack of English foxhounds. With the assistance of the noted secretary of the Masters of Foxhounds Association of England and Ireland, George Evans, Esq. (who later said that R. K. had "at once impress.d me as a fine young gentleman"), R. K. collected the nucleus of his fine pack. He developed it at home with the judicious advice of W. Plunket Stewart, president of the Masters of Foxhounds Association of America. In 1924 the Rolling Rock fox hunt attained the pinnacle when it was formally "recognized" by the Masters of Foxhounds Association, a mere four years after its inception,

---

*The mere thought of Rolling Rock Club made the colorful liberal Fiorello LaGuardia foam at the mouth. He complained about it in such terms to his aide Ernest Cuneo as to give Cuneo grave concern that if LaGuardia were "to make his anger public we would never, never be invited to this wonderful place."

and R. K. emerged as one of the youngest MFs' (as they were known) in
the history of either association. The sources are consistent: he had made
it on his own. In the most valuable study of the subject, *The Story of Rolling
Rock,* J. Blan van Urk put this achievement in its proper prospective:

> The significant point to be emphasized in connection with the quality of
> Richard King Mellon's accomplishment as a Master of Foxhounds is that he
> established orthodox foxhunting in a locality where this field sport was practi-
> cally unknown to the inhabitants. To bring the style, technique, finesse and
> spirit of hunting to such heights under the existing conditions, and in so short
> a time, was indeed an achievement.

Later the Rolling Rock steeplechase was inaugurated and quickly received
appropriate acclaim. R. K.'s own racehorses were often famous winners.
The Mellons had come a long way from 1885, when the Judge had written
(incomprehensibly, with pride) that he had never attended a horse race!

R. B. also had a younger child, a daughter, Sarah, born in 1903 and
named in honor of Jennie's mother, Sarah Cordelia King. Sarah was a shy
little girl, outshone by her brother and seemingly unnoticed by her parents.
Her looks were lamentably reminiscent of her father's.

Of all the Judge's sons, A. W. most totally devoted his life to business
pursuits. In a rare lapse from his customary self-effacement, he later described himself to a Senate investigating committee as having been, in 1920,
"Pittsburgh's leading banker." There was not much else in his life. He took
pleasure in horseback riding and golf, but without a family of his own
always at home, he could not rationalize the maintenance of such wonderful
retreats as his brothers enjoyed. When his children were with him, W. L.
tells us that A. W. took his greatest pleasures:

> With his children this quiet, reserved man was a different being from the
> financier the world knew. If the children slid down the banisters, he would slide
> with them. He would play hide-and-seek until they were tired of the game.
> Often he would refuse to join a game of poker with old friends because he was
> going to play cards with Paul and Ailsa. When Ailsa asked for a playhouse
> he built a wonderful playhouse on the porch of his home.
> At that Woodland Road place he assembled all kinds of pets, from rabbits
> to ponies. His children besides their sleds had a father who went coasting with
> them. A. W. would go shopping with them in the ten-cent store. If he didn't
> actually ride a bicycle he trotted along when they went whooping around on
> their bicycles. With the children and Rover, their dog, he would play in the
> snow or romp on the grass. He would play ball or ride in a pony cart and he

earnestly set to work to learn again how to fly a kite. He was never too tired at night to play blind man's bluff or to read aloud to his children. He entered whole-heartedly and with touching delight into every department of their lives.

As a toy-shopper at F. A. O. Schwarz in New York, he became a connoisseur because he, himself, played with the toys; with the hook and ladder, the electric train and the dolls, too. He trimmed the Christmas trees of his children. He made sure there were candles on their birthday cakes. He took them to the zoo. He took them to the circus. If they played house he could enter into the pretense as merrily as his children.

As the city's most important financial figure, it is no wonder that A. W. was in demand in civic and philanthropic circles. He permitted himself to become involved in several such activities and served on the boards of trustees and as chairman of the finance committees of both of Pittsburgh's important institutions of higher learning—Carnegie Institute of Technology (now Carnegie-Mellon University) and the University of Pittsburgh. He was vice president of the great Carnegie Library, a director of a settlement-house association and of the Tuberculosis League, and a generous contributor to the Children's Hospital of Pittsburgh. His principal "philanthropy," however, was the Mellon Institute of Industrial Research, founded by himself and R. B. in memory of the Judge.

The Mellon Institute was an ideal venture for A. W., the demigod of the 1920s, to undertake in honor of Judge Thomas Mellon, man of the 1870s. Over the centuries the relations between science and industry have varied as the emphasis of scientists, in response to community interest and attitudes, has moved back and forth between the "pure" and the "practical." In the 1870s, and then again in the 1920s, men of affairs thought about science and its promises; the scientists themselves responded by shifting into "practical" gears. In such periods science became the servant of business and viewed its function as assisting business to make more things better cheaper for greater profits. With the erection of the Mellon Institute, science pledged to love, honor, and obey business.

The Mellon Institute was conceived around 1910, when Gulf's general manager introduced the Mellons to a new book, *The Chemistry of Commerce,* by Robert K. Duncan, a University of Kansas chemistry professor. Duncan argued that commerce had been negligent in failing to utilize science to its fullest. Almost no businesses maintained serious research facilities. Every plant, of course, might not be able to support the expensive research laboratories necessary to properly consider complex technical problems, but that was not an insurmountable problem. At the University of Kansas, Duncan had opened the university's research facilities to industry. He had permitted select industries to underwrite the salary of one or more research technicians who might consider a particular problem of the sponsor and utilize the university's facilities, equipment, library, supervisory and broad intellectual resources in a search for the sponsor's solution. Duncan envisioned the institutionalization of the cooperation between industry and the scientific community that he had established in Kansas on a more systematic basis and a larger scale. Initial costs for establishing an up-to-date all-purpose laboratory complex might be. high, but thereafter its operating expenses would largely be covered by industrial sponsors.

A. W. was looking for a suitable memorial to his father; Duncan's book promised the solution to A. W.'s problem. At his urging, Duncan relocated to Pittsburgh, where he affiliated with the University of Pittsburgh and inaugurated his cooperative program in its laboratories while perfecting the design for what would become the triumph of his life's work. The success of Duncan's pilot program convinced A. W. to go forward on Duncan's full-scale plan. Duncan died in 1914, shortly before the Mellon Institute of Industrial Research was to open its doors. For many years thereafter, Dr. Edward R. Weidlein, Duncan's aide and successor, served as its head and became an important figure in Pittsburgh's business and academic communities.

Over the years between 1914 and 1967, when Mellon Institute merged with Carnegie Tech to become Carnegie-Mellon University, the institute solved thousands of problems for numerous "donors," as it euphemistically referred to its clients. Business was especially grateful to it for its "independence," as it was called. Any and all discoveries made in the course of a project became the property of the project's donor, and no publicity would be had without the donor's consent. A. W. told C. W. Barron how it worked:

> My company, Gulf Oil, for instance, bought the rights to results from research in oil and natural gas. We are not largely in the natural gas business but when we found a new gas of greater intensity than had yet been discovered, we sold it to Mr. Trees of Benedum-Trees. He incorporated a company and I believe has made considerable money out of it. We stumbled on something that was the basis for the cure of epilepsy, and we turned that over to somebody else.

If a donor wanted to merchandise the new discovery himself, the institute was willing to help further. W. L. explained in *Judge Mellon's Sons:*

> When there appears out of a research project something new that can be exploited commercially, it is customary at the Institute to proceed with the inquiry to the point of creating a pilot plant. In consequence, over and over,

there has moved out of the organization a fully-formed, infant business ready to grow as fast as that business develops and finds a market for its product.

According to him, there was "always a waiting list of companies prepared to become donors in support of new fellowships." Science paid a price for the opportunity to be of such service. It surrendered in the battle between its supposed dedication to the spread of knowledge and business's dedication to the preservation of patent rights and business secrecy.

Although most of the Mellon companies had their own thoroughly adequate research laboratories, they also endowed temporary fellowships for specific projects and permanent fellowships for ongoing research. For many years Gulf Oil located its own principal lab close by the institute, and the two laboratories functioned almost as adjuncts.

No doubt during its life the Mellon Institute made many great contributions. W. L. cites as examples its metallurgical discoveries, which enabled Gulf to drill deeper into the earth in its search for oil, and the institute's innovations in gas-purification processes, which facilitated profitable conversion by the Koppers Company from wartime production of toluol to production of peacetime by-products. It did pioneering research on smoke control—a public-service matter. Some of its work, however, was of arguable social utility. Its scientists, for example, discovered a process that enabled a bread company to reduce substantially the yeast content of its bread, giving the donor a patent that increased its profitability to the same extent as it reduced the nutrient value of its product. The institute occasionally permitted itself to be used in blatantly commercial fashion, as when it "established" that it was perfectly safe to eat food cooked in aluminum pots, or demonstrated the preferability of aluminum cans over tin cans for large milk containers. Their "donor" did not object to publication of these discoveries.

It is difficult today to understand why the Mellon Institute should have received greater accolades than any lab for hire would receive today. At the time it was founded, though, there were not other major labs for hire. In the climate of the day its establishment struck more men than just A. W. Mellon as a truly eleemosynary venture, promising better living, as well as bigger profits, through chemistry.

When the United States entered the great war in 1917, the Judge's descendants ignored the ghost's admonition that only fools become cannon fodder and did their part, or at least were willing to do their part. The period of active United States involvement in the war was so brief that the Ameri-

can forces produced correspondingly few heroes, none of them Mellons.
Only two of the Judge's descendants were of an age to take military roles;
W. L.'s son Matthew was the first to do so.

Matthew Mellon was an unlikely soldier. He begins his privately printed
War Log, 1917–18: "To me, a box of tin soldiers under the Christmas tree
was like an apple in the toe of my stocking—mere filling!" He had never
played with toy soldiers or had any desire to be a soldier, but when he was
fifteen W. L. shipped him off to a military school—according to Matthew,
in hope that "they would 'make a man out of me' before it was too late."
Shortly before graduation in June of 1917, Matthew, like many of his
classmates, enlisted in the Naval Reserve, so that his service in the war was
inevitable.

At the time it was possible for those who built vessels for the Navy to
man them with their own crews of enlisted men, so a group of fifteen
well-to-do Pittsburgh lads grouped together to build a submarine chaser
that they would man, each paying a portion of the cost. Gulf Oil put a vessel
at their disposal for training while their ship was being built. Snags in
construction prevented the group from carrying out their plan. One by one
they dropped out, and Matthew ended up in training at Cape May, New
Jersey, and was commissioned an ensign in January of 1918.

The easy life at Cape May did not sit well with Matthew. He wrote
W. L., "I have a strong desire to go overseas where the action is. After all,
it makes little difference what uniform a person wears as long as he plays
a man's part in this war, and I feel very much like a slacker staying over
on this side." He was given a London assignment, survived a perilous
sixteen-day transatlantic ship ride that cost the lives of many from pneumonia and influenza, and finally arrived in London in October of 1918. There
he passed the brief remainder of the war as a code clerk. From the diary
entries in *War Log* he seems to have spent most of his time attending the
theater, opera, and ballet, enjoying London's fine restaurants, browsing in
the collectors' stalls, and exploring the city in his flowing cape, flaunting
the marvelous silver-knobbed cane that he bought. He acknowledged the
cane to be "a terrific affectation at home," but it was nicely British, and his
diary reflects the delight he took in "Strolling along the Strand/Waving my
cane in my hand." Words like "bloke" and "jolly" crept into his diary; he
was beginning to feel very much at home by the time of Armistice Day, not
a month after his arrival in England. That night he danced the night away
with an Armistice Day girl friend. He was home by January 1919.

Richard King Mellon was a more enthusiastic enlistee than Matthew,
though his role in the ultimate victory was even less significant than Mat-

thew's. R. K., who later rose to the rank of general in the reserves, loved the military from his earliest days. He enlisted with the Third Pennsylvania Militia and then transferred to be a student pilot with the Naval Aviation Corps at the Great Lakes Training Center. The authorities there discharged him when they discovered that he was under age. Later he enlisted in the Army, but the war was over before he had finished his training at officers' school in Virginia.

Even Thomas Mellon II, thirty-seven, did his part as best he could. He enlisted in the Y—the YMCA—to participate in its seemingly hopeless battle to maintain what he described as "the props and restraints to an upright life" among military personnel. Stationed in the greater Washington area, his duties included selling chocolates, keeping track of pool cues, and rounding up the mail (diary entry of October 20, 1918: "Am out of humor when I have to go for the mail in the rain"). He caused his war diary to be privately printed in 1920 as *Army "Y" Diary,* devoting one of its few pages to a dedication to his mother. There he recorded his day-by-day duties; his colds and illnesses (October 28, 1918: "The other secretaries are not convinced that I am ill, and urge me to keep on at sign painting, for the educational movies tonight"); detailed accounts of sermons; and potentially useful maxims ("If every man in this country used profane language, the country wouldn't last ten years"). He terminated after three months, shortly before his nephew Matthew returned from London.

At home in Pittsburgh, A. W. lent his name to several committees involved in furthering aspects of the war efforts, and the Mellon banks did more than their part in subscribing to war bonds.

By 1921, A. W. was ready for a change. The election of Warren G. Harding opened the door to a new world for him, and a new life. His previous political activity had been minimal. Though his business interests made him vitally concerned with a host of public policy questions—tariffs, state and federal tax and labor policies—Frick, whose policy interests were on all points compatible with his own, had followed such matters and candidates whose views might be acceptable to them, relieving A. W. of the burden of keeping track of political doings. In those days of casual reporting of political contributions, he was no doubt an important contributor to countless campaigns on local, state, and national levels, though his reported contributions were insignificant. Only occasionally does his name appear in any public reports. He is listed, for example, as having donated $2500 to President William Howard Taft's pre-convention campaign chest in Taft's 1912 re-election bid against the challenge of his predecessor, President

Theodore Roosevelt. R. B. was reported as giving a like sum, and even H. C.—McEldowney down at Union Trust—dug deep and contributed a disproportionate $500. Taft's presidency had proven acceptable only to old-guard industrialists like themselves; and even Taft was very far from ideal for them, as his tariff policy was unsatisfactory and his administration had been responsible for innumerable anti-trust prosecutions. Still, he was surely preferable to anyone who might speak irresponsibly about "malefactors of great wealth." Malefactors of great wealth? To whom could Roosevelt have been referring? A. W. was not interested in trying on the shoe.

In 1916, when Charles Evans Hughes was the candidate, the issues were clearer, and the Mellons increased their public contributions to $6000 each.

Such sums were probably the tip of the iceberg. The close business relations of the Mellons with Magee and Flinn required Mellon help in oiling the bosses' Pittsburgh political machine, while Frick spoke, and no doubt spent, for the Mellon brothers on state and national levels. After Frick's passing, a story made the rounds of a fanciful conversation between A. W. and the state's biggest Republican power, Boies Penrose, in which Penrose had told A. W. that he needed $250,000 for an upcoming campaign. "Can't you get along with $150,000?" asked the banker. When Penrose finally agreed to try, Mellon quipped that he had "just made $100,000."

The Mellons gave not only in election campaigns but also to funds designed to influence public policy other than through the election process. A. W. is known to have contributed substantially, for example, to a private fund raised by Senator Philander C. Knox and Frick to finance anti–League of Nations efforts, though it is not clear whether he contributed because of personal opposition to the League or out of loyalty to the other members of the big-business political clique that went to bat for his interests, virtually all of whom were opposing the League. He also contributed to the American Association of Foreign Language Newspapers, a non-profit syndicate of the superrich who had acquired foreign-language newspapers for the purpose of inculcating new immigrants with those principles of "Americanism" dearest to the hearts of people like the Du Ponts, Morgans, and Mellons.

A. W. was personally acquainted with Knox, an old luncheon-club and card-playing crony, partner of Judge Reed, and one of the most influential political leaders in America. In the early part of the century he had served as Attorney General in the cabinets of Presidents William McKinley and Theodore Roosevelt, and had become known, at least among progressives, as "Sleepy Phil" because of his lethargic approach to anti-trust violations. Later he had become Secretary of State in President Taft's cabinet, and ended up in the United States Senate. Knox's brother Alfred was an officer at the Mellon National Bank.

In the Senate Knox joined Penrose, the senior senator from Pennsylvania. Penrose entered the Senate in 1897, and remained there until his death from overeating twenty-four years later. In that time Penrose became one of the two or three most powerful senators, more from the force of his personality than because of his seniority. For twenty-four years he stood for reprehensibly narrow policies. He was expansive only in his efforts to expand the limits and varieties of gluttony. A huge Rabelaisian man, Penrose was possibly the most dissolute person ever to rise to major national importance in an American political party, and he was surely the most forthright man to do so. His total absence of shame about himself and his ways, coupled with a tremendous sense of personal loyalty, make him one of the more appealing rascals in the history of American politics. By hindsight, his most important accomplishment is clear: he fathered the oil-depletion allowance so favorable to wealthy Pennsylvanian (now Texan) oil men. Penrose has been described traditionally as the "boss" of Pennsylvania, as heir to the power of the state's legendary boss Matthew S. Quay. At the time of the controversy over the Scott divorce law Penrose, a United States senator, but one exercising real or supposed dominance over the Pennsylvania state legislature, was named by its critics, possibly properly so, as the divorce law's unseen sponsor. He was Frick's intimate, but on his frequent trips to Pittsburgh he always visited the Mellons as well. One of his biographers, Robert D. Bowden, has written that after Frick's death and that of Rhode Island's reactionary senator Nelson Aldrich, A. W. "was the fair god of Penrose's industrial devotion."

With Frick's passing in 1919, A. W. found himself pushed to a larger role in state Republican affairs, though he was still almost entirely a background figure, unknown personally to all but a handful of people, political or otherwise. In 1920 he was named one of Pennsylvania's delegates to the Republican National Convention, which would surely be an exciting gathering, and especially so for Pennsylvanians, as Knox himself was a potent dark-horse prospect for the presidential nomination. A. W. was sincerely sympathetic to such possibilities. If things took the proper turn, perhaps he might be able to help Knox with power brokers from the world of high finance.

According to contemporary stories, A. W. learned of his selection as a delegate from the newspapers and immediately called his attorney, Judge Reed, to ask if he might decline the seat. Yes, he might beg off, replied the judge, but he stressed to A. W. that a Mellon had a public duty to accept the seat and to participate. To make it less onerous, the judge himself would accompany A. W. to the convention, so if some business emergency required A. W. to leave on short notice, someone would be available to fulfill A. W.'s public duty for him and act as his alternate. A. W. attended and managed to stay throughout the exciting convention, which finally produced the candidate from "the smoke-filled room," as the distinguished-looking senator from Ohio, Warren G. Harding, is commonly if incorrectly known. Massachusetts governor Calvin Coolidge emerged as Harding's running mate. During the Harding-Coolidge campaign against Democrat James M. Cox and his vice presidential running mate, Franklin D. Roosevelt, A. W. did a little fund raising for the Republicans, collecting more than the $150,000 quota that Republican National Chairman Will Hays asked him to raise in greater Pittsburgh. His own contribution at the time was a modest $2000—the maximum amount that Hays wanted shown under any one name. R. B. and W. L. gave the same. A. W. appreciated that there would be a campaign debt and intended to make a more substantial contribution when the magnitude of the debt became clear. He did too.

Harding's sweeping victory in the election of 1920 is generally interpreted as a rejection of calls for "reform" in favor of a return to what Harding himself signified and described as "normalcy."

When the President-elect began recruiting his cabinet, A. W. Mellon was not the first name that came to his mind. There is considerable dispute about who first broached Mellon's name to Harding as a possible Secretary of the Treasury—many have claimed the distinction—but there is no dispute as to Harding's initial reaction to the suggestion: "Who?" It is not surprising that the President-elect had never heard of A. W. Mellon; other than those with a long memory for scandal, scarcely anybody had. Though he and his family were the principal owners of the only significant producer of aluminum in America, and of one of the country's major oil companies, A. W.'s penchant for privacy had made him probably the least-seen influential man in the United States. In Pittsburgh he was widely known of among the city's elite, but little known, and scarcely anyone in Buffalo, Little Rock, or Port Arthur had even heard of him, though he was the most powerful man in their communities if he had cared to exercise that power. He was in the running with Henry Ford for the distinction of being America's second-richest man. Rockefeller was first and Ford was almost certainly second, but J. P. Morgan was dead, while the Du Pont fortune was dispersed in many hands. At his poorest, A. W. would have ranked third, with his brother R. B. just a notch below. Still, the Mellon names had not appeared on a recently published roster of the country's hundred richest men, and had been omitted from Bertie Forbes's 1916 bible of wealth, *Men Who Are*

Making America, though A. W. was certainly one of them. It has frequently been reported that until his selection as Secretary of the Treasury his name had never been mentioned in the New York *Times,* and though he had in fact been mentioned in the *Times* on numerous occasions, in those days before publication of the *Times* index, few could have recalled any context.

"Who?" "A. W. Mellon."

As a combination, no state had a more powerful duo in Washington than Knox and Penrose. Charles "Hell and Maria" Dawes (so known from the original expletive he had once used at a congressional hearing) was Harding's earliest choice for Secretary of the Treasury and perhaps his final preference as well; Harding was somewhat concerned about possible adverse reactions of "the little man" to the appointment of such a Croesus as Mellon. Still, he was not about to begin his presidency by treating the nominee of such men as Knox and Penrose lightly. The least he could do was to look interested, so on January 2, 1921, he wrote Mellon,

> If you can find a convenient day on the sixth, seventh, or eighth instant, to run out to Marion for a short interview, I will be more than grateful to see you. I feel very much that I want to know you, and I do have some matters concerning which I very much wish to have your advice.

A. W. found it convenient. He took the train, unaccompanied, to Marion. At the station he was unable to find a cab. As the story (possibly incorrect) goes, A. W., always self-effacing and unwilling to impose, did not phone but walked to the home of the President-elect and then waited, unannounced, interminably, until finally noticed. His visit with Harding was cordial and pleasant but nothing was resolved.

There were other men in whom Harding took greater interest. Particularly he was interested in having some place in the cabinet for that maverick youngster Herbert Hoover, already widely known for his war relief work during and after World War I. For all of Harding's myopia, he saw either Hoover's touch of greatness or his popularity with large numbers of Americans. Today Hoover's popular position on the political spectrum is pegged principally by reference to his narrow views of later years. He occupied a very different spot in 1921, when his progressive past and his record of undependability for party loyalty made him anathema to conservative Republican leaders like Knox, Penrose, and the circle around them. Quietly they began stirring up opposition to a cabinet seat for Hoover.

Dawes ultimately announced his unavailability for the cabinet, leaving the field for Secretary of the Treasury to A. W., but Harding put off announcing his selection while making clear to Mellon's backers that it would have to be a package: Mellon for Secretary of the Treasury and Hoover for Secretary of Commerce, or neither. According to Harry Daugherty, when it was put to Penrose the senator "rose to heights of profanity I have never heard equalled. He swore in every mood and tense." But the conservatives bought the deal, and on that basis both Hoover and Mellon entered the cabinet, raising one of the interesting "what if's" of American history: What would have been the subsequent course of the United States had the Republican right wing opted for "neither"?

On his own part, the great honor was not an unmixed blessing for A. W. He was simultaneously repelled by the thought of the position, its responsibilities and its exposure, and at the same time strangely attracted by it. For sixty-five years he had made a fetish of his privacy; not lightly would he sacrifice it. According to W. L., A. W. sent word back to Knox early in discussions not to take further steps by way of encouragement of his candidacy. A. W. himself later claimed to have told the President-elect at his first meeting with Harding, "I have just one personal favor to ask of you and that is that you find someone else for the Treasury and relieve me from going to Washington."

He was also concerned about his possible ineligibility for the position due to his myriad of business interests, and potential embarrassments to the administration should some irresponsible persons attempt to make political hay out of them. Judge Reed called A. W.'s attention to a 1789 statute that prohibited the Secretary of the Treasury from "directly or indirectly being concerned or interested in carrying on the business of trade or commerce." On the face of things it seemed impossible for A. W. to cleanse himself of indirect involvement in commerce. The Secretary of the Treasury sat as an ex officio member of the Federal Reserve Board, and another statute prohibited members of the board from owning banking stocks. That surely included A. W. He later said that the discovery of these statutes "relieved my mind. There was a door that I could go through gracefully, and not become Secretary of the Treasury." He set off for Washington to explain the situation to Knox, who would have to tell Harding "that I was not eligible for the office." "Oh, there is nothing to that" was Knox's reaction. He was unimpressed with the supposed legal obstacles and was satisfied that the matter of A. W.'s involvement in "the business of trade or commerce" could be overcome by Mellon's resignation from the boards of directors on which he held seats—something that he might have felt obliged to do in any event. Only the Union Trust stock would have to be sold. Knox rounded up a legal opinion to that extent on the impressive letterhead of the Washington law

firm of Faust and Wilson, while Reed drafted the terms of an agreement
between A. W. and a prospective purchaser for his bank stock, one R. B.
Mellon. No dollars would even have to change hands. The situation had
taken such a turn, as A. W. later explained, "that all of my opportunity [to
refuse the office] was gone."

On the other side, A. W. did not want to refuse the office. With Frick
gone, he was losing interest in business, but simple retirement was out of
the question. He knew that like his father he would be incapable of inactivity. The Judge had given some of his life to "public service"; should he
not do likewise? What better way to cap his career in the world of finance
than to retire as Secretary of the Treasury? The glamour of life in Washington compared favorably with that of drab Pittsburgh, and though he had
never been a "social" person, A. W. could take some pleasure by osmosis,
simply by being in the more exciting atmosphere. He had to think of his
children as well. Ailsa, eighteen, was eager for him to accept the position;
there would be advantages for her if he were to do so; and it would probably
be a better environment for young Paul, thirteen, as well. Removed from
the distractions and demands of Pittsburgh business, perhaps he would be
able to establish a closer relationship with the children. By the time the offer
finally came, there was no hesitation in his acceptance. According to his
friend Chancellor John G. Bowman of the University of Pittsburgh, he had
become "enthralled" with the prospect of going to what he had regarded
as "a city of mystery." He told Ailsa that he was accepting the position on
her account, but years later he explained that he had accepted because "I
felt that some day I must break away from my business and corporation
connections, and thought that this would be a good time." He resigned from
the boards of directors of

> Aluminum Company of America
> Aluminum Cooking Utensil Company
> Aluminum Ore Company
> American Locomotive Company
> American Metal Company Ltd.
> American Surety Company of New York
> Apollo (Pa.) Water Works Company
> Baltimore Car & Foundry Company
> Burrell Improvement Company
> Butler Bolt & Rivet Company
> Butler Car Wheel Company
> Carborundum Company

Electric Carbon Company
Forged Steel Wheel Company
Gulf Oil Corporation
H. Kleinhans Company
J. J. McCormick & Company
Koppers Company
Leechburg (Pa.) Water Works Company
Long Sault Development Company
Lyndora Land and Improvement Company
McClintic-Marshall Company
McClintic-Marshall Construction Company
Mellon-Stuart Company
Middleton Car Company
Minnesota By-Products Coke Company
Monongahela Light & Power Company
Monongahela River Consolidated Coal & Coke Company
Monongahela Street Railway Company
National Union Fire Insurance Company
Pennsylvania Water Company
Pittsburgh By-Products Coke Company
Pittsburgh Coal Company
Pittsburgh Modern Engine Company
Pittsburgh & Birmingham Traction Company
Pressed Metal Radiator Company
Riter-Conley Company
Riter-Conley Manufacturing Company
Robert Grace Constructing Company
Seaboard By-Products Coke Company
Standard Motor Truck Company
Standard Steel Car Company
Tri-Cities Water Company
Union Fidelity Title Insurance Company of Pittsburgh
Union Improvement Company
Union Insurance Company
Union Savings Bank
Union Shipbuilding Company
Union Trust Company of Pittsburgh
United States Aluminum Company, and
Verona Steel Castings Company,

and boarded the night train for Washington to begin the new life. "Who?" asked the American public. "A. G. Mellon" was the answer. It took a while for the press to get the middle initial straight, and by the time it did, Mellon's correct middle initial had become academic. In the minds and hearts of most Americans, A. W. Mellon had ceased to exist; this strange, distant, and cloistered person had become "Andy" Mellon.

BOOK III

⟶⟋⟶

The Greatest Secretary of the Treasury Since Hamilton

It is always a mistake for a good
business man to take public office.

—A. W. MELLON

"Andy" Mellon's selection as Secretary of the Treasury was firmed up only eight days before the new President's inauguration, allowing scant time to smooth out a transition of administrations in the Treasury Department. This deprived A. W. of any reasonable opportunity to feel his way around before taking over, and heightened his other and more significant disadvantage—that he was not well equipped for the new job. His own life in the worlds of business and banking gave him little to draw upon for worthwhile guidance when he was confronted with national problems. He began with no well-developed ideas as to national economic policies, and his prior experiences were not such as would enable him to develop any thought-through approach to them. The only "internal" direction he had as policy questions arose came from his attachment to "trickle-down theory." Mellon believed that favors placed at the economic top would trickle down, so that what was directly good for the business community at the highest economic stratum would inevitably be good for everyone, whereas what was directly good for the little man at the bottom would have a lesser beneficial impact on the nation at large. Crudely translated, it meant that what was good for the rich was really better for all than what was good for the poor. No one would be a bigger beneficiary from a wholesale application of trickle-down theory than A. W. Mellon himself, but A. W. was not a cynical man, and this author does not question the sincerity with which he advocated the approach. It took courage for him to do so.

Trickle-down theory may have appropriate applications in certain economic settings, but hindsight makes clear that it went wild in the 1920s, contributing to a great extent to the depression that brought down the whole deck of 1920s playing cards.

More immediately serious, because more pressing, A. W. knew almost nothing about the Treasury Department itself as an institution, or about its mechanics. He knew that the job was an awesome one and that his areas of responsibility did not end with the formulation of national economic policy but extended to a dozen unrelated and troublesome activities. When he met his predecessor, Wilson's outgoing Treasury Secretary David F. Houston, Houston told diarist Charles Hamlin that Mellon had "modestly" disavowed any knowledge of Treasury matters; he had "seemed very shy and almost frightened; was almost in a perspiration." A. W. always seemed shy, frequently showed nervous perspiration, and sometimes might have appeared frightened. In this case the signs probably had greater than usual indicative value. A. W. was over his head and knew it. He "seemed almost aghast" when Houston pointed out that the terms of the Democratic assistant secretaries would momentarily lapse. A. W.'s position as a brand-new secretary with brand new underlings would be like that of an honorary ship captain attempting to run a huge vessel with inexperienced staff. It would surely hit rocks. Mellon was not so innocent as to be unaware of the time-honored political rule about victors and spoils, yet he implored Houston to use his good offices to induce the assistant secretaries to remain, giving him assurances that he would ask President Harding to send in their names for reappointment. And so it came to pass that the most important second-level officials of the early Mellon period, most notably S. Parker Gilbert, were Wilson administration holdovers, dedicated to the policies of the outgoing administration. Most important of those holdover policies was the tax-reform policy for postwar America that had been formulated largely by Gilbert under Houston's leadership. It was a policy with which A. W. could feel entirely comfortable, as the key to it was reduction of taxes on the rich. A. W.'s successful salesmanship of the "Mellon Plan," as the refinement of Houston's tax policy came to be known, made for Mellon's greatest impact on the 1920s.

Mellon remembered the press. At first the journalists scared him. The Senate confirmed his initial appointment without a dissenting vote, but the press would play an even more important role than the Senate in making his life pleasant or miserable. He nurtured his memories, and they could only have been unsettling. Sure enough, A. W. and the press seemed to get off to a bad start at first. The New York *World*—just about everyone read it, and a lot of people clipped it—had called his nomination "an unfit appointment" and A. W. himself "an obscure Pittsburgh millionaire who has nothing to recommend him except his wealth and his reactionary environment." Though the New York *Times* was more nearly gracious, even it had described him as "a Republican of stand-pat variety." "Stand-pat variety" was probably not a favorable reference. More and more A. W. discovered that things were different as an important government official than they had been as a private businessman. For one thing, it was harder to avoid the journalists—probably couldn't be done, probably shouldn't be done. After all, he explained to W. L.,

> he always wished to know as much as possible about the character and the background of anyone who worked for him in an important position, there was

fairness in the desire of the people to know about him since he had become their employee.

He had to see the reporters, but he did not look forward to it. W. M. Kiplinger, then a New York *Times* correspondent, wrote that Mellon "quailed in his early press conferences"; Thomas Stokes found him at first "a shy and timid and uncertain man before us in his press conferences"; and another journalist participant, William H. Crawford, privately noted that the new Secretary was "a colorless, spineless individual who apparently lacked self-confidence." At a private background briefing with Kiplinger, A. W. did a little better, until Kiplinger asked, "What have you to say about being a rich man?" A. W. "stopped, looked out the window, then spoke with the hesitancy, almost a stutter, which was his mannerism":

> "Why . . . I . . . I . . . don't know what to say. I . . . I . . . suppose I am . . . what they call a rich man. . . . They tell me so. . . . I'm not particularly conscious of it. . . . I don't use money . . . for myself. . . . I don't spend much . . . on myself. . . . I have always . . . just worked . . . done what needed to be done . . . in business. . . . I didn't try to make money . . . especially . . . I'm not interested in it . . . in money. . . . I don't care . . . but . . . well . . . I . . . I can't think of anything to say about it."

Other journalists quoted him on the subject of his rank alongside Rockefeller and Ford as having said "Really, I'm a poor man, comparatively."

With time, A. W. conquered the press; the press helped him to conquer it. By the mid-1920s, newspaper coverage of his activities and policies was almost uniformly favorable, which loosened him up when he met the journalists. Mellon could never have been accused of seeking publicity—he did not retain a "press officer" or anyone else to steam up favorable publicity about him—but still it was nice to get favorable publicity. Stokes reported that A. W.

> marvelled that his hesitant "Yes" or "No" could become columns on the front page. I remember one day when he held up the front page of a newspaper and pointed to a story about the soldiers' bonus. Almost plaintively he said that he only had said one word "No" when asked whether he would favor passage of the soldiers' bonus, and look!, there was a whole column on the subject. I have often thought that, in time, these front-page stories became like a drug to him, that, figuratively, he hugged the newspaper to his breast and conned it avidly. It made him a master mind, a man of destiny—for a time. Life again was worth living. It had a purpose.

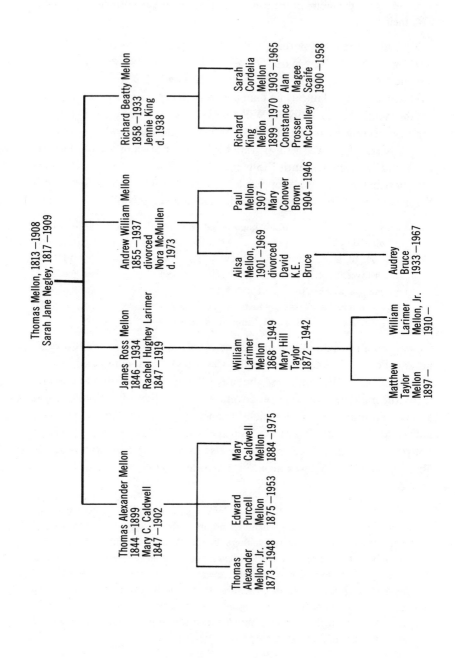

Thomas Mellon, 1813–1908
Sarah Jane Negley, 1817–1909

Thomas Alexander Mellon
1844–1899
Mary C. Caldwell
1847–1902

James Ross Mellon
1846–1934
Rachel Hughey Larimer
1847–1919

Andrew William Mellon
1855–1937
divorced
Nora McMullen
d. 1973

Richard Beatty Mellon
1858–1933
Jennie King
d. 1938

Thomas
Alexander
Mellon, Jr.
1873–1948

Edward
Purcell
Mellon
1875–1953

Mary
Caldwell
Mellon
1884–1975

William
Larimer
Mellon
1868–1949
Mary Hill
Taylor
1872–1942

Matthew
Taylor
Mellon
1897–

William
Larimer
Mellon, Jr.
1910–

Ailsa
Mellon,
1901–1969
divorced
David
K.E.
Bruce

Paul
Mellon
1907–
Mary
Conover
Brown
1904–1946

Richard
King
Mellon
1899–1970
Constance
Prosser
McCaulley

Sarah
Cordelia
Mellon 1903–1965
Alan
Magee
Scaife
1900–1958

Audrey
Bruce
1933–1967

He forgot the sins that had been perpetrated against him by the Philadelphia *North American.*

Most of the reporters were much younger men, and in many ways A. W. demonstrated a powerful paternal interest in younger men. He indulged the journalists and himself with them. One reported this personal vignette:

> He is perfectly approachable. A young reporter who has been studying law on the side rushes in to tell him that he has passed his bar examination. The reporter receives the warmest congratulations, Mr. Mellon showing the liveliest personal interest. "I might have been a lawyer," says Mr. Mellon. "I used to work in my father's law office and look up cases for him. I planned to enter the bar." With a wistful glance back at his youth, he adds, "I might have been a better lawyer than banker."

That is an anecdote about a nice man, and journalists like nice men. They also like honest men, and A. W. was "honest" with them, that is, he found great difficulty in being less than candid with them.

There was often something slightly awkward about him, but it was most pronounced when he was called upon to be less than thoroughly open. On such occasions, wrote Clinton W. Gilbert in *Current History,* "he becomes a little more hesitant in speech than ordinarily. The perspiration nervously breaks out upon his face. He is unwilling to mislead them. He conceals what he feels must be concealed with obvious reluctance." Otherwise he loosened up. Always best in a small setting, he began to give more one-to-one interviews, and though he generally asked the right to "review" the fruit of such interviews prior to publication, he "red-penciled" almost nothing. His unfriendly biographer, Harvey O'Connor, reported that he spoke openly and hostilely about the prohibition act that he was charged with enforcing to a *Saturday Evening Post* reporter:

> The astonished editor sent the manuscript to Mellon to make sure that a high public official had not only dared to be frank—but to be quoted. He certified the article, but the *Post,* semi-official organ of the administration, never saw fit to publish it.

With time, A. W. became completely comfortable with the journalists, and the warmth that he developed for them—fed by the warmth that they developed first for the seeming successes of his policies and then for himself —helped them to cloak his "businessman's" policies with an aura of the wisdom that they probably lacked. The press conferences became a delight for all. There, Stokes wrote, Mellon "indulged in that dry wit which often pricked the pretensions of the world, slyly, showing that he knew within him that all was vanity and vexation of the spirit." Journalists liked that too, and they rewarded him.

Public speaking was the thing A. W. dreaded most, but it was not always possible to refuse. He probably made fewer speeches than any other cabinet member of the decade, but such as he made were nightmares for himself and his audiences. Generally his speeches were inaudible more than a few feet from the podium, and he was so nervous about their delivery that he sometimes became discombobulated in the course of them. Frank Kent described one of his appearances before the House Ways and Means Committee:

> His reading of his long prepared statement was almost unintelligible and when he was through, and the Committeemen started to question him, he looked appealingly and pathetically around for the alert [undersecretary] Mr. Winston, who quickly stepped forward and answered for him.

O'Connor described a similar experience at an important fund-raising dinner for Carnegie Tech (now Carnegie-Mellon University):

> The honored guest, introduced as Pittsburgh's most illustrious citizen, began reading his speech in a voice hardly audible beyond the first row. Midway, he was seen to fumble among the pages. He had lost the continuity. Nervously, he fingered through the manuscript prepared by the faithful Finley [his closest aide], lost his patience, announced abruptly, "That's all," and retired to his seat.

In a small intimate group he had no such problems, and according to O. O. Kahn, onetime director of WABC's *National Radio Forum,* he was somewhat better on radio than in his live appearances.

With time, A. W. altered his approach before congressional committees; he would take the witness stand himself but would have an assistant read the prepared statement. He was then able to remain composed and could take an active part in the subsequent discussion. Clinton Gilbert quoted an unidentified Democratic congressman on A. W.'s quickness on one such occasion when "the Secretary's" speech was being read into the record by an assistant:

> You could see . . . that he had never seen the statement that was being read for him. But when its author was headed toward an assumption that I was ready to pounce upon, Mr. Mellon every time would break in and testify himself, taking another line and avoiding the embarrassment that he could see coming.

A. W. found the complexities of running the Treasury Department as baffling as any other man would have found the complexities of stepping into his network of varied businesses. For him the problems were worse in public life. "We do not function as smoothly in public life as in private," he once remarked; "the machine is more complicated, conditions more complex, the factors which we have to deal with are more uncertain." He was on numberless Washington boards, usually as an ex officio member, many of which were concerned with matters totally unrelated to financing of government. He sat, for example, as a member of the Interdepartmental Social Hygiene Board; it is hard to imagine anyone in 1920s Washington less suited than A. W. to be on such a board. No man could possibly have known all about the many varied things for which A. W. was to be saddled with a share of responsibility, and at his stage of life he was not really interested in becoming expert in most of them. After his first year on the job he told Dawes that he had been able to touch only the fringe of the office's routine activities.

Early in his administration Mellon reorganized the departmental chain of command into the corporate format with which he was familiar. A. W., the Secretary, functioned as chairman of the board; Gilbert, the first undersecretary, and his successors Garrard B. Winston (1923–27) and Ogden L. Mills (1927–32) were the "presidents" who actively administered the department. The assistant secretaries fulfilled the roles of corporate vice presidents, each overseeing distinct functions of the department. Mellon relied most heavily on his chief executives, and especially on Gilbert.

After Harvard Law School, Parker Gilbert was brought into the Treasury Department by Russell G. Leffingwell, Secretary Houston's closest adviser. He rose rapidly. A. W. was right when he decided that he needed Gilbert. Soon after A. W. was sworn in, Gilbert, then twenty-nine years old, was given his new title of undersecretary, and his salary doubled from $5000 to $10,000. Mellon presented Gilbert with the elaborate parchment document of appointment as undersecretary at a brief ceremony with a few informal words:

> Here is your commission, Mr. Gilbert. Usually such a commission is tied with pink baby ribbon, but we are out of pink baby ribbon at present, and since the policy of the Administration is for economy, we have used a rubber band. But it is a perfectly good commission, Mr. Gilbert.

Then it was back to work, in what developed into a warm working relationship. Though they remained always "Mr. Mellon" and "Mr. Gilbert," an affection developed between them. When Washington papers somehow

printed a groundless rumor—apparently inspired by Gilbert's eager mother
—of an impending engagement between Gilbert and Ailsa Mellon, Gilbert
rushed to the Secretary to make his explanations that he had never anywhere intimated that he was to be the Secretary's son-in-law. A. W. responded, "I don't know but I'd just as soon have you for one."

His relations with Gilbert's successors were less close but still more than
cordial. The good relations arose principally from the implicit and explicit
respect that he showed for them and trust that he put in them. Witness his
approach to decision making, as Chester N. Morrill, attorney for various
Treasury-connected agencies, described it to a Columbia University Oral
History interviewer:

> He always seemed dispassionate and always relaxed, and whenever any ques-
> tion came up he seemed to be quite willing to listen, to defer to the judgment
> of other people, and then say what he thought, but not expecting necessarily
> that everybody would agree with him. So that one can imagine how under
> those conditions the relationship would be agreeable.

Mellon made no effort to discourage his underlings from supporting
political candidates other than those of his own preference. Winston told
Columbia's interviewers that Mellon "had a great capacity for delegating
work—more than any man I've ever seen." Winston was not as close to
Mellon as was his predecessor, Gilbert, or his successor, Mills, but he was
given what he described as "nearly carte blanche authority." Matters of
negotiations were almost invariably left to the undersecretaries. Only broad
policy questions concerned the Secretary, and even those were initially
formulated by the undersecretaries. This was especially the case in the early
period, when the "Mellon policies" that were to shape the decade were
refined by Gilbert from the policies of the Wilson administration, and in the
later period, when Undersecretary Mills virtually supplanted A. W. as the
actual Secretary.

Most of the undersecretaries' letters went out without Mellon's clearance;
and the initial drafts of virtually all his important position papers, preserved
in the National Archives, are in the handwriting of the underlings. Their
initials appear on the copies of the lengthy, detailed, and often deadly dull
policy letters that emerged from the Secretary's office in an unending river,
indicating that they had been checked and "cleared" with the staff, if not
drafted by them, before they got to A. W.'s desk for signature. He signed
many of those drafted by the undersecretaries without reading them.

The surface formality among the members of Mellon's inner staff is clear
from the handwritten notes on the documents in Treasury archives, and it

is startling. Even the notes between Mellon and David E. Finley, the staff member who became closest to Mellon, were always to and from "Mr. Finley" and "Mr. Mellon." Finley's 1973 book, *A Standard of Excellence: Andrew W. Mellon Founds the National Gallery of Art at Washington, D.C.,* maintained the formality of his relationship with his long dead benefactor, "Mr. Mellon." The notes between the younger men in the department never presume to refer to the Secretary as "A. W." or the "Chief." Nonetheless, the deference to these younger men that A. W. demonstrated, and the respect that he showed to them, commanded a loyalty that belies all the "Misters." Finley later said that Mellon's treatment of them "had a way of making you feel badly if you failed him."

The retention of Gilbert and other Wilson holdovers, all presumably Democrats, rankled more than one Republican Party loyalist. It didn't rankle A. W. He was interested in the public needs and in his own needs. He was interested in substance (a subjective consideration). As things turned out, Gilbert himself, the first and hardest bone for Republican regulars to swallow, turned out to be a Republican. He had been a "merit" appointee of the Democratic administration. A. W. did not know it until months after he had pushed Gilbert through; it was not a relevant consideration to him. He was not interested in party labels. A responsible Democrat like, say, Maryland's Senator William Cabell Bruce, who viewed public policy questions as honorably as Henry Clay Frick himself, was surely preferable to a left-oriented Republican like, say, Senator James Couzens, the millionaire populist from Michigan. In the congressional elections of 1922 A. W. was the only cabinet member who failed to go out on the hustings for the party's candidates. He had too much of the Judge in him ever to be party to electioneering claptrap.

Nonetheless, A. W. appreciated the demands of party organization. He had used up about all the indulgence that he had coming to him in pushing through the appointments of the holdover assistant secretaries, and for a while he would have to let the spoilsmen have their day, at least on appointments that were not crucial to the proper functioning of the department. Comptroller of the Currency was one such appointment. It was a grand title, but the title was more important than the function itself. There was a position made for a patronage appointee. At first A. W. had told the Federal Reserve Board that he expected to delay the appointment of a Comptroller of the Currency and would be back to them about it before doing so. But the President himself had a candidate—Daniel R. Crissinger, a Marion lawyer and sometime small-town banker whose relations with the President dated back to boyhood watermelon thefts. The only disadvantage to Crissinger's nomination was possible temporary loss of face with those Federal Reserve Board holier-than-thous who ignored important political and personal considerations. A. W. seemed downcast when he discussed the dilemma with Hamlin, an influential member of the board (possibly a ploy on A. W.'s part). Ultimately, Mellon appointed Crissinger.

On more important issues, more significant appointments, A. W. would make the fight. One such was the appointment of a Commissioner of Internal Revenue. Now there was an office that mattered, an appointment that was not to be lightly made. The front runner was so much ahead of the field as to have made his ultimate appointment seem inevitable. President Harding himself had written A. W. that he intended to name so-and-so "if" A. W. had no objection. As far as A. W. was concerned, the President's implicit preference was not the end of the matter. He brought in one of W. L.'s ablest underlings from Gulf, Colonel J. Frank Drake, to scout out whatever he could about the possible candidates. After Drake's investigations, A. W. did have objections, and he pushed hard instead for the appointment of one of the men further down the list, North Carolina lawyer David Blair. Blair was appointed to the most important position of Commissioner of Internal Revenue; Crissinger was appointed to a post with an equally impressive title but a less important function. It was a good bargain for propriety in the conflict inevitable in political government between the forces of "good" and the forces of "evil."

The conflict between politics and "qualifications" in selection of appointees came to a head subsequent to the nomination in December 1921 of Elmer Dover as an assistant secretary of the Treasury. Dover was another member of the Harding gang, a onetime confidant of the legendary congressional kingpin, Ohio's Mark Hanna, and former secretary of the Republican National Committee. Republican leaders wanted someone in the Treasury Department to keep an eye open for patronage opportunities. No one was better qualified than Dover. Dutifully, A. W. nominated Dover to the post of assistant secretary. Dover was dedicated to his task of rewarding the party faithful. A. W. was dedicated to his task of running the Treasury Department to the best of his abilities. A blowup was inevitable.

The first major battle came in April 1922, when Harding issued an executive order dismissing twenty-seven executives from the Bureau of Engraving and Printing "for the good of the service." Rumor circulated by Republican "party people" had it that outright dishonesty was involved. Most of those fired were longtime civil servants; they included the director of the bureau, James L. Wilmeth, a man who had had twenty-four years of government service, and the assistant director. Their replacements were empowered by the order to replace the other dismissed employees. Twenty-seven party regulars were rewarded. A. W., together with Assistant Secretary Eliot Wadsworth, went to the White House to protest, but the President was resolute. According to W. L., A. W. regarded "the replacing of such expert people with inferior human material [as] outrageous. I know he pondered earnestly on his course." His determination was not to make an open break over the matter, and he was quoted in the newspapers in support of the "reorganization." His statement defended the severed civil servants from any imputation of improper conduct.

Days after the announcement of the executive order, Dover let it be known that the Internal Revenue Service would likewise be "Hardingized," as he called it. The newspapers reported as much. That was a more important matter to A. W.; he would not stand for it. He immediately issued a statement that "These reports do not emanate from any official source and are absolutely without foundation. No such reorganization is now nor has been at any time contemplated." Undaunted, for several months Dover made continued efforts to fill Internal Revenue with his people; Blair, Dover's underling in the departmental chain of command, resolutely protected established employees and resisted the appointment of the more obviously unqualified to vacancies. A. W. himself began firing people—Dover's appointees.

Dover was not without muscle. Out of nowhere appeared a widely circulated "Survey of the Personnel of the Bureau of Internal Revenue," which listed 150 key employees who were supposed Democrats (many were not) who were "causing embarrassment for the Republican administration." The survey was sent to Harding with a petition signed by more than 150 Republican congressmen and senators supporting Dover's efforts and demanding Blair's removal and rectification of the situation. The spoilsmen gave A. W. the opportunity to become the hero of good-government proponents. When the reporters asked his comment on the survey he said,

> The affairs of the Treasury are of too great importance to allow of interference to its proper conduct through the introduction of petty politics. . . . Those Democrats who hold positions in the Treasury have been retained because of their qualifications for the offices they hold, and I have had no evidence of partisan activity on their part.

The President himself was a spoilsman from way back, and no doubt was entirely sympathetic with the needs of his patronage-starved party. He early complained to William P. G. Harding, governor of the Federal Reserve Board, a Democrat unrelated to the President, that Mellon was a "fine man,

but doesn't know a damn thing about politics; you Democrats run everything, and Mellon praises each of you by name every day and wants me to
retain you all." Still, Harding needed Mellon, and the Secretary obviously
felt strongly about the matter—perhaps strongly enough to resign over it.
Mellon's resignation might poison the entire business community against
the administration. According to W. L., when the Secretary met to discuss
the situation with the President, Harding left the handling of the matter
entirely within A. W.'s discretion.

In another month Dover resigned, according to the press as a result of
an ultimatum given Harding by the Secretary. He became the victim of his
own purge. A year and a half later A. W. publicly offered to restore Wilmeth
as director of the Bureau of Engraving, but the offer was refused for "private
reasons."

The passing of Dover did not mean the end of patronage-related problems
for the Secretary. At the same time as Dover left, so did Governor Harding
of the Federal Reserve. When the governor's term expired, A. W. strongly
urged his reappointment, but the President refused to get into a discussion
about it. A. W. told Hamlin that the President "threw up his hands and said
he was too busy with the railroad and coal strike to think of anything else."
Governor Harding was replaced by Crissinger, to the disgust of both A. W.
and the members of the Federal Reserve Board. The board members liked
to think of themselves as a kind of fiscal Supreme Court that functioned
outside of the political arena. Some of them were already getting uncomfortable about Mellon's acknowledgment of political considerations, and the
replacement of Governor Harding by Crissinger unfairly lowered A. W.
another notch in the board's collective judgment. Ailsa Mellon told Governor Harding's daughter Margaret, one of the few friends of Ailsa's lifetime,
that her father had been left very angry over the matter. More importantly,
the board was seriously weakened by the change.

Governor of the Federal Reserve Board, however, was a presidential
appointment to an independent agency, not a branch of the Treasury Department; the confrontation over Dover at least left A. W. in charge of
running his own ship. Thereafter the documents and manuscripts reflect
that A. W. made frequent queries as to the political affiliations of prospective nominees for office, but nowhere do the sources indicate that he ever
permitted the objectives of the political community, with which he had to
work, to outweigh his objective of getting the significant work done as he
thought it ought to be done.

At first A. W. stayed at the Hotel Willard, until he found a suitable
apartment in the penthouse of the McCormick Apartments on Massachu-

setts Avenue. Paul was away at schools, but Ailsa was with him most of the time until her marriage in 1926, after which A. W. usually rattled about the apartment's fifteen rooms alone except for the servants. His daily routine became fairly fixed. It was early to rise, a lumberjack's breakfast, and then a mile walk to the office, arriving early. Usually he walked home for a heavy lunch and then walked back to work, and walked home again after staying late at the office. He became a common sight walking along Massachusetts Avenue in his chinchilla overcoat. As time went on, and A. W. aged from sixty-five to seventy-six during his term at Treasury, one or two of those walks (but no more) might be omitted, especially on bad weather days. The stride slowed down.

Supper was usually sparse. Throughout the day A. W. drank substantial quantities of water—according to Walter Davenport in an "approved" *Colliers* piece, a great deal more water than most men drink. The evenings were not long; it was early to bed. He usually passed them reading, but never fiction. Most would have thought the evenings lonely, but there were people in the paintings with which A. W. surrounded himself. A. W. burgeoned as an art collector during his period as Secretary, acquiring more paintings and more-expensive paintings. Some of them were masterpieces of the greatest importance. Many of them were soft portraits of nice people, lovely ladies and unmistakable gentlemen. They were people with whom A. W. felt very comfortable.

At work his office had a rich feel to it, which *Time* wrote was unequaled in Washington. In the center of it was his massive orderly desk. He sat behind it, his legs usually crossed. Occasionally, when he thought himself unobserved, he would tuck one leg beneath his buttock and sit on one foot, a habit less common with him now than had been the case in earlier, spryer days. Always the ubiquitous little cigar burned, its smoke sometimes duplicating the little circles that A. W. made with his hand when he spoke.

According to his later sworn testimony, A. W. had just about closed out the business phase of his life; his new job took virtually all of his attention. Johnson sent him regular accounts and reports, but he scarcely looked at them. Later he testified that after going to Washington "I don't believe I thought of the Aluminum Company once in six months." He ceased to have any knowledge at all of goings on at Union Trust, and the periodic reports of the other companies went unread. His testimony was that he almost lost contact with R. B., his near-constant companion until his appointment as Secretary; A. W. was seldom in Pittsburgh and R. B. seldom in Washington. There were occasions when A. W. might play some part in one of the businesses, and on such occasions his participation sometimes involved implicit conflict of interest, but they were conflicts that would only have been apparent to one attuned to the potential for conflict of interest in one's own picture. A. W. was not so attuned.

Mellon found a new thing in Washington: social life. He had avoided it in Pittsburgh. In Washington, relieved of the burdens of his busy business life and expanded by sympathetic recognition, he found that he rather liked social life. He was a much sought after man in Washington's social scene, both for the stature that his presence would lend to any gathering and because his acceptance of an engagement would likely bring a return invitation to that apartment of his, the decoration of which, and especially the paintings, awed all who were privileged to be invited there. W. L. wrote that "A. W. delighted in the sensation that his pictures made. He was as happy when the pictures were being admired as he was unhappy when attention was focused on himself." He was inundated with invitations, which he would carefully sort out with the assistance of Miss Anne Randolph, a legendary social secretary in the world's most social-climbing city. Few were accepted. He found official state functions deadly, and except when called upon to escort some visiting Rumanian princess, he would attend only to retreat into a corner with Charles Dawes (erstwhile director of the Bureau of the Budget, Vice President, and ambassador to Great Britain) and similar big-business types. He joined the Metropolitan Club, but was seldom seen there.

Outside of his home, his first preference for a night out was a good poker game. The Judge wrote in his memoirs that he had never played a game of cards. It was his son's favorite recreation. He was an occasional participant in the twice-a-week poker games that took place at the Harding White House, when "the boys" would assemble, take off their jackets, snap their suspenders, light up their cigars, pour themselves a good belt of contraband drink, and play the night away. He must have felt out of place in such a crowd, but he played there and, according to Samuel Hopkins Adams's account of the Harding era, usually won. More often he played in more polite company, with people like the reactionary New Jersey senator Walter Edge; Speaker of the House Nicholas Longworth and his brilliant, acerbic wife, the Rough Rider's daughter Alice Roosevelt Longworth; and Ogden Mills. Though A. W. protested his ignorance of the finer points of the game, according to W. L.

> A. W. in a poker game had few peers. He was a masterly poker player, who abandoned a weak hand as fast as if his fortune had depended on it, and who exercised every trading instinct when he was competing for a pot. In a poker game he knew neither kinsmen, partners nor friends. He competed earnestly but merrily.

Mrs. Theodore Roosevelt Jr. recounted an anecdote of one of those "hands that will live forever" that A. W. did not win:

> I shall never forget a hand I watched one evening when the players were the Longworths, Charlie Curtis, Andrew Mellon, Secretary of the Treasury, John Weeks, Secretary of War, Albert Lasker, head of the Shipping Board, and Ted. It was a jack pot opened on the dealer's left by a pat full house. No one raised and everyone came in. The pat full naturally stood pat. Mr. Mellon drew a card. So did Charlie Curtis. I forget what the others did, but it didn't matter. The full house bet the limit, was raised by Mr. Mellon and again by Charlie. The rest couldn't throw in their hands fast enough. Even the pat full dropped. Mr. Mellon raised; Charlie raised. Mr. Mellon raised again, refusing to believe he was beaten. Charlie raised back. Mr. Mellon, remarking that he always had to pay for his experience, called and laid down four queens. Charlie had four kings and an ace.
>
> At the end of the evening Mr. Mellon, a gentle, shy man, laid forty cents on the table. "That's all I have left," he said in a soft voice. Albert Lasker, who in addition to his government post was head of Lord and Thomas, one of the big public relations firms of the day, suddenly sat up straight. "Mr. Secretary! If you can contrive to be held up on your way home, I'll guarantee you space on the front page of every newspaper in the country tomorrow!"

Mellon most enjoyed hosting dinner parties of twelve to fifteen guests. The menus were as choice as the paintings, though the host himself usually partook little. At his side as hostess was usually the beautiful Ailsa, or sometimes Mrs. Edward Purcell Mellon, wife of his nephew, T. A.'s younger son. E. P. had already achieved some renown as an architect, and he and his wife fit in nicely. A. W.'s undersecretaries were often included in his social life, as was Pennsylvania senator David A. Reed, and in the later period David Finley was invariably present. He was often invited to the same social functions as A. W., perhaps to increase the likelihood that A. W. himself might attend.

David E. Finley was born in 1890 to a prominent South Carolina family. His father spent his last eighteen years as a conservative Democratic congressman. After graduating from George Washington University Law School in Washington in 1913, Finley was a Philadelphia lawyer until service in World War I, and after the war practiced tax law in Washington until 1922, when his friend Parker Gilbert brought him into the Treasury Department. There he had increasing contact with the Secretary. In many ways he was more like the Secretary than A. W.'s own son. Finley also was of Scotch-Irish background, but his more important similarities with A. W. were his soft ways, his gentlemanly bearing, his small slender stature and fine birdlike features, his love for Old Master paintings. Principally at his urging, A. W. undertook *Taxation: The People's Business,* largely drafted by Finley and published in 1924 as an exposition of A. W.'s tax policy. Thereafter he became Mellon's principal man Friday and confidant. Finley also echoed Mellon's modesty. He told Professor Lawrence L. Murray, whose doctoral dissertation, *Andrew W. Mellon, Secretary of the Treasury, 1921–1932: A Study in Policy,* is the most thorough study of the subject, that his role at Treasury had been that of a mere functionary. Murray's researches in the National Archives convinced him to the contrary. He wrote that

> of the records retained, every item of import that crossed Mellon's desk after 1923 was either written or initialed by [Finley] . . . No one saw the Secretary without first going through him and it was Finley who passed on all directives to underlings. More importantly, it was Finley who followed up on decisions to see that they were carried out.

Finley served A. W. until Mellon's death, when he became the first director of the National Gallery of Art, given by A. W. as the storehouse of the fine collection that he, with Finley's help and guidance, had brought together.

At this time Ailsa was the Secretary's principal "child." She had grown to be a willowy girl, taller than her father and conventionally beautiful. A graceful form, soft blue eyes, and light brown hair gave her a delicate appearance belied by her excellence as a horseperson. Her "finishing" at Miss Porter's School prepared her to be a polished hostess for her father. According to a yellowed Baltimore *Sun* clipping, her debut soon after graduation "furnished history for such events in Pittsburgh, and set a standard not often reached."

In Washington, Ailsa's companions were largely wives of Supreme Court justices and cabinet members, elderly women and too rarely people of her own age. Washington rumor had it that she was often bored. Her own very great reserve—possibly exceeding even that of her father—combined with the demands of her duties as her father's hostess to insure that her friends would be very few in number. Like her father, she was generally uncommunicative. When she did speak, her first words revealed the English accent acquired from her mother.

Ailsa's beauty, refinement, and position on the social ladder made it inevitable that she would be one of the most sought after girls in Washington. She selected her engagements with the help of social secretary Anne

Randolph, and on her evenings out with gentlemen she was usually chaperoned by a Miss Alice Sylvester, identified in the press as being from "an old and well-known Pittsburgh family." Her suitors were varied and often titled, including among them Prince Otto Bismarck, grandson of Germany's "Iron Chancellor," but her preference was for the exciting and talented son of Maryland's Senator William C. Bruce.

A strong Churchillian aura surrounds the story of the life and career of diplomat David K. E. Bruce. His was not an "American" life but one more typical of many brilliant English aristocrats from gone-by periods. He was born to wealth and power as the son of Senator Bruce. He attended Princeton and the University of Maryland Law School and ranked first when he took the Maryland Bar examinations in November of 1921. Though independently wealthy, he became affiliated with a Baltimore law firm. A couple of years later he entered politics himself as a Democratic candidate for the Maryland legislature. He campaigned as what he described as an "unqualified wet." He favored repeal of the federal prohibition act and leaving the matter of prohibition enforcement entirely to the states, and he himself would vote against any proposed Maryland prohibition statute. He favored "clean" horseracing (some would say Maryland never got it) and he opposed Sunday blue laws. "We have entirely too many moral and uplift laws already," he said. He did not envision a political career for himself but said that he would like to be elected to a term in the Maryland legislature: "It'll be a sort of mid-winter frolic for me, I guess." As the son of the most powerful Democratic leader in an overwhelmingly Democratic state, it is not surprising that the voters indulged his fancy.

After a term in the legislature Bruce dabbled at the law and began preparing himself for a career in the State Department at its foreign service school. In January 1925, without fanfare or previous announcement he went down to the Baltimore city hall and took out a license to wed Miss Regina Mellon of Philadelphia. When the *Sun* reporters called for the story, they reached an irate senator. No, his son was not married and was not going to be married, and no, the senator was not going to say anything further about the matter! The younger Mr. Bruce could not be reached for comment. As best the *Sun* could determine, the fiance "had prepared to go hunting in Abyssinia today but has changed plans and is now at his parents' home in Washington." They could not get through to him there, and Miss Regina Mellon was equally elusive; it seems that there was no such lady in Philadelphia and no one seemed to know of any such person anywhere along the eastern seaboard. She never did appear. Instead, in

May of 1926 David Bruce married Ailsa Mellon.

The wedding was held in a small chapel at Washington's Episcopal Cathedral, with room for only a couple of hundred. Ailsa was attended by R. B.'s daughter, Sarah; W. L.'s daughter Margaret; and three other girls. More than a few eyebrows were raised during the ceremony when somehow the word "obey" got left out of it. The United Press wire reported that the bride herself had decided against that particular promise.

The reception at the Pan-American Union was somewhat less private. Press reports on the attendance varied from 2000 to 3000, including the President and his wife, most of the high-ranking leaders of government and of Washington society, and innumerable members of the Mellon and Bruce families.

A. W. imported ten New York chefs who spent three days preparing a little luncheon for the guests. Depending on which newspaper one read, the Secretary had spent $100,000 or $1 million on the show. The newspapers confidently ranked it as the best Washington wedding since Alice Roosevelt had married Nicholas Longworth twenty years earlier. For days the Washington *Post* and the Baltimore *Sun* filled their society pages with vignettes of the wedding and reports on what the ladies had worn.

The string of pearls that A. W. gave Ailsa for her wedding was reported to be worth $100,000. Soon after, he bought her another present, a little place at Syosset, Long Island, an Italian stucco mansion nicely snuggled amidst its 121 acres.

After the wedding the Bruces set out on their new life together. He was to be vice consul in Rome, not a bad assignment for a foreign service officer just beginning his career.

Paul was away at schools during most of his father's Washington period: Choate, a preparatory school in Wallingford, Connecticut, and then Yale, where he developed his considerable literary talent. When W. L. would visit the Secretary in Washington, A. W. "would produce from an inside pocket some papers. These documents concerned matters that made him feel extremely proud. Usually they were cuttings from the Yale *News*—sometimes a poem, sometimes an editorial. Paul Mellon had written them." A. W. contrived to spend vacations with Paul whenever possible; several times they went to Bermuda together in the spring, sometimes joined by some of Paul's classmates. He enjoyed being around the young people and strived mightily to cement a relationship with a son who described himself as "more McMullen than Mellon."

Warren G. Harding has been regarded until recent times as America's worst President. He was a poor judge of character (if, indeed, he was interested in character), which together with his easy-going ways invited the corruption that permeated his administration. Many of the traits that contributed to his weakness as a President made a very likable person. Harding was probably the only humble man ever to be elected President. An apt description of him as "a man of limited talents from a small town," was authored by himself. "I knew this job would be too much for me," the President once lamented to Nicholas Murray Butler, the Republican bigwig who served as president of Columbia University. Harding was also probably the nicest man ever to sit in the White House. It was the administration of that great liberal Woodrow Wilson that jailed the kindly Socialist Eugene V. Debs; it was the conservative President Warren G. Harding who gave Debs a Christmas Day pardon over the objections of the President's wife, those of his closest confidant, Attorney General Daugherty, and probably those of the American public at large. Harding asked that Debs stop at the White House on his way north from the federal prison in Atlanta, Georgia. Only the President's greeting survives their historic meeting: "Well, I have heard so much about you, Mr. Debs, that now I am very glad to meet you personally." Harding has probably suffered worse than he deserves. The 1920s tolerance for corruption and its repressive spirit, predated his inauguration. As Socialist Louis Waldman points out in *The Good Fight,* "Harding did not create the era over which he presided . . . he was simply its product."

The Harding administration and the Coolidge administration that followed and perpetuated its policies could best be characterized as the era of big business. Harding himself said, "We want less government in business and more business in government," a precursor of Coolidge's many parallel comments. Both men got more business in government with A. W. Mellon. In all ways but one, A. W. was out of step with the flashy fast 1920s, but the one consonant beat was all important. He symbolized big business, and he could speak for the "desires" of big business, whether or not those desires represented "needs" of big business. Better than any other American, better than Rockefeller, Ford, or the ghost of Morgan, A. W. could say what was best for big business; and what was best for big business was best for America. Harding once complained,

> I can't make a damn thing out of this tax problem. . . . I listen to one side and they seem right, and then—God!—I talk to the other side and they seem just

as right, and here I am where I started. I know somewhere there is a book that will give me the truth, but hell! I couldn't read the book.

President Harding did not need the book. He could turn to A. W. Mellon, and he usually did.

Other men had more direct influence on Harding, but on the most significant administration policies Mellon was the key man. Economy in government and tax reduction were probably the most important policy goals of the administration, and in those areas A. W.'s influence was felt. The drive for economy in government was formalized by the establishment of the Bureau of the Budget, ostensibly a branch of the Treasury Department but really an independent agency under the direction of Charles Dawes. In the course of its history the bureau has certainly had a positive effect on the conduct of American government. Factors beyond the control of either the Bureau of the Budget or the Secretary of the Treasury were largely responsible for its earliest successes after its institution. Frank Kent pointed out in the *New Republic* that "The expenses of government were automatically and swiftly receding from the war peak, the crumbling and dismantling of the war machine was gradually taking place and the systematic reduction of the national debt through sinking funds had begun. No sane person will attribute any of those things to Mr. Mellon." Still, they were credited to Mellon. The matter of tax reduction can more appropriately be attributed to him.

Natural slowdown in the demand for national spending, coupled with increased revenue to the Treasury generated by the 1920s boom economy, made reduction of taxes easy. The question was which segment of society would have its burdens lightened? A. W. had the answer. Before his election as President, Senator Harding had declared for heavier income tax rates on large incomes. Mellon converted him, and before the end of his term Harding was an understanding if soft-spoken advocate for reduction of "confiscatory" taxes on the superrich.

At cabinet meetings Mellon said little, confining his comments to matters of economics, in which field his personal experiences seemingly extended to every area of the world of finance. Should the United States scrap a war plant that had cost $12 million, or should it spend as much again to rehabilitate it? Finally it came Mellon's turn to discuss the question. Edward Lowry reported in a 1921 sketch that

> Mr. Mellon was hesitant. Then he spoke up in his low, quiet, dry voice. The matter was not exactly in his department; he had not given the problem any study; he was not familiar with all the conditions and the full situation; it was

a question of some importance; he did not wish to be understood as giving his final opinion unless he had opportunity to go into the whole matter more fully, but he thought he could indicate possibly what his final judgment might be, if allowed to tell what he had done in a somewhat similar and personal case. He owned a war plant that stood him about fifteen or sixteen millions, and just the other day the question had come up whether to spend that much more money on it or to wipe it off. "I told 'em to scrap it," concluded Mr. Mellon.

The government scrapped its plant. The *Saturday Evening Post* reported in 1923 what happened when the cabinet turned to a delicate matter of international relations involving the Chinese Eastern Railway:

> The President leaned over to Attorney General Daugherty and whispered, "Now we've got him. Surely he wasn't in this.
>
> "I don't suppose, Mellon," said President Harding, winking at Daugherty, and assuming a most casual manner, "that you were interested in the Chinese Eastern Railway, were you?"
>
> "Oh, yes," Mr. Mellon replied placidly; "we had a million or a million and a half of the bonds." And he told the cabinet all about the road; all about it —not part—all.
>
> "It's no use," said the President, "no use. He's the ubiquitous financier of the universe."

When it came to matters of finance or economics, A. W. was deferred to not so much because of the persuasiveness of his arguments or his wealth as because his economic views paralleled those of his fellow members of the cabinet. Scholar Robert K. Murray has said that he was "their spokesman, not their persuader."

Personally, Mellon was not close to Harding or to any member of the President's inner circle. Direct contact between Mellon and the President, official or otherwise, was minimal and always formal. At cabinet meetings Harding addressed his cronies by their first names; but Mellon, Hoover, and Secretary of State Charles Evans Hughes were customarily addressed as "Mr. Secretary," reflecting the varying degrees of formality in the relations between the President and the members of his team. The personal correspondence between Mellon and Harding is similarly stiff, crisp, and businesslike.

Privately, Harding's attitude toward his Secretary of the Treasury was informal. When he spoke of Mellon in his inner office, it was of "ol' Andy Mellon," or "ol' man Mellon." When someone mentioned the poor condition of the sidewalk in front of the Treasury Building to the President, Harding said to Secret Service man Edmund W. Starling, "the Treasury

Department ought to fix it. If they don't, some day my Secretary, ol' Andy Mellon, will come walking along here counting his coupons and stub his toe."

Harding's dependence on Mellon is sometimes overstated. The President went along with those of Mellon's policy suggestions that were within the Secretary's supposed sphere of expertise, but he failed to give the Secretary's proposals the active support of the White House. On matters only tangentially related to the Treasury, he was independent. When Secretary of Agriculture Henry C. Wallace proposed a national conference on agriculture both Mellon and Hoover opposed the idea for fear that the conference would heighten an impression that Harding was more interested in agriculture than in industry, but Harding gave Wallace his approval. Though Harding ultimately permitted Mellon to run the Treasury without the interference of patronage seekers, he insisted on maintaining his own discretionary rights as to those appointments that were the President's to make.

Mellon was in Europe at the time of Harding's premature death in 1923. Gilbert wired Mellon not to hurry back, and Mellon didn't but stayed another couple of weeks vacationing, which perhaps reflects Mellon's personal opinion of his departed chief. W. L. wrote,

> I am sure that A. W. never would have hired Harding to run any company in which he was interested. He once told me that when any matter in his department required the attention of Harding as President, he would go to the White House with the pertinent facts in concisely stated, typewritten sentences, almost invariably on a single sheet of paper. Whatever the matter was, A. W. would discuss it with the President and then, for Mr. Harding's convenience, hand him the memorandum sheet. Habitually, Harding would take the paper almost as if it were an unpleasant bill and tuck it into the mound of other papers on his disordered desk. Then by way of dismissing the matter he would say, "I'll look into this."
>
> Such procedure was shocking to A. W. who was puritanical about the day's work.

A. W.'s public statement on the President's demise was polite, formalistic, and emotionless. Years later he urged the members of the Harding Memorial Committee to abandon the idea of holding a formal dedication of the monument to their hero.

The Harding administration will always be remembered for its corruptions and the revelation of them. They began to come to light early in 1923, when Harding's crony Charles R. Forbes, director of the Veterans Bureau, resigned and moved to Europe. Soon after it was discovered that Forbes, through thefts and waste, had robbed the bureau of some $200 million. Before the resulting investigations were over, it was clear that there were also serious irregularities in Daugherty's Justice Department, and in the Departments of the Interior and the Navy. Daugherty's intimate, bootlegger-procurer Jess Smith, and Forbes's attorney committed suicide. The last of the corruptions to come to be extensively probed was the celebrated Teapot Dome scandal.

The United States Navy owned valuable oil lands at Elk Hills, California, and Teapot Dome, Wyoming. Secretary of the Interior Albert B. Fall induced his weak buddy Navy Secretary Edwin Denby to transfer jurisdiction over these assets to the Interior Department; Harding himself signed the order effectuating the transfer. Soon after, in April 1922, the Interior Department, without competitive bidding, leased the government lands to Edward L. Doheny and Harry F. Sinclair. Black bags full of money and bonds changed hands.

From the start Senator Robert M. La Follette, the progressive Republican from Wisconsin, didn't like the smell of things and called for a Senate investigation of the oil leases but the inquiry did not get under way until October of 1923. Ultimately it disclosed the corruption involved in granting the leases and led to their being set aside, imprisonment for Fall, humiliation for Denby, and the revelation of the peripheral involvement of many, among them A. W. Mellon.

At about the time that the Senate was getting started on its inquiry, Will Hays completed tabulating the Republican Party's 1920 campaign debt. It came to over a million dollars. Who should come to help with a generous contribution at just the right time but Sinclair! It was beginning to look as if Sinclair was going to need continued help from important party friends. He gave Hays some $185,000 in U.S. bonds toward the campaign debt, but his generosity could not be acknowledged. So Hays set out to visit the party's most wealthy backers—men from whom a substantial contribution would not arouse suspicion, men like A. W. Mellon. Hays had a messenger deliver a fat packet of $50,000 worth of Sinclair's bonds to Mellon, and then he stopped in on the Secretary to make his request: Would Mellon take Sinclair's bonds and "lend" the Republican National Committee a like sum toward its debt? A. W. was not about to taint himself with that kind of involvement. He later testified that the bonds "had come for a purpose which did not suit me so far as I was concerned." It took him ten days to reach that conclusion, but after ten days he had Gilbert return the bonds to Hays in New York. He assured Hays that he would otherwise make a substantial contribution and a few days later sent off his own $50,000 toward the party's debt.

The Senate's investigations continued long after Hays disposed of Sinclair's bonds. Sinclair's bribing of Fall shortly came to light. A. W. remained quiet about what he knew, although his information might have been helpful not only to the Senate's investigators (with whom A. W. might have been able to rationalize an unwillingness to cooperate) but also to federal attorneys attempting to set aside the leases, and to Internal Revenue Service agents—A. W.'s own men—who were attempting to collect unpaid income taxes owed by Sinclair's Continental Trading Company. Hays testified and swore that Sinclair's sole contribution to the party was $75,000. A. W. must have known better—he knew about the bonds. In any case he remained quiet. The Senate's committee asked the Treasury's cooperation in tracing bonds that were known to have once been property of Continental Trading. By all means, the Treasury would assist, and it did. While his operatives laboriously pored over the records of banks and bureaucracies, the Treasury's head remained quiet about what he himself knew as to the course of some of those bonds. Hays returned to the committee for a second unpleasant round of interrogation; this time he told more, but what he did tell defied belief. He did not mention his abortive visit to Mellon. If Hays hadn't mentioned him, why should Mellon have bothered to involve himself?

With time, those who had become involved with Sinclair's bonds were ferreted out and the story of the "laundering" of Sinclair's spectacular secret contribution to the party came to light. Among the witnesses was V. E. Hommel, an employee of the deceased John T. Pratt, a prominent Republican with Standard Oil ties who had taken some of the tainted bonds. Among Pratt's papers was a scrap with a cryptic notation of it. In pencil Pratt had scribbled "$50,000," followed by a list of names. Senator Gerald Nye handed Hommel a magnifying glass and asked the witness's assistance in deciphering the names:

> "Take that first notation on the slip there and see if you cannot translate it for us," Senator Nye requested. "The first one is, 'Weeks,' that is clear enough."
> " 'Weeks; yes, sir," Mr. Hommel answered.
> "What is the next one?"
> "I am trying to read it; see if that is 'Candy.' "
> "Candy?" Senator Nye asked.
> "That is what it looks like," Mr. Hommel said.
> "Might it not be 'Andy'?"
> "Possibly."

"Possibly, you say?"

"That is quite possible, from his writing here."

"And just what might the notations of those names mean there?"

"I have not the slightest idea."

"Might it be to write a letter to the individuals named on there, addressing a letter to each of them of what he had done?"

"I would not presume to say what a notation of that kind would mean."

"You think it quite possible, though, that that second name is Andy?"

"It is quite possible."

"You would not venture to say who Andy was?"

"I have no idea."

The large audience had no difficulty in deciding to whom "Andy" referred; they howled with laughter.

"You said it was quite likely that it was Andy?"

"It is quite likely that that is the name; yes."

"If it were 'Candy,' would it have any added significance to you?" Senator Nye asked.

"None, whatever."

"You have no recollection of a name of that kind?"

"No."

The Nation editorialized that it was not the first time that a man had been betrayed by a single word.

The committee's leading inquisitor, Montana's progressive Democratic senator, Thomas J. Walsh, sent a copy of the Pratt note to Mellon, without elaboration as to his purpose in doing so; Mellon correctly read the senator's communication as a request for an explanation. The time had come when Mellon's continued silence would make his role actively conspiratorial. He sent back a written explanation providing the outline of his contact with Hays about the bonds. Three days later A. W. was before the Senate's investigating committee testifying himself. He testified that he had drawn no inferences of impropriety from Hays's approach to him: "I had not any knowledge of any sinister nature in connection with it." The identity of the secret donor had not aroused any particular suspicion in him at the time. True, the investigations had begun the month before amid widespread publicity, and Sinclair's name had been in the newspapers almost daily in connection with the inquiry; the scandal was a frequent topic of conversation, but Mellon explained, "I do not follow all the investigations that are started. I have plenty of troubles of my own there to keep me busy and I had no knowledge of it personally at the time." He had rejected Hays's proposition only because he had felt under an obligation to make a bona fide contribution himself. His only previous contribution to the 1920 presidential campaign had been $2000, and as he put it to the committee, "I felt that in my position there was something more due." He had planned on giving a substantial amount toward the end of the drive to wipe out the campaign debt, when he might have played a significant role in cleaning up the balance, but instead he had taken Hays's visit as the opportunity to make his contribution. One of the others who had received the Sinclair bonds had testified that he had been "incensed" with the proposal. Senator Walsh asked whether the Secretary's reaction had been similar.

> Mr. Mellon: I do not know that I am of that temperament, and I do not become incensed. If you take things in this world as they are, and according to your own conscience, I do not see that there is much use in getting incensed. At least I do not recall anything of that nature particularly.

When the committee had zeroed in on the bonds, he acknowledged that he "had the impression that anyone would have that it was likely that they may have been bonds connected with the Continental Trading Co.," but at that point he had failed to see any purpose in calling himself to anyone's attention; after all, he had not taken any of the bonds. As for Hays's failure to mention his approach to Mellon in Hays's earlier testimony, that was a matter "between the committee and Mr. Hays." Toward the end of his testimony, New York senator Robert Wagner commented on the fact that no one had volunteered any information about Sinclair's relations with the Republican National Committee. "Was it my responsibility?" asked the Secretary. "I was not connected with the national committee."

The New York *Times,* as consistently unsympathetic to the Senate's Teapot Dome investigation as it was consistently favorable in its coverage of Mellon's doings, called the Secretary's testimony "a complete explanation" in its editorial, and perhaps it was, but it was an unsatisfactory explanation for the progressive elements that instigated and pursued the investigation of the corruption that permeated the Harding administration. It is indeed difficult to believe that A. W. had not immediately detected the sinister reasons behind the desire to launder Sinclair's contribution. Even if he had been unaware of Sinclair's involvement in the breaking scandal —which is difficult to believe—surely he must have thought it odd that such a one as Sinclair should feel a compunction to contribute a sum which Hays had represented to Mellon to have been $300,000, when Mellon himself regarded $50,000 as a suitable contribution from a cabinet officer who was one of the country's richest men. The progressives found him guilty of a

"An old picture may be a very poor likeness of the original," complained Judge Thomas Mellon, family founder, above, "and at best can show nothing of his true character or qualities; but still, natural affection clings to it." Below is the Judge's wife of sixty-five years, Sarah Jane Negley.

Two of the Judge's four branches. Above: The Judge, left, his son J. R., right, J. R.'s son W. L., standing, and W. L.'s son Matthew, held by the Judge. Below: The Judge, his grandson Thomas Alexander Mellon Jr. holding baby T. A. III, and the baby's maternal grandfather, the Reverend Mr. Wightman.

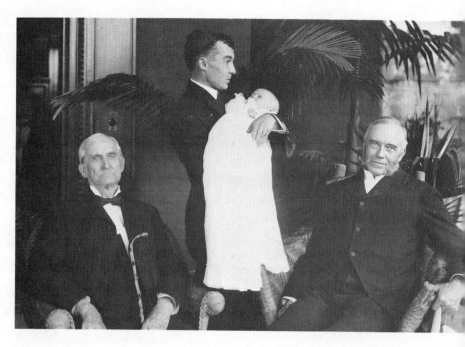

When himself an old man, the Judge's grandson W. L. could still picture "my grandfather wearing a black, long-skirted frock coat of the same style he had worn when he was on the bench, and which he wore always thereafter. His shirt front invariably was glossy and stiff from starch and his collar was equally stiff, its points, however, not meeting by an inch, so that you could see his Adam's apple rise and fall beneath his strong chin."

The Judge was a highly rational man, but he could not help wondering, could the spiritualists, perhaps, bring back his beloved son Selwyn?

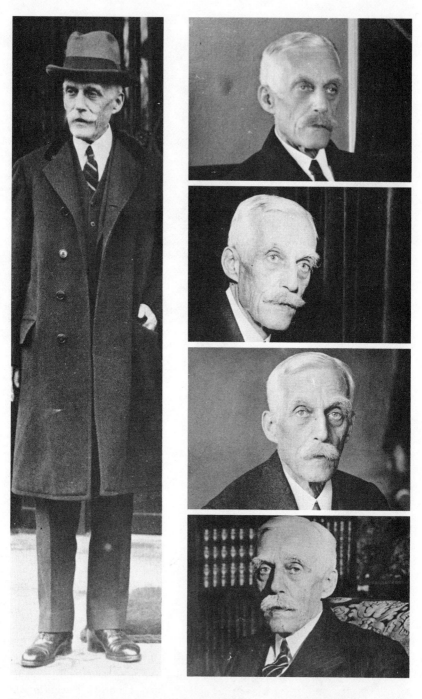

The most famous of the Judge's sons, A. W. could look elegant—dignity and taste personified (left)—but more often he looked haggard or ill. The pictures on the right are, unfortunately, more representative.

In the 1920s A. W. was known as "the greatest Secretary of the Treasury since Alexander Hamilton." At right, he lays a wreath at Hamilton's statue. To the left of A. W. is Secretary of Commerce Herbert Hoover.

Below, A. W. greets the "gold-watch" employees of the United States Treasury Department's Bureau of Engraving.

A. W.'s wife, Nora. At upper right is a photograph of her with their children, Ailsa and Paul (infant), which her lawyers circulated at the time of their divorce in 1911 in an effort to arouse public sympathy for her. Until A. W.'s death in 1937, Paul attempted to reconcile his parents. Photo below shows Paul, A. W., and Nora at Dinard, France, 1926, fourteen years after the divorce.

Nora's son, Paul Mellon.

Nora's lover, Alfred George Curphey.

Men important in the founding of the Mellon empire. Upper left: The colorful Colonel James M. Guffey, strong man of Gulf Oil, until, as he later put it, the Mellons "throwed me out."

Upper right: Coke king Henry Clay Frick, after the Judge, the principal mentor of A. W. Mellon.

At mid-left: Charles Martin Hall, inventor of aluminum, and Arthur Vining Davis, the administrative genius who built Alcoa.

Lower left: Edward G. Acheson, inventor of Carborundum, and Heinrich Koppers, inventor of the Koppers coke oven.

Above: Bigwigs of Alcoa, 1920s. Seated at the left end in the front row is George Clapp, who, together with his partner, Captain Alfred E. Hunt, was important in the original organization of Alcoa. Next to Clapp, wearing cap, is A. W. Behind A. W., without vest, is A. W.'s brother and partner, R. B. Mellon. To the right of R. B. is Arthur Vining Davis.

At right: A.W. strolls with H. C. McEldowney, operative head of the Mellon banking enterprises. 1930.

Above left: James Ross Mellon, "J. R.," age 19 (1865). Above right: J. R. in full flower. The photo shows a dynamic, forceful and productive man—traits which no one who knew J. R. would ascribe to him. His grandson Matthew T. Mellon, recalls J. R. as a timid man. His nephew Ned Mellon says that "J. R. never did a damn thing in his life except have a helluvah good time."

Matthew recalls "Grandma," J. R.'s wife, Rachel Hughey Larimer Mellon (left), as "short and stout and rather pompous." She had a veritable *passion* for genealogy.

Judge Mellon urged his progeny to leave soldiering to others, but upon the outbreak of World War I, his grandson, J. R.'s boy Thomas Mellon II, threw caution to the winds and rushed to join the "Y"—the YMCA—in its seemingly hopeless fight to maintain what he called "the props and restraints of an upright life" among military personnel. At right he is shown in battle garb.

J. R.'s daughter, Sarah Lucille (left), about seventeen, modeling her mother's wedding gown in a 1902 photograph.

"R. B.," the outgoing, hail-fellow-well-met partner of the withdrawn and retiring A. W., had all of those positive social traits that A. W. lacked. He also had a nasty streak in him that was foreign to his brother.

In the 1918 picture at left R. B. is shown with his daughter, Sarah, and his son, R. K., together with three children of his friend John M. Phillips.

208

R. B.'s wife, Jennie, combined some striving-class pretensions with a lot of lower-class decency. Jennie was real people. Upper left: Jennie and their son, R. K., dressed for a 1923 costume ball. Upper right: Jennie and daughter, Sarah, leaving church. Lower left: Jennie and R. B. Lower right: at the opening of the East Liberty Presbyterian Church, descending staircase, architect Ralph Adams Cram, R. K., Jennie, Sarah, and Sarah's husband, Alan Scaife.

W. L., oldest and most successful of J. R.'s children, became the guiding light of Gulf Oil and the ostensible czar of Pennsylvania politics in the 1920s. He looked very much the caricature of the company president, and he was. Above left, W. L. formal; above right, W. L. informal.

W. L. was the only Mellon of his day to appreciate yachting. His *Vagabondia* was one of the legendary yachts in the history of American wealth.

Descendants of the Judge's first-born son, Thomas Alexander Mellon. Above, the family of T. A. Jr. leaves A. W.'s funeral, 1937. From left, Mrs. T. A. Jr., T. A. Jr., their daughter "Patsy" (Helen, Mrs. Adolph Schmidt), daughter "E" (Elizabeth, Mrs. John Sellers), son, "Ned" (Edward P. Mellon II), in double-breasted suit, T. A. Jr.'s sister-in-law, and Sellers.

At left: T. A. Jr.'s younger brother, architect Edward P. Mellon, and wife, out for a stroll at Southampton, Long Island, early 1930s.

Villains in the Mellon story. Upper left: Pennsylvania Republican Governor Gifford Pinchot, who spent most of the 1920s bad mouthing W. L. and A. W. Upper right: Michigan's Republican Senator James Couzens, the "millionaire radical" who engaged A. W. in "the battle of the millionaires." Lower left: Texas Democratic Congressman Wright Patman, the populist who "got" A. W. Lower right: Robert H. Jackson, later a member of the United States Supreme Court, who led the New Deal's vendetta against A. W.

Mellon ladies in the 1930s. Above: Mrs. T. A. Mellon Jr. and daughter "Patsy" (Helen, to become Mrs. Adolph Schmidt) in 1934. Below: "Peggy" Hitchcock, one of W. L.'s daughters, with her second husband, the celebrated polo player Thomas Hitchcock Jr., and her son by her first marriage, Alex Laughlin.

Upper left: A. W.'s children, Paul and Ailsa, early 1920s. Upper right: Ailsa in riding gear, around 1922. Below: Paul and A. W. at Paul's Cambridge graduation, 1931.

Possibly the most important wedding in Washington social history: David K. E. Bruce
and Ailsa Mellon, 1926. Lower right photo shows the couple's parents, Senator and Mrs.
William C. Bruce and Secretary of the Treasury A. W. Mellon.

Second Lieutenant Paul Mellon at Fort Riley, Kansas, around 1942.

Horses have meant a lot in Paul Mellon's life; at sixty-nine he is still winning long-distance endurance contests.

Jumping in the '50s.

Ned Mellon still enjoys the outdoor life. Dean of the "poor" branch of the Judge's descendants, Ned is a "self-made" millionaire, but his face shows that it hasn't been easy.

Matthew T. Mellon, elder of W. L.'s two sons, as a young man in the 1930s, and on the beach in Jamaica with his second wife, Jane, in the late 1950s. Below: Matthew in 1976.

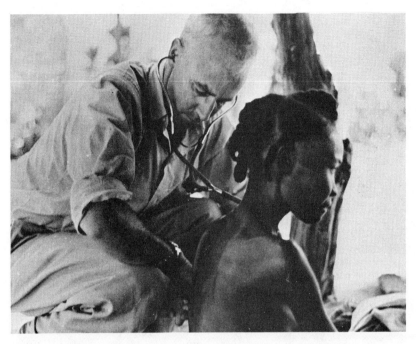

Larry, Dr. Mellon of Haiti, an Albert Schweitzer protégé, prefers it when his wife, Gwen, is in front.

"The General," Richard King Mellon, last cohesive force in the family, as a young man and at his peak.

The General's family. Above: Prossie, Cassie, Dickie, and Connie, circa 1946. Below left: The General's wife, Constance, with daughters Constance (formerly Mrs. J. Carter Brown) and Cassandra (Mrs. George M. Henderson) in the late 1960s. Below right: Sons Richard Prosser Mellon (standing) and Seward Prosser Mellon.

Today Seward Prosser Mellon, "Pross," is the best-known Mellon because of the publicity he received as the "kidnapper" in his adventure-story custody battle with his former wife, Karen. At left, Pross and Karen in happier times. Below, Pross and second wife, Sandra Springer Stout, at the Rolling Rock races, 1976.

Dickie Scaife, who gave $1 million to re-elect President Richard Nixon in 1972, was having a good time at the 1976 Rolling Rock races until he sensed that someone was watching him. Below: Dickie's wife, Frances, with two of his kin, first cousin once removed Paul Mellon (seated) and second-cousin once removed James Mellon Walton, head of the Carnegie Institute.

Matthew's sons: Karl (bearded) and Jay (tuxedoed) represent very different traditions.

Other contemporary young men. Above: from the T. A. line, Charles N. Abernethy III, engineer (left), and Thomas Alexander Mellon IV, photographer.

At left: W. L.'s grandson Billy Hitchcock, at the age of 18 in 1957. Billy was to transform the manufacture of L S D from a cottage industry into big business.

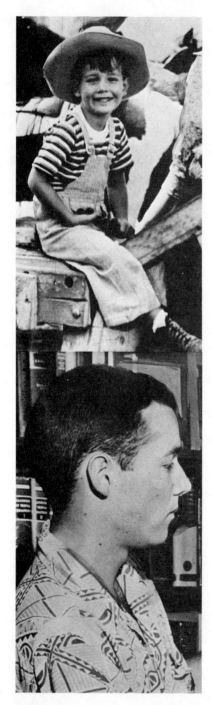

Two of the most promising of the Judge's descendants took their own lives. At left, William Larimer Mellon III, Princeton; at right, John Sellers, Yale.

Almost certainly the richest living Mellon woman, "Cordie" Scaife is shown above in baby photo and at the Rolling Rock races in the mid-sixties.

At left: Helen Claire, possibly the only one of the Judge's "daughters" to feel the cause of the women's movement.

Christopher Karl Mellon, 1957- . The name "Mellon," the Judge tells us, "originated among the Greeks, where, in the Theban dialect, it meant 'future hope.'...Therefore, in the language where it originated, every young Mellon may be truthfully regarded as a 'young hopeful.'"

major crime: silence. *The Nation* captioned its editorial "Silent in the Presence of Sin." Senator Thaddeus Caraway, an Arkansas Democrat, described Hays's role as that of a "fence" trying to market stolen goods, with Mellon's role scarcely better: "Although he declined to aid in the marketing of the goods, after he had knowledge of what they were he refused to disclose this information, but handed them back so that the fence could find somebody who would act for him."

The progressives demanded Mellon's resignation because of his role, but scarcely anybody paid any attention. It is indicative of the temper of the times that most of the indignation roused by the Senate's Teapot Dome investigation was directed at the investigators rather than at the grafters. It is little wonder that A. W.'s relatively minor role in the story should have had no significant impact on his public standing in such a climate.

Whether or not A. W.'s silence was proper, he could rationalize it by separating his various roles to an extraordinary degree and by putting in and taking out ear plugs as he switched his hats. A. W. Mellon was conventionally honest, but he was an unimaginative man, and especially so when considering ethical questions. A tolerant man, he found it easy to tolerate that misconduct for which he bore no direct responsibility.

Despite several perceptive biographies, Calvin Coolidge remains one of the most enigmatic of American Presidents. Born in 1872 to a small Vermont merchant, he went to Amherst College, studied law, and then worked his way up the political ladder from the lowest rung in Northampton, Massachusetts, to the state's governor's mansion. There he sat when the Boston policemen affiliated with the American Federation of Labor and went out on a strike in 1919. His disordered responses to the crisis are now generally accepted to have had a deleterious effect on the situation, but his widely publicized telegram to Samuel Gompers, president of the A.F. of L., insisting that "There is no right to strike against the public safety by anybody, anywhere, any time" brought him national acclaim and a place as Harding's running mate in 1920.

Now he was President. When Parker Gilbert wired the news to Mellon abroad, he assured him that the new President was "well informed and absolutely sound" on all of the policy positions that the Treasury had taken or been formulating, and that Coolidge was most favorably impressed with A. W.'s administration of the department. From the start Coolidge made the same kind of impression on A. W. On his return, Mellon made the perfunctory offer of resignation that high administration officials make to a new chief executive; it was refused. According to A. W.'s confidant

Senator George Wharton Pepper, Coolidge greatly impressed the Secretary on that occasion with his understanding of the economic situation and basic economic principles. If true, that came only when their discussion was well under way. Before they reached that point, A. W. had already noticed the top of the desk that had only recently been Harding's. The messy piles of papers in which Harding had buried the most important of business were gone. Instead of the decent bumbler, the man behind the neat desk radiated all the root principles that had guided the life of Judge Thomas Mellon himself. He seemed to give Mellon the undivided attention that A. W. himself invariably gave to others. The relationship between the new President and the old Secretary of the Treasury would be a good one.

The surface differences between Mellon's elegance and wealth and Coolidge's provincialism and poverty are more apparent but less significant than the similarities between the two. As a lawyer, the President had done Mellon stuff; he had devoted himself principally to matters of land titles and mortgages, settling estates and problems of creditors and debtors. He had been counsel to a bank. The work habits of the two were similar. Both men were driven by their work ethic; both were creatures of their routines; both were good delegators of authority; both were essentially practical men, slow and narrow in their thought processes. The two were men of real if limited sagacity. The President and the Secretary were both men of "solid character," with all of the virtues and limitations that such a phrase conveys.

Coolidge's legendary taciturnity gave rise to the moniker by which he is most commonly remembered, but it would have been equally appropriate to have called Mellon "Silent A. W." Cleveland Amory writes that the two must have conversed "almost entirely in pauses." Coolidge's crusty silence and Mellon's Tibetan silence suggested a profundity that neither had. Louis Waldman was not far from the mark when he wrote that " 'Silent Cal' was silent because he had nothing to say." The silence was probably also a function of the great reserve that Coolidge and Mellon shared, which was in turn a function of their basic shyness. One last explanation for the silence —and possibly the most nearly complete explanation of them all—was the one that Coolidge himself put forth: "I have never been hurt by anything I didn't say." A. W. was similarly sensible.

For history, the most important similarity between Mellon and Coolidge was their view as to the appropriate relationships between business, government, and society. Herbert Hoover has written that Coolidge was "a real conservative, probably the equal of Benjamin Harrison. . . . He was a fundamentalist in religion, in the economic and social order, and in fishing." In his approach to the most important of those fields of study, A. W. was similarly Harrisonian.

Coolidge's attitude was capsulated in his famous statement "The business of America is business." As he saw things, it was the function of government to aid and promote business in any way possible, and surely not to interfere with it. A prosperous business climate would make all the other problems disappear. His attitude became operative in many ways; an example would be his influence on the history of the Federal Trade Commission. In the course of its life the F.T.C. had been one of the most useful vehicles for anti-trust enforcement. Under Harding's administration it had initiated numerous investigations, including one against Alcoa. The Alcoa hearings were proceeding in due course when Coolidge succeeded to the presidency. Coolidge's Attorney General, Harlan F. Stone, was taking a conscientious attitude toward the Alcoa case, completely uninfluenced by the presence of the company's major stockholder at his elbow at cabinet meetings. Coolidge was openly critical of the F.T.C.'s attitude and actions, and he restaffed it with men sympathetic to the "needs" of business. Its investigations became perfunctory, and as often as not it was the friend of "consolidation" in business. Attorney General Stone was promoted to the Supreme Court (the left insisted that he was "kicked upstairs" to protect Mellon's companies), and his successor took a more friendly attitude toward anti-trust matters, including the Alcoa case. Coolidge supported high tariffs favorable to big business. All of his political attitudes were consonant with A. W. Mellon's. Even more important, Coolidge, unlike Harding, backed his views and his Secretary of the Treasury openly and forcefully with Congress. A. W. never campaigned for Harding or the Harding administration, but in 1924 he publicly endorsed President Coolidge for re-election. His speech is more notable today for its "endorsement" of Benito Mussolini, a well-regarded statesman to many Americans of the 1920s: "A strong hand has since come in and re-established the Italian government on sound principles and government by party, not by bargain."

Coolidge's policies were so thoroughly compatible with Mellon's policies and with the best interests of the Mellon interests that the impression persists that he was a mere tool of his Secretary of the Treasury. In fact, Coolidge kept his own counsel—from his family and from A. W. Mellon. With the departure of Charles Evans Hughes from the cabinet in 1925, Mellon was clearly the "first minister," but not even the first minister had that much direct influence on the President. Coolidge's support for the Mellon policies must be attributed to the fact that they were also Coolidge policies.

Mellon first took office in the Harding administration in the midst of a minor economic crisis. After the war, pent-up consumer demands kept American industry working at near-wartime levels, but inevitably came a slacking off, and with it the economic recession of 1920–22. Countless small businesses folded, including the haberdashery across the street from the Muehlebach Hotel in Kansas City. As he locked its doors for the last time, its proprietor, Harry (later to be known as Harry S) Truman, cursed "Old Mellon" for having "engineered" the recession. The national economic setback was short-lived and was overcome through no efforts of the U.S. Treasury Department. Thereafter the national economy took off on the "boom" which enabled the attainment of Mellon's policy objectives. The highlights of his policies were economy in government, reduction of the national debt generated by the war, and reduction of income tax rates, especially those applicable to the highest tax brackets. Most of Mellon's positions on public questions of the 1920s were determined with an eye on those three ultimate goals.

It was easy to institute relative economy in government in the 1920s, as it had never been systematically pursued prior to the Mellon period. With the end of wartime and immediate postwar demands, the federal government's financial needs automatically lightened, and the economies instituted by the Bureau of the Budget helped to further the cause of economy. Mellon opposed any substantial new expenditure, most notably an unsuccessful proposal by Senator George Norris to help farmers by buying up surplus farm produce and shipping it abroad to starving foreigners. He also opposed a proposition to give a bonus to veterans of the war. The "bonus bill" was the more serious threat and the more hotly debated matter. Mellon opposed it as "class legislation," a subsidy to a special-interest group at the expense of the rest of the nation and one that threatened his hopes for reduction of the national debt and reduction of income tax rates. The bonus proposition must have struck A. W. as the live-world realization of Judge Mellon's worst nightmare—the rabble attempting to rob men of property under the guise of democracy. Veterans' groups, coordinated by the American Legion, saw things somewhat differently and pointed out that Mellon's public argument boiled down to an assertion that government should lighten the load of the high-bracket taxpayer rather than the load of the bottom-bracket patriot. Ultimately a bonus bill was passed in 1924, an election year, over Mellon's objections and President Coolidge's veto, reinforcing for the Secretary the wisdom of his great teacher, the Judge: "Those who have nothing to pay with and are indifferent have the numerical majority of votes and elect their own class to office." At least Congress put off payment of the bonus until 1945, when, in all likelihood, it would no longer be A. W.'s problem.

By dint of circumstances and the economy effort, Mellon was able to reduce the country's annual budget from over $6 billion a year during the last year of the Wilson administration to $3.5 billion in 1927.

Reduction in federal spending coincided with the influx of greater tax revenues generated by the bustling economy to enable the Treasury Department to proceed on both a systematic reduction in the national debt and reducing income tax rates. Over the period between 1921 and 1929, Mellon reduced the national debt at a respectable rate, bringing it down from over $24 billion to $16 billion. In addition to lightening the debt upon future generations, this accomplishment annually saved the government increasing millions of dollars in interest expense, thereby assisting the effort to reduce the nation's annual budget. Mellon's efforts at "tax reform," as he would have called it, were equally successful.

The income tax has been with mankind since A.D. 1435 in England. It was first adopted in the United States during the Civil War, was abandoned in 1872, was readopted in 1894, and was thereupon declared "unconstitutional" by the United States Supreme Court. In the first year of President Taft's tenure, a constitutional amendment led the way to its re-enactment, and by 1916 its progressive nature had been introduced, with a rate of tax ranging up to a maximum of 15 per cent. The war led to the imposition of higher taxes, and the maximum was increased to 73 per cent. An excess-profits tax was imposed on the "abnormal" profits of corporations, presumed to be attributable to war conditions and therefore presumably less worthy of retention by their generators. A wealthy conservative might live with a 15 per cent maximum tax on his personal income, but a 73 percent bite out of the upper reaches of it was surely socialistic. There were, of course, ways around it. A wealthy taxpayer might channel his funds into state and local bonds, commonly known as "municipals," the interest from which was (and still is) constitutionally exempt from federal income taxes, or into investment in capital assets, profits from the disposition of which were taxed at the time at 12.5 per cent. Still, the idea of taking more than two-thirds of any man's "ordinary" earnings, no matter how rich, was conceptually offensive to many people, rich and poor. Now, many years later, when the maximum federal income tax rate stands at 70 per cent, 73 per cent no longer seems that much higher; but when A. W. Mellon took office, the increase in the maximum from 15 per cent to 73 per cent had only been in effect a few years. It had been increased so radically only in response to war needs, and it might reasonably have appeared to be a grossly unfair and excessive imposition on anyone. To A. W. Mellon it represented a real social problem crying for reform.

Mellon's opponents charged that he would be one—if not the biggest—
of the beneficiaries of the reforms that he advocated over the next several
years. Their charge was especially true by virtue of the kinds of investments
that A. W. made. Unlike so many rich men then and now, he had not
generally traded in tax-exempt municipals* but preferred to put his money
into more dynamic investments. He did utilize the "capital gains" escape
hatch to some extent, but he does not seem to have ever attempted to
maximize that particular loophole. A greater percentage of his income
actually reached the highest tax bracket than was true of most wealthy men.

In the session of Congress following Harding's inauguration, A. W.
Mellon's first tax-reform package was introduced. He called for repeal of
the excess-profits tax altogether—it had outlived its supposed rationale—
and immediate reduction of the maximum tax to 40 per cent, with further
reductions in the maximum to come over time. At that time he enumerated
most of the arguments that would make up his tax pronouncements
throughout the 1920s.

Mellon's most important argument was that the high surtaxes were unproductive and probably counterproductive. With statistical corroboration,
he insisted that the surtaxes had passed the point where they could be
collected. They forced wealthy people into tax-exempt bonds and similar
legal tax-avoidance devices, so that their money ended up in protected
rather than taxed investments. The net effect was that the wealthy as a
group were paying less in taxes to the federal Treasury than they would be
paying if the tax on ordinary income were smaller. He insisted that his call
for a reduction of the surtax on the rich "is not designed to lighten the tax
burden of the rich. On the contrary it should eventually have the effect of
increasing the aggregate amount of taxes received from large incomes when
they have again been diverted into taxable business."† Not only was the
situation producing less tax revenue for the country than more moderate
rates would produce, the high surtaxes discouraged both men and money
from the kind of enterprise that had made the country great. The high
surtaxes

---

*When R. B. died in 1933, the inventory of his estate included no tax-exempts at all. When
A. W. died four years later, his inventory included $8 million in tax-exempts, probably
acquired subsequent to R. B.'s death in response to the New Deal's increases in the income
tax rates. W. L.'s estate, processed in 1948, also included significant holdings in tax-exempt
municipals.

†This and the next two Mellon quotations come not from his 1921 arguments but from his
statements on later tax bills. The author selects them as representative of the arguments that
Mellon made throughout the 1920s.

tend to destroy individual initiative and enterprise, and seriously impede the development of productive industry. Taxpayers subject to higher rates cannot afford to invest in American railroads or industries or embark upon new enterprises in the face of taxes that will take 50 per cent of any return that may be realized. These taxpayers are withdrawing their capital from productive business and investing it instead in tax-exempt securities and adopting other lawful methods of avoiding the realization of taxable income. The result is to stop business transactions that would normally go through, and to discourage men of wealth from taking the risks which are incidental to the development of new business.

He insisted that investments in tax-exempt municipal securities had a much lesser effect in stimulating the economy as a whole than direct investments in industry, and that their principal effect was undesirable, since they encouraged municipalities to "extravagance and reckless expenditure on the part of local authorities." Echoes of Thomas Mellon!

Senator La Follette characterized Mellon's argument uncharitably but correctly as one that insisted that "wealth will not and cannot be made to bear its full share of taxation." La Follette was outraged and called for Mellon's resignation, though the Secretary's great sin would appear to have been describing the situation as many reasonable men might have seen it. La Follette led the battle against. Aided by veteran and farm groups, he limited Mellon's victory. Congress reduced the maximum surtax, but only to a maximum of 50 per cent; it repealed the excess-profits tax, but simultaneously increased the basic corporation tax from 10 to 12.5 per cent. Mellon would go back for more the next time.

The highlight of Mellon's proposal for a 1924 Revenue Act was its call for halving the maximum surtax from 50 to 25 per cent. His suggested tax package was well received by the public but hit rough sledding in Congress. Progressive Republicans like La Follette and Congressman Fiorello La Guardia joined with populist Democrats, notably Congressman (later Vice President) John Nance Garner, to come up with a very different set of proposals that gave the smallest taxpayer a much bigger reduction than A. W. had proposed, while allowing the big man a proportionately smaller reduction, from 50 to 40 per cent. Even worse for A. W. Mellon, they called for an increase in the maximum inheritance tax, from 25 to 40 per cent on estates of over $10 million, and to add teeth to their death-tax proposal they proposed for the first time the imposition of a federal gift tax, to prevent the rich from escaping the death tax by giving their assets to children, grandchildren, and unborn great-grandchildren prior to their death. The liberals' act also proposed that everyone's income tax return be open for public inspection, a provision that could only lead to the embarrassment of wealthier (or aspiring but not so wealthy) taxpayers, and which the rich appropriately regarded as an invasion of their privacy.

The alternate bill was an almost unmixed horror for Mellon. As a man of sixty-nine, and the most visible of those Americans whose estates might approach $10 million, he might have thought that the estate and gift tax proposals were directed against him personally. He spoke out most strongly against the estate tax proposal: "Estate taxes, carried to an excess, in no way differ from the methods of the revolutionists in Russia." Forty per cent was an excess.

Congress adopted the alternate tax bill with all of its repugnant terms. After a lot of grumbling, President Coolidge signed the bill. At least income taxes had been reduced again, this time to a maximum of 40 per cent of taxable income, so that at last the large earner would be able to keep more than half of his total income. Mellon could take some solace in that, and he could come back again to Congress in brighter times.

The election of 1924 paved the way for the brighter times. Mellon and his policies were the major issue. Bitter attacks on him by Democratic presidential candidate John W. Davis, and by La Follette, the presidential candidate of the new and short-lived Progressive Party, were indeed counterproductive. Coolidge's triumphant re-election was taken—probably properly so—as a national endorsement of Mellon and everything for which he stood. When he next returned to Congress it was with irresistible muscle given to him by the American electorate.

The progressive-populist coalition that had carried the day in 1924 could fight Mellon but it could not fight the nation and especially not without La Follette himself, who died in 1925 before what he might have made his last great fight. The election returns tamed Garner, who gave the Secretary no opposition on what A. W. would have regarded as the important points. With or without La Follette and Garner, by 1926 it was clear that the Mellon Plan was the national plan. Congressmen of both parties vied to cut taxes still further in support of the Mellon principles. Democrats insisted that Mellon was reducing the national debt much too rapidly and that more of the Treasury's surplus should be channeled into tax reductions.

The Revenue Act adopted that year reduced the maximum surtax to 20 per cent (which, together with a basic 5 per cent charge, made for a maximum tax rate of 25 per cent of taxable income), and it increased exemptions sufficiently to remove the lower earners from its effects. The result was to shift tax burdens to the middle class. The hateful estate tax was rolled back from the 40 per cent maximum that the previous Congress had foisted on Mellon, to a tamer 20 per cent, lower even than the tax that had preceded the progressives' intemperance. The gift tax, La Follette's pet tax, was repealed outright, thereby rubberizing such teeth as the estate tax would otherwise have had. The outrageous public-disclosure clause of the 1924 act was repealed forever. A. W. had won an uncompromised victory. He had turned back what he would have regarded as the "threat to the American way of life," if such a phrase had been known at the time. With a practical tax exemption on every household's first $4000 of income, there was no income tax at all for most Americans, and the rich could live with such as their taxes were.

Best of all, almost, was the benefit to the American economy that the success of the Mellon Plan brought about. The Treasury's receipts seemed to bear out the wisdom of the plan; the statistics did not lie. W. L. no doubt spoke for A. W. when he reported them, and they proved that though the rich were paying "less" (on a percentage basis) they were really paying very much more. As W. L. wrote, A. W. had

> assumed that anyone with an assured income of $300,000 probably had a capital fortune of about $6,000,000. In 1922, before his reforms had affected this situation, this class of people who could be assumed to have $6,000,000 fortunes reported, in their tax returns, a total income of only $154,000,000; but five years later, in 1927, when the Mellon tax plan had been in force for a couple of years, this same group was being taxed on an income of $1,153,000,000. It had worked out as A. W. had predicted.
>
> Most of those millionaires had been glad to get their money out of unexciting municipal and state bonds and into fields of investment where their returns were larger, with the effect that the whole economy was made more ruddy. With a surtax of 50 per cent, as was levied in 1922, this group paid $77,000,000 into the government; but, in 1927, when the rate was only 20 per cent, the returns of the group had grown to $230,000,000.

For progressives, who understood the needs of the coal miners, the farmers, and the poor of America, and who disapproved of the social implications of a relatively minor tax on the superrich, the success of the Mellon Plan signified, wrote Pittsburgh poet Haniel Long, "a moment of terror. It was like the Black Death in Europe in the XIV Century. We did not die, but something in us was dying. We were forgetting our fellow men. . . . Great causes were as unheeded as the legend of the Grail." Long spoke only to the coal miners, the farmers, and the poor.

There were incidental benefits for everyone (excepting the coal miners, etc.). Of course, that included A. W. and the Mellons; they were citizens too. As Will Rogers put it in his 1928 "Presidential Message": "Mellon has saved some money for the country, and done very well for himself."

Income tax returns give a hint as to just how well Mellon may have done for himself. Comparative figures are available for the two years during which the public-disclosure clause was applicable. In 1923, A. W. was the nation's third-largest taxpayer with his tax payment of $1,173,987. John D. Rockefeller Jr., was the biggest taxpayer at $7,435,169, followed by Henry Ford, who paid $2,467,000. That year R. B. was far out of the running with his modest $348,646 payment. (W. L. paid almost as much, $225,843.)

The following year A. W.'s tax bill was larger still, $1,882,609, but his rank dropped to fourth. John D. Jr. and Ford both far outstripped the pack, and Henry's son Edsel slipped in for show. But R. B. had a better year, and his $1,180,699 contribution made him the nation's seventh biggest taxpayer, behind the four front runners and Harry Payne Whitney and Edward S. Harkness.

A. W.'s attorney announced in 1935 that from the inception of the income tax in 1913 through and including the year 1933, A. W. had paid total income taxes of $21,223,473.87. Government spokesmen added that his income during the period had exceeded $100 million.

With income of that magnitude, and income taxes of that magnitude, it is easy enough to appreciate the substantial savings that the progressive reduction in the maximum income tax rate from 73 per cent to 25 per cent meant for A. W. and for his family.

Even more important for A. W. were the changes in the estate and gift tax situation. At seventy-one, the income tax rate was not likely to have direct effect on him very much longer. Sophisticated about the vicissitudes of both politics and economic cycles, he appreciated that his "accomplishment" would not live forever. The death tax would again be increased in some hard time; the gift tax was not forever dead, and its ghost would ultimately be resurrected. Now was the time for him, for R. B., aged sixty-eight, and for young W. L., fifty-eight, to act. During the period 1926 to 1932, A. W. funneled off much of his wealth to Paul and Ailsa, with many of the gifts made in the closing days of 1931 and the first half of 1932, when the imminent reimposition of a gift tax was foreseeable.

Mellon's identification of his own self-interest with the national interest on the matter of taxes, if inappropriate, was nonetheless one that he was entitled rationally to have indulged. With regard to other legislative propositions, though, his seemingly instinctive identification of his own self-interest with the public interest appears to be less rationally justifiable. Compare, for example, his position on the McNary-Haugen bills of the 1920s with his position on tariffs.

Senator Charles McNary and Congressman Gilbert Haugen were two farm-oriented legislators who proposed a solution to the farmer's great problem: overproduction that kept farm prices depressed and that yielded to the farmer a continually decreasing portion of the American pie. McNary and Haugen proposed the establishment of a new federal agency that would set a minimum price for sales in the United States of five basic commodities. The agency would purchase any quantities of these commodities that could not be sold in the United States at the minimum price and would sell the excess abroad at whatever the world market price might be. The losses would be borne not by the government but by the farmers themselves, who would have to pay an "equalization fee." The system would have enabled farmers to get a higher price for their domestically sold produce than they would otherwise have received. Farm-bloc supporters likened the proposal to a tariff because it involved governmental action to maintain an artificially high price in the United States of an American product, thereby enabling a vital domestic enterprise, farming, to survive against world price competition. Like the tariff, it necessarily involved increased costs to American consumers.

The McNary-Haugen proposals were subject to objection on a number of bases—some nicely phrased by Coolidge and Herbert Hoover—but A. W.'s opposition to them was framed in terms that were particularly inappropriate for him. He argued against the McNary-Haugen bill on the grounds that the bill would raise the price to American consumers, who would have to pay an artificially high price, greater than their European counterparts would have to pay. This situation would tend to reduce costs of foreign industrial production, enabling foreign producers to compete better against American industries in world and domestic markets. The proposal ran counter to natural economic laws.

All of this was equally true regarding the high protective tariffs that Mellon favored for industry. The Fordney-McCumber Tariff Act of 1922 established a new commission authorized to set tariffs, ostensibly to nurture and protect nascent or threatened American industries. It led to the highest tariffs that had ever been collected in America. Among the industries that benefited by the tariff act was the aluminum industry, already an entrenched American monopoly that Arthur Vining Davis testified was earning a thoroughly respectable return. The tariff on aluminum was increased by three cents a pound—from two cents to five cents—whereupon Alcoa promptly increased its domestic price by three cents a pound. Alcoa's action graphically demonstrated that the tariff represented a government-enforced subsidy that the American consumer had to pay to an American monopoly. Any aluminum that Alcoa could not sell domestically at its new price it

could of course "dump" on the world market for whatever it might fetch.
A. W. Mellon made no objection; there were no comments about violation
of natural economic laws or the effect of the tariff on America's ability to
compete in world markets. He consistently supported the high tariff policy
for industry.

The contrast between Mellon's farm and tariff policies was seized upon
by farm-bloc spokesmen, notably Senator William Borah, who read Mellon's McNary-Haugen position paper on the floor of the Senate substituting
the words "tariff law" for "Haugen Bill" with telling effect. The contrast
was also disturbing to those without an immediate stake in the McNary-
Haugen fight. The New York *World* wrote that Mellon's McNary-Haugen
position paper coming from anyone else would have been "excellent," but
that from a man who had so benefited from the tariffs it was "preposterous";
it offended "an instinct for fair play." The *World* acknowledged Mellon to
be an honest and sincere man but suggested that the Secretary was "a man
who has never been taught to question the premises supplied by his own
self-interest." His position was "not the product of cynical self-interest but
of naive self-interest."

By January of 1919 the required number of states had ratified the "prohibition amendment" to the United States Constitution, and Congress quickly
provided the enforcement machinery for the elimination of liquor, beer, and
wine in America, by passage over President Woodrow Wilson's veto of the
Volstead Act. Illogically, enforcement of the act was delegated principally
to the Treasury Department. Mellon's predecessor, David Houston, urged
Congress to transfer it instead to the Justice Department. When Boies
Penrose early discussed A. W.'s possible appointment as Secretary with
Mellon, one of the reasons for Mellon's reluctance was that he wanted no
part of prohibition enforcement, but Penrose assured him that in a matter
of months prohibition enforcement would be into the Justice Department
and out of Mellon's hair. As things turned out, it was not quite so simple.
Year after year Mellon went back to the Congress to make his sensible
argument that the Treasury Department should be concerned principally
with fiscal matters and that Justice was the more appropriate repository for
law enforcement responsibilities. It was to be nine years before Mellon was
free of the prohibition bugaboo, during all of which he was the nominal
head of the country's anti-liquor establishment.

No one was less in sympathy with the prohibition movement or the
concept of prohibition than A. W. Mellon. Liquor had a long and respect-

able place in his family's traditions. Historically, western Pennsylvania farmers "banked" their excess farm products by converting them into more easily stored and transported whiskey. Typical of his neighbors, Judge Mellon's father maintained a home distillery. The Judge wrote that children of his day and world were "dosed" with whiskey every morning, and when he took his long walk from the farm to Pittsburgh at the age of ten, he carried a half-pint flask back with him and nipped at it along the way. Though he despised drunkenness, the Judge clearly believed that a wholesome introduction to drink was likely to breed moderation, and his own household was as permissive as his father's had been. "Old Mrs. Cox," the Judge's housekeeper, rewarded his little boys with a wonderful spruce beer that she made, the taste of which lingered in W. L.'s mouth many years later when he spoke of it in *Judge Mellon's Sons.* The Judge's obituary mentioned that he had been an early investor in the whiskey industry.

A. W. himself had been a stockholder in Overholt, an investment that he had disposed of long before prohibition became law, but he expected that his appointment as Secretary of the Treasury would be criticized by "drys" on the basis of his former Overholt connection. It was. Dry senator Matthew M. Neely, Democrat of West Virginia, argued that "a thought, a hope or a dream of satisfactory enforcement of prohibition" with Mellon in charge was "as idle as a painted ship upon a painted ocean. Obviously, a thief will never enforce the law against larceny; a pyromaniac will never enforce the law against arson; a distiller will never enforce the Volstead Act."

A. W. did not try to enforce the Volstead Act. Instead, he let the "drys" take that responsibility by placing unimpeachable drys at the head of the Treasury Department's prohibition efforts. Perhaps he theorized that the drys and their leaders should properly bear responsibility for the inevitable failure of their great experiment. In any event their presence at the top of active enforcement efforts might kosher to some extent Treasury's doings and his own role. Wayne Wheeler, America's most potent prohibitionist, had a sidekick, Roy Haynes, who was appointed to head Treasury's prohibition unit. Later, when prohibition enforcement had become so disorganized as to bring disrepute upon the Secretary of the Treasury himself, Mellon appointed Brigadier General Lincoln C. Andrews as assistant secretary of the Treasury with supervisory powers over the Coast Guard, Customs, and prohibition units, with the idea that Andrews would "militarize" prohibition into order. That failed, partly because of friction between Haynes and Andrews, and Mellon replaced both men with similarly "respectable" heads. Other than selecting as the top men in prohibition people who would be acceptable to the drys, Mellon essentially washed his hands of prohibition. An "as told to" article by Mellon in *Colliers* was captioned "Prohibition Is Up to You," reflecting Mellon's personal attitude that prohibition enforcement was up to the public and the drys; it was not up to A. W. Mellon. Attorney General Stone, whose Justice Department was charged with prosecuting the offenses uncovered by Mellon's prohibition unit, became concerned about the caliber of the prohibition unit's agents, and concluded that Mellon took no interest in the appointment of agents or the activity of the executives who supervised them. He complained in disgust, "Law enforcement agents shouldn't be under that man."

Professional drys were not satisfied with Mellon's cop-out. His policy positions on prohibition-related matters were often anathema to them, though they seemed to make good sense. Early in his tenure he ruled that light beer and wines could be allowed for medicinal purposes on prescription; he declined to reveal the quantities of alcoholic beverages imported by foreign officials exempt from the Volstead Act on the grounds that it would be "improper" for him to do so; he extended "freedom of the port" to congressmen returning from abroad, whose personal baggage was sometimes transported in small curiously cubic-shaped wooden crates; he opposed efforts to make wood alcohol more certainly fatal by adding further poisons to it; and in 1929 he opposed a substantial increase in the budgetary appropriation for prohibition enforcement on the grounds that the prohibition unit could not use the additional monies "wisely and effectively." Prohibition zealots believed that Treasury's regular snoops were watching them as closely as the prohibition unit was watching Messrs. Capone and Schultz, and though Treasury denied it, it did maintain "personal" files on an awful lot of people, including some dry spokesmen. Quite early on, Mellon announced that a temporary two-thirds cut in prohibition field agents would have little adverse effect on enforcement—they would be replaced at the start of the next fiscal year when more funds were available. The caliber of replacements was noticeably lower than that of the men in Internal Revenue. The patronage hacks who were scrupulously weeded out of Treasury's "regular" departments seemed to be welcomed in the prohibition unit, and when Andrews attempted to beef up the unit with retired military officers, Mellon urged him not to close his ears to congressional suggestions on prospective appointees—something Mellon himself regularly did when considering appointees to "important" departments. Corruption could not be tolerated anywhere within the Treasury Department, but there were differences in corruption, perhaps turning on the relative importance attached to the function being corrupted. A clue as to the department attitude on corruption in prohibition may be gleaned from a letter that Undersecretary Garrard Winston wrote to Mellon, who was vacationing in Europe in July 1926:

> It has been very hot in Washington, and the usual troubles seem to break out on liquor enforcement. I have had to suspend the California administrator [of prohibition], who will probably be indicted by the Grand Jury this week for appropriating to his own use seized liquor. He seems to be a good deal of a fool but not a knave.

To the undersecretary, and probably to the Secretary, corrupting prohibition enforcement was "fool"-ish, but not worse.

The drys were not blinded by A. W.'s pushing of Haynes, Andrews, and their successors to the fore. The New York *Times* indexes for the years 1921 to 1930 are cluttered with columns of citations of articles in which assorted dry spokesmen attacked Mellon in particularities and in generalities for Treasury's enforcement of prohibition and Mellon's stands on prohibition-related issues. Prohibitionists began to see his every move as part of a conscious effort to sabotage prohibition, though Mellon was too busy to waste any effort supplementing the drys' own unconscious efforts in that direction. Later, in 1934, after it was all over, the famed Methodist bishop James Cannon (the "Dry Messiah") put the principal blame for the failure of prohibition on Mellon: "When Prohibition control was turned over to the Treasury Department under Andrew W. Mellon, it was doomed." The drys were too harsh on Mellon. The American experience in prohibition of marijuana, for years conscientiously enforced by relatively corruption-free agents, leads one to conclude that prohibition of alcohol could not have been accomplished even if there had been an able "dry" Secretary of the Treasury blessed with optimum enforcement machinery. Mellon did nothing actively to retard the prohibitionists' cause; he was indifferent to it. Indifferent, that is, except insofar as it might impinge on his own freedoms.

One of the hidden costs to American society of the prohibition effort was its characterological cost. Prohibition institutionalized hypocrisy, rather than prohibition. President Harding set the standard for observation of the prohibition law when he ignored it. His enforcer followed the President's example. In *The Big Spenders,* Paul Mellon's friend Lucius Beebe described a prohibition-era visit to Pittsburgh, where

> three separate parties, all involving bottled matters, were in progress at the Mellon manse. In one wing the Secretary was entertaining a group of personal friends; in another his brother Richard B. Mellon was conferring with a group

of Pittsburgh bankers on topics so dry as to require liberal lubrication, and in
Paul's personal apartments a group of friends from New Haven were simply
drinking without the fabrication of any excuse for doing so. It was a time when
drinking was admired among college boys as a full-time occupation.

So vast were the Mellon premises that three separate parties could be in
progress attended by suitable servants without one of them infringing on the
privacy of another, but during an only temporary lull in the chaos which
reigned in Paul's room there was a timid knock at the door and there was the
Secretary. We tried without notable success to look sober and intelligent but
Mr. Mellon had no intention of joining us.

"I just thought to warn you, Paul, about throwing bottles out the window,"
he said in his mildest whisper. "You remember last Christmas when you had
a party and when the snow melted in January there were all those bottles on
the lawn. There was talk, you know."

Beebe wrote that "under the Mellon homestead were literally acres of
cellars filled with the best of everything." It must indeed have been a great
hoard. Matthew Mellon recalls that years later, in the 1960s, Ailsa Bruce
once offered him cases from her own vast reserve of Old Overholt—by then
very old Overholt—an unused portion of her father's legacy.

In Washington, Mellon was discreet but not dry. In his biography of
Albert Lasker, John Gunther reported that Lasker despised prohibition but
felt that as a government official (he was chairman of the United States
Shipping Board) he had a moral duty to obey the law even if the President
declined to do so. Lasker served no alcoholic beverages but permitted his
guests to bring their own, and when Mellon came on several occasions, he
would bring one bottle of beer with him. According to Matthew Mellon,
the Secretary brought "a suitcase of liquor" with him to a Republican
convention. "Dry" and "left-wing" critics of the Secretary rumored that his
personal secretary, Arthur D. Sixsmith, functioned for Mellon as shady Jess
Smith had for Attorney General Daugherty, arranging raucous entertain-
ments at which important visiting firemen might disport themselves in an
undignified manner with free liquor and freer women.

The rest of the Mellon family paralleled the enforcer's, and the nation's,
observance of the law. According to Matthew, his father, W. L., always had
a drink in the evening. Matthew himself, like W. L. before him, was brought
up with drink, and his diary entries from the 1920s, published in *Watermellons,* make clear that neither he nor any of the other Mellons of his generation wanted to be the only dullard in America. Slightly younger Mellons,
W. L. Jr. and Ned Mellon, set up stills at their prep schools. According to
Ned, W. L. Junior's was the better, until it exploded.

In the 1920s A. W. Mellon emerged as the boss of Pennsylvania as the head of the "Mellon machine" that dominated the state—or at least dominated it in the reportage of most state and national political columnists. A. W. had not wanted to become a key political power in Pennsylvania state politics; that role was forced upon him by the deaths of Boies Penrose and Philander Knox within ten weeks of each other in the fall of 1921, only months after A. W. had assumed his responsibilities as Secretary of the Treasury. He might well have viewed his possibilities for success as Secretary as dependent on the support that his programs would receive from congressmen influenced by two such powerful men. With them gone, the success of his stay in Washington was much less certain. At the least he needed someone who would be his strong right arm through thick and thin in the United States Senate. Such considerations prompted him to involve himself and his hapless nephew W. L. in the family's series of ill-advised bumblings in Pennsylvania state politics, which gave rise to the myth of the Mellon machine.

W. L. was about the only man in Pennsylvania less suited for the political world than A. W. Mellon. His son Matthew insists that W. L. was never interested in politics, yet somehow there he was in the thick of things, as operating manager of the Mellon machine; two unhappy years as chairman of the Pennsylvania Republican Party (1926–28); many years thereafter being blamed as the "man behind" his successor as state chairman; sometimes mentioned as a likely treasurer of the Republican National Committee. Frank Kent described W. L.'s savvy: "It is obvious he knows little about practical politics . . . all he knows about politics is that it takes a lot of money to run campaigns." Kent characterized the leadership of the Mellon team in a crucial primary as "a bumble puppy management."

W. L.'s role on behalf of the Mellon interests was essentially that of "harmonizer"; he would be the fellow who attempted to get the top big boys together to make peace, avoid expensive and disruptive primaries, and keep a friendly senator, or possibly two, in Washington to speak for A. W. in Congress. More often he found himself in the middle of state and local fractional bloodlettings, with himself as the principal target.

Against the Mellons was arrayed an unusually talented circle of "political animals," all vying for control of the Republican Party in a one-party state. In Philadelphia was the city's great boss, William A. Vare, a caricature of the big city boss. At a "peace conference" between Vare and A. W. himself, the Secretary offered the boss one of his elegant little cigars. Harvey O'Connor reported that Vare contemptuously "scooped a half dozen in his paw, tied a rubber band around them and grunted, 'A fair smoke, Mr. Secretary.' " The Mellons could, and sometimes did, get in bed with Vare. Joseph Grundy, though, was more to their liking. The president of the Pennsylvania Manufacturers Association, Grundy was just beginning to assert himself in Pennsylvania politics at the time of A. W.'s accession to the Treasury. With time he was to become the unrivaled Republican leader in the state, with influence sometimes approaching the power that Penrose had exercised. Vare's only policy interest was a virulent opposition to prohibition; Grundy's policy interests covered the spectrum, and were almost uniformly compatible with those of the Mellons. Unlike the Mellons, though, Grundy was interested not only in public policy questions but also in power for power's sake; and with that interest Grundy could—and sometimes did—get in bed with the devil.

The devil was Gifford Pinchot. Pinchot had first become well known as a pioneer forester and conservationist; his dismissal in 1910 as head of the United States Forest Service by President Taft had been a cause célèbre. Thereafter he entered Pennsylvania politics as a Teddy Roosevelt progressive. As governor in the mid-1920s and early '30s, he cut his own salary, threw open the doors of his office to the public, appointed a woman to high state office, and invited every state employee to a dance. On some issues he was downright radical, and he often sounded far left when he got around to discussing "the interests." He was without a doubt the independent good-government star of Pennsylvania politics of his era. He was also a dedicated and crusading "dry," and was twice elected governor with the support of the right-wing Grundy and that of the most intolerant church ladies of the state. He drove around in a battered Ford auto, though he owned some fancy European makes, and he reportedly mussed his expensive suits before each public appearance. Pinchot had two hobbies. His favorite was attacking A. W. Mellon's enforcement of prohibition; when he needed a change of scene he would busy himself lambasting W. L. Mellon, whom he blamed for every piece of anti-social legislation that passed the state legislature. His private papers at the Library of Congress include an elaborate chart which Pinchot had periodically updated, tabulating the Mellon financial interests and indicating thereon what people were, or might be, entangled in the Mellon web. In one of his most celebrated polemics Pinchot said,

> For many years politics in this state has been run as a part of the business of
> certain moneyed interests. These interests invest in politics as they do in mills
> or mines or banks, and for the same purpose—to make money. But instead of

property, they buy men and votes, favors and legislation. What these interests buy is non-interference, tax exemption, extortionate rates allowed public utilities and other special privileges for themselves at the expense of the people.

In case anyone missed his point, he mentioned the "Mellon machine."

In a crowd of W. L., Vare, Grundy, and Pinchot, there could be no question about who was the most inept. W. L. knew well that he was a fish out of water, and he repeatedly "retired," or at least announced his retirement from politics; but each time an opportunity to further A. W.'s cause appeared, he was back in the fray. Mark Shields, political columnist for the Pittsburgh *Sun-Telegraph* commented that "the retirements of W. L. Mellon from politics are much like the farewell tours of Adelina Patti or Sarah Bernhardt. One succeeds the other, and there seems to be no permanency to seclusion." Each time he re-entered, almost always to suffer public insults, bruises, and defeat.

The most significant involvement of the Mellon machine in Pennsylvania politics was its role in the Republican primary for United States senator in 1926, most significant because that battle, and the staggering sums spent in it, attracted national attention and gave a clue to the value of the Mellon role in the clinch.

After Penrose's death, George Wharton Pepper was chosen to fill his unexpired term. Pepper titled his autobiography *Philadelphia Lawyer,* which just about tells his whole story. Though he was somewhat more liberal than the Mellons (his opposition to child labor laws was tempered, and he spoke out against what he regarded as too-frequent grants of injunctions by federal judges in labor disputes), on the balance he looked to be acceptable to the Mellon interests. Vare stepped forward as a candidate and was looking to make a package with a gubernatorial hopeful. Pinchot, serving as governor but ineligible for re-election as such by virtue of Pennsylvania constitutional restrictions, also announced. Grundy was unimpressed with all three—possibly most hostile to Pepper—but he took greater interest in securing the gubernatorial nomination for his appropriately neanderthal ally, John S. Fisher. Such a man was entirely satisfactory to the Mellons, and they agreed to go with Fisher in exchange for Grundy's support for their senatorial choice.

As Pepper told it in *Philadelphia Lawyer,* A. W. summoned the senator to his office to offer Pepper the senatorial slot on a ticket with Fisher. Pepper wanted to run alone and resisted, but he reported that A. W. taunted him with "Of course I can get along very well with Mr. Vare." Against his better judgment (Pepper claimed) he made the pact and threw his lot in with the

fat cats. In the exciting primary that followed, Pepper and Fisher confronted Vare and his gubernatorial running mate, Edward E. Beidleman,
with Pinchot running for the Senate alone. W. L. was identified in press
reports as the "Field Marshal" of the Pepper-Fisher forces; the national
press took notice and observed that A. W.'s national political reputation
might turn on the primary outcome.

Principally the battle devolved into a contest between Vare's big city
Philadelphia machine, and all the vulgar corruptions that it stood for, and
what the New York *Times* characterized as "its pretentious and heavier
pursed enemies, devoted to virtue and the tariff." In the closing days of the
campaign, the Field Marshal brought out the heaviest guns. A. W. Mellon
himself came to Pittsburgh to deliver what the Judge would have called a
"claptrap declamation" for Pepper and Fisher. It was a mixed blessing.
Kent, covering the campaign for the *Sun,* reported that among the thousands of employees of the various Mellon enterprises,

> there is a pretty general idea that the Mellons are a cold-blooded hard-boiled
> lot, intent only on piling up more millions for themselves and eager now for
> political domination because of the protection it means to their financial inter-
> ests.

All three Senate hopefuls fought hard, and more to the point, spent hard.
When the dollars were counted, the victorious Vare had spent, together
with his running mate, $788,943 to garner his 598,000 votes, well over a
dollar a vote and a staggering price to pay in 1926. His budget was dwarfed
by that of the Pepper-Fisher people, who spent a *reported* $1,804,979 for
Pepper's 515,000 votes, more than three dollars apiece. Even Pinchot paid
half a dollar each—$187,029 for 339,000 votes. The vast amount of money
spent by the two front runners was not the only thing to lift eyebrows;
intimidation at the polls, perpetrated by Vare supporters in Philadelphia
and Pepper people in Pittsburgh, and obvious irregularities in the mechanics of the polling in both cities made the whole primary stink. Pepper's
running mate for governor, Fisher, edged Vare's companion, giving each of
the "regular" factions half a loaf. Both Vare and Fisher easily bested the
nominal Democratic opposition on election day, and when the smoke
cleared, W. L. Mellon emerged as state chairman of the Pennsylvania
Republican Party. In certifying Vare's election as senator to the federal
officials, outgoing Governor Pinchot reported that Vare had won on the
basis of a nomination that had been "partly bought and partly stolen."

The Mellon value to the Pepper forces seems to have been almost entirely
financial. In his analysis of "The Mellons, Their Money, and the Mythical

Machine" published in *Pennsylvania History,* Professor Lawrence L. Murray concluded that the Mellons could never "deliver" any votes other than their own, and that the financial and big business backing that they could round up was the extent of their political usefulness. Even as to money, Louise Overacker, the pioneer analyst of money in politics, concluded that Grundy was the fatter cat in 1926. A. W. and his brother R. B. were both listed as contributing $25,000 to the Pepper forces; W. L. as giving $40,500. In addition to which W. L. "guaranteed" a committee debt of $83,000, and a Mellon bank made a portion of a $75,000 loan to another committee. Even assuming that the Mellons were ultimately stuck for all of those sums, their total investment was a paltry $248,500. Grundy—who had silent businessmen backing him—contributed $31,250; lent another $291,575, and "guaranteed" a portion of another committee debt of $90,000.

The United States Senate was aghast—or so it claimed to be—at the vast amounts of money spent in the primary; and at the urging of Senator Norris and populist Democratic senator James A. Reed of Missouri, the Senate denied Vare admission to its hall pending results of an investigation. At that point the rest of the Pennsylvania party regulars rallied behind Vare. If Vare was to be denied because he had spent a mere $788,943, what moral judgments were to be made as to the spending of $1,804,979? At one point in the long Vare proceedings Pennsylvania's "seated" senator, David A. Reed, who had supported Pepper in the primary, filibustered to prevent a vote adverse to Vare. Both A. W. and W. L. defended the amounts spent on the grounds that Pennsylvania was a large state with a varied population, thereby requiring much greater expenditures than in some state like Nebraska or Missouri. A. W. likened giving for such a worthy purpose as the re-election of Pepper to "giving money to a church." Journalists were horrified at the analogy. Even the New York *Times,* customarily friendly to Mellon, commented that "the real Pennsylvania scandal is the fact that Pennsylvania did not seem to know that it was doing anything scandalous." The New York *World* was less charitable. It calculated that in Allegheny County, the Mellons' home territory, where Pepper had collected 80,346 votes, his forces had "hired" 35,350 "poll watchers" at ten dollars each. Assuming that each "poll watcher" had lent only his own and his spouse's vote, "we reach the conclusion that practically the whole Mellon-Pepper electorate in Allegheny County was purchased."

The investigation dragged on for three years, ultimately resulting in the refusal of the Senate to seat Vare, ostensibly because his "buying" of the nomination would reflect adversely on the Senate and was contrary to public policy. In his place, to serve until the next general election, Governor

Fisher appointed Grundy, key man in the Pepper spending that had greatly dwarfed Vare's. His policies were even more acceptable to the Mellons than Pepper's.

All in all, the Mellons' active involvement in state politics was not a happy experience. For years the Mellons and their machine were the best possible target for every insurgent politician, whether a progressive like Pinchot or a hopeless fringe party (Democratic) spokesman like the little known "leader" of Allegheny County Democrats, David Lawrence. Their support for candidates over the years was invariably attributed to their desire to insure another vote against old-age pensions and minimum-wage bills (probably an accurate if loaded explanation for Mellon backing). Their public endorsement of any candidate was surely a mixed blessing, as it invited the labeling of their "horse" as a "tool" of the Mellon interests. "Mellonism" was the issue in too many campaigns to suit any Mellon. Time after time "their" candidates for office—governor, U. S. senator, important Allegheny County positions—were defeated in primaries or, in the early 1930s, in elections. In their home town Republican presidential contenders after 1920 did progressively worse. Hoover barely carried Allegheny County in his big sweep in 1928. The net effect on the family was to deprive it of some of the dignity that was born of its aloofness, and in history to give A. W. and W. L. their share of credit for the devastation in the 1920s of the once irresistible power of the Pennsylvania Republican Party. For W. L., the Mellons' supposed dominance of state politics produced only a mountain of yellowing, crumbling press clippings, most of them uncomplimentary to him, and an occasional bewildered nod of the head. In his memoirs he did not discuss his period as "kingpin" of the Pennsylvania Republican Party. He included only one brief comment that might hint at the lesson of his political period: "Politics is a fantastic business where truth almost never triumphs." There was, however, one consolation for the Mellons in their involvement in state politics. They got that one strong right arm that they had wanted in the election of Senator David A. Reed.

After Knox's death in October of 1921 his unexpired term was filled by William A. Crow, Republican state chairman, an infirm man whose hold on the position was clearly tenuous from the start. A political unknown arose to challenge Crow for the Republican nomination for a full six-year term in the Knox seat in 1922: David A. Reed. Reed, son of Judge Reed, himself a onetime law partner of Philander Knox and sometime chief counsel for United States Steel, was a wealthy, relatively young man (he was forty-two in 1922) with no prior political background at all. His principal qualification was his complete acceptability to the most traditional Pittsburgh business elements. Reed made clear in his announcement of candidacy that he was not the creature of any particular party faction. Crow backed out of the race, and the back-room boys insured "harmony" by trading the nomination of Reed, from Pittsburgh, for the full six-year Senate term, with that of Philadelphia's Pepper for the four-year sitting that would complete the balance of Penrose's unexpired term. Reed's support for the seating of Vare after the 1926 election insured him the Philadelphia support when Reed's first term expired in 1928, and he was renominated that year without opposition. In both 1922 and 1928 his nomination was tantamount to election, allowing him twelve years in which to serve as A. W.'s strong right arm. And serve he did. He not only carried the ball for Mellon's programs, he carried it for Mellon personally and for the Mellon financial interests. Whenever a progressive made a personal attack on A. W., or on his eligibility to serve as Secretary of the Treasury, or on his Teapot Dome silence, or on the "Aluminum Trust," or on tax refunds to Gulf, Reed was on his feet with a ready response. He always seemed to know the details, almost as if he had been briefed in advance to make the defense. In fact, he almost surely needed no such briefings; he knew the details himself from years of close involvement with the Mellons and their interests.

Reed's loyalty was so great as to override any competing claims. When, for example, Mellon's antagonist Senator Thomas Walsh sought unanimous consent of the Senate to consider a resolution affecting Alcoa, Reed withheld his vote. Sometimes his homage carried to such lengths as to cause embarrassment to both master and servant. On one such occasion Reed defended the Mellon banks against the charges of one of A. W.'s regular critics, Senator Norris. Union Trust and Mellon National had filed separate tax returns, when, it was argued by Norris's ally, Senator James Couzens, they should have filed a consolidated tax return that would have called for a higher tax payment to the government. Norris got his side's argument mixed up. He erroneously attacked the banks for having filed a consolidated tax return instead of separate returns. Reed arrived during Norris's presentation and true to form rose to make the defense. He delivered a powerful argument based on his own personal knowledge of the structure and working of the banks to the effect that it was entirely proper for them to have filed a consolidated tax return. "In every sense these corporations are one enterprise," he insisted, thereby clinching the progressives' argument. On another occasion involving the propriety of a $91,000 tax refund to the Mellon banks, he argued that the money could not be returned to the Treasury because the Treasury had "closed" their file. The Treasury's spokesmen corrected him soon after. They *could* reopen the file. Silas Bent, a distinguished journalist of the 1920s, referred to Reed's position in the Senate as "as near cabinet representation on the legislative floor as anything we have seen in this country." Drew Pearson and Robert S. Allen were closer to the mark when they described Reed in their *Washington Merry-Go-Round* as Mellon's "senatorial office boy."

When Reed's second term expired in 1934, Pinchot challenged him for the Republican nomination, and made Reed's service to the Mellons and their interests his principal campaign issue. Reed carried the primary, and made a gentlemanly acceptance speech at his victory party at the Rolling Rock Club, but it was academic. The time had run out for the Pennsylvania Republican Party. Joseph Guffey, Democrat, defeated Reed for re-election.

It should be plain from the above sections that throughout the early 1920s A. W. Mellon was almost always under attack on one front or another—from veterans disgruntled over his opposition to their bonus; farmers upset over his positions on proposals to aid their plight; progressive Republicans and Democrats who, whether from vision or partisanship, disputed the mathematics or denied the social desirability of his fiscal policies; "drys," usually incorrect on the particulars but quite justified in their overview that the Secretary of the Treasury was indifferent to the performance of the only one of his duties that meant anything to them. As in all times, however, most men of the 1920s were not primarily farmers or veterans or tax reformers or drys—or politically aware on broader planes. Most men were, and are, generally apolitical, and political only insofar as they are creatures of "the temper of their times." The temper of the 1920s was with A. W. Mellon.

The "Coolidge era" was one of the most materialistic periods in the history of the United States, when wealth was venerated and success in its accumulation was regarded as the plainest mark of the moral worth of its possessor. By the time of Harding's election A. W. Mellon had the number on the "unco squad." He knew the standard to be shallow, and in little ways —such as lending his "byline" to a probably ghosted piece speaking out against conspicuous consumption—he rebelled in his quiet manner. But he was not at the core a rebel, and his opposition to the mores of the 1920s was as soft-spoken as he was himself. He was not a man of the 1920s, though he was one of the heroes of the 1920s.

In a period when a million dollars represented greatness, wealth of Mellon's magnitude approached sacredness. When its possessor's wisdom was demonstrated in solid public accomplishments, the benefits of which devolved upon all of his countrymen, he was entitled to a respect approaching veneration. A. W. Mellon was entitled to such respect. He had abandoned infinitely better-paying pursuits to devote himself to public service and had led the nation in overcoming the recession of 1920–22. Thereafter he had simultaneously reduced both the national debt and the rate of taxes; and, as he had predicted, the lower tax rates had indeed prompted an increase in the river of revenues flowing into the national Treasury rather than a decline in the volume. Except for pockets of special interest groups—such as the poor—the nation was grateful to this Solomon-Croesus.

Several politicians claimed the distinction of coining the characterization of "Andy" as "the greatest Secretary of the Treasury since Alexander Hamilton," which was to become a cliché, and later, after the onset of the depression, a taunt. Mellon's great admirer Reed Smoot—the all-purpose reactionary memorialized by Ogden Nash in "Senator Smoot (Republican, Ut.)"—was almost certainly the first to go one better with the insistence that Mellon was the greatest Secretary of the Treasury including Hamilton. The *Saturday Evening Post* agreed: "Admitting the genius of Hamilton and the value of his constructive work on the rudimentary governmental financial system at the birth of the Republic," and of his many able successors, none "was so completely the master of finance as Mellon, nor any, of course, who had problems one-tenth the size and complexity of his problems since 1921." By 1923 A. W.'s prestige was already probably the highest of any member of the cabinet. The following year the New York *Times* editorialized that "No one is more applauded at public meetings. Even in the movies, the picture of Mr. Mellon excites more cheering and enthusiasm than that of any other man shown." William Allen White reported in *A Puritan in Babylon* that at the dull 1924 Republican National Convention "the ovation of the hour came when a frail, gray-haired wisp of a man rose in the Pennsylvania delegation waving some sort of a paper. Instantly the convention recognized Andrew W. Mellon, Secretary of the Treasury." The cheers and cries and applause provided the only genuine excitement of the convention. A. W., always reticent, responded to the demands of the crowd— "Platform! Platform! Platform!"—only when, as W. L. wrote, he and others in the Pennsylvania delegation, "closed in on him and almost forcibly escorted him up the ramp and steps of the platform." White continued, "He mounted the steps and stood bashfully revealed as some subterranean creature unused to the light." He described the crowd's reaction as representing "a paroxysm of joy at seeing in the flesh so rich and powerful a being." A. W. was awkward about his reception, but W. L.'s "feelings of pride were almost those of a parent."

In that presidential election year, Coolidge's challengers for the presidency failed to read the obvious signs. They attacked the sacred cow himself, but they paid the price on election day. Thereafter only fools and the foolhardy dared to make political hay out of attacking "Andy." One such hopeless one, Franklin D. Roosevelt, addressing the New York State Democratic Convention in 1926, included in his uninspired claptrap declamation "Calvin Coolidge would like to have God on his side, but he must have Andrew Mellon"; sounder heads, like the chairman of the Democratic National Committee, privately acknowledged, "If we could only take Mellon away from the Republicans we could win easily."

The adulation given to "the greatest Secretary of the Treasury since . . ." was revolting to most of the intellectual community. Kent, Silas Bent, Pearson and Allen, and Walter Lippmann each analyzed Mellon's "greatness" in contemporary magazine pieces that attributed the apparent successes of the 1920s economy to factors other than A. W. Mellon's policies or his administration of the Treasury, and that pointed to potentially disastrous elements in the seemingly bright economic picture. The disdainful H. L. Mencken found Mellon unworthy of such analysis and dismissed him abruptly in his *Prejudices: Sixth Series* (1927): "I know of no other country in which . . . so preposterous a vacuum as Andy Mellon would be venerated as a great statesman." Most people ignored such criticisms, or dismissed them uncharitably. One of Ailsa's friends assured her that responsible people were satisfied that a naked-emperor piece by Kent—a thoroughly honorable journalist—had been bought and paid for by her father's enemies within the progressive wing of the Republican Party, probably by Senator James Couzens and Secretary of Commerce Herbert Hoover.

In an unsigned New York *World* editorial, Walter Lippmann wrote that Mellon was "surrounded by an adulation which would sicken a man of finer sensibilities." Mellon was not easily sickened, but he was easily bewildered, and the adulation was as bewildering to him as it was sickening to Lippmann. He knew that he was not "Andy"; he appreciated that he was not entitled to the credit extended to him; and though he was not sickened, he was embarrassed by the comparisons with Hamilton: "I think that each successive Secretary of the Treasury at some time during his incumbency of office enjoys the distinction of being 'the greatest Secretary of the Treasury since Alexander Hamilton'; however, he goes out of office and his glory has departed." He declined to participate in the writing of a sycophantic biography by Philip H. Love, *Andrew W. Mellon: The Man and His Work* (1929), and took steps to disassociate himself from it and to denigrate its "authoritativeness." He could not understand the attention, but as a methodical character, he recorded it, and kept an album of political cartoons that had been drawn about him. "Why are they so interested in making cartoons of me?" he asked Candler Cobb. He could not fathom Cobb's explanation. Always uncomfortable about recognition, he was more than usually so at the recognition extended him at the 1924 Republican Convention. W. L. wrote that "A. W.'s hands were wringing to pieces the sheets of paper on which was typewritten the motion he was expected to read." When he finally read his routine motion to establish a resolutions committee, it was "in the faintest of voices."

A year before the Republican Convention that would pick the party's 1928 presidential nominee, Coolidge made the announcement that he did not choose to run again. A. W. was vacationing in Europe at the time of the announcement, but Pennsylvania political leaders, fronted by Governor John Fisher and backed by state party chairman W. L. Mellon, lost no time in inaugurating the "Mellon for President" boom. Asked whether the Secretary might indeed be "available," W. L. insisted that the Secretary himself would have to make the announcement and decision on that. On his return from vacation, A. W. played coy; he insisted that he did not seriously take note of the mention of his name as a possible contender, but he said nothing to take himself clearly out of the running. Support for him from important sources began to mount. William Randolph Hearst and his newspapers gave A. W. a powerful endorsement, as did independent papers from every section of the country. He may never have seriously entertained the possibility of his candidacy, but he did nothing to discourage the efforts on his behalf for several months. In December 1927 the New York *Times* editorialized that the nomination of a man of A. W.'s age—he was seventy-two —would be "absurd to the point of impossibility"; perhaps A. W. agreed, for soon after he removed himself from consideration. W. L. was greatly disappointed, and called his uncle "and chided him a little, explaining that his statement to the newspapers had undone a lot of good work. I said it had been poor politics to discourage our organization so early. . . . He soothed my ruffled feelings."

Had A. W. elected to make the challenge, it is entirely possible that he would have disproved the *Times*. He would have gone to the convention with the solid support of Pennsylvania, a key state; Hearst would likely have been able to deliver the California delegation to him; he had powerful ties with the party organizations throughout the northeast, notably in New York, New Jersey, and Massachusetts; he would almost certainly have had President Coolidge's backing; and he commanded the loyalty of every dedicated "party man" in the country, most of whom detested the ultimate nominee, Herbert Hoover. Hoover's impressive victory on election day, founded on Coolidge-Mellon prosperity, warrants the conclusion that Mellon himself could at least have sneaked through, even if his advanced age were to have cost him a large portion of Hoover's ample plurality.

In order of A. W.'s preferences for President, Herbert Hoover must have come fairly close to the bottom. Their personalities were very different. As self-effacing as A. W. was, Hoover was the contrary—a boastful, publicity-seeking upstart. His crispness and the tone of infallibility with which he expressed his opinions—and his opinions extended to just about everything —were irritating not alone to Mellon. Coolidge sometimes called his Secretary of Commerce "wonder boy." Mellon more charitably complained that "Hoover is an engineer; he wants to run a straight line, just one line, and then say to everyone, 'This is the only line there is, and you must keep up to it, or else keep out.' " A. W. was a gentleman, and by his standards, Hoover . . . well, A. W. was not one to denigrate another person.

Since 1921 the two had sat together in the Presidents' cabinets. During all that time Mellon had confined himself to the Treasury's business; Hoover had confined himself to everyone else's business. His busybodying in "Treasury" matters was a frequent irritation to Mellon. On policy matters Hoover was frequently on the "wrong" side. When he defended collective bargaining and the right to strike he sounded a little too convincing. He endorsed a public works program that threatened A. W.'s policies. He was critical of the "loose money" policies with which A. W. was associated, and stood for higher rates of interest and for a curtailment of American loans abroad. His ally on the Federal Reserve Board, Adolph Miller, regularly opposed A. W.'s positions; Mellon ultimately concluded that Miller was acting in cahoots with Hoover in consciously trying to "embarrass the Board."

Hoover's progressivism can be overstated but he was the nearest thing to a progressive in the Harding or Coolidge cabinet. It was to him that liberals looked for an influence to offset Mellon. His personal friends included many progressives and most of the most repugnant Republicans in Washington, notably Senator Couzens, who did to Mellon in Washington what Pinchot did to Mellon in Pennsylvania. In every way Hoover seemed to be closer to Republicans of the Couzens stripe than he was to that inner circle of Republicanism of which A. W. Mellon was the prime minister.

From the moment of Coolidge's announcement, Hoover was off and running and remained the front-runner from the start until he clinched the nomination. Given the differences between them, Mellon can hardly be blamed for participation in the regulars' stop-Hoover movement. His candidate was anyone else. His first choice was Coolidge, and he, together with other key party higher-ups, repeatedly urged Coolidge to reconsider. Cal gave no direct encouragement. A. W.'s second choice was the regulars' other great hope, the distinguished Charles Evans Hughes, who was similarly distant.

Mellon's Treasury underlings Undersecretary Ogden Mills and Commissioner of Internal Revenue David Blair were both openly for Hoover, and may have spoken to their chief on his behalf. Hoover himself closeted with A. W., only to be told, according to W. L., that A. W. "proposed to remain neutral and would not commit himself, but he also told him that he expected that he might be supporting him later on." A. W. stubbornly declined to jump aboard. He shied away from discussion with journalists that would put him in a position of opposition to the front-runner, but he pointedly abjured any statement that could be taken as a commitment to him. As the time grew near, Hoover's strength looked to be becoming irresistible, but A. W. hoped against hope that Coolidge would "rescue" the party or perhaps that Hughes might have a change of heart.

When Mellon left Washington to return to Pittsburgh prior to going to the convention, Coolidge's innocent enough parting words, "Bon voyage," encouraged Mellon to think that perhaps the President was indeed susceptible to a draft. He urged the Pennsylvania delegation to remain uncommited, just in case. It agreed. According to W. L., as of June 8, 1928, just days before the convention to select the Republican nominee, A. W. was still urging Coolidge to give him a sign.

The press ascribed the ultimate decision as to whom the nominee would be to Mellon, whose influence within the Pennsylvania delegation and beyond would make the difference. *Time* magazine's pre-convention scuttlebutt issue featured a cover photo of A. W.; their text was to the effect that A. W. would be the President maker. The New York *Times* also reported that he held the key to the nomination. Had Mellon been of the Penrose mold, quite possibly he might by skillful trading have been able to dominate the convention and might have brokered the nomination of someone other than Hoover. But he was not of the mold. In comparing the two, *Colliers* wrote a year before the convention that "Penrose was at home among the delegates, bound to them by a hundred personal ties. Mellon isn't that. The hardest thing Mellon does is meet men. . . . Mr. Mellon looks like a poet in a convention of washing machine manufacturers."

By the time the Pittsburgh delegation boarded the train for the Kansas City convention on June 10, A. W. had nowhere to go but to Hoover. Enroute, Mills boarded the train to do missionary work for Hoover with Mellon. When the train arrived in Kansas City, he passed word among his cohorts that his efforts had been successful, that Mellon would endorse Hoover. Soon after, Mellon called Hoover to report that he would urge the Pennsylvania delegation to support him when it caucused the following morning. Mellon's public statement the next day put an end to all speculation, but by that time it would have been an inevitability even without Mellon. He later explained to fellow regular Senator James E. Watson that he had acted in recognition of the inevitability, that any other course would have jeopardized his position as leader of the Pennsylvania Republican Party. According to Watson's memoirs, he responded, "You are not the party leader in Pennsylvania now."

In fact Mellon had been too late, and everyone knew it. Scholar Lawrence Murray wrote that

> the platform, exhibiting the pens of Reed Smoot and Ogden Mills, praised his record as "unrivaled and unsurpassed," but the man whose appearance was the highlight of the last quadrennial meeting passed by unnoticed. No longer was he kingmaker; no longer was he important . . . the "greatest Secretary of the Treasury since Alexander Hamilton" had succumbed to his prejudices and committed political suicide. It appeared that the old guard was changing.

In the election between Hoover and Democrat Al Smith, A. W. went through the motions, and a few more of them than he had shown four years earlier for Coolidge. Then his dedication to the slate had been above question; in 1928, after his obvious reluctance to accept Hoover's nomination, it required a little proof. He twice delivered radio addresses on Hoover's behalf, and he issued a press release calling for the election of Republican congressmen who would support Hoover's policies. He and R. B. made their customarily modest contributions, $25,000 and $27,000. At Yale, Paul Mellon lent his name as head of Yale's Hoover-Curtis Club. How could he say no, and what would Yale's Hoover-Curtis Club matter anyway?

The family was, however, split, as no doubt were A. W.'s private loyalties in the 1928 election. Smith represented the conservative tradition in the Democratic party. It was an election between a Republican "liberal" and a Democratic "conservative," in which if either was the more explicitly progressive candidate, it would have to have been Hoover. Al Smith learned from the errors of 1924. He at no time attacked A. W. Mellon or any of his policies, either expressly or by implication. Ailsa's husband, David Bruce, actively supported Smith, working on a fairly high level with Herbert Lehman, later governor of New York, and James W. ("Jimmy") Gerard, Wilson's ambassador to Germany and long a financial mainstay of the Democratic Party. As everyone is aware, Hoover swept the election.

Notwithstanding past and continued policy differences, Herbert Hoover had considerable respect for Andrew Mellon. His attitudes, however, were very different. He describes Mellon in his memoirs as "in every instinct a country banker," which Hoover no doubt realized was other than an unmixed compliment. Perhaps he viewed their differences as generational. In his memoirs he wrote, "in Mellon's day," thereby indicating that "Mellon's day" was a different day than that with which Hoover himself identified.

If anyone should have been ready for retirement, it was A. W. Mellon, seventy-four in 1929. At the time of his first appointment as Secretary of the Treasury in 1921 he had thought of a brief tenure—a couple of years, possibly one full term at most—just enough to cap a career. At first he checked off the months of his "obligation" on the calendar. But as each day of intended retirement came, he put it off. In 1928 he had told the reporters that he was going to call it a day when Coolidge's term expired. And then? "Oh, Providence will look after me," he answered. But Coolidge's term expired, and again he put off the retirement. Mellon remembered his father's retirement: the Judge's years and years of fidgeting, the frustrations of a great mind limited to little matters. "Providence" had not looked after the Judge. A. W. was a man of courage, but he did have one dread: retirement—dread of the rich as well as of the not-so-rich.

Hoover unquestionably gave serious consideration to an involuntary retirement for Mellon. Couzens and the Republican senators of his ilk had somehow gotten the impression that their candidate for President would replace A. W., but Hoover appreciated that large segments of the business community would be repelled if Hoover failed to keep the greatest Secretary of the Treasury since Hamilton in his cabinet. And so he offered to retain A. W. Mellon, and the offer was accepted. "At my age," Mellon told the journalists, "I might as well work here as anywhere else. I have no plans about retiring."

No doubt Hoover discussed Mellon's continued tenure as Secretary with Hoover's early supporter, Undersecretary Ogden Mills. He discussed many things with Mills. Mills had served three terms in Congress, where his brilliance had brought him influence far beyond his seniority, and especially so on matters of taxation and finance. In 1926 he had made himself available for slaughter as the Republican candidate for governor of New York, and after being slaughtered by Al Smith he had replaced Winston as Mellon's undersecretary. Mills was of aristocratic background, and were this not a book about the Mellons, his financial standing would be described as "fabulously wealthy"; he had scarcely more of the "common touch" than A. W. had. Nonetheless, he was articulate and extroverted, and he enjoyed excellent relationships with many key congressmen. Among his close friends was Mellon's erstwhile nemesis, Congressman John Nance Garner, who by the late 1920s had become one of the most powerful Democrats in Congress, and was soon to become Speaker of the House. It is a tribute to the rich aristocrat (and to the populist Texan) that Garner knew Mills affectionately as "Little Auggie." Given his milieu, Mills was relatively liberal. As a member of the New York State Senate in the early part of the century, he was one of a handful of "respectables" to protest the expulsion of duly elected Socialist Party candidates from the New York legislature. Frank Kent, whose attitude toward the Mellons is reflected above, wrote that Mills was "one of the ablest men in public life. Clear-headed, informed, experienced, he is a man of character, courage and capacity."

Mellon had always relied heavily on his undersecretaries, but none more so than Mills. The Secretary's advancing age, Mills's expansive ways, and the greater rapport that Mills had with the President all contributed to Mellon's increased dependence on him. It was apparent to reporters who covered Treasury press conferences. Mills would sit beside Mellon, and after A. W. had mumbled his answer to a question Mills would interject, "The Secretary means thus-and-so." When it came to dealing with the White House, Hoover wrote in his memoirs that he was "relieved" whenever A. W. was on vacation, so that the President was "able to deal directly with Mr. Mills [who] had a younger and more vigorous mind than Mr. Mellon." Without knowing the titles that each man held, when one reads the transcribed phone conversations between Mellon and Mills that are preserved in the National Archives, one would assume that Mills was the Secretary of the Treasury, and Mellon one of his higher-ranking underlings. Little by little Mills supplanted A. W. as Secretary of the Treasury in all but title, and then in 1932 he supplanted him in title as well.

By nature, Hoover was an interfering man, and he kept a much more active eye on the operations of his various departments than Coolidge had, and played a more important role in their day-to-day operations. He involved himself in Treasury Department matters to the point of naming a Commissioner of Internal Revenue and an assistant secretary of the Treasury, over A. W.'s objections. Hoover's close supervision of the departments, and particularly the Treasury Department, coupled with Mills's position and influence with Mellon, enabled Hoover to permit Mellon's continued tenure in office, notwithstanding their differences. When Mellon, despite Mills's influence, offered unwelcome advice, it was simply ignored. In the Harding period A. W. would have resigned. Now, other than an occasional complaint to W. L., he was silent as his role was reduced to that of a cipher. At a later Gridiron Dinner of the Washington Press Club the journalists included a skit portraying John D. Rockefeller and A. W. as janitors, bantering as they swept up. "Well, Andy, when did you recognize your talent for janitor service?" asked Rockefeller. "To tell you the truth, John D., it was very early in the Hoover administration."

Then came the stock market crash and the Great Depression that followed, throughout which A. W. served as a lightning rod for the administration, paying, as a price for the privilege of serving, the total devastation of the reputation of the greatest Secretary of the Treasury since. Pearson and Allen captioned their 1931 *Washington Merry-Go-Round* sketch of Mellon as "The Man Who Stayed Too Long."

In October 1929 the bottom fell out of the stock market. From the mid-1920s on, it had been spiraling upward seemingly without end, fed by a speculative frenzy that had previously been seen in America only as a prelude to depressions of the past. By early 1928 stock prices were wildly out of proportion to actual or reasonably anticipatable corporate earnings, and many if not most responsible economists thought the situation unwholesome. The Secretary of the Treasury no doubt disapproved of excessive speculation—it was repugnant to everything that the Judge had taught him—but he was never fully satisfied that the speculation had reached "excessive" levels, and insofar as its effect on the nation was concerned, he told Charles Hamlin of the Federal Reserve Board that he did not foresee any harm from the speculation. His private opinion to Hamlin in April of 1929—six months from disaster—was that "expansion" in the market would continue for a long time.*

The market began its catastrophic descent on October 19, 1929, taking Mellon by surprise, but his reaction was delayed, as his father's had been to the 1873 crash. The market had been of little proper concern for the federal government or the Treasury Department, and personally no concern at all of Mellon. He had never been a "Wall Street type"—a market plunger and manipulator—and had never speculated himself. He had been a responsible man, an industrialist, a banker. The fellows who had gotten caught in the crash had been the gamblers, the knaves, and the fools—but mostly the knaves. Herbert Hoover has written that Mellon "had no use for certain varieties of New York banking, which he deemed were too often devoted

---

*The above characterization of A. W.'s attitudes is based on Hamlin's unpublished diary. W. L., however, wrote that A. W. had long seen danger signals and had regarded the speculation as excessive, but that he was afraid to take any steps that might set off a panic.

to tearing men down and picking their bones. When the boom broke he said, 'They deserved it.' " Mellon remembered, however, how the stock market panic of 1873 had seemingly precipitated a full-scale depression. When he saw Hamlin on October 29, 1929, the day that the market took its third and fatal submerging, he was depressed. He had thought that the New York "interests" would prevent what had happened, as J. P. Morgan had salvaged the situation during the panic of 1907. Indeed, the Morgan affiliates had attempted to do so again in 1929, only to abandon the task. Now Mellon feared that the market collapse would be the first act in a depression —as it had been in 1873.

In ascribing blame for the depression, liberals have always known to whom to look, and many responsible conservatives have agreed with the left's indictment of A. W. Arthur Krock wrote in his *Consent of the Governed and Other Deceits* that "by Coolidge's total reliance on the economic and monetary counsels of Secretary of the Treasury Andrew W. Mellon, he invited the deluge of 1929" and that the Mellon-Coolidge policies "led directly to the crash of the stock market in 1929 and the Great Depression."

Many "causes" have been suggested for the Great Depression, and many of the most commonly cited ones would seem to have involved A. W. Mellon: easy credit and "low" interest rates; official statements that might have been taken as an encouragement of the unwholesome trend of the stock market; and top-heavy distribution of wealth.

Easy credit and "low" interest rates have often been charged with encouraging the stock market speculation, premature overexpansion of industry, and other forms of unwise borrowing by all segments of the community, all of which were important to the ultimate crash and depression. Judge Mellon, who lived through the depressions of 1819 and 1873, wrote that both of them had resulted "from the same cause—excessive extension of credit and consequent expansion of values . . . The vitals of trade were destroyed by the canker work of credit; bloated inflation spread and increased until the decayed carcass dropped dead." He would probably have blamed easy money as the principal cause for what happened in 1929. If he were to have done so, he would have had to put a good share of the blame on his son, the Secretary of the Treasury. On balance, he would have been mistaken.

Mellon sat as an ex officio member of the Federal Reserve Board; but because of his status as Secretary of the Treasury he could wield very great influence on the board's doings, and from the start of his tenure he supported lower interest rates in board discussions. In his earliest talks with board officials in the spring of 1921 he supported a reduction in the Federal

Reserve discount rate—the rate on short-term loans made by the Federal Reserve to member banks—from 7 per cent to 6 per cent. To Governor William Harding's suggestion that the cut might revive speculation in the stock market, A. W. replied that a little speculation in the market would not be harmful, that the number of loans would not be greatly expanded, and that the decrease would have a good psychological effect. For 1921, in the midst of the recession of 1920–22, A. W.'s position almost certainly made good sense. Over time, the rates dropped. In a minor national economic retreat in 1926, Mellon's remedy remained the same: that the Federal Reserve should encourage a policy of liberality, looking toward easier money conditions and more credit.

After the slump of 1926 everything continued upward except for interest rates. By early 1929 President Hoover and a majority on the Federal Reserve Board favored increasing interest rates, principally as an effort to check stock market speculation. Mellon was opposed in general. He argued that the market speculation was not to any considerable extent dependent on interest rates, that it was beyond control of Federal Reserve policies, and that speculation would continue unabated regardless of the Federal Reserve's rates. He was not invariably opposed to increasing the Federal Reserve rate, though, and supported some proposals affecting specific areas, where that rate was out of line with prevailing local rates. Ultimately the board did raise the rates, with Mellon in active or passive dissent, but whether too late, too little, or irrelevantly, the crash came on anyway.

A.W. was almost certainly correct in his assumption that increasing the Federal Reserve rate would do nothing to check market speculation. Interest rates in the late 1920s were by previous standards on the high side. Rates on "margin loans"—loans by brokers to customers secured by the customers' stock holdings—were usually exorbitant during the wildest periods of the boom, and bore no relation to anything that the Federal Reserve was doing or might do. While increasing interest rates might have had some chilling effect on other forms of excessive borrowing, this effect would have been minimized by the influx of European capital seeking more advantageous interest rates than were available in lower-interest Europe. Attracting foreign investment capital to the United States would probably have had other adverse effects on the economic picture in America. Mellon was unquestionably a restraint on the raising of interest rates, but the net effect of his position on the subject was at most minimal, and probably totally irrelevant to the coming of the depression.

On other counts, Mellon does not fare so well.

In August of 1928, a full year before the crash, a Columbia University banking expert, Dr. Ralph W. Robey, writing in *Atlantic,* attributed the bull market to the optimistic statements of Mellon and Coolidge, made in what Robey regarded as an unfavorable economic climate. After the crash the bright statements were looked at more closely. The first of them came in the midst of the setback of 1926, when Mellon made the first of his optimistic forecasts, the net effect of which was to spark a market revival. Thereafter he made other encouraging statements. March 1927 (a full year before the start of the spectacular market rises): "The stock market seems to be going along in a very orderly fashion and I see no evidence of over-speculation." September 1928 (after the market was already out of hand): "There is no cause for worry. The high tide of prosperity will continue." January 1, 1929: Another bright picture for the year ahead. The market seemed to react to each statement with another upward move. A statement seemed to come from either Mellon or Coolidge after any major downturn, to reverse the trend and push it up yet another tick. By hindsight the statements were ill-advised, but at the time their actual content seemed relatively innocuous. In view of Mellon's private comments to Hamlin mentioned above, they were almost certainly sincere, not an effort to maintain an artificial prosperity for as long as possible.

Mellon also made some counterinflationary statements, none of which seem to have been picked up by historians of the period. In January of 1924 he lent his by-line to a "Thrift Week" article entitled "Success," which despite its nineteenth-century homilies included some good advice for the little man: Don't speculate unless you are rich; keep away from mines, oil wells, swamps (the Florida boom was under way), and mail order businesses; and most important, save—"If youth did know what age did crave, many a penny it would save." A year later he spoke out by implication against the Florida land bubble, which was crying to be burst, when he said that real estate speculation in some communities was threatening to "undermine the spirit of caution in business." Soon after, the bubble burst, destroying the life savings of thousands of big and little men. At the same time that Mellon warned against Florida speculations, he also spoke against "overexpansion," and against the "tendency of the consuming public to buy every conceivable commodity 'on time' and mortgage future earnings." His defenders might point to those statements as examples of sound advice that ran against the current of the times. Insofar as his public statements related to the stock market, however, they were not helpful.

Hoover was seriously concerned about the trend of the market, and thought that the federal government should take steps to put a damper on it before it exploded. At his insistence, the Secretary of the Treasury commented "informally" in March 1929 that bonds had become an especially attractive investment vehicle, inferentially steering investors away from the stock market. It was done so obliquely that its impact was minimal and quickly forgotten: "This does not mean that many stocks are not good investments. Some, however, are too high in price to be good buys. For prudent investors I would say, if making a suggestion, that now is the time to buy good bonds." With obvious annoyance, he told Federal Reserve member Eugene Meyer that he had made the statement only in response to presidential pressure. A more direct statement against stock speculation by the Federal Reserve Board, in the form of a directive against Federal Reserve credits being used for securities speculation, met with Mellon's disapproval. He regarded it as a form of radical control over stock exchange transactions, and probably as an unwarranted interference with private banking.

Perhaps the most important factor in causing the depression was the distribution of spendable money in the United States. An inordinate proportion of the wealth of the country was in the hands of the rich, who could put it to no good use. At best they could use it to build factories the output of which could not be bought because the bulk of potential consumers lacked the purchasing power to buy. Otherwise the wealthy could only put their money into speculations, aggravating the stock market. This state of affairs was at least in part the result of the Mellon tax policies, which freed up vast amounts of rich men's monies for unproductive uses.

Mellon's attitude as to the proper way of confronting the depression was founded on his fifty-six-year-old experience in the depression of 1873. At that time he had liquidated his lumber yard, and so had survived the crisis. The old experience provided a clue to his attitude toward minimizing the adverse effects of the depression of 1929. President Hoover wrote in his memoirs that Mellon

> felt that government must keep its hands off and let the slump liquidate itself. Mr. Mellon had only one formula: "Liquidate labor, liquidate stocks, liquidate the farmers, liquidate real estate." He insisted that, when the people get an inflation brainstorm, the only way to get it out of their blood is to let it collapse. He held that even a panic was not altogether a bad thing. He said: "It will purge the rottenness out of the system. High costs of living and high living will come down. People will work harder, live a more moral life. Values will be adjusted, and enterprising people will pick up the wrecks from less competent people."

It sounded like the lesson of the Great Teacher, the Judge:

> Nothing but a process of general liquidation could determine what any man
> owned or was worth. The stock had to be boiled down to evaporate the water
> from it. Real and fictitious wealth had become so mixed up that the refining
> process of bankruptcy and sheriff's sales became necessary to separate the
> dross from the true metal. And when in this way the real owners of property
> and wealth were ascertained, they were found to be only the few who had paid
> as they went, or confined their business and speculative operations to what was
> clearly within their power to hold.

Hoover went on to say that Mellon "often used the expression 'There is a
mighty lot of real estate lying around the United States which does not
know who owns it,' referring to excessive mortgages." The Judge said,
"Property of all kinds remained, but it was set afloat in search of its true
owners."

A. W. recounted for Hoover the experience of 1873, and the lessons of
it. The same wistful recollections he shared with others. Thomas L. Stokes
recalled in *Chip off My Shoulder* a press conference on the heels of a healthy
crop report at which A. W. was "chatty and optimistic":

> Agricultural recovery had lifted the country from the great and terrible
> depression that began in 1873 and lasted into 1881. Off he went into the past.
> He related how, in that time, he had been sent out to Colorado by his father
> to sell wagons, a young man with a business career. The present vanished for
> him. He lived in his youth as he talked and talked. America had come from
> that depression.

America had come from that depression, and it would come from this one
as well; recovery would come, as it always had, because it always had.
Unless, that is, governmental action were to interfere with natural economic
doctoring. The "boiling out" process had to be permitted its run, and the
sooner the better. Artificial supports of prices or wages would only prolong
everyone's agony and the deprivation of the most wretched. Hoover's Secretary of State, Henry L. Stimson, who had considerable admiration and
affection for Mellon, characterized a Mellon discourse on the subject at a
cabinet meeting as "childlike."

Hoover was of a very different mind than Mellon:

> I, of course, reminded the secretary that back in the seventies an untold
> amount of suffering did take place which might have been prevented; that our
> economy had been far simpler sixty years ago, when we were 75 per cent an
> agricultural people contrasted with 30 per cent now; that unemployment dur-

ing the earlier crisis had been mitigated by the return of large numbers of the unemployed to relatives on the farms; and that farm economy itself had been largely self-contained. But he shook his head with the observation that human nature had not changed in sixty years.

Secretary Mellon was not hard-hearted. In fact he was generous and sympathetic with all suffering. He felt there would be less suffering if his course were pursued.

Hoover was the first President in American history to recognize a role for the federal government in grappling directly with an economic crisis. He was unwilling simply to permit nature to take its course. Many of his efforts were ones with which A. W. could and did sympathize. His first reaction was to cut interest rates and income taxes, in the hope that greater abundance of money would encourage increased production, thereby lessening unemployment, increasing spendable wages, and thus generally stimulating the depressed economy. Mellon supported these wise proposals. Later, in 1931, with the government falling more deeply into debt and the federal budget into increasingly more alarming disbalance, Hoover called for retrenchment and a radical increase in taxes. Even at the time, such a position should have been recognized as representing the worst possible counter-depression strategy, but it was strongly supported by Democratic House Speaker Garner and implicitly supported by New York's Governor Franklin D. Roosevelt, as well as by Mellon.

The Secretary called for approaches that would "broaden the base" of the income tax—make more people subject to it—and impose some unprogressive taxes; but he also supported a substantial increase in the maximum surtax on the rich. According to Hoover, he privately urged the President to tax the rich even more heavily than the President proposed. At first he was out of sympathy with Hoover's 1931 proposal for a "moratorium" on intergovernmental debt payments, but after personal study of the economic situation in Europe he became an enthusiastic supporter of the President's plan.

For the most part, however, Mellon was much out of step with the President. Hoover characterized one difference between them for Stimson, who recorded it in his diary: "He told me that he always believed in going out to meet a situation rather than to let it come and commented on Mellon's habit of doing the other thing." The President had oversimplified. It was not that A. W. did not believe in going out to meet a situation; it was that he believed that the depression should not be "met" actively. He believed in the cyclical nature of the capitalist economy. Automatic "rightings" of the economic wheel were inevitable when they were needed to purge the system, and though sometimes very painful, they were ultimately beneficial. There was nothing that could or should be done other, perhaps, than to relieve some suffering through temporary welfare assistance, which could best be handled—and financed—on a local level. In the historical perspective, Hoover's contrary attitude made him, not Mellon, out of step.

The relations between the President and his ostensible Secretary grew more distant and, ultimately, strained and sour. A. W.'s advice was treated with a studied neglect. In a discussion with W. L. in November 1929 about one of the President's "erroneous" moves, "A. W. shrugged his shoulders. By that time he was getting used to having his advice ignored." According to W. L., A.W. "was disappointed rather than irked whenever this happened."

Later the President became bitter toward the Secretary for failure of the Mellon enterprises to respond to administration pleas for business cooperation in battling the depression. Early in the depression Hoover asked business and industry not to cut wages but to hold the line, thereby preserving the purchasing power of their employees. Wage cuts would only aggravate the downward spiral of the economy. American business did hold the line for as long as it otherwise suited the business community to do so—and no longer. It ceased to suit business around 1931. One of the first major employers to begin systematic wage cuts was Alcoa. In October of 1931 it ordered a 10 per cent across-the-board pay cut, which it followed with another 10 per cent cut the following June. Gulf also imposed a 10 per cent pay cut in June of 1932, and the rest of the Mellon companies—like most American employers—followed suit. At a time when the federal government was embarking on major public works in a pump-priming effort and urging private enterprise to undertake capital projects with the same thought in mind, Gulf announced the day after the 1930 elections that it would begin a gradual slowdown of work on its gigantic Gulfport construction project at Staten Island, New York, which would put 2500 construction workers out of work. A group of labor leaders journeyed to Washington to seek A. W.'s intervention with Gulf to keep the Gulfport project going. They got as far as Colonel Arthur Woods, chairman of Hoover's Emergency Employment Committee, but Woods's committee member, A. W. Mellon, was out to them. Gulf's shutdown was a major blow to the Staten Island community, outbalancing the beneficial effect of the construction of a dozen post offices. Before the end of Hoover's term all of the Mellon companies had laid off large percentages of their regular work forces. (In Pittsburgh, however, A. W. and R. B. sponsored two major construction projects—the East Liberty Presbyterian Church and a new Mellon Institute building—both of which employed large numbers of men over long periods.) At a time when the administration, speaking through the Secretary of the Treasury, was urging public cooperation to make stepped-up income tax rates effective, A. W. was devising ways to reduce his own taxes to levels that he himself might regard as "fair."

Hoover was especially concerned about the bad effect of bank failures. He urged the banking community to support its own to preserve any and all banks from folding. When the Bank of Pittsburgh, the only substantial competitor of Union Trust and Mellon National, looked to be going under, Hoover personally took an interest in putting together a syndicate to rescue it. They fell a million or so short. Though R. B. and his son R. K. were inclined to help bail out their competitor, A. W. said no. Hoover was outraged in reporting to Stimson that "Mr. Mellon had allowed the big Bank of Pittsburgh to fail just because he was unwilling to subscribe his million dollars when three of the four million had already been made up by others. That, the President said, had thrown a tremendous waterblanket upon the efforts of other bankers to stay the situation." Hoover opposed recognition of the Soviet Union, while the Koppers Company sold the Russians engineering services. Hoover could hardly expect voluntary cooperation from the business community when his own Secretary of the Treasury and the Secretary's businesses declined to cooperate on every front.

Personal charity to alleviate personal suffering was another matter. The Mellons contributed significantly. In 1931 A. W., R. B., and W. L. contributed a total of $1,090,000 to the Allegheny County Welfare Fund, largely as a "challenge" contribution, more than one-sixth of its total budget. The following year A. W. and R. B. each gave $100,000. R. B.'s wife, Jennie, an expansive and generous person, hired an extra cook and provided a dining room for the homeless, hopeless men who knocked at the door of R. B.'s mansion. She personally prepared the menus for her "guests." No doubt the Mellons performed many such quiet acts of charity. One of those reported was to the effect that A. W. had personally paid the return fare from Washington to Pittsburgh of 276 stranded members of "Father Cox's Army," the remainder of 12,000 who had staged a hunger march principally from Allegheny County to Washington.

One of those to whom A. W. offered help refused it: William Andrew Mellon, aged son of the Judge's brother Samuel. William Andrew sometimes served as the Judge's clerk, and was associated with him in Kansas City at the *Leader*. In 1934 a Pittsburgh "relief worker" discovered him living shabbily in a back alley cluttered with discarded packagings and rusting cans. He had no coal. A. W. immediately offered him a comfortable home, but the cousin told the press, "I like it here and would not consent. I work, dream, read and think. What more could a man want?" He accepted one gift from the world's third-richest man: a typewriter.

The world's third-richest man fared less well. The depression knocked the rich man off his pedestal; the confidence of the masses in the business elite was shattered forever. The Mellons were probably the first of the rich to be recognized as fallible. Frank Kent, during a trip to Pittsburgh, noted the change in local attitudes toward Allegheny's first family:

> Today the respect is diluted, the reverence confined to a much smaller group and the influence vastly diminished. Three years ago a visitor here could not fail to be impressed with the high regard in which the Mellons were held. The name of Mellon—particularly that of Andrew W. Mellon—was almost a sacred name. There is nothing sacred about it now. Men spoke of him then in confidential whispers. Such little criticism as was heard came from unimportant persons and was cautious and restrained. The Mellon interests were above real criticism. The family could do no wrong.
>
> Today the town is full of uncomplimentary stories about them. Men sit around tables in clubs and relate one unpleasant incident after another about this Mellon and that Mellon, which are apparently enjoyed by one and all. . . . The awe is gone; the worship has ended; the glamour has utterly disappeared.

Of course the opprobrium was heaped mostly upon A. W., just as he had enjoyed the acclaim of the good years. In the period 1929 to 1932 he became the most abused Secretary of the Treasury since Alexander Hamilton (who was also very much abused in his day). The economists did the most devastating job on him. The "apparent" folly of his tax policies was pounced upon by men who had not commented on the apparent when Mellon had been riding high. And why had he not paid off the national debt in the mid-1920s, when it could have been done, the interest on which was so crushing during the depression? Kindlier Democrats took to calling him "the greatest Secretary of the Treasury since Carter Glass," Wilson's Secretary of the Treasury from 1918 to 1920. Less kindly critics spoke of him less kindly. "A thief and a scalawag," cried the colorful Oklahoma governor, "Alfalfa Bill" Murray. The Kingfish, Huey Long, made "Mellonism" one of his favorite speech topics; and the nobody congressman from Texarkana, Wright Patman, bellowed at 2000 at a Lamar County, Texas, rally, "Now that we have just gotten rid of Al Capone, let's get rid of another public enemy!" The crowd roared its approval. When a Republican congressman attempted at the close of the 71st Congress to invoke the name and supposed influence of "the greatest Secretary of the Treasury since Alexander Hamilton," Congress howled in derision. Mellon had never been comfortable about that label, and thereafter toastmasters were cautioned against using it in introductions. Depression-related suicides were not as common as they would seem to have been from the folk literature of the 1920s, but at least one witty twenty-five-year-old, Wellington Lytle, wrote a note bequeathing "my soul to Andrew W. Mellon and my sympathy to my creditors" before putting a bullet through his head in a Milwaukee hotel room.

The good times and the acclaim had brought A. W. Mellon out of his shell. The bad times brought derision, and a retreat from the limelight to which he had so recently become accustomed. Stokes wrote that

> in the early thirties when the depression enveloped Washington like a clammy fog that would not lift but only got heavier, he again became the uncertain little man. His economic theories wouldn't fit, his words no longer would act like magic. He propounded into the encircling gloom in vain. Once more he was the lonely and tragic figure wandering down the street at night peering into the windows.

He had come to enjoy his bantering with the newsmen. Now the visits from the journalists were again painful experiences for him. And who was this Mencken? Where did anyone get the gall to write things referring to "a senile country banker like Andy"—and to publish them in a supposedly respectable newspaper like the *Sun?* And "Andy." Andy? No, he would not grant an interview, he told the journalists as he disembarked in Europe in July of 1931. He did not grant interviews outside of the United States— "and as few as possible therein," he added.

Almost from the start of his career as Secretary of the Treasury A. W. had difficulty with different elements within Congress on isolated policy issues. There was also a continuing strain of hostility toward him from progressive Republicans and populist Democrats which transcended specific issues. Georgia's Democratic Senator Tom Watson, twice the populist People's Party candidate for President, was the first to raise the question in Congress that A. W. had anticipated from the outset: Was Mellon even eligible to hold the office of Secretary? Were not his staggering investments an indirect interest in carrying on trade, making him ineligible to serve as Secretary of the Treasury consistent with the 1789 law? Watson was not satisfied with the legalistic response of A. W.'s defenders, but most people were.*A couple of years later Democratic Senator Kenneth McKellar of

---

*Watson was an interesting fellow, sometime publisher of the *Weekly Jeffersonian* and other magazines and the author of biographies of Jefferson, Jackson, and Bonaparte and of a history of France. He frequently peppered his attacks against industrialists and financiers with out-

Tennessee raised the same question. Senator David Reed's authoritative response seemed to cover the ground, McKellar's motion to investigate died, and the question seemed ended once and for all. A. W. was less fortunate when he locked horns with Senator James Couzens at about the same time.

James Couzens was poor born in Canada in 1872, but by 1903 he had risen to the position of general manager and second-in-command of Henry Ford's company. In 1914 he had a falling out with Ford which ultimately led to Ford buying out Couzens's interest in the Ford Motor Company for almost $30 million. He became active in Republican politics and in 1918 was elected mayor of Detroit. Re-elected in 1920, in 1922 he was appointed to a vacant seat in the United States Senate. There he fell in with the La Follette-Norris progressives on most issues and became their leader on matters of taxation and finance. Couzens was forceful, hot-tempered, and abrupt; and as the richest man in Congress he was not impressed by money or by those who had money. He became known as the "millionaire radical," principally because of his support for high taxes on the rich. He viewed Mellon's tax plan as an effort to shift the burden of paying for government from those who could afford to pay to those who could not. He didn't much like Mellon either.

In 1924 Couzens inaugurated a correspondence with Mellon over tax policy with a letter that, for Couzens, was uncharacteristically polite. Mellon responded with one that was uncharacteristically unpolite. Couzens sent one back a little nastier, to which A. W. responded with real venom. Couzens had invested virtually all of his many millions in tax-free state and local bonds, he explained, so that he would be free from any possible conflict of interest. Mellon's letter clearly implied that that was not the reason at all. It pointed out that Couzens paid no income tax whatsoever, despite his million-dollar-a-year income, because of the exemption from federal income tax of state and local bonds, and suggested that "some change in the law might render [Couzens's investments] much less valuable." He cited Couzens's supposed investment strategy as evidence that the surtax against the rich had become "uncollectible." Couzens responded with an equally undiplomatic letter implying, as Mellon had, that his correspondent was motivated solely by self-interest. ("Will you please tell . . . how much you will benefit by the reduction of surtaxes as proposed by you?") Mellon's heated

---

bursts against blacks and Catholics. By the time of his attack on A. W. he was most noted for his virulent anti-Semitism, which caused the Post Office to bar his publications from the mails. He died in 1922, not long after his attack on A. W., to the satisfaction not alone of A. W. Mellon.

response to Couzens's first letter was entirely out of character for him; it became an open secret in Washington that the Secretary's coterie of "bright young men" had been responsible for embroiling him in what was to become known as "the battle of the millionaires."

Couzens escalated the feud by introducing a resolution in the Senate calling for an investigation of the Internal Revenue Service, and particularly of its refunds to large corporate taxpayers. An Internal Revenue code lays out the basic law as to what is and is not taxable income, and what are or are not proper deductions from income, but administrative regulations and determinations must flesh out the broad outline of the statute book. Those determinations are invariably influenced by departmental policy biases. The administration's policy during the Mellon era was decidedly pro-business, and lopsidedly in favor of megabusiness. During Mellon's administration the nation's major corporations were largely relieved of paying gray-area taxes by I.R.S.'s friendly attitudes and rulings. Many of the biggest took advantage of the favorable climate to right past wrongs by filing amended tax returns for years gone by, requesting rebates of "excessive" tax payments "erroneously" made in prior years. Matthew Josephson later wrote that the I.R.S. became "cluttered up with mobs of corporation accountants and lawyers, all demonstrating how oddly 'stupid' they had been in other times, what whimsical errors of overpayments of taxes had been made, the sum of which they drew up and had duly honored by the treasurer."

Lamentable errors had been made by U.S. Steel, Standard Oil of California, Bethlehem Steel, Du Pont, the Hearst newspapers, and countless others, including a few Mellon businesses—Gulf, Alcoa, Standard Steel Car, Union Trust and Mellon National. Among those individual (as opposed to corporate) taxpayers who had made sloppy errors in the past was one A. W. Mellon of Pittsburgh, who received $72,000 in rebates. The bulk of that $72,000, rebated on A. W.'s 1926 return, arose from his having included the same income entry twice, thereby resulting in an overpayment by him, which was properly refunded. The propriety of the refund was never seriously questioned by his enemies, but they occasionally mentioned it, no doubt for its embarrassment value.

In the period 1922–26 the Treasury paid out rebates of over a billion dollars for "overpaid" taxes to the nation's leading businesses—plus 6 per cent interest. Though the line of corporate mendicants outside the Treasury's doors became so long as to attract the attention of the well informed, there was not a word of it in the daily papers. Couzens was outraged. He determined to expose what he regarded as secret government charity to the unneedy. The Senate authorized an investigating committee to proceed, with Couzens as one of its members, and at his inducement the committee began its task by taking a close look at the rebates made to the Mellon companies. The Couzens hearings went on and on, filling several fat volumes with testimony. The upshot of it all was that few if any of the Treasury's positions were clearly inconsistent with the statute. The Mellon companies had not received greater consideration than that extended to the other giants, all of whom, to Couzens's way of thinking, had received much too much consideration. The fault was in the department's policy orientation and its lack (since remedied) of written guidelines. But that was a matter of policy, and as to matters of policy, Couzens was out of step with the majority and with the times.

It was clear to Mellon that the sole purpose of Couzens's inquest was to embarrass him—a not wholly unwarranted conclusion when one considers the senator's point of departure with Gulf, Alcoa, and Mellon National. Mellon too could pull out stops. Couzens's interim appointment would expire in 1924, at which time he would have to stand for re-election. Two "regulars" stepped forward to challenge him in the Michigan Republican primary for the Senate seat. Mellon permitted, if indeed he did not encourage, Undersecretary Garrard Winston, to take an active part in behind-the-scenes maneuverings to get one of the two regulars to withdraw, thereby increasing possibilities for unseating Couzens. When that failed and Couzens was re-elected by a majority of enormous proportions, the Internal Revenue Service at last undertook its duty to investigate Couzens. He had no monopoly on such courses.

At the time that Couzens sold his stock in Ford Motor Company to Henry Ford, the government was entitled to a tax on the "profit" that Couzens had realized from his sale. Usually profit is easy enough to figure —it is the difference between selling price and cost—but because Couzens had owned his Ford stock long prior to the adoption of the income tax, his "cost" basis was the value of his Ford stock at the time of adoption of the income tax in 1913. A high 1913 value meant a lower "profit" for tax purposes, and a lower tax to pay; a low 1913 valuation would cost Couzens a higher final tax. In 1913 Ford stock was not publicly traded; its value as of 1913 was something on which reasonable men could reasonably disagree. Especially so if they made their computations years later. When Couzens sold in 1919, he declined to do the figuring but invited I.R.S. to make its own valuations, offering to accept their figures. Commissioner of Internal Revenue Daniel C. Roper, one of the all-time great commissioners of Internal Revenue, ultimately valued the Couzens Ford stock as of 1913 at $20,686,761.20. As the selling price to Ford was $29,308,857.90, Couzens's tax was computed on a profit of $8,622,096.70. With a maximum tax in 1919 of 73 per cent, Couzens's tax bill came pretty close to his entire "profit"; and with his other income, he paid a tax for the year of the sale totaling $7,229,161.75.

Just a few days before the statute of limitations would have barred reconsideration of the case, Mellon's I.R.S. notified Couzens that it felt Roper's 1913 valuation was inordinately high, and presented him with a bill for an additional $10,861,131.50 in taxes, computed at the high 1919 tax rates. The bill threatened to eat up half of Couzens's fortune. He screamed that Internal Revenue's conduct in attempting to upset its former determinations at such a time constituted bald reprisal, designed to punish him for his interest in I.R.S.'s activities. Virginia's conservative Democratic senator, Carter Glass, who generally supported Mellon policies, had been Secretary of the Treasury at the time of Roper's determination, and stood by it. He insisted that the matter had been reopened "simply because [Mellon] and the senator from Michigan hate each other." Commissioner David Blair defended the department against such charges; the Secretary himself, of course, took no interest in the matter.

The Couzens tax case dragged on before the Board of Tax Appeals for as long as did the Couzens investigation. Now Mellon seemed to take a greater interest in assisting his Internal Revenue Service than he had taken in helping it to trace the Teapot Dome bonds. Among the unpublished letters in the Treasury's files is correspondence from none other than A. W. himself to H. C. McEldowney at Union Trust, seeking McEldowney's assistance in scouting out the best possible witnesses for the government to testify as to the 1913 value of Ford stock. Similar correspondence went to Mellon's crony at Bethlehem Steel, Charles M. Schwab, and to General Motors head John J. Raskob, a Democrat but a reactionary likely to disapprove of the likes of Couzens. For the Secretary of the Treasury to take such a role in a routine collection matter warrants the conclusion that it was not at all a routine matter, lending weight to a conclusion that Mellon kept his "hats" most neatly separated when it most suited him, and to Couzens's insistence that he was persecuted because of his friction with the Treasury Department and its chief. The Board of Tax Appeals, presided over by a conservative Republican, Ernest H. Van Fossen, finally resolved the Couzens case with a determination that Roper had *under*valued the stock as of 1913, which thereby increased the 1919 "profit" (for tax purposes) to Couzens and the tax bill that he had paid. The senator, therefore, was now entitled to a rebate of $900,000! He regarded it as something of a victory, but it was a mixed victory, as his expenses of litigation probably absorbed much of the rebate.

When Couzens announced the Treasury's move against him on the floor of the Senate, he was interrupted by Senator McKellar: "Does the Senator regard this as a sort of effort to intimidate him, and will it have any effect upon the further investigation of that department?" Yes, Couzens regarded it as an attempt to intimidate him, but no, no he would not be intimidated. Indeed, he said, the Treasury's action would only make him more energetic. And it did. When it looked as if he had about exhausted the matter of the corporate rebates, at the suggestion of Pennsylvania governor Gifford Pinchot he began to turn his attention to the Treasury Department's enforcement of prohibition (he was a "wet" himself), retaining as his special investigator Francis J. Heney, a celebrated California prosecutor who came to him with Pinchot's highest possible recommendation. Pinchot and Couzens disagreed about prohibition, but they agreed about Mellon. As the investigating committee had not been allowed a budget for staff, Couzens personally paid Heney's salary. Mellon made public protest that the Couzens investigation was an effort to "vent some personal grievance," and that its effect would be to "threaten the institution of government itself." President Coolidge followed up with his own protest of the course of "Government by lawlessness," in an overcharged letter couched in muddled constitutional argument. Couzens seemingly brought out the worst in men. Ultimately Congress passed an appropriation for the hiring of a staff to pursue the investigation, with the understanding that Heney would not be part of it. Nothing came of it, or of the battle of the millionaires, except considerable unhappiness for A. W. Mellon. Unhappiness was something to which Mellon had long been accustomed.

Sniping, as A. W. would have regarded it, continued after the close of the Couzens hearings. In the Senate, Couzens and McKellar kept up their attacks on him, sometimes relieved by Mississippi's Democratic Senator Pat Harrison, who was upset about prohibition enforcement. In the House, Garner took a renewed interest in the Secretary—about as friendly an interest as his old interest had been—his troops rallied by the ostensibly Republican congressman from New York City, Fiorello La Guardia, and by that crazy upstart Patman. After Hoover's election, Couzens, McKellar, Republican Senator Gerald P. Nye of South Dakota, and Democratic Senator Burton K. Wheeler of Montana made clear that they would lead a fight against Senate confirmation of Mellon as Hoover's Secretary of the Treasury.

Hoover's response was his announcement that he did not have to resubmit A. W.'s name. As the Senate had once confirmed Mellon, there was no need for him to send the name back to it for "reconfirmation," and he did not propose to do so. A. W. would simply continue to serve in the office for which he had previously been confirmed. The progressives' motion to have the Judiciary Committee consider the propriety of Hoover's position, and Mellon's eligibility to serve as Secretary of the Treasury, carried; but as the bull market was still on the upswing, the move against Mellon was still premature. The Judiciary Committee's brief majority report, signed by nine now-forgotten senators, resolved both questions in favor of Hoover and Mellon, but the lengthy and well-reasoned separate dissents of progressives George Norris and William E. Borah (Idaho Republican), and that of the Teapot Dome inquisitor Thomas Walsh, provided much of the argument and recapitulation of evidence that would enable Patman to mount the successful assault when times were "brighter" in 1932.

Wright Patman was born in 1893 in a log cabin at a tiny Texas settlement that no longer exists. As a young man he worked on a cotton farm. After World War I service he pursued law studies at a small Tennessee college, and then began practice in Cass County, Texas. He rose to be district attorney for his judicial district, and then entered the Texas House of Representatives, where he shared a desk with Representative Sam Johnson, whose son Lyndon was to become something of a someone. Patman entered Congress in 1929 (and left it on death in 1976) and there he devoted himself to seemingly hopeless causes, such as his advocacy of a cash bonus for World War I veterans (it passed in 1936), and to denouncing the outrages perpetrated against the nation and mankind by Andrew W. Mellon. In January 1932 he rose on the floor of the House to demand the impeachment of the Secretary of the Treasury. His long impeachment resolution dragged out all the tired charges that had previously been aired by Watson and McKellar and put to rest. There was nothing new of any significance. Most commentators agreed with the Baltimore *Sun:* "No one is likely to get very excited over Representative Patman's move to impeach Secretary Mellon except Mr. Patman himself." There were some differences, though—not in the charges but in the setting. Previously the demands for impeachment had originated in the Senate, the wrong chamber for initiation of impeachment proceedings. This was the first time that the demand had arisen in the appropriate body. More important, until the early 1930s A. W. Mellon had been "unimpeachable." His public standing had been so high that few could seriously consider such a ridiculous proposition as impeachment. That situation had been changed by the Great Depression. The hunter was different too. He was a "rube" Texan like Garner; but Garner's warm personal relationship with "respectable" people like Ogden Mills and the great Speaker of the House Longworth lulled one into a sweet, secret confidence that Garner's numerous attacks on "Uncle Andy," as he called Mellon, were made with crossed fingers. None of Garner's forays had ever done the Secretary himself any harm. But this Patman was something else. He was resolute and determined.

The Patman hearings began on January 13, 1932, and in their brief life recapitulated all the old charges that had been made against the Secretary. The thrust of Patman's charge was that Mellon's vast holdings, including dominant interest in key elements of key industries, indirectly "concerned" him "in carrying on the business of trade or commerce." The purpose of the old law had been explained by President James K. Polk's Attorney General, Nathan Clifford, as

> to withdraw from the accounting officers of the Treasury every motive of private interest in the performance of their public duties and to guard the Nation from the consequences frequently to be apprehended when the business affairs of public officers are suffered to lie commingled with the financial concerns of the country.

In his presentation Patman presented examples of how that "commingling" had manifested itself in the Treasury under Mellon: in the refunds to Mellon companies; the vastly increased use of aluminum in public buildings; the ratification by the Republic of Colombia of a disputed oil concession that had been acquired by Gulf Oil, at a time that Colombia was hard pressed for American banking credits; in the setting of tariffs. In the final analysis, however, there was no proof of any direct improprieties, and the central question lay as a question of law. No one gave a more comprehensible answer to the question than Senator Norris, whose comment was incorporated into the Patman hearing transcript:

> The question might be simplified by asking: Is a person owning stock in a corporation even indirectly concerned or interested in the business of such corporation? In this simplified form the question answers itself.
>
> To deny that the owner of stock in a corporation is interested in the business of such corporation is a violation of all logic and reason; and to assert that the owner of such stock is not even indirectly "concerned or interested" in the business of the corporation must impress the minds of honest people as being ridiculous. When we add to this the proposition that the ownership of stock in a corporation is substantial and that in connection with the stock owned by relatives and close business associates it constitutes a controlling interest in the corporation, and in some cases constitutes the ownership of practically all the

outstanding stock of the corporation, we have reached a point where no reasonable mind, by any possibility, can conceive that the owner of such stock is not only indirectly, but directly and positively interested in the business of the corporation.

A. W.'s case was presented by Alexander W. Gregg, former chief counsel of the Internal Revenue Service, who had presented the Treasury's case against Couzens at the Board of Tax Appeals. While Patman took a broad "practical" approach, Gregg tried to walk a fine line of legality that required blindness to realities. His presentation showed a quick legal mind adept at devising the forms necessary to surmount technical hurdles which might obstruct the route to forbidden ends.

Gregg conceded that the corporations in which Mellon owned stock were involved in trade, but A. W. was not a majority stockholder in any single enterprise. He placed special significance on the fact that A. W. was just another stockholder, and he relied upon what lawyers call "the corporate veil" to insulate A. W. from any interest in trade or commerce. In an exchange with the young New York congressman Emanuel Celler he said that

The ownership of a large block of stock, so long as it be a minority of the stock; it does not make any difference whether you own, say five shares, or own 49 per cent of the stock. And that is the case with Mr. Mellon. He does not own more than 50 per cent of any of the stock. As to control of more than 50 per cent, it might be a different question. Personally, I do not think it would

Mr. Celler. Do you not think that where stock is widely scattered, 30 per cent of it, or even 20 per cent, might give control, particularly where there are a great many stockholders who are scattered and unorganized? They might control it with 25 per cent of the stock, and there are cases where even 20 per cent is sufficient to control.

Mr. Gregg. It would give them control over the election of directors and officers, and over the very few things that have to come before the stockholders, such as a sale of the assets of the corporation, or dissolution, consolidation, or merger. But while the corporation is operating a 99 per cent ownership is not any better, as a matter of law, than a 1 per cent ownership.

Mr. Celler. Except that if they have the power to elect directors, and then they have that minority interest which is unified, they have the power to control the operations of the company?

Mr. Gregg. That is very true. They have the power to elect directors. But after the directors are elected they have no power whatever over them, whether they have 99 per cent or 1 per cent of the stock.

He did a lot of question begging. West Virginia Congressman Carl G. Bachmann asked him,

> Do I infer from what you say, Mr. Gregg, that Mr. Mellon and his family do not own the control in any of these corporations?
> Mr. Gregg. I do not know.
> Mr. Bachmann. You do not know?
> Mr. Gregg. I know that Mr. Mellon does not.
> Mr. Bachmann. Mr. Mellon himself controls no corporation at all?
> Mr. Gregg. He, himself, controls no corporations at all; no.
> Mr. Bachmann. But whether his family do you do not know?
> Mr. Gregg. Whether his family and his business associates do, I do not know; whether he and his family do, I do not know.

Sometimes he was less than candid, as in his discussion of the I.R.S.'s independence from the rest of the Treasury and its secretary:

> I was in the Treasury Department from 1920 to 1927, and never yet have I known the secretary to indicate any opinion or desire—or to consider, as a matter of fact, any individual tax case. I have gone to him on matters of policy, naturally; but never have I asked him to consider a specific case, and never have I known of his doing it.

He feigned ignorance about who might have purchased A. W.'s interests in Union Trust at the time that A. W. had become Secretary, but he knew enough of the transaction to be able to assert categorically that the same had been an outright sale, and that the stock was not being "held for his interest, even remotely—that he has no interest in it at all."

A. W. decided at that time to advise the committee that R. B. Mellon had been the purchaser of the stock; it was a detail that the committee was almost certain to find out about anyway. He did not disclose the particulars of the sale and purchase until testifying on another matter years later. A. W. "sold" the stock to R. B. but carried full financing of the sale price at a rate of interest equal to what the dividend yield had been on the stock. R. B. never paid anything at all on the principal debt due for the purchase price, but as Union's yield increased, R. B. voluntarily and without any pre-agreement to do so increased his interest payments to A. W. so that the interest payment to A. W. would exactly equal the amount of dividends that the former A. W. block of Union Trust was paying to R. B. The net effect was that A. W. continued to receive precisely the same amount of income in the form of interest from his former Union Trust holdings as he would have received as dividends if he had continued to hold Union Trust's stock. The dates on which the interest payments were due were changed to coincide with the date on which Union Trust paid its dividends. When Union issued new shares, A. W. lent R. B. exactly as much money as would be necessary to purchase enough of the new issue to maintain the proportionate share in Union of the former A. W. block, on the same terms as the initial sale to R. B.

Ultimately R. B. sold the former A. W. block to A. W.'s son, Paul, for exactly the same price as he had "paid" A. W. (though the market price of Union had doubled in the interim)—the full amount of which was still an outstanding debt—with Paul to take over the debt to his father. A. W. later "forgave" most of the debt on the purchase price. He later testified that there had never been any understanding that that was how things were to turn out; they had just worked out that way. By the time of Patman's inquiry they had already worked out that way. The course of A. W.'s block in Union Trust makes it very difficult to believe that A. W. could have taken no interest in Union's well-being while Secretary of the Treasury and member of the Federal Reserve Board.

In any event it is clear that, except insofar as legal title was concerned (not an important matter as between brothers and lifelong partners), his interest in Union Trust after the "sale" to R. B. remained exactly what it had been before the sale. Had Patman's inquiry proceeded, the history of A. W.'s Union Trust stock would almost certainly have come out at the time. The practical—even if unintended—sham of his divestiture of Union Trust would have been apparent to everyone but Senator Smoot (Republican, Ut.). Patman was just warming up when the issue became moot.

A. W. Mellon was seventy-six when Patman was getting under way. He had suffered more than two years of constant abuse for having "caused" the depression, but he had been permitted no input in its cure. W. L. wrote that

> the work was obviously becoming too much for him. It was apparent to all of us who loved A. W. that he was being completely worn out by the pressure of his treasury duties . . . with the country plunged into one of the worst depressions in history. . . . I think A. W. felt that it was time a younger man took over.

Charles Dawes was returning from his recent post as ambassador to Great Britain; the position was open. The author cannot say whether Mellon was "kicked upstairs" by Hoover or whether A. W. requested the transfer. Contemporary Pittsburgh newspaper reports insist that it was Hoover's decision, that the President enlisted Senator Reed's assistance to hard-sell A. W. the ambassadorship, and that A. W.'s only alternative was to be shown the exit. In any case, on February 3, 1932, the President announced that

> The critical situation facing all countries in their international relations, the manifold economic and other problems demanding wise solution in our national interests calls for experience and judgment of the highest order. The importance to our country of the sound determination of these world-wide difficulties needs no emphasis.
>
> I have decided therefore to call upon one of our wisest and most experienced public servants to accept a position which will enable him after many years of distinguished public service at home to render equal service to his country in the foreign field.
>
> I have asked Mr. Mellon to undertake the Ambassadorship to Great Britain. I am happy to say he has now expressed his willingness to serve.

In years past the stock market had trembled at any suggestion that A. W. might leave his post. Now it ignored his departure. For the day that his resignation was announced, the New York *Times* characterized trading on the New York Stock Exchange as having been "the dullest in the last five or six years." News of the resignation had caused "not even a ripple."

A. W. told Secretary of State Stimson that he was a little worried about the new assignment, especially about his health (the English climate never agreed with A. W.), but that he had made up his mind to go. As he explained it to the journalists,

> We have to change about in this world. You cannot keep going on in the same channel all the time.
>
> There is not a great deal of difference between being occupied in London and in Washington. The problem of life is where you can be the most useful.
>
> The main satisfaction—the main pleasure—is in carrying on, in being able to accomplish results.

As he said "I do" to the oath upon being sworn in as ambassador, A. W. quipped to the assembled, "This is not a marriage ceremony; this is a divorce," which commentators, perhaps improperly, took to be a "telling" remark. The Pittsburgh *Press* reported that "many in Washington are feeling today that Mellon's passing is a tragedy—a tragedy of a broken and disillusioned man." His family, however, had no misgivings. W. L. wrote that he was "relieved knowing that A. W. now could rest."

A. W. was succeeded as Secretary of the Treasury by Ogden Mills. W. L.'s resentment toward the successor is apparent from his "innocent" comment that Mills "visibly glowed with satisfaction." Charles Hamlin was also upset with the thought that Mills had "forced Mellon out" (an unrealistic appraisal). A. W. felt no such resentment. He had affection for Mills and regarded him as the logical and appropriate successor. Mills repaid the friendship extended by "the old man," as he privately called the Secretary. According to David Finley, Mills was a devoted friend to his chief. Hoover was happiest of all at the change; he wrote that "the shift to Mills as secretary was of great help, for he warmly supported my views on handling the depression. He had one of the finest intellects in the country."

Patman naturally claimed credit for the appointment. Hoover's appointment of A. W. to England was nothing less than "a presidential pardon." But for the appointment, his investigation would have revealed Teapot Dome to have been a minor episode and would have established that "Mr. Mellon has violated more laws, caused more human suffering, and illegally acquired more property to satisfy his personal greed than any other person on earth." It might have seemed as if Patman were kicking a downed man.

Patman went on to become one of the few significant congressmen of the twentieth century, devoting most of his career to battling the concentration of economic power in the hands of the few. By the close of his long career, he was generally regarded as the most cantankerous of the grand old men of Congress—surely a distinction of sorts. He never forgot A. W. Mellon. Mellon was more than a man to him. He wrote President Eisenhower's Postmaster General Arthur Summerfield in 1955 in an unsuccessful protest against the issuance of an A. W. Mellon commemorative postage stamp that "he was a symbol, and as a symbol I do not like to perpetuate that type memory." In his later years he occasionally referred on the floor of Congress to his great battle with Mellon. His last such statement, on November 19, 1975, was to have been a tirade against evils in the Federal Reserve System but devolved into a nostalgic, chatty reminiscence of the great fight of 1932—how "I was sitting on one side with my books and papers at this table, and Mr. Mellon and his thirteen lawyers on the other side. Of course, I was considerably outnumbered in most every way, I suppose . . ." On and on he rambled about those days gone by—until he recalled that he was making a speech about the Federal Reserve System. On March 7, 1976, in his forty-eighth year in Congress, the last populist died.

To a great extent Patman, the progressives, and the populists were correct in their insistence that the mere extent, diversity, and total size of Mellon's varied private interests made it impossible for him not to be "indirectly concerned" with "carrying on the business of trade or commerce," and impossible for him to purge himself of his conflicts, as the statute seemingly required.

With or without the direct or indirect incentive of their chief, it was inevitable that Internal Revenue auditors would be on their kindliest behavior in perusing the books of Gulf, Alcoa, or other Mellon concerns. In one Alcoa-related tax-refund case, a field auditor's memorandum carried a notation: "This is a Mellon company." At the Patman hearings Gregg insisted that the notation did not indicate any sanctioned department policy: "The chief of his section . . . as soon as he saw that memorandum, reprimanded the engineer for having put it in the file, and crossed it out." (As Gregg stated the matter, the reprimand had been for making a written record that such considerations had been entertained, which is a different matter than a reprimand for entertaining such considerations.) Stephen T. De La Mater, once chief engineer on questions of amortization at the Internal Revenue Service, testified at Senator Couzens's hearings that there was no "list" of Mellon companies: "The only way I ever knew that a case was a Mellon case was from the underground route. There was never anything to indicate that a case was a Mellon case. There was a great deal of gossip circulating through the bureau when it was intimated that a case was a Mellon case." It is inconceivable that some auditors—such as the one who made the embarrassing notation—did not attempt to curry favor with higher-ups by showing favoritism for the Secretary's private interests.

As Garner put it on the floor of Congress, "Do you think the government is going to get the best of it when the Aluminum Company of America starts in to compromise with the Secretary of the Treasury?" A 1922 New York Times article reported that the government was pressing a disputed claim against W. L. Mellon for back taxes. It cannot be imagined that the department took the same attitude toward a gray area when it was dealing with W. L. Mellon that it took when it was dealing with a Couzens. There may have been nothing that Mellon should or could reasonably have done to insure that his family and his businesses would be treated without favoritism; in any case he made no attempt. One former I.R.S. auditor wrote Patman that he had been fired as a result of having made too vigorous an audit of a west coast utility that he later learned was 51 per cent Mellon owned.

Patman could talk for hours (and sometimes did) about possible architectural uses for aluminum, and of the many ways and the many times that it had been employed in government buildings built under Treasury Department supervision during Mellon's tenure. It is inconceivable that stepped-up specification of aluminum in federal projects came in response to any directive from Mellon. The "federal triangle" buildings built in the late 1920s and early '30s, in which A. W. himself took a direct and active interest, did not make any substantial use of it. It is not inconceivable, though—indeed, it is likely—that some of the "smart" architects and engineers, hoping for further government assignments, might resolve competing alternatives in favor of the product that was made only by the "boss's" company. Congressman Patman's expertise on the subject came from his close perusal of the back issues of *Federal Architect,* a quarterly magazine published from the Treasury Building by architects on the Treasury staff, which regularly touted the many uses for the miracle metal and carried photos of its sometimes novel uses in federal buildings.

It also seems likely that A. W. himself might have been at least subconsciously influenced on tariff questions by his important stake in Alcoa, or that others with significant authority on tariff questions might have been so influenced. During the 1924 presidential campaign Democrats repeatedly referred to the increases in the aluminum tariff imposed after the Fordney-McCumber Tariff Act of 1922, and cited Arthur Vining Davis's testimony at the Federal Trade Commission, that Alcoa

> really consists of A. W. Mellon and R. B. Mellon. Of course, A. W. Mellon resigned as a member of the board of directors when he went into the government, and we now have six directors instead of seven. When he has finished his work in Washington he will again become a member of the board of directors.

A. W.'s role in the revalidation of Gulf's oil rights in the Republic of Colombia in 1928 was most circumspect but the course and the outcome of the controversy warrant a conclusion that government decisions—particularly those of the Republic of Colombia—were probably influenced by the fact that the highest fiscal officer of the Colossus of the North had a personal stake in the matter.

In the early part of the century the Republic of Colombia rewarded her patriot General Virgilio de Barco by granting him certain potentially valuable oil concessions in the easterly portion of Colombia. His rights became known as the Barco Concession. By 1925 the Barco Concession was still undeveloped and had been acquired by Colombia Petroleum Company, a corporation controlled principally by United States interests. That year Gulf took an option giving it the right to purchase a 75 per cent interest in Colombia Petroleum at a price of $1,250,000. Before Gulf exercised the option the Colombian congress in a fit of nationalism adopted a law that was adverse to foreign oil interests, and in particular, that purported to cancel the Barco Concession. The legislation made both the concession and ownership of Colombia Petroleum Company seemingly worthless. Notwithstanding this unfortunate turn, Gulf determined to exercise its option. It paid the $1,250,000 purchase price that had been set at a time when the interests appeared valuable, for interests that now, on the face of things, appeared to be without value. According to conversations of Gulf agents preserved in the State Department's archives, the decision to purchase was made by W. L. Mellon himself, who, until the matter was resolved a few years later, remained the only Gulf officer who took the matter of the concession seriously. Gulf brought suit in the Colombian courts to have the legislature's revocation of the concession declared invalid, and the suit dragged out awhile.

Meanwhile, back in the United States, the Republic of Colombia found her credits in American banks drying up. A "confidential" Department of Commerce memorandum to bankers suggested that Colombia was overborrowed, thereby discouraging the making of further American loans to the republic. State Department official Jefferson Caffery led Colombia's ambassador to the United States, Dr. Enrique Olaya Herrera, to think that dissatisfaction in America over Colombia's actions against the Barco Concession was the principal source of difficulties between their nations, and sophisticated Colombians thought they saw some tie-in between the Barco matter and their credits.

Olaya Herrera was shortly after elected president of his country. Secretary of State Stimson hosted a dinner for the president-elect at which Olaya Herrera was seated next to the Secretary of the Treasury, who commiserated with him about the problems of his country. Mellon had hopeful, fatherly, and prophetic words for the new president. As Olaya Herrera recounted it to *El Tiempo*, a leading Colombian newspaper, when he got back to the Republic, Mellon had assured him that

> After you settle those questions pending in matters of oil; after you solve in
> a just and equitable manner the difficulties confronting you in this respect; and
> as soon as you adopt a policy to give stability to the industrial activities of those
> enterprises, there will be open for Colombia without any doubt wide roads for
> its economic progress and its financial restoration.

Olaya Herrera seems to have thought that Mellon was alluding to the status of the Barco Concession. The reports of the diplomatic conversations between Olaya Herrera and Caffery in the State Department files make clear that Olaya Herrera regarded Barco and American loans as intertwined: that if Colombia altered its position on Barco, American bankers would alter their position on loans, an attitude which, according to the State Department files, Caffery neither encouraged nor discouraged. Whenever he got the chance, Gulf's South American representative mentioned to Olaya Herrera Secretary Mellon's continuing interest in the problems of Colombia. Ultimately Olaya Herrera prevailed upon his congress to adopt a bill which, with minor face-saving provisions, restored the Barco Concession. Almost immediately the National City Bank of New York reopened Colombia's credit line. A National City vice president later testified before a Senate committee headed by California's progressive Republican senator, Hiram Johnson, that the State Department had called National City and urged a liberal attitude toward the Republic of Colombia, and had pointed to the republic's friendly attitude toward American business as exemplified by its restoration of the Barco Concession.

Senator Johnson began investigating the matter of American loans to Colombia almost simultaneously with the beginning of the hearings on Patman's move to impeach Mellon. "Clarifications" were issued. Olaya Herrera sent an unsolicited message to the State Department, which, though it did not retract anything from the *El Tiempo* interview, did put things in a somewhat "better" light:

> I never discussed nor even spoke with Secretary Mellon regarding the Barco concession nor regarding any matters of the American Government in order that Colombia might obtain credits, and the conversation with Mr. Mellon referred to in the report of *El Tiempo,* of Bogota, of August 8 of last year, was in the nature of general appreciations regarding economic conditions in Colombia, and the mention made in it by the Secretary regarding the possibilities that the petroleum riches of Colombia offer for its economic restoration were incidental, and I considered it then and have considered it ever since as a mere general opinion in estimating the elements which constitute the riches available for the progress of the country but never as a hint or suggestion regarding a specific litigation.

On behalf of A. W., Alexander Gregg made an artful statement at the Patman hearings which when closely read does not deny the substantial accuracy of the newspaper's account of the friendly advice that the Secretary had reportedly given to the Colombian president-elect:

> Mr. Mellon had no conversation with President Olaya that had to do with the so-called Barco concession, nor the Gulf Oil Corporation, nor with any suggestion whatever, alleged or implied, as to any support or assistance on the part of the Government with respect to Colombia obtaining credit.
>
> Mr. Mellon has never had any conversation with officials of our State Department concerning the Colombian loan, nor has he had any conversation with bankers with respect to this loan.

Asked whether he was denying any discussion about the Barco Concession between Mellon and Gulf officials, Gregg said, "No, sir; I did not say
that at all. That is what I was very careful not to say." The State Department officially announced that there had been no connection whatsoever
between the resumption of American loans and the favorable action of the
Colombian congress on the Barco Concession, an insistence that Stimson
repeated in his diary.

The effects of A. W.'s private interests on governmental actions were not
only indirect; sometimes they were direct. Mellon was sufficiently satisfied
as to his own "integrity"—his ability to keep his private interests from
conflicting with his public duties—that he was sloppy about keeping his
private and public roles apart. The documents available in the Treasury and
State Department archives and in the Library of Congress warrant a conclusion that where his own interests were concerned A. W. had no sense of
propriety whatsoever. It did not strike him as inappropriate to ask the
Internal Revenue Service to recommend someone from their office for hire
onto his private staff (in part to serve as his personal tax attorney), though
the least detrimental of the possible effects of honoring his request would
have been (and was) to remove the ablest civil servant from public employment and transfer him to private employment. Similar requests came to
high department underlings from W. L. Mellon when Gulf Oil needed men
of particular qualifications, though presumably no non-Mellon companies
utilized the Treasury Department as a manpower reservoir or employment
agency.

It probably never occurred to Mellon that it was improper for him to take
a personal interest in the dispute between his Internal Revenue Service and
his art dealer, Baron Duveen of Milbank, though he did. And a 1925 memo
from Undersecretary Garrard Winston to Commissioner of Internal Revenue Blair on the subject of the 1925 World Series baseball games asks, "I
am wondering if some of your revenue agents are not in pretty close touch
with the ballpark and could arrange for an upper box for Secretary Mellon,
well inside of either first or third base"—as had been arranged the previous
year. This "innocent" request involved the compromising of an auditor for
the personal pleasure of the Secretary. A. W. either knew or should have
found out how he came to enjoy such wonderful tickets. There were some
things that he preferred not to know.

W. L. wrote that after A. W. went to Washington, his involvement with
the Mellon businesses came "only as one or another of us forced it on him,"
and that the demands were infrequent. When they came, though, they too

often involved Mellon directly in the relations of his businesses with the United States government, sometimes with the Treasury Department itself.

Early in the 1920s the Federal Reserve Board had its consulting architect, Alexander B. Trowbridge, conduct tests and make a report on walling for bank vaults. Carborundum Company's subsidiary American Abrasive Metals Company made walls for bank safes. Their product ranked fairly low in Trowbridge's opinion, and hopelessly far behind the "Steelcrete" walling that he ranked first. His testing showed that a Steelcrete wall costing $5.82 a square foot could withstand five hours of the most imaginative efforts that a yegg could bring to bear. The American Abrasives product was better. It could take an extra half hour of yegging, but for that minimal extra durability the banker would have to pay $117.52 a square foot. The conclusions of an independent test conducted for the Federal Reserve Board by its consulting architect would carry insuperable weight. It could fatally affect the product line for American Abrasives—even Union Trust might opt for Steelcrete. Trowbridge's report was not made available to inquirers, but curious bankers in the United States and Canada were told of his conclusions. Among the banks that asked for his report was the Mellon National Bank of Pittsburgh. Somehow Trowbridge's conclusions came to the attention of the officials down at American Abrasives, and they did not much like them. Carborundum Company joined American Abrasives in asking for an end to the dissemination of Trowbridge's data, insisting that his testing had been unfair, incomplete, inconclusive, and that it had resulted in the recommendation of a "manifestly inferior" wall. Their letter of protest was delivered to the highest Federal Reserve officials by the Secretary of the Treasury. Charles Hamlin, who liked A. W. immensely, noted in his diary that Mellon had

> said he was interested in the companies. I am surprised that Secretary Mellon sent in this letter to the Board, the companies should have sent it direct; by sending it through Secretary Mellon they are evidently trying to use his influence with the Board. He should have refused to send it to us, but should have made the companies do it themselves.

In evaluating Mellon's overtures for Carborundum there are three alternatives: 1) he was improperly attempting to influence the board's position; 2) he was hopelessly naive; and 3) he satisfied himself that corporate citizens had been subjected to an injustice which ought to be corrected. He was good at convincing himself of the moral propriety of courses which comported with his self-interest; he was experienced at it.

Governor William Harding summoned a special meeting of the Federal

Reserve Board to consider the matter and to hear from the American Abrasives and Carborundum representatives. The upshot of it was, Governor Harding wrote American Abrasives, that

> the Board has instructed Mr. Trowbridge, as its Consulting Architect, to refrain in future from advising member banks as to the kind of vaults they should construct. The Board takes the position that while Mr. Trowbridge may properly inform any member bank as to the character of construction of the vaults of its Federal Reserve banks, he should make it clear that opinions differ and that he does not put himself in the attitude of giving advice to member banks. Since receiving these instructions Mr. Trowbridge has received letters from two member banks and has sent us copies of his replies which show that he understands and appreciates the instructions given him by the Board.

"Justice" had triumphed. Later A. W. urged the President to reappoint Governor Harding, notwithstanding his Democratic Party affiliation.

Somehow Alcoa's attorneys, Gordon, Smith, Buchanan & Scott (address: Union Trust Building), thought it appropriate to write this compromising letter dated January 6, 1926, to the Secretary of the Treasury, taken from Treasury archives:

> Dear Mr. Mellon:
>
> I enclose a letter which I have addressed to you concerning the claim of the War Department against the Aluminum Company of American in the sum of $1,540,473.57, together with an extra copy of the letter. I shall be very glad if you will submit the matter to Mr. Winston in order that we may have the benefit of his views as to the proper procedure. If the procedure outlined by my letter is carried out, it will result in a suit by the Government against the Aluminum Company to recover the Government's claim of $1,540,473.57. Such a suit can only be instituted in the United States District Court, where the rights of both the Government and the Aluminum Company will receive proper consideration. The only alternative that I can see to the procedure suggested in my letter is for the Aluminum Company to bring suit against the Government in the Court of Claims to recover the amounts which are being withheld by the Government. In my judgment it would be very much against the company's interests to proceed in the Court of Claims.
>
> Yours very truly,
> William Watson Smith

Essentially the letter asks that the Secretary of the Treasury use his official position to influence the conduct of the federal government in a manner that, in the opinion of its author, would be advantageous to a company in which the Secretary himself had a substantial personal interest. If A. W.

thought the suggestion highly improper, he failed to communicate his indignation. Several months later Arthur Vining Davis wrote Winston asking the undersecretary to refer to Smith's previous letter to Mellon of January 6, "and permit me to call you about it tomorrow."

Gulf was not neglected. An unrevealing memorandum in the Treasury archives from Undersecretary Winston to A. W. dated March 29, 1924, says simply, "No new developments today. Think it advisable we have conference on Gulf nine-o'clock Monday morning." Its only significance today is that it indicates that Mellon failed to divorce himself from his businesses even in their dealings with the Treasury Department itself. It would probably have been impossible for him to have sold his vast Gulf interests to a bona fide non-family purchaser for fair value. It would not have been impossible for him to have told Winston that the department should conduct its relations with Gulf in accordance with established or emerging policy, without reference to himself or consideration for himself, and without his own involvement in any way. He failed to do so. Instead he took an ongoing interest in the government's relations with an entity that he identified to Clarence W. Barron as "my company, the Gulf Oil."

The purpose of the law prohibiting a member of the Federal Reserve Board from owning banking stocks is that at every possible turn the private banker's interests conflict with those of the Federal Reserve. A. W.'s "divestiture" of his banking stock may have sufficed legally (there was never a need to determine whether it did), but the sale to R. B. was at best a mere color of compliance with the statute. It did not have the slightest effect in divorcing the interests of A. W. as a member of the Federal Reserve, with duties owed to it, from the interests of A. W. as a private businessman. The conflict survived full-blown. No one can say whether or to what extent it influenced his determinations on Federal Reserve policies, but A. W. was at least as adept as the next man in convincing himself that what was good for Citizen Mellon was really best for the nation at large.

Two clichés were commonly applied to Mellon during his tenure. Pinchot, Norris, and Couzens all claimed the distinction of having labeled him "the man under whom three presidents served." It was a clever identification, but the evidence does not support it. "The greatest Secretary of the Treasury since Alexander Hamilton" probably stood on firmer ground, as few American Treasury secretaries have had even a tinge of greatness to them.

There were some undeniably positive effects from A. W.'s years in Washington. He was perhaps most proud of his work in beautifying the capital with architectural monuments. The federal government erected many of its most important office buildings in the 1920s, and the Treasury supervised the program. A. W. himself personally took great interest in the selection of architects. His classical tastes guided him and them. He explained that his goal was "to provide a magnificent setting for the requirements of modern civilizations." Whether or not he succeeded is a matter of taste. Elizabeth Stevenson called them "ponderous buildings" in her *Babbitts and Bohemians,* and Harvey O'Connor said that "all the structures look like the Mellon National Bank in Pittsburgh except that they cover more ground and are consequently more depressing." Those whose tastes run to "Mellon Gothic" would disagree. A. W. liked Mellon Gothic.

Also during his administration the organization of the Treasury Department was modernized and streamlined in a manner that has survived, with some modification, until today. Segregation between the department's 5000 black employees and its more numerous white employees was kept to a minimum; under Mellon the Treasury was far more advanced in its civil rights attitudes than most Washington bureaucracies. During this period the size of American paper money was reduced from franc-sized notes to the smaller size still in use. This change provided a relatively small but continuing savings to the government. Smaller bills require less paper and ink to print; and because they require much less folding, they have a substantially longer life span.

On more theoretical matters, A. W.'s record reads less well. The accomplishment of his early period—reduction simultaneously of both tax rates and the national debt—was a result of increased revenues generated by a more active business climate together with the slowdown in the needs of government, factors beyond the control of any Secretary of the Treasury, greater or lesser. Just as the success of his administration coincided with the upswing in the economy, so too did the failure of his administration coincide with the downturn in it. A.W. was probably as irrelevant to the one as he was to the other.

Mellon's role in the coming of the depression and his attitude toward grappling with it have been fully discussed. Our inability to forecast what-might-have-beens saves A. W. from conclusions that would probably be unfavorable as to the wisdom of his approach to ending the depression. Hoover's attempts to combat the depression were succeeded by Roosevelt's attempts, which while greater in variety, volume, and visibility, were scarcely more successful in their effects on the economy. Both presidents attempted to utilize an expansionist financial policy to cure the depression, but neither used the expansionist approach with sufficient consistency or intensity for the approach to work. It took the demands of the Second World War to generate enough economic activity to "cure" the depression. There was another approach that might have been followed. Instead of inconsistent and inadequate attempts to spend the country to recovery, the nation might have tried A. W.'s—or more accurately, the Judge's—nineteenth-century laissez-faire approach, kept hands off, and permitted a general liquidation. As neither the expansionist nor the laissez-faire tack was taken, it is still possible to argue that Mellon's approach—archaic, unsentimental, and arguably shortsighted—was nonetheless more nearly correct than that of either president, and that it might have yielded faster as well as less costly results for the nation.

The Mellon Plan of taxation was surely the most important of A. W.'s policies. It cannot be viewed merely as an attempt to favor the superrich by reduction of their taxes. Mellon also argued strongly for removal of the exemption from federal income tax of the interest on municipal bonds, a limitation on the deduction allowed for capital losses, and a favored tax rate for "earned" income as opposed to income generated by investments. All of these suggestions were unfriendly to taxpayers of his own economic class. At one time he proposed imposition of a two-cent tax on bank checks (which were not so widely used then as now), a suggestion that could not have been welcomed by the banking community with which his own family identified. He stood as a brake on efforts by the Chamber of Commerce to have surtaxes reduced still lower in 1927–28.

As a package, A. W. could fairly have regarded his proposals as an effort to eliminate some loopholes, thereby helping to enable an overall reduction of tax rates—a comprehensive "reform" package. The reductions would accrue principally where they would do the "most good"—in the highest brackets. But after his first visit to Congress his plans always provided some frosting for those further down the economic ladder. Virtually all of his suggestions were implemented, and especially the substantial reduction of tax rates imposed on the highest brackets. Oddly, the benefits failed to "trickle down." Much of the rich men's freed monies did go into expansion of industry, but the workingman's wage did not increase substantially enough to enable him to purchase the increased production. Steelworkers, for example, received not a penny wage increase between 1924 and 1929, the period of most apparent prosperity and economic progress, while the pockets of poverty that have always been with America became large reservoirs. The freed money that did not go into superfluous factories went into stock market speculations of no value to society at large, or, in the end, to the rich man himself.

In any case, it is clear that little would have been different for America had Mellon never been Secretary of the Treasury. As has been pointed out above, the Mellon Plan was inherited from the Wilson administration. Its refinements through the 1920s were dictated first by S. Parker Gilbert, a Wilson-administration holdover, then by Gilbert's personally selected successor, Garrard B. Winston. There is no reason to believe that anything would have been different had those who had selected Gilbert in the first instance remained in power themselves after 1920. There is very good reason to believe that the fiscal policies of the nation would have remained thoroughly Coolidge-era even if Democrat John W. Davis had defeated Coolidge in 1924. Of the 1928 contenders, Democrat Al Smith may well have been more in tune with Mellon's fiscal policies than Hoover was.

Only in one sense was Secretary Mellon "great." He was great in that he fulfilled the ideas and ideals of his time and place. In perhaps the most materialistic period in American history he was the finest symbol for a country. Then things took a bad turn for him. When he left office in 1932, he left the country with the highest national debt in its history, and he would live to see it go very much higher. Before the end of his tenure he saw tax rates increased substantially, and he would live to see them increased to higher levels even than those that had been in existence when he began. He lived to see the rejection of the milieu in which he had been "great," and of the values upon which his greatness had been dependent; and with the rejection of that milieu and of those values, he lived to see his greatness evaporate.

No one was ever better suited to be ambassador to Great Britain than A. W. Mellon. His tastes and inclinations were markedly British, and he had become something of an Anglophile from his many sojourns in Great Britain. With his quiet manner and soft speech, his clothes of the finest cloth, which for years he had had cut in the English manner, the "American mogul" seemed very much more typically an old-family English aristocrat. Ailsa joined him in Britain as his companion and official hostess, and David Finley came along as his personal assistant, at a cost to the United States government of a dollar a year. After a month in Britain, Finley wrote Ogden Mills that "Mr. Mellon is really most happy about the whole situation. It could not be better, just as you predicted, and I think he is going to enjoy his life here far more than would have been possible in Washington."

In London, A. W. was able to come out of the closet as a "wet." Asked at the time of his appointment whether he would serve alcoholic drinks at the American Embassy, Mellon responded that he would "follow the custom of the country." England was very "wet." Press reports early in his tenure that the Ambassador himself had publicly consumed "whisky and soda" brought some of the last gasps of outrage from the temperance people before the "Great Experiment" was put to rest.

The wires available in the State Department's archives, as well as then Secretary of State Stimson's manuscript diary available at Yale, make clear that A. W. was an active, working ambassador, involved in representations on a wide range of issues, and useful to the Secretary of State. But his period as ambassador was interrupted by several vacations, and, as at the Treasury, he had competent underlings upon whom he might rely and did. On his arrival in England the press asked him whether he feared that London's fog and rain would adversely affect his health. He smiled and waved his cigar, but when it appeared that he would have no further answer, Ray Atherton, the embassy's highest-ranking civil servant, interposed a determined no. It sounded like Mills all over again, but that was what Mellon would have wanted. Most important, he was out of firing range.

Probably Mellon's most important services to Mellon came in his assistance in obtaining for Gulf an interest in Kuwait oil. His active efforts in the matter took place from his ambassadorial office. During the many years that Kuwait had been a protectorate of the British government, B.P. (British Petroleum, largely owned by the British government) had never indicated more than passing interest in the sheikdom's possible oil resources. In the early 1930s Major Frank Holmes, as much as any other man responsible for the development of Arabia's oil wealth, interested Gulf in Kuwait oil rights. When Gulf began to show an interest, B.P. at last sat up and took notice, probably more in an effort to keep out the competition than because of any desire to develop a new oil field. Because of Kuwait's protectorate status and the connection between B.P. and the British government, Gulf reasonably concluded that its competitor had the inside track.

Gulf decided to interest the United States government in insuring fair play for an American corporate citizen. A State Department memorandum of November 1931 records that "At the request of Mr. Mellon [then serving as Secretary of the Treasury] the secretary received at 11 o'clock today Messrs. Wallace, Stone and Stevens of the Gulf Oil Corporation of Pennsylvania." A note of the following day includes the words "in connection with the assistance which Mr. Mellon has asked us to render the representatives of the Gulf Oil Corporation . . ." It goes on to say that the official United States position should be to insist on equality of opportunity in the Arab states, and cables to the United States embassy in London outlined the fight that the government was to make for its citizen.

When Mellon was about to be appointed ambassador to Great Britain early in 1932, the State Department made special efforts to resolve the matter before his arrival in England, on the entirely unfounded theory that it would embarrass A. W. as ambassador to have his embassy involved in representations on behalf of a business in which he had a large personal interest with the country to which he was officially assigned. A. W. did not embarrass easily. In any case, negotiations were still unresolved when he sailed for his new assignment. Undersecretary of State William Castle wired Chargé Ray Atherton that

> the Ambassador may want you to handle the matter without any reference to him. If this should be the case, you may, of course, take full and sole charge of it. . . . It is quite obvious that in this whole matter, all the Department is doing is the protection and prosecution of the rights of American citizens and it is merely accidental that the Mellon family has an interest in the Gulf Oil Company. Under circumstances of this kind it would always be very easy to lean over backward too far for the sake of preventing criticism. In all that we do, therefore, we must accord the Gulf Oil Company no more or no less, but precisely the same, assistance that we should accord to any other bona fide American company under similar circumstances.

Castle was on the wrong track entirely. A. W. did not in any way intend to shirk his responsibilities to any American citizen, whether a breathing citizen or a corporate citizen—not even if that citizen were his own child. The British document books available at the Public Record Office in London report at least three visits between A. W. and Sir Robert Vansittart, the highest-ranking civil servant at the British Foreign Office, in which A. W. broached the subject of Gulf's interest in Kuwait. A. W. could be quite forceful on the subject. Vansittart's memorandum of November 3, 1932, reports that

> The Ambassador was perfectly polite throughout, but it was quite plain that he considered that we were acting with deliberate dilatoriness, and indeed with duplicity, and that the infinite delays of this matter had resulted in his compatriots getting the reverse of a square deal.

In reviewing the history of B.P.'s interests in Kuwait, Vansittart noted that "The Ambassador was bitter on this point."

Vansittart's memorandum makes clear that he was entirely in sympathy with Mellon on the matter of delays occasioned by the various departments of the British government concerned with the problem. He wrote that "they expect me to do their work and encounter foreign representatives who practically accuse HMG [His Majesty's Government] of dishonesty, and into whose hands their dilatoriness plays." At the time, the British government was involved in discussions with Mellon and the United States of vastly greater importance to Britain than Gulf and B.P.—matters involving Britain's huge debt to the United States arising from World War I. Vansittart's memorandum continues: "Apart from this, for reasons of considerably higher policy I do not wish to have acrimonious disputes with the U.S.A. at this moment."

The British are circumspect about such matters. Vansittart was talking about quid pro quos, about hands washing hands. That day he wrote the director of the Petroleum Department of the Mines Department, "The Secretary of Mines will no doubt appreciate that the unfortunate atmosphere created at such an interview may well have important repercussions on questions of major political importance under discussion with the Ambassador." It was only to be expected that in their dealings with Mr. Mellon over what their memoranda sometimes refer to as "Mr. Mellon's company" the British diplomats would keep those "important repercussions on questions of major political importance" well in mind.

It is clear from the State Department archives that Castle and Wallace Murray, chief of the Division of Near Eastern Affairs, thought it unwise (if not improper) for the Ambassador to take an active role in representations on the Gulf-B.P. matter. Though the British were much too gentlemanly to mention personal improprieties in their files, references in their memoranda to "the Mellon group," "Mr. Mellon's company," the Ambassador's discussions about "his" company, and to the implications that the Gulf-B.P. discussions might have for greater issues in Anglo-American relations, make clear that they appreciated the compromising nature of A. W.'s position.

A State Department memorandum of December 27, 1932, notes that "the Ambassador is not at all bashful in pressing this matter himself. Possibly Mr. Castle or the Secretary may wish to suggest to him that he go easy on the question." The next day Murray addressed a strong letter on the subject to Secretary of State Stimson himself:

> Ordinarily there would of course be no objection to such action on the part of the Ambassador but the situation in this case is altered by the fact that Mr. Mellon and his family are understood to have a controlling interest in the Gulf Oil Company. As pointed out above it was originally agreed that negotiations in this case had best be carried on by Mr. Atherton. The more I see of the case the more I am convinced that this was a wise decision. Under the circumstances it occurred to me that you might wish to mention the matter to Mr. Mellon with a view to seeing whether he does not agree that the necessary

negotiations in the case be left in Mr. Atherton's hands. Unless this is done I very much fear that the Department, the Ambassador and the Administration may be open to serious criticism.

There is no indication in the British or American document books of any further role by A. W. on behalf of Gulf in the matter. Stimson probably spoke to him diplomatically about the "problem."

Ultimately the matter was resolved when Gulf and B.P. got together and made a joint offer to the Sheik of Kuwait, which he accepted. Kuwait was to become, and remains to the day of this writing, Gulf's principal source of crude oil.

In assessing A. W.'s role in the Kuwait negotiations, Richard O'Connor wrote in *The Oil Barons* that Mellon combined "national and personal concerns, more the latter than the former." It may or may not be an unfair assessment; it is unquestionably a reasonable one. The manifest impropriety of A. W.'s involvement was clear to all but to A. W. Mellon. He was just doing his duty.

A. W. declined a seat at the Republican National Convention of 1932, pleading the demands of his duties in London. In the election campaign between Hoover and the Democratic contender, Franklin D. Roosevelt, the Mellons made their customary modest donations, totaling $45,000. As almost everyone knows, F.D.R. won. His vice presidential running mate, the new Vice President, was John Nance Garner. Mellon served as ambassador through the balance of the Hoover administration, which did not terminate until March of 1933. A final note from Mellon to Hoover shows that notwithstanding the friction between them, Mellon was usually a man of balance: "I value your friendship and want to thank you now, on the eve of my departure from London and public life, for the courtesy and consideration which you have always shown towards me." As he got off the boat in New York on his seventy-eighth birthday the reporters asked if he was ready for a rest after his years of public service. "Well, I don't know about a rest," he said. "Nobody rests. But I will be free, and I think I have reached an age when I am entitled to be free." In a short time he was aboard the Pittsburgh train, and the following day he granted one of his last interviews to the reporter from the Pittsburgh *Press:* "It's good to be home again," he said. "Yes, it certainly is good to be home." The *Press* reported that "Mellon hasn't changed much in the 12 years that saw him Secretary of the Treasury under three Presidents, Harding, Coolidge and Hoover, and finally Ambassador to the Court of St. James."

The 1920s were good to business, and the Mellon enterprises flourished.

Alcoa blossomed in the 1920s with the benefit of the tariff and the boom in construction and consumption. The tariff really smoothed Alcoa's way. Aluminum's raw material, bauxite, was imported into the United States substantially duty free (a dollar per ton), whereas foreign aluminum and aluminum products were almost "dutied" out of the American market. After Attorney General Harlan Stone was promoted out of the way, and Coolidge attacked the Federal Trade Commission for its report on Alcoa as "letting itself be used for political purposes," the anti-trust foolishness pretty much ceased. Private anti-trust suits against Alcoa were resolved in its favor.

Throughout the period, Alcoa maintained its dominant position in the American hydroelectric picture. Henry Ford had shown some interest in developing the government's huge Muscle Shoals hydroelectric power site in the Tennessee Valley, almost certainly with production of aluminum in the back of his mind, but then he strangely lost interest in the proposition. Presidential vetoes prevented the government from developing Muscle Shoals itself, while Alcoa bought up tobacco magnate James Duke's big hydroelectric site in the wilds of Quebec. The company's dominance of cheap power made the possibility remote that any significant competitor might emerge in the western hemisphere. The Democrats had tried to make a political issue of the "Aluminum Trust" in the 1924 presidential campaign, but it had not done them any good.

Things got tougher for Alcoa, as for everyone, after the depression came. Its profits declined from $10,868,000 in 1930 to $4,595,000 in 1931, and in 1932 it suffered a $6,763,000 loss (after payment of dividends to preferred stockholders, of whom the Mellons were the largest). But it cut wages, laid off half of its New Kensington work force, cut hours for the rest, and instituted similar cuts in its installations across the country. It reached a friendly "understanding" with the major foreign aluminum producers. With its very substantial assets and capital reserves, its situation was well under control.

Gulf did well too. Boies Penrose's masterpiece, the oil-depletion allowance, successfully withstood the attacks of Senator Couzens. The industry's historic problem, overproduction, promised to be brought under control by "understandings" that were reached by the major world oil producers at conferences in Scotland attended by W. L. on behalf of Gulf. There were some turbulent moments over Gulf's Mexican holdings, but these were ultimately resolved satisfactorily, and Gulf went on to acquire important rights in Venezuela, Colombia, and Kuwait.

The depression caused problems with Gulf also. It lost $23,658,000 in 1931, but layoffs and pay cuts—some wages slashed to 60 per cent of 1929 levels—helped stabilize the balance sheet. In 1932, generally a worse year for business than 1931, Gulf turned a small $2,743,000 profit. Its stock dropped from a high of 209 to 25, but those were just numbers; the Mellons weren't interested in selling.

Venezuelan oil could be produced and shipped to east coast ports for less than the cost of transporting inland American oil to the coast. Under the circumstances, the small independent producer could not compete with outfits like Gulf or the Rockefeller companies. There was no tariff to bother the importers until 1932, when the "independents" forced through a tax of twenty-one-cents a barrel on imported oil; but not even that was enough to make up the difference. Plenty of little men's oil-bearing properties and rights could be picked up cheap in the hard moments, and Gulf made the most of the opportunities.

Koppers sometimes caused the family a little embarrassment in the 1920s. Labor spokesmen focused on Koppers's West Virginia coal mines as among the most dangerous and poorly paid in the nation. Its sales of engineering services to the Soviet Union were seized upon by A. W.'s enemies as running counter to President Hoover's foreign policy, and were cited as a violation of the nation's slave-labor statute. No one but the virulent anti-communists paid any attention to that kind of talk. As Koppers Company made clear in its press release, if Koppers hadn't sold the Russians the services someone in Europe would have.

Koppers's growth was gratifying, but not an unmixed blessing. W. L. wrote that "it grew too fast and too big and to some extent in the wrong directions," for which he blamed Koppers president Henry B. Rust. He explained its growth this way:

> If his staff failed in attempts to sell Koppers equipment to some gas company in need of modernization, Mr. Rust would step in and his way was to engineer a purchase of some of that company's stock—not necessarily enough for control but enough usually to get for Koppers the equipment business it was seeking. Time and again, as a result of this scheme of getting contracts to build ovens, Koppers found itself obliged in the end to purchase control of some utility company which was being not too well managed. It had to do this, in effect, to take over the customer for which it had built the by-product ovens in order to make sure of getting paid for its ovens. The business, after some twenty years, had grown from $1,500,000 to over $400,000,000 but since so much of that growth had resulted from the kind of expansions I mention, it is no wonder poor Mr. Rust's health failed.

Its corporate structure became dizzying. The Koppers Company of Delaware that emerged in the 1920s controlled eleven subsidiaries, most of which had subsidiaries which in turn had subsidiaries, some of which had subsidiaries. For example, one of the eleven components of Koppers Company of Delaware was Koppers Gas and Coke, which had twelve subsidiaries itself, one of which, Eastern Gas and Fuel, had seven subsidiaries, including Massachusetts Gas, parent corporation of Boston Consolidated Gas. Koppers gobbled up corporations, mostly in the public utilities field, but also in other related lines. Its enterprises included Alan Wood Steel, American Tar Products, and Mystic Iron Works. The collapse of utility mogul Samuel Insull's pyramid of holding companies discredited corporate structures such as Koppers's, and thereafter the company pulled back and consolidated.

Koppers made money, and aided by wage cuts it weathered the depression second best of all. Its assets increased in the depression years, and its profits for 1930, 1931, and 1932 were respectable each year.

Best of all were the banks—R. B.'s principal business interest. Union Trust and Mellon National had financed much of the great growth that greater Pittsburgh experienced in the 1920s. At the end of the era, R. B.'s boy, R. K., together with young Frank Denton, had inaugurated the Mellbank Security Company, which could claim considerable part of the credit for saving countless smaller banks in the area. One of their small-town affiliate banks stemmed a run on it by posting a sign in the window: "This bank is owned by the Mellons of Pittsburgh." Union Trust and Mellon National were never in trouble; their earnings in 1931 and 1932 were $6,208,000 and $5,438,000, and they continued their regular dividends. The Mellons had learned their lesson away back in 1873; they were sufficiently liquid and had one of the highest ratios—if not the highest—of cash to deposits of any major bank in the country. Other banks—including their principal competitor, the great Bank of Pittsburgh—were less fortunate.

Union and Mellon National never suffered any great run on them, but such run as there was contained something of a tribute to the family name. Much of the money that panicky Union depositors withdrew, they placed instead in a "safer" institution—Mellon National. As the crowd surged into the bank, R. B. grumbled, "I told those damn architects to make more room in the lobby."

Those were all manageable businesses. Two businesses that promised to become unmanageable were liquidated.

By the summer of 1929 the Mellons were ready to retire Standard Steel Car. By that time Diamond Jim Brady had long gone to the great jeweler in the sky; Hanson had been "kicked upstairs" to become chairman of the board and was clearly nearing death. The Mellons themselves were no longer young and perhaps sensed that the country was in for one of those periodic economic setbacks that might conceivably outlast A. W. and R.B. They opened negotiations for sale of Standard to J. P. Morgan's Pullman Company, the only other major producer at the time. An understanding was reached with Morgan for sale and purchase of Standard shortly before the stock market crash of October 1929. With the crash, the Mellons expected that Morgan might cite "unsettled market conditions" and refuse to close the deal. There was a period of uncertainty during which Hanson died of what the obituaries described as "apoplexy." Morgan, however, honored the agreement, and in March 1930 Pullman absorbed Standard at a price for the Mellon interests reported by W. L. as $38,700,000. The Mellons came out of the deal with some $4,342,000 in cash and about 400,000 shares of Pullman, which was trading as of March 1 at $82.50. Standard's president, J. Francis Drake, a "Mellon" man who had been with the family's enterprises since 1919, became chief executive of Pullman; and R. B.'s son, R. K., and his son-in-law, Alan Scaife, joined Mr. Morgan (Jr.) on Pullman's board of directors.

At last, the Mellons' investment in railroad cars was liquid, and over the long haul it was liquidated. Until the early 1970s, however, the family still retained a representative on Pullman's board of directors.

McClintic-Marshall was a great business, and a big business, but by 1931 it was still a "partnership" of four old men. Wisdom dictated that the four convert their interests into an investment that was more liquid and that relieved them of ongoing responsibilities. That year, two years into the depression, they sold out virtually all of McClintic-Marshall's assets to Bethlehem Steel in exchange for Bethlehem stock and bonds, and conveyed some of its property to Koppers Company for security interests in Koppers. McClintic-Marshall's liquid assets were divided equally among its four stockholders in proportion to their stock interests in the company. In A. W.'s later difficulties with the Internal Revenue Service, the government and A. W. stipulated that the cash value of the distribution to A. W. was $19,823,478.04. R. B.'s interest would have been the same, with McClintic and Marshall receiving some $13,200,000 each.

The 1920s had been good to R. B. In 1927 he saw his daughter Sarah marry Alan Scaife, well born and well educated, handsome and charming, in Pittsburgh's society wedding of the decade. It was a union—and a wedding party—in which R. B. could take pride. All—well, almost all— of the family businesses had prospered in the '20s without A. W., and that reflected well on R. B. too. Reflected very well on R. B.

Of course you can't expect everything to be rosy; one of the businesses had not done all that well. R. B. took his lumps on that one.

The '20s prosperity passed by one great enterprise—coal. Of the many large coal companies, the two biggest were Consolidated Coal, principally a Rockefeller concern, and Pittsburgh Coal, which in the 1920s became increasingly Mellon owned. Largely that was R. B.'s fault. To hear A. W. tell it, it *was* R. B.'s fault. At R. B.'s urging the brothers kept buying more and more Pittsburgh Coal stock. Until 1927 their interests had been relatively modest. That year they increased their holdings to about 25 per cent. Even A. W. had to admit that "those were prosperous years, and we had the income."

In 1923 R. B. became chairman of the board of Pittsburgh Coal, an office that he held when the company and most of the major coal producers signed a three-year contract with John L. Lewis's United Mine Workers for a $7.50 daily wage. The economics of the situation made it an impossible contract for management to honor. There were twice as many coal mines as demand warranted and twice as many miners as there were jobs. The big companies tied to the U.M.W. could not compete with non-union mines in southern West Virginia. They were losing money. In 1925 Rockefeller's Consolidated Coal repudiated the agreement; so did Charles Schwab's Bethlehem mining subsidiary. Pittsburgh Coal simply closed up its operations. The mines did not have to be closed very long to make mining-town people realistic. Four months later Pittsburgh Coal reopened as an "open" shop paying six dollars a day, implicitly repudiating the contract with the U.M.W. In the interim R. B. resigned as chairman of the board to be replaced by an unabashed anti-union man. The Mellons were not about to take the heat for what was to follow.

Management came out on top—the natural economic laws had made that inevitable—but there was a lot of unpleasantness in the strikes that followed. A miner was beaten to death in a Pittsburgh Coal Company office by the company police. The company doctor had protested, "This will have to stop now because his condition is serious." They hadn't listened, the doctor had salved his own conscience and left, and before they were done the man was too far gone to be revived. Everything that could be broken had been broken and the rest had been crushed. The district attorney had described it as one of the most brutal murders he had ever investigated. Well, the company lawyers did a good job and the men were only convicted of "involuntary manslaughter," but still, that kind of thing . . . Pittsburgh Coal gave the fellow's widow $13,500.

Such happenings and the destitution of the miners' families dominated the coal industry in the late 1920s, and were not easy to ignore. When Senator Burton K. Wheeler got around to questioning R. B. at a 1928 Senate investigation into conditions in the coal country, he asked the Secretary's brother, "Have you ever been out there yourself and seen the conditions that exist out there?" "I am not in the operating department" was about the best answer R. B. could give, so he gave it.

> Senator Wheeler. But, Mr. Mellon, you have not been out there to look at what the conditions are under which those employees of yours and their families are living, have you?
> Mr. Mellon. I have not been out there; no.
> Senator Wheeler. And you are not interested in them to that extent?
> Mr. Mellon. Oh, yes.
> Senator Wheeler. And do you not think, Mr. Mellon, that you as one of the substantial investors in the Pittsburgh Coal Company, owe it to yourself to go out there and see under just what conditions—
> Mr. Mellon. I have perfect confidence in the men that are operating the business.

He did too. Throughout the period of turmoil the Mellons were increasing their proportionate ownership of Pittsburgh Coal.

The mine owners won their battle with John L. Lewis and his U.M.W., but maybe that hadn't been so wise either. The labor sympathizers had said that if management got rid of Lewis's crowd the *real* commies would come in, and the bosses would come to find out that there was something worse than the U.M.W. When the National Mine Workers Union got started, things did get worse: more violence, more shootings. One of the company's policemen was actually convicted of murder after a 1931 shooting. R. B. did not approve of that. And he did not say, "You can't run a coal mine without machine guns." He had never said that. That was something that the left-wing press had twisted. What he had said in his exchange with miners' counsel O. K. Eaton was

> Mr. Eaton. You never heard of the question of machine guns being bought for [the police]?
> Mr. Mellon. I never heard of that. They may have.
> Mr. Eaton. Would you approve of them having machine guns—
> Mr. Mellon. Such as the police here have them?
> Mr. Eaton. I beg your pardon?
> Mr. Mellon. Such as the police have them?
> Mr. Eaton. Well, would you approve of that?
> Mr. Mellon. It is necessary. You could not run without them.
> Mr. Eaton. You could not run a coal company without machine guns?

Mr. Mellon. No, I didn't say without machine guns.

Mr. Eaton. Well, I am asking you about machine guns.

Mr. Mellon. Well, I don't know anything about machine guns. I don't know whether the police have them here.

In January 1930 Pittsburgh Coal was still trading as high as 78½. By December of 1931 it was trading at around 4, and by A. W.'s figuring it had no intrinsic value whatsoever. No one could remember the last time it had paid a dividend. By that time the two brothers owned a 52 per cent interest in the company. Even a Mellon couldn't be right about everything.

R. B. devoted much of his time in his last years to his civic interests. R. B. really loved Pittsburgh. In the 1920s Gulf, Koppers, Mellon National, and Union Trust all built magnificent (by the standards of the day) new buildings in downtown Pittsburgh, which did much to spark up the center of town. Farther out, the Mellon Institute undertook construction of its huge, somber Hellenic monument in the early 1930s.

Other than the Mellon Institute, R. B.'s philanthropies were principally church-related. In 1926 R. B. was one of the chief sponsors of a drive to establish a $15 million pension fund for aged Presbyterian ministers. The climax of his philanthropic career was the East Liberty Presbyterian Church. First announced in 1930, the vast neo-Gothic structure was estimated to cost between three and four million dollars. Whatever it finally came to, R. B.—and Jennie—paid almost the full freight, giving the new church as a memorial to their mothers. According to O'Connor, many called it "Mellon fire insurance." When its plans were first announced, the New York *Herald Tribune* predicted that the completed edifice would rank "as the outstanding structure of Presbyterianism." It was well under way at the time of R. B.'s death.

R. B. died at the end of 1933 at the age of seventy-five. The younger brother had predeceased two older ones. R. B. had been in failing health for about six months before his end, but a few days prior to his death he had gone on an inspection tour of a water project related to one of the family's businesses. He caught a cold that led to pneumonia. On December 1, 1933, he was dead. The mayor of Pittsburgh ordered the flags flown at half mast as a symbol of the city's mourning. The newspapers carried columns upon columns of panegyrics from civic and business leaders praising the deceased, no doubt solicited by the journalists, including a tribute from the ubiquitous Mrs. Enoch Rauh.*

R. B. was laid to rest on a bitter December day in a receiving vault, where

*Page 135 *supra*.

his remains would be held until his final resting place within the East Liberty Presbyterian Church was ready for him. A large crowd of mourners accompanied him from his mansion to the cemetery. As their impressive caravan of depression-era vehicles emerged from the winding driveway to his estate, the mourners were surprised to find the street outside thronged with spectators attracted by some incomprehensible curiosity powerful enough to overcome the chill and the unrelenting rain and bring them out. Before the funeral the mansion had been opened to the public for a sort of wake. Why had they not come to pay their last respects to their banker and benefactor at that appropriate time as so many hundreds had? A Mellon woman in one of the limousines never forgot the faces that lined the street that eerie day, peering from beneath umbrellas in at the city's leading family in their coaches—"glowering" at them, as she recalled it. She was frightened.

R. B. had channeled off the bulk of his fortune before his death; the inventory of his estate showed that he died with insignificant interests in the great Mellon enterprises. Nevertheless, he failed to divest himself of as much as he might have or could have, and he died with an estate of $200 million, on which the tax collectors would assess their levies. His lengthy inventory included some colorful items, such as a 1925 Hispano Suiza seven-passenger "Town Car," described as "antiquated" and valued at $75; but the bulk of the $200 million still standing in R. B.'s name at time of death was in real estate. The inventory listed numerous "one-half interests" in vast, scattered real estate holdings in and around Pittsburgh; the other half stood in A. W.'s name.

The first bequests in R. B.'s will included $250,000 to be divided between his domestic servants and his business employees, none specifically named in the will. The will then said that R. B. had taken care of charitable considerations during his lifetime and that he was therefore leaving only a relatively modest $1.1 million for further charity, all for the Mellon Institute. The balance he left equally to Jennie and to his children, R. K. and Sarah—one-third each. After taxes, the net to each of the children probably did not add much of significance to the many fortunes that R. B. had given them during his lifetime.

Gifford Pinchot, once again Pennsylvania's governor, announced that the state would use the inheritance taxes received from R. B.'s estate for pay raises to state employees. His papers at the Library of Congress indicate that he took a personal interest in rounding up Caesar's share, which ultimately brought Pennsylvania $13,309,000.

James Ross Mellon, second of the Judge's sons, followed R. B. the next year. He had been sick for almost a year with the complications of old age, and died in his sleep in October 1934 at the age of eighty-eight. His daughter, Sarah Lucille, by then Mrs. George S. Hasbrouck Jr., and his son, Thomas Mellon II, were with him at the last moment. In the preface to a book of old letters between himself and the Judge published shortly after his death, he was fortunate to have been able to write that his life had been "almost one hundred per cent sunshine and very little shadow." His grand-nephew Ned Mellon, with an exaggeration born of his considerable affection for J. R. , says that "J. R. never did a damn thing in his whole life but have a helluvah good time." Ned knew J. R. only in retirement, long after the days in which the uncle had gone through the motions of being a true son of the Judge. Fortunately, he had stopped early enough to allow plenty of time for enjoyment.

A nicely done account of the funeral in the Pittsburgh *Press* reported the presence of the same curious crowd that had assembled for R. B.'s funeral, "stretching necks and straining eyes for a glimpse of 'The Mellons,' " but

> Only a few curious eyes followed the casket from the hearse to its last resting place in the modest mausoleum in Homewood Cemetery. The Mellon men, led by former Secretary Andrew, ignored the outsiders. The Mellon women—the older ones shielded by black veils and gowned from head to foot in funeral black—wore an air of studied reserve.
>
> Andrew Mellon led the family into the dim crypt. A few minutes later he led the way out and to the cars. The funeral for James Ross Mellon was over.

A. W.'s last years were not happy ones. He busied himself about the bank, as his father had done before him, bought a little stock—just "to see whether my judgment was still good," he explained to W. L.—and tried to be productive. But according to his neighbors, he found time to play with the squirrels on the front lawn of his Woodland Avenue home. He kept his apartment in Washington and was there often. To contemporary Pittsburghers he seemed to be involved in some secret project at the Capitol—probably just a way for an old man to fill up his days. There was a little joy: Ailsa gave birth to A. W.'s first grandchild, Audrey, in 1933, and a couple of years later Paul got married to a nice girl, Mary Conover Brown, recently divorced from her first husband. But there was more turmoil and sadness.

Most upsetting to A. W. was the publication in the summer of 1933 of Harvey O'Connor's *Mellon's Millions,* a lengthy and well-researched (if occasionally incorrect) polemic infused with O'Connor's left liberalism, which filled in any possible gaps in the evidence in a manner hostile to Mellon. In an intemperate statement, A. W. commented publicly,

> I have tried to read the so-called biography of myself entitled *Mellon's Millions* . . . the book is obviously a travesty of truth and appears in the nature of literary racketeering, still it is a serious injustice that such false statements in respect to private affairs, and such malevolent innuendos in respect to personality should have to be submitted to.

A. W. experienced the kind of outrage over *Mellon's Millions* that family and friends had rarely seen. Some had seen it only once, many years before, when J. R.'s wife, Rachel, had playfully clipped the end of A. W.'s mustache. Both were the same kind of offense—they were assaults on A. W.'s dignity. O'Connor's was worse only because it was malicious.

It was only to be expected that such a sensational book would become a best seller; but at least in Pittsburgh, home town of both author and subject, most of the booksellers were honorable, principled men who naturally refused to carry such a vicious volume. The letters to the editors of the Pittsburgh newspapers showed that most of the burghers had the right number on the "recognized red," as one correspondent called O'Connor* and the important librarian of the Carnegie Institute denounced the book as well: "I personally think the book most unfair, but as a librarian I have no other choice but to obtain it. Sometime I hope someone will write a really fair and judicial biography of Mellon which we can put beside this one by O'Connor."

It served O'Connor right when shortly after publication of *Mellon's Millions,* the Pittsburgh police arrested him at his home on the charge of being a "suspicious person." He certainly was that! It almost made one question whether there was any justice in this world when the court immediately discharged O'Connor.

Then there were the deaths: R. B. in 1933, J. R. in 1934, and H. C.— Henry Clay McEldowney—in 1935.

Throughout the period of his retirement, when he was supposed to be at peace, A. W. was haunted by that old matter, that old forgotten matter: Who "owned" T. Mellon & Sons after the death of the Judge? The land on

---

*O'Connor was not a communist, but he had a refined and profound sense of injustice which in the socio-economic milieu necessarily impelled him to take positions which were often compatible with those of the radical left. His five-cent pamphlet, *How Mellon Got Rich,* was published in the same year as *Mellon's Millions* by International Pamphlets, which often published pro-communist tracts.

which the old bank had sat (and on which its successor sits) had been passed on equally to the four branches of the Judge's tree. By what token had not the banking business itself been similarly devised? By what rights did A. W. and R. B. "own" it to the exclusion of the T. A. and J. R. branches?

A. W. could give a short answer to the question: The Judge gave the banking business to him by his "Proposition to son Andrew" in 1882, and he, in turn, had later given a half interest in it to R. B. But the short answer was not an adequate one. The "Proposition" was not a conveyance of the banking business to A. W., it merely set forth the compensation that A. W. was to receive for his managerial services "till superseded by another [agreement] or annulled by either party." Insofar as the legal documents told the story, at the time of the Judge's death in 1908 he still held title to the banking business associated with the family except for the 20 per cent interest in it that he had indeed conveyed to A. W. in 1874. Were not J. R. and the heirs of T. A. entitled to their quarter shares of the Judge's 80 per cent interest?

T. A.'s heirs pondered their course. They discussed it with J. R., still living. Yes, J. R. said, he too had sometimes asked himself the same question, but no, no he would not take part in any confrontation with his brothers over it; A. W. and R. B. had been good to his son, W. L. When T. A.'s heirs looked at their own situations, they could not see that A. W. or R. B. had been good to any of them—A. W. had not even waived the fees for handling the estate left behind by their father, and he had invested the estate's money in relatively unproductive channels. Sure, he had set T. A. Junior up in the Mellon-Stuart Construction Company, but ever since then T. A. Junior had drained himself running, running, running just to keep up with the interest payments owed to dear Uncle Andy.

T. A. Junior was not eager for a fight with his rich uncles. He was basically a timid man, and he was wary of the emotional scars that the battle would leave on the whole family. His younger brother, Edward P., the architect, was away from Pittsburgh and gave little encouragement to his branch of the family. Their spirited sister, Mary McClung, however, retained the same tough instincts that she had shown when she had deserted her first husband years before. On behalf of herself and her brothers, she was ready to ask the hard questions and she did so through her attorney husband Sam McClung. By that time T. Mellon & Sons was long gone, and what the question really meant was "Who owns the valuable and imposing successor to T. Mellon & Sons?" The stakes were high.

What transpired at the confrontation in A. W.'s office between the nation's third richest man and one of Pittsburgh's less-important lawyers has been variously reported to the author. Harsh words were exchanged, and there was no offer of compromise. If all that had been involved had been money, A. W. might have tossed off a few millions, but implicit in the claim of T. A.'s descendants was an accusation that A. W. had taken advantage of the orphans of his dead brother. He could not acknowledge that there was even a tinge of validity to such a claim by making a cash settlement of it. T. A.'s branch backed down from bringing suit, but the bitterness, the bad taste, lingered and poisoned the last few years for A. W.

The final great trauma of A. W.'s life might be called Couzens's revenge: A. W.'s painful and prolonged difficulties with the Internal Revenue Service. In May of 1933 Louis T. McFadden, an influential maverick Republican congressman from Pennsylvania who had a long history of bad blood with A. W., charged on the floor of Congress that Mellon's 1931 income tax return was riddled with fraudulent transactions designed to cheat on Mellon's income tax. He called upon the Department of Justice to investigate his claim. Roosevelt's Attorney General, Homer S. Cummings, announced that he would do so, but from all that A. W. could see, Cummings did not seem to be proceeding on any investigation further than to make regular comments to the press that his department was "looking into it." Each time that it was brought up, the newspapers reiterated McFadden's charge, using his cruel words, "fraud" and "cheat." In June 1933, no doubt on the advice of counsel, A. W. wrote Cummings demanding that the inquiries Cummings mentioned to the press actually proceed or be laid to rest, and offering his full cooperation. He got no response, but in October 1933 three government accountants showed up and began perusing his books. After three weeks of auditing and consultations with A. W.'s chief accountant, Howard Johnson, they were satisfied. Everything added up correctly.* The differences between Mellon and the New Deal involved the propriety of transactions and questions of law, not "forgotten" items of income or misplaced decimal points. Nevertheless, A. W. took some satisfaction that the administration's accountants had "exonerated" him, a fact that he repeatedly mentioned in the subsequent proceedings, for he found that the exit of the investigators was just the beginning, and not the end of his difficulties.

Notwithstanding the favorable attitude of the government's accountants, the Attorney General continued to answer press queries to the effect that

---

*Almost everything. The federal accountants determined that A. W. owed R. B. twenty-five dollars.

his investigation was continuing. He did not, however, indicate to Mellon or to the press specific areas of concern, nor did he or the Treasury Department specifically challenge the correctness of A. W.'s returns. He ignored Mellon's written demands that the government proceed or put the matter to an end, and stop the "campaign of character-wrecking and abuse against me" to which he had been and was being subjected. The Attorney General's only response to A. W.'s requests came in March of 1934, when in a seemingly unprecedented press release he announced that he was submitting a number of tax matters, including the matter of A. W. Mellon's 1931 return, to grand juries. He would seek criminal indictment of the old man —to some still the greatest Secretary of the Treasury since Alexander Hamilton—for income tax fraud! Mellon was in for the most important fight of his career, a fight in which his very character was to be tried in the courts and, more important, in the press. A. W. began the grand jury phase of the campaign with a lengthy statement outlining the history of the matter and of his repeated unanswered requests of Cummings, in a manner impelling the conclusion that he was being politically persecuted. The administration made no response. As the grand jury sat down, A. W. followed up with another attack on the manner in which he had been singled out for "railroading." It was the reverse of the situation in his old divorce case. He was now taking the offensive in the press, while the government, after a lot of early tantalizing loose talk, was now handicapped by the ethics of the legal profession, which prohibited it from "trying its case in the press" by revelation of its specific charges and its evidence. A. W. was scoring the victories in the court of public opinion.

The grand jury met in Pittsburgh in early May 1934 to consider only the government's evidence and determine whether there was sufficient cause on the basis of the government's case to indict the accused and bring him to trial for fraud. No representative or attorney for the accused was entitled or permitted to be present. The proceedings were supposed to be secret throughout. Among the grand jury's twenty-four members, its foreman, William B. Beeson, was a bank clerk, but the bulk of its membership performed such occupations as might warrant a presumption of hostility to Mellon: a carpenter, a plumber, another clerk, two farmers, two mechanics, a writer, and five whose occupation was simply "day laborer." After hearing the government's capsulated case, the grand jury deliberated five hours. As they did, A. W. sat down for lunch with W. L., who later recalled that A. W. was "as calm and unmoved as on any other day. This was because he had been so certain that honest, sensible men would find him guiltless."

For dessert they had the grand jury's decision: "Not a true bill." They had refused to indict!

The press sweetened A. W.'s victory in the first round. Virtually every significant paper in the United States editorialized on it, generally applauding his victory as a victory for democracy. The Philadelphia *Inquirer's* editorial was typical: "The politically minded Cummings has failed in his raid, which is well, because if he had succeeded with Mellon he could have cited any political enemy into court upon the slightest provocation." Rallying to A. W.'s side were such unexpected newspaper allies as the Detroit *Free Press,* staunch supporter of Senator Couzens, which had attacked A. W. for the Treasury's role in the Couzens tax case ("The action of the grand jury deserves applause and appreciation"), and the Baltimore *Sun,* newspaper of Frank Kent and H. L. Mencken ("The swing of the political pendulum away from Mellonism is not to be taken as an excuse for persecution"). The family was most gratified by Walter Lippmann's comment in his popular New York *World* column, lambasting the administration for Cummings's "act of profound injustice." W. L. included the whole piece in *Judge Mellon's Sons.*

The matter was far from over. The Treasury Department then served on Mellon a notice of tax deficiency for the year 1931—the same kind of letter that Commissioner Blair had caused to be served on Couzens ten years earlier—announcing that the Treasury had found A. W.'s 1931 return to be deficient and claiming additional income taxes for that year of $3 million. Unlike the notice served on Couzens, however, this one included a penalty assessment for fraud, which the government included despite the reservations of the general counsel of the Internal Revenue Service, Robert H. Jackson, later a member of the United States Supreme Court. According to Jackson's biographer, Eugene C. Gerhart, the way Jackson saw things,

> To charge Mellon with fraud would put government counsel at a disadvantage because legally the burden of proof would then be on the government. If fraud were not charged, the burden of proof would be on the taxpayer to prove he did not owe the tax claimed by the Commissioner of Internal Revenue. Jackson argued that if a large tax was ultimately found to be due the Treasury, that, in effect, was equivalent to finding its former Secretary guilty of fraud. Also, citizens are reluctant to make such findings of fraud; and the criminal indictment had already failed. Then, too, Mellon was an old man, an obviously successful businessman and banker, who had apparently been a faithful public servant. To charge him with fraud now would arouse a great deal of sympathy for him. Nevertheless, Jackson was informed later that the President had decided that Mellon should be charged with fraud.

The failure of the government to get a criminal conviction—or even an indictment—for fraud weakened its fraud charge but did not make it "illegal" for the administration to keep the issue alive in civil proceedings. The government ultimately claimed a total of $3,089,261.24 balance due, including the penalty. A. W. told the press that he "would rather spend the rest of my days in jail than submit to such tyranny."

A. W. publicly claimed, and no doubt believed, that the Roosevelt administration's moves against him were "politics of the crudest sort," as he put it to the press. He probably recalled Roosevelt's foolish speech of 1926 in which the future President had called A. W. "the master mind among the malefactors of great wealth." Roosevelt's Vice President Garner had gone even further and had once said on the floor of Congress that when the Democrats took power, he would like to "look into Uncle Andy's books." As a private attorney years before, Attorney General Cummings had wasted thousands of his hours in *Baush Machine Tool Company* v. *Aluminum Company of America,* and *Haskell* v. *Perkins,* both unsuccessful private anti-trust cases directed against A. W.'s aluminum business. It was easy enough for A. W. to see what was going on. These three malevolents were perverting their offices by using their powers to single out and persecute him for private purposes. A. W.'s friends (or Roosevelt's enemies) were of like mind. Herbert Hoover wrote in his memoirs that the prosecution of A. W. Mellon "was an ugly blot on the decencies of democracy," and W. L. lamented in *Judge Mellon's Sons* that in A. W.'s last years "he was fated to be persecuted and humiliated by conspirators. . . . It is difficult for me to review the events of that time without bitterness."

An objective eye (the author's) would have to conclude that A. W. was right, that the New Deal was furthering a vendetta against him. On the basis of the precedents, the Roosevelt administration should have realized that their case would boil down to highly technical questions. They could not have foreseen that A. W. would prevail on most of those technical disputes as he did, but they should have foreseen that no judge was going to find someone guilty of fraud for having resolved a technical question incorrectly. They should have seen that their battle to hold A. W. for fraud was almost unwinnable, and that from a political viewpoint the administration would suffer a serious public relations setback were they to lose in an assault on A. W.'s character. All of that the Roosevelt administration should have foreseen, unless they had been blinded by crusader's zeal.

A. W. was correct in characterizing the administration's move against him as "politics," but it was not "politics of the crudest sort"; it was not a matter of discrediting the Republican administrations by discrediting

Mellon. It was politics of the least crude (but worst) sort: ideological politics. The administration was attempting to discredit the values of the 1920s, attempting to discredit Mellon as a symbol, not as an individual or as an important Republican. This becomes clear from reading the voluminous diary of Roosevelt's Secretary of the Treasury, Henry Morgenthau, mostly unpublished but available at the Roosevelt Library in Hyde Park, New York. Morgenthau, as successor to A. W., also acceded to his role as chief officer of the Internal Revenue Service. In a conversation with Robert H. Jackson recorded and included in Morgenthau's diary, Jackson questioned his chief as to whether Morgenthau thought he was being too hardheaded. Morgenthau's answer tells the story of the administration's motive: "You can't be too tough in this trial to suit me. . . . I consider that Mr. Mellon is not on trial but democracy and the privileged rich and I want to see who will win."

Jackson no doubt felt the same way. If he did not think A. W. guilty of "fraud," his contemporary correspondence with Morgenthau makes clear that he did regard Mellon's tax planning as reprehensible. He lost all objectivity and fell in love with his own case. By the time that he wrote his autobiographical notes years later, Jackson was satisfied that Mellon had not proceeded fraudulently, but he still mentioned Mellon's "avarice to save money." Why was it avarice for A. W. to have attempted to minimize his tax bill? How many who are aware of the possibilities of tax planning fail to utilize it to the fullest possible extent that their situations, imaginations, and bravado permit? The principal check on any man's avarice is his own sense of fairness—and A. W. wanted to pay a tax that he could regard as "fair," and he did pay a large tax for 1931, though he could easily have created enough "paper" losses in that year to have wiped out his entire tax. A. W.'s efforts, or those of his staff, to reduce his tax bill could appear as "avarice" only to a social crusader likely to agree with Morgenthau that the issue was democracy vs. the privileged rich.

The kind of vendetta conducted by the New Deal against Mellon, justified on ideological bases, is the "worst" kind of politics because it is backed by a sense of moral righteousness that obscures not only objectivity (as it did in New Deal vs. Mellon) but also competing values. Moral righteousness enabled honorable people of the orientation of Morgenthau and Jackson to fill the newspaper pages with irresponsible charges of fraud and dishonesty —with a clear conscience. Elmer Irey, who was director of the Internal Revenue Service's intelligence unit at the time of the Mellon investigation, never for a moment believed that A. W. had committed any fraud. He had a sour taste in his mouth throughout the investigation, but at the same time he was completely satisfied as to the good faith on which his higher-ups were proceeding.

By objective standards, A. W.'s action against Couzens would also have to be regarded as a vendetta. No doubt A. W., like Morgenthau and Jackson, was able to rationalize it on some basis other than simple politics. A. W.'s private papers, unlike Morgenthau's, are not available, so we cannot know the basis on which A. W. justified what, objectively, would have to be regarded as a "wrongdoing" visited upon Senator Couzens. Perhaps A. W.'s papers would justify it on a basis no more profound than "just doing my job." The author suspects that A. W.'s real motive in proceeding against Couzens was politics of the crudest (best) sort: A. W. stopped short of attacking Couzens's character with loud claims of fraud.

Perhaps Morgenthau and Jackson can be forgiven to some extent on the theory that their hearts were pure, but Franklin D. Roosevelt was a more cynical man. From the start Roosevelt personally insisted on taking the route that was most injurious to Mellon's reputation. A handwritten memorandum by him to the Department of Justice, undated but almost certainly predating the request for an indictment, says that a report on A. W.'s taxes "has been there since Nov. Why not have Cummings read it and make it public." Just prior to the request for a grand jury indictment, the cabinet met and, according to the published diary of Interior Secretary Harold L. Ickes, discussed whether the case should be sent for consideration by the grand jury. All conceded that the case involved close questions. The President himself, though, took the position that it would be better to let Mellon's and other close cases go to the grand jury, because that course would minimize criticism that the administration had favored the rich and the powerful over relatively insignificant taxpayers.

Publicly, though, the President attempted to lay low. In an off-the-record comment at his press conference he gave an unconvincing explanation why an honorable precedent had been broken and the names of Mellon and a few other well-known suspected citizens had been given to the press before the grand jury could consider the evidence:

> I think the reason there was an announcement of names the other day—and of course there are a great many other names—was because if there had not been an announcement from here the story about these particular names would have broken in each of the districts very shortly and therefore it was easier to announce them from here. Now, these actions are by no means confined to the names announced. There are several hundred cases in exactly the same category.

He attempted (unsuccessfully) to minimize his own role, and to lead the influential Arthur Krock of the New York *Times,* and no doubt other journalists, to believe that he had known nothing about the Mellon case proceedings, or the request for an indictment, until the matter broke.

After the grand jury failed to indict, Stimson, who had served as Hoover's Secretary of State and then retained influence during the Roosevelt administration, had lunch with Roosevelt and took the opportunity to give the President a piece of his mind. According to Stimson's diary:

> I brought up the Mellon cases. I pointed out to him the essential difference between property rights and personal rights; how in the case of the former it was usually only the question of a better distribution of the highly profitable results of the industrial revolution, but that in the case of the latter, personal rights, these were the rights which had been hammered out in seven centuries of leadership by our own race and that I felt that if the American people thought there was any danger of those being trampled on, it would produce a tremendous revulsion of feeling. He said he agreed perfectly.

Roosevelt put the blame on a mixup at the Treasury, but Stimson was not to be gotten off the subject so easily:

> I pointed out how outraged I had felt as a former prosecutor at the publication of names of the defendants before the grand jury had acted. He said he agreed perfectly. He said it was a case of bad work by the publicity man of the department. I said that if that was the case they ought to get a new one. He said they already had.

Subsequently the administration proceeded with its civil case, still including the claim of fraud, according to Jackson's autobiographical note, as the result of a decision made by the President himself.

The notice of tax deficiency that Internal Revenue served on A. W. required that he either accept the I.R.S.'s position or appeal to the Board of Tax Appeals, the same judicial body that had passed on the Couzens case. He appealed. By then the fifteen-member panel included only six Coolidge-Hoover holdovers; the majority of its members were Roosevelt appointees. The Mellon case was heard principally in Pittsburgh by a hearing panel composed of three of the board's members, presided over by Ernest Van Fossen, the Ohio Republican who had presided over the Couzens case ten years earlier, together with Charles M. Trammell, an old-school Florida Democrat, and Bolon B. Turner, an Arkansas Democrat who fit the New Deal mold.

The trial began in Pittsburgh on February 18, 1935. Jackson himself tried the case for the government, while A. W.'s battery of counsel was headed by the famed and flamboyant Washington trial lawyer Frank J. Hogan, author of the quip that "an ideal client is a very rich man, thoroughly scared." Hogan began with an impassioned opening statement attacking the political persecution of his client, and revealing for the first time that his client would build, and had all along been planning to build, a great national gallery of art, to which he had already dedicated many priceless paintings. His principal defense would be that "God Almighty in his infinite wisdom does not place in one heart and one mind those divers characters which would make such a gift for such a purpose to the people of his country, at the very time that with deliberate and willful intent he was planning to defraud those people of taxes." It was the kind of speech that one might have expected to be made to a jury, but seemed strangely inappropriate as an opening statement to a panel of three dry judges. Jackson responded in his opening:

> I have been so charmed by the eloquence of my friend, Mr. Hogan, that at times I have almost forgotten that a great deal of it was entirely irrelevant to the issues we are here to determine. Being somewhat of a jury lawyer myself, if anything at times I have looked to see where the jury was, and I found them in the box.

He turned to the jury box—filled to overflowing not by jurors but by journalists—and made a reverent bow. Over the next eleven weeks of trial at Pittsburgh both sides tried to win their case with the judges, but with at least one eye on the great jury beyond. A. W. sat there most of the time, usually with Ailsa or David Bruce close by. The Bruces moved to Pittsburgh to give the old man moral support; but Pittsburgh-based Paul— almost certainly to avoid the subpoena that Jackson had prepared for him —took a honeymoon abroad that went on and on, and that could and did last as long as the trial itself.

Often the trial was exciting, as when Van Fossen exploded at Jackson that a government argument was "false, ill-tempered and not useful." Often it was humorous, as when Jackson, the "country lawyer" matched wits with the consummate English gentleman, Lord Duveen, the celebrated art dealer whose polished ways of salesmanship combined with his mind-boggling price tags to make him appear something of a con artist. The packed courtroom howled when the Englishman referred to the site of Mellon's proposed museum in the capital as "by the obelisk near the pond"—where, indeed, it now stands close by the Washington Monument and its reflecting pool. Duveen was at his best in discussing the "value" of the works that

Mellon had donated to the A. W. Mellon Educational and Charitable Trust.
The testimony as carried in the transcript does not read as nicely as S. N.
Behrman's account of it in his biography *Duveen:*

> Jackson asked about the value of van Eyck's panel "The Annunciation."
> Duveen looked at him reprovingly, as you could not help looking at a man who
> would ask a question about a thing like that. "Perhaps you don't realize that
> there are only three small van Eycks in America," he said. "And they cannot
> compare with Mr. Mellon's van Eyck." He threw a compliment at Mellon for
> his shrewdness in getting this panel for a mere $503,010. It was worth a
> million, he said, and added, "Why, even I would give $750,000 for it now."
> He was asked about the "Cowper Madonna" of Raphael, which he had sold
> Mellon. This turned out to be another example of Mellon's shrewdness; he had
> wrested it from Duveen for $836,000. "I thought it a very low price. Mr.
> Mellon thought it a very high price. One day after lunch, I gave way," said
> Duveen, with the candor of a man who was not above admitting defeat. He
> beamed at Mellon to show that he bore no grudge. Mellon nodded in acknowl-
> edgment.

Gently Jackson exploded the baron's pomposities with questions about
Duveen's own taxes, and an embarrassing memorandum in Duveen's own
I.R.S. file that contained a powerful inference that A. W. had been Lord
Duveen's principal "mark." When the Englishman failed to catch the title
of the painting "The Praying Pilgrim," Jackson repeated it: " 'the *Praying
Pilgrim*,' P-R-*A*-Y . . ."

Often the trial was whimsical, and especially so during the five days that
A. W. himself spent on the witness stand. On the opening day of trial the
New York *Times* wrote that A. W. "appeared self-conscious like arriving
late for church and marching to the front pew." When his own testimony
got under way, the witness seemed like the A. W. Mellon who had been
traumatized by his speechmaking duties as Secretary of the Treasury. The
Times reported that

> Mr. Mellon was a diffident, almost shy, witness, who gave his answers to the
> questions by Mr. Hogan and by Robert H. Jackson, Federal counsel, in a voice
> so soft and low that spectators ten feet away could scarcely hear him and the
> three members of the board acting as his judges leaned forward with hands
> cupped behind their ears.
>
> At times he stammered and groped for words to express the exact shade of
> meaning he desired.

But as he continued in subsequent days, guided by the designedly delicate
cross-examination of Jackson, he relaxed and opened up. He began to enjoy

himself. Often he grinned broadly or chuckled out loud as he chatted on, almost as if to himself, about the days of long ago. He talked much more freely than anyone had ever imagined him capable of talking, and much more freely than Hogan would have wanted. A. W. regularly ignored Hogan's objections to questions posed by Jackson, and continued his discussion oblivious to his attorney's efforts. It was about the only time in the history of jurisprudence that the client knew better than his attorney. A. W.'s presentation was engaging and disarming. The trial showed Pittsburgh a man that few had ever realized existed. His mild and gentlemanly answers, and his frequent "philosophical" commentaries, transformed him from a name into an individual, and a likable one.

Often the trial was tense. In one of his telegrams to Morgenthau, Jackson wrote, "We here are all weary and on edge and all need to be viewed with an indulgent eye." He developed shingles, frequently a tension-related illness.

More often, though, the trial was deadly dull as it heard forty-five witnesses over a period of four months at hearings in Pittsburgh and Washington, producing a transcript of 10,345 pages plus another 847 incomprehensible exhibits. Day after day accountants reviewed unending columns of figures. Corporation officials "explained" the intricacies of corporate finance and the complex details of the sale of McClintic-Marshall to Bethlehem Steel. Bankers traced the course of stock sold by A. W. to Union Trust, which in turn sold the stock to Ascalot and Coalesced, holding companies controlled by A. W.'s children. As the witnesses droned on and on, one of the journalists—name unknown and undiscoverable—stopped attempting to follow the confusing web and instead set himself to drafting the following poem, a copy of which the author found in Morgenthau's papers:

> Come now the Board of Tax Appeals,
> To hear of Andy's daffy deals.
> It hears of sales, of dough in bales,
> It hears of stock, but somehow fails,
> Although unbiased, quite impartial,
> To comprehend McClintic-Marshall.
>
> Take Coalesced and Ascalot,
> Sales to them were sometimes not,
> Even solemn Judge Van Fossen,
> Couldn't reason for a loss in,
> But harken to Judge Trammel's thrust,
> "What's that to do with Union Trust?"

The questions involved in the A. W. Mellon tax case are somewhat complex. In an effort to keep each of the major issues straight, and more nearly comprehensible, as the author outlines each issue he will discuss the ultimate judicial resolution of each.*

Tax treatment of the sale of McClintic-Marshall to Bethlehem Steel is both the least interesting and one of the more interesting aspects of the suit. It is least interesting, except for those readers who would ponder such matters as whether the sale constituted a "reorganization" within the meaning of Section 112(i)(1)(A) of the Revenue Code of 1928. That and related questions occupied as much of the trial panel's attention as any other issue. It was ultimately to be resolved "no," thereby producing no net impact on the case.

More interesting, because of its poetic implications, was the question: In computing A. W.'s "profits" on the sale, how much was McClintic-Marshall's stock worth as of 1913?—precisely the kind of question that the Treasury Department under A. W. Mellon had used to plague Senator Couzens many years before. Couzens, still sitting in the Senate, had more than won that litigation. He had come out with a refund. He must have felt some satisfaction in seeing his old nemesis now hoisted on the same petard.

In computing his "profits" on the sale of stock to Bethlehem, A. W. had included a high valuation as of 1913 of $353 per share of common stock and $148 per share of preferred stock, thereby minimizing his "profit" and the amount of tax due. His return included a reservation as to his valuations: "In the computation of gain . . . a tentative value as of 1913 has been adopted. It is believed that the gain so computed and returned is in excess of the gain actually realized. In due course a proper basis will be presented and claims for refund filed." As the parties confronted the question, A. W. argued for a $500-a-share valuation of the common stock as of 1913, which would have resulted in a refund due him, while the government argued for

*The author is eliminating discussion of purely technical questions and of the "issue" of whether A. W. had made a bona fide divestiture of his banking stock when he became Secretary in 1921, discussed pages 280–281, a question the answer to which involved insignificant impact on A. W.'s 1931 taxes, and which the government almost certainly threw in only for its embarrassment value. Also eliminated has been any discussion of the "Blair Memorandum," a memo from the Commissioner of Internal Revenue to A. W. as Secretary setting forth various tax-avoidance techniques, which began with a statement that it was being sent pursuant to A. W.'s request. The government pointed to the memorandum as evidence that A. W. had used his official position as Secretary to get personal "how to" advice directly from the I.R.S. At the trial, A. W. categorically denied having requested any such memorandum, and denied any recollection of having received it. It is not out of the question that one of his underlings requested it for him, and then passed it along directly to A. W.'s Pittsburgh office without Mellon himself ever being aware of it. That was the kind of detail to which Winston attended.

a valuation of $158 as of 1913, which would have made for a much greater "profit" to A. W. and a substantially greater tax due the government than he had paid. The parties stipulated that the preferred stock as of 1913 should have been valued at $130 a share, meaning, in essence, that A. W. had underpaid his tax at least in that aspect of his figuring.

After dizzying testimony from accountants and financial experts, the Board of Tax Appeals set the value of McClintic-Marshall common stock as of 1913 at $300 a share. That aspect of the decision made for a significant increase in the taxes due the government; it was the only major issue in the case that was resolved in favor of the government. Couzens died before the board's decision, so he never had the opportunity to savor his full triumph.*

Valuation of McClintic-Marshall stock as of 1913 was obviously a matter on which reasonable opinions could differ, and the board's scaling down by a mere 15 per cent the value that A. W.'s tax preparers had placed on it as of 1913 when preparing his 1931 tax return eighteen years later could not properly cast any ill reflection on A. W.'s character. The more important issue from that standpoint involved what the government alleged to have been "phony" sales of stock, made with an eye to cheating the government. Toward the end of the year 1931 A. W. had made a number of sales of stock that did seem to be somewhat suspicious.

In the closing months of 1931 Johnson called to A. W.'s attention that his income that year had been substantial, though the value of his assets had declined. He suggested that A. W. consider liquidating some of his holdings in order to establish capital losses that could offset some of his income, thereby reducing his taxes. A. W. agreed that that would be a fine idea. On the witness stand he later described his thought process:

> I had the estimate of my tax return, although without any offsetting deductions, and I knew that was wrong, that is, I mean that it would be—I don't know the word, but unjustifiable to pay the taxes on profits that were capital gain profits when the law which made that obligatory upon me provided for deductions for the losses, and consequently I looked for something to make that deduction, and the amount was rather to my mind what would be a fair amount. Of course, to have wiped out all the tax would have been justifiable, would have been legal, but I did not realize that the next year was going to be worse and the next year worse, and that I was not still going to have a substantial income, and therefore I wanted to pay a substantial tax.
>
> So I, without making any calculation in figures or anything that way, but

---

*Couzens's term expired in 1936. That year he declined the Democratic nomination for his seat, and lost the Republican endorsement because of his independent ways. It didn't matter; he died before election day. The Board of Tax Appeals rendered its opinion late in 1937.

I just in my mind came to the conclusion that I would stop at a certain place in taking deductions and pay the amount of tax which would result, and that amount, the final amount that was reported, was a large amount. . . . I did not want to take any further losses; I wanted to pay a substantial tax. I considered that I was able to do that, and I was arriving at in my mind what was fair— I was going to use the word honest, but fair, a fair amount to pay to the government.

Of the several issues that he decided to sell and did sell to establish his losses, the largest block was his common stock in Pittsburgh Coal. He sought out McEldowney at a board meeting and offered to sell Union Trust 123,622 shares of Pittsburgh Coal that had cost him a total of $6,177,-956.25, for $500,000, little more than four dollars a share, but about what it was trading at on the stock market. After a moment's reflection McEldowney said, "All right. Send it up and we will take it." On December 31 Johnson delivered the stock and received Union's check, thereby establishing A. W.'s loss on the sale of $5,677,956.25, which reduced his tax bill by $710,177. If that were all there had been to the matter, there could be no question as to the propriety of the transaction and the legitimacy of his deduction for the losses he had suffered on Pittsburgh Coal, but the fuller background and the subsequent history of the block of Pittsburgh Coal stock created a powerful inference that the sale to Union had been a sham.

Sometime in the spring of 1929 or 1930 (the testimony was unclear), Frank E. Taplin, an important man in railroads, offered A. W. $100 a share for 100,000 shares of Pittsburgh Coal, or $10 million. As he made his offer he handed A. W. a certified check for $500,000 as a deposit. A. W. turned him down. When he later decided to sell his holdings, he did not seek out Taplin, who had offered almost twenty-five times as much a couple of years earlier. To Taplin the stock had much greater than market value, because a block of that size would have insured traffic for his railroads. He would certainly have declined to honor his old offer, but he would surely have paid in excess of four dollars a share. But A. W. did not approach Taplin or any possible purchaser other than Union Trust, and he offered it to Union at $4.044 a share. At the time, Pittsburgh Coal had not paid dividends in years; and if it were ever to pay dividends again, common stockholders would have to stand in line behind preferred stockholders awaiting unpaid accrued dividends. Pittsburgh Coal was the very worst possible investment that Union Trust could have made. McEldowney, however, quickly agreed to purchase, and his decision was ratified by Union's executive committee on December 31, 1931. Members present and voting were R. B. Mellon, W. L. Mellon, Roy Hunt (of Alcoa), McEldowney, William B. Schiller, and J. H. Lockhart.

One hundred and eighteen days later McEldowney decided to sell A. W.'s block of Pittsburgh Coal, and told his assistant Carl R. Korb to see if he could find a buyer. Korb made only one phone call, but it turned out to be the right one. He called Howard Johnson. It just so happened that Johnson did know of a possible purchaser: Coalesced Company. Coalesced was a holding company with two classes of stock: common stock, which paid no dividends, but which had voting rights; and preferred stock, which did not have voting rights but which was entitled to receive all dividends. Coalesced's common stock was owned half and half by Paul and Ailsa Mellon; all of its preferred stock was owned by A. W. Mellon. Virtually all of its $97 million in assets had come to it directly or indirectly by gift from A. W.

The agents agreed upon a price: 123,622 shares of Pittsburgh Coal for $500,000 plus a sum representing 6 per cent per year interest on $500,000 for 118 days. Korb called no other possible purchasers. Union's executive committee met to consider the transaction (members present: R. B. Mellon, W. L. Mellon, McEldowney, and Schiller) and approved the sale. Coalesced's board of directors (Paul, Ailsa, Johnson himself, family tax attorney David D. Shepard, and another longtime family employee, Henry A. Phillips) voted for acquisition, whereupon the transaction was consummated. On April 25, 1932, Johnson went back to Union Trust to retrieve the stock certificates. At about the same time A. W. made a gift to Paul and Ailsa of the preferred stock that he had held in Pittsburgh Coal. They immediately conveyed it to Coalesced Company.

At the time, Union Trust maintained a daily printed list of its security holdings. At no time during the 118 days that it "owned" A. W.'s block did the 123,622 shares appear on the list. When produced at the trial, the lists carried Pittsburgh Coal typewritten at the bottom. During those 118 days, a new board member joined the board of trustees of Pittsburgh Coal: Paul Mellon. At the end of the following tax year, on December 29, 1932, A. W. sold five blocks of stock to Union Trust, producing a loss to him of $2,958,782.42. On February 29, 1933, Union Trust sold and Coalesced bought the batch of them.

The evidence adduced at the trial established a pattern of A. W. making gifts to his children that found their way into Coalesced, demonstrating a desire or a possible plan on the part of A. W. to transfer his assets to Coalesced over time, the dividends from which would come to him during his lifetime, with the assets themselves otherwise controlled and owned by his children. The overall picture justified the government in concluding that A. W.'s sale of Pittsburgh Coal to Union Trust had not been a bona fide transaction, and that there must have been some private understanding that

A. W. would get Union off the hook at a later date, all as part of a stratagem to give A. W. a tax "loss" while furthering his overall plan. The government contended that Union served as a conduit by which A. W. had attempted to accomplish his scheme. Even Korb admitted under oath that in his twenty years at Union he could not recall any instances—other than those at issue—in which the bank had purchased stock in a company that was neither producing earnings nor paying dividends, without an agreement that the seller would arrange for repurchase.

Pittsburgh Coal was the most substantial of the "sham" sales, as the government characterized them, that A. W. made in 1931, but there were others. Also near the close of that year, on December 2, 1931, R. B. Mellon sold from the joint account of A. W. and R. B. Mellon 54,000 shares of Western Public Service at the four-dollar-a-share market price to Union Trust, a sale that meant a loss of $402,000 to each of the two brothers. On January 8, 1932, thirty-seven days later, R. B. Mellon purchased from Union Trust 57,000 shares of Western Public Service for the joint account of A. W. and R. B. Mellon, at a price of $4.075 a share. A. W. also sold assorted stocks at the close of the year to the Ascalot Corporation, netting losses to himself of $445,307.50. Ascalot was a holding company whose sole stockholder was Ailsa Mellon Bruce. Family members and their retainers composed its board of directors and made up its roster of officers.

A. W. did not just liquidate in 1931; he also acquired some stock for his portfolio: 2000 shares of Pennsylvania Railroad and 800 shares of Republic Steel. The seller of those issues, Ascalot, suffered a $57,176.31 loss on the transaction! In the many dealings between A. W. and his daughter during the early 1930s, sometimes A. W. realized the loss, sometimes Ailsa realized the loss, but invariably there was only one real loser, the United States Treasury. Ailsa's "losses" in 1933 reduced her taxable income to eighty-six dollars, thereby completely wiping out her income tax for that year, principally because she realized a loss on the sale of a cooperative apartment at 1 Beekman Place, New York, and her husband sustained a loss on the sale of some bank stock. The buyer of both the apartment and the stock was one A. W. Mellon, who never occupied the apartment. When this testimony emerged, Jackson asked the witness, Howard Johnson, whether Ascalot should be spelled with a "k" or a "c." With a deprecating smile, Johnson replied that it had always been spelled with a "c."

In his testimony A. W. readily acknowledged the tax motive behind his selling, but he insisted that his sale of Pittsburgh Coal and the stocks sold to Ascalot had been bona fide transactions. He personally regarded Pittsburgh Coal to be intrinsically worthless. He had no understanding with

McEldowney or with anyone else at Union Trust that the stock would be held for his repurchase, and he had no idea at all of Coalesced later becoming the owner of it. "I was not thinking of it ever coming back into the family at all." He had never thereafter discussed the matter with McEldowney, and he had had no knowledge of its subsequent acquisition by Coalesced until after the stock had been purchased by it: "I was not concerning myself about the Coalesced investments and I never have." If he had concerned himself with such matters, "I would not have advised the Coalesced to buy the property, although when I learned about it, I thought it was all right." Despite the family's dominance of Union Trust Company, he resisted any conclusion that the dealings between his office and McEldowney had been anything other than arm's-length transactions: "No one who knew Mr. McEldowney would consider that he could be influenced by anyone. He was a positive character, a masterful man, and he did his own thinking." As for his unwillingness to deal with Taplin, A. W. explained that Taplin was interested in acquiring control of Pittsburgh Coal in order to generate traffic for his railroad by hauling the coal away from western Pennsylvania, where it was needed as the motive power for Pittsburgh industry. A. W.'s loyalty to Pittsburgh prevented him from profiting at the expense of the well-being of his home town. As for the sale and repurchase of Western Public Service, he had never been aware of that transaction at all.

The court viewed the question essentially as one of credibility. Whether or not the sales were bona fide transactions without any understanding as to repurchase turned upon whether or not A. W. was to be believed. By a vote of eight to seven the majority, speaking through Van Fossen, found for Mellon: "This study leads us to the conclusion that petitioner's testimony is entitled to full credence." The mere fact that the transactions had been motivated by tax considerations was irrelevant, they concluded, citing respectable precedent: "Anyone may so arrange his affairs that his taxes shall be as low as possible; he is not bound to choose a pattern which will best pay the treasury; there is not even a patriotic duty to increase one's taxes." The majority's terse conclusions were that

> The sale by petitioner of stock of the Pittsburgh Coal Co. to the Union Trust Co. of Pittsburgh was a complete and valid sale, giving rise to a legal deduction. . . . Sales of stock by petitioner to a corporation all of the stock of which was owned by his daughter were valid sales and under the law as it existed in 1931, gave rise to legal deductions.

The Western Public Service sales—the smallest of the allegedly "sham" sales in question—was resolved against A. W. It was Mellon's burden to establish that there had been no understanding at the time of the sale with regard to possible reacquisition. The deaths of R. B. and McEldowney, the only parties to the Western Public Service sale and repurchase, made it impossible for him to meet that burden. The decision against him on that transaction, under those circumstances, could not be taken as any ill reflection on him.

Seven dissenters on the Board of Tax Appeals, speaking through Bolon B. Turner, would have held against Mellon on the Pittsburgh Coal transaction. The evidence, to Turner's eye, "to state the conclusion most leniently for the petitioner, casts a definite cloud of doubt on his claim that he made an outright and bona fide sale of the stock to Union Trust Co." As Mellon had had the burden of proof on that issue, the seven dissenters would have found against him. They were most influenced by the seeming incomprehensibility of Union Trust's position. Turner reviewed Pittsburgh Coal's dismal picture as of December 1931 as that picture had been presented by A. W. and Johnson in their testimony, and then continued:

> Undoubtedly McEldowney was also fully aware of these facts . . . Yet we are asked to find as a fact that the Union Trust Co. actually purchased, with the funds of its investors and depositors and as an investment, 123,622 shares of that stock, a stock which had no dividend prospects and which the bank had never seen fit to invest in even during the prosperous days of the Pittsburgh Coal Co., if it had ever known such days. . . .
>
> I am able to reach no other conclusion than that the Union Trust Co. throughout the transaction looked to the petitioner to take up or to provide a taker for the Pittsburgh Coal Co. stock and to pay a reasonable sum for services rendered.

Both majority and minority were looking at the subject much too narrowly. They were looking at A. W. Mellon's personal intentions—an important consideration in determining whether or not he was guilty of fraud, but of little significance in determining the tax status of a transaction. They should have been considering the intentions of those who were acting for and on behalf of A. W. Mellon. A. W. may or may not have had any personal intention of bailing the bank out of Pittsburgh Coal, but the probability is that his staff—Johnson or the tax counselor Shepard—recognized some obligation to relieve the bank of the undesirable stock either by reacquisition of it by A. W. himself, or by arranging for the purchase of it by one of A. W.'s avatars, Coalesced or Ascalot, after their employer had enjoyed the benefit of the tax loss. There was no point to compromising A. W. by discussing the full strategy with him. He would probably want it done, but he might not want to know. Nor was there any need to make explicit commitments with McEldowney, who could figure such things out for himself, and who appreciated that when gentlemen deal with gentlemen, some things do not have to be pinned down, and some things are better left unsaid.

Had such a view been taken, A. W. would have suffered the tax, but his personal integrity would have remained above reproach. The board's decision would not have had to depend on a finding of a silent conspiracy; it could have turned on failure of A. W. to meet the burden of proof, the basis on which the entire board found against him on the Western Public Service transaction. This line of argument, however, was not developed by the government, perhaps because its efforts were not directed so much at collecting the money as at exposing Mellon personally for his "criminal" role. It was too much to ask fifteen members of the Board of Tax Appeals to find that A. W. Mellon was a liar.

Probably the most colorful issue in the trial revolved around A. W.'s "gift" to "charity" of five valuable paintings in 1931. Were they "gifts"? And was the A. W. Mellon Educational and Charitable Trust a real "charity"? On his original income tax return for 1931 A. W. claimed a deduction for various "routine" charities, but he made no claim for any deduction for gifts to the trust, probably because it would not have made any difference had he done so. At the time, deductions for charitable contributions were limited to 15 per cent of adjusted gross income; as A. W.'s "regular" contributions totaling $580,078 exceeded 15 per cent of what his return showed to be adjusted gross income, there was nothing to be gained by including a recitation of further contributions that might or might not be looked at askance. When the Roosevelt administration claimed that his adjusted gross income for 1931 was very much higher than what he had shown on his 1931 return, the matter of his contributions to the Trust began to become relevant. If a court were to find for the administration, then a portion of his contributions to the trust might become deductible, and so reduce the adverse effect on A. W. of such findings as might be made in favor of the government. That, no doubt, is what the accountants said when urging him to file an amended return claiming a deduction for the paintings. His lawyers were interested in other strategic considerations. If the government were to challenge the deduction for the paintings, the lawyers would then have an opportunity to drag out, at great length, the benefactions of

their client, and thereby paint him as a philanthropist. It would be inconceivable that such a philanthropist would cheat on his income taxes! So,
after the government challenged his 1931 return, A. W. filed an amended
return claiming a deduction in the amount of $3,247,695 for the gift of the
five paintings to a charity, the A. W. Mellon Educational and Charitable
Trust. The government denied the propriety of the deduction. Jackson, who
tried the case for the government, later quipped that when the trial got
under way, every time he would score a point A. W.'s lawyer "would drag
out another Madonna. I was literally smothered by Madonnas!"

As the evidence developed, it appeared that at the very end of the 1930
tax year, on December 30, 1930, A. W. established a charity, the A. W.
Mellon Educational and Charitable Trust, devoted to educational and charitable purposes. Its board of directors was made up of A. W. Mellon, Paul
Mellon, David Bruce, and D. D. Shepard the tax counselor. Anyone who
cared to make a contribution to charity might make one to the the trust.
So long as not in excess of 15 per cent of adjusted gross income, that
contribution would be deductible from the income upon which the benefactor would otherwise be taxed. By the time of trial only two citizens had
decided that the A. W. Mellon Educational and Charitable Trust was their
kind of charity: Paul Mellon, who had made relatively modest cash contributions to it, and A. W. Mellon, who had made relatively modest cash
contributions to it and some staggering gifts of works of art. In the last
minutes of 1930, seconds after the trust was established, A. W. contributed
$10,000 to it plus one painting valued (probably conservatively) at $800,-
000. That year A. W. claimed a deduction for charitable contributions to
the trust of $810,000.*

In the year in question at the trial, 1931, he gave the trust five significant
paintings: Raphael's "Alba Madonna," Botticelli's "Adoration of the
Magi," Titian's "Toilet of Venus," Van Eyck's "Annunciation," and a
Perugino "Crucifixion." He had acquired these paintings from the government of the Soviet Union at a total price of $3,247,695. Almost immediately
thereafter he had given them to the trust by deed and a letter addressed to
each trustee (including himself). They were stored in a secure storage area
at the Corcoran Gallery of Art in Washington, a public gallery of the United
States government, by agreement between A. W. and the gallery's director.
In his amended 1931 return A. W. claimed a deduction for the paintings

---

*This sounds worse than it was. Further along the author attempts to make clear that
though A. W. did keep an eye on tax consequences of his benefactions, they were not the
principal motivation for his gifts of art to the public.

in the amount of the purchase price. In subsequent years prior to trial, 1932 and 1934, he gave more paintings to the trust of substantial value: $6 million in 1932 and $9 million in 1934. Most of those paintings, however, were not removed to the Corcoran Gallery's storage rooms, but were left hanging right where they had always hung—on the walls of A. W.'s Washington apartment or in Ailsa's New York apartment. Title to the objects changed hands, and A. W. became entitled (or so he successfully claimed) to his tax deductions to the limit to which they were deductible, while actual enjoyment of the paintings remained completely unaffected. By the time of the trial none of the paintings owned by the trust had ever been displayed to the public, who to some extent had paid for them by reduction of the taxes that A. W. would otherwise have paid.

The government opposed the deduction, claiming that only formalistic gifts had been made to a "charity" dominated by A. W.'s own family. As Jackson put it in a telegram to Morgenthau, it was inconceivable that a man could "claim that pictures still hanging on the walls of his private residence have been given to education and charity just by a deed to himself and others of his family and employees as trustees." To his eye, it was just another tax dodge, this one cloaked in a phony garb of philanthropy.

The Board of Tax Appeals disagreed, and disposed of the issue briefly. The trust could be regarded as a charity; the gifts had been completed ones, and insofar as A. W. or Ailsa had kept physical possession of the paintings, they had done so only as an accommodation to the trust. The gifts gave rise to legitimate charitable deductions to the extent that the 15 per cent limit permitted. There was no dissent.

The last of the major issues confronting the board was the matter of A. W.'s alleged fraud. The government limited its fraud charge to the claim that the Pittsburgh Coal and Western Public Service transactions had been fraudulent. Not even Jackson was much persuaded by the government's claim. He later told his biographer that in the course of the trial "I became convinced that the fraud, if any, had been perpetrated by some of his lawyers, not by the old man himself." In his unpublished autobiographical notes, quoted by Gerhart in his published biography, Jackson wrote

> From watching him and from what I knew of him and men of his type I was satisfied that the sharp practice in his tax return was the work of a tax adviser and that Mr. Mellon's contribution to it was his avarice to save money. If he had been told it was wrong or illegal, he would not have done it. . . . My impression of Mr. Mellon is that he did not intend to cheat the government.

Given the board's determinations on the propriety of the Pittsburgh Coal and Western Public Service transactions, they were not prone to give serious consideration to the fraud claim. They dismissed it with an abrupt finding of fact: "Petitioner did not file a false and fraudulent return, with the purpose of evading taxes. No part of the deficiency, if any, resulting from the recomputation consequent hereon, is due to fraud with intent to evade taxes." There was no dissent on that aspect of the case. A. W. won all fifteen votes on the only question that mattered to him.

Essentially, the government had argued that A. W.'s tax-avoidance plans (or those of his agents) went beyond "honest" tax planning. In fact, A. W.'s counselors employed most of the devices then known to tax planners; they had pushed their engineering to the nth degree. But the legitimacy of their plans had been upheld by the board; they had not been in error, let alone had they entered the area of fraud. Those aspects of the board's decision that were resolved against A. W.—the valuation of McClintic-Marshall stock as of 1913 and the disallowance of the deduction for the losses in Western Public Service—turned on purely technical considerations that involved no hint of moral turpitude on anyone's part.

The board's decision meant a balance of taxes owed by Mellon of some $400,000 or so, probably less than the cost to the taxpayers of conducting all of the investigations, the grand jury proceedings, and the Board of Tax Appeals hearings. Thereafter, both sides made preliminary motions to appeal those aspects of the board's decision that had been adverse to them, but neither got very far. With minor modifications, the case was settled on the basis of the board's decision for $485,809 plus interest, a small fraction of what the government had claimed. By then, however, A. W. had passed away. Like Couzens, he had been cheated by death of savoring the full delight of his essential victory.

After the close of the trial, A. W. devoted himself to his great monument, the National Gallery of Art.

Until Frick's death in 1919 A. W. was known to the major dealers in New York and London as Frick's friend, but they saved their important canvases for Frick and other more discriminating, less tight-fisted buyers than A. W. Mellon. While Frick was acquiring works of art of major importance, A. W. was accumulating mediocre "Barbizon" works such as Constant Troyon's "Cows in a Meadow," his major purchase of 1899, acquired from Knoedler and Company for $17,000. Later A. W. asked Roland Knoedler, "When I first started buying pictures why didn't you offer me Gainsboroughs, Rembrandts, Frans Hals, et cetera?" Knoedler responded, "Because you would not have bought them." The likelier explanation was that it was easier to sell important works to people like Frick, and Frick might have been offended had a dealer offered first pickings to his "sidekick."

In 1916 A. W. moved to a slightly less austere home on Woodland Road, Pittsburgh, but it too was dark most of the time. There he hung his collection. In one of his college-day poems, Paul Mellon alluded to

> . . . paintings hidden in a long dark hall,
> Only alive when the sun's beams of gold
> Slant, at day's ending, where they were confined
> In shadows?

In 1920 A. W. approved an appraisal of his collection at a relatively modest $900,000.

With Frick's passing in 1919, A. W. became a somewhat more "worthwhile" person to international art dealers like Knoedler and Duveen. Perhaps they recalled how Frick had introduced his friend: "This man will someday be a great collector." To a man, they hoped so. Mellon had met the flamboyant Duveen at Frick's in 1919. In *Duveen,* Behrman recounts how the baron renewed their acquaintanceship in England in 1921:

> Although Mellon knew very little about Duveen, apart from the fact that he didn't want to deal with him [Duveen was substantially more expensive than Knoedler], Duveen was thoroughly informed about Mellon. Duveen was much better prepared to know Mellon than Mellon was to know Duveen. For another thing, the mechanics of the meeting were so much simpler than they would have been had Duveen been an unfriendly man. The meeting was effected by a delicate feat of co-ordination. Duveen could not depend on coincidence unless he himself created it. In 1921, Mellon, visiting London, occupied a suite on the third floor of Claridge's. Duveen had a permanent suite on the fourth floor of Claridge's. Stirred suddenly by premonitions of intimacy, he had himself moved to the floor below Mellon. Duveen's valet was, inevitably, a friend of Mellon's; the two valets seem to have wished the contagion of their friendship to spread to their masters. One afternoon, Duveen was apprised by his valet that Mellon's valet was helping Mellon on with his overcoat and was about to start down the corridor with him for the lift. Duveen's valet hastily performed the same services for Duveen. The timing of the valets was so exquisite that Duveen stepped into the descending lift that contained Mellon. Duveen was not only surprised, he was charmed. "How do you do, Mr. Mellon?" he said, and introduced himself, adding, as he later recalled, "I am on my way to the National Gallery to look at some pictures. My great refreshment is to look at pictures." Taken unawares, Mellon admitted that he, too, was in need of a little refreshment. They went to the National Gallery together,

and after they had been refreshed, Mellon discovered that Duveen had an inventory of Old Masters of his own that, although smaller than the museum's, was, Duveen thought, comparable in quality.

The dealers, principally Knoedler, together with David Finley, educated Mellon to an appreciation of works of infinitely greater artistic merit than those that he had previously been accustomed to acquiring. They were costlier too.

Throughout the 1920s A. W. was acquiring important art. Mostly they were pieces that reflected his personal tastes—paintings that he liked and liked to live with. According to Finley, he had strict ideas about what could be hung in one's home. He did not like contemporary paintings, he would not own nudes, and he disliked paintings of unpleasant scenes, paintings done in gaudy colors, or "dark" paintings with black backgrounds. He was not enthusiastic about religious paintings, but such as he acquired he insisted be displayed respectfully—away from areas where company might be smoking or drinking. What he really liked, and principally what he bought, were pleasant, placid paintings.

In 1925 A. W. purchased his first fabulously expensive canvas, Holbein's "Portrait of Edward VI as a Child," bought from Knoedler for $437,000. Thereafter Knoedler and Duveen vied to get their canvases on the walls of his Washington apartment "on approval." A. W. would discuss a new arrival over a long lunch with Finley, live with it for a while, and if after several months he decided that he liked it he would haggle over price. Paintings that he did not like, regardless of importance or price, were returned. W. L. reported this anecdote in *Judge Mellon's Sons:*

> For a while A. W. had on the wall above the mantel-piece in the drawing room of his apartment Raphael's portrait of Giuliano de Medici. Experts, and among them A. W., generally considered this to be one of the best of all Raphaels. Nevertheless, A. W. was disturbed by the picture. One time he was asked why.
> "The man has an evil face and it is not particularly attractive to live with."
> He returned the picture to Duveen. The absence of that Raphael attracted rather more attention than had its presence. One evening when he was having a dinner party, the Princesse de Ligne, wife of the Belgian ambassador, was going about the apartment on the arm of David Finley. They were looking at A. W.'s pictures. The princess asked, "Where is the Raphael?"
> "Mr. Mellon sent it away."
> "But why?"
> "Because he did not like it."
> The eyes of the princess widened as she gasped: "How wonderful! To be able to say, 'Take away that Raphael. I don't like it.' Who but Mr. Mellon could do that?"

After A. W. conceived the idea of a national gallery of art, he began buying more and more pictures, at higher and higher prices, with an eye focused more on depth, breadth, and "importance" of the collection, than on his own personal tastes. He bought crucifixions, dark paintings, unpleasant scenes, and even semi-nudes. His most important acquisitions were probably the paintings that he bought from the Soviet Union between 1929 and 1931, through intricate and exciting negotiations in which he was represented principally by Knoedler. Ultimately he acquired twenty-one paintings, most of the truly important "Old Masters" in the Russians' Hermitage Gallery, at a total cost of $6,654,000. Later the administrators of the National Gallery of Art would regret the few important Old Masters, including two Leonardos and a Giorgione, that he passed up as "overpriced" on Knoedler's advice. At the time, his purchases were kept as secret as possible. The United States government did not recognize the Soviet Union and officially discouraged dealings with the communists. Almost more importantly, publicity about the payment of large sums of money for paintings during the worst periods of the Great Depression could only be embarrassing. Inevitably, though, news leaked to the press.

Exactly when A. W. began buying for a national gallery of art is not completely clear. In 1926 he wrote the Duchess of Rutland that in his collecting "I have not had occasion to consider acquisition of [works of art] for public purposes." The following year, though, when Finley was considering leaving government service, A. W. pressed him to remain, promising him an important role in some national art gallery that he envisioned. That year he put his personal attorney, David Shepard, to work studying the organizational documents of important public art galleries. His diary after 1928 includes regular discussions of possible sites for the gallery.

In his memoirs Herbert Hoover reported that

> While Mr. Mellon was in my Cabinet the question of a certain site for a public building came up. After the Cabinet meeting he came to me and asked that that particular site be kept vacant. He disclosed to me his purpose to build a great national art gallery in Washington, to present to it his own collection which was to include the large number of old masters which he was then purchasing from the Soviet Government. He said he would amply endow it and thought it might altogether amount to $75,000,000. I urged that he announce it at once, and have the pleasure of seeing it built in his lifetime. He was a shy and modest man. The only reason he told me at all was that he wanted that site reserved. He asked me to keep it in confidence. Had he made this magnificent benefaction public at that time, public opinion would have protected him from the scandalous persecution under the New Deal.

A. W.'s gift of the Hermitage art to the A. W. Mellon Educational and Charitable Trust, while not a commitment to build what was to become the National Gallery of Art, nonetheless constituted an irrevocable dedication of the specific works to some public purpose, which could be delayed indefinitely but could not be defeated without tampering with the documents. Still, Mellon refused to make a complete and public commitment, and as late as 1934 he publicly denied any such commitment. In his tax trial he had this exchange with Jackson:

> Q. Mr. Mellon, from photostat copies of the newspapers of November 13th of 1934 it appears that you issued a statement on that day saying:
> "The report that I have arranged to build an art gallery at Washington is entirely unfounded. I have engaged no architects, have caused no plans to be drawn, and have made no commitment to build or endow a gallery at Washington, Pittsburgh, or elsewhere."
> You made such a statement, did you not, on that date?
> A. I was waylaid by a reporter, and I think what I told him was substantially true. My impression is that in the sense of "commitment" I had not made any commitment at that time, and I do not recall whether—I got that word "commitment" from what you have read, but I do not think—I do not just recall that being a part of the conversation. But I had not, and have not yet, engaged an architect, or—I have forgotten what the other questions were.
> Q. Have caused no plans to be drawn.
> A. That is true.
> Q. And have made no commitment to build or endow a gallery at Washington, Pittsburgh, or elsewhere.
> A. That is substantially true.

According to Finley's affectionate remembrance, *A Standard of Excellence: Andrew W. Mellon Founds the National Gallery of Art at Washington, D. C.,* after the trial some of A. W.'s friends

> tried to deter him. "Why do you give your collection to Washington when you have been treated so badly by the New Deal Administration?" Mr. Mellon replied firmly: "I am not going to be deterred from building the National Gallery in Washington. Eventually the people now in power in Washington will be dead and I will be dead, but the National Gallery, I hope, will be there and that is something the country needs."

In 1935 or 1936 A. W. engaged an architect, John Russell Pope, who had considerable experience in designing art museums and had supervised the conversion of the New York mansion of Mellon's mentor, Frick, into an art museum. A. W. wanted the kind of palatial Palladian-inspired building to which Pope himself gravitated. They agreed to cap it with just what Washington didn't need—another dome. Mellon himself gave personal attention to every detail of the museum. He was not concerned with avoiding expense, though he was concerned with avoiding ostentation. In discussing the decoration of interior rooms, he told Finley, "I don't care how expensive they are if they don't look expensive." He personally specified the (expensive) pink-hued Tennessee marble that sheaths the building's exterior. Behrman says that he "decided on Tennessee marble because it was, like himself, unostentatious and austere. He chose it because it didn't look like marble. Here, too, perhaps, his choice indicated an expression of his desire for silence; he didn't want the marble to admit that it was marble."

Together, Mellon, Finley, and Pope designed one of the world's truly great examples of routine monumental architecture. It is an impressive building. According to Paul Mellon's friend John Walker, second director of the National Gallery, Mellon felt that Americans needed more magnificent, less utilitarian buildings than the small apartments and homes in which they lived.

A. W. also embarked on a radical expansion of his collection. According to Behrman's *Duveen,* the Englishman told Mellon

"You and I are getting on. We don't want to run around. I have some beautiful things for you, things you ought to have. I have gathered them specially for you. You don't want to keep running to New York to see them; I haven't the energy to keep running to Washington. I shall arrange matters so that you can see these things at your convenience and at your leisure." Then, in an allusion to the National Gallery, he added, "Of course, these things don't really belong to us. They belong to the people." Mellon lived in an apartment house near Dupont Circle. Duveen prevailed upon the family living below Mellon to transfer its lease to him, and then moved in the wonderful things that belonged to the people. The result was very beautiful and very expensive. He installed a caretaker, engaged several guards to keep an eye on the apartment, gave Mellon the key, and went back to New York.

Duveen kept in touch with his caretaker in Washington. The caretaker confided charming vignettes of the tenant on the upper floor, in dressing-gown and carpet slippers, leaving his own apartment to bask in Duveen's more opulent environment. Sometimes, the caretaker reported, Mellon found it more agreeable to entertain guests in Duveen's place than in his own. Gradually, Mellon must have begun to feel that the paintings he showed off to his friends as Duveen's were his own. There came a moment when he felt he couldn't go on living a double life. He sent for Duveen and bought the contents of his apartment, lock, stock, and barrel. This was the largest transaction ever consummated in the world of art. Duveen had easily outdone the Soviets.

There were twenty-one items in the Soviet deal, forty-two in Duveen's. Mellon
paid the Soviets seven million dollars; he paid Duveen twenty-one million.*

The deal included eighteen important pieces of Renaissance sculpture.
A. W. did not particularly like sculpture, but Finley did, and Duveen was
overloaded with it. According to Walker, Duveen was responsible for providing sculpture galleries in the plans for the National Gallery. Mellon also
acquired a large and important collection of American portraits.

Still, A. W. did not actually make a dedication of his collection to a
national gallery until the year of his demise. He began the process of making
a formal gift to the nation in December 1936, probably with the encouragement of his children. The decision in his tax case was still pending, and no
one could be completely certain as to its ultimate outcome. If he were to
pass away before its resolution (as was to occur), and if the court were to
deny the tax-exempt status of the A. W. Mellon Educational and Charitable
Trust (which did not occur), then the effect of those combined circumstances would be particularly disastrous for his heirs.

In a letter to President Roosevelt, A. W. finally made a formal offer to
the nation of his collection, the expense of constructing the building, and
an endowment of $5 million (later increased to $10 million) for future
acquisitions and the salaries of key employees. He imposed two restrictions
on his grant. First he insisted that the new art museum was not to bear his
name but was to be known by some designation such as the "National
Gallery of Art." This condition was consistent with A. W.'s modesty, but
even as to that A. W. deprecated his modesty. Who, he asked, could identify
the Mr. Smithson who had established the Smithsonian Institution? Further, he suggested that if the gallery were to be known as the "Mellon
Gallery," others would be unlikely to give their collections to it, whereas
the "National Gallery of Art" would probably attract other significant gifts.
The second restriction was that the new gallery be directed by a self-
perpetuating board of directors composed of four ex officio members from
the highest echelons of government and five "public" members, with Mellon
himself to name the initial five.

In his discussions with government representatives, David Bruce urged

---

*Behrman's wonderful prose should not be edited, but does require a little correction. At
A. W.'s direction, Finley preselected the items to be sent to Washington, and a few of them
were ultimately rejected by Mellon and returned to Duveen. Finley was present when it came
time for A. W. and Duveen to discuss price; he reported that at one point A. W. lamented,
"Well, Lord Duveen, I think you will have to take all these things back to New York," to
which the public-spirited dealer responded, "I would give you these things for the National
Gallery rather than take them away."

dispatch, and let it be known that "though he did not want it in his words, 'his family is worried about inheritance taxes on these pictures in the event that Mr. Mellon, whose health has been none too good, passes on.' " President Roosevelt responded affirmatively in January, and even passed a teatime with the donor. While Roosevelt and Mellon sipped their tea, their respective attorneys were contriving to paint each other in the worst possible light in their Board of Tax Appeals briefs.

Congress went along, with only insignificant objections voiced by Congressman Patman in the House and Senators Norris and La Follette Jr. in the Senate. The building cost some $16 million, and A. W.'s nucleus collection, for which he had paid $32,490,155, was reasonably valued at approximately $50 million, probably the largest single gift to the American people in the nation's history. The National Gallery of Art opened to the public in 1941, with Finley as its director. By that time A. W. Mellon was long gone.

Several years after the opening of the National Gallery, Congress (over the objections of Congressman Patman) authorized a group of A. W.'s friends to erect a $300,000 fountain in his honor on public lands. The tasteful monument can be visited today at the busy intersection of Pennsylvania and Constitution Avenues, opposite the rear entrance to the gallery. (A. W. would not have wanted it in front.) It is as understated as he was himself. Off to the side, a granite bench bears the inscription "1855 Andrew W. Mellon 1937."

A. W. is difficult to evaluate as an art collector. In his outstanding study of *The Age of the Moguls,* Stewart H. Holbrook wrote that neither Mellon nor Frick really cared for art, without any discussion of how he reaches his conclusion. Finley refers to his master's "love of art" with a similar lack of supporting data. The author's own conclusion is that A. W. loved something in the paintings, but doubts that that something was "art."

By superficial tests A. W. would fail as a connoisseur. His home can be visited on the grounds of Chatham College in Pittsburgh. It is not the "dark" house described by Paul Mellon on page 127, but a second home acquired in 1916 that had been built several years before for Alexander Laughlin of the Jones and Laughlin steel interests. While it is more welcoming than the "dark" house, it is none too light itself. From the street side it is decidedly austere and cold. The other side, probably intended as the main façade, is somewhat better, sporting some "half-timbering" as was common for its period, but still it is the least rich, the least warm, the least lush, of the several lovely mansions that grace the campus and its immediate vicinity. It is not the house of a man of remarkable taste. It is a rich man's home, but it is not a connoisseur's home. The structures built with Mellon's inspiration, notably the National Gallery and the federal office buildings erected during his tenure as Secretary of the Treasury are for the most part conventionally majestic and unimaginative.

As for his paintings, John Walker, who succeeded Finley as director of the National Gallery, wrote that A. W. was "inarticulate on the subject of art. Even the names of the artists whose works he owned occasionally escaped him."

A. W.'s selections were not particularly to his credit. His early paintings were plainly mediocre. No one would dispute that his later acquisitions were paintings of the highest artistic merit, but similarly no one could dispute that they were unimaginative purchases. The early A. W. bought only "bad" paintings; the later A. W. bought only "proven" paintings, paintings that "the ages" (as opposed to his own subjective evaluations) had irrevocably determined to be "great." It seems almost certain that A. W. never acquired a painting by a living artist, and it is certain that he did no pioneering, made no discoveries, and patronized no creative people in the world of fine arts. He was only interested in the blue chips—the Rembrandts, Holbeins, Raphaels—not the speculative new issues, the wild Valmincks and the oriental Matisses. These latter had not stood the test of time, and he left the newer schools for his son and daughter to accumulate when the faddists and nobodies were themselves well on the way to becoming blue chips. By then Knoedler was selling them.

Today when one walks through the National Gallery, one visits A. W.'s fine Old Masters in the same company with the works that A. W. rejected (or more accurately, never considered): the warm canvases by Degas and the impressionists, the sad paintings of the dissolute Toulouse-Lautrec, disturbing landscapes by the madman Van Gogh, eerie blue scenes by the unknown Spaniard Picasso, all mostly depicting a life and a world unrecognizably foreign to anyone who might think of himself as "A. W." Today these rejects, acquired instead by Chester Dale, who gave them to the National Gallery at Finley's behest, find their places in A. W.'s great museum, where they dwarf his heavy Dutch treasures.

With the notable exception of Goya's "Marquesa de Pontejos," which he purchased direct from the Pontejos family, A. W. bought all of his significant works from Knoedler or Duveen, the two most "establishment" dealers in the world, thereby insulating himself from possible exposure to the real art world of his day. He explained to Colonel Candler Cobb that if one buys from a major dealer, if "anything goes wrong," the dealer would have to take the painting back, whereas lesser dealers might weasel on their obligations. The chances are excellent that he never even heard of the Paris dealer Ambroise Vollard, already very important in the art world, who sold the vibrant "new" canvases to mad Russians and lesbians (and possibly even to Chester Dale) and who was destined to have a greater impact on the history of art than the gentlemen at Knoedler and Company and Lord Duveen combined.

But art collecting was more to A. W. Mellon than just an expensive hobby. Walker says that "from the way he looked at his paintings, from the sheer intensity of his scrutiny, I knew that he had a deep feeling for what he collected, a relationship to his pictures which I have rarely found in the many collectors I have known." But what was that relationship? Was it a love of art—an appreciation of artistic merit? University of Pittsburgh Chancellor John Bowman once asked A. W. why he collected art. As Bowman later recounted it, A. W. stared at him during a long pause, and then spoke slowly: "Every man wants to connect his life with something that he thinks eternal. If you turn that over in your mind you will find the answer to your question." And also the answer to why Mellon could not purchase moderns: Rembrandt was eternal. Picasso? Who could say?

Otherwise A. W. busied himself in his last years with the work of his other favorite charity, the Mellon Institute, and followed the progress of its great new $10 million mausoleum on Fifth Avenue, in Pittsburgh's Oakland section, the heart of the city's complex of universities and libraries. He lived to see the new building dedicated and opened in May of 1937, and to make the presentation address. By that time, though, A. W. was obviously becoming feeble. The Pittsburgh *Sun-Telegraph* reported that his delivery had been "badly rattled"; he left his glasses on the rostrum, forgot his hat, and then got lost in the Carnegie Museum. Three months later he died at the age of eighty-two on August 26, 1937, at Ailsa's Southampton estate. Paul and Ailsa were present with him. David Bruce gave the press a brief statement: "The end was perfectly peaceful." There were no final words or requests. There was one surprise attendee among the mob at the funeral: Nora. Most of the family shunned her. A. W. was buried in Pittsburgh, where he remained until the late 1940s, when Paul Mellon moved him to a plot on Paul's Rokeby Farms in Upperville, Virginia. Relations between father and son had never been entirely comfortable; at last they were close.

A. W. had done a more thorough job than R. B. in divesting himself of his assets. Howard Johnson estimated A. W.'s net worth as of 1931 during the tax trial at $200 million—that during the worst days of the depression when stock prices were close to their lowest. By then he had already given many fortunes to his children. By 1933 things had picked up somewhat. When R. B. died that year, most of his stock in the Mellon companies had already been transferred out of his name; still, R. B.'s estate, consisting mostly of half-interests in real estate holdings owned half by A. W., came to $200 million. By the time that A. W. himself died, however, he had managed to get everything out of his own name except for a paltry $37 million, mostly in stocks and bonds. He left his personal effects to his children, $180,000 to various employees, and the rest to the A. W. Mellon Educational and Charitable Trust, thereby making virtually his entire estate exempt from federal death taxes. To the New Deal, it was his final tax dodge.

The accomplishments of A. W.'s life were measurable and impressive, but withal A. W. Mellon was a hapless man. If ever he had a close friend, it was Frick, but even Frick remained "Mr. Frick" to him throughout their relationship. He probably never developed any real closeness with anyone. Mostly, he longed for a closeness with Paul , and Paul for a closeness with A. W., that eluded them despite the best efforts of both. He took interest in and showed great kindness to other young men—Parker Gilbert, David Finley, journalists—and one of his favorite charities was a Washington institution that provided clothes and lodging for what the New York *Times* described as "young men of the better class" who were attempting to find positions in the capital. These interests perhaps gave partial satisfaction to the paternal instincts left over within him, but only partial satisfaction. His was a lonely life. Many of those who knew him have commented on his loneliness, none more poetically than journalist Thomas Stokes, who remembered him "as he sat among his luxuries, nursing his loneliness, and conversed with his soul." Others have commented as well upon his "conversations with his soul." Chancellor Bowman of the University of Pittsburgh suggests that A. W. might have wondered as he contemplated the paintings whether there was "in the paintings any illumination of the great riddle?" And according to W. L., A. W. was a dreamer about "the still unrealized potentialities of men, the limitlessness of our universe and the riddle of time." The profound wistfulness that always surrounded A. W. makes one suspect that his waters probably ran very deep; indeed, it makes one suspect that his waters ran much deeper than they probably ran. He was aware of the great questions, but put them aside with a wry smile and a delicate butting of the ash from his ubiquitous little cigar.

Perhaps as an antidote to his blue aura, or to his own subtleties, A. W. enjoyed having more exuberant people around him. At all times there was someone not too far away of more vibrant spirit, hearty gusto, or flamboyance such as Diamond Jim Brady, Frick, or Alice Roosevelt Longworth. While he did not speak freely, A. W. had a certain grace to his speech when he did talk, and an occasional inelegant phrase from him seems like a misquote. His testimony in the tax trial sometimes includes some truly superb diction, as in his characterization of McEldowney: "a positive character, a masterful man, and he did his own thinking." Elsewhere in the trial he described what happens when a slow-moving stock suddenly becomes active: "Then the habitual speculator gets after that stock, just like a moth will go to a light, thinking somewhere that he may be able to make a turn." To C. W. Barron he expressed a rather pedestrian thought about credit most elegantly:

> Credit is the larger part of the whole structure in finance. Before the revolution, Russia was one of the wealthiest countries of the world. Then the Soviets thought they would grab this wealth, and they destroyed the structure of credit, and found only the dregs of gold. The wealth had evaporated. It was as if you had burned down the house to get the nails.

A. W. was not noted for his wit, but he had a fine dry humor exemplified by this anecdote from the memoirs of Nicholas Murray Butler. At the 1924 Republican Convention, a self-appointed inner cabal gathered in A. W.'s room to weed out possible vice presidential running mates for Coolidge. Word came through that Coolidge was leaning to Senator William E. Borah, the Idaho progressive who, from A. W.'s point of view, was wrong about everything. As Butler related it, one of the potentates

> turned to Secretary Mellon and said to him: "Mr. Secretary, what do you think of Borah?" The Secretary, looking dreamily off in the distance, took his characteristic little cigar from his mouth and said placidly: "I never think of him unless somebody mentions his name."

The same lack of imagination that A. W. exhibited in his career at the Treasury, in his art collecting, and possibly even in his business life, he exhibited in his personal ethics. He was capable of vindictiveness, as in his dealings with Couzens, but more often than not he had a balanced approach toward others. The Judge instilled a sense of fairness in his sons,* and A. W. tried to be true to his standard of fairness. Colonel Guffey of Gulf,

---

*In an unpublished letter to J. R., at Jefferson College, the Judge exhorted him not to move lightly out on one landlord to go to another's lodgings. College boys, he wrote, change their lodgings too often, inconveniencing boardinghouse keepers for scant reasons. "A boy of gentlemanly feeling won't do it."

Acheson of Carborundum, probably Nora, Senator Couzens, advocates of a bonus for World War I veterans, farm spokesmen, would-be aluminum producers, labor organizers, and Harvey O'Connor would all have insisted that Mellon was the unfairest of men, but Mellon himself would not have agreed. He never did anything that he did not truly and sincerely believe to be fair, honest, and proper. Even Frank Kent acknowledged that Mellon was "incapable of deliberately using his powers as Secretary of the Treasury to put money in his pocket which would not otherwise have accrued." There was "nothing cheap or false about him," his great critic wrote. By his own standards, he could fairly have regarded himself as a man of integrity, though that integrity often depended on his great ability to weigh the questions only to resolve them in favor of his own self-interest.

To some extent A. W. had an awareness of proprieties in business dealings. Correspondence between himself and Philander Knox pertaining to Mellon investments in South America dated 1909, when Knox was serving as Taft's Secretary of State, indicates a sense of propriety with regard to influence peddling by Knox's State Department underlings. Later, as Secretary of the Treasury, Mellon was greatly disturbed that the Federal Reserve Bank of Cleveland had leased rooms to the Republican National Committee, feeling that doing so might tend to compromise the non-partisanship of the Federal Reserve System. In 1929, when a Federal Reserve Board meeting was to consider possible purchase of Treasury Department certificates, Mellon declined to attend that particular meeting on the grounds that the interests of the Treasury and those of the board might not be the same. During his administration of the Treasury, regulations were adopted prohibiting former Treasury Department employees from representing private interests before the Treasury for two years after termination of their public employment, in an effort to limit the effect that "cronyism" might have on public decision making.

Where his own private interests were concerned, though, Mellon was not tuned to detect conflicts of interest and was seemingly unsympathetic to the concept. In the days of Crescent Oil, Pennsylvania law provided extraordinary rights of eminent domain for pipeline companies on the theory that they were "common carriers" operating for the common good. The law provided that they could not be in any branch of the oil production business. The theory behind the law was that if a pipeline were also in the production end of things, it might give its own product preferential treatment, to the disadvantage of other citizens. There would be a conflict between the company's interests and duties as a common carrier, and its interests as a producer. The Mellon route around was simple—to have two totally distinct and separate corporations, Crescent Pipeline Company, and Crescent Oil Company, both owned and officered by Mellons. The law was satisfied, but the potential for unfairness survived intact.

The same laws aimed at avoidance of the appearance of conflicts gave birth to the Union Trust Company. Its parent corporation, Fidelity, was not permitted to represent conflicting or potentially conflicting interests in administration of its trusts, so it spawned an "independent" entity to pick up the conflicting side of its files. Fidelity and Union were totally independent of each other—except that they had the same stockholders and directors. The law was satisfied, but the conflicts survived.

When the Gulf Oil Company approached the Mellon Institute, a charitable enterprise, with a project, Gulf's proposals were passed upon by a board of directors consisting of A. W. and R. B.; their "man," Henry A. Phillips; their beneficiary, Mellon Institute's director E. R. Weidlein; and Chancellor Bowman, whose own institution was crucially dependent upon Mellon beneficence for its continued existence. As a public charitable institution, the Mellon Institute's interests should have been somewhat different than those of Gulf Oil, but who among the five members of its board was capable of making an independent determination as to what the charity's interests were?

The same, of course, can be said of the later business dealings between A. W. Mellon and the A. W. Mellon Educational and Charitable Trust. As Mellon's business involvements increased in number, he went onto the boards of directors of some fifty-one business corporations (plus the boards of many philanthropic organizations). He was honor bound to follow the course of each business, and to make determinations for each in accord with the best interests of it as a separate entity. His is the classic case of the overcommitted director; in the nature of things, it was impossible for him to seriously consider the workings of each of the fifty-one corporations. The best that he could do was to tend the fifty-one conflicts of interest that those seats represented. A. W.'s handling of his conflicts of interest as a public official has been amply discussed in previous sections of this book, without credit to Mellon.

None of this is to say that A. W. was in any way immoral or dishonest, but only that he was unimaginative about ethical questions. His standards were not out of step with those of his day, as codified by the statutory laws established by legislatures, pursuant to which he and his businesses guided themselves. More often than not, what was or was not "legal" held the answer for him to the moral questions with which he might be directly confronted. He refused to take any responsibility for the resolution of moral or ethical questions that might confront others, whether it was the president of Pittsburgh Coal in "settling" labor disputes, Arthur Vining Davis in reaching an "understanding" with foreign aluminum producers, McEldowney in determining to underwrite an overwatered stock issue, Frick in his dealings for the joint Mellon-Frick interests with the city's corrupt bosses, Bowman in his discipline of liberal dissenters on the University of Pittsburgh faculty, or Will Hays in merchandising his satchelful of Teapot Dome bonds. It was not to A. W. Mellon's interest to worry about other people's moral dilemmas, or to be innovative in resolving his own.

A. W. was not without generosity, which for the most part does not appear to have been tax motivated. In the last days of 1930 he established his private charitable foundation and quickly gave it an $800,000 painting, which provided for an $800,000 tax write-off. In 1933, probably the "worst" year in Mellon's adult life, his adjusted gross income was scarcely more than a million dollars, and he made no contribution at all to the A. W. Mellon Educational and Charitable Trust. Significantly, though, the contributions of important paintings that he made to the trust in 1931 and 1932, reasonably valued at over $9 million, and for which he had paid over $9 million, were not written off his income tax for those years. His contributions to public charities more than ate up the limits of his charitable deduction in those years. Equally significant, the 1931 and 1932 conveyances of the paintings to the trust were made at a time prior to the reinstitution of the gift tax. Had Mellon's eye been focused principally on depriving the tax collector, he might simply have given the paintings to his children, thereby saving on his death taxes. Or he might have reduced his "other" charities so as to realize the tax benefits of the gifts of paintings to the trust. Or he might even have tempted death by putting off the gift of paintings to some later year in which he might have been able to realize the deduction for them on his income tax. The Judge, prior to imposition of either death or gift taxes, had divested himself of all of his assets long before his death; A. W. might have done the same and transferred his entire fortune during the period 1926–32, when there was no gift tax, thereby preserving his entire fortune free from all transfer taxes. The fact that he did not do so indicates that he wanted the tax collector to have the tax collector's "fair" share, as A. W. might determine it to be.

A. W.'s contributions to institutionalized charities were substantial,* but like the Judge he took greater delight in small personal charities, some of which were discreetly referred to in magazine articles of the 1920. Holbrook, summarizing a conversation he had had with Lucius Beebe, wrote in *The Age of the Moguls* that

> the more personal [charities] were kept hidden out of his "patrician" hatred for anything savoring of personal popularity or seeming to cater to "good will." [Beebe] had understood, too, that Mellon's benevolences such as hospital care, college educations, pianos for music students, and all sorts of generosities, were shrouded with scrupulous secrecy; and that every Christmas time, he had a sort of private celebration of his own. This consisted of burning the notes of small debtors and telling them to forget it.

Mellon was also capable of personal generosity: he gave a Yugoslav autograph collector not only an autograph, but a forty-five-minute visit.

At the same time countless less successful businessmen would have described Mellon as a cold man, the chill within him sometimes visible through his eyes. Matthew Mellon wrote in *Watermellons* that A. W. enjoyed shooting alligators from the boat deck.

A. W.'s most endearing trait was his modesty. It was not a false modesty (he acknowledged himself to be Pittsburgh's leading banker), but a sincere modesty, the result either of having grown up in the shadow of the mighty oak, the Judge, or of his historical perspective. He was always reluctant to call attention to himself. The spectacle and vulgarity of the "Pittsburgh millionaires" created by Carnegie's munificence must have horrified him and steeled him in the quiet ways that he had already set for himself. When he traveled he always stayed at the quietest hotel, in a room other than the presidential suite. He ate his meals in the dark corner of the dining room,

---

*Year-by-year tallies for the years 1930 to 1934 were brought out during the tax trial, as follows:

YEAR	MELLON TRUST	OTHERS	TAX DEDUCTIONS TAKEN
1930	$ 810,000	$ 693,266	$1,497,255
1931	3,241,250	580,078	340,079
1932	6,070,000	1,308,941	208,396
1933	none	701,578	173,198
1934	9,465,965	740,550	—
Total	$19,587,215	$4,024,413	

The amount of the deduction for 1934 was not clear at the time of the trial; A. W.'s 1934 return had been a preliminary one only, and had not included a claim for deduction for charitable contributions pending his final return.

where he would be unlikely to be noticed. His dress was always conservative and unobtrusive. In an early sketch of him, Edward Lowry wrote that "he complies so closely and rigidly to the standards of well-dressed men that it requires a distinct effort of attention and memory to remember anything about his personal appearance." W. L. recounted this story about A. W.'s silk hat, and its container:

> While he and Henry C. Frick were in London during their first trip abroad, when Mr. Frick was newly a millionaire, these two young men had purchased silk hats and that purchase had entailed for A. W. a further purchase of a hatbox. In Scott's hat store the row of new and shiny leather boxes had made him cringe. However, on the floor in a corner of the store, he had spied an old and travel-worn brown leather case, and he asked the salesman to let him see that one.
>
> "But it belongs to a customer. It's here for repairs."
>
> "Well, couldn't you ask your customer if he wouldn't prefer to have a new hatbox, which I will buy? Then you could let me have his old case."
>
> "But the customer is Lord Soandso."
>
> It turned out that it was possible to seduce his lordship from allegiance to his old hatbox by the gift of a new one. I still retain a vivid memory, out of my boyhood, of Mr. Frick and A. W. confronting us at home on Negley Avenue in the grandeur of London-made silk hats. Within a day or so A. W. had put his hat away, to be worn thereafter only in situations where it might keep him inconspicuous.

His only lapse into ostentation seems to have been in his all-aluminum automobile, which may have been foisted on him by R. B. Unlike many wealthy people (including his children), he did not accumulate residences, but limited himself to one in Pittsburgh and one in Washington, both quite necessary. In them the paintings were the only hint of his fabulous wealth, and paintings of that caliber could not be regarded as "ostentatious." He probably would have regarded his introduction as guest of honor at the 1923 dinner of the Pennsylvania Society of New York as his finest tribute: "Mr. Mellon is not spectacular at any time, but is a fine listener and a keen observer."

The first impression that A. W. made was consistent with his modesty and self-effacement. Too often he looked like a bookkeeper's clerk, abused, scorned by so many higher-ups. When he spoke, the first impression was confirmed. You had to strain to hear that weak voice, to decipher the words through the slight stammer. He looked like Herman Melville's Bartleby: "Pallidly neat, pitiably respectable, incurably forlorn." It was inconceivable to most strangers that he was in fact Andrew W. Mellon, one of the three or four most powerful men in America, one of the richest men in the world. At social events he was sometimes rudely greeted by security guards assigned to keep out gate crashers. When he found himself in a Washington taxicab without the fare (he frequently neglected to carry pocket money), a cab driver refused to believe that Mellon was the Secretary of the Treasury and identified himself as "Cleopatra" and treated A. W. rudely. He seemed to invite rudeness from any passing bully. During his tax trial, when he thoughtlessly lit his ever-present cigar in the courtroom during a recess, the bailiff bellowed at him, "You can't smoke in here!" "Oh, I'm sorry," the Secretary meekly responded.

A. W.'s modesty, together with his perspectives, accounted for the fact that he was a remarkably undominating man (outside the business world). He permitted his Treasury Department underlings full freedom in their personal choices as to presidential contenders, even when they opted for Herbert Hoover. According to Hamlin's diary, Mellon never attempted to dictate Federal Reserve Board policies, as other secretaries had, and even urged the reappointment to the Board of Dr. Adolph Miller, the only professional economist on the board, whose opinions, personality, and associates were all fairly repugnant to Mellon.

A. W.'s even temperament was consistent with his modesty. Its hallmarks of steadiness and calm were rarely broken. One of his associates described him in a 1924 *World's Week* sketch as "the most imperturbable man." He viewed friction as a waste of time and energy; avoidance of it was a useful and workable means of economizing one's faculties for better purposes. This temperament (and balance) enabled Mellon to be a gentleman under trying circumstances. Frank Kent reported a party at which an inept hostess had invited both Mellon and Senator and Mrs. Couzens. A. W. went out of his way to be cordial to Mrs. Couzens. Kent quoted her as saying, "Jim always has to fight with people I like." Kent was satisfied that Mellon was a "gentleman"—"also a man."

It is surprising that such a one was in fact a vital man, even in advanced age, with tremendous physical vigor, a need to be ever active, and a remarkable optimism that survived both the depression with the humiliation that it visited upon him, and the New Deal's tax inquiries. In 1930, at a seventy-fifth birthday dinner for him, he said that if he could choose to live another seventy-five years he would choose to live the next seventy-five, and to live them in America. Five years later a reporter asked whether he still felt the same. There was no hesitation in his reply: "Certainly I do!" His self-effacement never extended to compromising out the Mellon interests or the Mellon policies.

Though he was a highly rational man like his father, like his father he also had a sentimental streak. On one summer vacation while Secretary, he made a long, unnecessary detour from Dinard to Lormont, France, to meet a wine merchant who had written him of a strange coincidence: the merchant's name was Paul Mellon, and his father's name had been André Mellon.

The key to A. W.'s remarkably appealing personality was his vista, which put everything in its proper perspective. A hint of it can be found in his comment to Lucius Beebe on the horses' hooves in London, quoted in abbreviated form much earlier in this book. Mellon had remembered from his first trip to London with Frick

> listening when I awoke in the morning to the clopping of horses' hooves on the wooden blocks which paved the street under my window at Brown's. It seemed to me they were the everlasting voice of London, those horses' hooves, and I thought, as a melancholy boy will, that they would still be clopping on the pavements long after I, and perhaps my money, were gone. Now I've outlasted the horses in the streets of London. It makes me feel very old indeed.

Indeed he was very old, older even than the cobbled streets of London. The sphinx and the pyramids were the framework of his perspective; all pleasures and pains were viewed from within that perspective. Only one who measured time by sweeps of the great brush could have described the depression as he did, as "a bad quarter of an hour." He applied the same standard to himself and to his place in history, impelling him to the same conclusion that his father had reached: All is vanity.

In 1956 Mellon was honored with the issuance of the A. W. Mellon commemorative postage stamp. The Postmaster General presented souvenir albums of the stamp to Paul and his children and stepchildren, Ailsa and her daughter, the children of R. B. Mellon, to Finley, Shepard, and to the leaders of the Mellon businesses: Davis and Hunt from Alcoa, Drake from Gulf, Denton from Mellon National. Though the issuance of the stamp merely inducted Mellon into the ranks of hundreds of others so honored, it was marked by an impressive ceremony at which Pennsylvania senator Edward Martin insisted that "This stamp is of the greatest significance to all Americans." A. W. would have viewed the stamp and the ceremony with more whimsy than pride. In his speech on the occasion, Paul Mellon said that his father would have pointed out "the ephemeral quality of individual fame which, like every likeness on a stamp, is in the end dated, postmarked, and canceled out."

Only a couple of the "founding" generation of Mellons survived A. W. Jennie, R. B.'s widow, died the following year. Jennie combined some striving-class pretensions with a lot of lower-class decency, making her a likable if sometimes comical character. Jennie liked people. Dozens of department store clerks could brag that they "knew" Mrs. R. B. Mellon because she visited with them over the counter. Her hairdresser and the corner grocer could fairly regard themselves as "friends" with her. Anyone who had had any contact with her could approach her, and she was a "soft touch" in times of need. Much of Jennie's spirit died with R. B. five years earlier, but she continued to attend concerts and benefit balls and community functions out of a sense of duty, and by so doing she encouraged many constructive efforts. Three weeks before her death in November 1938 she worked at a rummage sale run by the Women's Industrial Exchange, which she served as vice president. Though she was the "front man" of Mr. and Mrs. R. B. Mellon socially, she was modest when it came to the public. Her funeral was private. Today she and R. B. can be visited in a small plain chapel off to one side of the nave of the East Liberty Presbyterian Church, where they lie in huge stone boxes that are relatively free of ornamentation when compared with their European prototypes. Jennie's will made a lot of small personal bequests to friends and servants, and she left the bulk of the rest to charities.

Jennie made one dying request. She asked that the press not reveal her age. All of her life Jennie played games about her age, stealing a year here and a year there, even on official documents such as her marriage license, which was sworn to only by the groom. Perhaps not even he knew the real truth. The press honored her request, and the author has decided to do likewise.

W. L., though technically a third-generation Mellon as a grandson of the Judge, felt more at home with the second generation. He was only eight years younger than his youngest uncle, George, while he was thirty-nine years older than his generational contemporary, Paul, also a grandson of the Judge. The Judge's important early influence on W. L.; his close working relationship, occasionally approaching that of equal with A. W. and R. B.; and his important role with them in the development and history of the Mellon family fortune, all link him more closely with the Judge's sons than grandsons, and it is clear from *Judge Mellon's Sons* that W. L. regarded himself as part of the older generation. He properly counts as one of the "founding" Mellons.

W. L. spent much of his last twenty years enjoying himself. In 1930 he became chairman of the board of Gulf Oil, and was succeeded as president by J. Francis Drake. He continued to exercise a dominant role in the business for many years thereafter, but it ceased to preoccupy him.

Around 1900 many well-to-do Pittsburghers began to summer at Beaumaris, Canada, about a hundred miles north of Toronto. The W. L. family went to visit friends there in 1909, and began making it their summer home the following year. He and William H. Donner, the Union Steel man, divided Squirrel Island between them, and W. L. built a "camp" there for his family. As Matthew describes it, the camp "turned out to be a complete summer resort," a string of dwelling houses and utility structures. He recounts the pleasant life for all at Beaumaris in *Watermellons.*

Winters were usually passed cruising southern waters. Of the founding Mellons, only W. L. cared much for yachting. First of his important boats was *Vagabondia,* a large paddle-wheel houseboat propelled by a wood-burning engine, on which the W. L.s wintered from 1902 to 1916. *Vagabondia* was followed by a number of lesser vessels, mostly named *Vagabondia,* until finally replaced by one of the great yachts in the history of American wealth, *Vagabondia,* an ocean-going steel vessel, 224 feet long, built in the Krupp shipyard at Kiel, Germany. It took over two years to complete the yacht, but it was finally delivered in December 1928. *Big Vag,* as it was known in the family to distinguish it from the lesser Vags, required a crew of thirty-two.

Often *Big Vag* carried naturalists from the Carnegie Museum on its cruises, notably Professor Arthur L. Twomey, who collected and catalogued shells, birds, insects, and other forms of natural life observed on *Big Vag*'s journeys to little-visited areas of the world. Twomey was good company, and his presence made at least part of the voyage expenses tax deductible for W. L. as a contribution to the Carnegie Museum, a charitable organization. W. L.'s first cousin, Edward P. Mellon, the architect, was frequently a guest on the cruises. E. P. was seven years younger than W. L., a big gap in childhood that narrowed to insignificance in old age. They were increasingly together in their later years. Despite the stylistic differences between the polished architect and the more basic industrialist, E. P.'s daughter Mary Mellon Wise says that the two were good company for each other.

In 1941 *Big Vag* was given for war duty to the government, and the W. L.s settled down into a relatively modest 134-foot cruising houseboat, reportedly the largest cruising houseboat ever built, though it required only fourteen crew members. Inexplicably, it was named *Old River.* It exploded and burned to water's edge in the Florida Keys in 1947, and though it was replaced by a somewhat smaller houseboat, *Vagabondia III,* by then W. L.

was seventy-nine and his sea-going days were essentially over.

W. L.'s cruises offered non-stop fishing opportunities, which he enjoyed. He loved hunting almost as much as he loved fishing. Together with A. W., R. B., and a few others, he bought a huge area of wilds near what today is Cape Canaveral, Florida, for private hunts in a (previously) unspoiled preserve.* W. L. hunted deer and wild turkey, and sometimes they would hunt alligators at night with the aid of spotlights. Aboard ship W. L. would sometimes "hunt" sea life by shooting huge prehistoric mantas and other oversized varieties of marine life that in those days still populated Florida waters. A photo in *Watermellons* appropriately captioned "Standby for Murder!" shows R. B. shooting at what are described in an adjacent photo caption as "These friendly porpoise came to play/But never lived another day." Matthew wrote that "The 'conservation nuts' had not yet raised their ugly heads, or they would have been shot too!"

May, as W. L.'s wife Mary Taylor was known, died in 1942. A quiet lady, May was personally unostentatious and rarely wore jewelry. She avoided the social circuit and spent most of her time attending to her family or to the doings of the Shadyside Presbyterian Church or the Industrial Home for Crippled Children. Her father had encouraged a love of music in all of his offspring, and May was a creditable soprano. In addition to her formal charitable work, she was devoted to little charities. For example, she would save all of the family's old newspapers and magazines and would disburse them to the lonely men who tended the lighthouses along the coasts that they cruised. In a pioneering attempt at environmentalism, she personally planted hundreds of Australian pine seedlings throughout the Florida Keys.

May suffered from cancer for years, and finally died aboard the *Old River* in Miami Bay. Her family was with her.

Thereafter, W. L. went down hill. In his last couple of years he spent a lot of time rambling with Boyden Sparkes for *Judge Mellon's Sons,* from which most of the quotes attributed in this book to W. L. were taken. *Judge Mellon's Sons* is folksy, charming, and highly readable, and for some aspects of the Mellon family history it is indispensable, but it wasn't "W. L.," and he knew it and was dissatisfied that his ghost writer had pushed him out of his own book. He retired as chairman of the board of Gulf Oil in 1948 after forty-six years with the company, just prior to his eightieth birthday. By that time Gulf was the world's fourth largest oil producer, with 42,000

---

*Matthew chuckled when he related a recent conversation with a Florida "local." The Floridian had told him that if his family had kept their Cape Canaveral holdings, "you'd all be rich today!"

employees and total assets of $839 million. But he had endured a figurehead status for several years before his exit, and being a figurehead was a difficult role for him to play. It sat poorly with W. L. when Drake and the others —with the complicity of his "young" cousins (once removed) R. K. (son of R. B.) and Paul (son of A. W.)—worked around him and "humored" him. W. L. had long been the controlling force of Gulf; he was used to controlling, producing, exercising power, and it was hard and frustrating for him to see the change in his role. Sometimes he was irritable.

His sons were his biggest heartbreak. From his era of Mellons, only for W. L. was there a painful generation gap. There was no gap between R. B. and his son, R. K.; and A. W. could be philosophical about his boy, Paul; but W. L. wasn't the philosophical sort. W. L. had lived to see his sons grow to manhood, but that wasn't a terrific consolation, given the sons. Matthew, the older, had become a genuine intellectual. Imagine that. Took after his mother's side. Matt's public support for the young Nazi regime in Germany in the early 1930s had caused the family some embarrassment. W. L. could live with that; that kind of price must always be paid by the families of brilliant thinkers. But W. L. had never felt much at home in the company of intellectuals or brilliant thinkers. The other boy, W. L. Jr. (Larry), well, call him what he was—a failure. Both had turned their backs on business.

W. L. looked very much the caricature of the company president, and he was. He was proud to be a businessman. He protested that

> Though all the adventures of Sinbad the Sailor usually ended in the enrichment of Sinbad, he never is regarded as a money-grubber because we remember the adventures rather than the riches. Yet, for some perverse reason, successful business men are differently regarded.
>
> It is a curious thing to me that so many people outside of business fail to sense its thrilling excitement, and regard it most of the time as a dull routine which men endure simply for money.

Business wasn't a matter of money, not really:

> As I see it, there is no other scheme known to man except business whereby such able fellows as A. W. and R. B. Mellon could have generated for our country what they did generate. They were builders. They were creative. They were not actuated solely by profit, but profit was the proof they were right.

Matt and Larry weren't listening.

> Observing various younger persons in our family who turn from business to some other field of activity, I am bound to say that I should hate to discover any one of them doing this in the belief that business was in some way ignoble.

Matt didn't think that business was ignoble, though he thought it ignoble to insist on the nobility of business. Larry probably thought it was ignoble. W. L. couldn't relate to either. He could not be philosophical about it, but he could be tolerant, and he was. Matthew says, "If I had had a son like me I'd have been less understanding."

W. L. died a relative pauper on October 8, 1949, at the age of eighty-one. He had given most of his fortune to trusts for his progeny long before his death, but still his estate in Pennsylvania (which did not include his Canadian real estate or his ships registered outside of Pennsylvania) came to over $22 million. It included a large number of tax-exempt municipal bonds and substantial blocks of stock not only in Gulf but also in Gulf's "competitors" —Standard Oil of New Jersey, Standard Oil of California, Socony Vacuum, and Texaco—as well as significant holdings in all the other Mellon companies, Bethlehem Steel, Pullman, and Pittsburgh Plate Glass. The tax collectors took all but slightly over $6 million of it.

He left all of his Canadian property to his daughter Peggy (Margaret, Mrs. Thomas Hitchcock Jr.); $100,000 to his son-in-law John F. Walton Jr.; $50,000 to William S. Moorhead, his lawyer and golfing buddy; $50,000 to his sister, Sarah Lucille Hasbrouck; a pension for his black companion Dave; and $75,000 to be divided among his other employees. The rest he divided into four equal trusts that were mechanically identical to those that he established during his lifetime. Each trust paid its income to one of his four children, with the provision that upon the death of the last of the four, the principal was to be divided equally among all of W. L.'s grandchildren. As of this writing, all of W. L.'s four children are still alive and well. He has eleven surviving grandchildren. Each of the four trusts established pursuant to the will started off with assets valued at $1,461,203—plus a one-quarter interest in *Big Vag*, which the government gave back to the family after the war. By then it was the whitest elephant afloat.

The Judge's first born, T. A., died in 1899. Over the years the rest of his children passed on, R. B., J. R., and A. W. W. L. was the last of those who grew up under the shade of his limbs. With his passing, that older generation that had turned the Judge's millions into a fortune with the potential to crush its possessors died out. The next generation might or might not be crushed by it.

BOOK IV

Young Men in Search
of Themselves

I have no doubt the ragged newsboy
derives more satisfaction from the
few extra pennies of a good day's sale
of his papers, and the encouragement
of his poor mother, than the boy
pampered and indulged in all the
ease and luxury wealth can afford.

—JUDGE THOMAS MELLON

T his section of the book considers what might loosely be called the third generation of Mellons, some the Judge's grandsons and some his great-grandsons, but all of roughly the same generational period, born within a thirteen-year time span. The oldest of them, W. L.'s son Matthew, was born in 1897; R. B.'s son, Richard King Mellon ("R. K." or "the General" or "the King"), was born two years later; A. W.'s son, Paul, in 1907; T. A.'s grandson Edward Purcell Mellon II ("Ned"), 1908; and the youngest of the principal characters of this section, W. L.'s younger son, W. L. Jr. ("Larry" or "Dr. Mellon of Haiti"), was born in 1910. For the most part, this section is about males.

There were, of course, females, but to the thinking of Mellons of this era, male and female alike, a woman's place was in the mansion. Neither the Judge's *Thomas Mellon and His Times* nor W. L.'s *Judge Mellon's Sons* gives any significant attention to the family females, and over time the women themselves have principally been a cloistered lot, breaking into print only when they have been divorced or when their jewels have been burgled. Imbued from birth with a Victorian concept of their roles in life, most of the Mellon women (both then and now) never seem to have done much "searching" for themselves.

The ladies from all four branches of the family tree grew up insulated by their wealth. Money, of course, was never discussed. Polite people did not talk about such things. Money and the advantages that accompanied money were simply taken for granted, and women, especially, were shielded from such vulgar discussions as they might be shielded from other coarse talk.

A similar, possibly related hallmark of the Mellon "lady" of the period —still surviving though to a diminished extent among her daughters—was her attitude toward her privacy. It was her most valued possession. Publicity was to be avoided. Period. Young Mellon girls of today still recall their mothers' advice to them as children: Do not permit your photograph to be taken. Your photograph is private.

We will visit with the females more briefly than the males: R. B.'s daughter, Sarah, born in 1903; A. W.'s Ailsa, 1901; T. A.'s Mary, 1884; and W. L.'s two daughters, Rachel, 1899, and Margaret ("Peggy"), 1901.

Sarah, daughter of R. B. and Jennie, was surely one of the nicest of them. She always took the back seat to her dynamic older brother, R. K., and was relatively neglected by her parents, and almost totally neglected by her father. Her "shyness" was not simply a family trait, but was probably a function of her role in the family or of her striking homeliness. The high point of her life was probably her marriage to lively Alan Scaife.

In the early 1800s the Scaife family had established themselves as tin fabricators in Pittsburgh. Their Scaife Company (as it ultimately came to be known) was sometimes touted as the oldest continually operated manufacturing enterprise west of the Allegheny Mountains. They were in manufacturing when Thomas Mellon arrived in America. By the 1920s they were probably the "oldest" respectable family in the city. Alan himself grew up on what was known as "Millionaire's Row" in Pittsburgh's Old Allegheny section. He went to the right schools, capped by Yale ('20), where he was an editor of the *Yale Daily News* and a member of St. Anthony's Society. He was tall and very handsome, and quite charming and nice, if not overly profound.

The marriage of Sarah Mellon and Alan Scaife in 1927 was described in the Philadelphia *Inquirer* under the head "Orient Outshone at Mellon Home as Daughter Weds." The wedding was held in a pavilion constructed especially for the occasion, at a cost reported in the press (possibly without reasonable basis) of $100,000. It was "a scene rivaling the beauty of a fairyland bower," at least to the journalists: "The Mellons challenged the elements. Although there was no moon tonight, there was synthetic moonlight serene and mellow, from all four sides of the pavilion." The one thousand guests included someone identified in the press as "Princess Lebkowitz," and they came bearing gifts valued (by the journalists) at half a million dollars. After their marriage, Scaife continued to dabble in his family's business as chairman of the board. He liked business because he liked people and dealing with people, and because it gave him the excuse for the business trips in which he took so much pleasure. He was personally known to many American businessmen that dealt with Scaife Company as an outgoing, egalitarian type.

Alan easily took up his new role as a Mellon. He succeeded R. B. on the board of Pittsburgh Coal and was to become its chairman. For a time he served on the boards of Gulf (once as a vice president), Mellon National Bank (once as its chairman), the Mellon Institute, Magee Hospital (another family charity, though principally of the Scaife as opposed to Mellon families), and also as a member of the Yale Corporation, the governing body of Yale University, all without particular distinction. During World War II he was a Lieutenant Colonel with the O.S.S. (the Office of Strategic Services, predecessor to the C.I.A.) under Colonel William "Wild Bill" Donovan,

and earned himself a Bronze Star and the French Croix de Guerre, neither
for heroism of the life-risking variety.

In 1949 the Pittsburgh Junior Chamber of Commerce selected him as
their "Man of the Year." (Their dinner in honor of Richard King Mellon
the previous year had been a grand success.) From 1949 until his death in
1958, Alan was chairman of the board of trustees of the University of
Pittsburgh, generally regarded at the time as a Mellon family trust. His
tenure coincided with that of Pitt's controversial chancellor, Edward H.
Litchfield, whose radical ideas about university expansion caused conster-
nation in the Oakland neighborhood and in downtown financial centers.
Litchfield's partisans—like Pittsburgh's business leaders—regarded Alan as
"charming but ineffectual." Still, he gave the chancellor lip service, which
was probably responsible for keeping Litchfield afloat for as long as he
managed to keep afloat. After Alan's death Sarah's brother, the General,
pulled the rug out from under Litchfield and his plans, a matter that left
considerable bitterness between Pittsburgh's intelligentsia and its rich.

One gets a good glimpse of Alan as a person from reading his privately
printed booklets about two of his incessant travels with Sarah, *Travelog:
Notes of a Trip through Africa, the Middle East, the Mediterranean, and
Europe, January–April, 1950* and *Arabian Interlude: Notes of a Brief Trip
in the Interior of Little-Known Southern Arabia*. They were not intended for
general circulation, and Alan let his hair down in them. He showed himself
as socially conscious (in the vulgar sense), but not without social conscience.
He was sympathetic to the situation of the blacks in Kenya and South
Africa. Both books regularly comment on unpleasant odors encountered
along the way, usually directly and sometimes crudely, but occasionally by
implication only ("Bedouins attached to the caravans camp right in the
camel park with their families during their stay in Mukalla. We didn't see
how the camels stood it"). Though he had a great sense of decorum, he also
had an adolescent appreciation for "naughty" things. He titillated over the
name of a steamship steward, a Mr. Hoare, and included a humorous and
subtly related anecdote about the size of one of the male passenger's geni-
talia. He also included a full-page picture of Brussels's overrated fountain,
the "Mannekin Pis." *Arabian Interlude*, about a trip to visit some archeological excavations, financed in part by the Sarah Mellon Scaife Foundation,
includes no substantial discussion of the excavations. Alan was a hail fellow
well met with a deep Rotarian strain in him. He was also a creditable writer,
witty, with a good eye for a story, a hearty and likable locker-room type
who was probably the best company at Rolling Rock. His death in 1958 of
heart problems at the age of fifty-eight deprived his many friends of a

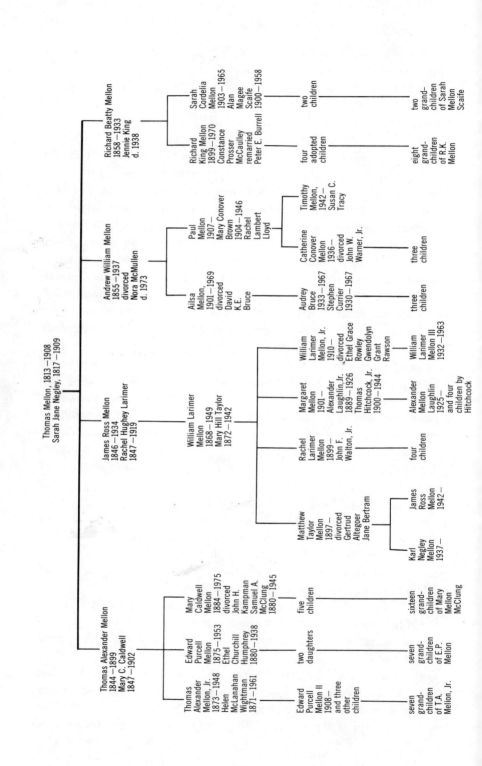

Thomas Mellon, 1813–1908
Sarah Jane Negley, 1817–1909

Thomas Alexander Mellon
1844–1899
Mary C. Caldwell
1847–1902

Thomas Alexander Mellon, Jr.
1873–1948
Helen McLanahan Wightman
1871–1961

seven grand-children of T.A. Mellon, Jr.

Edward Purcell Mellon
1875–1953
Ethel Churchill Humphrey
1880–1938

Edward Purcell Mellon II
1908–
and three other children

seven grand-children of E.P. Mellon

Mary Caldwell Mellon
1884–1975
divorced
John H. Kampman
Samuel A. McClung
1880–1945

five children

sixteen grand-children of Mary Mellon McClung

two daughters

James Ross Mellon
1846–1934
Rachel Hughey Larimer
1847–1919

William Larimer Mellon
1868–1949
Mary Hill Taylor
1872–1942

Matthew Taylor Mellon
1897–
divorced
Gertrud Altegoer
Jane Bertram

Karl Negley Mellon
1937–

James Ross Mellon
1942–

Rachel Larimer Mellon
1899–
John F. Walton, Jr.

four children

Margaret Mellon
1901–
Alexander Laughlin, Jr.
1889–1926
Thomas Hitchcock, Jr.
1900–1944

Alexander Mellon Laughlin
1925–
and four children by Hitchcock

William Larimer Mellon, Jr.
1910–
divorced
Ethel Grace Rowley
Gwendolyn Grant Rawson

William Larimer Mellon III
1932–1963

Andrew William Mellon
1855–1937
divorced
Nora McMullen
d. 1973

Ailsa Mellon,
1901–1969
divorced
David K.E. Bruce

Audrey Bruce
1933–1967
Stephen Currier
1930–1967

three children

Paul Mellon
1907–
Mary Conover Brown
1904–1946
Rachel Lambert Lloyd

Catherine Conover Mellon
1936–
divorced
John W. Warner, Jr.

three children

Timothy Mellon,
1942–
Susan C. Tracy

Richard Beatty Mellon
1858–1933
Jennie King
d. 1938

Richard King Mellon
1899–1970
Constance Prosser McCauley
remarried
Peter E. Burrell

four adopted children

eight grand-children of R.K. Mellon

Sarah Cordelia Mellon
1903–1965
Alan Magee Scaife
1900–1958

two children

two grand-children of Sarah Mellon Scaife

good-natured, decent fellow, whose failings, such as they were, were all-American.

Alan made good cover for a shrinking violet. After finishing at Miss Spence's school in New York City, Sarah was presented to the Queen (the Judge would have said that his children were aping the "shoddyocracy") and then returned to Pittsburgh to busy herself with the kinds of things with which young ladies of socially prominent families were expected to busy themselves. She became the third president of the Junior League of Pittsburgh in 1926, but after her marriage to Alan in 1927 she retired to her homes on Shady Avenue and in Ligonier, and to her children Cordie (Cordelia Mellon Scaife), born the year following the marriage, and Dickie (Richard Mellon Scaife), born four years later.

In 1962, at the time of some significant gifts of art to the Carnegie Museum, Sarah finally consented to a newspaper interview, and the report of the well-connected society columnist Mary O'Hara in the Pittsburgh *Press* constitutes the only published personal vignette of Sarah. Sarah is described as five feet seven inches, salt-and-pepper hair, with "fine" blue-green eyes. Ms. O'Hara detailed how beautiful Sarah's hands were. Her homes were traditionally furnished in English antiques, dotted with fine non-abstract paintings, the walls painted in light pastels. Sarah had said that she preferred simple clothes, preferably "store-bought" (though she made the "Ten Best Dressed" list in 1957). Her favorite flower was identified as lily of the valley, her favorite jewel rubies, and her constant companion was identified as Pamplemousse, her French poodle. She admitted to having no interest whatsoever in cooking; she liked gardens but was not keen on gardening. She did do a little needlepoint herself. O'Hara described her as a "sentimentalist," and noted the "scrapbooks and favorite family photographs where they can be seen." According to Ms. O'Hara, Sarah's abiding interest was people, even though, she quoted Sarah, "they usually do the opposite of what you expect them to do."* She especially loved children, and discussed at some length with O'Hara her friendship with the ten-year-old daughter of a menial at the zoo that Sarah gave to the city. A good clue as to Sarah's attitude about her role in the world can be found in her thoughts on hats: "I'm not keen about hats for myself although I like to see a pretty hat on someone else." The interview concluded, "Sensitive and shy, Mrs. Scaife shuns the limelight. She is more interested in observing other

---

*"Sense of Mellonhood" in any particular Mellon can be gauged by degree of familiarity with *Thomas Mellon and His Times*. Sarah's comment, an echo of "Ye'll find mankind an unco squad," is a sign that Sarah knew whence she came.

people than in having them observe her." It was not a searching article, but it showed a nice lady. Sarah was a nice lady, but she also had a lot of bitterness pent up within her, which she tried to wash away in drink, and which sometimes cropped out in edged jokes. She died in 1965 at the age of sixty-two of unreported causes. Her obituary described her as being "of retiring nature."

By the time of her demise, Sarah's Sarah Mellon Scaife Foundation had given $26 million to various charities, virtually all of it to Pittsburgh universities, hospitals, and museums. Her most notable outside gift was $750,000 in 1964 for a building at Stanford's Hoover Institute to house papers related to President Herbert Hoover, one of her son's heroes. The University of Pittsburgh, principal recipient of her benefactions, awarded her an honorary Ph.D. for her "sincerity, integrity, and friendship." The president of the foundation, of course, was Alan rather than herself.

Much of Sarah's art collection, and several very fine paintings that she purchased for the Carnegie Institute's museum, provide the nucleus of the collection of the Sarah Scaife Gallery. The gallery, a wing of the Carnegie Institute's museum-library complex, was built and opened in 1974 at a cost of $12.5 million as a gift from her foundation and other Scaife family foundations and members. It includes paintings donated by a wide variety of Mellons and allied families, together with notable contributions from Pittsburgh's Heinz family and others. At its entrance the visitor is greeted by a discombobulating painting-sculpture by contemporary French artist Jean Dubuffet, which Sarah herself would almost certainly have viewed as modernist junk, possibly correctly so. Inside, though, it becomes clear that the Scaifes, along with other members of the community, have provided Pittsburgh with a fine gallery for a city of its size, including a broad sampling of schools and periods, highlighted by a few very fine impressionist canvases. There is a small memorial alcove away from the main corridors which bears a plaque: "In memory of Sarah Scaife for her many contributions to the arts, this building is presented to the Pittsburgh community by the Scaife Family Foundation, 1974." Of course the alcove includes the inevitable oil painting of Sarah, striking a pose reminiscent of the one that her father, R. B., would strike for the portrait painters. One other work of art shares the alcove with Sarah, Rodin's bronze portrait-bust of Eleonora Duse, the legendary Italian actress and mistress of Gabriele D'Annunzio, the poet and intellectual father of Italian fascism. Rodin's bust is titled "Head of Sorrow."

Sarah's was a happy and fulfilled life when compared with that of her cousin, A. W.'s daughter, the sad, strange Ailsa. Her brother, Paul, has said that Ailsa "led a life of quiet introspection . . . even tinged with a touch of melancholy." She could also, however, be a difficult woman. Her imperious and inflexible qualities (as well as her undeniable beauty, wealth, and social station) made her an intriguing and challenging woman for any man of spirit to attempt to tame. But she was untamable. She picked a husband with a potential for greatness but refused to permit him to develop that greatness. A silly Pittsburgh *Press* piece at the time of her marriage in 1926 to David Bruce reported that she had resolved that the couple would "live on his income" as the most junior secretary at the American embassy in Rome. It wasn't true; there was no such resolution. The manner in which she insisted on living as the wife of a beginning foreign service career officer could only cause embarrassment to him and to the higher-ranking men at the post. After a few months in Rome Bruce resigned from the State Department, assigning the ill effect of Rome's climate on his wife's health as the reason. Thereafter he entered the business world as an "apprentice" in the bond department at Bankers Trust, and was soon representing the Mellon family interests on a baker's dozen of corporate and philanthropic boards of directors.

In the battle of the wills, Ailsa won until, that is, the early 1940s, after A. W.'s death, when Bruce reached early middle age. Washington promised a much more fulfilling life for him than the world of corporate directors' meetings, but no, Ailsa liked her existence precisely as it was. She was not about to move. Life was drifting by him, and the couple drifted apart. The gossip columns began reporting friction in their marriage. Working out the separation of the two from each other was staggeringly complex because of the extent to which their tremendous interests had in fact become merged. When they were finally divorced at Palm Beach, Florida, in 1945, letters from Bruce to Ailsa dated 1943, probably written by prearrangement for use in a divorce action, mentioned his love for another woman. Three days after the divorce, Bruce was married to Evangeline Bell. Appreciating that Ailsa had been a stubborn and sometimes unreasonable empress, the Mellon clan went out of their way to impress upon Bruce their continued good will for him.

Bruce went on to become President Truman's ambassador to France, President Eisenhower's ambassador to West Germany, and President Kennedy's ambassador to Great Britain. He assisted in negotiations to end the Vietnam war under President Nixon, and finally retired as President Ford's representative to NATO at the beginning of 1976 at the age of seventy-seven. When he died in December of 1977, his place as one of the consummate diplomats in American history was already secure. There was a woman behind him. Evangeline made the perfect diplomat's wife. *The*

New York Times Magazine later called her "the model of an American First Lady abroad." She was educated not only in the social graces but in the ways of the diplomatic community. Her father, Edward Bell, had been a career officer with the State Department and she held a minor position there herself at the time of her marriage to Bruce. Her French and German were faultless, her Italian and Swedish almost as good, and her Hungarian was passable, though she had to make some apologies for her Japanese. Evangeline was not "beautiful," but she had a wistful Garboesque look and feel to her that compared quite favorably to Ailsa's bloodless prettiness.

Ailsa's shyness was more a matter of insulating herself from hurt by shielding herself with aloofness. After the divorce she retreated still further from the world outside and limited her society severely. Her circle was composed of a very small number of very old friends, most of them dating from childhood. Among the closest of them was her cousin (once removed) Peggy Hitchcock. On those infrequent occasions when she went out after the later 1940s, she was usually accompanied by George Lauder Greenway, a one-time Navy officer and official of the Metropolitan Opera, who became her near-constant companion for the rest of her life. He served as chairman of the board of trustees of her Avalon Foundation, and continues to sit on the board of Avalon's successor, the Andrew W. Mellon Foundation.

Essentially Ailsa became a recluse. She filled up her life with apartments, and the apartments with things—fancy things: overornate furniture and porcelains, the kinds of things that peaked in price just before the French Revolution, and then again just prior to the great stock market crash of 1929. When she was bored she might stroll over to the shop of the world-respected porcelain dealers, Jas. A. Lewis & Sons (now defunct), just off Madison Avenue on Fifty-seventh Street, where she would purchase a figurine, or perhaps a little candlestick ornamented with a superfluous pale pink rose. Superfluous pink roses typified her collection. Every once in a while she would buy herself just one more set of fine antique china to add to the sets upon sets of fine antique china that she already owned. She had enough plates and saucers to serve several hundred people on rare china, and continued to accumulate it, though after the divorce she rarely saw more than a handful of people at the same time.

Ailsa, like her father and her brother, Paul, also collected paintings, and after 1951 concentrated on impressionists and post-impressionists. That year she acquired over ninety examples from the famous French dress designer Edward F. Molyneux, who had become seized with the perverse desire to begin a new collection of works by unknown young artists. Thereafter she accumulated more and more impressionists. She was addicted to delicate little "boudoir" paintings, which she would cluster on her walls in groups or display on tabletops.

By that time it was no longer easy to collect French impressionist paintings, though. As John Rewald wrote in the preface to the catalogue *French Paintings from the Collections of Mr. and Mrs. Paul Mellon and Mrs. Mellon Bruce,* published by the National Gallery in 1966, "Times have changed since the days when Albert Barnes or Chester Dale could leisurely make their choices from among abundant offers." Her indecision as to possible purchases was both complicating and expensive for dealers, so they saved first crack at their more desirable canvases for less difficult, more decisive collectors like her brother, with the result that her collection was valuable, but not choice when compared to Paul's French paintings.

Highlights from both collections are reproduced in the National Gallery's catalogue, which includes some of the most wonderful canvases ever painted. Virtually all of the more evocative works by Degas, Manet, Monet, Toulouse-Lautrec, Renoir, Cezanne, Seurat, and all of the Gauguins, Rousseaus, and Picassos come from Paul's collection. The only field in which Ailsa outstripped her brother was in the field of dog portraiture. The catalogue includes dog portraits by Toulouse and Renoir, and two by Manet, all owned by Ailsa, all four of cocker-spaniely lovables. What her collection lacked in quality, though, it made up in quantities sufficiently large that she could not keep track of them herself. At the time of her death she owned some two hundred impressionist and post-impressionist paintings, scattered about her homes and apartments, or hidden in the back rooms of various art dealers.

Ailsa's charities were numerous, but not particularly engrossing for her. The National Gallery was the charity she most generously aided; many of its most important purchases were paid for by her. Former National Gallery director John Walker related in *Self-Portrait with Donors* the story of the acquisition of "La Liseuse," a fine, fussy, and delicate Fragonard painted around 1776, just before the deluge, which was especially appealing to the ladies of the ancien régime and to Ailsa. "La Liseuse" was to be auctioned at Parke-Bernet Galleries, predecessor to today's Sotheby Parke Bernet, and Walker called Ailsa to ask her to buy it for the National Gallery. She admitted that she wanted it very much for herself, but instead she bought it for the National Gallery, at $875,000, establishing a new world record for Fragonards. Walker suggested that she keep possession of it herself throughout her lifetime, but she declined, echoing her father, because it was too important a painting for private ownership. She refused to permit her generosity to be publicly acknowledged when she bought the National

Gallery a multimillion-dollar Leonardo, "Ginevra de' Benci" because she did not want to appear ostentatious. She shunned publicity as much as any Mellon ever; Walker said that she "dreaded" it.

Most of her benefactions during her lifetime were made through her Avalon Foundation, named after a summer "cottage" that had once been a family retreat in Pride's Crossing, Massachusetts, near Frick's summer home. She religiously attended the meetings of Avalon's board of trustees, but according to Paul she was a very infrequent contributor to the discussions. She was generally quite removed from her benefactions. She was an important financial mainstay of a refuge founded by the daughter of Leo Tolstoy for White Russian émigrés, but she felt put upon when Madame Tolstoy invited her to actually visit the institution that her generosity was keeping afloat.

Apartments was Ailsa's greatest collection; but they were more than apartments, they were places to live. At one time she owned three New York apartments, two houses in Greenwich, Connecticut, her fabulous estate at Syosset, Long Island, and a Palm Beach residence. Her great triumph was to have been her magnificent apartment at 960 Park Avenue. Furnishing and decorating it preoccupied the last few years of her life, and enabled her to drive numberless decorators and art dealers crazy with her exercise of the rich woman's prerogative of changing her mind. Plans and items acquired for it cluttered the homes in which she was living. It was to be the finest apartment in the world, and she was a little obvious about her wish to outdo the "Joneses." When it was ready, she asked Walker, Would it compare favorably with the Charles Wrightsman apartment? Walker put her mind at ease. It was just about finished in high French style when she died of cancer in 1969 at the age of sixty-eight.

For years before her death Ailsa was touted, probably on the basis of *Fortune*'s periodic rosters of the wealthiest, as the richest woman in the world. They were probably right. A. W. was somewhat richer than R. B., which would warrant a conclusion that Ailsa was richer than Sarah. *Fortune* estimated Ailsa's wealth in 1968 at between a half-billion and a billion. When she died the following year her estate totaled $570 million, *after* substantial but inestimable gifts to her daughter Audrey (who is discussed in the next section of this book) and Audrey's three children, and after her many gifts to the Avalon Foundation and other charities. Reckoning Ailsa's "share" at about one-fifth of the total assets transferred by A. W., R. B., and W. L. to their children, one begins to get some feel for the significant wealth controlled by the family as a unit.

Ailsa made bequests for thirty-two servants and provided unimpressive pensions for six former employees. She left her jewelry (reportedly quite staggering, but little seen) equally to her two granddaughters, and she made a bequest of money to her grandson equal to the value of the jewels being left to each of his sisters. She had warned Walker not to expect that the National Gallery would get all of her paintings, that she would leave some of them to her grandchildren, but she apparently had a change of heart and gave all of her paintings, drawings, and watercolors to the National Gallery. At Paul's suggestion she had willed her furniture, porcelains, silver, and decorative effects to the Carnegie Institute. (In 1977 the Carnegie Institute "deaccessioned" many of her porcelains at a Sotheby Parke Bernet auction in New York. There were no bidders at all for many of her items.) All the rest was willed to the Avalon Foundation, which because of its charitable status removed the great bulk of her estate from the reach of the tax collectors.

Despite her millions and the luxuries they bought her, Ailsa's was not a happy life. Walker said that she was always surrounded by an "aura of sadness." Her childhood was traumatized by the vicious divorce in which her parents vied for discredit. As a young lady in Washington, she had two dear and close friends: Federal Reserve Governor William Harding's daughter Margaret, who committed suicide in 1924 by shooting herself, and Charles Hamlin's daughter Anna, who died a few months later of unreported causes. After her marriage she was almost constantly plagued by ill-health, by undeniable illnesses that defied diagnosis and by other "illnesses" that hinted at hypochondria. She developed bizarre phobias. She saw her husband blossom only after he had been freed of her—something that she never resented. Family sources told the author that she loved him to the grave, and they remained friends. Their only daughter, Audrey, married a man whose values were as opposed to Ailsa's as was humanly possible, and she saw the daughter adopt those values. She lived through the daughter's death in an airplane crash, and the reading of her daughter's will, which bequeathed the only possession of value—the guardianship of Ailsa's three orphaned grandchildren—to a "stranger," a Yale Law School professor. Everything that she might have held dear was taken from her except her houses and her things, the bibelots that people sold her. In her later life she suffered constant discomfort and near constant pain from premature arthritis. She accepted all of the sadnesses that were visited upon her with a noble and heroic dignity.

While Ailsa had a petulant streak to her, she did no rebelling; Mary McClung, T. A.'s only daughter and the oldest of the Judge's granddaughters, was a rebel. She rebelled when she "deserted" her first husband, John H. Kampman, and in her aborted fight to establish the rights of T. A.'s branch of the family to an interest in the family banking business. Otherwise, Mary had much in common with other well-to-do ladies of her time. She ran a big house in Pittsburgh, another in New York, and a third at Summer Haven, the Florida home of her father and the original winter retreat of the entire Mellon clan. When her children were young, her odd son, John Kampman, required most of her attention. There was clearly something "different" about Jack but it probably was not just simple retardation. In many ways he was almost "normal." He became a very good and sensitive pianist, and would play the piano hauntingly, until of a sudden something would snap in him, and then he would play the same notes over and over again, tinkle tonkle, tinkle tonkle, tinkle tonkle. Tinkle. Jack needed her most, and Mary was devoted to him, relying on the servants to rear her other four children. By the time of Jack's death in 1940 at the age of thirty-three, Mary's other children, another by Kampman and three by her second husband, Samuel A. McClung Jr., were fully grown and largely strangers to her. It probably did not matter; she probably would have been true to the child-rearing approach of the wealthy of her day anyway and have had the children reared by surrogates even if she had not been preoccupied with Jack. She made up for it by lavishing attention on her grandchildren.

In Florida Mary became friendly with Marjorie Kinnan Rawlings, author of *The Yearling,* who encouraged Mary to write. Mary's first novel, *Sheepshead Point,* was published by a "subsidy press" (less kindly known as a "vanity press") a year after she became widowed, in 1946, when Mary herself was sixty-one years old.

Sheepshead Point was a brief novel tracing the course of the lives of beachcomber "Thomas Selden" (a name suggestive of Thomas Mellon but probably inspired by a Mr. Morse, who was the beachcomber at Summer Haven), his wife, son, daughter-in-law, and granddaughter. It is a melodramatic, sentimental book, further marred by deficient editing, occasional gone-with-the-wind dialogue, and plenty of just plain corn, such as having the protagonist expire at the precise moment that the sun sets. The book also indicates Mary's truly limited understanding of the reality of day-to-day life for non-Mellons. The beachcomber, it seems, becomes fairly prosperous repairing fishermen's nets and retailing flotsam and jetsam, and ends up sending his granddaughter Gloria to a ladies' boarding school, where she takes up "her sketching and her painting." She rubs elbows with the island's fashionable winter colony and with the kindly Mellonesque banker in nearby St. Augustine. The beachcomber's granddaughter is welcomed at the socialites' "gay house parties" (Mary's words) and ends up hobnobbing with people with names like "Betsy Lawrence" and her brother "Ronnie," and Ron's pal "Keith Barclay" (Gloria "cared for him deeply"). Mary describes Keith as "rich, very rich," and inasmuch as "rich" is a relative concept, when Mary says "very rich," we can assume that she knows of what she writes. There is virtually no outward sign of affection between the young lovers (let alone of passion), and such as there is makes clear that Mary was no Erica Jong: " 'Oh Keith, why ever did you come. I'm so wretched,' and Gloria threw herself on the sand and wept bitterly." He was too much the gentleman to take advantage of the situation.

Notwithstanding all of the above, the book is fast-moving, sometimes charming, often evocative, and occasionally touching, if in a soap-operary way. It neither deserved nor received any recognition, but still it was a passable attempt at fiction writing.

After *Sheepshead Point* Mary worked on other writings—a novel set in Texas and a family history—neither published. In later life she liquidated two of her homes, necessitating the apportionment of a pharaonic quantity of personal belongings. She grew thin and frail and had pneumonia twice, but she was a tough old bird, almost impossible to kill, and maintained an inspirational existence until the end in 1974 at the age of ninety.

The fourth of the Judge's sons, J. R., had only one daughter, Sarah Lucille, previously introduced, who spent most of her life riding with the three husbands that she outlived. J. R.'s son W. L. had two daughters, both of whom fall within the same "generational" period as the daughters of A. W. and R. B. Though neither Rachel, the older, nor Peggy (Margaret), the younger, could ever have been called beautiful by conventional standards, both have strong faces with creditable features. They never had any public identification other than as daughters of their father and as wives of their husbands; and as Rachel's husband was the lesser-known, she is the lesser-known.

She married John F. Walton Jr. from a well-to-do Pittsburgh family of coal merchants. He went to fashionable St. Paul's School in Concord, New Hampshire, and then to Yale ('15), where he was on the staff of the Yale newspaper and was a member of Berzelius Society. After their marriage he entered the Mellon family businesses, working first with Alcoa and later as a vice president of Gulf. Over the years he was a director of assorted Mellon interests: Gulf, T. Mellon & Sons (a family coordinating group organized in 1946), and the Ligonier Valley Railroad. He was a trustee of the Carnegie

Institute and of Carnegie-Mellon University. In 1964 he served as co-chairman of the Committee of 100,000 Pennsylvanians for Goldwater, which proved to be fairly aptly named. He died in 1974 at the age of eighty-one. Rachel now lives at Pittsburgh's Royal York apartments, one of the most "respectable" apartment houses in town, which houses the city's most nearly gourmet restaurant, the Park Schenley. Born in 1899, Rachel is now well along in years, but she is still an impressive, smartly dressed woman, whom one would not consider to be an "old" lady. She is a woman of strong beliefs and opinions and a strict moral code, to which she clings inflexibly. Her modest Rachel Mellon Walton Foundation, with assets of about a million, makes grants of $1000 to $10,000 to Pittsburgh-area charities.

Most of W. L.'s twelve grandchildren have either expressed themselves in an unconventional manner or have had personality difficulties. Fortunately for Rachel, all of her four children have led relatively "normal," "wholesome" lives. The oldest, Anne, is married to Joshua C. Whetzel Jr., head of the Western Pennsylvania Conservancy, an organization concerned with conservation and environmental protection. A chemist by training, Whetzel brings a scientist's temper to a field overrun by zealots, but his own dedication to the cause is unimpeachable.

Rachel's next daughter, Mary, is the wife of New York investment banker Walter J. P. Curley, who served as chief of protocol for New York mayor John Lindsay, and then as United States ambassador to Ireland under President Ford. If anyone in Ireland realized that Curley's wife was the great-great-granddaughter of a man who had written virulent attacks on the Irish ethnic group, the Curleys could defuse the situation by pointing out that Mrs. Curley had herself married a "South" (Catholic) Irishman. "Jack," John F. Walton III, the older of Rachel's two sons, comes as close to a "rebel" as she produced. He moved to the southwest and became a rancher at Kirkland, Arizona. In the fall of 1977 he sold his Arizona holdings, and as of this writing is apparently at loose ends. The youngest of Rachel's children, James Mellon Walton, is the most active of them on the Pittsburgh scene today. He went to St. Paul's, Yale ('53) and then got a master's in business administration at Harvard, after which he spent several years with Gulf in scattered cities, among them Rome and Tokyo. Since 1968 he has served as head of the wonderful Carnegie Institute complex of library, natural history museum, and fine arts galleries including but not limited to the Sarah Scaife Gallery. He "represents" the heirs of W. L. on the board of directors of Gulf Oil, and was credited as one of the strong men of the "cleanup" of Gulf after the corporation's illegal "gifts" and "campaign contributions," discussed further along, were uncovered.

Only one of Rachel's four children has ever been divorced, and each of her children has given her four grandchildren. Rachel is the only one of W. L.'s four children who has not suffered some pain from her own sons and daughters.

Her sister, Margaret, known as Peggy, was fated to suffer more sadness, though at least by superficial standards she has enjoyed a more interesting life. Her first husband, Alexander Laughlin, was the scion of a wealthy Pittsburgh steel family, Yale-educated, who fought in World War I as a major. By 1926 he was the head of his own steel-related business, Central Tube Company. That year, at the age of thirty-six, he had a toothache, so he stopped in at the hospital to have his tooth pulled. He died there from an overdose of anesthesia. Laughlin left Peggy with an infant son, Alex. Two years later Peggy married again, this time to Thomas Hitchcock Jr., already a famous man if in a limited circle, destined to become famous in a somewhat wider circle, and to leave his wife widowed again at an early age.

Thomas Hitchcock Jr. is probably unknown to well over 99 per cent of living Americans. He remains, however, the best-known American polo player in history. For eighteen years he carried the highest "handicap" assigned in polo, making him, objectively, the best player for the longest time. No one would have guessed that Hitchcock was a great athlete from his photographs. The one included in this book is typical and shows a somewhat dumpy man who looks like he never was physically fit—the very opposite of most people's conception of the debonair polo player. He did not photograph well. He was all muscle, with arms like a blacksmith, and at the same time flexible. Polo was in his blood (as it probably must be). His father, like himself, once carried a "ten-goal handicap," and his remarkable mother organized a women's polo team. When her boy was thirteen, she put together and coached the Meadow Larks, a team of adolescent polo players affiliated with the Meadow Brook Club on Long Island, the spiritual center of American polo. Meadow Brook remained Hitchcock's home base throughout his polo career. At the age of sixteen he began competing in major polo tournaments.

Hitchcock's parents were the leading citizens of Aiken, South Carolina, where they owned thousands of acres for riding and hunting. His father lived on inherited wealth; his mother was the daughter of a United States senator. He was sent off to St. Paul's, but when the United States entered World War I he rushed to enlist. The Americans rejected him as under age, so he went to France and joined the French air service. He shot down three

German aircraft before his own plane was hit behind German lines, leading to his capture. After five months in captivity, he escaped by jumping off a fast-moving train, and then limping eighty miles to neutral Switzerland, from which he made his way back to France. He was awarded the Croix de Guerre.

After the war Hitchock returned to school at Harvard and Oxford, and to the polo fields. By the time of his marriage to Peggy, he was already the most celebrated polo player in America, and he continued to lead the American teams in international competitions until 1939. He devised new techniques and strategies for the sport, and played it so aggressively himself that he was utterly exhausted at the end of a game. His style and approach brought unprecedented attention to polo in the United States, and his participation in a tournament attracted tens of thousands, crowds never before or since equaled at American polo matches. Hundreds of thousands of sports fans knew of him as "Tommy," or "Hitch."

Hitchcock entered the coal refining business briefly, and then found his niche at Lehman Brothers, the important firm of New York investment bankers. According to his father-in-law, W. L., "He would have been, had he lived, a really great and creative man in business. He had discovered that there is an excitement in business which transcends even that of the polo field."

In a 1938 interview Hitchcock said, "Polo is exciting, but you can't compare it to flying in wartime. But you've got to be young to fight in the air. I wouldn't enjoy it now. It would be a painful duty." When Pearl Harbor was bombed, he was almost forty-two years old, but again he rushed down to the recruiting office seeking flying duty. He was placed in charge of an airborne combat group stationed in England, and died there in an airplane crash in 1944. The New York *Times* noted his death in an obituary, an editorial, a letter to the editor from Arthur Krock, and a strangely prophetic sports-page eulogy: "His memory will live as long as man swings the polo mallet."

Hitchcock left Peggy, then forty-three years old, with four more fatherless children: Louise, fourteen; Margaret, eleven; and twin sons Tommy III and William Mellon Hitchcock, aged five. W. L. wrote that he lost a friend and a son, but he consoled himself: "I am sure his valor was contagious. It is impossible for me to believe that any [of his children] will ever cease to try to be as fine and courageous as was Tommy Hitchcock."

Since Hitchcock's death, Peggy has lived at Gracie Square, in the fashionable Upper East Side of New York City, making a fetish of avoiding publicity of any kind. When the sons and daughters of Thomas Mellon gathered at his cottage in Northern Ireland in 1968 for their first of two major reunions, she chided one young Mellon for having given an interview to a London newspaper: "We don't like publicity and we don't want any of that!" She calmed down when the boy told her that he had consented to visit with the journalist only at the request of her brother Matthew.

Early photos of Peggy show her to be a handsome, possibly exciting woman, with a lot of spirit and independence. Though she has shunned the public eye, she never became a recluse. She still spends some time every summer at W. L.'s Camp Vagabondia in Beaumaris, Canada.

The men are more interesting in their own rights, and none more so than Matthew Taylor Mellon, W. L.'s oldest son and brother to Rachel, Peggy, and W. L. Jr. Matthew's charming trilogy, *The Grand Tour, War Log, 1917–18,* and *Watermellons,* all privately printed, give a good picture of growing up rich in the early part of the century, and should be consulted by social historians as well as family biographers. Most of the text of them was taken verbatim from his contemporary diaries. Like dozens of Mellons, Matthew was a compulsive diarist for much of his life, and even at the age of sixteen he was remarkably well-written. He had a greater incentive than most to be complete. He wrote in the preface to *The Grand Tour,* "Thinking he was doomed to become a business man in Pittsburgh for the rest of his life, the boy wrote desperately about everything he saw and did each day." The rest Matthew has filled in more recently. Matthew is a chatty person. The warmth of his nostalgia occasionally approaches that of Dylan Thomas's *Child's Christmas in Wales,* and belies his insistence that his books would hold no interest for outsiders. In *Watermellons* he recalled his trips as a small boy on the railroad train to Florida:

> I remember seeing skinny little Negro girls in white dresses and pink stockings waving from the platforms. . . .
> We children were kept in the stateroom at the end of the car. During the day we would look out of the windows and try to spot a razorback hog among the endless scrub pines and palmettos. Once we had a big stuffed teddy bear that we were tossing around in the stateroom when it got caught on the bell rope that ran through the train to the locomotive. My sister and I were really scared when the train began to slow down, but when it finally stopped and the irate conductor came through the car, we were both safely locked in the toilet!

At the hotel in Miami:

I remember the huge dining room with its colored waiters in their white coats balancing heavy trays of steaming dishes. I remember the big dance floor opposite the main entrance where Miglionico's band would play and the Negroes put on cakewalks for our amusement. . . . Upstairs, every room had a long coil of rope by the window "in case of fire." I sometimes dreamed of fat ladies climbing down those ropes in their nightgowns, but was never fortunate enough to witness the event.

On longer stays:

We went around with a gang of boys about our own age who attended the little school up the hill back of the hotel. There was Walter Peacock, Landon Carney, Frank Frow, and Fraser Noble, to name a few of them. We spent most of our time looking for gophers or snakes and the rest of the time pulling the burrs out of our feet.

On the first of W. L.'s *Vagabondias*:

Often, when we were at anchor on still nights, my oldest sister and I would steal down to the lower deck to hear old Roy, the engineer, play his guitar. Soon the voices of other darkies would join in the singing.

> If all my money was stacked up high
> I'm sure that the coins would reach the sky.
> I'd brush my teeth with diamond dust
> And I wouldn't give a damn if the bank would bust.

Later Matthew would recall that "These rich low voices singing to the chords of old Roy's guitar were, up to that time, the greatest aesthetic experience of my young life."

In *The Grand Tour* Matthew recounted the tour that the W. L.s and their entourage made of Europe in the summer of 1914. In addition to all of the W. L.s, there was Fräulein, the governess of the older children; Herr Reichlin, a German Swiss who had guided the R. B. contingent the previous summer; a nurse for Baby Larimer; a chauffeur; and sometimes other attendants. By then sixteen, Matthew included in his diary the pranks of boyhood. He climbed the ladder within a huge bronze statue of Cardinal Borromeo and while "inside the head, I went out into the nose and let my handkerchief hang out Borromeo's nostril. Peals of laughter could be heard from the people standing below. It looked as if he needed to blow his nose badly." Also, the insensitivities of adolescence: "We had a fat man in our compartment who couldn't speak English and we had lots of fun making raw remarks about him to his face." He touches upon his romance with a Rumanian princess—"Her favorite color is tango, too. She is knitting a tango pull-over for me"—and the romances of his sister: "Rachel's beau seems just as scared of Rachel as she is of him." He enjoyed the pleasure of marching behind a big brass band, and the disappointment of having two lizards stolen that he had had in a bottle. They hit all of the important cultural highlights of a trip to Europe, including a visit to the grave of Geeds:

> Fräulein said she planned to visit the Forum with us tomorrow, but there might be time to visit the grave of the great Geeds. We had never heard of Geeds, so we asked her who he had been. She admitted that she didn't really know but told us, in her slight German accent, that all the Americans and English go there. I racked my brains to know who she was talking about and finally I had an idea. She must mean Captain Kidd, the famous pirate I had just been reading about, the man who buried a fortune somewhere in Long Island Sound. I asked her whether it wasn't the great Captain Kidd she was talking about and, in desperation, she admitted that it probably was. So, we trotted off to the Protestant cemetery, a small plot surrounded by a high wall. I couldn't wait to get home and tell the boys I had seen the grave of this colorful character. Even the girls got excited when I told them whose grave they were about to see. Arriving at the gate we rang a bell for a long time before the watchman came and let us in. He led us through a narrow path to the grave. We all leaned over and read the name on the gravestone. It read:
>
> JOHN KEATS
> 1795–1821
>
> We looked at each other in disgust. To think we had come all this way for nothing!

There was low culture too. W. L. took him to the Folies Bergère (Matthew had previously been to "the old Academy Burlesque in Pittsburgh, which was thought to be the wildest show in town") and pointed out to him bars where women loitered. The outbreak of World War I made for vast complications for the W. L.s in arranging return passage, encouraging Matthew to hope that he would be late for school. On their return,

> I spotted Grandfather Mellon [J. R.] standing in the front row of those assembled on the dock. He had his Panama hat and white waistcoat on and carried a huge basket of fruit, rolls and sandwiches on his arm. It looked as though he thought we were returning from the prison camps of Siberia. Grandma was there, too, with the usual contingent of Taylors, all weeping as the band played the Star Spangled Banner and other patriotic airs.

The above selections, picked for their nostalgic value, do not reflect that Matthew was unusually intellectual almost from the time of his birth in

1897. As a child he worried his father, who caught him reading a book when he should have been watching the bait on the other end of his fishing pole. "That was conduct he couldn't understand," Matthew wrote; Matthew felt a little guilty about it himself. Photos of him as a little boy show him in typical Huck Finn attire, but wearing eyeglasses. At the age of thirteen he was sent off to St. Paul's. In *War Log* he wrote that "The names of the boys in my class at St. Paul's read like a condensed volume of the Social Register. There was 'Ribbs' McAdoo, Bill du Pont, Cornelius Vanderbilt, Bobby Strawbridge, Tony Biddle and Freddy Church, just to throw a few names around." At the age of twenty-one, he would describe the English boys at Eton in a diary entry as "a snobbish set of little rascals like the handpicked spawn of the American rich at St. Paul's."

Matthew enjoyed a number of athletic endeavors but despised organized sports of any kind, and he would sneak off the playing fields to retreat to the library. He wrote in *War Log* that "The masters were always trying to push me into 'sports' but the more they pushed the more I escaped to the library where I could hide out and enjoy reading." Music was as great a love for him as reading. The W. L.s' "French" governess turned out to be a German governess, and she introduced Matthew to the glories of German music and especially to Wagner. At St. Paul's his greatest enjoyment became singing in the choir, and he wrote that "It was a sad day for me when nature took my soprano voice from me and substituted for it the voice of a bull frog!"

Oddly, Matthew's grades were unimpressive. He did well in English and geography, but poorly in Latin and French, and he had to repeat his first year at St. Paul's. From W. L.'s vantage, Matthew's picture and prognosis were disturbing:

> As time went on, father became afraid that I would become a worthless "dreamer," destroying his hopes that I would some day follow him as a successful Pittsburgh businessman. So, with father's fears and the [headmaster] on my back, the day arrived when they agreed that I should be transferred to a military school where they would "make a man out of me" before it was too late.

He was sent to St. John's Military School, where he "shaped up" under military discipline, becoming a creditable horseman (almost a prerequisite to family acceptance among Mellons of his day). Still his intellectual bent was irradicable. He became editor of the school newspaper and escaped from military drilling by joining the school band as a saxophone and clarinet player. He brought his clarinet with him on the grand tour.

Matthew was four years at St. John's, finishing at the age of twenty, just in time for his World War I service previously discussed. The demands of his wartime duties left plenty of time for the opera, the ballet, and the theater, and for reading Shakespeare. He bought a guitar and entertained himself with it. The high point of his military career came on December 28, 1918, when President Woodrow Wilson visited the American embassy in London and greeted everyone attached to it: "When he took my hand he seemed to be pushing me on at the same time, and I remember he was talking to someone else when he did it, which added to the perfunctory nature of the occasion."

After the war Matthew entered Princeton in February 1919, majoring in philosophy, and graduated with the class of 1922. He played in the college orchestra and wrote much of the music for a college play, a production which Matthew now recalls to have been "a lot of damn nonsense." He seems to have been something of a loner at school, always residing alone. His classbook says that his future course would be studying philosophy at graduate school, but it was not to be. After a summer's respite in Europe, where he climbed the Matterhorn from the more difficult Italian side, he returned to Pittsburgh to begin his working life as a Pittsburgh businessman with the Gulf Oil Company. In a 1931 lecture on American values delivered to a German audience in Freiburg, Germany, he said, autobiographically, though not to the knowledge of his listeners,

> it is also essential for the rich young man in America to at least pretend that he works. He must have an office and visit it occasionally to maintain his appearance, no matter how rich his father is. But if a man is rich and his physical needs are satisfied, why does he demand still more money? The answer is that he considers important not more money but the respect of his fellow creatures. We Americans have no titles to strive for, no reward to satisfy our ambition. The only way to prove our excellence and so to acquire the respect of our fellow beings is to earn money. Our bank accounts are our titles. They determine our place in the respect of our fellow man—not with all, that is true, but with the majority.

That was a very accurate analysis of the ethos of the 1920s, and as of 1922 Matthew was not yet ready to rebel against that ethos. For four years he filled various roles with Gulf, auditing minor and later important branches of the business, running an asphalt plant, and helping to develop new product lines. From the reports of his many long cruises in *Watermellons,* it does not appear to have been an onerous life. He visited the office occasionally and maintained appearances. But it was not an intellectually stimulating life, and Pittsburgh was not an intellectually stimulating community. He now recalls the essence of his discussions with his father in 1926 about his life and his future as having been "If I had had two lives, I would have stayed." W. L. wrote in *Judge Mellon's Sons,*

> I supposed we were going to make a business man out of him, and for a while he gave himself fully to business—generously, as I now see it. . . . As president of the company I was honestly pleased with his work. But when it devolved on him to take up the selling end, Matthew told me he was through.
>
> In a kind of apology he explained that by giving him an income sufficient for all needs I had taken the profit motive out of business for him.

It was a sign of Matthew's emancipation from the dominant mores of the 1920s. He was no longer willing to let the respect that others might have for him turn upon his work or his status as a "big businessman." In the fall of 1926 he entered Harvard to study philosophy with the greats of his day, most notably Alfred North Whitehead. He became particularly interested in the history and philosophy of religion, developing a view of the subject that put the values of and the prognosis for Christianity in their anthropological place, and that is reflected in his published essay "How God Became Moral."

Matthew received his master's degree in 1928, and went on to study for his doctorate at the Albert-Ludwig University in Freiburg, Germany, one of the important philosophical centers of the time. The university's great luminary Martin Heidegger, now often cited as the spiritual father of French existentialism, was already recognized as one of the world's leading living philosophers.

Matthew had planned to write his doctoral dissertation on pragmatism, but university officials steered him elsewhere and encouraged him to select a historical topic for his thesis, specifically early American views on Negro slavery. He followed their guidance. He now believes that his advisers had suggested the topic thinking that his thesis might have some potential propagandistic value for Germany's National Socialist (Nazi) movement.

The thesis consists principally of excerpts taken from the writings of the Founding Fathers revealing their views on slavery, and includes concise recapitulations by Matthew of the views of each, together with his own overview of the subject. Its message was necessarily disconcerting to those who viewed the American experience as in some way morally superior to the European experience. It is written in formal "dissertation" prose, and Matthew kept himself fairly well in the background, generally revealing his personal opinions only by implication. *Early American Views on Negro*

Slavery was published by an obscure Boston publisher in 1934, but because it touched on an interesting and previously unmined area of American history, as well as because of its quality, it received the recognition of a highly favorable review in *The New York Times Book Review*. In 1969 it was reprinted by the respectable Mentor paperback house, with an introduction by the distinguished Columbia University historian Richard B. Morris:

> Matthew Mellon must be considered a pioneer in his explanation of the racial attitudes of early American statesmen. Writing as he did in the 1930s, when there was a trend toward hypercritical reassessment of the roots of the American tradition, Mr. Mellon reflected the disillusionment of his generation. At the same time he placed the focus of his research upon the subjects of slavery and race, subjects which had been shunted into a dark corner of the historical record. For the pitiless illumination which he has shed upon these controversial topics and the thoroughness and candor of his analysis, present-day readers will be very much in his debt.

Matthew remained associated with the university for ten years, 1928–38, sometimes as a student or faculty member and sometimes only informally as a member of the university circle. By the time that Matthew arrived there, Adolf Hitler could no longer be dismissed as the ludicrous Charlie Chaplin look-alike. Did his Nazi Party with its unthinkable philosophy represent the wave of the future? By the close of Matthew's German period, it seemed certain that it did. They were a difficult ten years to spend in Germany, whether or not one was a citizen of the Third Reich. Every thinking resident of the country was forced to formulate an attitude involving serious moral judgments on the course of German politics. Much in Matthew's intellectual and cultural background foreshadowed the stand that he was to take.

H. L. Mencken was the most powerful stimulant to the bright young people of the 1920s. He spawned what might be called the Mencken generation of intellectuals. Matthew was typical of them. He devoured Mencken's writings and invariably found himself in agreement. Much of that was very positive, as in the rebellion of the Menckenists against the materialism of the times. Unlike most of his peers, Mellon and his family were among the beneficiaries of that materialism, but as much as any he disapproved of the values of the American money culture that induced veneration of his father and his uncles. "It is not to be pardoned," he told a German audience in 1931, that we often pay our respects more to wealth than to art or intellectual or scientific strivings. . . . I personally believe that if the possibility to make large fortunes is taken away, our ideals would turn to more worthy and intellectual aims than the mere accumulation of money; and if we use the same energy for the realization of these new ideals, as we used for the previous, naive ones, then a whole lot can be expected from the American culture of the future.

He saw the income tax as a step in the right direction, as promising a means for effectuating "a more just distribution of wealth." Had W. L. spoken German, he would have disowned Matthew for such traitorous talk.

Also positive was the debunking tradition of the Mencken intellectual, insofar as it was a stimulant to challenging thought. Mellon contributed to that tradition with his thesis by pointing up the less-than-complete dedication of the Founding Fathers to their proclamation about all men being created equal. Washington himself, Matthew demonstrated, "was a very human 'plaster-saint' and a good deal of moral casuistry lay behind those pious, dignified features." In the debunking vein, Matthew's view of "the rich man," the 1920s hero, can be gleaned from a 1927 diary comment on railroad magnate Henry Huntington: "a man who first got on, then got honor, and finally got honest. He moved to California, bought everything in Duveen's art store, as well as the much overrated 'Blue Boy' of Gainsborough from the National Gallery in London, and died a gentleman of 'culture and refinement.' "

Until Matthew was himself well advanced in age, his comments to family members made clear that he was scarcely more impressed with the greatest Secretary of the Treasury since Alexander Hamilton. A comment in his thesis that Benjamin Franklin, "by extolling the virtues of commonsense, thrift and making a success of the world (which meant, making money), endeared himself to the middle classes in America and has served them ever since as their model," constituted a subtle slap at the patron saint of Mellonhood.

His attitude toward the priestly class is exhibited in this *Watermellons* comment on the ancient Maya: "A powerful cult of priests took advantage of the ignorant, as they still do today." His thesis includes other unfriendly commentary on the clerics: "Many of the [American Colonization Society's] members were good citizens who were themselves ignorant of its real purposes. The real blame for the deception is now known to have been the reverend clergy who were benefiting by the contributions." He was typically cynical about the effect of idealism on man's actions, and noted in his thesis that the support of the southern clergy for the institution of slavery "only shows how weak and futile principles are when confronted with the economic desires of a people." As for all of these attitudes, Mencken himself would have mounted the maximum enthusiasm of which he was capable.

Despite the wonderful flavor of the hundreds of quotes that survive the acerbic Baltimore iconoclast, at the bottom Mencken's philosophy was dark. Its essential hallmarks were a contempt for the common man, for the American culture, and for "boobocracy," as he described the American form of government, and a skepticism about (if not a rejection of) traditional "Christian" values. His own favorite philosopher was the nineteenth-century German Friedrich Nietzsche, who shared Mencken's contempts but whose rejection of the traditional values was crystal clear. The emptiness of Mencken's nihilistic world is reflected in this 1962 writing by Matthew included in *Watermellons,* inspired by a cruise among the Greek islands:

> The Greek gods themselves have descended from Olympus and passed into folklore, and Christianity, like every other religion or institution of men, will some day pass into oblivion. The universe we live in is completely indifferent to individual human lives, and it is frightening but true that, in the end, we are, each one of us, alone and utterly helpless, in a world of unending chance and unpredictable future!

Mencken was an "anti-humanist." The principal foil to him among thinking people of his day were the "New Humanists," most notably Harvard's Irving Babbitt, who were scarcely more democratic than Mencken, and who were also strongly Nietzschean. With the cataclysm of the Great Depression many young intellectuals, already long disenchanted with democracy on a theoretical basis, more or less openly committed themselves to totalitarianism, usually but not exclusively to totalitarianism of the left. Some moved to totalitarianism of the other stripe—Mencken's own *American Mercury,* long after Mencken's disassociation from it, devolved into an obscure journal catering to the far right. For many intellectuals of the period, what began as a revolt against the dominant businessmen's values of the 1920s ended as a revolt against democracy.

Mencken's deprecation of the American culture was superfluous for one such as Matthew, who had been steeped in the glories of German culture by his governess. In 1935 he wrote about his Germanic background:

> My admiration for Germany began in childhood. Translations of Grimm's fairy tales carried me first into an enchanted land of rare imagination. Pyle's "Otto of the Silver Hand" was one of my favorites, as well as many other tales of life in the feudal castles along the Rhine. Later I read a series of books— I have forgotten by whom—depicting life at the Prussian Court in the time of Frederick the Great. Accounts of the crowning of Wilhelm I by Bismarck in

the great Hall of Mirrors at Versailles, the reading of Goethe's "Wilhelm Meister," all helped to kindle my admiration for this great country.

By his own account, though, music, and especially Wagner, was much more important in inculcating a German orientation in Matthew. Adolf Hitler told William L. Shirer, "Whoever wants to understand National Socialist Germany must know Wagner." Wagner was the music of the strident Germany. Wagner himself was virulently anti-Semitic, anti-democratic, anti-materialistic, and if not anti-Christian, he was at least pro pre-Christian. Matthew "knew" Wagner:

> I was deeply impressed by the beauties of Wagner's Music Dramas. At every opportunity I visited opera houses and made many pilgrimages to Bayreuth to be near the source. On these visits I met delightful and cultivated German people . . .
> If you had been with me on a certain evening at Bayreuth and seen the audience rise together, tears streaming down their cheeks, during the last measures of the "Die Meistersinger" . . . you mightn't be so quick to dismiss this great people as a band of "barbarians" or "huns."

Wagner was fairly close in tune with the thinking of his good friend Nietzsche. Nietzsche was not anti-Semitic, but he was decidedly opposed to the "Christian" values of the "weak" that stood in the way of will and power. He represented in philosophy the pre-Christian ideals embodied in Wagner's operas. Much in his philosophy would strike a respondent chord in Matthew Mellon, and especially his glorification of raw power, perhaps the most important element of Nietzschean philosophy. Even before he knew of Mencken, let alone of Nietzsche, as a schoolboy of fifteen Matthew ended a poem about Easter Island

> Oh, distant, independent Easter Isle!
> No nation yet has gripped thee in its maw.
> I'm glad there still remains upon the earth
> One unmolested place where will is law.

The devotion of both Nietzsche and Wagner to antiquity was also consistent with Matthew's orientation. His studies of religion convinced him that traditional Christianity was no more "sacred" than the religions that had gone before, and entitled to no greater veneration. In a 1927 diary entry he discusses his liking for his nephew's name, Alexander: "It pleases me because of its pagan and particularly its Greek connotations." For a couple of years his constant companion was "Plotinus, the neo-platonist cat," and he was fascinated by archeology, just as the Nazis were fascinated by their own ancient roots.

At the time of Matthew's arrival in Freiburg in 1928, Nietzsche and Wagner were both enjoying a revival under the aegis of the adolescent Nazi Party. Together, they might be regarded as the spiritual fathers of Nazism, and they well represented its ideals.

University circles in Germany at the time were markedly anti-liberal, anti-democratic, and anti-Semitic. Most professors were strongly nationalistic. Though the Nazis were somewhat rowdy for the refined tastes of most university people, most German academics of the period were philosophically close to Nazism. The experience of the American intellectual of the 1920s led him as well to anti-democratic conclusions. The author has no reason to suspect that Matthew had any anti-Semitism ingrained in him. From his thesis it appears that Matthew of the period was not unsympathetic to Negroes, and though the "issues" might be somewhat different between Negroes and Jews, the Mellons have enjoyed a good rapport over the years with Pittsburgh's Jewish community and A. W. had good relations with many Jews. Still, Matthew was at least aware that Jews were "different" than most people. In a diary entry in *The Grand Tour,* one of the steamship passengers is identified as "the Jew."

What Matthew did have ingrained in him was an anti-"sentimentalism." *The Grand Tour* is a fairly brief book, in which at at least three places Matthew refers to someone employed in a humble role as a "flunky." On the grand tour, W. L. took his children to the Paris morgue, once open as a tourist attraction, only to find that it was closed. Matthew recorded that "father said that when he was a boy anyone could go in and that the stiffs were all laid out on marble slabs for inspection." When W. L. showed Matthew a lower class bar, "I looked in and saw some poor old hags sitting around and as it was nearly midnight, father said they would have to go out and hunt a hole to crawl into as the saloons close at midnight."

The somewhat cold attitude toward his fellow man reflected in the sixteen-year-old's grand tour diary was reinforced by the American intellectual milieu of the 1920s. George Jean Nathan, long Mencken's collaborator at *Smart Set* and *American Mercury,* wrote that "If all the Armenians were to be killed tomorrow [as seemed likely in the 1920s] it would not matter to me in the least. . . . What concerns me alone is myself, and the interests of a few close friends." The "New Humanists" were only marginally more humanistic; Irving Babbitt insisted that he had no use for "sickly sentimentalizing over the lot of the underdog."

Nietzsche's world was not as empty as Mencken's; Nietzsche filled his world with the concept of the superman, an idea that lent itself nicely to Nazi adaptation as the concept of the super race—it filled a "moral" void for many. Hitler came to power as chancellor peaceably and by constitutional means in January 1933 and solidified his position that spring by the "revolution" of 1933, after which university circles fell in line behind him. Heidegger himself publicly pledged his support for and loyalty to the Nazi regime. Matthew Mellon had married Gertrud Altegoer, the daughter of a Freiburg professor, in December 1931, a year before Hitler's first selection as chancellor, and had settled down in a lovely house overlooking the city. There was no reason to move. On the great issue of his day he was prepared to take his stand, and in May 1935 he took it publicly in the Pittsburgh *Press* with an unrestrained endorsement of the Hitler regime:

> Regarding the National Socialistic Government and Germany's future, I have nothing but strong approval and the highest of hopes for its ultimate success. Being a property owner in Germany I regard Adolf Hitler as having saved my home from the Communistic rabble that would have spread all over Europe had he not come into power in 1933. He has fought constantly to free Germany from the slavery imposed on her by the Treaty of Versailles.
>
> The German people, with the exception of a few loud-crying minorities who do not matter much, have the utmost faith in him as the one man who can bring Germany back to a respectable place in the brotherhood of nations.

He was not opposed to democracy in the abstract, but insisted that it was not necessarily the best form of government for all people at all times:

> It has always seemed to me that different peoples are temperamentally and psychologically suited to different types of government. That is why I cannot believe that our American democracy should be forced on any other people holding different views. It is not apparent that the ideal type of government has yet been worked out, and in the meanwhile the course of tolerance would be to remain at home and perfect our own Government.

In particular, it was inappropriate for the Germany of his day:

> Democracy as I witnessed it off and on in Germany from its inception until the last revolution, could hardly be described truthfully as a desirable form of government, certainly not a safe one. . . . It was unity that was needed in Germany more than anything else, and Adolf Hitler was the man that brought this miracle about and to whom the great majority of Germans are truly thankful. . . . A strong man who shows the way is at this time preferable to the eternal chewing of the Congressional cud [in Germany].

Hitler had "marked the end of a dangerous democratic regime," and had created "one united German front in a heroic effort to win back a respected place among the nations!"

Typical of pro-Nazi propagandists, Matthew heaped scorn on the Versailles Treaty that ended World War I, urged restoration to Germany of her former colonies before Germany's population pressures became "unbearable," and particularly defended Germany's rearmament efforts:

> Personally I rejoice when I hear that Germany is again re-arming, that she's building an air force and submarines, that she's using her inalienable right to defend herself against the whims of her dangerous and heavily armed neighbors—neighbors who have broken their sacred word and have been re-arming while Germany lay defenseless. . . .
>
> Sitting on the veranda of my house in the Black Forest one can look west across the Rhine Valley and over into Alsace as far as the Vosges Mountains. With the aid of glasses it is not hard to detect the white concrete openings of French underground fortifications and huge cement gun bases covered sometimes by wooden shacks or smoke stacks in a childish attempt to make the Germans forget that they exist.
>
> Long military roads stretch out from the Rhine into the mountains beyond. Our German side of the Rhine lies in the demilitarized zone. Sometimes when watching a sunset over these mountains I think how easy it would be for these over-armed Frenchmen to destroy our town, the university, my house and everything I own in it.
>
> I long for the days when the watch will again stand on the Rhine—the watch which will protect the German people from their dangerous enemies!

In another piece, Pittsburgh's *Bulletin-Index* of March 1934 quoted him as saying

> "No one could look you in the eye" before the days of Hitler, because of the doubt and skepticism of the older German generations: "But today you get a full eye from every one, especially from the youths of Germany who now are more hopeful of the future under the leadership of Germany."

In discussing disputes within the Protestant Church of Germany, he said that "Premier Hitler has missed a grand opportunity to eliminate the Old Testament entirely" from future reprints of the Bible: "After all, the Old Testament is principally nothing but a history of the Hebrews, so why don't they begin with the advent of the Christian era and use only the New Testament?"

Throughout the later 1930s Matthew spent much of his time in Germany and the rest of it vacationing in America. When the reporters saw him on his comings and goings, they noticed signs hinting at loyalties: a Nazi flag draped over his steamship berth when embarking for Germany in September 1935, a pair of discreet lapel pins—one an American flag, the other a swastika—ornamenting his coat as he disembarked from the first transatlantic dirigible flight in the spring of 1936.

Matthew's support was no doubt responsible for his being invited, on the recommendation of the rector of Freiburg University, to attend Nuremberg Day exercises—the Third Reich's week-long annual celebration of the Nazi deliverance—in the fall of 1936, as the personal guest (along with several dozen others) of the Führer. When he discusses Nuremberg Day today, he does so with a scientific detachment free from any hint of either entrancement or of moral judgment. His contemporary diary notes showed more enthusiasm:

> Tonight I attended a special performance of The Meistersanger as a guest of Hitler. I was given a place in a box, next but one to the Führer. I have heard Die Meistersanger many times before in various countries with better voices and with grander pageantry in the last act, but never have I heard it under more inspiring conditions. To be here in the very city of Nürnberg as a guest of Germany's present ruler, surrounded by all his devoted followers and invited to witness a scene which tomorrow will be enacted on the very meadow depicted in the third act; this combination of the old and the new order stimulated by the inspired music of the great master; is this not an occasion to arouse the imagination and bring great joy to one's heart?

He continued to be impressed with German morale: "Surely this fine, healthy, slender race of men and women do not fit the image we Americans have of Germans. This is a new generation with the look of hope on their faces and something heroic in their mien." The social events were among the highlights of the week, including a dinner at which

> I sat next to Count von Rosen, Equerry to the King of Sweden, and Trude Moor, head of the Federation of German Maidens, sat on my other side. She told us she had 2,500,000 virgins under her, which caused a ripple of laughter when von Rosen hinted he would be satisfied with just one or two under him!

His introduction to Hitler was reminiscent of his introduction to President Wilson years earlier: "When I reached the Führer he took my hand and at the same time moved me on. I looked for a moment into his eyes and passed on without a word."

At the same time his diary notes indicate that he was tiring of some aspects of Nazism. He sat through long speeches by Dr. Alfred Rosenberg, Nazism's leading exponent of anti-Semitism, and by Dr. Paul Joseph Goebbels, propaganda minister of the regime, and noted that "After these hot air volcanoes had blown their gas, a fine trickle of lava appeared which seemed to be attempting to link up Communism with world Jewery using the events in Spain as an example." He skipped personal attendance at another Goebbels address and listened to it instead on the radio:

The speech was being broadcast in the dining room and during the duller moments our table would converse on other subjects. An enraged waiter came over and told us all to be quiet. So deep down has fanaticism spread that it was unthinkable for this indoctrinated flunky to imagine anyone not breathless to take in the immortal words of the little doctor from Heidelberg.

Invited to a party with the head of "the National Socialist Power Corps," he was unimpressed to find the head "in a rather advanced state of inebriety," and surrounded by a group characterized by "lusty laughs and dirty jokes." He found a display of military might to be "a never-to-be-forgotten sight that seemed to belie much of Hitler's insistence of Germany's peaceful intentions." He clicked tongues with Dr. Jacob Schurman, onetime American ambassador to Germany, over "crude misrepresentations" about the Jews in Nuremberg's Nazi weekly, *Der Stuermer.* The anti-Semitism most nearly bothered him. As he now recalls it, the Nazis' anti-Semitic policies in education were very bad for the university: "We were losing all these good men, especially in the medical school." Around 1936 he went with Freiburg's "British professor" (Matthew himself was its "American" faculty member) and a couple of other teachers to the regional head of education to protest that the state's attitude was detrimental to the university, and to ask for an end to the policies, or at least an end to the application of them at Freiburg, in the interests of maintaining the quality of education. The gentleman with whom they spoke exploded: "If you don't like it, get out!"

The heil-ing didn't wear well, and is still imprinted in his mind. He told the author, "Yes, we were heil-ing everything. 'Heil Hitler!' 'Heil Hitler!' everywhere. It got to be very tiresome." Even W. L., to Matthew's puzzlement, on a visit to his son in Germany joined in the heils on a when-in-Rome rationale.

But Germany had become home to Matthew, and the relativism that had been ingrained in him by his studies in America and by the intellectual milieu of his era made it easy for him to ignore the Nazis' lapses from traditional Christian values. His notes from Nuremberg Day mention running into "my friend Baron von Guinant from Freiburg, who proudly wears the black shirt of an S.S. man."

Matthew left Germany in December 1938. W. L. had written him that the war clouds were too dark (as indeed they were), essentially summoning him home. Matthew obeyed the order of higher authority. He made clear that he left Germany on good terms: "We were getting along quite well." After his return to the United States, his circle was composed largely of people with backgrounds paralleling his own. German was the principal language of his household, and when his son Karl, born during one of

Matthew's United States sojourns in 1937, but whose name is spelled in the German manner, entered school during the Second World War, he did so speaking virtually no English. Karl now recalls that the other children "picked on me because I was a kraut. I couldn't help it that I was a kraut."

When the war broke out, Matthew did his part, or attempted to. Given his past, it could not be expected that he would be assigned to a high-security role, but he was permitted to enlist in the Coast Guard Reserve— "about the lowest thing you can get," he now says with a twinkle. He did not see active service.

Matthew has remained a Germanophile. For many years he served as an adviser to Harvard's German department, and as an associate editor of the *American-German Review*. In 1950 he donated an organ to the chapel at Colby College that was a replica of one that he had donated to Freiburg University, which had been destroyed during the war. A plaque on Colby's organ reads, "May the voice of this organ bring to Colby something of the greatness and genius of that Germany the world once loved and admired." Until the end of his yachting days, his personal yachting flag pictured a black symmetrical eagle against a white background, the eagle a traditional German symbol (though his was not in the traditional Germanic form), the colors being the colors of Prussia. In 1958 Matthew was awarded the Commander's Cross of the Order of Merit of the Federal Republic of Germany, in recognition of his efforts to maintain and advance cultural relations between the United States and Germany.

Matthew Mellon is a generous man. He gave the author several long interviews, during which the author shied away from broaching the potentially touchy topic of Matthew's flirtation with Nazism. Finally Mellon looked the author straight in the eye and said, "You know, if there's anything you want to ask me, go ahead. If you're going to write a book, it might as well be accurate." So the author broached the subject. With a pause between each word, Mellon began: "I . . . was . . . just . . . duped." Hitler had built the autobahns and had accomplished some other tangible benefits; he had kept saying that he did not want war. Matthew had believed him. "I was taken in by a lot of this stuff." He had felt sorry for what the Jews were going through. Probably to his credit, Matthew did not mention that the German citizen of his day did not imagine what the ultimate outcome of the government's anti-Semitic campaign would be. Mellon gave the author a Xerox of an essay entitled "1936 Nürnberg 'Party Day,'" written by him around 1972, which ends with a recapitulation of the relations between France and Germany over history, intertwined with a discussion of the self-concept of the "little man" in Germany, that may shed fuller light on Mellon's matured attitude toward the Nazi era:

> Suddenly another "little man" appeared who not only felt the same way about things, but had developed a technique to reach the masses. He took over the government in 1933 and three years later sent German soldiers to occupy the Rhineland. He formed the work battalions that built a new network of auto highways which the world copied. He cleaned the museums of lot of worthless crackpot canvases and replaced them with sentimental and realistic ones that were just about as bad, for this "little man" considered himself an artist too! He revived Nietzsche's Superman, confining him to the Aryan race, and this gave the "little man" dignity instead of humiliation. The Jews were his scape-goats. Everything that bothered the little people was blamed on them. This was terribly unfair and Germany lost many good Jews such as Einstein, but all in all this devilish scheme worked. The Führer had a psychological technique that was new to the little man. He dazzled him with floodlights, loud speakers, flags, uniforms and medals. Propaganda was pounded into his skull by the radio and press. He was told he was a great fellow; given a title like Ober Gauleiter, and assured of a place in the Thousand Year Reich. Old Barbarossa, the Kaiser Frederick, had awakened and left his cave! And later it was the Führer's turn to dance at the old railway car while French generals, too cowardly to fight for their own country, were forced to look on! The Maginot Line, costing France millions of francs, was made useless by a brilliant "end run" maneuver, which proved that this "impregnable" fortress was just another example of Gallic stupidity! Thus, as Tennyson said, "the old order changeth, yielding place to new."

Matthew T. Mellon

After December 1938 Matthew never "worked" again. For that matter, he hadn't much worked during his German period. He had pursued his doctorate in a leisurely manner. Both before and after receiving it, he taught off and on at Freiburg, but American society columns of the 1930s reporting his comings and goings make it apparent that his teaching schedule must have been more off than on. Still they identified him as a faculty member at Freiburg University. After 1938 there was no effort to maintain appearances. He was "retired." If the superman had filled any kind of void for Matthew, hedonism replaced it; in a couple of spots in *Watermellons* he mentioned a "search for that elusive thing called pleasure."

Thereafter Matthew and Gertrud (known in the family as "Gerda" or "Trudy") lived prototype existences for the superrich, shuttling back and forth between homes in Palm Beach, the less known but equally fashionable retreat at Northeast Harbor near Bar Harbor, Maine, and a house on

Nipowin Island in the well-to-do community of Greenwich, Connecticut, long a refuge for tax exiles from New York City. There was a house in Baden, Germany, as well. Much of the time they were cruising on one of the series of yachts that Matthew owned or leased. Everywhere their lives revolved around "the colony." In Palm Beach, Matthew became a leader of it as the longtime president of the Society of the Four Arts, the driving force behind just about anything cultural that took place there during the 1940s. Matthew took his duties to it quite seriously, even to the point of interrupting an expedition in Honduras for a brief trip back to Palm Beach to attend a meeting of the society. Neither Paul, Ailsa, nor the Scaifes, all part of the Palm Beach world, got into the whirl of the social season as did Matthew and Gertrud.

Like his father before him (and his son Jay after him), Matthew sponsored Carnegie Museum expeditions, sometimes but not always accompanying naturalist Arthur Twomey and his entourage on their wanderings. For a time Matthew appeared slated to become head of the Carnegie complex, a position now held by his sister Rachel's son James Walton Jr., but for reasons sufficient unto himself, his father's cousin R. K., a vital financial mainstay of the Carnegie Institute, put a damper on the suggestion with Carnegie decision makers.

Matthew and Gertrud had two sons—Karl, born in 1937, and Jay, born in 1942—both attractive youngsters, nice to have around. Matthew enjoyed reading the funnies to them and introducing them to the joys of yachting. But for the most part it was an authoritarian household, the parents distant, and usually formal. Most of the child rearing was done by the domestics, with the parents functioning as overseers, not always approachable. The mother was more nearly responsible for the tone of the relationships. Karl recalls that when his father left him as a teenager at the Menninger Institute, Matthew cried. Gertrud's emotions were much better controlled.

Matthew and Gertrud were divorced in Nevada in 1951, on terms undisclosed but described in the New York *Times* as "substantial." It was an amicable separation; they have remained friends since, and Gertrud remains close to many members of the Mellon family. She now lives close by the Metropolitan Museum on New York's Fifth Avenue. Subsequent to the divorce she became interested in primitive art and served on the board of directors of New York's Museum of Primitive Art. She has accumulated a distinguished collection of African artifacts as well as an important sampling of German expressionist graphics. Two years after their divorce, Matthew married the former Jane Bartram, newly divorced from her husband Rensselaer W. Bartram Jr. The Bartrams had been neighbors and close social friends of the Mellons at both Greenwich, where their properties adjoined, and at Palm Beach.

After his remarriage Matthew and his new wife lived most of the next eleven years (1953–1964) aboard a new yacht that Matthew had built for him in the Netherlands, principally cruising about the Mediterranean, where Matthew enjoyed visiting archeological sites. Symbolically, he named his yacht *Vagabondia,* after the series of yachts owned by the father with whom he had never been quite able to communicate. He liquidated his other homes, and they wintered on a 100-acre plantation that he bought at Runaway Bay on the north coast of Jamaica in the West Indies. By 1964 problems of staffing the vessel had become overwhelming, and the political climate in Jamaica had become worrisome. Both properties were sold.

Today Matthew divides his year between his houses—Haus Mellon in Kitzbühel, Austria, and a home at Coconut Grove, just south of Miami, Florida—living a somewhat different lifestyle at each. Haus Mellon, his "main" house, built in the early 1950s, he describes as an ornate baroque house. His impressive philosophical library, his collection of musical manuscripts, and most of his family memorabilia are kept there. There is also a prominently displayed portrait of the once-scorned Andrew W. Mellon, flanked by a pair of record-size elephant tusks, trophies of one of his son Jay's hunts. His chauffeur-driven Mercedes-Benz is one of the more impressive in the neighborhood. His days are occupied with Hapsburg and Hohenzollern leftovers. Mellon denies any gourmet leanings, but he tends to put on weight in Austria because of the typical Austrian menu. "They don't know anything about nutrition there," he says.

He prefers his Coconut Grove home. At its entrance the visitor is greeted by a richly colored ornate portrait of the owner seated by a window beyond which one sees a typical Tyrolean scene. In the background of the painting is a picture of Richard Wagner. Other than the portrait, both the architecture and the furnishings of the house are decidedly "thin-look." It is a large, crisp southern-contemporary home, decorated in starkly modern furniture of lucite and chrome. The green and white color schemes are cooling in the hot climate. Floors are covered with fine contemporary area rugs, unostentatious though only marginally less expensive than semi-antique orientals of similar size. The main wall of the living room is ornamented with a Mondrian-like abstract. In his bedroom there is a clock, a row of Mellon family books, his own and others, a sketch of Alfred North Whitehead, a framed print of a proposed layout for an Ulster-American Folk Park, and very little else. His study is almost as sparse and decidedly modern.

When the author asked why, with his interest in archeology, he did not surround himself with Greek vases and Roman marbles, he explained his decorating tastes: "I despise clutter." Surrounded by "things" all of his life, he has liberated himself from them. As for the archeological remnants, he said, "I think that things like that ought to be in museums. I like contemporary things." His Florida library is small, just "books people give me." His Coconut Grove chauffeur drives a late-model station wagon, much more appropriate than a "showy" car in a society that frowns on displays of wealth. In Florida his diet would strike a fashion model as spartan, and it enables him to shed a few of his Austrian pounds each winter. His wife, Jane, tall and slender, with long straight hair and no discernible makeup, appears very much younger than her age must compute out to be, and has a fresh air to her. Together they spend their days at one or another of the clubs to which they belong.

Matthew devotes some time—less now than formerly—to writing and compiling more books on aspects of the family history. He says that it is "nice to write it down, and it doesn't cost much to print." He quickly adds that "there's not much there of interest to anyone." He also busies himself with his principal charitable endeavor, the Ulster-American Folk Park at Camp Hill, Tyrone County, Northern Ireland, the site of the Judge's birthplace. His interest in it springs from the mid-1960s, when he visited the Judge's birthplace and was dismayed to find "the run-down condition of the cottage and the filth and disorder of its surroundings." With the encouragement of the Northern Ireland government and some financial assistance from the wealthier branches of the family, he acquired the cottage and its immediate area from the farmers who then owned it, and restored the Judge's birthplace to typical early-nineteenth-century state, and presented it as a gift to the government of Northern Ireland. For its official opening in June of 1968 Matthew organized the first of two Mellon family reunions. A party of about fifty, including twenty-seven of the Judge's descendants, representing all branches of the family tree, journeyed to Ulster for the official ceremonies and a series of parties. Matthew told the press, "I don't think people want to see where the Mellons came from particularly, but it's a very beautiful farmhouse of the period."

Since then, the Matthew T. Mellon Foundation has continued an interest in developing the area immediately around the farmhouse as a kind of Sturbridge Village with new world and old world areas, showing life in the early 1800s in both hemispheres. The proposed plan shows a number of "period" buildings and displays plus a cafeteria building and the Matthew T. Mellon Information Building.

Matthew has also been a benefactor of Colby College. The longtime president of Colby, Julius S. Bixler, was a fellow student with Matthew and

Gertrud at Freiburg University, and has remained close to both of them. Both have aided the college generously, and Matthew has served on its board of directors over the years.

He still enjoys listening to music, though he no longer plays much himself. There is a guitar propped up in a corner of his study, and he said that he plays it mostly for the entertainment of his grandchildren. Wagner continues to be one of his favorites. Wagner's is "the music of the strong will," as he calls it, "with the power of bringing you back into an age that's gone." But he now prefers Strauss, he says, and Puccini and other "modern" Italian composers (as from his perspective they are), excepting Verdi, whose music he does not like.

Every day he reads his daily newspaper, the New York *Daily News*, and he still occasionally samples old volumes of Mencken's writings.

He sees relatively little of his two sons—almost nothing of his elder son, Karl. (Both are discussed in some detail in the next section of this book.) Both Matthew and Karl acknowledge something of a gap in values between them, though they share a mutual respect. Matthew has four grandchildren, two from Karl's first of three marriages, to whom Matthew writes grandfatherly letters, and two from Karl's second marriage, boys too young for letters, but not yet too old for grandfatherly affection and indulgence. The younger pair live in Palm Beach, and Matthew sees much of them when he is in Florida. He has maintained excellent relations with their mother, his former daughter-in-law. When she remarried, the widely read gossip columnist "Suzy" reported that at her engagement party "Anne's ex in-laws with whom she remains very close, the Matthew Mellons of Coconut Grove, Florida, and Kitzbühel, Austria, were very much on hand." He has almost no contact with his brother, Larry, or with his sister Rachel Walton, but he sees something of his sister Peggy Hitchcock.

Politically, Matthew describes himself as "very conservative." His talk of 1931 about the desirability of ending the possibility of accumulating large fortunes, and the value of the income tax as an instrument of social policy, has been replaced by words like these:

> We Americans, who own property in this country and plan to increase it, are being cleverly bullied into the idea that we should feel guilty about it! It seems that the purveyors of Socialism and Welfare are trying to tell us we should be ashamed to enjoy the fruits of our labors or those of our fore-fathers. The "have-nots" who are setting these winds of doctrine loose in the land, have the impertinence to call capitalism a "dirty" word, hinting that the accumulation of wealth is morally wrong. They ignore the fact that the very greatness of America is based on the production and accumulation of wealth.

He is quick about "idlers and welfare termites," and "the 'share the wealth' minority." He wishes that left-wing radicals would work through the democratic process or, "failing to do this, they should get to work and above all, keep quiet!" Unhappy experiences in Jamaica have made him unreceptive to the problems of emerging nations, or the problems of their racial brothers wherever located, and his language is peppered with ethnic slang.*

When the author visited him in May of 1976, Matthew expected that he would probably support President Ford for re-election. "Not too clever a man himself, but he has good men around him." There is no self-consciousness about him as he says that he votes his interests. He is more honest with himself and with others than most men are where their own motives are concerned. For the most part, "his interests" means oil: What's good for Gulf is good for Matthew.

He has become somewhat more conservative in his appraisal of people. Yachting in the 1920s, he would pick up a nautical hitchhiker *because* the man was an obvious oddball. A 1927 *Watermellons* note shows a tolerant man:

> . . . we noticed some Gulf products on the shelves. I asked the man whether they were really any good and it was amusing to hear him tell me the virtues of our sewing machine oil and spot remover just as I had written it for the use of salesmen. Little did he know that the perspiring riverman before him had written the sweet sounding words that appeared lithographed on the cans and tubes. All of which shows what a strange thing Life is; how little we know of each other; how little we can judge others by their outward appearances. This crude little shopkeeper might, for all I knew, have been the greatest authority on caterpillars or Kantian philosophy in all Kentucky!

Now he is quick to formulate unfavorable opinions on superficial bases, and speaks sharply about "bearded freaks" and like types. Though he is still a theological libertine, if not a skeptic, in the 1960s his Matthew T. Mellon Foundation became an important contributor to the Missionary Society of the Protestant Episcopal Church, a group which Matthew of the 1920s and '30s would have regarded uncharitably.

Where the family is concerned, Matthew says that he is a "sentimentalist." Until well along in years himself, he was harsh about many of his relatives. Now "that old drunk so-and-so" of the 1920s, '30s, and '40s has

---

*Matthew is a gentleman and a gentleman does not use "swear words." In four days of visits, he did not use a four-letter word, though there were occasions when one might have been appropriate. Gentlemen of his day did not use four-letter words, though they might employ an ethnic slur. Today everything is reversed. Today's gentleman will use an occasional four-letter word; the ethnic slur has become taboo.

become "dear old so-and-so." Except insofar as time has softened his remembrances, though, he is coldly objective in his discussions of his relatives, and totally open. Even where the family is concerned, he is unwilling to indulge in artifice, and incapable of shading truths. He takes an Olympian view of the foibles of his kinsmen (and himself), and he does not often make moral judgments. When he does, they are without compassion.

Matthew Mellon had a great potential for creativity. His doctoral thesis demonstrated an ability to sift and evaluate historical evidence, and revealed an incisive mind. The thesis was properly acclaimed. He was also a gifted writer. Few have better celebrated the industrial city than Matthew did in this 1927 diary entry:

> I love old Pittsburgh, perhaps because my roots were nourished in her smoke and dirt. To me the glow of her furnaces against the clouds on a winter's night, the rumblings and screams of her gigantic mills bring peace to my mind. Pittsburgh, a great drama being enacted by sweating and striving individuals —a drama not of an age of heroes, made romantic merely because their defects are forgotten, but a drama of terrifying reality, obviously including, yet heroically surmounting, its own defects. Many a night have I lain awake and listened to those distant whistles—big ones with deep bass voices, shrill sopranos, and rich sonorous baritones—and wondered whether steel mills, locomotives, and steamboats do not converse in a language of their own.

Looking back on his life, Matthew says, "I've been pretty well off, and didn't have to work, but I've always been active. I've traveled a lot, and spent a lot of time writing these squibs about the family. I've had a good life." He enjoys reminiscing—the only sign of his eighty years—and he reminisces nicely. He regrets (from the foreword to *Watermellons*) "how little of our lives we can communicate to others, and how very much of it we must carry with us to our graves." Otherwise, there are no regrets.

Most people would think that Matthew's brother, Larry—William Larimer Mellon Jr.—has made a greater success of his life than any other member of the "third" or any other generation of Mellons. No two brothers could be less alike temperamentally, culturally, or philosophically. Matthew was imbued with the cynicism of the 1920s intellectual; Larry matured in the different climate of the depression era.

Larry Mellon has spent the better part of his life and fortune doctoring the neglected Haitian country folk, who number among the most wretched of mankind. At the time of W. L.'s death thirty years ago, Larry had just begun to show signs of his future role as the Haitian Albert Schweitzer. By any man's standards, and especially W. L.'s, Larry Mellon at the age of thirty was still an all-around failure.

The last of W. L.'s four children, Larry was born in 1910, nine years after his nearest sibling, at a time when W. L. was forty-two and May was thirty-eight years old.

May Mellon told her little boy that being a medical missionary was the highest of callings, and instilled in him a child's passing interest in doctoring. W. L., however, did not have much interest in doctoring; he no doubt shared the Judge's view that the sons of Hippocrates were a hypocritic lot. For W. L., business was the only path for his sons, and every child's passing interest in doctoring passed, for the moment, from Larry Mellon.

Larry and his second cousin Ned shared a mischievous boyhood until each was sent off to a separate boarding school, Larry to Choate in Wallingford, Connecticut, where his father's cousin Paul (just three years older than Larry) had preceded him. Though Larry was never particularly articulate, he had a curious knack for languages, the only sign of brilliance in his picture. His earliest tutor, a Swiss governess, had taught him French, and at Choate he mastered Spanish in classes and in contact with a Cuban roommate, and picked up respectable Portuguese from a Brazilian boy whom the school administration assigned to Larry in hopes that the Brazilian might easier learn English. In later years Larry became proficient in the Basque language of northern Spain, and acquired passable familiarity with Arabic and Hebrew. Today Creole, the Haitian natives' corruption of French, is his second language, if not his first.

During the most sinister portion of the Capone era, at a time when his grand-uncle was in charge of the nation's prohibition enforcement, the Choate student paralleled his father's early feat of electrifying the Judge's house, and W. L.'s boyhood trips to market to sell the produce from the Judge's farm: he set up and operated an elaborate first-class still and sold its product to students and area farmers alike. W. L. was upset when the still exploded and the matter came to the attention of school officials.

Larry went on to Princeton, where his much older brother, Matthew, had studied, but it wasn't for him. He felt uncomfortable with classmates whom he later characterized as wanting to sell bonds and "belong to the right clubs." He did poorly and dropped out after a year, much as his father's "Cousin Dick" (R. K.) had done. A friend later ventured that if Larry had had to work his way through, he might have stayed at Princeton. W. L. was sorry. Like "Cousin Dick," Larry entered the Mellon National Bank, ten years behind him.

He married not long after. Grace Rowley was of "lower class" background; her father made artificial limbs. Hers was a warm, welcoming family in American middle-class surroundings that strongly appealed to the poor little rich boy. Larry later said of his youth that there had been "times when I felt ashamed to be from a family that was known only for wealth. I felt more at home with chambermaids than with people in my own group." The distance between Larry and "the rich" was perhaps greatest in his relationship with his own father. "We never really got along," he says. Grace's humbler background heightened for Larry her undeniable beauty.

The Rowleys were not without social pretensions. They pointed with pride to their descent from John Hancock, and made sacrifices to send their daughter to a "fashionable" girls' boarding school, Ogontz, near Philadelphia. Her mother saw Larry as fitting nicely into her family picture, and showered him with attention and affection. In November of 1929 Larry, at the age of nineteen, and his intended, eighteen, eloped to West Virginia.* For a year they kept the marriage secret from all but Larry's brother, Matthew. Matthew strongly disapproved of the match and attributes it to an excess of morality on his brother's part: "With that moral streak of his, Larry wouldn't live with the girl unless he married her." But Matthew kept the secret.

Months later the formal engagement of Miss Rowley and Mr. Mellon was announced with the marriage scheduled for November 1930. That November a Pittsburgh society column discussing the wedding preparations caught the eye of an obscure cleric, the Reverend Milton M. Allison, down in Wellsburg, West Virginia, who called the papers to say that he had married a William Larimer Mellon Jr., "aged twenty-six," and a Grace Rowley, "aged twenty-one," the year before. Were these the same parties? The newspaper's calls were answered by incredulous parents.

The wedding party had begun rehearsals, and guests from all over the eastern seaboard, including the Secretary of the Treasury, were enroute to Pittsburgh for the ceremony. The Rowley house was packed with elegant presents, and a pipe organ was being installed there—to play the wedding march—when Mrs. Rowley was called to the phone by the Pittsburgh *Press.* No, there had to be some mistake on the clergyman's part. Her daughter had been at school in Philadelphia at the time of the supposed wedding. ("Why, that school is so strict that girls can't even get permission to go to downtown Philadelphia to see a movie.")

"It just can't be true," agreed Mrs. Mellon. But it was.

---

*"Level-headed young people avoid escapades and elopements . . . such courses are for weaklings." *Thomas Mellon and His Times.*

"They will have to be married over again, before my eyes, before I will believe it," said the bride's eager mother, but the Mellon family had already been sufficiently embarrassed over the matter. W. L. was outraged. The wedding was canceled. Many of the invited guests demanded the return of their gifts.

It was a bad start, but on paper things soon looked good again for Larry Mellon. He found that he did not like the clerical work at Mellon National Bank, so he left it (to the displeasure of W. L.) and took a position at Gulf Oil. His wife gave birth to a son, William Larimer Mellon III, in 1932; and in 1935 they remodeled and moved into an eleven-room house in the heart of Pittsburgh's fashionable but conservative suburb of Sewickley, Pennsylvania, after transforming the house with steel, aluminum, glass, and cork into a modern showplace. Evelyn Burke of the Pittsburgh *Press* compared it favorably with earlier Mellons' "Victorian palaces, huge piles of stone." Their social life seemed active and appropriate for people of their standing.

Only a couple of insignificant driving scrapes gave hints of any underlying malaise. In August of 1931 the press reported that Larry had received a stop-sign ticket in a suburban town after he had sped past a corner, causing a near pileup of vehicles that had the right of way on the intersecting street. According to the police report, Larry had told the arresting officer, "If you had driven as far as I have you wouldn't give a damn for stop signs or anything else." A couple of years later he was stopped for turning left at a no-left-turn intersection in McKeesport, Pennsylvania, home of a major Gulf installation, and after exchanging words with the arresting officer, found himself arrested as well for "disorderly conduct," and hauled off to the police station to await bond. When Gulf's agent, Jack Fade, arrived to bail him out, he asked the McKeesport police chief, "Do you know that you have W. L. Mellon's son under arrest?" Words like that would sting anyone with any sensitivity; most of all they stung Larry Mellon, both when he heard them spoken and again as he read them reported in the Pittsburgh *Press.* W. L. was embarrassed.

Just as he had not felt quite right at the Mellon National Bank, Larry felt out of place at Gulf Oil. He later explained,

> It was my feeling that a man should try to do something on his own. He could be a professional baseball player or a carpenter. It didn't matter what, just so long as a man was using his own talents. Nobody has much respect for a kept woman, and neither should they have for a kept man. He doesn't deserve respect.

Larry Mellon knew that he was a kept man.

The marriage was no better. The homespun atmosphere that had helped attract him to Grace was not to last. When W. L. offered the newlyweds a home of their own as a wedding gift, the teenaged bride expressed her preference for French château architecture. She seemed to enjoy the upper-class life, while Larry, as he later explained it, "hated all those parties. Year after year the same people danced with the same people and they had the same conversations. I came to despise that jaded group of remittance people who lived on trust accounts and did little else."

Though W. L. thought that ranching was a bad business, and especially so for one of his sons, Larry bought the huge Apache Maid Ranch near Rimrock, Arizona. He was dropping out. "I was running from an unhappy marriage and from Pittsburgh," he later explained to a journalist. He would make a new life for himself, as himself, even to the point of abjuring Gulf's experts' advice as to where ranchlands were most likely to prove oil-bearing. (Gulf's advice turned out to have been correct.) On December 1, 1935, he stuck his head in the living room of their newly completed Sewickley home while Grace was entertaining a friend and said, "Good-bye, I'm leaving; I'm not coming back." He didn't.

By prearrangement, Grace brought suit on grounds of desertion in August of 1937, and the marriage was dissolved the following January. On the witness stand, her lawyer asked her whether Larry had arranged for her support, to which she replied, "No. My father-in-law has been very kind to me." Too kind, to Matthew's thinking: "Father went overboard being nice to her; he felt she was young, and he was forgiving."

Larry worked hard at every aspect of the manual labor of ranching: fencing, branding, riding herd. At the main outpost he built for himself what his sister Peggy Hitchcock later described as a "one-peg" shack, but usually he was out on the range, sleeping in the open with his men. His wardrobe was soon stripped of everything but dungarees, and W. L.'s present to him of two suits left him embarrassed because he did not own any clothes hangers. When May came to see him on her first visit, cowhands were around to record her reaction to her son's material situation: "Oh, son, really!" Photographs of him from his early ranching period show him as rangy, square-jawed, and ruggedly handsome in his Levi's and cowboy hat. His current pictures show a very different face: open, kind, notable for its unashamed decency.

Larry expanded his holdings with the acquisition of the 128,000-acre Fort Rock Ranch, which he bought in 1937 in partnership with W. L. at a reported price of $100,000. Much of his holdings were used for fattening cattle on consignment for Mexican cattlemen; ultimately he acquired his own herds in partnership with W. L. Larry Mellon became a success at ranching, almost entirely his own success.

When Pearl Harbor was bombed, Larry rushed to enlist. Getting into the service was almost as hard as the war itself. Though the vigorous cowboy was as fit as he looked, because of a series of Navy slip-ups he was subjected to five separate complete physicals and endless delays, and by the time he received his acceptance, all positions with his preferred naval intelligence had been filled. Finally his well-connected brother-in-law, Tommy Hitchcock, arranged an assignment for him with the O.S.S., but then he was stuck interminably in Washington. At last, he was sent to Europe and, according to W. L., rose to head the U.S. intelligence network in Spain and later in Switzerland. Larry himself won't discuss that period of his life, explaining that it was secret than and he supposes it still is secret.

After his return from the war, Larry remarried. Gwendolyn Grant was the daughter of a successful construction engineer in New Jersey. She went to Shipley, an expensive girls' boarding school, with a year off for traveling the world at the age of sixteen with her family. When she graduated from Smith College she almost accepted a job as a welfare worker in the Virgin Islands; instead she became Mrs. John Rawson, and quickly gave birth to three children. Her marriage went sour, and she and the children moved to Arizona early in the 1940s to establish residence for an Arizona divorce. For support, she took a job as a riding instructor on a dude ranch close to Larry's property. She was also strikingly beautiful. Larry was only a new friend to her when Gwen came down with pneumonia, but he was already a good friend. During her hospitalization he washed and fed and put her children to bed and brought them daily to the hospital for a visit with their mother, the daughter's hair carefully braided each day. Gwen and Larry were apart during the war, but not out of touch, and married in February 1946.

Gwen roughed it on the ranch too, but with W. L.'s encouragement, gradually eased her husband into a spacious modern home on the ranch, complete with swimming pool. Larry could now "afford" such a luxury. He had proved himself. But he was uncomfortable in his new role. "I had become a domesticated cowboy, a dude, and that spoiled the whole thing," he later said. Now that he had made a success of ranching—and of himself —the ranches had become as meaningless to him as the family empire had been. He began to busy himself with studying Arabic and had a Syrian instructor come to the ranch to help him. When the Syrian departed, he left behind some literature for Larry to translate from Arabic to English: the

Gospel of St. Luke. Dutifully, Larry translated into English "It is easier for a camel to go through the eye of a needle than for a rich man to enter the kingdom of God." (Luke 18:25.) It kind of made one think.

He was ready for a change in his life when *Life* arrived in the mail soon after with a compelling spread on "the greatest man in the world"—Albert Schweitzer. The famed organist and theologian had changed careers in middle age; with no relevant background or experience, he had entered medical school, become a doctor, abandoned Europe, and was spending his life as a medical missionary in Africa. His pattern was inspirational. A few days later came a letter from Matthew that unintentionally reminded Larry of Schweitzer's work. It contained a discussion of Bach's music and of the great organist's interpretations of Bach. When Larry's ranch manager soon after complained of exhaustion and requested time off, Larry urged him to take a novel vacation, to go to visit Schweitzer in French West Africa. The manager went, and his reports of the doctor and of his work further inspired Larry. It took a while for everything to fall in place, but at the age of thirty-seven, Larry Mellon decided to follow Schweitzer's example. After he recounted the course of his interest in Schweitzer's work to a representative from the influential liberal Protestant journal *Christian Century,* the reporter concluded that Mellon's case history carried "all the cardinal symptoms of conversion."

Gwen was enthusiastic about the idea, and Schweitzer answered Larry's letter of inquiry with a lengthy encouraging response. The ranch was sold at a substantial profit. Even that made for difficulties with his aged father. Larry later explained that the ranch had brought father and son "closer together than we'd ever been [but] for tax purposes at the time my father would have preferred a [paper] loss. I never seemed to be able to give him what he wanted."

Larry and Gwen and the children moved to New Orleans, where Larry began six years of study at Tulane undergraduate and medical schools in the summer of 1948. Schweitzer wrote him not to try to do more than just get by in his medical studies—just enough to get the necessary diploma— that the real education would come in the field. But merely getting by was a big problem at Larry's age; formal studies were hard for "Grandpa," as his fellow students knew him, and Larry studied himself sick in the process. By virtue of her age and the fact that she already had a highly respected college diploma, Gwen might have had an easier time of medical school, but Larry's disposition required that he be the boss, and it would be better for them as a family unit if he never had to feel or to sense subconsciously that he was competing with his wife in his profession. She spent her time at Tulane preparing to be a lab technician and operating-room nurse. While in New Orleans, the couple became Disciples of Christ, largely through the influence of Dr. Emory Ross, a missionary friend of Schweitzer's.

While the Mellons studied, they also surveyed backward areas of the world in search of that place most in need of medical help which was suited for establishment of a new hospital. They found it in the Artibonite Valley of Haiti, whose natives lived as poorly as those anywhere in the world, and markedly worse than those in Schweitzer's region of Africa. The Artibonite area was densely populated and rampant with disease so that whatever facilities the Mellons might bring to it could be utilized to the fullest.

While still a medical student, Larry opened discussions with Haitian President Paul Magloire about the possibility of purchasing a site for a hospital. His timing was perfect. United Fruit was closing down an installation at Deschapelles in the very center of the Artibonite Valley, and the president offered Larry its property as a welcoming gift from Haiti, so long as Larry might use it for his proposed hospital. Before the hospital was built, Magloire had been overthrown in a coup and replaced by a kindly country physician, François Duvalier, who had led a successful one-man campaign against yaws in his country, and who in his new and ill-suited role as Haitian president was to become world renowned as the odd, crazy "Papa Doc," who governed as the prototype tyrant. Duvalier, however, did not repudiate Mellon's understanding with his predecessor. In the many years since, Mellon has maintained excellent relations with the Haitian government, both under Papa Doc, and under Papa's son and successor, Baby Doc, principally because Mellon has given much, asked nothing in return for himself, and mostly because he has minded his own business. Haiti, he believes, is for the Haitians to govern or misgovern. He had eagerly looked forward to attending the Mellon family reunion in Ireland in 1968, but at the last moment Papa Doc suspected an imminent invasion of Haiti and banned all travel. Rather than ask even one small personal dispensation, Larry Mellon stayed at home.

The hospital was designed by John Lord King, an expert on the design of hospitals for tropical climates, and construction began in 1953. Gwen moved to Haiti to oversee construction from a rat-and-roach-infested house in Saint Marc. When they were not in school, the Rawson children, raised as Larry's own, and Larry himself, joined her there, and the whole family assisted in the manual labor of construction. The Mellons were the best workers on the job. Unskilled Haitian peasants recruited for the work force knew nothing of responsibility and refused to learn about it; they had to be shown the simplest of tasks over and over again. Fortunes in cement "disappeared." The pace of construction was maddening. Meanwhile, Larry finished his studies at Tulane, completed the necessary internship, and then joined Gwen permanently in Haiti. In 1956 the complex was completed: a network of low buildings of concrete and native gray fieldstone set upon a hill, air-conditioned only in the operating room and library. From the start Mellon envisioned it as a Haitian place, and commissioned an unschooled native "sculptor" to design bas-reliefs to ornament interior screening walls. They acquired a 100-acre farm adjacent to the hospital grounds that enabled the installation to provide most of its own foodstuffs. Gwen designed a fine low rambling house for themselves, with a lovely view and a swimming pool, though without air conditioning.

On June 26, 1956, Dr. Mellon celebrated his forty-sixth birthday by opening L'Hôpital Albert Schweitzer, named for his great inspiration. Now clearly middle-aged, Larry Mellon was embarking on a new career in a bizarre and frightening environment that was dominated by a psychotic. The overall circumstances seemed to defy success, but Larry Mellon had to make it a success. He had burned most of his bridges. The hospital had cost the Grant Foundation, which Larry established and named after Gwen, close to $2 million. Establishing an endowment to meet the projected annual operating deficit of $200,000 a year took much of the rest of his assets. Mellon was not at all pessimistic. He spoke hopefully of the day when Haitian personnel would be ready and willing to take over the hospital, when he and his family might move "to wherever we might be useful." He is still there.

The initial staff consisted of Mellon and four other doctors from around the globe, an X-ray technician, and a lab technician. Mellon recruited Miss Walborg L. Peterson, "Miss Pete," from her position as executive assistant to the director of the prestigious Massachusetts Eye and Ear Infirmary to be chief of five nurses. While staff has come and gone over twenty years, Miss Pete is still there. There was also an engineer to keep the mechanical equipment operating and a business manager—Mellon's former ranch manager who had made the first inspection trip to Schweitzer's African hospital. While Mellon was going to medical school, he too was furthering his education as a student of hospital management.

Mellon's principal fear was that the white man's hospital would be unable to compete with the black man's *bocor,* the witch doctor. Papa Doc himself had practiced "white-man's" medicine, and perhaps his example smoothed the way for easy acceptance of the hospital. In any case, the Mellons were soon busy enough to keep themselves working to the point of exhaustion on the three clinic days of each week. The hospital grounds would fill up each night before clinic day with peasants, many of whom had traveled great distances, to await their turn the next morning. Draining as clinic days were, they brought satisfactions for the hospital staff. Clinic days attracted large numbers of the kind of serious but treatable problems that allow a doctor to see near-immediate improvement. In deference to the hospital's success, the region's most famed *bocor,* Monsieur Paul, came to Mellon to announce his retirement.

The hospital was a success every way but financially. To preserve the dignity of his patients, Mellon decided that the hospital would not be a "charity." He established a fee schedule calling for payment of the equivalent of sixty cents for the first visit, forty cents for follow-ups, and six dollars a day for in-patient care. Yes, he would accept payment in the form of fruit, vegetables, or livestock; indeed, in appropriate cases the fee might even be waived. In computation of the barter, an item of produce might be valued a trifle on the high side. "Anything will do," Mellon told American reporters, "just to satisfy their pride in themselves." Over the years most of his patients have paid little more than an occasional mango, on account.

Mellon extends his personal humility to his professional schooling, which has facilitated acceptable relations with the *bocors.* His respectful attitude toward them is reflected by his reference to them as "leaf doctors," rather than as "witch doctors." He is quick to point out their contributions:

> We must remember that these leaf doctors have borne most of the burden of country medicine since French colonial days. . . . Sure, they mistreat patients, but so do all doctors sometimes. The *bocors* do know how to treat malaria and average cuts and pains. And they understand the psychiatric problems here better than we do. I've seen a broken leg perfectly set by a *bocor.* They recommend bed rest for tubercular patients, and this is okay.

The Mellons and the *bocors* have established what sometimes approaches a working relationship. Many *bocors* have themselves been patients at the Mellons' hospital, and the Mellons have utilized the leaf doctors in their health education programs, and for treatments in that field of medicine, important in Haiti, in which the *bocors* can appropriately be regarded as the specialists: the cure of those plagued by evil spirits.

The hospital was presented with cases of every imaginable type, but the most common diseases and those most disturbing to Dr. Mellon were the illnesses that accompany poverty, ignorance, and deprivation—malnutrition, typhoid, tetanus. He viewed his training in perspective, and when doing so, he saw clearly the wisdom of Schweitzer's advice. "It burns me

up sometimes to think I spent five years at medical school. I could have been
here five years earlier. A doctor has no special magic for a place like this.
An intelligent layman could diagnose ninety per cent of the cases of sickness
. . . the greater want goes beyond medicine and it can be filled by a variety
of men." There was great satisfaction in treating the acutely ill; there was
prompt, visible reward. The environmental disease was a more difficult
matter, and Mellon's own focus turned more and more to that.

Over the years Mellon and his hospital staff, without significant outside
help, have brought about vital public health improvements in the valley.
Until they came, no one in the valley appreciated the importance to public
health of sanitary disposal of human excrement. Mellon taught the Haitians
to dig latrines in their villages—by digging them for them. He encouraged
villages to secure sanitary water supplies, principally by buying pipe and
laying it to springs himself. A generation of midwives trained at the hospital
has virtually ended in Haiti the ancient African custom of smearing a
newborn's navel with dung, long a principal cause of infant mortality on
the island. Mellon has also taken an interest in the more purely economic
well-being of the Haitians. A veterinarian clinic was added to the hospital,
and Mellon's vets and his agronomists in the field have been teaching the
natives how to raise healthier, more profitable animals. Mellon imported a
talented Guatemalan weaver to Haiti to teach a new trade to the natives,
and he inaugurated sewing classes. He sponsored reforestation efforts. Hos-
pital-related schools have taught illiterate adults to read and write in Creole.
Though Dr. Mellon still closely follows the purely medical aspects of the
hospital's work, for many years the greater part of his attention has been
devoted to a macro approach to his patients' problems. None of his positive
results have come easy, and too often the fruits of his efforts have been
disappointing, the blossoms short-lived, principally because of the Haitians'
generations-bred inertia.

After twenty years the hospital's plant and layout have not changed
significantly, but its staffing has. Mellon now has an arrangement with the
Yale and the University of Vermont medical schools that puts a number of
their recent graduates into two-month residencies at the hospital; otherwise,
H.A.S., as staff commonly refer to the hospital, has ceased to be dependent
upon doctors who might contribute only a couple of weeks or months.
Mellon has built up a permanent staff of seventy to eighty dedicated people.
Given the embarrasingly modest pay for an overworked physician, he can
be certain of their dedication. The staff has been selected with an eye to
picking people who will be able to accept the Haitians as individuals and

human beings rather than as a vehicle by which a concerned applicant might do his part to carry the white man's burden. Those who treat the patients as charity cases (which they are) are weeded out. Staff accommodations are adequate if spartan; the pace of the work prevents the staff from missing greater comforts. At last many of the staff are Haitians. As much as possible Mellon has attempted to push them forward and place them in positions of responsibility. Many hospital departments are now headed by Haitians. When Mellon was decorated by Papa Doc, he brought only Haitians to the ceremony. In The Grant Foundation's fund-raising brochure the only photo of the staff at work shows a black doctor assisted by a barefoot black paramedic. Now sixty-eight, Larry still hopes that they will relieve him.

Working conditions are far from optimum, and unless a doctor keeps his eye on the greatest good for the greatest number the hospital's shortcomings would make it impossible for some conscientious physicians to function. As one University of Vermont resident put it, "When you see sixty people a day, you're going to miss something." The hospital has continually lacked a permanent full-time pathologist, which some would regard as a prerequisite for a modern hospital. Its simple equipment meets 90 per cent of the needs, but that still leaves some needs unmet. In short, H.A.S. is a jungle hospital, not a big-city medical complex. Those who have served there insist that the enthusiasm and dedication of the staff more than make up for the hospital's material shortcomings.

Clinic days are still marked by caravans of peasants making their way to the hospital the night before, and by work to and past the point of exhaustion.

The esprit at H.A.S. is diversely but profoundly religious—even among the hospital's agnostics—as is reflected by the common practice of saying some form of grace before meals. Mellon's own religious views, though surely profound, are now amorphous. "I like to think I'm a Christian, but I don't know any church that would testify to that," he told a journalist. He has refused to be party to any effort that might subvert the pagan religion of his patients. He appreciates that voodoo is about all that the peasants have left of their heritage, and seems to regard any attempt to replace it with Christianity as an unwarranted attack on the natives' dignity. His own example has dampened the missionary spirit of those around him, and there is no proselytizing. If anything, Mellon is countermissionary. "To me," he says, "religion is a means of sustaining one's self and is not to be talked about or disseminated."

Mellon himself, currently preoccupied with road-building projects, is not much seen at the hospital. Beyond hosting a welcoming dinner for new doctors, he has taken almost no part in the hospital's social life, and he has ceased to have regular ongoing contact with most of the hospital staff. One University of Vermont doctor—who approved of Mellon's choice of emphasis—never saw him on the hospital floor once during his two-month residency. He saw the evidence of Mellon's presence, though—notations on medical records, made at some unknown hour—and he felt the powerful moral tone that the founder set and still maintains.

"Madame Mellon," as Gwen is known, and appears to enjoy being known, is the Mellon in evidence. She is at the desk every morning at six A.M., registering patients, translating for "foreign" doctors, writing up case notes, and sharing hospital administrative duties with Dr. Leperaux, a professional hospital administrator. From the start, she has been the "front man" of the Mellons, more available and much more assertive (as well as more gregarious) than her husband. For just about everything, she has been the court of last resort. Many of the staff—and some of the family—regard her as the more formidable of the partners and the dominant personality, as do the natives, who know the Hôpital Albert Schweitzer as "Madame Mellon's Hospital." The *National Observer*'s reporter described her as "a combination of Cinderella's Fairy Godmother and Lady Macbeth." Her current photos show that she makes no effort to cover the lines of age and work. While she is still a handsome woman at a well-preserved sixty-seven, wisdom and strength are now the more striking qualities in her face.

Financial problems have put an increasingly serious squeeze on the Mellons' operations. Few things are more expensive to run than a hospital. The international energy crunch has caused a heavy direct burden for the hospital as costs of operating its diesel-powered electric plant have spiraled with the price of oil. Greatly increased shipping costs have aggravated the inflationary prices of many imports. The hospital still receives the income from Dr. Mellon's original endowment, supplemented by many small contributions from those who know of its work, gifts from CARE, and gifts in kind from pharmaceutical manufacturers and others. But the income of the Grant Foundation (P.O. Box 1138, Pittsburgh, Pennsylvania 15230) has not kept pace with increased costs; so cutbacks have had to be instituted, with others projected.

Matthew Mellon has never been sympathetic with his brother's cause, for philosophical reasons which cannot be isolated without doing injustice to Matthew's fuller thought process. Still, his Matthew T. Mellon Foundation has made infrequent contributions at particularly tight moments, as have the Margaret Mellon Hitchcock Foundation, the Rachel Mellon Walton

Foundation and the Laurel Foundation established by Sarah Scaife's daughter, Cordelia. For the most part, however, the family has not been generous toward Dr. Mellon's work.

Early in the hospital's life, one physician quit in desperation, explaining to Mellon, "What you're doing here is trying to empty an ocean of misery with a teacup. You're not getting anywhere." Since then, Mellon has been responsible for improvements in the quality of life in his region, but wretchedness still dominates the Artibonite Valley. Poverty, filth, and sicknesses both superficial and profound remain its most apparent characteristics. Various forms of malnutrition in children still require an inordinate proportion of the hospital's resources. Many years later, the quitter's characterization seems to have proven more true than false.

Mellon is still there bailing with his teacup. His humanistic approach enables him to keep functioning. Though he takes a macro view of the problems, he views his brothers micro, not as a vast horde of faceless blacks but as separate individuals each with his own identity. He is satisfied knowing that he has eased the pain or reduced the load of an individual, even if only temporarily, even if his efforts have little altered the big picture.

Mellon has built his personal creed around Schweitzer's philosophy, and particularly Schweitzer's "reverence for life." At the dedication of the Hôpital Albert Schweitzer he prayed, "May the spark of 'reverence for life' which came to us from across the Atlantic Ocean continue to burn until it has consumed us with real and deep concern for every living creature that suffers." Larry has extended the philosophy from man to all living things, and declines to hunt or fish or intentionally step on a bug.

Humility and self-effacement are the most obvious of Larry Mellon's personality traits. He has resisted all efforts at giving himself or his work any publicity. He has been embarrassed to the point of horror at the few pieces—all eulogistic—that have been printed about him, and has been happy when other jungle doctors, such as the late Dr. Tom Dooley (whose sacrifices were dwarfed by Mellon's), have taken the spotlight and kept it off himself. When intruded upon by journalists, he has pushed his wife forward. Dr. James Hennessy, a Hartford internist who has spent considerable time over the years as a volunteer at H.A.S., says, "He's the real McCoy, so's she; they don't want any recognition." It is almost as if recognition would somehow ruin it all for Larry Mellon. He has scribbled in a little notebook a quote from Schweitzer: "There are no heroes of action, only heroes of renunciation and suffering. Of such there are plenty. But few of them are known and even these not to the crowd but to the few."

This humility is the most obvious difference between Mellon and his spiritual mentor. Schweitzer was a domineering man with a low regard for those he healed. Mellon has never acted like a boss, and more striking is his attitude toward his patients. The author asked Dr. Hennessy whether Mellon showed any hint of superiority to his charges. "Not at all," came Hennessy's quick response. "If anything, he feels two steps beneath them." He has insisted that his staff treat the Haitians with dignity, as he has himself. While tourists to Haiti insist on visiting a voodoo ceremony and a cockfight, Mellon and his family have declined to do either, feeling that to do so would be a voyeuristic intrusion on the Haitians' dignity. Their children, however, were permitted to attend a nearby black men's night-club, and to dance the meringue as equals until late hours. The Mellons' son, Ian Rawson, ultimately married a Haitian girl.

The Mellons find it difficult to verbalize why they have abandoned the easy life that they could have shared with Brother Matthew or Cousin Paul. They came to regard that kind of life as being victimized by one's own wealth. When Mellon says, "I was born to opulence," it is with obvious disdain. He fled it like a medieval monk. Today his lifestyle and financial statement would probably compare unfavorably with those of the average "orthopedics" man on Long Island, a fact that seems to cause no dissatisfaction for Dr. Mellon. Beyond that, he is not articulate in dissecting his motives and compulsions. His work has given Larry Mellon a sense of brotherhood with the most destitute of men and has impelled him to follow Schweitzer's commandment: "One who escapes misfortune should render thanks by doing something to relieve suffering." It has given some recogniz-able, commendable meaning to Dr. Mellon's life.

One might expect that such an intensely spiritual man would not be very good company. "He's not," says one who has worked closely with him and greatly admires him. He is a contemplative, driven man; informal but uncommunicative. He talks little about himself. Some who have worked long periods with him feel that they know him scarcely at all. While he rarely frowns, his smiles are equally infrequent. His stepdaughter Jenny says, "He can be great fun to be with, but there are times when you can't even make contact at all."

Mellon today continues to rise before dawn and to work a long, full day in the field. His usual garb is dungarees, and invariably his head is covered with either a straw hat or with the pith helmet that Caucasians often wear in the tropics as protection from the heat. Sometimes he carries a huge golf umbrella for further cover from the sun. By now he is the Artibonite's best-known citizen. As he moves about the valley he is greeted by adults with an affectionate "Bon jour, Doc," and with a loving "Bon jour, Papa," by the children. At night he gets what diversion he gets playing music. Gwen, the only person at all close to him, sometimes joins him in duets. He plays six instruments with respectable proficiency, but he gravitates to the cello and the oboe, a string and a wind which share the same sad, lonely tone.

Ned Mellon (Edward P. Mellon II), Larry's contemporary and boyhood companion, has lived a very different life. Though a philosophical and reflective sort, until recent years Ned did not have the leisure to ruminate about questions on the meaning of life, or the financial security necessary to consider changing courses. Ned has always been a "poor" Mellon. Never so poor as to fall so low as the ranks of the upper middle class, but poor in the sense that until his early middleage he and his father lived with heavy business debts over their heads, and through almost all of his life he has had to work hard in the most draining and competitive of businesses for what he has attained.

The Judge believed that the "ragged newsboy" had greater opportunities for satisfaction than the sons of the well-to-do. Ned comes as close as anyone in this book does to the Judge's hypothetical ragged newsboy. Today Ned is obviously financially well off—a millionaire without too many "multis" in front of it. He is now a handsome older man, but his face shows a line for every dollar.

Ned's father, Thomas Alexander Mellon Jr., was the eldest son of the Judge's oldest son. T. A. the first did not approve of college, and none of his children went. None suffered from the loss. A letter from Ned's father to Senator Philander Knox in Knox's papers at the Library of Congress could have been written by a Wall Street lawyer. T. A.'s other son, Edward Purcell Mellon, later became a well-respected architect; and his daughter, Mary, was thoroughly literate. T. A. left a respectable estate for the day when he died in 1899, but not a huge one. In its administration, and the administration of its trust funds, A. W. and R. B., like responsible estate administrators, invested it principally in interest-bearing obligations, as opposed to riskier equity positions, so that it never grew to any significant size. When the remainder of the estate was distributed, it did not give enough to any of the three children of T. A. to enable anyone to coast through life.

Of T. A.'s three children, Edward P. felt himself confined by the life of Pittsburgh of his day and oppressed by his clan; so he escaped to make a life as an architect. After living away, he could never make Pittsburgh his home again. Mary went off with her first husband, John H. Kampman, to

Texas. Ned's father, T. A. Jr., remained behind to make his life in Pittsburgh. T. A. Jr. was twenty-six when his father died, but he had always been close to his uncles, A. W., R. B., and J. R., and the uncles continued to take a fatherly interest in him. At the time of his father's death, T. A. Jr. was already married to Helen McLanahan Wightman, daughter of a Presbyterian minister, and was soon to be a father. T. A. Jr. raised his family—Ned, two sisters, and a son, T. A. III, who died at the age of eleven—in the Judge's mansion at 401 Negley Avenue. He became associated with A. W. and R. B.'s business interests.

The uncles had a 51 per cent interest in the Grace Construction Company, an important contracting firm in Pittsburgh, and they put T. A. Jr. in the business to keep an eye on their interests. After two or three years, in 1917, the Mellons discovered financial irregularities in Grace's books, so they took complete control of Grace Construction Company and sold it lock, stock and barrel—on credit—to T. A. Jr. and his partner, James L. Stuart, for $3 million. Grace Construction became the Mellon-Stuart Company. Stuart became concerned about his health a couple of years later, got out of the business, "and then outlived all the rest of them," Ned told the author.

No doubt the uncles thought they were doing their nephew a great favor in allowing him the promising opportunity of owning his own substantial business without a penny's investment of his own, but to the nephew the great debt was a moral obligation. Payments on it proved a heavy stone around his neck for twenty-four years, until 1941, when T. A. Junior's profitable speculations in water companies enabled him to retire the last of the ancient obligation. By that time he was sixty-seven years old and had only another seven years to live.

Ned was born in 1908, the third of T. A. Junior's four children. His closest boyhood friend was his second cousin Larry, and the two egged each other on in their misbehaviors, beginning with the time when they were eleven or twelve and destroyed Miss Oliver's Dancing School. Most of the boys at Miss Oliver's wore blue serge outfits, but Ned's mother had sent him and Larry off for their first dancing lesson dressed up "in ruffles." Miss Oliver began the class—"Boys form a ring; girls in the center of the ring" —and directed Ned and Larry to the center. They proved that they were "all boy" in a riot of destruction that had Mamma trooping Ned off to what he describes as "a headshrinker." The diagnosis: perfectly normal.

Ned attended Shadyside Academy, then and still Pittsburgh's leading private day school, after which, he says, "I went to every school in the U. S." It wasn't simply that Ned "wasn't much of a student," as he puts it; he was also something of a hell raiser. He ended up at Milford, in Milford, Connecticut, where he roomed with Albie Booth, later to become one of Yale's most famous football players. As he looks back on his youth, Ned shakes his head in disbelief and says, "This generation is damn good. We were the prohibition generation, and I don't know how we lived through it."

At the same time he developed what he describes as "a delicate, beautiful relationship" with his father. He recalls fondly his vacations with T. A. Junior at the father's club in Idaho—"where the youngest guy was sixty" —but he was never bored. Both father and son had terrible tempers, and often they argued; but they were "lovers' quarrels," as Ned now calls them, and at the end of them they would argue over who had started the argument. Ned remembers his father with great affection as a shy man, "never really very much of a businessman."

After Milford, Ned worked at a foundry in Philadelphia for a year, and then returned to Pittsburgh to begin his life with the Mellon-Stuart Company. He was started as a jackhammer operator on one of the company's important jobs, the Mellon Institute Building, then under way, and went through most of the paces before assuming executive responsibilities. He also married in November 1930, for Ned too young at the age of twenty-two. Marian Stone, twenty-one, was the daughter of Judge Stephen Stone, granddaughter of Governor William A. Stone. A Mellon-Stone match naturally called for a big and important society wedding, followed by a grand honeymoon trip abroad.

After the trip the young couple settled down in a modest home in a modest neighborhood—the house across the street was owned by R. B.'s butler. Ned recalls that shortly after their return R. B. invited the newlyweds to his mansion for tea. The great-uncle took the young man aside and asked him about his financial situation. He nodded soberly as Ned replied. Finally R. B. got to the point. With a flourish he presented the groom with a small, light, narrow currency-sized box. At his first private moment, Ned ripped off the wrappings and opened the box—within: a gadget for squeezing lemons.

Ned was never much interested in horses, but his mother was eager for him to participate in gentlemanly doings and pushed him to ride at Rolling Rock. He went—once. After being thrown by the horse, he picked himself up off the ground and didn't go back. Baseball was his great sport and hobby, and the Mellon-Stuart baseball team became a highly successful amateur ball club. ("We were almost as good as a major league team," Ned insists.) His mother accepted his preference but laid down two rules: "Don't play on Sunday, and don't play niggers." The second rule was honored principally in the breach; Ned was never as interested in the color of the other team as in their quality as ballplayers, and some of his fondest memories of the great games of the 1930s involved contests with all-black teams, supervised by two umpires, one white and one black. (Ned was an important backer of Camp Achievement, a summer camp for disadvantaged youngsters from Pittsburgh's Hill District, a matter which he did not mention, but which the author picked up from newspaper clippings of the 1940s.) One of the black teams, the Buffalo (New York) Bisons, once wrote Ned offering a hundred dollars if the Mellon-Stuart team would come to Buffalo for a game. Somehow their letter was misdelivered and ended up on the desk of A. W. Mellon. Ned recalls that A. W. had the Bisons' proposition costed out, and the great-uncle "advised me to get out of baseball and into something else if there wasn't any more money than that in the game. He said it wouldn't be a paying proposition." They went to Buffalo and had a "helluva good time," though Ned didn't tell A. W.

Ned was also (and still is) an avid fisherman, and until about the age of forty was a well-regarded hunter of North American big game. At that time he shot his last big game. He still remembers the day quite clearly, with a big deer with beautiful eyes fairly close to him. When he pulled the trigger, "it shrieked like a woman." He hasn't hunted since. Ned says that advances over the years in the science and engineering of firearms have removed any hint of "sport" from big game hunting, and he speaks feelingly about the decimation of rare species and about the greater value and sport in collecting what he describes as "trophies on film." This rugged man has also had a lifelong love for another outdoor activity: butterfly collecting. Ultimately he gave his collection of 12,500 butterflies to the Carnegie Institute. From his discussion of butterflies and moths, it is obvious that he is quite learned about them. In his early days at Mellon-Stuart he says that he had to force himself to work. "I didn't want to work, I wanted to chase butterflies." But he did work.

From 1930 until T. A. Junior's death at the age of seventy-four in 1948, Mellon-Stuart was a father-and-son company that got most of the big construction contracts in the Pittsburgh area for commercial buildings, industrial plants, hospitals, churches, bridges, and railroad spurs, whether the job was with a Mellon family enterprise or not. But they were mostly "low bid" jobs, in which the margin of profit too often fell below one per cent. Sometimes the bid was too low and produced a loss for the business. Labor problems increased as time went on. Ned was away a lot, and cantankerous when he wasn't. His marriage fell apart. He and Marian were divorced in the spring of 1945. Soon after he married Louise Keeble Grubbs, also recently divorced.

After T. A. Junior's death Ned brought Donald C. Peters into the business, a man who had the necessary enginering expertise that Ned never pretended to have. Other principals have also joined the firm in the years since. Over time, Mellon-Stuart has continued its growth and maintained its position as the leading contractor of its kind in the Pittsburgh area, and it has sprouted four subsidiaries in the construction field in West Virginia, Ohio, and Kentucky. Ned himself became "chairman emeritus" of its board in 1972, at the age of sixty-four, succeeded by Peters as the head of the company. One of the speakers at a "surprise" retirement dinner for Ned was identified in the Pittsburgh *Post-Gazette* as " 'Buck' Lahey," who presented Ned with a plaque on behalf of that segment of the American work force known as "the construction bums."

Ned still has large interests in Mellon-Stuart, but he pays little attention to its ongoing business. Mellon-Stuart now ranks as the forty-fourth largest construction company of its type in the United States. When Ned insists that only accounting peculiarities deprived it of the thirty-eighth spot, the listener senses that his greatest interest in the firm is paternal rather than financial.

Today Ned lives permanently in Summer Haven, Florida, the island where Thomas Alexander Mellon established the first Mellon family vacation home in 1873. Ned's house was once Summer Haven's Inn, mentioned in Mary McClung's novel (Summer Haven no longer has an inn). He has other significant real estate holdings in the immediate vicinity. Ned has been coming to Summer Haven since long before the causeway was built connecting it to the mainland and to the next piece of land beyond, and beyond, pretty much all the way down the coast of Florida. His father, he says, was the first man—"maybe the only man"—to swim to the island. He has seen a lot of changes since he has been coming to Summer Haven, most of which he regrets. It isn't just the cars. The "fogging" for bugs has killed the bird life and the butterflies and even reduced the number of fish, and for what? "We lived with the mosquitoes," he says. His family fought the linking of Summer Haven with the mainland, and he still hopes that his paradise can be saved from the high-rises that have taken over most of the coast of Florida. He has a lot of admiration for his less affluent neighbors, who have resisted temptations much more powerful to them than they would be even to a "poor" Mellon. So far the only sign of commercialism at Summer Haven is a rusted out Gulf sign on a long-closed filling station.

Ned's house is a rambling structure with a vacation-home ambience, cluttered with favorite treasures from his heritage. A tasteful bronze knocker bearing the name "Mellon" ornaments his front door and is only one of several mementos that he salvaged from "401" before the Judge's mansion was demolished.

Ned's second wife died after a long illness at the age of fifty-one in 1965, and Ned has since married again, to Grace Granger McCrady, known as Bernice, a gracious blond lady who looks to be middle-middle-aged, though presumably she is somewhat older. When the author saw Ned, he was surrounded by his third wife, a son by his second wife, and a daughter by his first wife. They looked very much at home with one another.

Ned himself was wearing an open green sports shirt, plaid pants, no socks but well-polished black loafers. He was easy-spoken in his gravelly voice. He smoked throughout our long visit in May 1976, but since a heart attack the following month, he has changed his brand from Camels to Kents. He projects an odd mixture of western-hero qualities with a decency reflected in his diction. He inclines to words like "sensitive" and "lovely." (He once wrote nice poetry himself.) He is a self-effacing man without any trace of pretense. He fishes some, reads a lot—he used to love Hemingway until he met the great man and found him "a bore and a bully"—and he ruminates some. He tends to ramble a little in his conversation: "The good Lord's been good," he begins to say . . .

A. W.'s son, Paul, is a man of belles lettres, and in that respect is unlike any of the others of his generation of Judge Mellon's descendants. His only familial competitor as an intellectual, Matthew, who was born in 1897, ten years before Paul, enjoyed a more traditionally classical education than Paul, whose studies indulged a bent for romanticism inherited from his British mother, Nora McMullen. While Matthew is also a very fine writer, Paul's prose more often approaches poetry, and some of his unabashed poetry is very good indeed. Paul has also enjoyed the "belle vie." The Judge would have cited Paul as living proof that "novel reading . . . unhinges the mind entirely for manly employment." Today Paul is the richest living Mellon, almost certainly worth something in the range of one billion dollars.

Paul spent much of his early years in Pittsburgh, occasionally attending Shadyside Academy. Much of the time and most of the summers were passed in England, where he grew to love the countryside and the English life. He later recalled the England of his childhood:

I remember huge dark trees in rolling parks, herds of small friendly deer, flotillas of white swans on the Thames, dappled tan cows in soft green fields, the grey mass of Windsor Castle towering in the distance against a background of huge golden summer clouds; soldiers in scarlet and bright metal, drums and bugles, troops of grey horses; laughing ladies in white with gay parasols, men in impeccable white flannels and striped blazers, and always behind them and behind everything the grass was green, green, green . . . somehow at this great distance it all melts into a sunny and imperturbable English summer landscape. There seemed to be a tranquility in those days that has never again been found, and a quietness as detached from life as the memory itself.

At the age of twelve he was sent off to Choate, according to Charles J. V. Murphy's *Fortune* sketch, in part because A. W. had been favorably impressed by the rather stern, Spartan character of one of the Choate teachers who ran a summer boys' camp that Paul had attended. Paul remained at Choate for six years, and says that he came awake there to literature and writing. In his final year, he told *Sports Illustrated,*

They had just built a new chapel and I don't know whether I was feeling very religious or whether I thought it was a good way to win the Sixth Form poetry prize. I can still remember being alone at night in a classroom and writing the verse on the blackboard:

From dreams and visions heaven-sent,
From simple faith and Godly trust
Great empires, yea, each continent,
Has risen from the dust.

To those who saw this spire arise,
This composition out of nought
Is like a light from Christ's own eyes,
A glimpse of Christ's own thought. . . .

Years later I found the poem pasted in the school hymnal and the boys singing it. But I never received the poetry prize. Instead, they gave me the most insulting thing—a leather-bound biography of Lincoln with the inscription, "For earnest and persistent effort."

Paul was all set to follow his older cousins, Matthew (cousin once removed) and R. K., to Princeton when he had a change of heart. He was impressed by Yale's English department, without question America's finest at the time, and he has recently recalled that the Princeton freshman yearbook "looked too much a prayer book. I'd said too many prayers at Choate." Yale never regretted his decision to go there.

At Yale Paul fell under the sway of its now-legendary greats, Chauncey

B. Tinker and "Billy" (William Lyon) Phelps, who heightened his appreciation for literature and for things English. He continued his own writing.
While he was a first-term freshman, the respected *Yale Literary Magazine*
published in November 1925 the first of several of his poems that it would
publish during his four years at Yale; this earliest college effort was later
included in the anthology *Art and the Craftsman: The Best of the Yale
Literary Magazine, 1836–1961.* At the end of the year he was awarded the
McLaughlin Memorial Prize, an annual award given for the best piece of
freshman writing, for his study "Donn Byrne, His Place in Literature."
(Byrne, a young Irish-American writer much in vogue in the early 1920s,
has since yielded his place to others.) With time Paul became vice chairman
of the *Yale Daily News* and a member of the *Lit* board.

The biographer invariably looks for autobiographical signs in the poetry
or fiction written by his subject, and perhaps finds them where they are not.
Paul's undergraduate writings published in the *Lit* give many possibly
autobiographical signals, and if they are, they show a diminishing of the gulf
between his romantic self and his businessman father over his four years at
Yale. For example, the message of Paul's first published poem, "All Told,"
appears to be the futility of the search for wealth that had preoccupied his
father for too much of the father's life:

> A hundred and one
> In an iron-bound box,
> All glittering, round, all bright, pure gold—
> In an old, carven chest picked up on the rocks,
> A hundred and one, all told.
>
> The dark sea was raging,
> The wind had a whine,
> The cabin was shadowy, weird and damp.
> But a hundred and one—and they all were mine,
> And they gleamed by the cabin lamp.
>
> Then a creak of the hatch
> And a flare of the flame,
> A flash of bright steel—so sharp, so cold!
> And the wind seemed to shriek out an old, ghostly name.
> A hundred and one, all told.

Autobiographical references also appear in "To Sail Beyond the Sunset,"
a fairly bad short story published in the *Lit*'s March 1929 issue, during
Paul's senior year. In part it details the friction between Robin Bennett, a
well-to-do artistic young man who returns home from college, and his rich

businessman father, upon whose continued generosity Robin's continued artistic occupations depend. Robin is greeted at the door of the mansion by Parkes, the butler.

> "I suppose the old man's in the library. Has he dined?"
>
> "Yes, sir."
>
> "Thank God," said Robin. . . . As Robin entered the dark-paneled library, Mr. Bennett looked over the top of the evening papers. Then he gradually laid them on the small table beside his chair. It was all as Robin had expected— his father deep in the easy-chair before the fire, the flickering light playing upon his stern face, and all about the walls of the room the same immaculately arranged and never-touched books reaching endlessly up into the shadows of the ceiling. Robin glanced at the papers and smiled. "Stocks and bonds and columns of figures still, eh Dad? Sort of dry for a liqueur, isn't it?"
>
> He walked straight across to him, silently on the soft carpet, leaned down to kiss him. Then he stood up with his hands on his hips, looking down. Robin was not small, and Mr. Bennett gazed up at the towering form above him.
>
> "You'll love them yourself soon, my dear boy. You'll soon forget those phantasies floating in the back of your mind that you are about to spring on me, and come down to earth. You'll be living from now on, Robin, not studying, or scribbling, or dabbling in paints. Is that what you've come to talk about—or have you forgotten those pipedreams?"
>
> Robin suddenly became wistful, serious. He walked over in front of the fire, turned about, and leaned his broad back against the mantelpiece.
>
> "I suppose it's that business of ours still, Dad. That damn business."
>
> Mr. Bennett watched him for a moment through the thick, steel-rimmed glasses which magnified his cold blue eyes. He clenched his teeth momentarily.
>
> "Robin, you're a fool. You'll enter the business eventually and you know it."

Among the less obvious similarities between the Bennetts and the Mellons: Paul was very much bigger than A. W.; also, while A. W. did not wear "thick steel-rimmed glasses which magnified his cold blue eyes," more than one person commented on the "coldness" of his eyes, and Paul himself mentioned his father's "ice-water smile" to Lucius Beebe. Despite their differences, though, Paul maintained an affectionate relationship with his father; Robin's kiss was not foreign to him. Still, he and A. W. were as he described the Bennetts Senior and Junior in his story: "sparks struck from far different anvils." Robin seems to have enjoyed a better relationship with Parkes, the butler, just as Paul enjoyed an easy rapport with A. W.'s valet, Flore, co-conspirator in some of Paul's early pranks. Mr. Bennett allows Robin one final year of independence before demanding that he settle into business, just as A. W.—at about the time of the publication of "To Sail" —agreed to allow Paul a final year.

"To Sail" doesn't indicate who won the battle of the wills between the Bennetts, but temporary victory was ultimately to be won by A. W., and held until the father's death freed the son. Paul's last published poem in the *Lit* indicates a change in his view toward "treasure hunting":

> I never saw a stranger face than his,
> Ruddy and wrinkled, yet not seeming old;
> And as I watched the ticker-tape unfold
> One busy day, he came and whispered this
> Into my ear, with curious emphasis—
> "On Spanish Point there lies a chest of gold,
> And though you are the hundredth I have told
> No one believes me. But I know there is."
> He babbled of an old lost chart we'd find
> To trace the cypress swamp, where pirates hid
> A chest of jewels and many a gold doubloon.
> And then, I knew I'd have no peace of mind
> Until I'd lifted up the creaking lid
> And seen the treasure shining in the moon.

He ended his college literary career convinced by a "wrinkled yet not seeming old" face at least to try for the treasure that four years earlier had seemed fruitless to seek.

It all seems much clearer from the poems than in fact it was. Paul never did become comfortable seeking the chest of doubloons, but the poems at least indicate that he gave serious consideration to doing so, and the short story must at the least be taken as a sign of his own awareness of his problems with his father—and of a willingness to expose those problems publicly. We do not know what if any inner turmoil accompanied the college boy as he pondered such things. Whatever his own adjustment problems may have been, we do know that in 1949 he gave Yale $2 million (today's purchasing power $6 million) earmarked to provide psychiatric and personal counseling for students.

From Paul's first day at Yale, A. W. was generous to the school and its institutions in quiet and indirect ways such as by "guaranteeing" that a Yale musical production would at least "break even." The Carborundum Company reached the remarkable conclusion that it could increase the sale of grinding wheels by advertising in the *Yale Literary Magazine,* and Gulf and Alcoa made similar evaluations as to the advertising value of the *Yale Record.* A. W. was also generous to Paul's fellow students, or at least was willing to be. Lucius Beebe and a few of Paul's Yale classmates accompanied Paul and A. W. to Bermuda one season, probably as A. W.'s guests. Beebe later recounted the visit of their entourage to the English clothiers for the selection of Paul's polo coat:

> When Paul had been fitted and the old gentleman was counting out the square English banknotes, he turned with his timid frosty smile to a group of at least five of us and said hesitantly: "Wouldn't you boys each like a polo coat? I'd admire to stand treat." Of course we all swore we had polo coats at home by the dozen (which we hadn't) and all wanted desperately to have one, but the quaint old-fashioned remark stuck in my mind because the treat wouldn't have cost him more than about a thousand dollars—just as though it were a round of sodas!

It must have been very difficult for Paul to have won any acceptance on his own under such circumstances, but he appears to have overcome the hurdle of wealth and done so. The senior class poll ranked him seventh under "most modest," and he polled a few votes for "most gentlemanly," both greater tributes than the likely tongue-in-cheek ranking his fellows gave him as second-highest vote getter for "most likely to succeed." (The "most likely" never made *Who's Who*.) He was active in an array of extracurricular activities, of which his senior society selection meant most to him.

Every spring at Yale the elite of the junior class are invited to join a senior society. During Paul's day, the Ins and the Outs were decided in the emotion-charged proceedings of "tap day." Paul was "tapped" by the two most prestigious societies; he passed up Skull and Bones in favor of the slightly less renowned Scroll and Key. In a 1931 article about A. W. Mellon, Beebe pointed out the significance of Paul's choice. Paul had

> joined a senior society noted for emphasis on the casual aspects of life rather than that organization as famous in the business world as on the Yale campus for its objectives of contacts, achievement and purposefulness in life.
>
> Paul Mellon's acceptance of election to Scroll and Key rather than to Skull and Bones, the traditional choice of young men on the commercial "make," whose dedication to success may be spelled in upper case, was clearly an indication of distaste for a career in the world of finance and may well have marked an epoch in the progress of the Mellon dynasty.

Paul wrote his father that tap day's happenings had been the finest that he had known in college. Among those entering Scroll and Key with Paul was George W. Wyckoff of Elmira, New York, who was to become a key executive in the Mellon family empire.

After Yale, A. W. agreed to just one more year before Paul would settle down, and the son went off for further study at Cambridge, England. He found the Cambridge lectures dull—"dull as dishwater after the heady wine of Yale," he said at a recent Yale gathering. He did little studying there but indulged his fond remembrances of England from his childhood. His love for the life and the ways of the English gentry matured; he became, as he later described himself, "a galloping Anglophile." He had long enjoyed horseback riding, but he found a new dimension to it at Cambridge—fox hunting. Though his older cousin R. K. had already established fox hunting at Rolling Rock, Paul had not participated in it. At Cambridge he hired a horse and began to ride to the hounds. He began to keep a horse of his own, and then he became a regular in the hunt. The fox hunting led him into collecting. He later said, "It was through horses that I really got interested in art, at Cambridge." He began buying color-plate books on horse racing and fox hunting, what the English call "sporting books," long a passion of the English country gentleman. Then he bought his first painting, "Pumpkin," a picture of a horse by the then little known painter George Stubbs. "I didn't pay much for it," he later recalled, "a few hundred pounds, I'd guess. I loved horses and that was the start of my passion for Stubbs." Over the years Paul would acquire dozens of Stubbs's paintings of horses; his patronage of the long-deceased artist prompted an astronomical increase in the price of Stubbs's works, and correspondingly closer and more favorable critical attention. Almost entirely because of Paul's interest, Stubbs has at last assumed his rightful place as one of the greats of English art. "Pumpkin" remains Paul's favorite Stubbs.

As the first year at Cambridge drew to a close, A. W. got a letter from his son. The father testified at his tax trial that Paul "wrote me from abroad giving me reasons why he wanted to stay another year and he could not get a degree in one year, but he could in the two, and . . . so I wrote to him and I made a bargain with him that he should come home and go to work in the bank for his vacation. Well, he proposed that himself in order to get that other year." The bargain was made—Paul would work the summer at the bank and could then return for a last year at Cambridge. The press reported on June 30, 1930, that the Secretary of the Treasury would spend his annual summer vacation in Pittsburgh instructing his son. Dutifully the son returned in early July to keep his part of the bargain and get his first taste of work. After disembarking he agreed to see the journalists and received them at the Bruces' New York apartment. He chatted amiably with them. "I do not think I would be a great success as a banker or an industrialist," he told them. "Commerce and industry hold no particular interest for me and I think it is wiser to enter a field which is more attractive." In an apparent reference to his older, business-oriented cousin R. K., he said, "There are other members of our family who are far better fitted than I am to look after the family interests." He speculated that he would probably enter publishing, long one of his principal interests, an intellectually stimulating "business," which to the way of thinking of most bankers was no business at all. Two days later the New York *Times* reported that he had been escorted into the Mellon National Bank by his father.

Paul fulfilled his part of the bargain; he stuck out the summer getting a taste of each of the bank's departments, and then returned to Cambridge for his final year. In June of 1931 he received his Cambridge bachelor's degree at an ancient ceremony attended by his father.

By then A. W. had either mellowed on Paul's "phantasies" (as old Mr. Bennett had regarded Robin's predilections) or had made a sensible strategic decision. He well knew that his son was "more McMullen than Mellon," as Paul described himself. If A. W. were to go for broke and attempt to force his son into the mold of the Pittsburgh businessman, he risked an irrevocable routing of himself and the way of life that he had inherited from the Judge by the forces of McMullenism. Or he could make a truce with the competing values, possibly the kind of truce that he had made with Nora McMullen years before. Perhaps the ways of life could share Paul just as he and Nora had shared custody. A. W. was not a personally domineering man; he could compromise to maintain his relationship with his son.

In any case, while Paul was still at Cambridge in the spring of 1931, A. W. purchased Rokeby, a famous horse-breeding farm in famous horse country near Upperville, Virginia, as a country estate for Paul. The New York *Times* reported that Rokeby was "one of the most beautiful and oldest estates in that part of Virginia, widely known among turfmen. . . . It has been famous throughout the Virginia region as an assembly place for hunters during the season, as well as for the breed of its horses." It was the kind of place to which Paul might periodically retreat from the business world of Pittsburgh and enjoy the English country life in America. The *Times* reported that the Secretary's former wife had been living in England to be near her son, Paul, while he was at Cambridge, and that she "would spend a part of her time at Rokeby. Mrs. Mellon was said to be greatly interested in the horse farm." Paul returned from England with his mother, passed a wonderful fall hunt season with her at Rokeby, and then, on December 1, 1932, showed up to begin his life's work at the Mellon National Bank. The newspapers reported that the Secretary of the Treasury took the night train from Washington to Pittsburgh to be with his son personally on the important day. Harvey O'Connor speculated in his 1933 *Mellon's Millions* that "Paul was playing the game. Perhaps in a few years it would be called off and he would be free."

Paul's first day at work was continually interrupted by the newspaper people. Asked about the old reports of his literary ambitions, he answered, "That's all old stuff, and it's all been explained." He was weary of the interruptions by the end of the day, but still cordial to the last reporter into the bank, a delegate from the Pittsburgh *Press.* "I didn't do much, really, just looked around mostly. I just haven't got a job yet. I haven't the slightest idea what I'm to do." He was embarrassed by the request for another photograph:

> Really, no more pictures, I just can't, that's all. I've had others today and it simply just disrupts business so. I simply can't. And besides, my father—my father—well, my father just doesn't like that sort of thing at all. It's a nuisance, you know, this fuss every time I come to Pittsburgh. I do wish people wouldn't make such a to-do.

Finally, the newsman coaxed him into a final pose:

> He seated himself at a desk when the photographer asked him to, but that business of putting a writing pad before him and pretending to work on it, was —well, just too much entirely.
> "Oh, no, no, no," he laughed. "Why everybody on earth would know it was a dreadful fake. They know it isn't my desk. They know I haven't any desk. I'm not a banker, and everybody knows it."

Things settled down quickly, and Paul began to make his new life as a banker. After six weeks he began going on boards of directors, the first of them being the board of the First National Bank of Donora, Pennsylvania —Heywood Broun cited his selection as belying talk that advancement was closed to the American young. Thereafter came the boards of Union Trust and Pittsburgh Coal. A. W. believed that the myriad problems confronting the coal industry would make Paul's involvement with Pittsburgh Coal a particularly rich learning experience. Soon he sat on an array of Mellon boards. In the spring of 1933 he moved temporarily to New York to work on the staff of the Mellon-connected Bankers Trust Company, the bank where David Bruce had received his initiation. There Paul might get another exposure to the world of investment banking. When he registered to vote in Pittsburgh in 1934, he listed his occupation as "banker." For a while it looked as if the "my brother and I" of A. W. and R. B. might become the "my cousin and I" of a Pittsburgh era dominated by Paul and R. K. A. W. had made the right decision.

One of Paul's regular callers at the bank was a young schoolboy, Tony Grosso, who delivered newspapers around the bank and took bets from the tellers and the secretaries as he made his rounds. Grosso, later to become boss of Pittsburgh's numbers racket, recalled in the fall of 1977 his relations with Paul:

> I think Paul Mellon knew what I was doing in his bank. But I did it in such a nice, clean way that he had to like me. I would sit and talk with Paul Mellon sometimes a half hour, 45 minutes. He wouldn't let me go home. He was a very thoughtful person, strictly for the underdog. He had a warm heart. Rich people are very lonely people. . . . I tried to make him the last of my newspaper deliveries because I knew he wanted to talk. I enjoyed talking to him. He was a tall, lanky man. He used to put his legs across the table, and we'd talk about my life, the environment that I lived in, the conditions of the poor people up in the Hill District. He knew about that, because the bank owned practically all those homes up there.

And Paul found time for pleasure: fox hunting at Rokeby, and running flat races with other amateurs; marlin fishing with Ernest Hemingway in the Bahamas; and fun and courtship. The New York papers carried a "nostalgia" item in late December 1933 about how Paul Mellon had inspired the rebirth of a beloved pre-prohibition custom—a sleigh race across Central Park to the Central Park Casino to welcome the season's first heavy snowfall, the winner of which had traditionally been awarded a magnum of champagne. The Paul Mellon sleigh captured the magnum in the low-keyed contest, just a nose ahead of the Eddie Duchin sleigh. Passengers with Paul in the winning sleigh were identified in the New York *Herald Tribune* as "Mrs. Karl S. Brown, manager of the John Beckert Art Gallery, and Lucius Beebe, bon vivant."

"Mrs. Karl S. Brown" (soon to be Mrs. Paul Mellon) was born Mary Conover, three years ahead of Paul, to a Kansas City physician. Her social credentials were well in order, but she was much more than a society girl. She had been educated at Vassar and the Sorbonne, appreciated art, and, like Paul, she loved the literary world. Later she was to be instrumental in the founding of Pantheon Press, publishers of quality but "uncommercial" literature. She had married Karl S. Brown, a stockbroker whose interests, like Paul's, lay more in the publishing world. The Browns got an amicable Nevada divorce in 1933. At the time of Mary's marriage to Paul, Brown was working at *Newsweek,* in which Paul had taken a significant financial interest. Brown wired his best wishes.

Paul and Mary were married at a private ceremony at the Bruces' Sutton Place apartment in New York City in February 1935. Only A. W., Nora, the bride's parents, and a small group of close friends and relatives were present. Other weddings reported in the Pittsburgh newspapers on the same day included the marriage of Greta Wenngien, Swedish-born maid at the Paul Mellon residence, to Robert Higgins, Scottish-born valet to Mr. R. K. Mellon.

After a prolonged honeymoon abroad, Paul took Mary back to Pittsburgh, where she felt as much at home as his mother Nora had felt. Paul's lifelong friend John Walker, former director of the National Gallery, wrote that Mary "had been part of a society whose members were less parochial and more bohemian than most of Paul's Pittsburgh friends." There was "a slight feeling of estrangement" that did not dissipate, but that particular problem was to become largely inoperative when the Pittsburgh umbilical cord was severed with the death of A. W.

A. W. was in his most productive period during Paul's earliest years and was not around much. Paul later told a commencement day audience that "modern psychological theory more and more leans to the conclusion that it is not just childhood in general which shapes each one of us almost irrevocably, but the very earliest years, between birth and five." Paul's adolescence was passed at Choate. During all of the more important formative years, father and son had minimal contact. Even when they were not apart, the father was fifty-two years older than the son. Vacation periods together must have resembled other boys' visits to a grandfather, but they were devoid of grandfatherly indulgences. In the last four years of A. W.'s life, however, the two resided together much of the time at the Woodland Road mansion that they shared. The physical closeness meant a lot to the father, and he believed that at the last he had made contact with his son —not by indoctrinating the son as the Judge had done, but by becoming friends, even if they were friends of different orientations. The New York *Times* observer wrote that the father's "voice quavered and he blinked beneath his bushy white eyebrows" when he spoke of their relationship at the tax trial:

> Q. And of course, on those occasions you had frequent and long visits with your son about all the affairs that he was interested in and all that you were?
>
> A. Yes. Young men are not so much interested in affairs to talk any more about them than may be required.

Q. Well, so far as you could you were interesting him in the affairs of business?

A. Oh, yes, and he became interested.

Q. And you were trying to cultivate in Paul Mellon the tradition of the Mellon family?

A. That word "trying" . . . I could not say that I was making an effort. We hadn't any—he was very responsive to all my wishes and suggestions, and there wasn't any question about any particular drilling in any direction or anything in that way.

Q. That is he was entirely responsive to your wishes in his course of life?

A. Yes, and I was as responsive as a father could be in his wishes and decency or desires.

Q. And on those occasions you discussed the various business transactions, and the relations of the Mellon family to the different industries, I take it?

A. I do not think we ever discussed questions such as you have indicated. That is not usual between father and son. What I mean by that is that we were congenial, and I do not like the word, but say, comrades. I mean we discussed matters which were of interest.

Q. Well, that included of course, the business interests to which you had given a large part of your life?

A. Very little of it.

In the father's last months, Paul worked with him regularly on the plans for the National Gallery of Art.

The death of A. W. marked the beginning of the end of Paul's Pittsburgh phase. He became president of the National Gallery trustees, and his duties as such during construction of the gallery's great building required his presence more and more in Washington, and gave cover to his evacuation from Pittsburgh. One by one he got off of the various boards that he had joined—Pittsburgh Coal was among the first to go. Rokeby became the principal residence of Paul, Mary, and their infant daughter, Catherine, born in 1936. He began construction there of a lovely brick Georgian style mansion, designed by his friend William A. Delano. In a matter of months after the father's funeral, Paul had largely extricated himself from Pittsburgh and from the burdens of Mellonism; death gave the victory to McMullenism.

In July 1939, two years after his father's death, Paul resigned from the National Gallery's board before completion of its building—the New York *Times* reported because of the press of private business—and was succeeded as its president by David Bruce. Ten months later Paul again appeared in a *Times* report as one of a horde of evacuees from the European war returning to the United States aboard the S.S. *Washington*. The *Times* reported that he had spent the previous nine months in Zurich.

From the account of his friend Walker, it seems that Paul's months with the famed Swiss psychiatrist Carl Jung in 1939 and 1940 were the most valuable of his life. Jung had worked closely with Freud until 1912 when they separated, largely over matters of emphasis. Jung put much less emphasis on sexuality than Freud, and much more on inherited tendencies. Freud was quite old by 1939 and died that year; so by the time of Paul's selection, Jung was clearly the world's foremost psychiatrist. According to Walker, Paul, "perhaps as a result of Jung's analytical psychology, became one of the best balanced and, as far as an outsider can ever know, one of the happiest of human beings." Paul certainly thought the time well spent, as he named the more creative of the two foundations he founded—the Bollingen Foundation—after the site of Jung's retreat, where he had visited the great man; and he established the estimable Bollingen series of Princeton University Press for the purpose of publishing Jung's writings and Jung's extensive correspondence with Freud. At Yale he established the Bollingen Prize for poetry. One of his first acts on return was perhaps symbolic. He donated A. W.'s Woodland Road estate—Paul's home in Pittsburgh—to Chatham College. He ceased to have a permanent address in Pittsburgh.

Paul was starting over. Paul Mellon, Yale '29, Cambridge '31, was ready to begin college. That fall he entered as a freshman, St. John's College, the ancient institution at Annapolis, Maryland, that three years before had introduced its "great books" course of study. He had come, he explained to the press, "to make up, to some extent, important gaps in my education." He would live alone at Annapolis and return weekends to Rokeby, where his wife and daughter would reside. It was a difficult time for a boy—and Paul seemed to be proceeding as a boy—to begin his college education. As Paul was registering at St. John's in September 1940, Hitler had already stormed the European continent, and the Battle of Britain was under way; by the end of his first year of college, American entry in the conflict seemed inevitable. Like so many other college boys of the day, he took leave of his education to enlist in the Army. To go from the end of the freshman year of college into the Army was a very natural progression for a young man to have made in July of 1941, and especially so for young men fifteen years younger than Paul. Though his age and his family status made him virtually assured of deferment from the newly instituted draft, Paul said in answer to newsmen's queries that he had "thought it was the right thing for me, personally, to do." Thirteen weeks later, in September of 1941, still several months before the bombing of the American fleet at Pearl Harbor, Paul completed basic training. He was eligible for release to return him home. No, he would not accept release; the press reported that he had decided to remain in the Army a year. That December Pearl Harbor was bombed, and the United States and Paul were into a war.

It was not an arduous military career. Paul later recalled that before joining the service he had consulted "the only person I knew in the whole U.S. Army," General George S. Patton Jr. Paul and Patton had fox-hunted together. Patton had encouraged Paul to enlist, thereby assuring his choice of branch of the service. Paul's choice was the cavalry, the horse-mounted troops, and off he went to Fort Riley, Kansas, the great American cavalry center. There he found others of similar interests and often of similar background; reporter George Cantwell wrote in *Sports Illustrated* that "To the cavalry post in the heart of Kansas came the country's foremost horsemen, suddenly soldiers but as keen as ever for gentlemanly sport."

Arriving before Pearl Harbor, Paul was one of the first, but still his training was stalled behind a group consisting of three Oxford graduates, seventeen lawyers, a chiropractor, and a man whose education had stopped after grammar school. After Pearl Harbor, Cantwell wrote, "almost every Union Pacific train that stopped at Junction City brought a celebrated fox hunter, jockey, polo player, rodeo performer, or Western movie star," and Fort Riley became "a *Who's Who* of American horsemanship." The "fox" hunts—with the hounds usually chasing coyotes—and the polo matches continued, under the auspices of the United States Army.

Paul was "trained" and then remained at Fort Riley as an instructor in the horsemanship department. Designer Oleg Cassini, also an instructor, described their life for Cantwell: "I often think it was like India in the time of the Empire. There was a group that socialized together, an ingroup of jumpers, famous horse people who stuck together and created an elite. It was not unpleasant." Paul recalled that "even after Pearl Harbor, we were allowed to bring our horses. I had three hunters shipped from Virginia."

But the life of Riley was not to last. The idea of a saber-carrying horse-mounted cavalry in 1940 was already a quaint anachronism in the day of the tank and the howitzer, one that could be supported only in peacetime. A quarter of the cavalry had already been "mechanized" by the time of Paul's arrival at Fort Riley; a year later the horse cavalry had all but ceased to exist. In 1943 Paul was transferred to the O.S.S., and largely through David Bruce's connections an assignment was arranged for him in England. From there he went on to Patton's Third Army in France, but according to W. L.'s *Judge Mellon's Sons,* "As the American Third Army surged across France, exposure and exhaustion brought him down as surely as a bullet. Even before the French capital was securely won, Paul, feverish and delirious, was lying on a stretcher in an Army field hospital. He had pneumonia." He was mustered out a major. Paul later told *Fortune*'s Charles J. V. Murphy, "Junior officers do a great deal of sitting around and waiting in a war. It's a good time for collecting one's thoughts."

Home in 1945, essentially for the first time in five years, Paul rejoined his wife and family, increased by the addition of his son, Timothy, born in 1942. Mary was not well. She had suffered asthma for years, which appeared somehow to be related to her husband's great love, horses. Thinking that it was somehow psychosomatically related, she had encouraged them to go to see Jung in 1939, and her own time with Jung was so helpful that she seemed cured of her asthma and was able to share Paul's favorite pastime without ill effect. By the time of his return from the war, though, the asthma had recurred. According to John Walker, the asthma attacks were so severe that they had strained her heart, and "she was told by her doctor that she must never again go near a horse. It was characteristic that she rejected this diagnosis, refusing to be separated from Paul's greatest pleasure." Her obituaries indicate that she died unexpectedly in October 1946 at the age of forty-one of a heart attack only a few hours after she had been fox hunting with the Piedmont Hunt. She left a daughter, Catherine, nine, and a son, Timothy, four.

Paul has remained loyal to her memory. A beautiful Norman-style church that he donated to the Episcopal community of Upperville in 1960 contains a series of stained-glass memorial windows in her honor, and he has continued to make contributions to her college, Vassar, including in 1949 a gift of $2 million that was used by the college to establish the Mary Conover Mellon Fund for the Advancement of Education. His next wife, though, whom he married a year and a half after Mary's passing, was a woman of different tastes, values, and aspirations.

Rachel, known as "Bunny" ("I used not to like it but now I am reconciled to it," she told the New York *Times* of her nickname), was born three years after Paul, daughter of Mr. and Mrs. Gerard B. Lambert of Lantana, Florida, and Princeton, New Jersey. Early press clips identified her as "heiress to the Listerine fortune." She grew up at Carter Hall, a masterpiece of ante-bellum southern mansions in Millwood, Virginia, not far from Upperville. She finished in nearby Middleburg at Foxcroft School, keenest rival to Miss Porter's School as the country's most fashionable girls' boarding school, and debuted in the 1929–30 season.

In 1932 she married Stacy Barecroft Lloyd Jr., son of a Philadelphia banker, rich and good-looking, educated at St. Paul's and Princeton, class of '30. His pedigree was of the very best as a descendant of Captain Samuel Morris, aide to George Washington, a matter in which he took no little pride. Their marriage was described in the Philadelphia *Record* as "one of the most important weddings of the winter season." The Lloyds had two children—a son, Stacy III, about Catherine's age, and a daughter, Eliza, about Timothy's age—before they separated in 1947. When their divorce was finalized at Palm Beach in March of 1948, friends told reporters that Rachel's supposed romance with Paul Mellon was "only a rumor." They were married on May Day that year at a private ceremony at the New York home of their friends Mr. and Mrs. Henry Parish II.

Bunny brought Paul out socially. He was never "shy" but he was and remains of a retiring nature, and his and Mary's social life had been as subdued as he was himself. Bunny and Paul became social lions. The sign of their blossom was apparent when in 1957 the Queen of England and Prince Philip, touring the United States, picked Rokeby as their hunt-country stop for tea; it reached full flower with the accession to the White House of First Lady Jacqueline B. Kennedy. "Of course," Bunny told a New York *Times* interviewer in 1969, "Jacqueline was an old and true and loyal friend of mine a long time before she went in the White House. I can't say anything but good of her."

In the White House, Mrs. Kennedy relied heavily on Bunny's decorating advice, which seemingly covered the whole range of the decorative arts. Bunny was responsible even for such matters as the appointment of Larry Arata to the position of White House Upholsterer. Mostly the First Lady depended on Bunny for her tasteful floral arrangements and for horticultural and landscaping advice. Bunny's skills in the gardening department were almost entirely self-taught, but dated back a long time: "I transplanted wildflowers when I was six. By eleven or twelve I did gardening designs," she recalled for the *Times* reporter. By the time of her maturity she had become, by John Walker's high standards, "a brilliant horticulturalist and landscape gardener, the equal of any professional." At the request of the Kennedys, she redesigned the White House Rose Garden and supervised the execution of her design by members of her own personal staff; once completed, she often tended the Rose Garden herself. She was always a working gardener, and not simply a patron of gardening. Later she undertook similar work on the White House's East Garden (also known, at Bunny's insistence, as the Jacqueline Kennedy Garden), completed during the Johnson administration. Later, in 1966, the Department of the Interior presented her with one of five Conservation Service Awards for her work on the White House gardens, but a modest lady, she insisted, "Really, this whole award should go to President Kennedy and not to me," explaining that she had proceeded only at his request. During President Kennedy's tenure, the Mellons made a number of contributions to the White House art collections, most notably a highly important portrait of Thomas Jefferson, generally accepted as having been painted by Rembrandt Peale, and Rachel's father donated a historically significant portrait of Andrew Jackson.

Bunny's public service did not end with the assassination of John F. Kennedy. While Lyndon Johnson was seeking tactful ways to ease out the Kennedy crowd, Lady Bird was confronted with precisely the opposite problem. "My main hope," she confided in her diary, "is to have the grounds and the flowers in the house continue to profit by Mrs. Mellon's hand." Bunny's devotion to cause transcended intra-party factional lines, and she continued her interest in White House horticulture—"Gardens aren't political," she told reporters. The Nixon administration was less forgiving. "Of course I would be happy to help Mrs. Nixon," she volunteered to the *Times* reporter, "but she hasn't asked me."

Bunny and Mme. Onassis have remained close over the years since, their friendship documented in unending gossip-column and society-page entries. The friendship has meant a lot to Bunny. When she submitted to the New York *Times* interview in 1969, she ebulliently displayed one of her proudest possessions; it was

> a large squarish book, a bit larger than a newspaper page, bound in a green stripe and boxed in matching paper.
>
> "I couldn't sleep all the night that Jacqueline Kennedy gave me this wonderful scrapbook tracing the history of the gardens—the Rose Garden and the Jacqueline Kennedy Garden I did for the White House.
>
> "When all that William Manchester business was happening, Jacqueline Kennedy was serenely pasting these pictures of Jack Kennedy in the book for me.
>
> "Look at those pressed flowers from the Rose Gardens. See, here are the first sketches I drew for the garden."

As a special tribute to the then First Lady, Bunny's daughter Eliza's coming-out party in 1961 was in French motif and decor (Mrs. Kennedy was a Francophile). President Kennedy begged off attending, citing his intermittent back difficulties, but Mrs. Kennedy came escorted by William Walton, Washington artist and gentleman. Reports of the affair in the Pittsburgh *Press* estimated the cost of the party at one million dollars, and from the *Press*'s account it looks to have been a bargain at that. The network of party sites on the estate grounds were linked by a series of roads paved especially for the occasion, and thereafter torn up so as not to detract from Rokeby's rustic beauties. It was one of the most unashamed displays of money since the regime of Louis XVI, at least to the eye of anyone who was not invited to it.

When Bunny's daughter, Eliza, was married in the spring of 1968 to Viscount Moore, son of the eleventh Earl of Drogheda, Caroline Kennedy was a flower girl, and John F. Kennedy Jr. was one of two pages. It was a nice wedding.

The friendship of Bunny and Mme. Onassis has been founded on their mutual interests: luxury life and country life, horses, art and antiques, and homes—lots of homes.

The Mellon homes grew in number from one to several. Maxine Cheshire reported in 1968 that "the tropical horticultural Eden which [Bunny] has created around her Antigua home reportedly requires a private water supply larger than the public reservoirs that service every other kitchen, bathroom, swimming pool and lawn-sprinkling system on the arid island." Their Osterville, Cape Cod, home was lacking in one vital respect: dunes. There were none. So the Mellons trucked in some 2000 tons of soft clean sand from a more generously endowed site ten miles away to create their own dunes. The brownstone in New York's East Seventies wasn't quite right—"It got sort of bedraggled," Paul told *The New Yorker*—so it was torn down and a more suitable structure erected on its site, a two-person residence, not a place for major entertaining, and the brownstone across the street was acquired as a kind of auxiliary building to service it. The account by "Suzy" of the decoration of the Mellons' Paris apartment near the Bois de Boulogne must rank as a classic of gossip-column reportage. She wrote that Bunny's Paris flat was being decorated by Carlos Ortiz of New York, who "created fold-up furniture and draperies for it that went up *tout de suite* upon Bunny's arrival and came down for storage even tout-er-de suite upon her departure. Rather like a tent indoors, do you see? What could be more divine? Gardens, that's what. And gardens there will be!" There is also a Washington residence.

Upperville remains the "main" home. Over the years Paul has increased his holdings to some 4000 acres of rolling fields and farms amidst historic Civil War country. The estate at large is now known as "Oak Spring," with "Rokeby" used to identify the stable and horse-breeding enterprises situated at Oak Spring. In addition to Rokeby, Oak Spring includes a network of gardens, an airstrip, farmed lands, and a gaggle of residential buildings and outbuildings. Paul feels a responsibility to keep his grounds as unspoiled as possible, and according to *Fortune*'s Charles Murphy worries that he has perhaps done too much tampering with nature already. Murphy reports that "the honeysuckle deliberately has been left to climb the stone walls and split-rail fences." The brick house has been converted into their private museum and the Mellons now live well inside the grounds in a rambling stone country house that has grown by additions. Besides the main kitchen staffed by chefs, it includes a smaller kitchen for Bunny herself; she likes to cook and describes herself as "a Sunday cook." Much of their produce is raised on the estate. The French impressionist paintings seem very much at home there. Among the other buildings is a small brick one-room schoolhouse where the four children received their pre–boarding school educations. Occasionally large groups are permitted to visit—like the Herbs Society of America or a convention of veterinarians or a delegation from an organization of Pittsburgh bibliophiles—and enjoy a refreshing light lunch courtesy of the Mellons. The estate's staff of over 200 includes librarians and art curators and a private security force.

Bunny has always been attuned to new decoration; Maxine Cheshire reported in 1968 that she kept two theater set designers on her staff to attend to details of her various homes. Still, Murphy describes the Mellon homes as "characterized by a deceptive air of simplicity—simplicity of the costliest kind."

Today Paul and Bunny live largely separate lives, Bunny principally on Antigua, where the climate is more favorable for the exotic varieties of plant life to which she inclines ("Gardens have always been my life"). He lives principally in the Upperville and New York homes, but travels a great deal.

Paul did not abandon all interest in the family's concerns when his father died, and for many years journeyed regularly to Pittsburgh for consultations. Around 1960 he became more involved personally when he joined the board of Mellon National Bank and succeeded General Matthew B. Ridgway as the head of the Mellon Institute. He merged the institute, by then mainly engaged in fundamental research, into Carnegie Tech in 1967, to form Carnegie-Mellon University. In 1976 he declined to stand for reelection to the bank's board of directors, citing his age, sixty-nine, and his desire to devote time to other interests. Throughout, his financial affairs have been managed by a team of competent money managers that was long headed by George Wyckoff, who retired a few years ago, and is now directed by Nathan Pearson. Pearson, stationed in Pittsburgh, was Dartmouth '32 and Harvard Business School '34. After service with Carborundum he joined Paul's staff in 1947. Today he sits on the boards of the Mellon companies and other corporations in which Paul has made sizable invest-ments—Ampex, Hanna Mining, and CertainTeed Products—to cast the vote of Paul's interests. He is a lean, trim, efficient-looking person and identifies himself as Republican and Presbyterian. Paul told a reporter in 1963, "I'm active in business in an overseeing capacity. I have excellent advisers. Fundamentally, I have never been terribly interested in business, but I do like to know what's going on."

In January 1963 Paul resumed the presidency of the National Gallery, a position that he still holds. It requires his personal attention on a regular basis, and has imposed some burden of official entertaining whenever the gallery has a new opening of significance. On each such occasion he delivers one of his good-natured, low-keyed, and witty speeches. He raised a few eyebrows at the dinner marking the opening of an exhibition of Chinese archeological items loaned by the government of Communist China in 1974 by toasting "the good health of Chairman Mao and Premier Chou." Work on an addition to the gallery under construction as of this writing, and scheduled to open during 1978, has required a lot of Paul's time and attention recently.

Much of his time over the years has been required in supervising and coordinating a dozen personal staffs—his business staff, a staff for each of his houses and philanthropies, staffs for the stables at Rokeby and in En-gland, and other staffs to catalogue and maintain his varied collections.

His philanthropies have also required much of his time. For years Paul funded two separate foundations, Old Dominion, established in 1941 with traditional philanthropic purposes, and the smaller Bollingen Foundation, established in 1945 with an emphasis on encouraging scholarship in the humanities. In 1969 both were merged with Ailsa's Avalon Foundation to form the Andrew W. Mellon Foundation, with assets of $664 million as of January 1, 1977. He also maintains ongoing interest in his father's A. W. Mellon Educational and Charitable Trust, which now generally confines its benefactions to Pittsburgh-area concerns. Its assets, now dwarfed by those of the Andrew W. Mellon Foundation, were $18 million as of January 1, 1977.

Paul regards major philanthropy as a heavy responsibility. He told the press that "giving large sums of money away nowadays is a soul-searching problem. You can cause as much damage with it as you may do good." On the other hand, "Foundations and individuals can make decisions to act on things that are slightly controversial faster than governments because the machinery is less. I think that's the usefulness of private wealth."

According to Walker, who serves on the board of the A. W. Mellon

Educational and Charitable Trust, Paul spends at least three days a week on philanthropic work. Paul says that he looks for "regenerative" philanthropies, and those in which his foundations would be cooperating rather than carrying the whole freight. Business details of a benefaction are handled in a businesslike manner. The detailed demands made by his staff during the recent construction of the Yale Center for British Art that Paul sponsored drove officefuls of Yale administrators and accountants crazy (though not so crazy as to have wished that Paul had gone to Princeton after all). He discusses particular proposed grants not only with his own staff but also with knowledgeable outsiders. Ernest Brooks Jr., onetime head of Old Dominion, described Paul as an ideal philanthropist, "alert to ideas, objective in judgment, unafraid of controversy but not given to charging after trouble for its own sake." His lack of fear of controversy is borne out by the first presentation of his Bollingen Prize for Poetry in 1948; it was awarded to the brilliant if enigmatic Ezra Pound, at the time confined to a mental institution and under indictment for treason as a result of his pro-Fascist and anti-Semitic propaganda broadcasts from Italy during World War II. Despite Pound's repugnant politics, it seems likely that no one was a more important force in the development of modern English language poetry.

In the world of education Paul has been the mainstay of his prep school. The family's major capital gifts to Choate date back to his senior year there, when A. W. gave the school a new library designed by Edward P. Mellon. Since then, Paul has given the school several millions for other capital improvements, including Choate's Paul Mellon Center for the Arts, an exciting modern building. St. Johns has also benefited by several millions. Yale has been his most favored charity. In addition to dozens of routine grants for this or that, and gifts of this or that (such as his collection of manuscripts pertaining to alchemy and the occult), he paid for a major expansion of Yale's undergraduate residential facilities in 1958, when Yale built its Morse and Stiles colleges at a cost of $15 million. More recently he gave Yale its Yale Center for British Arts, together with most of his collection of British paintings, drawings, prints and books, discussed below. A hint as to his importance to Yale's ongoing vitality is apparent from a scanning of the *Yale Alumni Magazine* of March 1977, which includes an article on the appointment of the paper conservator at the Yale Center for British Arts (no identification of the center's donor), another on the opening of the center, and another announcing the award of the Bollingen Prize, administered by the Yale University Library—an award endowed by Paul. A spread of photographs of some of Yale's distinguished collections includes a page of pictures of twelve of the donors, the picture of early American artist John Trumbull being ever so slightly larger than that of Paul, probably in response to dictates of format.

Paul also gave a 420-acre farm to Virginia Polytechnic Institute for agricultural research. "I do not claim to be a dirt farmer, or a knowledgeable cattleman, or a soil scientist, but the soil is in my blood, and I feel a deep debt of gratitude to the soil of America," he said upon making the presentation. To Oxford University's Bodleian Library, owner of half of the personal books of John Locke, Paul presented—the other half. Pittsburgh universities have also received significant aid, as has Harvard, and a large number of lesser colleges have received lesser grants. One of the relatively insignificant grants, $200,000 to Grinnell College in 1975 to support a program offering retraining opportunities for tenured faculty, demonstrates an awareness of emerging social problems.

Paul has also been much devoted to conservation efforts and has given strong support to the Western Pennsylvania Conservancy, now headed by his cousin twice removed in-law, Joshua Whetzel. His most useful contribution to conservation was probably a gift of a little over $7 million made jointly by his Old Dominion Foundation and Ailsa's Avalon Foundation, matched by funds of the State of North Carolina, to buy up the Outer Banks, the islands off the shore of North Carolina, to form the Cape Hatteras National Seashore as a national parks facility. At the official dedication of the seashore in 1952 Paul delivered one of his finer speeches. In it, he traced his interest in the project as dating from his first look at a map of the project:

> There was a magic emanating from that lifeless map that none of us who have been concerned in the project could ever have resisted: the magic of sunlight on the waves and the white froth of surf, sea birds, salt winds, the gold of warm and seemingly endless sands, the silver-green of dune grass waving in the wind; pirate legends, skeletons of old ships, hostile Indians, rum, and murder. It was the magic of names from history: Raleigh, Drake, Ralph Lane, John White, Virginia Dare, Blackbeard. It was the magic of the hardy and precarious life of fisher folk and other men of the sea, and the timeless resourcefulness and individualism of the men of these islands, even to today. In fact, the map gave out an aroma, a kind of distilled essence of Nature, man, America and history.

He regarded it as an investment in the future:

> I am sure that the real value of this area (not its monetary value, but its real value) will not be fully realized for another 50 to 100 years, by which time so many more wild and beautiful areas will have disappeared under the waves of population, pollution, profligacy, but what many call progress.

Its worth is already clear.

The National Gallery received $20 million in 1967 from Paul and Ailsa for an addition, and Paul has made other less substantial gifts to it, including a portrait by Cezanne of the artist's father, acquired by Paul for the National Gallery in 1970 at a cost reported to be $1,600,000. John Walker, former director of the National Gallery, played the gracious loser in his *Self-Portrait with Donors* when he discussed Paul's gift to Yale of his important British collections; Walker well knows that there are still a couple of pretty nice pictures at the house in Upperville, yet to be devised.

The Norman-style church that Paul donated to the Upperville Episcopal community at a cost of about $2.5 million must also be regarded as a contribution to art. It is an authentic medieval gem (though updated by unobtrusive heating, air conditioning, and sound and lighting equipment). As a touch of authenticity there is a noticeably off-centered beam, true to the ancient tradition that no work of man is perfect. The church was designed by architect Page Cross, who has worked on a number of Mellon's architectural projects, assisted, according to the newspapers, by Bunny.

Over the years, Paul's foundations have spent a proportionately small but significant total amount in encouragement of esoteric scholarship, such as a study of the iconography on medieval Bosnian and Herzegovinian tombstones, and more recently, and much more spectacularly, a $950,000 grant to help speed completion of a dictionary of the pre-Elizabethan English language. Congressman Wright Patman, a foe of charitable foundations because of their economic impact on the country and its tax base, as well as a foe of A. W. Mellon, characterized Paul's Bollingen Foundation with considerable exaggeration as "an organization that seems to specialize in sending thousands of dollars abroad for the development of trivia into nonsense."

Otherwise, Paul's time has been divided between his great loves, horses and collecting.

Fox hunting has been an important pleasure for Paul and has heightened his love of nature. At the Foxcroft School commencement in 1964, he spoke of the joys of the hunt in terms of

> a frosty morning in October with the air clear and cold, corn in golden hillocks in the harvested fields, the trees turning to bronze, yellow, scarlet, and gold, the deepening bell-like wave of hound cries coming from the woods, the far horn and its echo and a distant "tallyho!"
>
> And speaking of the joys of hunting, let's not forget the warmth of a hot cup of tea, or a toddy, or both, and a long hot bath, after a long, cold, wet day.

As a younger man Paul was a sometime competitor in amateur point-to-point horse racing, and he followed steeplechase racing closely enough to have discussed the relative merits of the sport in England and America on a Pittsburgh radio station in 1935. By the late 1940s he was America's leading steeplechase owner. At that time he was becoming seriously interested in handicap racing on the major tracks and began acquiring expensive horses in England and Kentucky. As in his financial affairs, he seldom interferes with the operations of his able trainers, but he participates in important buying decisions. Some of his purchases of promising horses have set new price records. He personally selects the name for each horse; many have been given Yale-related names. Rokeby has produced a number of famous horses over the past several years, notably Mill Reef, Quadrangle, Arts and Letters, Run the Gauntlet, and Fort Marcy.

Paul has been active in a number of racing organizations, and he enjoys the camaraderie of the small upper-crust segment of the racing world of two continents.

Though he no longer enters speed races himself, as recently as May of 1977 he jockeyed Christmas Goose to win the annual three-day hundred-mile horse-endurance contest conducted annually by the Virginia Trail Riders Association. "It was exhausting for the horse," he said. It was the third time that Paul had ridden the winning horse over the difficult course. After his victory he told the sportswriters, "Well, I'll be seventy in June but I'm reasonably fit. I usually get down to the farm in Virginia in time to ride Friday and Saturday, and sometimes Sunday and Monday morning. I got in three to three and a half hours like that for about two months before the ride. But to tell the truth, I was pretty tired at the finish."

Prior to his marriage to Bunny, Paul had been a desultory collector, principally of rare books and manuscripts, largely but not exclusively related to England and the country life. His tastes in paintings also gravitated to the English, but he was not an important buyer. After his marriage, his book collecting increased in intensity and his collection in importance. Largely from Bunny's urgings, he began buying French impressionist and post-impressionist paintings. Highlights from his collection, exhibited at the National Gallery in 1966, can leave little room for doubt that his is the finest collection of paintings of the schools still in private ownership, and one that surpasses all but a few public collections of French paintings of the period in breadth and depth. It includes important works by all of the key painters of the period; some canvases that have by now been reproduced almost to the point of triteness, and many lesser-known works, unpublished until the

National Gallery's catalogue, which are more powerful still. His own preference is to the more subdued Boudins, and especially Boudin's beach scenes.

Many of his French paintings were acquired at auction, including Cezanne's "Houses in Provence," acquired in 1965 for $800,000; others he has bought through dealers. Acquiring a desired painting at auction gives him "the great sense of triumph, plus a sleepless night before." All of the French paintings have been selected by himself and Bunny with an eye to their own tastes. Several years ago he told the New York *Times,* "Bunny and I are not systematic collectors of French painters. We are interested chiefly in those works that please the eye and please us—things we like to see on the wall." At the time of the opening of the National Gallery's exhibit of his and Ailsa's French collections, he wrote in the same vein:

> Our pictures . . . are lived with, constantly looked at, and loved. They are more than decorative, or merely attributes of the general style and atmosphere of each house. They have become companions and friends, and are part of the life lived in the house, part of our own lives. . . . I have never bought pictures as an investment, except as an investment in pleasure, as treasures to the eye.

Though his personal forte was to become collecting British paintings, Paul also appreciated what he has described as

> The lift in the heart and the joy to the eyes that blew in with that new wind which swept across France during the nineteenth century; earlier, over Courbet's wild waves, later, more gently across Boudin's placid beach at Trouville . . . then gently up the quiet reaches of the Seine for Monet, Renoir, Sisley and many others. It was a fresh and delicious wind.

Paul was not breaking any new ground when he entered the field of the French impressionists, but he was when he began acquiring British paintings in a grand manner in 1961. Until that year his own collection of British paintings was relatively modest—perhaps a dozen good pictures, dwarfed in number and importance by his French works. That year the Virginia Museum of Fine Arts, on whose board Paul sat as a trustee, held an exhibition of English sporting pictures. The museum had had Paul head the selection committee, and had recruited Basil Taylor, librarian of Britain's Royal College of Art, to assist him. The exhibition inspired Paul, and over the next several years he acquired hundreds of British paintings with Taylor's advice and assistance, mostly from the period between the birth of Hogarth and the death of Turner (1697–1851), which Paul regards as the greatest age of British art.

Besides sporting paintings, Paul said, his tastes "were not the stately formal paintings so much admired by museums, but rather intimate, informal, revealing paintings that are pleasing to the eye—what are called conversation pieces." In practice it broke down to genre painting, with a heavy preference for the genre of the English upper classes. The appeal to him of such works surely revolved around his happy reminiscences of the good days he had enjoyed in England long before, the days of the laughing ladies and of the men in their impeccable white flannels, and of the grass that was green, green, green, and mostly the days of tranquillity. When he began his serious buying in 1961, he ceased collecting on the basis of his personal tastes, and began buying to create a great public collection, acquiring those stately formal paintings not particularly to his liking, such as the important Van Dyck portrait of Mountjoy Blount, Earl of Newport.

At first his buying was rapacious, and Walker wrote that London's dealers

> were spellbound by the magnitude of the orders they received. Photographs, transparencies, drawings, paintings arrived in America by the plane-load. The available supply of British art, accumulated over a long period of disregard, was so great that prices for a surprising time remained at the same low level.

Walker said that Paul's purchases were "like repeated shots of Vitamin B, to which the English market finally responded." To the dismay of less affluent aficionados, his demand pushed the prices of British art upward from the levels to which long neglect had depressed them, to such levels that now even Paul regards the prices as "inflated." One side effect of the price rise was the birth of a new respect for English art. Walker, who should know, says that "in America and England undue neglect has changed to an almost exaggerated esteem."

A year after Paul began buying, the collection had reached sufficient size that the National Gallery could devote an entire exhibit to English drawings and watercolors from his collection. By the following year, only two years into the market, he had amassed over four hundred British paintings, enough to fill another Virginia Museum exhibit of British art, this time with paintings entirely from the collection of Paul Mellon. He explained at that time that his motivation had been to assemble a representative collection of English art between 1700 and 1850 so fine that it would cause a revaluation of the underrated period. It had that effect. *Apollo,* the English collectors' magazine, dedicated its April 1963 issue to him in appreciation of what he had done for English art, and devoted most of its issue to a review of the Virginia Museum's exhibit. *Time* and many lesser publications gave the exhibit major coverage.

Several hundred more paintings arrived before the exhibit of his English collection the following year at London's Royal Academy, and many, many more before the collection was shown at Yale in 1965. The following year, in 1966, it was announced that Paul would donate the entire British hoard to Yale, together with a building to house it. At the time, the collection consisted of 1000 paintings, 3000 drawings, and 4000 rare books, valued at a total of $35 million. Paul was just getting started.

By the time that his Yale Center for British Art opened in 1977, his collection had further swelled to 120 Constables, 42 Hogarths, and 70 Turners. ("This is Mr. Mellon's twenty-fourth Wooton," says the guide at the Yale Center, "which proves that more *is* better, because this is Wooton's best.") The total gift came to over 1800 paintings, about 7000 drawings, 5000 prints, over 20,000 rare books, 10,000 art history books, and over 60,000 photographs for art history research. *Time* magazine valued the gift at close to $200 million. Paul also paid for the gallery portions of the building, some $10 million, and gave further endowments of sufficient size to cover most operating costs for the near future, and to enable the center to sponsor research and publications in art history.

The net result of Paul's effort, almost all since 1961, is that he assembled a collection of British art that Walker ranks as the equal of the combined collections of Britain's three greatest museums, and it is virtually all now ensconced at the Yale Center. While its emphasis is on the period and the subject matter personally most favored by Paul, the center's collection includes fine examples of British painting dating back to pre-Elizabethan times. Its many featured attractions include Hogarth's "Beggar's Opera," Turner's "View of Dordrecht" (regrettably only one of Turner's later "impressionist" or "abstract" canvases is on view, though Paul owned several), Constable's "Hadleigh Castle," and the world's finest collection of works by Stubbs. In addition to major works by the world-renowned artists, there are many important canvases by lesser-known painters that Paul "discovered," such as Joseph Wright of Derby, whose Caravaggio-esque lighting makes his paintings among the most appealing of the collection. The center's library includes thirteen volumes printed by William Caxton, England's first printer; a famous group of color-plate books acquired by Paul as a unit; and the only copy of Blake's poem *Jerusalem* that was printed, illustrated, and hand-colored by Blake himself. At the time of its creation Blake had written, "It will cost twenty guineas but it is not likely that I shall get a customer for it." It was a good buy when Paul bought it for $60,000.

The building, last work of the late architect Louis Kahn, is not inspiring from the outside: a four-story glass and steel building of rather typical modern design. Its interior is exciting, a bold use of stark materials and light

that makes a fine museum setting. The street-side portions of the bottom
floor are rented by Yale to commercial tenants, thereby leaving a part of
the building and land value on the tax rolls of the city of New Haven, a
concession made by the university (with Paul's concurrence) in response to
the city's wishes.

The center must be visited at least a couple of times, and its purpose as
an educational tool kept in mind, for it to be properly appreciated. The
collection and the displays are not limited to the "great" works, but include
numerous representative canvases, consistent with the purpose of the Yale
Center as a teaching and research institution. Some 500 of the lesser oils
that most museums would store away in the basement are hung for public
viewing—from floor to ceiling, as closely together as possible, along a long
corridor and in a series of small rooms that are almost completely wallpa-
pered with "surplus" paintings. In such a setting, those seeking out "masterpieces" are likely to come away unimpressed with the overall quality of
the collection—though its finest works would unquestionably make a great
museum alone. The center's architecturally important enclosed courtyard
features two monumental canvases, one depicting a lion attacking a horse
and the other a lion attacking a stag—paintings of the size and theme that
one encounters on the back stairways of European museums. Because of the
jumble of greats, near greats, and misses, it takes a moment's contemplation
to appreciate that these are not simply oversized uglies and realize why the
artist, Stubbs, is regarded as one of the greatest painters of animal anatomy.

There is also sculpture. The visitor is greeted at the center's entrance by
a silly larger-than-life "Roman" figure of King William III ($23,520)—
whose features are vaguely reminiscent of Paul's own. William, together
with the marble busts of homely males scattered throughout the Yale
Center, well demonstrates the poverty of British sculpture. But that too is
a part of British art and the British cultural heritage, and appropriate for
a great teaching institution, now enriched with another magnificent educational tool through Paul's generosity.

Paul still has a few English paintings "at home" to keep the impressionists company. The impressionists are almost certain to join Chester Dale's
collection at the National Gallery. Some of the English works are also
earmarked for it, some for the Virginia Museum, some for London's Tate
Gallery—and perhaps some for his children. He also has a scattering of
other works. When a New York *Times* reporter visited him at his National
Gallery office in 1966, he noticed that it was hung with four large paintings
by George Bellows, painter of robust American life of the early twentieth
century, and one by the great American seascape painter Winslow Homer.

"Yes, they are all mine," Paul said, "I happen to like these paintings. They don't mean that I now intend to specialize in a new field of collection."

Around 1969 the Mellons, and especially Bunny, became interested in abstract art, and bought a work by the Dutch artist Piet Mondrian (1872–1944), still one of the most important abstractionists. Soon after the suicide of Mark Rothko in 1970, Bunny bought six of his canvases for $525,000 from New York's Marlborough Gallery.* Their collecting has slowed down, but it hasn't stopped. Still, the Mellons have yet to give significant encouragement to any living painter who has needed it (which excludes the recently deceased Pablo Picasso, whose early works they bought when Picasso was an old man). Paul's most fabulous philanthropies have been in encouragement of art *history,* and they dwarf the large but by comparison modest assistance that his Andrew W. Mellon Foundation gives to the symphony and the ballet.

Walker, who probably knows Paul as well as anyone, wrote that

> If one were to speculate on the period in which he would have chosen to live, I think one would select the time between the ministry of Sir Robert Walpole and that of Lord Melbourne [coinciding with the Hogarth-to-Turner period]. Paul would have been at home with those urbane, cultivated gentlemen, living in their Georgian town houses or on their country estates. We see them in pictures by Stubbs, Zoffany, Devis, Marshall, and others, painters who convey the charm of the country: the exhilaration of foxhunting, the excitement of shooting driven birds, the satisfaction of catching a salmon, and always as a recurring theme, the delight of seeing beautifully groomed horses in their cool paddocks. Little wonder that these gentlemen of Georgian England are so often portrayed walking with obvious self-satisfaction across the velvety lawns of their lovely country houses. Their way of life, as mirrored in English painting, must have exerted a strong attraction for Paul long before he became a collector.

It was a great period in history for the privileged classes. British historian George Macaulay Trevelyan pointed to its "fullness of life . . . Perhaps no set of men and women since the world began enjoyed so many different sides of life, with so much zest, as the English upper classes at this period." As much as possible, Paul has lived in that era and enjoyed the Georgian life, notably the life of horses, hounds, and field, and the life of the collector.

---

*Marlborough personnel were involved in the administration of Rothko's estate, and his daughter later brought suit against the gallery, pointing out that paintings it bought from the estate for $18,000 were within six months thereafter sold to Bunny for $180,000, and claiming that the estate had been robbed. It seems reasonable to conclude that *someone* had been robbed.

It has been impossible for him to totally re-create the Georgian life, but he has enjoyed it vicariously in the pictures. He enjoys looking at the pictures, at a favorite "doll house" of a stable, and at life.

His personal philosophy, as it may be gleaned from the commencement address that he delivered to Foxcroft graduates in 1964, is typically Georgian. At a time when young people were becoming increasingly preoccupied with the burning moral causes of the 1960s, he urged his listeners to keep a sense of humor, a sense of proportion, and especially a sense of pleasure. He characterized his speech as a "protest on my part against what I consider to be an overseriousness and overconscientiousness on the part of many parents, educators, and the clergy," and against "the cult of intellect, of intellect divorced entirely from emotion, of pure intellect refined to its brilliant but icy splendor [which] has somehow swept over the world with a dismaying, chilling effect." By way of antidote, "What this country needs is a good five-cent reverie." He was not suborning "selfish overindulgences or wild bacchanalian excitements," but only urging that his audience "do unto yourselves what you would like others to do unto you—that is, treat yourselves with kindness and consideration and sympathy." It was a delightful speech, erudite while puckish, probably his finest, and a masterpiece among commencement addresses. Its advice was much needed at the time on the campuses at Berkeley and Columbia, if somewhat less vital for the recently "finished" daughters of Foxcroft. It reflected the Georgian philosophy of the life that Paul himself has led.

In tone, Paul's life has not been the "zestful" life that Trevelyan ascribes to the Georgian aristocrats; it is not so much the zest of that England that has appealed to Paul as its freedom from worry, its confidence that the good life would go on forever, and its emotional tranquillity. The Georgian aristocrat never had to think about "the awful vistas of Infinity" that Paul contemplated in this 1928 sonnet:

> It is not often that such moments come.
> For all the world seems but a solitude
> Of vast primordial quiet, as though the rude
> Incessant beat of a last battle drum
> Has faltered finally, and now is dumb.
> Today for us has been an interlude
> Of peace profound, and an infinitude
> Of deepest calm, to which we must succumb.
>
> Majestic as the silence we revere,
> A golden cloud floats slowly down the west

Into the depths of the eternal sea.
And now we feel no longer any fear
That suddenly there may be manifest
The awful vistas of Infinity.

Personally, Paul is reserved and somewhat distant. The English paintings in which he has delighted reflect a reticence that typifies Paul himself. English painting excites fewer passions because it is, like the English, subdued; it does, however, excite the passions of those whose passions tend to the subdued. In his relations with people, Walker writes that Paul "likes to see others equally happy but with a minimum of personal involvement . . . fundamentally he is a loner." He avoids emotional involvements in general. His well-known modesty is more a matter of gentlemanly unwillingness to call attention to himself. Though he declined to permit the Yale Center to carry his name—probably in emulation of his father's decision on naming the National Gallery—he did allow its use by Yale's allied institution, the Paul Mellon Foundation for British Art, which he founded in London in the mid-1960s, and by the Paul Mellon Center for the Arts at Choate. Few modest men have commissioned so many portraits of themselves, though to his credit his favorite portraitist, William F. Draper, who has now done five portraits of Paul, does not flatter Paul in the warts-and-all portrayals that he has done of the sitter.

Paul is a "good" employer, well liked by his staff, generous to them not only financially but personally. An exchange of telegrams between himself and his secretaries Miss Tross and Miss Rye reflects the warmth between them: when Rokeby's horse Fort Marcy won an important race, the secretaries wired Paul in England, "Rokeby's colors flying high say the same for Tross and Rye," to which Paul responded, "The attitude of Rye and Tross is far outdistanced by the boss whatever state of joy they dwell in is more than matched by Mister Mellon."

The author had an opportunity to see and hear Paul at a special "Class of '29" dinner during the week of opening ceremonies of the Yale Center in May of 1977. Perhaps 200 survivors of '29, their wives, and a couple of their sons assembled at the center for a bustling evening of cocktails, a supper, the unveiling of Draper's fourth portrait of Paul, donated to the center by '29—and one of Paul's whimsical speeches.

Paul is of medium height (five ten), trim, and obviously in excellent physical condition. He is not a handsome man; his most noticeable feature is an oversized hawklike nose, which swoops downward menacingly, as if about to make a lunge for his protruding chin. His face is vapid in repose, but when stimulated it is lively and interesting—the more so the broader his grin. He has a fairly full head of hair, most of it gray. Time hasn't been hard on Paul, or at least no harder on him than it has been on the rest of '29.

He was dressed immaculately in the height of late 1950s fashion: a pin-striped blue suit, pale yellow shirt, and blue-and-white-striped tie pushed a little forward by the now-dated collar pin.

His handshake was uninspired—a British handshake, not an American one.

The dinner was a light cold buffet, with modest French white wines, during which a few of the class "rowdies" (now almost seventy years old) broke out into a song, which startled Paul for a moment. Before the speaking, '29 was treated to a medley by the Duke's Men, one of Yale's innumerable undergraduate singing groups. They did not inspire much interest in the audience or in the guest of honor, who intermittently continued his chat with Mrs. Kingman Brewster, wife of the outgoing Yale president, current American ambassador to England. Everyone joined in the singing of "Bright College Years"; though his voice was not audible, Paul's lips were moving, and he joined in the traditional waving of his napkin in the last phrase of the song: "for God, for country, and for Yale."

After introductions and comments, the painting was unveiled, a rather unattractive portrait of Paul in white tie and tails, with a medal draped on his chest. Then it was Paul's turn. As he rose to speak, Milton M. Koskoff, '29, whispered to his son that "Exhibit A looks like he was just embalmed by the undertaker," but by the close of the speech the elder Koskoff was captivated by the charm, wit, erudition, and grace of the speaker, and even the son had to admit that it was impossible not to like and even admire the man very much.

Paul is not a facile speaker; his prose is better than his delivery, though he recovered nicely when he came upon a page out of order in his prepared text. He has a trace of an accent that might be taken to be British, though it is not; it is the non-geographic intonation of refinement. It was not a "great" speech—there were none of the evocative lists and series that mark Paul's better orations—but then, it would not have been fitting to have delivered a great speech on the occasion.

It was a low-keyed, informal speech, warm and friendly. He began by commenting on his "modesty," which had been referred to by the speaker who introduced him, saying that he had a lot about which to be modest. He discussed the portrait, and explained the background of the "doohickey," as he called it, hanging on his chest in the painting—it had been given to him by the Queen of England as a quid pro quo for his gift of the other half of Locke's library to Oxford. As for the formal dress in which he was portrayed, he said that "the stuffed shirt needs no explanation; it is symbolic of its wearer." He called the work "a beautifully idealized notion of what the donor looked like," and said that he liked Draper because, "as I grow older, he constantly makes me look younger." He spoke about his time at Yale during its golden era. He talked fondly and at some length about "Whit"—the late A. Whitney Griswold, '29, Brewster's predecessor as president of Yale—and quite a bit about Brewster and Brewster's own devotion to '29, which Brewster, so Paul said, had grown to know and love through his long association with Whit. A lot of gray heads in the audience moved up and down in agreement with the speaker. He did not mention his wife or his son, Timothy, Yale '64, who lives in nearby Guilford, Connecticut. Neither was present. Most of his speech was devoted to discussing the development of his love for British art, which he attributed to a nostalgia for "an age and a way of life gone by." As he spoke, the author recalled Paul's Foxcroft commencement speech, in which he had speculated that his audience might remember him as "a kindly graying man who told a mild joke or two, and said things in an odd way about life and art and motherhood."

Richard B.'s only son, Richard King Mellon (R. K.), was only two years younger than Matthew; culturally, they were light-years apart. No two "cousins" of roughly the same age could have been more different. There was never a touch of rebellion in R. K., never a hint of the intellectual— and also, never a sign of whatever is necessary to propel one down "forbidden" paths of thought. No two cousins of roughly the same age could have been more different, unless, that is, they were R. K. and Paul. If Paul was representative of the aristocratic English cognoscente, R. K. was equally representative of the American big businessman. He thought—and sometimes spoke—of Paul disdainfully as "the poet." R. K. was conventional man, luxury model.

R. K. was tutored at home until about the age of twelve, when he was sent to Shadyside Academy, from which he went to a military school. After his flirtation with World Word I military duty, discussed much earlier in this book, he entered Princeton in the same class as his "Cousin" Matthew, but left after brief exposure. He attended Carnegie Tech briefly, was tutored for a while by professors from the Carnegie faculty, and called an end to his formal education very early in the 1920s. Like his own father and his

"Uncle" W. L., he got his education listening to the business discussions of his elders, the most successful businessmen in America. R. B. wanted a businessman for a son. "It was taken for granted that I would follow him in the bank," R. K. told *Fortune*'s Murphy. He started on the bottom rung as a messenger at the bank in 1920, served in other lower-echelon positions, advanced to assistant cashier, and finally he became a vice president in 1928. Top Pittsburgh executives, and those who pretended to be, knew him paternally as "young Dick."

Until his father's death in 1933, R. K. was not at the job all that much. He was exploring the 18,000 acres of his father's Ligonier estate, riding with the horses and the hounds chasing the fox, racing his thoroughbreds at tracks far and wide and winning this or that trophy with now-forgotten horses, or enjoying the good life abroad. A full-length portrait of a playboy can be found in a May 1934 *Country Life* article about him, "Full-length Portrait of a Country Gentleman." He got seasick easily, so he never tried to compete in yachting circles.

R. K. was also building—building the Rolling Rock Club and especially its principal activity, the Rolling Rock Hunt. The great crisis for the hunt came in 1937, at about the end of R. K.'s "playboy" period, when the historic friction between squires and farmers, dating back to 1066 in England, erupted in the new world. As no one can quite know the direction that the fox will take, fox hunting requires the cooperation of the squire's lowlier neighbors for miles around, regardless of the extent of the squire's own holdings. The Rolling Rock Hunt required the cooperation of potentially 240 area farm owners. In England and America cooperating farmers have traditionally enjoyed various privileges in exchange for their damaged fences and trampled crops, particularly work for themselves and their sons on the lord's estate.

Relations between the classes have always been touchy, and R. K. said in 1937, "There has been an unfriendly feeling by the farmers toward us for years." That year the friction surfaced in the form of a labor dispute. Rolling Rock's labor force, virtually all farmers' boys, demanded a raise from their thirty cents an hour and went out on strike to get it. Their fathers and neighbors backed them by threatening to close their farms to the hunt. R. K. told the press of the ingratitude of his adversaries: "We distributed jobs on the farms, more jobs than we needed to have done. We paid them $3 a day for this unnecessary work—welfare work if you want to call it that." They had permitted the farmers to participate in the hunt "without a cent of cost." He would not stand for the injustice (or the impertinence) of their stance: "We've been holding the Rolling Rock Hunt for 18 years, but there will be no more hunts. We're going to close down the farm. We will dispose of the stock, move our stables, abandon the hunts and steeple-chases."

A foolhardy farmer was quoted as having told R. K., "Go ahead and close up the farm tight. The people at the hunt cut down our fences if they're in the [way] and they'll run over a wet field with 50 or 60 head of horses." But the merchant class sided with the aristocracy, as it traditionally did in such disputes in the mother country. The Ligonier Board of Trade cir-culated a petition asking farmers to permit the hunt to traverse their lands, and ultimately they prevailed upon all but six of the 240 farmers to agree. Board of Trade secretary Edward Gromback, owner of a harness and auto supply store, was quoted as saying, "We can't help what the strikers have done and we'd be mighty sorry to see Mr. Mellon go." Community pressure became focused on the strikers. They abandoned their strike and joined in asking the Master of Foxhounds to relent. He did. Applauding the outcome in *The Story of Rolling Rock,* J. Blan van Urk credited it to the fact that R. K. "acted with dispatch, intelligence and courage."

The Rolling Rock strike established the predominance of squire over farmer in the Ligonier Valley, and it was never again challenged. Four years later the hunt had another community relations problem, arising out of the introduction in the area of single-strand, mildly electrified wire fencing, cheaper and more effective for the farmers than alternate kinds of fencing, but ultrahazardous for the horse and hound circle. The hunt secretary wrote all area farmers,

> There is no need to impress on you a fact which is self-evident, namely, that without Rolling Rock there would be very little upon which the community at large could depend to bring cash into the Valley, and that through the Hunt the farmer is undoubtedly benefited either directly or indirectly.
>
> It might be of interest to give some consideration to the following:
> Rolling Rock, Annual payroll $200,000.00
> Labor preference given Hunting Country Farmers
> Steeplechase Races, Polo, Skiing, Fox Hunting and numerous other activities, at different times throughout the year, bring upwards of 1,000,000 people in and out of the Valley, who, it is estimated, spend on an average of, at least, $1.00 per head. Total cash brought in $1,000,000.00

His letter sufficed to turn back the wave of progress in Rolling Rock country.

After the death of R. B. in 1933, R. K. had to shoulder far greater responsibilities. His "Uncle Andy" was seventy-eight and unwilling to resume any active business role; and A. W.'s son, Paul, was eight years younger than R. K. and did not seem temperamentally suited for business. So R. K. was the only logical successor to his father as president of the Mellon National Bank. Already on the boards of directors of most of the Mellon companies and a dozen or so others, he became president of Mellon National early in 1934, and that year he also succeeded to his father's seat on the board of directors of the mighty Pennsylvania Railroad. When A. W. died three years later, R. K. was the only hope of the major Mellon branches for perpetuating the family's tradition in business. He became the operative Mellon in the Mellon family empire. There was still a little time for the horses and the hounds, and for the big game hunting in the Canadian Rockies and Alaska that he liked to undertake "for" the Carnegie Museum, or "for" New York's Museum of Natural History, but there was less and less time for such interests. After A. W.'s death, R. K. proved that he could work with the same resolution and intensity that he had once shown for play.

Prior to assuming the full burdens of business, R. K. married. Constance was the daughter of Seward Prosser, chairman of the board of Bankers Trust Company of New York, and a member of the boards of directors of General Motors and General Electric. She "finished" at the Bennett School in Millbrook, New York, and studied awhile in Paris. A first marriage to Vance McCaulley, a Yale-educated investment banker from a prominent Denver family, was unsuccessful. They separated in July 1935 but were still in touch two months later, when he put a bullet through his skull. Her engagement to R. K. was announced the following February, and they were married soon after. Still childless in 1939, they adopted the first of four children that they were to adopt through The Cradle, a "foundlings home" (as orphanages for white babies were then known) in Evanston, Illinois. Connie, as she is known in the family, shared R. K.'s love for the horses and hounds and became a fine shot herself on their big game expeditions. She grew up largely in Nassau, the Bahamas, and at Woods Hole on Cape Cod, and had acquired a love for the sea and for the yachting life that R. K. never had. She is a strong woman, both bright and personable, who commands respect in the business community in her own right, as well as the good will of some family members who felt less kindly toward R. K.

The R. K.s built a magnificent stone mansion, Huntland Downs, in the compound at Ligonier, and R. K. began the daily commute of almost fifty miles into downtown Pittsburgh. As he got more deeply involved in his work, there was less and less time for his family.

R. K. was forty-two years old at the time of American entry into World

War II. In April of 1942 he was commissioned a major in the Army and was quickly promoted to colonel in the finance section, stationed in Washington, and engaged in establishing banks in the armed forces and in promoting the show *This Is the Army*. Then he was assigned to central headquarters for the draft system. The R.K.s became lions on the Washington social scene. One of their parties was written up in the Philadelphia *Record* as having made a recent Bernard Baruch entertainment "look like something you would get at Joe's Coffee Pot around the corner." According to the clipping, there "supposedly was not a Democrat present, let alone a New Dealer." In the summer of 1943 he was named by the state's governor to head the Pennsylvania draft system, and he moved to Harrisburg for a couple of years before returning to a War Department slot in Washington close to war's end.

After the war R. K. remained interested in military matters. In 1950 he was named head of Pennsylvania's civil defense operations, with the title "major general." With time he rose to the rank of lieutenant general in the reserves. R. K. liked military things and military people. He infused his businesses with retired generals, named General Matthew B. Ridgway to be president of the Mellon Institute (predecessor to Paul), was a generous contributor to Valley Forge Military Academy, and wore his general's uniform whenever he could find a plausible excuse to do so.

After the war in 1946 R. K. brought about the creation of an informal clearing house for Mellon family interests—T. Mellon & Sons. T. Mellon & Sons was not a holding company, and family members were free to go their own ways; but it maintained a professional staff with a wide range of expertise, and it operated as an information and discussion center concerned with common interests of the family as a family in both business and philanthropic pursuits. Representatives of the A. W., R. B., and W. L. branches of the family sat on its board of governors, together with key family employees, often including Adolph W. Schmidt, who by virtue of his marriage to T. A. Jr.'s daughter, Helen (Ned's sister), gave that branch of the family a shade of representation as well. While it did not pretend to be a decision-making center, T. Mellon & Sons did give some cohesion to family decisions about financial matters until after R. K.'s death, when it was disbanded. R. K. was its strong man.

R. K. emerged as one of the important men of American business in the late 1940s and was included by *Forbes* in both its 1947 and 1957 rosters of the country's fifty foremost business leaders. In addition to his overlordship of the Mellon family businesses, with time he became a member of the executive committee of the Pennsylvania Railroad, and ultimately chairman of the executive committee, and a director of Pan American World Airways. His branch of the family took an important financial interest in General Motors, and he joined its board of directors as well. Asked his occupation, he once said, "I hire company presidents." His own involvement in day-to-day operations of the businesses with which he was associated was nonexistent, and control was generally informal; but according to one who knew him well, in business he was "tough as nails." A large professional staff kept track of the details for him, many of the members of which are still serving the interests of his branch of the family.

Also in the immediate postwar period R. K. made his great contribution to Pittsburgh as one of the two spearheads of its redevelopment, euphemistically known in the city's folklore as "the Pittsburgh renaissance." R. K., like his father before him, cared about Pittsburgh, and appreciated that his family's continued well-being was tied to its fate. In 1941 he was elected president of the Pittsburgh Regional Planning Agency. There he came in contact with it's chief operative, Wallace Richards, who, as the war was drawing to a close, painted pictures for him of the death of their city. The major corporations headquartered in the city, even Alcoa, were considering relocation to cleaner cities where the air was not visibly textured, where the landscape was not highlighted principally by decay, and where promising young executives might be willing to commit their lives. R. K. was moved.

Traditionally the redevelopment of an American city has depended for its success upon the cooperation of the city's elected leaders and the leaders of its economic community. In Pittsburgh that required cooperation between Mayor David Lawrence and Richard King Mellon. The only things that the two had in common were their generally cold personalities and their enlightened self-interest, which could fairly be translated to an understanding of their joint stake in the City of Pittsburgh. They never became intimates or "friends," and they communicated almost exclusively through the contacts of their respective agents; but they developed a mutual respect as leaders in different spheres that ultimately led the conservative Republican businessman to give the comparatively liberal Democrat his implicit political endorsement, and that prompted Lawrence to allocate a full measure of credit for the successes of the renaissance to "the Mellon economic power."

Largely at R. K.'s suggestion, the Allegheny Conference on Community Development was established, and it marshaled the economic power of the community and spoke for business in the redevelopment of Pittsburgh. R. K. loaned the Allegheny Conference two of its most important and effective operatives, Arthur van Buskirk and Adolph Schmidt, both from the staff of T. Mellon & Sons. More, he gave consistent support to the redevelopment effort, even when that required backing positions that cut against the short-run interests of the Mellons. He exercised the personal dominance that was born of his economic dominance. As Schmidt later explained,

> When Mr. Mellon asked, let's say the president of the Gulf Oil Corporation or of the Koppers Company or of the Aluminum Company or of the Duquesne Light Company, or other officers throughout the community, to participate in this effort, the associations through the bank and through family holdings were such that they were very pleased to assist and cooperate. It wasn't a question of him ordering or compelling anybody.

His phone calls kept the business community solidly in line behind the redevelopment efforts of the Lawrence administration, which was in turn largely guided by the input of the Allegheny Conference. Lawrence later described R. K. to Stefan Lorant as "sort of a bell cow in Pittsburgh; as he moves, many others move with him." When the Pennsylvania Railroad seemed about to promise defeat for anti-pollution legislation pending in the state legislature that was important to the Pittsburgh effort, R. K.'s calls to railroad executives, and to the presidents of its major freight customers, made the difference in the railroad's position.

The accomplishments of the renaissance were important and obvious. It improved the quality of life in Pittsburgh as it brought pollution control ordinances and enforcement that promised great benefits for the citizens while threatening serious adverse consequences for the coal industry, in which the Mellons were still heavily interested. Instead of opposing pollution control, R. K. sold it. The feared consequences did not materialize; the benefits to the city's atmosphere were immediate. Almost overnight Pittsburgh, traditionally one of the country's dirtiest cities, became one of its cleanest. The renaissance brought the transformation of the Golden Triangle—the tip of downtown Pittsburgh formed by the junction of the Allegheny and Monongahela Rivers—from a jumble of wharves and slums into one of the city's major assets, highlighted by Point Park and the abutting Gateway Center skyscrapers. Just a little uptown from the point, at Mellon Square, the Mellon family donated to the city a $4.5 million pocket park with a below-ground parking garage, and adjacent to it sponsored a major new office building for Mellon National Bank and an exciting new Alcoa skyscraper.

The principal shortcomings of the renaissance were those that generally accompany urban redevelopment in America: inadequate concern for meeting projected housing needs and, especially, inadequate provision for housing those whose homes were displaced by "progress." It did not concern itself sufficiently with public transportation, and especially with possibilities for a rapid transit system for the city. R. K. himself regarded that as part of its unfinished business. Redevelopment is usually "businessmen's" redevelopment, focused on creating an improved business climate, and it was especially so in the Pittsburgh of the R. K. and Lawrence period. R. K. insisted that enlightened self-interest was the cornerstone of his own dedication to redevelopment; the well-being of his portfolio required the restoration of the city to which it was inexorably tied. In his study of *Twentieth-Century Pittsburgh: Government, Business, and Environmental Change,* University of Pittsburgh professor Roy Lubove calls the renaissance a "reverse welfare state," in which the public power and public assets were marshaled for the promotion of private economic ends.

The renaissance has been the subject of considerable puffing, reflected in its name, and the poetry of its bards has invited a somewhat more convincing debunking backlash. Now, twenty years on, it is clear that there was no "renaissance" in Pittsburgh, but it is also clear that there was a physical redevelopment of much of the central business district (marred by many shortcomings even as a project in physical redevelopment) and a vital improvement in the city's air quality, which together saved the city from economic disaster. The renaissance transformed Pittsburgh from a substandard city into a standard city that is now once again ripe for further efforts at "renaissance."

Otherwise, R. K.'s dedication to his city was manifested in countless benefactions from himself and his sister, Sarah, and to a lesser extent from his cousins, the offspring of A. W., both to Pittsburgh as a city and to its institutions. Virtually every college in the city has received many Mellon millions. For years the University of Pittsburgh was the most favored of the academic institutions, but after Alan Scaife's death the Mellons, for reasons sufficient unto themselves and never made clear to the public, grew cold to Pitt. Chancellor Edward Litchfield's partisans blamed R. K.'s unresponsiveness to the school's needs in the mid-1960s for the financial crisis that led to the university's absorption into the state college system. The Mellon Institute merged with Carnegie Tech to form Carnegie-Mellon University at about the same time. Several Pittsburgh hospitals have also been generously aided, some spectacularly so. Only Carnegie-Mellon and the two Mellon parks—Mellon Square Park downtown and the larger Mellon Park far out Pittsburgh's Fifth Avenue—bear the family's name, but they are the lesser part of the many Mellon benefactions to the city that were encouraged by R. K. He took greatest satisfaction from one of his "smaller" grants. Together with the March of Dimes he financed the research that led to the discovery of the Salk vaccine that ended polio as a major crippler. He also was a significant donor to the Western Pennsylvania Conservancy, reflecting his own interest in problems of conservation and environmental protection. In 1946 he established his Richard King Mellon Foundation with an initial grant of Gulf Oil stock which he increased substantially over time. It has made most of its benefactions to Pittsburgh-area charities.

In his last years R. K. began withdrawing from active business. It was not an easy end. A few years before his death he suffered a heart attack, after which his competence declined markedly and noticeably. In 1967, at the age of sixty-six, he became "honorary" chairman of the board of Mellon National Bank, by then successor to Union Trust and Mellon National. For the first time "outsiders" filled all the top roles at the bank. Still he journeyed into his office on the thirty-ninth floor of the Mellon Bank Building daily to follow his affairs. "Short of being hopelessly incapacitated, there is no such thing as retirement for a man of property," he told Murphy in 1967. "One goes on and on, doing what one has done before, if only because all of the other choices seem less important." By then the ruggedly handsome looks of youth had long faded, and his face was marked with heavy jowls and sad eyes. Bottles of liquor within his apparent control began, simply, to disappear.

Write-ups about R. K. invariably mentioned his modesty, something that a journalist might reasonably assume from Mellon's reluctance to grant newspaper interviews. It was probably more a sign of aloofness. Even his great admirer J. Blan van Urk wrote that R. K. "stands off" familiarity. He liked the sound of "General Richard King Mellon" and encouraged others to refer to him as the "General." Out of his hearing, third-person references to him were more often borrowed from his middle name; the tone with which people said "the King" was often edged. The King surrounded himself with courtiers and sycophants, and enjoyed their flatteries. The red telephone on his yacht was a hand-me-down from his buddy General Dwight D. Eisenhower. In his report for the fortieth-reunion book for Princeton's class of '22, he listed paragraphs of "honors" of dubious value that had been bestowed upon him: academic degrees from little-known but hopeful colleges, man-of-the-year recognitions by self-important organizations, and plaques presented by such groups as the Western Pennsylvania Chapter of the Society of Industrial Realtors—the folks who peddle and solicit listings for high-priced real estate.

He was rigid, generally humorless, and like his father could be short-tempered when, as Van Urk wrote, "people fail to do what they are supposed to do." One of his infrequent speeches, inserted in the Congressional Record Appendix by an obsequious congressman, is boring even by the relaxed standards allowed men of his calling. As a businessman he was not particularly gifted, and he relied to a greater extent than most on his capable staff, notably Frank Denton, whom he had inherited from the A. W.-R. B. period.

He was on bad terms with most of his family, both immediate and removed. He was a difficult husband and a distant father. He shared a mutual disdain with his richest cousin, Paul; blackballed Matthew for a position as head of the Carnegie Institute; and shunned most of the T. A. branch of the family in response to McClung's impertinence in having questioned his father's title to the bank. Chancellor Litchfield's partisans suspected that R. K.'s unresponsiveness to Pitt's needs had something to do with a rivalry with his brother-in-law Alan Scaife, longtime head of the Pitt board of trustees. Scaife's son, Dickie (discussed in the next section), never made much attempt to hide his feelings about his "overblown" uncle, the "General."

R. K. died in June 1970, just short of his seventy-first birthday, of heart problems. His wife and four children were with him at the end. His funeral was held at the East Liberty Presbyterian Church built by his parents; the sole bell that tolled had been given to the original Presbyterian community of Negleystown by the Judge's mother-in-law in 1828. Over 1600 attended the services, including Secretary of the Treasury David M. Kennedy, appearing as the personal representative of President Nixon, and many other dignitaries. He was buried on the grounds of Huntland Downs.

R. K.'s will left half to his widow, and the other half to the Richard King Mellon Foundation, an apportionment which by virtue of the federal estate tax scheme made his estate totally exempt from federal death taxes. By that time he had already passed most of it on to his four adopted children anyway. A year later his wife of thirty-four years remarried, to Peter E. Burrell, an old friend of the General and herself, an Englishman and a noted horseman who has been accepted nicely by the family.

W. L. correctly characterized R. K. in *Judge Mellon's Sons* as "today [1946] the young Mellon I would nominate as best fitted to sit down in a conference, were such a thing possible, that would include my grandfather, Judge Mellon, and his five sons." R. K. was the last of the "initialed"

Mellons, and his passing marked the end of the family's dynastic momentum. Journalists interviewed Frank Denton shortly after the General's death and asked him who would replace R. K. as steward of the vast Mellon empire. His answer was No one.

BOOK V

—~*~—

Today: A Kaleidoscope

I believe in the evolution also of families. A family of particular cast and
character originates and grows to
perfection and decays and dies, just
as religions, governments, nationali-
ties and all other institutions. It is a
law of nature. A family of good,
healthy stock, and good mental and
moral qualities, rises from the common level, prospers till prosperity
produces the canker of deterioration
and decay, then sinks again and
eventually disappears.

—JUDGE THOMAS MELLON

othing remains of the "Mellon patch" far out North Negley Avenue. In 1955 Rippey Place, a cul-de-sac, was built running plumb through the living room of the Judge's twenty-two-room mansion. House, stables, and outbuildings were demolished, and the Judge's grounds divided into twenty-three modest lots for single-family homes. One of the houses, a well-tended cozy place, bears the Judge's old number, 401. When the author rang the bell at 401, the door was answered by a pleasant, plump older lady with an old-world accent. Yes, she had heard that her property had had something to do with the Mellon family, but she wasn't quite certain what. Next door to 401 is a synagogue of Palladian form. The Judge could have lived with that easily enough, but for the noisy banner strung across the temple's entablature pleading for American intervention on behalf of Soviet Jewry. Across from 401, the old J. R. mansion has been replaced by an apartment house of no-frills design.

The Judge's was the last of the great Mellon mansions to go. In 1940 R. B.'s mansion was demolished. Much of the marble and many of its nicer fixtures were rescued by a Father Nicola Fusco, who incorporated them into a new church for his parish in New Kensington, the Alcoa town. R. B.'s iron banister railings became an artistic and imaginative baldachino over Father Fusco's altar. In 1951 W. L.'s house of forty-five rooms and thirteen bathrooms was demolished. Its five and a half acres now accommodate a couple dozen houses. A. W.'s house, previously described, still stands, but it has been integrated into the Chatham College campus and has thereby lost its principal identification as a Mellon structure.

The Mellon Institute's building, now a part of Carnegie-Mellon University, can still be visited in the heart of Oakland, the research and academic center of Pittsburgh. Its space is now given over principally to classrooms, which is just as well, for it was never particularly well suited for its intended use as a laboratory complex. A historically inaccurate plaque in its foyer says that it was dedicated May 6, 1937, to A. W. and R. B. A. W. made the principal speech on the day of its dedication, and he would never have participated in a dedication of something in his own honor. The East Liberty Presbyterian Church, built as R. B.'s great benefaction, within which he and Jennie lie, can also be visited. It stands along the "mall" in East Liberty—Negleystown—a solid monolithic structure of neo-Gothic style, squat but surmounted by an Empire State appendage plunked atop it. Its interior fares much better; it is light, airy, elegant, with very fine stained-glass windows and a notable sculpted "Last Supper." A discreet signboard in front announces it as the East Liberty Presbyterian Church. From the appearance of the passers-by, the neighborhood does not seem to be Presbyterian any longer. Most of the doors to the church are locked all of the time, and all of the doors to it are locked most of the time.

In downtown Pittsburgh one can see all of the great structures of the Mellon business: the "old" Union Trust Building, a beautiful reproduction of classical Flemish architecture built in the 1920s; the Mellon Bank buildings, the "new" one an unexceptional skyscraper built during the renaissance, linked to the "old" one, a Parthenon-inspired classic of the 1920s. The wonderful bronze statue of Franklin that had graced the portal of the Judge's bank was melted down long ago.

Close by is Alcoa's aesthetically appealing skyscraper, probably one of the few attractive buildings in the whole world that is finished in "aluminum siding."

Alcoa and the bank buildings are all clustered about Mellon Square, one of the family's contributions to the renaissance. Only a few short blocks away is the Koppers Company Building, an art deco masterpiece that can best be appreciated from photographs. It is difficult to get the perspective on it in downtown Pittsburgh that is necessary for proper appreciation of its dated charm. Across from the Koppers Building is the Gulf Building, of similar style and period, if of lesser artistic merit. A few miles outside downtown, at Fifth and Shadyside, is Mellon Park, another of the family's benefactions, but not a notable park even in Pittsburgh. The principal physical reminder of the Mellon influence in Pittsburgh is none of the above but is rather the handsome and utilitarian calendar of the Mellon Bank, which one sees in every other office in Pittsburgh, and the bank's seemingly myriad branch offices.

Pittsburgh today is a hodgepodgy city that exerts a strange appeal. It is built in, amidst, on top of, and around prominent hills and ravines, topographical features that explain why it is not more regularly laid out. Downtown Pittsburgh is notable for its pockets of redevelopment, notably at the tip of the Golden Triangle, and then a little farther north at Mellon Square. Again a little northerly of Mellon Square are other appealing new buildings, most impressive of them being the U.S. Steel skyscraper. Because the great buildings are not clustered together, downtown Pittsburgh lacks the unified feel to it that vast stretches of Manhattan have. Outside the immediate boundaries of Mellon Square, for example, the area is still quite scruffy. Just a few hundred feet from the towering buildings of the Mellon empire is the city's "combat zone" of peep shows and prostitutes.

The arts have not been much acclaimed in Pittsburgh. The Pittsburgh Symphony has a distinguished reputation, but the city's once-celebrated Pittsburgh Playhouse has had a checkered recent history, and its ballet is still precariously established. Until the opening of the Sarah Scaife Gallery, there was no major focus for the city's important paintings. The Pittsburgh International Art Show founded by Andrew Carnegie became a triennial before finally shutting down completely in 1970. (As of 1977 it is being reinstituted as a biennial one-man show with the encouragement of the A. W. Mellon Educational and Charitable Trust.) Still, there is a strong artistic and intellectual climate in the city. At the corner of Mellon Park at Fifth and Shady Avenues is the Pittsburgh Arts and Crafts Center, a modestly named institution. It shows paintings, sculpture, and weavings of significant artistic merit, hinting that a full array of inspired talent is at work in the city. In Oakland, where Carnegie-Mellon, the Carnegie Institute, and the University of Pittsburgh interlace, the faces of the students compare favorably for intelligence and sensitivity with those of college students anywhere.

The city's atmosphere is today visibly one of the cleanest in the world. It seems ironic (and cosmically unjust) that both A. W. and Frick took their most valuable paintings away from the city to which they owed their wealth largely because they feared that Pittsburgh's foul atmosphere (which they had done at least their share to create) would have deleterious effects on their prized canvases. Those that Frick left behind in Pittsburgh have survived as well as those that he took with him, and today, because of strict pollution-control enforcement originated during the renaissance, the city is measurably cleaner than New York, where Frick's collection can be visited, or Washington, home of A. W.'s hoard.

Pittsburgh's place in American life has grown out of its industrialization between the Civil War and World War I. The Mellons, as much as anyone excepting possibly Carnegie himself, were responsible for that industrialization. The General, as much as anyone excepting possibly Mayor Lawrence, can be credited for the city's revitalization during the renaissance of the 1950s. Today the Mellon foundations, especially the Richard King Mellon Foundation, the Sarah Scaife Foundation, and to a lesser extent the A. W. Mellon Educational and Charitable Trust (older but now smaller than Paul and Ailsa's Andrew W. Mellon Foundation), are among the agencies first approached for support of newly proposed public projects intended to maintain the city's apparent vitality.

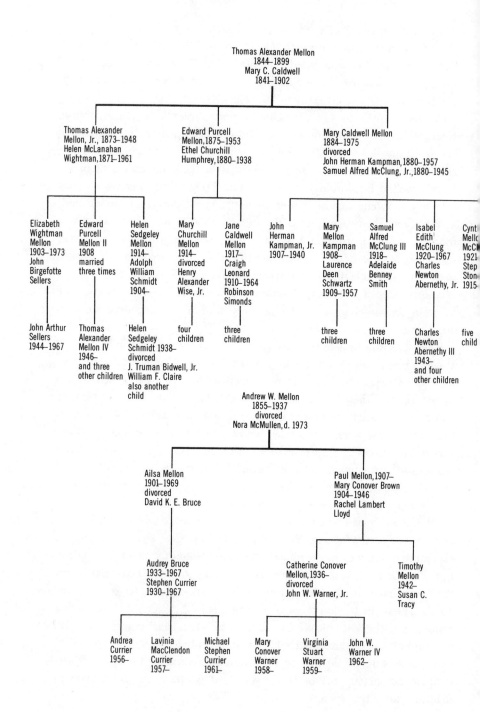

Thomas Alexander Mellon
1844–1899
Mary C. Caldwell
1841–1902

Thomas Alexander
Mellon, Jr., 1873–1948
Helen McLanahan
Wightman, 1871–1961

Edward Purcell
Mellon, 1875–1953
Ethel Churchill
Humphrey, 1880–1938

Mary Caldwell Mellon
1884–1975
divorced
John Herman Kampman, 1880–1957
Samuel Alfred McClung, Jr., 1880–1945

Elizabeth
Wightman
Mellon
1903–1973
John
Birgefotte
Sellers

Edward
Purcell
Mellon II
1908
married
three times

Helen
Sedgeley
Mellon
1914–
Adolph
William
Schmidt
1904–

Mary
Churchill
Mellon
1914–
divorced
Henry
Alexander
Wise, Jr.

Jane
Caldwell
Mellon
1917–
Craigh
Leonard
1910–1964
Robinson
Simonds

John
Herman
Kampman, Jr.
1907–1940

Mary
Mellon
Kampman
1908–
Laurence
Deen
Schwartz
1909–1957

Samuel
Alfred
McClung III
1918–
Adelaide
Benney
Smith

Isabel
Edith
McClung
1920–1967
Charles
Newton
Abernethy, Jr.

Cynt
Mellc
McC
1921
Step
Ston
1915

John Arthur
Sellers
1944–1967

Thomas
Alexander
Mellon IV
1946–
and three
other children

Helen
Sedgeley
Schmidt 1938–
divorced
J. Truman Bidwell, Jr.
William F. Claire
also another
child

four
children

three
children

three
children

three
children

Charles
Newton
Abernethy III
1943–
and four
other children

five
child

Andrew W. Mellon
1855–1937
divorced
Nora McMullen, d. 1973

Ailsa Mellon
1901–1969
divorced
David K. E. Bruce

Paul Mellon, 1907–
Mary Conover Brown
1904–1946
Rachel Lambert
Lloyd

Audrey Bruce
1933–1967
Stephen Currier
1930–1967

Catherine Conover
Mellon, 1936–
divorced
John W. Warner, Jr.

Timothy
Mellon
1942–
Susan C.
Tracy

Andrea
Currier
1956–

Lavinia
MacClendon
Currier
1957–

Michael
Stephen
Currier
1961–

Mary
Conover
Warner
1958–

Virginia
Stuart
Warner
1959–

John W.
Warner IV
1962–

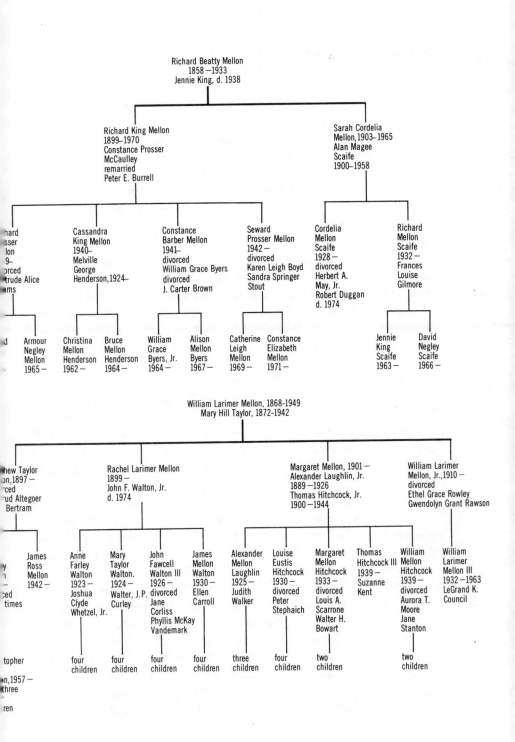

Richard Beatty Mellon
1858 –1933
Jennie King, d. 1938

Richard King Mellon
1899–1970
Constance Prosser
McCaulley
remarried
Peter E. Burrell

Sarah Cordelia
Mellon, 1903–1965
Alan Magee
Scaife
1900–1958

...hard
...sser
...lon
...9–
...orced
...trude Alice
...ms

Cassandra
King Mellon
1940–
Melville
George
Henderson, 1924–

Constance
Barber Mellon
1941–
divorced
William Grace Byers
divorced
J. Carter Brown

Seward
Prosser Mellon
1942 –
divorced
Karen Leigh Boyd
Sandra Springer
Stout

Cordelia
Mellon
Scaife
1928 –
divorced
Herbert A.
May, Jr.
Robert Duggan
d. 1974

Richard
Mellon
Scaife
1932 –
Frances
Louise
Gilmore

...d

Armour
Negley
Mellon
1965 –

Christina
Mellon
Henderson
1962 –

Bruce
Mellon
Henderson
1964 –

William
Grace
Byers, Jr.
1964 –

Alison
Mellon
Byers
1967 –

Catherine
Leigh
Mellon
1969 –

Constance
Elizabeth
Mellon
1971 –

Jennie
King
Scaife
1963 –

David
Negley
Scaife
1966 –

William Larimer Mellon, 1868-1949
Mary Hill Taylor, 1872-1942

...hew Taylor
...on,1897 –
...ced
...ud Altegoer
...Bertram

Rachel Larimer Mellon
1899 –
John F. Walton, Jr.
d. 1974

Margaret Mellon, 1901 –
Alexander Laughlin, Jr.
1889 –1926
Thomas Hitchcock, Jr.
1900 –1944

William Larimer
Mellon, Jr.,1910 –
divorced
Ethel Grace Rowley
Gwendolyn Grant Rawson

...y
...n
...–
...ced
...times

James
Ross
Mellon
1942 –

Anne
Farley
Walton
1923 –
Joshua
Clyde
Whetzel, Jr.

Mary
Taylor
Walton.
1924 –
Walter, J.P.
Curley

John
Fawcell
Walton III
1926 –
divorced
Jane
Corliss
Phyllis McKay
Vandemark

James
Mellon
Walton
1930 –
Ellen
Carroll

Alexander
Mellon
Laughlin
1925 –
Judith
Walker

Louise
Eustis
Hitchcock
1930 –
divorced
Peter
Stephaich

Margaret
Mellon
Hitchcock
1933 –
divorced
Louis A.
Scarrone
Walter H.
Bowart

Thomas
Hitchcock III
1939 –
Suzanne
Kent

William
Mellon
Hitchcock
1939 –
divorced
Aurora T.
Moore
Jane
Stanton

William
Larimer
Mellon III
1932 –1963
LeGrand K.
Council

...topher

...n,1957 –
...three

...ren

four
children

four
children

four
children

four
children

three
children

four
children

two
children

two
children

Of the fabulously wealthy Mellons, the only ones that still purport to be regularly active in the life of Pittsburgh are Richard Mellon Scaife, discussed further along, and the General's two adopted sons, Richard Prosser Mellon and Seward Prosser Mellon ("Pross"), both of whom live fifty miles out of town at homes on Rolling Rock Farms in Ligonier. Over the years the brothers have avoided journalists, which may explain, at least in part, why neither has had many nice words printed about him.

The elder of the two is Richard, born in 1939. He attended Valley Forge Military Academy, one of the General's important benefactions, where he rose to the rank of cadet captain. Then he went on to the University of Pittsburgh but dropped out somewhere along the line. At one time R. K. had thought of a military career for him, and Richard served for awhile in the Army and later as an officer in the reserves. He married and has since been divorced from Gertrude Alice Adams, a socially prominent girl whose father was president of Northern Bank and Trust Company of Lancaster, Pennsylvania. She was educated at Rosemary Hall in Greenwich, Connecticut, and Bennett College. Richard worked for a while at Mellon Bank, but for the last several years has been touted as the brother who follows the civic and philanthropic interests of the R. K. branch of the family. He lives at an estate on Rolling Rock Farms, where he keeps his extensive and important gun collection. He is little known.

His younger brother, Seward, known as "Pross," is presumably the abler of the two. It is Pross who holds the title of "president" of Richard K. Mellon & Sons, the organization that coordinates and represents the interests of the heirs of the General. Pross is also supposed to represent the interests of the family in the business world. He attended Choate and then Dartmouth, but transferred to the easier-going Susquehanna University, a small college in Selinsgrove, Pennsylvania, from which he graduated in 1965. He is as hardworking as the General was, arriving at work early in the morning. He long maintained homes in the Squirrel Hill section of Pittsburgh and in Ligonier, but in 1977 his twenty-four-room Pittsburgh residence went on the market, offered at $700,000.

Pross is the best-known Mellon today from the publicity that he received as the "kidnapper" in an adventure-story custody contest with his former wife Karen Leigh Boyd. The course of their battle sounds like a replay of the one of years before between Pross's granduncle and aunt, A. W. and Nora, but in the updated version the Victorian overlay of the earlier drama has been stripped away and replaced with the strong-arm antics of semi-comic mobsters of *Gang Who Couldn't Shoot Straight* caliber. Like Nora before her, Karen turned to the press for public support, and in the remake the role of the Philadelphia *North American* was played by the New York press.

Karen was of lesser social station, but from the well-to-do town of Berwyn, Pennsylvania, home of Pross's second cousin Alexandra Mellon Grange. She attended Marjorie Webster Junior College and then Susquehanna, where she and Pross met. Her friend Holly Jacobs told the *National Enquirer* that "Karen and Prosser got along right away. He was a pretty shy guy at first, but Karen was very outgoing, an easy-to-be-with girl, so she made up for his shyness." They were married in 1966 in the chapel at Valley Forge Military Academy, with a reception at the school's Mellon Hall.

Life at Ligonier was lush but unsatisfying for Karen. She told the press that her "household budget" for the two homes under her command was $750,000 a year, that Pross's "pocket money" was budgeted at $250,000 annually, and that there was even a $20,000 annual budget for the family dog. According to a security man from Huntland Downs quoted in the *Enquirer,* the General's wife looked down her nose at Karen. "When Karen's name was spoken, Mrs. Burrell had a tendency to turn away." Karen felt isolated and lonely. The security man said that she began to drink heavily. (Karen told the New York *Daily News* that her problems were caused by the combination of taking diet pills and tranquilizers at the same time.) The security man said that "She started to flirt with men openly—even in the presence of Prosser . . . I was told to start following her at night to gather information for Prosser. I followed her on several occasions. Often three or four nights would pass and she wouldn't return home."

Karen acknowledged to the *Daily News* reporter that her behavior became bizarre: "We had a $12,000 alarm system at the house and I would occasionally open the bedroom window on the second floor and toss the cat out so that I could watch the arrival of the security company and the police department. (The cat never got hurt.) I had this fantasy that they would shoot each other. They must have found it strange that I would greet them at 3 a.m. with my hair set and my eyelashes and makeup on perfectly."

According to the *Enquirer*'s source, she once slashed a particularly valuable painting at her mother-in-law's house, and she admitted to the *Daily News* reporter that she became extravagant in her spending: "The less love I got out of marriage the more often I shopped." Pross's spokesmen later said that Karen was under almost constant psychiatric attention and was institutionalized several times. She ended up at the Silver Hill Foundation, a private sanitarium in New Canaan, Connecticut. During her seven-month stay there Pross filed for and received a divorce. He was granted custody of their two daughters—Katherine, born in 1969, and Constance, born in 1971. Karen was given a settlement of undisclosed amount and a support allowance of $35,000 a year.

Karen later told the press that at the time of the divorce Pross had represented to her that when she was released from the sanitarium and had had a year to settle down emotionally, he would give her custody and put her and the daughters in an appropriate home, but that he reneged on the "promise" and it became increasingly difficult for her to enjoy visitations with her children. Late in 1975 she went to Duke University to participate in a special weight-reduction program sponsored by the university. Pross sent the daughters and a governess to visit Karen at Duke, and in early December 1975 Karen and the daughters, accompanied by a couple of men hired by Karen to assist in her plan, disappeared.

During the next four months Karen changed residence fourteen times, using nine different assumed names in an attempt to elude Pross's searching detectives. She ended up on the upper story of a two-family house in a middle-class neighborhood in Brooklyn, New York, using the name Roberts. For a while she maintained round-the-clock bodyguards until forced to cut back to less constant protection because, her chief heavy told the *Daily News,* "she didn't have any green." Her goons were linked to prominent New York criminal elements.

Custody matters are always subject to being reconsidered by the courts of the state in which the children "reside," and the day after the disappearance of Karen and the children her attorney filed a petition requesting custody on her behalf in the New York courts, representing that the children had become New York residents. Pross relied upon his prior Pennsylvania order and obtained a Pennsylvania contempt citation against Karen for violating its order. He ignored the New York proceedings and did not participate in them. Karen's lawyer was speaking with an eye on the media when he told the New York magistrate, "I don't have to kid the court. Whatever Mellon wants in Pennsylvania he can get."

As Pross did not acknowledge the New York proceedings, it inevitably followed that the New York court would give Karen custody by default, and it did in February of 1976. She therefore had custody in New York, he in Pennsylvania. The children were in New York. She continued in hiding with them.

Karen's efforts to elude Pross's private eyes were destined for failure. She told the press that only two days after her return to New York she, her children, and their security force were chased by unknown goons presumably in the employ of her husband. Soon, they found out where Karen and the girls were living.

On the morning of March 19, 1976, one of Karen's detectives loaded the daughters into a station wagon to set off for school. As he was about to pull away from the curb, two vehicles approached. One pulled over in front of his station wagon so as to block forward movement, while the other pulled alongside of him and stopped. Karen's bodyguard later told the press that two men jumped out of the car alongside him. One of them said that they were F.B.I. agents, and said "I know you have a gun. I have one too. Let's have yours." As he spoke, he simulated pointing a gun with his hand in his pocket. Karen's man yielded his gun, the "kidnappers" ordered the daughters into their vehicle, comforted one sobbing daughter ("Kathy, it's O.K."), and both of the assailants' cars sped off. The abduction might have been accomplished at a time of day when Karen's security force was off duty, thereby eliminating any possibility of violence. Karen's chief goon later criticized Pross's goons to the press: "I don't believe they were too smart."

Karen realized what was happening and alerted the police to watch the airports and the movements of Mellon-owned planes. At that very moment three Mellon planes were in the greater New York area, including one owned by Paul Mellon which was then approaching the city. Somehow the authorities decided to focus on Paul's plane and met it at the airport. Its pilot, according to the press, told the authorities that he had come to New York to pick up Seward Prosser Mellon and Pross's daughters. The police had nipped the abduction in the bud! Meanwhile the daughters were safely on another plane enroute to Pennsylvania.

Karen sobbed to the press, "My husband has stolen my children. He's taken them to Pennsylvania where he has more power and influence than anyone should have." She spoke feelingly of the never-to-be-forgotten trauma to which Pross had subjected the girls. Pross's lawyers insisted that the abduction had been necessary to establish a normal life for the daughters, which would have sounded pretty good but for the tongue-clicking that they did over the "dangerous criminal elements" to which Karen had been exposing the children. Both sides claimed to be motivated only by the best interests of the children.

Nora and A. W. had both been people of culture, and their story had "tragic" elements. The replay was more nearly sordid.

Today the daughters are with Pross, and seemed happy and sprightly when the author saw them at the Rolling Rock Races in October of 1976. They are continually guarded by unobtrusive security people, not so much for protection against Karen as against the acts of psychotics or criminal elements to whom the "kidnapping" might have given an idea. They also shield their charges from *paparazzi*.

Their father appeared to be an animated and likable sort. He is lean-built (though with a slight tendency to mid-section pudginess), dark-complected, with black hair, and he was wearing tinted glasses as he often does. He was dressed in a modish outfit of green jacket and green and white checkered pants. He looked to be in his early twenties (he was then thirty-four). He was the center of attention of the lively, laughing group of people in his box. He kept up a fairly steady stream of talk, accompanied by slightly over-refined gestures, to the apparent delight of his companions. There was an impish feel to him. He and his circle had good reason to be in good humor that day. His daughters were with him, and Brooklyn's district attorney had just announced that there would be no indictments arising out of the abduction. He had won.

In February 1977 Karen threw in the towel. By a written agreement she relinquished all rights and claims arising by virtue of the New York order, agreed to accept the courts of Westmoreland County, Pennsylvania—Pross's forum—as the appropriate body for any further consideration of the custody question, and promised that she would "not remove or attempt to remove the children from the father's custody without his consent." Pross agreed to pay her a further annuity of $20,000 a year in addition to the monies previously given her. Their battles are not over, however; as of October 1977 they were in court again arguing about which one was in violation of their agreement of only eight months earlier.

Pross was remarried shortly before the "kidnapping," to Sandra Springer Stout, a divorcee with children of her own. She had worked at the amusement park just outside of Ligonier, and her father runs a ski shop in the town. One small item in Karen's *Daily News* interview warrants a conclusion that Sandy, as she is known, is pretty decent. Karen told the *News* reporter that she had received Easter cards from her daughters that had been addressed to her in Sandy's hand.

Mellon is a common name in Pittsburgh, more common than in any other major American city, and the current Pittsburgh phone book lists many by that name; but except for the office telephones of Pross and Richard, none of the numbers are those of descendants of the Judge. The Mellons were never directly active in Pittsburgh "society." They, together with the Fricks and a very few other families, formed a society so "high" as to be beyond the dreams of most of "society." Today the Mellons are irrelevant to Pittsburgh society. Names like Hillman, another old Pittsburgh banking family, or Hunt, the Captain's descendants, have the magic ring to the socially aspiring that Mellon once had.

The Pittsburgh newspapers no longer give the deference that the dailies of 1912 gave to the first family. Both the *Press* and the *Post-Gazette* carried the wire-service stories of the abduction, though neither did any investigative reporting on their own as did the New York papers. Except for periodic scandals, the Mellon names are scarcely ever in the papers. Other family names that occasionally make the current press—Richard Mellon Scaife and James Mellon Walton—would be generally unknown as Mellons but for their middle names (and both prefer to use the middle initial "M"). Sometimes the names of Joshua Whetzel, head of the Western Pennsylvania Conservancy; former ambassador to Canada Adolph Schmidt; or former ambassador to Ireland Walter Curley appear in the newspaper but are unrecognizable to today's Pittsburghers as being in-laws of the "lesser" branches of the Mellon family. Office seekers in Allegheny County no longer bother to claim that their opponents have sold out to the "Mellon interests."

The author was in Pittsburgh when Karen Mellon charged that she could not get justice in the Pennsylvania courts because of the power of the Mellons, and he decided to test the current attitude of Pittsburghers toward the Mellons by getting man-on-the-street reactions to her claim. He stopped random people on the street and asked whether they thought Karen was correct. Of those who had any opinion, the yeses and the noes roughly equaled each other. To the author's surprise, responses indicating a cynicism about the independence of the judiciary when confronted with the supposed perniciousness of the Mellons, came more from older citizens than from younger ones ("No, no," said a skinny young black man with very thick eyeglasses, in disagreeing with Karen). More significant, both shades of opinion were far outnumbered by those who were not following the Mellon case at all, despite the front-page banner headlines that both Pittsburgh dailies were giving the story. There was a surprising lack of engrossment in the scandal, and the most representative comment was that of an older man outside an open-Sunday supermarket in Squirrel Hill: "Listen, Mister, I have my own troubles enough not to worry about Mister Mellon and Misiz Mellon."

Other Mellon towns have fared better or worse than Pittsburgh over the years. Butler, Pennsylvania, home of Standard Steel Car, has survived best of all of the "company" towns. Parking problems in downtown Butler make clear that the town is still prosperous. An Armco steel plant has replaced Pullman Standard as the most important economic force, but Pullman Standard still produces freight cars there. Its long drab metal buildings give the visitor his first view of Butler. The company has reduced the size of its Butler facilities since the great days of Standard Steel Car, but the areas once utilized by Standard now house other operating industries. Standard's "red row" of abysmal company houses was long ago demolished, and the children and grandchildren of the East European immigrants that lived there have been thoroughly assimilated into the life of Butler. Few people living there today are aware of the Mellons' role in the history of their town, and the only sign of them is the Mellon Bank, an old bank in Butler that has been at its current location for as long as anyone can remember. Only its shiny plaque—"Mellon Bank, N.A."—appears new.

It is easier to find a parking space in New Kensington, Pennsylvania, since Alcoa closed its plant there in 1972. From the time of the town's beginnings in the nineteenth century, Alcoa was the backbone of the New Kensington economy. The town and the company grew up together. Alcoa had been phasing out its operations at its home plant for many years, and its final evacuation from New Kensington left many hard feelings. Its former facilities now constitute the Schreiber Industrial District, where space is leased to assorted smaller industrial tenants. In 1976 Schreiber still had vacancies, and an experienced work force was still available for hire. As in Butler, the last sign of the Mellons in the community is the sign on the Mellon Bank, N.A.

The very name of Donora, Pennsylvania, is a reminder of its connection with the Mellon family. There is plenty of parking in Donora. Donora had some great days, but the trend was against her even before U.S. Steel closed down the Mellons' old Union Steel operations in the 1960s. The population figures tell the story. Donora's 1940 population was 13,180. In 1948 a cloud of poisonous gas settled over the town from the mills, took the lives of twenty, and sickened thousands. Two years later the census of 1950 put Donora's population at 11,818. The 1960 population was only six hundred less, but the closing of the mills in the 1960s meant the loss of over 4000 jobs for area residents, and by 1970 the population had dwindled to 8,825, many of them older people. Today the town supports four funeral parlors.

Donora looks like what it is—a mill town ten years after the mill has moved away. Most of its workingmen's houses, closely built on their small plots, could use a little paint. The bluffs that form their principal vistas have been eroded and discolored by the industrial pollution of the "good" days. Still, there is hope for Donora. The Middle Monongahela Industrial Development Association (MIDA) has taken over the vast abandoned industrial properties and is gradually wooing new industries to town. MIDA concentrates its efforts on attracting labor-intensive enterprises to Donora. Personnel from the local office of Mellon Bank are actively involved in MIDA's inspirational effort. MIDA's director, Robert C. Watson, says that migration from Donora has been stayed.

People in Donora—"Home of Champions"—take pride in their great local athletes, most famous of them being baseball star Stan Musial; and in their home-town actress, Jacquelin Ossko, who came to fame in the 1940s under the stage name "Donora Penn"; and in their restaurant, The Redwoods, which attracts diners from miles around. They are attempting to salvage their town through hard work and courage in what their talented local historian, John P. "Moon" Clark, calls "the American way, and the Donora way."

William Donner retained a sentimental attachment for Donora long after Union Steel had ceased to exist. Over the years he made many donations to local needs, and in 1945 gave the town its public library building. His role in its history is commemorated by the name of its park, Donner Park. Though the Mellons failed to show any parallel interest in Donora, their benefactions to the town of Ligonier, Pennsylvania, and particularly the benefactions of Richard King Mellon, have been essential to keeping Ligonier an up-to-date settlement for the Rolling Rock community.

The vistas that surround Ligonier are as lovely as those around Donora are saddening. Ligonier is nestled amid the kind of beautiful rolling hills that typify horse country everywhere. At the junction of the two "main" roads, Routes 711 and 30, there is a cemetery notable for its carefully modeled shrubbery. But for the manifest ill health of some of the bushes, one could think himself in the Cotswold countryside so loved by the Mellons of both the A. W. and R. B. branches of the family.

Ligonier's Main Street has a sleepy backwater ambience to it, in which the shiny new metal parking meters look markedly out of place. Main Street leads into and out of a rectangular-shaped central square, known locally as "the diamond," around which most of the businesses are clustered. The diamond is dominated by the architecturally uninspired Ligonier Town Hall, which is stylistically consistent with the nearby public library. Both were donated to the town by R. K. There are several banks in Ligonier, of which the Mellon Bank is not the most imposing in appearance. There are a surprising number of churches for such a small town, almost all of which have been generously aided by R. K. and his family.

Agriculture is still an important enterprise in the area around Ligonier, and there are a couple of grain dealers and farmers' supply houses in the town. Otherwise the town is largely dependent upon the tourist industry. During the season skiers flock to the area, to another of R. K.'s contributions. In 1939 he developed the Laurel Mountain Ski Resort, the first in the region, and later donated it to the state as a public facility. In the late 1940s the Chamber of Commerce instigated the restoration of Fort Ligonier, the first British fort west of the Allegheny Mountains, important during the

French and Indian Wars. R. K. was the most significant contributor to the restoration. About 92,000 people a year visit the fort, a plasticized colonial "tourist attraction." The Rolling Rock Races still draw the town's biggest crowds.

South of the town is Rolling Rock Farms, variously estimated at from 16,000 to 20,000 acres of woods, fields, and hills owned by the descendants of R. B.: the General's survivors and the son and daughter of the Scaifes. Dozens of luxurious houses and mansions dot Rolling Rock Farms, all built by family members or social or business associates on parcels leased to them on long-term leases. Rolling Rock Club is within its confines, as is the Valley School of Ligonier, created by the General to provide elementary school instruction for the children of Rolling Rock's "tenants," and the children of neighboring very-well-to-dos.

Public highway 381 runs through the heart of Rolling Rock Farms, and according to *Ligonier: The Town and the Valley,* "tourists are welcome provided they stay on Route 381." Except for a unique caution sign— "Horses and Hounds Ahead"—Route 381 is a typical back-country road, narrowly paved and not overly maintained, bordered by woods and fields on either side, the fields rimmed by split-rail fences. A network of private roads, some paved and some unpaved, runs off of 381, each marked with a rustic "Private—No Trespassing" sign. The private roads meet some-where in the interior, at wonderful junctions unseen by the author. None of the imposing structures are visible from the road, and there is no hint along the way of the great houses set far back and out of sight from 381. The only visible sign of the Rolling Rock complex along the highway is an undistinguished brick administration building of pseudo-English style across 381 from paddocks and horse jumps of varying heights and angles.

About eleven miles north of Rolling Rock is "Rachelwood," James Ross Mellon's old estate, acquired by the General in the 1940s. Its grounds, now swelled to over 20,000 acres, constitute the laboratory of the Rachelwood Wildlife Research Preserve, another of R. K.'s benefactions. There are no signs pointing to Rachelwood from the main road, and when arriving at its grounds the visitor is greeted by more "Keep Outs," beyond which one can see only rhododendrons of prehistoric size. J. R.'s "$1.98 Schloss" and his Church in the Wilderness have long since been demolished, and Rachel-wood's name is the only remnant of his influence.

Other than their benefactions, the Mellons keep a very low profile in Ligonier (as they do everywhere). Except for Pross, whose new wife links him to the town's mainstream life (lots of Ligonier people refer to him as "Pross"), they and their circle keep to themselves and are little known but much appreciated for the economic vitality that they give to the community. Twice a year horsing events are held on the grounds of Rolling Rock Farms, at which time the public is invited to those carefully defined sections of the property where the events are being held. In August there is a Horse and Breeders Show, followed in the fall by the Rolling Rock Races, held on a Wednesday and again on the following Saturday in early October of each year.

Racing at Rolling Rock is steeplechase racing, in which the horses race around a course intersected by rail fences and movable rows of shrubbery which horse and rider must jump. R. K. first sponsored the Rolling Rock Races in 1934, and since 1939 the meet has been operated as a benefit for Pittsburgh's Home for Crippled Children. The roster of its sponsors and contributors, printed alphabetically in the program together with the number for the parking space reserved for each, reads like a social register of Pittsburgh and beyond. The 1976 program, presumably representative, was replete with the names of Mellons and their associates: Burrell, Denton, Henderson (one of the General's daughters), McClung (he has a high-numbered parking space, far back from the course), Mathieson (a high-ranking adviser to the General's heirs), Cordelia Scaife May, Mellon, Mellon, Mellon, Mellon, Paul's chief financial executive, Nathan Pearson, Scaife, Adolph Schmidt (he has a low number), Taber (the "public" spokesman for the General's heirs), Walton, Walton, Whetzel (also a Walton), Paul's confidant George Wyckoff, and dozens of executives from the Mellon companies and every other important Pittsburgh corporation. Most people come in station wagons and enjoy a picnic lunch together with a few bottles of cold white wine from the wagon tailgate before, during, and after the races. Some of the picnics looked to be very nicely done up indeed. In addition to station wagons, there are occasional Bentleys and Rollses—some new, some classic—and a few sports cars, mostly driven by nicely sweatered lean-built fellows in their early twenties. There are some routine sedans but no Volkswagens at all. Tweeds are de rigueur.

The Mellon role in today's Rolling Rock Races is more impressive in the program than in person. For the 1976 running, Peter E. Burrell, spouse of the General's widow and a distinguished British horseman, was honorary chairman. Alfred M. Hunt, grandson of Alcoa's Captain Hunt and himself an Alcoa bigwig, together with Richard P. Mellon, the older of the General's sons, were co-chairmen (an "assistant to the chairmen," Dolores Sinopoli, ran the show), and Richard Mellon Scaife was one of the placing judges. The Race Committee of fourteen included Paul Mellon and his former son-in-law John Warner, both Richard Scaife and his sister, Cordelia Scaife May, Pross Mellon and J. Blan van Urk, author of *The Story of Rolling Rock* much quoted above. There was also a General Committee, which included Mrs. Burrell, Mrs. Mellon, Mrs. Mellon, Mrs. Mellon, and Mrs. Walton (the younger). The owners of the previous winners of the race's "important" cups are all rostered in the program, and many Mellon names occur and reoccur: Richard King Mellon, Mrs. Alan Scaife, Richard M. Scaife, Cordelia Scaife May, and Rokeby Stables, owned by Paul.

In 1976 the Mellons did not take much active interest, however. Rokeby's horses ran in several races on the first day, but its entries were generally undistinguished nags that ran close to the rear, indicating that Paul was giving the Rolling Rock meet only perfunctory support. His horses were scheduled to run on the second day but did not. Paul did not attend himself. The first day of the 1976 meet, a beautiful Indian summer day, the Seward P. Mellon family, the Richard M. Scaife family, and the senior Mrs. Walton (looking about thirty years younger than she is) were the only Mellons in attendance. Most of the parking spaces assigned to the Mellons and their allied families were vacant. The Paul Mellon and Cordelia Scaife May boxes were occupied by people who looked like poor relations of those to whom Paul and Cordie had given the tickets; those in Cordie's box were not even wearing tweeds. The second day of the races it rained and was cold all afternoon. Almost nobody came to the races, most of the boxes were empty, and the only Mellon to attend was Richard Scaife, who stood out in the wet drinking hot coffee and shifting from foot to foot to ward off the cold, while performing his official duties as a judge through sleet, rain and gloom.

Today the Mellon businesses, like most big enterprises, run themselves without particular distinction. They are all thoroughly professionalized and attuned to good public relations. "Ethnic" employees are on display in all of their operations. The Mellons themselves do not pay much attention to any of the businesses. Standard and Poor's 1975 *Directory of Directors* listed only two people named Mellon, neither a descendant of the Judge, though it had columns of Rockefellers and half a dozen Du Ponts.

Nathan Pearson, Paul's chief financial adviser, represents him on the boards of directors of the companies in which Paul maintains large investments; and Andrew W. Mathieson, finance man for the General's heirs, often sits for them. Both men work out of "the thirty-ninth floor," as the Mellon family offices on that floor of the Mellon Bank Building are known in business and philanthropic circles.

Most of the boards of the Mellon companies are dominated by company men, people who have spent much of their adult lives in the employ of the companies they now direct. Even Pearson and Mathieson do not follow day-to-day operations of the companies on whose boards they sit, and are unknown even to upper-echelon employees of "their" companies. Only at the bank is there any ongoing sense of Mellon presence, and there the aura lingers mostly because of the name of the enterprise.

The bank, while probably only the third most important of the family's holdings in terms of its "value," is still the center of its interests and a mighty institution. In 1946, at the suggestion of the General and his chief adviser, Frank Denton, Union Trust, which owned well over 99 per cent of Mellon National, completely merged with Mellon National and emerged under the name Mellon National Bank and Trust Company, which thereafter was "taken over" (a purely formalistic change in its corporate structure that did not affect actual ownership) by the Mellon National Corporation, a holding company, the principal component of which is Mellon Bank, N.A. The "N.A." stands for National Association. As of December 31, 1976, it had deposits of approximately $6.8 billion; 6200 employees; 105 branches in Pittsburgh and surrounding counties; branch offices in London, Tokyo, Frankfurt, and Grand Cayman in the British West Indies; representatives in Mexico City, Rio de Janeiro, the Philippines, and Melbourne, Australia. It has a Chicago subsidiary, Local Loan Company; and other subsidiaries conduct extensive mortgaging operations in Louisiana, Colorado, and Ohio. Its subsidiary Mellon Bank International (MBI) in New York City engages in international banking, and Mellon National owns portions of other foreign banking and underwriting enterprises. It ranks as about the thirteenth largest bank in the country in terms of capital funds, fifteenth in terms of deposits, and sixteenth in terms of total assets. Its ratio of capital funds to total assets is probably the highest in the country, denoting it as the "strongest" American bank.

It is certainly one of the most conservative banks in the country. In a day when most banks have attempted to portray themselves as "progressive," Mellon National has remained unashamedly conservative; and it reaped the rewards for its philosophies in 1975, when most of the "modern" banks found themselves embarrassed by involvements with financially troubled Real Estate Investment Trusts. With minor exceptions, Mellon National steered clear of the REIT's, gave its customers good advice in telling them to keep away from gold speculations, and otherwise has run its affairs in an updated style with an old-fashioned outlook. So far its attitude has fared it well. Not to say that it has not made errors. It was one of fourteen major banks that was caught in the collapse of W. T. Grant, and it found itself loaded with well over $40 million in New York City bonds at a time when one had to feel sorry for anybody that owned $40 million in New York City bonds.

Mellon Bank grew greatly in the period when Pittsburgh was growing greatly. Now the focus of American growth has moved elsewhere, and the growth of Mellon Bank has slowed when compared with that of financial institutions more fortuitously situated. Even if its growth were to cease however (and it shows no sign of ceasing, only of slowing down) it will remain an important institution in American finance.

The corporation's stockholder list includes all of the old names: Mellon, Frick, McEldowney, Knox, Reed, Hunt. Without doubt some portion of the interests of the Mellon and the other "great" families stands in the names of "nominees," names such as Lack & Lindsay, whose address is c/o Wilmington Trust Company. Lack & Lindsay's 1.2 per cent ownership of Mellon National represents the composite holdings in the Pittsburgh bank of all of the estates and trusts administered by Wilmington Trust. Precisely who is the real owner of how much of the stock standing in its name is known only to the executives at Wilmington Trust. (The beneficial owners of most of the Lack & Lindsay stock in Mellon National are probably heirs or beneficiaries of Ailsa. When Carborundum "went public" in 1953 it disclosed that some of Ailsa's stock in it stood in Lack & Lindsay's name, and that other family holdings were in the name of Mac & Co., the name used by the trust department at Mellon Bank.)

In addition to whatever the Mellons or their historic associates might own in the names of nominees, as of April 1977, when the author parsed the company's stockholder list, forty-one separate Mellon entities—Mellons, Mellon trusts, and Mellon foundations—owned 34.9 per cent of the bank; over sixty recognizable Frick family entities owned 8.1 per cent (and it is entirely likely that the author failed to recognize some of the Frick entities); and McEldowney entities owned 1.4 per cent. In 1971 the New York *Times* estimated Mellon family ownership of the bank at 40 per cent. The author's current estimate: someplace between 37 and 39 per cent. Among the bank's current directors are Pross Mellon, Paul's man Nathan Pearson, Richard M. Scaife, two Alcoa executives, the chairman of the Koppers board, and three Mellon Bank officers. Until 1976 Paul Mellon himself was an ostensible director.

Besides the big names, the bank has another 7900 stockholders of record, and though none of them "count," the corporation scrupulously adheres to the forms of corporate democracy. Its annual meeting in 1977 was the most nearly exciting meeting that the bank had ever had. About 200 stockholders attended; virtually all were on the far side of middle age. They were all well dressed—brokers and second-level leaders of Pittsburgh's financial community, most of whom had come to mingle with one another. Most of the directors (excluding Richard Scaife) attended the meeting as a body, did not mix with the stockholders at large, and sat in the front row to be introduced to the "stockholders" seriatim. Both Pross Mellon and Nathan Pearson attended, though the meeting was obviously "pro forma," and it was nice that they gave their time to participate in the same affair with the small guys.

Promptly at two P.M. the doors to the assembly room were closed and Board Chairman James H. Higgins began the meeting. Nominations for membership on the "new" board of directors were received (one man made all the nominations and another man seconded them all); Higgins appointed the election tellers; and then, while the tellers counted the ballots, he presented his annual message about the state of the business and business prospects. At the conclusion of his presentation the election results were announced. Stockholder Whitney Irons pointed out that the ballots distributed to stockholders in attendance had not been collected, so presumably had not been counted; but when everyone at the head table looked embarrassed about the oversight, Mr. Irons pointedly declined to press the point. All nominees were declared elected.

The questions and answers from the stockholders showed that Mellon National is now becoming subject to the kind of stockholders' examination and complaints to which more popularly owned corporations have long been subjected. Higgins's formal presentation had been uninspired, but he was flexible and articulate in his handling of the questions and of the audience. A gentleman who was a "remainderman" of a trust administered by the bank griped about the bank's services and its fees for processing the trust. Another gentleman asked what effect "Jimmy Carter's plans for energy" would have on the bank. A spokesman for retired bank employees asked consideration for increasing pensions (the matter was taken under advisement). An earnest, slightly awkward young man asked about the corporation's stand on the Arab boycott (the bank "assiduously adheres" to all United States laws and regulations with regard to the boycott; "we process letters of credit that conform to Commerce Department regulations and turn back those that don't"). A lady's question about the possibility of increasing dividends brought subdued applause from the audience.

Mr. Irons, a charming and often folksy raconteur who opposed and continues to oppose the transformation of the enterprise from a bank into a holding company, asked some sophisticated questions about the handling of conflicts of interest that arise when different components of the holding

company deal with each other, to which Higgins gave somewhat less sophisticated responses. Irons pressed him, but maintained a good-natured tone
and interspersed his argument with compliments to Higgins and the rest of
the bank's management. He was obviously well known and well liked by
the other "regulars" at the annual meeting—and by corporate officials as
well. Another less polite stockholder of the same view as Irons jumped in
on the repartee between Irons and Higgins to insist of corporate management, "You done it illegally!" Not so, responded the corporation counsel.

After a respectable period of discussion, the person that had made the
nominations moved that the meeting be adjourned, which motion was
seconded by the fellow who had seconded the nominations, and it was so
voted. Higgins had kept everything well in control throughout. The front
row of directors quickly filed out and disappeared before any might be
buttonholed. At least they had come. The officers remained to talk with
anyone who wanted to talk with them. Irons approached the podium, and
Higgins greeted him warmly and no doubt sincerely: "Whitney, I don't
know what we'd do without you!"

The bank's public image remains high, though tarnished by scuffles with
consumer groups and with Pennsylvania's Democratic governor, Milton J.
Shapp. The consumers have brought the bank to court alleging that the
bank and the other major Pittsburgh banks have charged usurious interest
rates on credit card transactions. The issues are more nearly technical than
"moral," and as the bank's leading local competitor is also named as a
defendant, regardless of its outcome the suit is not likely to have great
impact on the bank's reputation. Governor Shapp's charge that the bank
has been self-dealing with the state's monies and has "betrayed the public
trust" is the more damaging.

For many years the state and various of its agencies have been important
customers of Mellon Bank. In the middle of his 1974 campaign for re-
election Governor Shapp said that $3.4 billion in state retirement funds
were deposited with Mellon Bank, and that he would diversify the state's
investments if re-elected. Which was why, he explained, Richard Mellon
Scaife was spending so much money to defeat him with Republican gubernatorial candidate Andrew T. "Drew" Lewis. In the spring following
Shapp's re-election, the state authorized an investigation of the bank's
handling of the monies of the State Public School Building Authority, to
be conducted by Victor Wright, a Philadelphia lawyer, and Milt Lopus, an
economic consultant to the governor. Their report, publicized in April of
1976, cited three types of alleged wrongdoings by the bank: 1) it had
invested the state's monies only in certificates of deposit issued by Mellon

Bank, and not in CD's of other banks that sometimes paid higher rates, representing a loss to the state of additional interest of $1,444,000; 2) it had allowed an average daily sum of $4.3 million of state monies to remain uninvested throughout the period 1966 to 1974, thereby getting the use of the money without paying interest on it, representing a loss to the state of interest totaling $2.3 million; and 3) it had sometimes invested the state's money in Mellon Bank CD's at a lower rate of interest than the bank was then paying to private customers who bought similar CD's, meaning a loss to the public of $535,000. In reliance on the report, Shapp and the Public School Building Authority asked that the bank resign as trustee for the authority's monies, and that it "make up the difference."

Not surprisingly, the bank had its answers, at least two of them plausible answers. It contended that the terms of its trusteeship precluded it from investing the authority's money in CD's issued by any bank other than itself (Shapp's aides interpreted the relevant documents differently and contended that the bank was free to buy CD's elsewhere). The bank contended that public authorities, rather than itself, were responsible for so much of the state's money having lain around uninvested. Higgins did acknowledge, however, that there had occasionally been a differential between the interest rate that the bank paid to the state and what it paid to private individuals. He conceded that a 1973 letter from the bank to the authority to the effect that the state's money had "in every instance" received at least as favorable a rate of interest as the best rate of interest then being given, was "a mistake of fact with relation to some certificates previously issued. [But] it didn't create an obligation of the bank to adjust interest rates in respect to either past or future transactions." No, the bank would not "make up the difference"; no, the bank would not resign as trustee. The authority brought suit asking removal of the bank as trustee and claiming $5.9 million in damages. That litigation is still pending as of this writing. In the standard verbiage of "annual reports," the bank's 1976 report says of the matter that "Management believes that the Bank has performed its duties in a proper manner, that valid defenses exist to all the Authority's charges and that the Authority's actions will have no material impact on the financial position of the Bank or the Corporation." Given its stockholders' equity of $690 million, the bank is surely correct that the outcome of the litigation "will have no material impact" on its financial position.

"Nothing moves in Pittsburgh without the Mellons" was a cliché in the days of A. W. and R. B., and then again during the renaissance period when R. K.'s business people and Lawrence's political people joined in redevelopment efforts. If "the Mellons" means the Mellon Bank, then there is still much truth to the assertion that nothing moves in the Pittsburgh business world without the Mellons. By far the giant of Pittsburgh banking, Mellon Bank is still the key to finance in the city. Most major "moves" in the greater Pittsburgh area are financed by it, as well as many of the minor ones. It is quite possible to put together financing for even major projects in the steel city without Mellon Bank—some things in the Pittsburgh business world do move without Mellon Bank—but for one reason or another most Pittsburgh business moves move with the Mellon Bank.

The bank's power beyond routine and major business transactions of western Pennsylvania is little felt, not objectively measurable, and probably rarely if ever exercised in an unwholesome manner. It arises by virtue of the web of interests that its board of directors represents, and by virtue of the size of the assets administered by its trust department.

Insofar as it concerns itself with Pittsburgh, a 1967 study by Congressman Wright Patman's Banking and Currency Committee, *Commercial Banks and Their Trust Activities: Emerging Influence on the American Economy,* focused at some length on the number of *other* boards that Mellon Bank's directors graced. By the count of his staff, the twenty-eight Mellon Bank directors held a total of 239 seats (each seat an "interlock") on the boards of 185 different companies. Patman himself may have taken this fact to mean that Richard King Mellon himself had a handle on control of the American economy. It did not really mean that, but it is easy enough to appreciate the possibility that the economic power of those 185 corporations might, appropriately nurtured, be more or less marshaled in a manner detrimental to the common weal.

It may not be desirable to eliminate totally interlocks between corporations, and it would be impossible to do so short of congressional act. In any case, interlocks between the Mellon Bank's board and the boards of other companies have very greatly decreased in number and importance since Patman's staff counted. In addition to the seats that they hold on the bank's board, the twenty-two directors elected in April 1977 fill a total of ninety-nine other corporate board seats at eighty-three different corporations. The sharp decline in the number of interlocks over ten years arises from a combination of factors: reduction of the Mellon Bank board from twenty-eight to twenty-two, which accounts for a drop-off of a quarter of the interlocks; increased awareness on the part of directors of the liability that attaches to a corporate director for nonfeasance of his duties to oversee the corporation; and probably to ongoing efforts by both the Mellon family and the Mellon Bank to defuse what might otherwise become a politically explosive situation.

The corporations with which the Mellon board interlocks include most of the great Pittsburgh industries and a few outside giants: General Motors, Anaconda, Proctor & Gamble, Goodyear, Pullman. To keep the magnitude of its prospective power (or threat) in perspective, however, it is necessary to consider the companies with which it does not interlock. It does not interlock with U.S. Steel, Bethlehem, or any other major steel producer, nor with any major bank, railroad, insurance company, communications network, airline, food chain, or retail outlet, nor with any major oil company (excepting the "local" Gulf), nor with Du Pont, Ford, General Electric, IBM, or Xerox. Its web is almost exclusively a regional one.*

The other element in the bank's unobtrusive power arises from the size of its trust assets, the funds that it holds and manages as trustee for others. Patman's 1967 tabulations indicated that Mellon Bank controlled 32 per cent of all trust assets in Pennsylvania, dwarfing the state's second most influential trust department, that of Girard Trust Bank of Philadelphia. In recent years the total value of Mellon Bank's thousands of trust funds has run in fairly close consonance with the Dow Jones industrial average. If you want to know the total value of the bank's trust portfolio at any given moment, just take the Dow Jones average at the time, multiply by ten million, and you won't be too far wrong. Examples: On December 31, 1974, the Dow was 616, the Mellon portfolio was $6.8 billion; one year later the Dow stood at 852, Mellon at $8.1; on December 31, 1976, the Dow was at 1005, Mellon at $10.7.

This formula should still be valid in 1978 and 1979, but not for much longer thereafter, because of the unrelenting stream of dollars that every day flows into the pension funds that Mellon Bank administers. Already pension funds total just short of half of the bank's total trust assets, far outweighing the "rich men's monies" that the bank manages. The investment decisions that the bank makes for utilization of all of this money, together with the parallel decisions made by similarly oriented money managers at trust companies, mutual funds, and insurance companies across the country,

---

*There are still potential evils inherent in the situation. Four Mellon Bank directors sit on the boards of Allegheny-Ludlum and of Alcoa, three each on the H. J. Heinz and Koppers boards. Impressive chunks of the bank's trust assets are invested in the stock of these companies. When one of them needs financing and approaches Mellon Bank, will the parties be able to deal with each other as strangers? It seems at least possible (indeed, probably probable) that the stockholders, or the minority stockholders, of one or of the other are going to receive a lesser degree of fidelity than that to which they are entitled. The interlocks increase the possibilities of exchange of "inside information" for either personal or corporate advantage, to the disadvantage of outsiders, and increase the possibility that competitors who meet at board meetings will cease to compete. At the Mellon board meeting, a director from Colt sits with directors from Allegheny-Ludlum, who are competitors or potential competitors in some lines. Do they ever talk shop? In short, the more interlocks, the more opportunities will arise for men to act dishonorably.

have tremendous potential social and economic impact on the nation as a whole. That impact will be felt increasingly as pension funds mount.

To minimize the potential impact, Texas Senator Lloyd Bentsen, Patman's successor as the leading congressional watchdog on concentration of economic assets, proposes that no trust department be permitted to hold more than 10 per cent of the outstanding stock of any one company, and that no pension fund invest more than 5 per cent of its assets in any one corporation. These suggestions, if implemented, should be helpful in reducing the possibility of presumably undesirable consolidated control of the great American corporations, and would help to free money for investment in a wider range of enterprises. An analysis of the Mellon Bank's trust portfolio indicates that, at least as of June 30, 1975, in all but a few cases, Mellon Bank could meet the criteria that Bentsen would impose. The following discussion of the portfolio is based on the bank's trust department's "1975 Interim Report," which gives statistical data as of June 30, 1975. While the dollar amounts and percentages will be outdated by the time the reader reads this book, the data should suffice for illustrative purposes.

Most of the bank's trust money (63 per cent) is invested in common stocks, giving the bank notable influence on the affairs of a significant number of companies. Some of its individual pension fund portfolios may be overloaded with a particular security, but the largest element in its combined pension portfolios, IBM, represents only 2.8 per cent of total pension investments, so that all in all its pension trusts must be very well diversified. Only its holdings in Gulf exceed 5 per cent of its total trust assets; 5.5 per cent of its total trust assets are in Gulf. Virtually all of the Gulf stock, however, represents holdings of Mellon family trusts; whether that Gulf stock be held or sold will be determined by consideration of tax consequences and business outlook at any given moment. Regulating the operation of trust companies would not free any of that Gulf money for other investments.

The bank's combined portfolios give it a greater than 10 per cent interest in a small handful of corporations, but in most cases there is a reasonable historical explanation for the bank's "control" of these businesses, and in most cases the corporations would be "controlled," if not by the bank, then by the families that would control them anyway. The bank "owns" 25.24 per cent of Mellon National Corporation, almost all of it either Mellon or Frick family stock; 18.51 per cent of H. J. Heinz, virtually all of that in charitable or private trusts that are almost certainly the province of members of the Heinz family; and 10 per cent of Alcoa, the larger portion of that in charitable and private trusts probably connected with either the Mellon or Hunt families. In each of these cases, the degree of concentration of control does not depend upon the bank's role as overlord of many small contributions; the control would be almost equally centralized without the bank. It "owns" 10.51 per cent of Nalco Chemical, but its Nalco holdings are concentrated almost entirely in the portfolios of private foundations (not Mellon family foundations), and probably in the foundations of one family that would have controlled Nalco anyway. Only in the case of Armco Steel do the bank's holdings look surprisingly large and even there, there may be a reasonable explanation. With over 70,000 stockholders, the 12.47 per cent of Armco owned by Mellon Bank trusts probably gives the bank practical control of the nation's sixth largest steel producer. Virtually all of the bank's Armco holdings are concentrated in pension fund portfolios; its strong position in Armco seemingly arises from its centralization of many small contributions—the kind of situation upon which Senator Bentsen would look askance. One example arising out of combined investable assets of perhaps $8.5 billion (Dow as of this writing stands at 857) does not seem terribly alarming, at least not yet. Still, the pension monies come in every day, and every day bank officials are confronted with the recurring question How shall we invest them? How about Armco? Or Nalco? IBM is always safe.

The tendency of the combined Mellon Bank portfolios to move in tandem with the Dow gives a clue to the investment policies of its chief decision makers. To a large extent this remarkable quirk is explicable on the basis that much of the old Pittsburgh money that the bank manages in private trusts is in inherited portions of the great Pittsburgh industries—U.S. Steel, Gulf, Westinghouse, Heinz, Alcoa, Koppers, and PPG Industries (formerly known as Pittsburgh Plate Glass). These Pittsburgh industries are likely to move as a group not far out of tandem with the Dow. Otherwise, however, its major holdings are concentrated in blue chips (IBM is its largest holding in dollar amounts after Gulf) that are also likely to parallel the Dow. The bank's mid-1975 list of the eighty stocks in which it has its largest investments is composed almost entirely of companies as solid as Mellon Bank (well, nearly as solid). This indicates that the bank's policy setters take the same approach to investments as most institutional money managers: Play it safe and don't try to be a hero. Ride with the Dow. That is probably how it should be with those who invest other people's money, and furthermore no investment manager ever got sued for putting a client's money into IBM.

A side effect of this common approach is that it leads to the funneling of more and more money into the gigantic corporations which already have vast economic resources, and also tends to increase the market value of their securities unrealistically while leaving smaller business units relatively starved for equity financing necessary for growth. "Second-tier" companies are "red-lined" out of the money market. Working alone, Mellon Bank's several billions in trust assets do not have terrific impact on the total national picture, but when their approach is paralleled, as it is, by the professionals at trust departments, insurance companies, and other institutional investors across the nation, who already control untold billions and who as a group are given millions more in pension funds to invest every day, the implications for the country's social and economic future are significant and almost certainly undesirable.

Gulf remains the principal element in the Mellon family fortune. Today Gulf has 356,768 stockholders. More people own stock in Gulf than live in the State of Alaska. As of its 1976 annual report, its assets were valued at $13.5 billion, well in excess of the combined gross national products of all of the countries of Central America, and its revenues for that year of $18.5 billion dwarfed those of Illinois and exceeded the revenues of California or New York. Gulf directly employs 53,000 people, but the employment of many times that number is directly dependent on Gulf's well-being. In its 1977 tally of the biggest industrial corporations, *Fortune* ranked Gulf seventh largest in America, just ahead of IBM, and tenth largest in the world.

Over the years the Mellons have been steadily decreasing their percentage of ownership of Gulf. When Gulf first "went public" in 1943, its required filing with the S.E.C. indicated that R. K. owned 15.77 per cent of Gulf, Sarah 15.52 per cent, Paul 9.96 per cent, and Ailsa 9.84 per cent, with nine other individual Mellons, three Mellon foundations, and twenty-four different trusts established by various family members owning a combined 18.5 per cent, giving the family a total ownership of 69.6 per cent of Gulf. By the time of a 1956 S.E.C. filing the family had reduced its total interest to half that amount, 35 per cent, and by then no individual Mellon owned as much as the 10 per cent interest which would have required separate identification. Thereafter the filings show slow but steady decline in the family's interests. The last public filing in 1972 showed the family's combined holdings at 21 per cent. As of this writing the combined holdings of the family total about 18 per cent. Still, in a company where "majority" interest is scattered in the hands of hundreds of thousands of people with very small interests, an 18 per cent holding is more than enough to exercise working control, and from press reports it seems that the Mellons did so in grappling with the problem of cleaning up Gulf's post-Watergate picture.

When the Watergate investigations turned to the matter of campaign financing, the matter of Gulf's vast illegal political contributions began to come to light. First was the disclosure that Gulf had contributed $100,000 in cash to the Committee to Re-Elect the President, and made lesser contributions to Democratic possibles Henry M. Jackson and Wilbur Mills. After these initial revelations in 1973, Gulf's board was slow to react. It appointed a local law firm to make an internal investigation; but the inquiry was not very deep, and Mellon directors later claimed that they were not even advised of its results. Gulf also added to its board Sister Jane Scully, president of Carlow College (and its first woman director), who might either act as the company conscience or look as if she were acting as the company conscience. But the directors failed to ask the hard questions of who, when, where, how, how much, why, and why weren't we told; and as the questions went unasked, they remained unanswered. Among those sitting more or less silently were the three obvious "representatives" of the Mellon family: James Mellon Walton, Nathan Pearson, and Mellon Bank chairman James H. Higgins. The board perked up when the S.E.C. launched its own suit against Gulf arising out of its political contributions and demanded that Gulf undertake a full investigation of its own affairs. Thereafter, according to the *Wall Street Journal,* the Mellon family representatives played the leading roles in the effort to get to the bottom of the scandal and rectify the situation. A younger relative complained to the author that Walton had not been "on the job" when he should have been.

Gulf retained John J. McCloy, erstwhile public servant and high-powered New York lawyer who often acted as official spokesman for the oil industry, to undertake the investigation. McCloy's inquiry—completed and its results publicized in January 1976—established that in the period 1959 to 1973 a total of $12.3 million of Gulf's monies had been diverted for political contributions. Of that amount, $5.2 million went to United States politicians, virtually all of that in clear violation of federal statutes against corporate political giving. The rest went to foreign politicians, the biggest chunk of it being $4 million to the "Democratic Republic Party of South Korea" (Gulf board chairman Bob Dorsey claimed that South Korean "Democrats" veritably "shook him down" for the money). The status of the Korean grants under Korean law was uncertain. Most of the remainder went to politicians in Italy, Bolivia, Canada, and Sweden—gifts that were, for the most part, compatible with the laws of those countries.

McCloy's report established the history of the abuses going back to 1959, when Gulf began making illegal domestic political contributions at the inducement of its then chairman William K. Whiteford, who had decided that the company should beef up its political muscle. The early instructions were to the effect that the political efforts were to be handled as top secret, and, particularly, the Mellon family and its representatives were to be kept in the dark about them. And they were until the scandal broke.

After the board received McCloy's report, it closeted with him for two difficult days in which a wide range of moral questions, some close ones, had to be confronted. At the end the board asked for and received the resignations of Dorsey and several others. Walton, a close personal friend of Dorsey's, was credited in the press as having been the principal proponent of the hard line.

Gulf has made determined efforts to clean itself up and to keep itself clean. At two successive stockholders' meetings, in 1976 and 1977, Dorsey's successor Jerry McAfee has mentioned at the outset of his annual message the need "to restore our confidence in ourselves and our credibility with others," indicating that Gulf is not taking a bygones-be-bygones approach to the situation. It has established a reasonable "Code of Business Principles" and added as a regular committee of its board of directors a "Business Principles Committee" consisting of Walton, Dean George Kozmetsky of the University of Texas Business Schools, and, of course, Sister Jane.

The scandal established that in many ways businesses as large as nations can and do function as nations, with internal operations as covert and unknown even within the organization as the operations of a country's intelligence agencies are unknown to citizens and government officials alike. The activities of the Bahamas subsidiary through which Gulf was laundering most of its secret and illegal contributions were unknown to members of Gulf's board of directors, just as the nature of the South American adventures of the Central Intelligence Agency were unknown to the United States Congress. Even Dorsey was only marginally aware of the domestic contributions ("He perhaps chose to shut his eyes to what was going on," the McCloy report suggests), just as some American presidents may have preferred not to know precisely what the C.I.A. was up to. The auditors' painstaking annual studies of Gulf's accounts never turned up the $12.3 million misspent dollars, just as the money spent by the United States government supporting right-wing Chileans is nowhere to be found in the national budget.

Equally interesting (and also affording parallels with many public-sector examples) is consideration of what the money bought Gulf: little or nothing other than embarrassment, charges of attempts at corruption, and lawsuits. Richard Nixon, for example, took the money but never performed "for oil"

in the way that oil might have hoped. He permitted a reduction in the
oil-depletion allowance and he maintained a firm pro-Israeli position—
about the two most important issues to the world of the oil men. In effect,
he robbed Gulf. Other Gulf monies went to some of the most feckless people
on the American political scene. About the only "good" that the Gulf
crowd got out of the company's generosity at home was an occasional
invitation for its Washington lobbyist to a swank cocktail party. Perhaps
the money spent abroad accomplished more "good."

Like all of the other major oil companies and all of the nations of the
western world, Gulf has become almost totally dependent on foreign
sources of crude oil. In 1976 only 20 per cent of Gulf's crude came from
United States wells. For some reason oil seems to be found most often in
repugnant political climates; and Gulf, like the other six of the "Seven
Sisters" of world oil, has found itself involved in countries with repressive
social and political conditions, in the Middle East, Latin America, and
colonial Africa. Gulf's support has sometimes been important to the ability
of narrow oligarchies to hold on to their dominance in "their" countries,
most notably in the Portuguese colony of Angola. W. L. would have said
(and did) that one cannot operate a petroleum industry without petroleum.
Gulf—and the nations of the western world dependent on Gulf and her
sisters—probably had no easy alternative. In any event, the reliability of the
foreign sources has become increasingly shaky. For many years Kuwait has
been Gulf's principal source of crude. In 1975 the sheikdom nationalized
the Kuwait Oil Company, owned jointly by Gulf and British Petroleum,
paying the owners an unrealistically low "book value" for their property.
Though the Kuwait government has agreed to provide Gulf crude oil at a
favored price, the quantity has been limited. Gulf's purchases from Kuwait
in 1976 were a third of what Gulf was taking out of its "owned" wells there
in 1972. Important segments of informed opinion in Kuwait—today a
"minority" but tomorrow perhaps the dominant element in the country—
favor further limitations on production. Exactly the same story can be told
of Gulf's experiences in Venezuela. Things could be worse. The government
of Bolivia simply expropriated Gulf's holdings.

Gulf's troubles seem to have just started in Angola. In an effort to lessen
its dependence on Middle East oil, Gulf spent fortunes developing fields and
stations in the Portuguese colony in the 1960s. At the time, the political
situation there was so obviously explosive that investments of such magnitude might have seemed bad business, if not immoral on social conscience
bases. During the worst months of the Angolan war in 1976 Gulf closed
down its installation there to insure the safety of its personnel. It has since
reopened, but the Portuguese colonials with whom Gulf had worked so

comfortably have now been replaced by a government of African Fidelistas. As of this writing (September 1977) Gulf is operating its properties (for the moment still "its" properties) in Angola, negotiating with the new government over its future there, and attempting simultaneously to be a good Angolan citizen and a good American citizen. Its prognosis there cannot be viewed as bright. It is easy to say that Gulf has coming to it such beating as it may get; but before one takes undue satisfaction from Gulf's current or future difficulties it should be noted that because of its size and because of the parallel situations in which most of the major world oil companies either find themselves or will find themselves, what is good for Gulf is good for the United States.

Gulf's other foreign sources of crude, in order of importance, are Iran, Nigeria, Canada, Ecuador, Zaire, and Gabon. In none of them can one confidently predict long-run political stability.

Gulf is attempting to increase its domestic production. For years it saw an annual downslide in domestic production, which it halted in 1976. Recently Gulf has acquired important Louisiana offshore drilling rights and has acquired Kewanee Industries, a useful domestic producer. It is engaged in major exploration efforts in the United States and Canada. It has halted its work on development of the controversial nuclear breeder reactor, which provided hope for future cheap energy sources but which produced only staggering losses for Gulf. It continues to do research that it hopes will enable it to enter the nuclear energy market if and when OPEC prices foreign oil off the market, if such a thing is possible. It owns some valuable uranium-bearing properties, and also has sizable investments in good old coal lands.

On the domestic scene, Gulf is regularly threatened with congressional proposals to require the breakup of itself and the other large oil companies, either horizontally, vertically, or both.

Gulf is not one of the "comers" in the integrated oil industry, but then neither are any of the other giants of petroleum. Over the last fifteen years its earnings per share have increased from $1.64 in 1962 to a probable $4.50 for 1977, and dividends have increased steadily from 73 cents a share in 1962 to a current rate of $1.90 a year. Trading at 27⅛ a share as of September 1977, its annual earnings rate is a respectable 7 per cent; and with its unexcelled financial strength ($2.4 billion in cash or marketable securities as of July 1977), its dividend seems as secure as any. It is occasionally recommended by stock market handicappers. Conservationists insist that the world will sooner or later run out of oil. W. L. never believed it; he pushed the company to look farther and farther away and to drill deeper and deeper for sources. Gulf is still following his inspiration, and to a great extent the fate of the western world may hinge on the success of Gulf and her sisters in finding those sources.

Alcoa remains the second largest element in the Mellon family fortune. It has long ceased to have a monopoly of the American aluminum industry, though as a practical matter the introduction of hypothetical competition in the industry has made little difference to the American consumer and little difference to Alcoa. In 1937, at about the same time that the New Deal was harassing A. W. personally, it also instituted fresh anti-trust proceedings against A. W.'s "aluminum trust." Roosevelt's Secretary of the Treasury Henry Morgenthau noted in his diary that at a meeting of himself with Roosevelt and Attorney General Homer S. Cummings, Cummings had facetiously suggested to the President that if they were to institute the anti-trust case, "you might get another art gallery out of it!"

The suit was one of the longest in the history of American litigation. The basic issues of law were settled in favor of the government by a panel presided over by the distinguished jurist Learned Hand in 1945, but working out the details of the "remedy" took until 1951—fourteen years after the institution of the suit—and by then the situation in the aluminum industry had substantially changed from what it had been at the time that the suit had originally been brought. In the interim the government had inspired the creation of two "small" competitors to Alcoa, Kaiser Aluminum and Reynolds Metals. The anti-trust case did lead, however, to the complete separation of Alcoa and its important Canadian affiliate, Alcan Aluminium Ltd. The stockholders of the two had been almost completely overlapping. Among the final orders entered by the court in 1951 was one requiring that the major stockholders of Alcoa and Alcan divest themselves of ownership of either the one or of the other over a period of ten years. The Mellons opted to remain in Alcoa and began the process of selling their Alcan holdings, which they completed in 1960.

The Mellons have also divested themselves of a considerable portion of their holdings in the parent corporation. At one time A. W. and R. B. together owned 35.22 per cent of Alcoa. Prior to the first registration of the family's Alcoa holdings with the S.E.C., they could have sold some of their stock to other "insiders," but not to the general public. At the time of an S.E.C. registration in 1973 the New York *Times* estimated their then current holdings at about 30 per cent. At that time the family sold off 1,882,300 shares (since then Alcoa has split 3 for 2, so the shares sold represented 2,823,450 of today's shares). Assuming that the *Times* estimate was accurate, the sale reduced the family's ownership in Alcoa to about 21.4 per cent, which is about where it would stand today. Virtually all of the shares sold were sold by the R. B. branch of the family—by the trusts created by the General and by his sister, Sarah; by Sarah's daughter, Cordelia, and her Laurel Foundation; and by the Richard King Mellon Foundation. At this point the bulk of the family's interest in Alcoa is held by the A. W. branch of the family—by Paul; by the trusts established by Paul, Ailsa, and by A. W. himself; and by the foundations connected with A. W.'s branch of the family. The R. B. branch no longer has a representative on Alcoa's board. Currently the only "Mellon" representatives who sit on it are Pearson and John A. Mayer, retired chairman of the board of Mellon Bank.

While Alcoa no longer has a monopoly, it is still by far the world's largest integrated producer of aluminum and aluminum products. With total revenues of $2.9 billion in 1976 and about 43,300 employees in sixty-two plants scattered about the world, Alcoa is the dominant element in the aluminum oligopoly. It still owns many of its bauxite sources and relies on long-term agreements for most of the rest. It still owns about half of the facilities that generate its electricity, and it still sells most of its aluminum in the form of finished products. It still receives tariff protection, but usually at the modest rate of 4 cents a pound, about 7.5 per cent of the current domestic selling price of 53 cents a pound.

Other than operations directly and obviously related to the aluminum business, Alcoa's only important outside interest is in real estate developing. It owns and operates a number of important buildings and projects, most notably Century City Plaza in Los Angeles, with its architecturally inspiring Century Plaza Towers. Since the founding of Pittsburgh Reduction Company, scarcely a year has gone by without some new use for aluminum being discovered, and Alcoa's future continues to look bright. Early in 1977 the company entered into a new three-year contract with its unions that provided for expensive wage increases, but of course the company will not have to pay for them; it immediately increased the price for primary aluminum, thereby passing on the higher labor costs to the ultimate consumer. Its "competitors" were faced with and met similar union demands, and reacted with similar price increases.

Alcoa has also had its scandal, but the dollar amounts involved were minor when compared with the Gulf contributions, and no one paid much attention to the Alcoa case. Between 1962 and 1970 Alcoa made illegal domestic political contributions totaling $166,000 in fifteen states. Its method of keeping the contributions from appearing on its books was ingenious. It artificially increased the pay of selected employees in the total amount of $263,000, of which $166,000 was passed along to the political recipients, with the balance left for the funnels to compensate them for the increase in their personal tax liabilities. Alcoa also paid out $268,300 in bribes and quasi bribes to foreigners, and between 1970 and 1972 it made political contributions abroad totaling $80,000, which were disguised on the books of the subsidiaries involved. As in the case of Gulf, Alcoa's disclosure was inspired by the S.E.C. The company's filing with the regulatory body indicated that "some" unidentified corporation directors and officers had known what was going on, but that all of the "Alcoans" (as company employees are known) had proceeded "in good faith."

The other Mellon holdings are relatively insignificant in the total Mellon picture but still large in dollar amounts. The family's holdings in Koppers must still be substantial. Both Pearson, representing Paul's branch, and Andrew W. Mathieson, representing the General's branch of the family, sit on the Koppers board of directors and as members of both its executive committee and its audit committee, indicating the Mellons' substantial financial interest in the company. They would not otherwise devote the time and attention of these highest-ranking employees to its affairs. A perusal of the Koppers stockholders list, however, does not indicate the extent of their holdings. The annual report of the Andrew W. Mellon Foundation, for example, shows it to be a substantial stockholder in Koppers, but its name does not appear on the Koppers stockholders list. Most of the family's holdings in Koppers now stand in the names of anonymous and unidentifiable nominees. Only three "Mellon" names show up on the list: Paul, listed as owning in his own name 252,000 shares, a fraction of more than 1 per cent of the total stock outstanding; Richard Mellon Scaife, listed as owning in his own name 100 shares, or about 4/10,000 of 1 per cent of the total ownership; and a third Mellon, a Pittsburgh woman not a descendant of the Judge, whose 160 shares would seem to say that she has a 60 per cent greater influence in the company's affairs than does Scaife, the grandson of Richard Beatty Mellon. Her power is illusory only. In 1971 the New York *Times* estimated that actual Mellon family holdings in Koppers totaled 20 per cent, and it is unlikely that there have been significant changes in the family's Koppers position since then.

Koppers's principal business is still designing, building, and operating coke ovens, and refining and selling the by-products of the coking process. It has several other interests, many but not all of them related to the coking process. It is an important producer of timbers that have been pressure-treated with decay- and insect-repellent chemicals, which are used for railroad ties, telephone poles, and building-foundation piles. It also sells a broad line of other wooden building products and road-building materials.

It manufactures specialty equipment for the steel industry, parts for engines and motors, pollution control equipment, machines that make packagings, and machines that are used in mineral processing. In all it operates 241 plants.

Koppers has also had its scandal. Under pressure from the S.E.C., in 1976 an internal investigation headed by Pearson and Mathieson together with director Richard M. Cyert, president of Carnegie-Mellon University, disclosed that the company had given kickbacks to some of Koppers's foreign customers (a common if distasteful or unethical practice in international business) totalling $957,000 in the period 1970 to 1975. The tainted sales had totaled $13.4 million. Generally the kickbacks had been shown on Koppers's books as reductions in the amount of the sale, sometimes as a commission or selling expense, and in one case, as "exhibition expense." Often they had been paid in cash. The audit also disclosed instances of the company having issued phony invoices for more than the cost of the goods sold, with differences quietly "rebated" to either employees or principals of the recipient companies. It was discovered that during the 1972 presidential campaign one employee had worked intermittently for a total of forty-five days as an advance man for the Committee to Re-Elect the President, during which time his salary and benefits amounting to $2600 had been continued by the company with the tacit approval of three of the company's directors and top members of management. After the clean breast made by Gulf, Koppers's recitation seems somewhat less than candid. As to the knowledge of corporate higher-ups about the contribution to CREEP the Koppers "confession" says,

> It is possible that a member of Senior Management who is also a Director may have approved the action prior to its commencement, although he has no recollection of such approval; and another member of Senior Management was aware of the project. However, both persons state that they believed the employee had left the Company before joining the Committee. A third member of Senior Management who is also a Director became aware of the employee's activities just prior to their termination, and did not disapprove them. None of the above persons was aware that the continuation of the employee's compensation was a probable violation of Federal law.

In terms of the gross numbers, the Koppers disclosures were dwarfed by those in the Gulf scandal that exploded only shortly before, so that Koppers's revelations did not attract any particular attention or uproar. No one felt any compulsion to cleanse either the company or his own soul. On a percentage basis, however, the Koppers irregularities loomed much larger in Koppers's total picture than Gulf's $12.3 million had represented to that corporate behemoth.

For many years Koppers has been attempting to stimulate investor interest in it. Over the past twelve years it has had three 2-for-1 stock splits (one 1966 share now stands as eight 1977 shares) in an attempt to keep the price of the stock within the reach of the modest investor. In mid-1977 its investors relations department sent around a mailing touting the stock's impressive growth over the past ten years, demonstrating that Koppers stock had substantially outperformed the Dow Jones industrial average and other market indicators, and that it had run well ahead of inflation. (The charts showed that virtually all of the statistical success had come since 1975, representing two years of significant success following eight years of mediocre performance.) This may or may not indicate that the Mellons would like to draw others into the company, either to reduce their own interests in it or to create a more active and therefore more orderly and predictable market for Koppers stock. As of September 1977 the Value Line rating service gave a poor rating to the chemical industry, with which Value Line groups Koppers, and it rated Koppers itself as one of the least likely to show good performance in the year immediately ahead.

Carborundum, still an important producer of abrasives but with many seemingly unrelated lines as well, is in the process of ceasing to have an independent existence. In November of 1977 Kennecott Copper Corporation made a public offer to buy any and all shares in Carborundum that might be offered to it at $66 a share. Carborundum's directors voted unanimously to recommend that shareholders accept the Kennecott offer, and by the end of 1977 Kennecott had acquired majority ownership of Carborundum.

At the time of the Kennecott offer, the Mellon family still owned a 20 per cent interest in Carborundum, down from the 70 per cent interest that it owned when it first began selling off its shares in the company in 1953.

Kennecott has announced its intention ultimately to acquire ownership of 100 per cent of Carborundum's stock, and seems virtually certain to succeed. The favorable attitude toward merger held by two of Carborundum's directors, the ubiquitous Pearson and Thomas Beddall, front man in Paul's Washington office, would indicate that such interests in Carborundum as the Mellon family have not already sold to Kennecott, will be transfered to it either by sale or by exchange of stock in the immediate future.

Other enterprises have joined the historic Mellon businesses to become large elements of the family portfolios. In 1946 the General merged Mellon

Securities, an underwriting operation owned principally by the heirs of R. B., into First Boston, Inc., then and now an important underwriting and brokerage concern, for a 20 per cent interest in First Boston. His and Sarah's heirs have apparently little diluted the family's 20 per cent interest. Luther G. Holbrook, Mathieson's associate at the offices of the General's heirs, represents the family on the First Boston board.

At the same time that the General disengaged the family from underwriting, he got it out of insurance by merging Mellon Indemnity Company into General Reinsurance, again for a 20 per cent interest, still owned by his and Sarah's branches of the family. General Reinsurance and its subsidiaries rank thirtieth in volume as writers of fire and casualty insurance, and as the largest American "reinsurer," which insures risks already insured by other companies. At the time of this writing, stock in General Reinsurance could be bought at $177 a share. In 1977 it tripled its usual dividend to a rate of $1.20 per year, giving it a yield of something less than 1 per cent. It is a favorite with institutional money managers, but still has some way to go before it becomes attractive to most smaller investors. Both Holbrook and Mathieson sit on its board, and Mathieson sits on the boards of several of its more important subsidiaries.

Mathieson's presence on the board of directors of Hana Ranch, Inc., indicates that the General's side of the family has substantial interest in that enterprise. Hana is not a publicly traded corporation, and therefore its financial data is not public.

Nathan Pearson sits on the boards of CertainTeed Corporation, a leading manufacturer of building materials; Ampex, the manufacturer of top-of-the-line video and audio equipment; and Hanna Mining, an iron-mining enterprise which is also the only domestic producer of nickel. Pearson's presence on their boards means that Paul owns large parts of them, but less than the 10 per cent ownership in any one of them that would require the corporation to identify him as a principal owner in S.E.C. filings.

In sum, the family's combined portfolio is still topheavy in Gulf, Alcoa, and Mellon National, but to the extent that income tax consequences permit, they are making efforts to diversify. Probably the greater portion of the family's money is scattered among several dozen corporations in each of which they own insignificant portions.

Since the days of A. W. (and probably even then) the Mellon influence in politics has been slight, the Mellons themselves more givers than receivers. Over the years they have given to candidates whose positions were "right," regardless of how tenuous their interests might otherwise have been. In 1942, for example, the Mellons contributed a total of $9000 to re-elect a South Dakota Republican senator whose only distinction was that he had led the fight against ratification of the appointment of a progressive as rural electrification administrator, a position in which Alcoa took more than passing interest.

The General was the great political organizer for the family, and an important man in funding the state and county Republican Party. He was one of the few important regular contributors to the national Republican Party to increase his customary contribution in the year that Barry Goldwater sought the presidency. His alliance with Democratic Mayor Lawrence was about his only deviation from the Republican party line, and even as to that, it seems certain that he never made a financial contribution to the mayor's campaign chests. In 1962 he was mentioned as a possible "compromise candidate" for the Republican gubernatorial nomination when the party looked to be heading for a major battle for the nod. Nothing came of it.

His cousin Paul has never taken any real interest in the electoral process. He is a nominal Republican and probably a conservative one (he is close to former Texas governor John Connally), but the size of his contributions to the Republican Party reflects minimal enthusiasm.

Today the General's nephew Richard M. Scaife is the only Mellon who seems to take much interest in politics as such. Dickie Scaife was born in 1932, the only son of Alan and Sarah Mellon Scaife. Apparently not much of a scholar, he entered and dropped out of Yale, upon whose board his father sat. He then worked for a while on a Scaife Company project at the Mellon Institute, and ended up graduating from the University of Pittsburgh, whose board Alan chaired, at the age of twenty-five in 1957. The Pitt classbook, *The Owl,* lists no extracurricular involvements for him. He worked for a while at Gulf in the early 1960s. Late in 1969 he purchased the Greensburg, Pennsylvania, *Tribune-Review,* a small daily newspaper published at the Westmoreland County Seat, and since then he has been its "working" chief.

At the time that he bought the paper, Scaife stated that he regarded its editorial policy as "middle of the road to left," and that he expected to change that "but not overnight." As disgruntled former employees later outlined the transition to George Crile III for a 1975 *Washington Monthly* piece, Dickie began by encouraging reporters to "downplay 'liberals' like Hugh Scott." Then he ordered the destruction of all unflattering photos of Richard M. Nixon (only smiling pictures of the President were to be printed), and went on to insist that the wire-service stories about atrocities perpetrated by the pro-American military junta in Chile were not to be printed. According to Crile, the final blowup came when a young reporter,

Jude Dippold, covered a local political matter in a manner that offended one of Scaife's political cronies. The publisher ordered the night editor to fire Dippold, and when the editor balked he was fired himself. The staff went to Scaife to protest, and their spokesman, who had been one of Dickie's apologists, was told, "Your dismissal's accepted." Ten other reporters walked out in support of their brethren, and soon after the managing editor was presented with his own typed resignation.

Substantially the same account of the blowup was given two years earlier in the Philadelphia *Inquirer*, but the *Inquirer* attributed the crisis to a remark that Dippold had made when the resignation of Vice President Spiro Agnew had been announced, which had irritated Scaife: "One down, one to go." The night editor told the *Inquirer* that when he resisted firing Dippold, Dickie had "simply asked me when my resignation was effective." When visited by the staff, he had told their spokesman and those around him, "Your dismissal is accepted. Anybody else who feels the same way can leave too."

The slogan on the page-one masthead of the *Tribune-Review* proclaims it to be "Worthy of Western Pennsylvania," hinting at a parochialism that is both belied and confirmed by the paper itself. The issue of Sunday, March 16, 1976, is probably representative. It carried the popular national newspaper magazine *Family Weekly*, a section of color comics, a separate sports section, a TV guide, a "women's" section unashamedly proclaimed to be such, a hodgepodgey section titled "Sunday Life Styles," "front" sections, and the *T-R*'s own Sunday magazine, *Focus*. Its own editorials were largely explicative and noncontroversial. Its editorial pages also carried an eye-opening piece on Russian imperialism by the conservative British essayist Peregrin Worsthorne, no doubt syndicated though not credited as such, and a piece on the joys of capitalism by Michael Novak, syndicated by the Washington *Post*. But it also carried a glowing review of the operation of socialized medicine in Britain by Clancy Segal from the Los Angeles *Times* syndicate. All three were heavyweight pieces and together reflected both "right" and "left" political orientations.

Only in *Focus*, the *T-R*'s own weekly magazine (perhaps the soul of a newspaper), was there any down-home flavor. There was a color photo on its cover showing a Spencer Tracy–looking fellow seated in judge's robes, accompanied by a chubby lad with his arm wrapped around the jurist. Inside, the reader finds out who it is. "Judge Earl S. Kime, an Old Softy?" is the title of the article. In slightly smaller type the reader is introduced to his honor in the lead: "His reputation as a gruff, unapproachable jurist doesn't really tell the story." The article had a couple of boldface quotes from the judge: "Being an active member of the Loyal Order of the Moose has been gratifying"; and "I particularly like the work in the orphans' court." The judge's political slant is also revealed: "What is needed is to shut off the federal spigot . . . we've got to quit financing new projects and fight more taxes."

The *Tribune-Review* is probably the only newspaper of its size in the world that deems it a reasonable and necessary business expense to maintain its own DC-9.

Since the spring of 1977 Scaife has published another area publication, *Pittsburgher,* a slick and professional magazine that caters to Allegheny County's middle and upper-income readers. The magazine's financial difficulties led to a staff crisis there in November 1977. Scaife urged that the magazine's financial problems be confronted by institution of a weekly "advertising day" when the entire staff would spend the day making telephone advertising solicitations. Alternately, he suggested cuts in staff. Both ideas were resisted by *Pittsburgher* editor Pat Minarcin, who took the position that the magazine's costs were in line with expectations and that the young journal needed a period of growth before it could be expected to put in a brighter financial performance. In mid-November 1977 Minarcin, senior editor Harry Black, general manager Joseph S. Stelmack, and art director Martine Sheon all submitted their resignations. In capsulating the problems at *Pittsburgher* the Pittsburgh *Post-Gazette* reported that

> Minarcin said economic issues were only 20 per cent of the problems. He did not want to discuss the other ones. Other sources indicated there were strong personality clashes between the publisher and editor, that Scaife inserted himself into every facet of the magazine despite written and verbal agreements that he would not.

According to Jack Anderson, in the early 1970s Dickie tried to buy the Washington *Star,* the capital's "second" paper, but was unable to come to terms with its owners. In December, 1977, he acquired an interest in the Sacramento, California, *Union* and a chain of lesser northern California newspapers.

Scaife sits on two corporate boards of directors, that of Mellon National and the board of Air Tool Parts and Service Company, a small business (forty employees) province of his friend James L. Winokur, a right-wing-oriented leader of Pittsburgh's Jewish community, but he almost certainly follows the affairs of neither company. His philanthropies take a lot of his time. Off and on he has sat on various civic boards. In 1964, at the relatively young age of thirty-two, he was selected to become a member of the board of trustees of Carnegie Tech, soon to become Carnegie-Mellon, but he resigned in 1971, reportedly over campus demonstrations. He still retains some influence at Carnegie-Mellon, however. In 1973 C-M's president, Richard Cyert, confirmed that plans to use a C-M building in the Morewood-Shadyside area, not far from Scaife's own Shadyside house, as a rehabilitation center for women convicts were being scrapped after he had been approached by Scaife's representatives. He currently sits on the board of regents of Pepperdine College, a conservative California institution. Through someone's generosity, Pepperdine has come to own 10,000 shares of Mellon National, currently worth $500,000. Scaife lent his name for a while to the board of directors of Forum World Features, a London-based "news syndicate" run by the Central Intelligence Agency. Though he seems to have taken a greater interest in the Rolling Rock Races than the rest of his family, he does not personally go in for the more challenging aspects of riding, such as fox hunting. When he was nine, his horse News Girl shied at something, stumbled, and fell on him, knocking him unconscious, which required a period of hospitalization for him.

Scaife has taken an active interest in politics for years, generally backing conservative candidates like Barry Goldwater, Ronald Reagan, and Max Rafferty. He once described himself as a "Goldwater Republican," but after the demise of Goldwater as a national political figure his first allegiance was to Nixon. In 1968 Dickie was treasurer for the local Nixon fund-raising efforts, and spearheaded the total Mellon family contribution to the presidential contender of $215,000. Four years later Dickie outdid himself. He, all alone, contributed an even one million dollars to President Nixon's re-election drive. By then Nixon had already "let down" oil, and had shown himself as unfriendly to private charitable foundations.

The contributions were given quietly, 332 checks of $3000 each and two checks for $2000, adding up to an even million dollars, each made payable to a separate "dummy" Republican campaign committee, all delivered to Nixon's former law firm in New York. Many $3000 contributions made much better sense from a tax-planning point of view than one million-dollar check, because any gifts in excess of $3000 were liable for the federal gift tax as it then stood. Nelson Rockefeller's mother had contributed $1.43 million to Rockefeller's 1968 presidential effort, and had had to pay a bill for the gift tax of another $854,000. Dickie's mode of contributing saved all those taxes.

The matter of the contribution, of course, had to be kept secret at least until after the election, or the campaign issues might become clouded by irresponsible charges that the President was tainted with "oil money." The

Washington *Post* caught wind of it, though, and revealed Dickie's generosity only days before the election. Dickie's natural inclination would have been to decline comment about his spectacular gift, but if he refused comment the papers would print that, and it would make his contribution appear tainted. He was forced to respond to the journalists' queries. He told the Philadelphia *Inquirer,* "I did it because I want four more years of the leadership President Nixon can give us." He attributed the disclosure of his beneficence to "political espionage conducted by the McGovern forces." He described himself for the *Inquirer:* "I'm genial and I'm jovial . . . . I'm a golfer—I don't ride to the hounds or anything like that, though. No, I've never played golf with the president—or the vice president, either."

That year Dickie, his sister, Cordie (no doubt at his prompting), and the General's widow, gave a total of $187,500 to contenders in 108 different congressional races, backing 107 Republicans and one Independent. Roughly half of those that they supported were incumbent congressmen, the other half challengers. They supported candidates in virtually every state, and came up with seventy-six congressional winners plus a president. Or two presidents. One of the successful congressional candidates that they backed was Congressman Gerald R. Ford, Michigan Republican.

Scaife is still an important financial backer for the state and county party, but on a much diminished basis. He also had, and may still have, a flirtation with Pittsburgh's former Democratic Mayor Pete Flaherty. Flaherty is a clean, righteous fellow with no machine ties, generally "progressive" but with considerable appeal to conservatives arising out of his reputation as a tax cutter and anti-pornographer. The two have been on a first-name basis and speak well of each other. Flaherty appointed Scaife a member of the city's Zoo Committee. For a while it appeared that their relationship might develop into a latter-day parallel of that which had existed between the General and Mayor Lawrence.

The Mellons have not gotten much out of politics, certainly not directly. Such personal recognition as their involvement has brought them has not extended beyond occasional White House dinner invitations and appointments to relatively innocuous offices, such as that of the General's wife to be chairman of the Governor's Home Advisory Committee. There have been no "Mellon" ambassadors since A. W., though the General was surely as able as many other fat cats who have burnished their self-images in the diplomatic world. Adolph Schmidt, who married into the T. A. branch of the family, was appointed ambassador to Canada, and Walter Curley, who married into the J. R.-W. L. branch, was appointed ambassador to Ireland, both during the Nixon administration, but neither's entrée depended on family connections. Schmidt had worked with Nixon personally and was well known on his own in Republican foreign-policy discussion circles, while Curley was diplomatically well connected as chief of protocol for New York mayor John Lindsay. Their appointments did not constitute recognition for the family or for its contributions.

Even party recognition has largely eluded Scaife, who is about the only Mellon who ever cared much about party recognition. In 1964 he was named an alternate delegate to the Republican National Convention, a totally powerless, honorific acknowledgment generally reserved for loyal party workhorses just below the highest rank. In 1968 he was an alternate delegate to the state Republican convention, an even lesser nod, and that year intra-party maneuverings sidetracked him from a national convention seat even as an alternate. A good sport, he went anyway and hosted a fancy luncheon at which the Pennsylvania delegation might meet and mingle with the party's almost-certain presidential candidate: Nixon. Nobody came. The Pennsylvania delegation caucused on the morning of the luncheon; the caucus dragged on and on and on, and, well . . . In 1972 he was given what the Pittsburgh *Press* described in its write-up as one of the most "prestigious" Pennsylvania seats at the national convention as an at-large delegate. It may have been prestigious, but it was nothing more. The most nearly significant task confronting the Republican gathering that year was to consider whether to renominate an incumbent president who had no significant intra-party opposition. It was the year when state Republican hierarchies all across the nation recognized their Scaifes. Busy men did not attend. Scaife, however, is always the first one thought of when it comes to filling seats on party finance committees.

Any effect that the family might have had on public policy through direct influence on public officials has been unclear and imprecise. Indirectly, however, Mellons do influence things. To the extent that their influence might be pernicious, though, it is probably not because of any cynical effort on their part to "corrupt" the democratic process, but owing to the weaknesses inherent in mankind, and particularly men of the office-seeking genus: people tend to curry favor. It would be unreasonable and unfair to expect the Mellons to assist candidates who stand for policies repugnant to them, and it is easy and tempting for office holders or office seekers to rationalize the resolution of gray-area questions in favor of an outcome that will conform with the interests of an important contributor or potential contributor.

An example of how it works may (or may not) be found in the case of Westmoreland County Commissioner Robert Shirey. Westmoreland

County is one of Pennsylvania's larger counties. It lies just east of Allegheny County (the Pittsburgh county) and includes among its communities Ligonier, Greensburg, and New Kensington. In 1971 real estate in the county was revalued for tax purposes. Taxpayers who did not like the results banded together under the banner of the Association of Concerned Taxpayers (ACT) to point out that the newly revised valuations were markedly favorable to the vast Mellon holdings at Rolling Rock, thereby shifting tax burdens that should have fallen on the county's richest family to the county's less-rich families. ACT pointed to a number of curious statistics. Valuations on other property in Ligonier were increased 40 per cent on the total; those at Rolling Rock, they claimed, were increased only 2 per cent. ("Six per cent," officials responded.) Much of the Mellon acreage was valued at less than $100 an acre, and one 312-acre parcel was valued at sixty-four cents an acre. ("Mathematical error," the officials said, and revised the figure to bring it into line with other Mellon valuations.) A 178-acre piece bought by Scaife in the year of the re-evaluation for $590 an acre was assigned a full fair market value of $133 an acre. ACT convinced the Nader-affiliated Tax Reform Research Group of Washington of the justice of its cause, and it joined the local group in the activists' cause. Westmoreland County District Attorney John Scales was satisfied that something was amiss, and petitioned the county court to order a grand jury investigation of the reappraisal, but Judge David H. Weiss declined to authorize the inquest. The judge later explained that he thought the request was "just politics," and there may have been something to the judge's line of thinking, because at the time, ACT was fighting hard to elect its candidates, Dorothy Shope and Robert Shirey, to the Board of County Commissioners for Westmoreland County. Both won, giving ACT control of the three-man board. When the campaign contributions were published, it turned out that $9000 of Shirey's $12,000 campaign chest had been given by the Mellons, principally by Richard Scaife. ACT members were incredulous when they heard their champion, newly elected, speak about the

> great dangers involved in pushing the Mellons too hard on the assessment question. There was once a time when I could pick up a phone and get a grant for a library from the Mellon Foundation, but now it's dried up. . . . You've got to be careful, the family could leave the county.
>
> Now I know that there have been things carried out in this community that have been a little bit beneficial to them . . . but if there have been mistakes, they could have been corrected very quietly without all of the commotion. Maybe there are still some mistakes. I don't know. I'm not an assessor, but

I'm sure they'd like to have them corrected. . . . my goodness, a few tax dollars to the Mellons wouldn't mean anything.

He threatened to sue his running mate, Mrs. Shope, if the Mellons did leave the county, and he consistently voted against her and with the "establishment" member of the board on matters related to the reassessment.

Shirey was almost certainly telling the truth when he said that Scaife "has never once asked me to do a favor for him," and he may even have believed it himself when he insisted that he was still independent of "the interests." "I'm free. I really can do anything I want."

During the Mellon custody case (II), in evidence of her claim that she could not get justice in Pennsylvania, Karen told the press that she had once been present when a judge had called Pross for "directions" in how to decide a case. Even assuming for the sake of discussion that Karen told the truth, no further conclusion would be warranted than that the Judge who called was attempting to ingratiate himself with Pross or the Mellons. It does not follow that Pross made the ultimate decision in the case; it is more likely that the judge had already determined that the proper decision was one that would comport with what he anticipated Pross's reaction to be. By making the call the caller might pretend to be showing the ultimate in deference, all quite "harmlessly." Public decision makers in legislative, executive, administrative, and once in a great while even in the judicial arms of government, may sometimes be petty, but they are less often dishonest.

To the extent that public officials have given undue consideration to the Mellons and their interests, the Mellons are blameless; it is not incumbent on them to encourage public officials to lean over backwards to make determinations contrary to their interests. Scaife, specifically, holds straight and true to basic concepts of right and wrong where "dishonesty" is concerned. He is an honest and conventionally honorable man. When his childhood friend, Allegheny County district attorney Robert Duggan, was accused of corruption, he remained true to Duggan until the evidence against the D.A. became overwhelming. At that time he disassociated himself from Duggan. Just then Scaife's sister, Cordie, married the D.A. Pittsburgh sources close to Scaife were quoted in the Pittsburgh *Post-Gazette* as saying that "Dick was intensely upset" about the marriage; "he just went into orbit." His reaction to the Watergate scandal was similar. Early in the Watergate investigations he said that he was "appalled" by the revelations, but that he was reserving opinion on the President's role—a reasonable and decent position for any friend of the President to have taken. By May of 1974 it was impossible for any reasonable man to "reserve" opinion any longer. In what Scaife has described as a "composite" editorial, the *Tribune-Review* called for Congress to impeach Nixon, and for the President to step aside during the deliberations. The paper said that it was "sickened with Mr. Nixon's twisted sense of loyalty to those shadowy figures who have been close to him; this at the expense of a much higher form of loyalty we feel he owes to the good people of this country." There was something refreshing about the explanation for the editorial that Scaife gave to the New York *Times:* "My country comes first, my party comes second."

One of the greatest elements of Mellon power today, and certainly the most visible aspect of it, arises from the family's vast foundation assets. Most of the Mellons make charitable contributions privately and do not funnel all of their charity through foundations, so that it is not possible to judge their "generosity" by the size of their foundations.

Very few philanthropists—probably no Fords, Rockefellers, or Mellons —have been as personally generous as the simple parishioner who tithes himself weekly. According to the income tax returns of the foundations established by W. L.'s children, the Gulf stock that they gave to their foundations "cost" them ("cost" probably meaning the cost to W. L.) $1.70 a share. Assuming for the sake of illustration that one of them gave a share of Gulf stock to his foundation in 1965, when Gulf was trading at 28¼ (which is what it closed at on the day of this writing in 1977), then the donor was able to deduct $28.25 when computing his taxable income for stock that had cost the family $1.70. Assuming further that the particular Mellon was in the 70 per cent tax bracket, a reasonable assumption, then that $28.25 deduction meant $19.77 in his pocket for a donation of stock that had cost the family $1.70. If instead the philanthropist had sold the stock and paid the maximum 25 per cent capital gains tax, he would have ended up with $21.61 in the pocket. In short, many if not most of the charitable contributions made by living Mellons have cost them, substantially, nothing at all.

Charitable bequests made in the wills of deceased Mellons have been somewhat more expensive for the family. They have cost thirty cents on the dollar. Money left to a foundation escapes the federal death tax, whereas 70 per cent of the money left to the heir of a Mellon goes to Internal Revenue. When it goes to the foundation, at least one hundred cents on the dollar of it is still within family control, to be dispensed leisurely for favored causes.

If, however, one were to take a family's foundation activities as a hint of the degree of their basic generosity, then one might conclude with Waldemar Nielsen, author of the frequently cited study *The Big Foundations,* that the subjects of this book can be called "the middling Mellons." On the basis of their foundations' size and activity over the years, Nielsen says that the Mellons are less "generous" than the Rockefellers, but infinitely more so than the Du Ponts, a family that he characterizes as "niggling to deplorable" in the generosity department. As of January 1, 1977, the assorted Mellon foundations had handed out almost $800 million. At that time they still had, and were currently giving, as follows:*

	VALUE OF ASSETS AS OF JANUARY 1, 1977	CONTRIBUTIONS MADE IN 1976
Andrew W. Mellon Foundation	$ 664,274,741	$35,675,018
Richard King Mellon Foundation	263,177,769	12,669,261
Sarah Scaife Foundation	88,813,853	3,443,350
A. W. Mellon Educational and Charitable Trust	18,900,515	1,437,372
Allegheny Foundation (Donor: Richard M. Scaife)	12,402,642	2,842,964
Taconic Foundation (Donor: Audrey Bruce Currier)	11,982,169	491,605
Carthage Foundation (Donor: Richard M. Scaife)	5,133,338	1,750,560
Laurel Foundation (Donor: Cordelia Scaife May)	4,982,532	160,200
Sachem Fund (Donor: Timothy Mellon)	2,116,685	366,228
Rachel Mellon Walton Foundation	1,223,726	70,000
Cassandra Mellon Henderson Foundation	1,095,920	60,000
Margaret Mellon Hitchcock Foundation	1,015,062	44,000
Loyalhanna Foundation (Donor: Seward Prosser Mellon)	923,537	39,000
Rachelwood Foundation (Donor: Constance B. Mellon)	836,585	42,350
Landfall Foundation (Donor: Richard P. Mellon)	680,338	47,700
Matthew T. Mellon Foundation	300,223	80,000
Total	$1,077,859,635	$59,219,608

*Asset values for the Allegheny, Taconic, Carthage, Sachem, and Matthew T. Mellon Foundations are as of January 1, 1976; gifts stated for them were made during 1975.

The table omits a number of family-related philanthropies: Dr. Larry Mellon's Grant Foundation, which is a public charity as opposed to a private foundation; the Rachelwood Wildlife Research Preserve Fund, established by the General's heirs for the preserve and now almost exhausted; the modest foundation established by Peggy Hitchcock's son Alexander Mellon Laughlin; and, the slightly larger foundation established by Laughlin's paternal grandparents, who were Laughlins rather than Mellons.

Just over a billion dollars places the combined Mellon foundations far behind the nation's biggest, the Ford Foundation, whose $2.3 billion dwarfs all others, but only a hair behind the "second place" foundation, the Robert Wood Johnson Foundation.

A billion dollars for "good works" can have a major impact on the social direction that the nation takes. It can be spent to make the ballet an important art form in America or it can be spent to establish military training in American public high schools. It can be spent counseling returning Vietnam draft evaders or it can be spent furthering the educational efforts of anti-communist groups. It can be spent to develop "right-wing" schools like Pepperdine College, or left-oriented institutions like Howard University. A billion dollars spent in any particular direction can alter the national attitude and orientation. The Mellon foundations, however, are not coordinated. The Andrew W. Mellon Foundation's $1.4 million grant divided among ten dance companies in 1975 was important in keeping the dance alive, if not fiscally well, in America for a while longer; whether the dance flourishes in America may well depend upon Paul Mellon's whim. The generosity of Richard Mellon Scaife's Carthage and Allegheny foundations toward military training for teenagers, for anti-communist educational efforts, and for Pepperdine College, has been appreciated by those who appreciate such things. Howard University thinks more kindly of Audrey Bruce Currier's Taconic Foundation. Timothy Mellon's Sachem Fund has, in its small way, helped to ease the path home for the returning dissenters of the Vietnam era.

Various Mellon foundations occasionally cooperate to spearhead a common philanthropic venture (though less frequently than in the days when the General was living) or contribute to the same Pittsburgh area charities, but for the most part they go their own ways. There is virtually no overlapping among the officers and directors of the four largest Mellon family foundations. Paul Mellon sits on the boards of both the Andrew W. Mellon Foundation and the A. W. Mellon Educational and Charitable Trust, but the latter, compared to the former, is small to the point of insignificance. The General's son, Richard P. Mellon, sits on the boards of both the Richard King Mellon Foundation and the Sarah Scaife Foundation (as well as his own relatively minuscule Landfall Foundation), but Richard P., while sometimes personally imperious, is not generally a domineering sort. Otherwise the makeup of the most significant Mellon family foundations is mutually exclusive. Essentially each foundation has its own personality.

Biggest of them is the Andrew W. Mellon Foundation, formed as a consolidation of Ailsa's Avalon Foundation with Paul's Old Dominion and

Bollingen foundations in 1969. The Foundation Center's most recent tally ranks it as the seventh largest private foundation in America. Ailsa left virtually all of her half-billion estate to it, and it seems likely that Paul will follow her example. Until recently Paul could give his children and grandchildren untold millions, or millions told only to Internal Revenue, subject to the comparatively harmless gift tax rather than to the near-confiscatory 70 per cent death tax. Long ago he either gave them or should have given them whatever he intended for them to have, and they should not feel hurt when Paul's will is read. Assuming that he does leave all or virtually all to the foundation, it should easily slip into place as the second biggest foundation, right behind the Ford Foundation.

The list of the grants of the Andrew W. Mellon Foundation shows it to be involved in almost every aspect of modern philanthropy, with emphasis on preserving and fostering the humanities, cultural projects, conservation, and the environment. Its list of grants shows it to be well within the mainstream of enlightened American philanthropy. In *The Culture Barons* Faye Levine says that the foundation "can sound as liberal as the next fellow, putting a good bureaucratic face on it." She is critical of what she regards to be a less innovative approach to philanthropy in the arts than she feels the foundation should be taking. Occasionally the foundation funds in tandem with other major private foundations, or with the national endowments for the arts or humanities.

In 1971 Paul, emulating the Ford and Rockefeller foundations, which were already recruiting high-level academics to their top positions, brought Harvard president Nathan Pusey in to head the foundation. Pusey retired in 1975 and was succeeded by John E. Sawyer, former president of Williams College. Sitting with Paul on the foundation's board are Sawyer; Ailsa's friend Lauder Greenway; former Texas governor John Connally; William O. Baker, president of Bell Telephone Laboratories; John R. Stevenson, partner in the heavyweight law firm of Sullivan & Cromwell; and two others.

The foundation's portfolio is still weighted down with Mellon companies, and particularly Gulf. It owns some 5 per cent of Gulf Oil, an amount which, but for the other major blocks of Gulf owned by the Mellon family, would give it practical control of Gulf. As of January 1977 Gulf accounted for 44 per cent of the total value of the foundation's holdings. It also owns 4 per cent of Mellon National and large blocks of Alcoa, Koppers, Carborundum, and General Reinsurance. Otherwise its portfolio is diverse. As of January 1977 slightly over half of its holdings were in Mellon companies.

Its smaller relative, the A. W. Mellon Educational and Charitable Trust, founded by A. W. himself, is the grandfather of all Mellon foundations and the father of the National Gallery of Art. A. W., like John D. and Carnegie, disapproved of continuing large charitable trusts in perpetuity, and in 1946 the trustees of the E and C T (as it was known in the family) decided that they would spend the trust out of existence over the next fifteen years on Pittsburgh-oriented programs. In 1958, with the trust's assets depleted to about $21 million, they reversed direction and decided to keep it alive for the foreseeable future, limiting its size to about $20 million, where it still stands today. As Pittsburgh foundations go, it is dwarfed by several others, including both the Richard King Mellon Foundation and the Sarah Scaife Foundation. It now limits its benefactions to Pittsburgh area causes to promote The Arts (its annual report consistently capitalizes the "T" in "The Arts") and to education related to The Arts. Its board consists of Paul and Pittsburgh friends George Wyckoff, George Lockhart, Theodore L. Hazlett, and John Walker, the former director of the National Gallery, who is also a Pittsburgh native. Only about 14 per cent of its assets are still invested in Mellon companies.

The Foundation Center ranks the Richard King Mellon Foundation as the nation's thirteenth largest private foundation. Unlike the Andrew W. Mellon Foundation, whose board is now composed almost exclusively of outsiders, the trustees of the General's foundation are all family people: his widow, Mrs. Burrell ("chairman," as she is identified); Richard P. (president); Pross; their finance men Holbrook and Mathieson; and two other family employees. They are, however, assisted by a professional staff that channels their money into respectable if generally conventional and unimaginative channels. In 1976, 83 per cent of their grants went to charities oriented to Pittsburgh or western Pennsylvania. In their list of grants for 1974, studied by the author, not one of their many benefactions would be likely to offend anyone of whatever political slant, and an occasional grant appeared to the author to be decidedly laudatory, such as the foundation's $100,000 support for "Reading Is FUNdamental," a project to distribute free books in "deprived" neighborhoods, and to sell books to minority elementary school students at ten cents a copy. The foundation's report has a picture of the Reading Is FUNdamental bookmobile making a stop in a black neighborhood, with a caption pointing out that "Ownership of a book in a home unable to afford books can be the catalyst that begins a lifetime enhanced by reading skills." Other grants made in 1974 that struck the author as other than pedestrian included $21,000 for the Pittsburgh public schools earmarked for recruitment of "black teachers" and grants for inner-city restoration programs directed by the Pittsburgh History and Landmarks Foundation. Mostly, however, its grants were to very nice routine charities that ought to be supported by someone.

The Richard King Mellon Foundation's portfolio is still dominated by Mellon companies. As of January 1, 1977, it owned about 9 per cent of General Reinsurance, representing one-third of the foundation's total assets. As General Reinsurance pays practically no dividend, it is not a respectable holding for a foundation ostensibly concerned with generating charitable funds. Gulf made up another 19.5 per cent of the foundation's assets, and Alcoa and additional 5.5 per cent.

The Sarah Scaife Foundation, though of a much smaller size than the foundation established by Sarah's brother, the General, seems to take a more innovative approach to public giving. Its 1974 list of grants shows that its principal project in recent years was the establishment of the Sarah Scaife Gallery, but among its other contributions in 1974 were grants to bring black kids to see the Pittsburgh ballet, monies for agricultural education for adult American Indians, funding for counseling and job-placement services for women convicts, help to Planned Parenthood, to a non-profit group engaged in making high-risk mortgage loans, to a treatment center for "bad" boys, money to fund a study of potential public transportation facilities for Westmoreland County, and a grant to an organization to buy a special van to provide transportation for people confined to wheelchairs. The foundation made no grants to unabashedly right-wing causes. Its board, less inbred than that of the Richard King Mellon Foundation, consists of Richard M. Scaife, chairman; his friend James Winokur; Richard P. Mellon; James Bovard, the longtime head of Carnegie Institute; Francis Cheever, vice chancellor of the University of Pittsburgh; General Matthew B. Ridgway; a partner from Reed, Smith, Shaw, and McClay; and Charles Ford, an officer of the foundation. Its portfolio is top heavy in Mellon companies. Gulf and First Boston holdings amount to 60 per cent of the foundation's total assets. Except for the composition of its portfolio, by the usual tests of a foundation's respectability the Sarah Scaife Foundation ranks well.

Dickie's own foundations—Allegheny Foundation and the smaller Carthage Foundation—had total assets as of January 1, 1976, of $17,535,980, making Dickie the most "generous" (at least publicly so) of the Judge's great-grandchildren. Not quite half of their combined assets is invested, in order of importance, in Mellon National (a little over 1 per cent of total ownership in the bank), Gulf, Koppers, and First Boston. His grants tend to be more traditional than those of his mother's foundation. The ones that have the right-wing tinge to them, such as $200,000 in 1975 for the National

Strategy Information Center and $125,000 for Pepperdine College, are channeled through his Carthage Foundation. In 1969 Carthage was the principal support for a conference on communist strategies. Its grant for the funding of R.O.T.C. programs in high schools dates from 1973.

Dickie's sister Cordie's foundation, Laurel Foundation, is much smaller in size, which does not mean that Cordie is less generous, but only that she permits less of her charitable giving to pass before the public eye. Most of Laurel's recipient charities have a strong humanistic appeal to them. For reasons discussed further along, the author regards Cordie as the most generous of all Mellons.

A very different matter is the Taconic Foundation established by Ailsa's daughter, Audrey Bruce Currier. Audrey fell under the sway of her husband, Stephen Currier, a man whose background would give no clue to the making of a civil rights radical, but Currier became one and took Audrey along with him. Their Taconic Foundation, with assets as of January 1976 totaling $12 million, not a penny of it in Mellon companies, devotes itself principally to furthering "equal opportunity." The Curriers, discussed in greater detail below, died before the dimensions of "equal opportunity" were expanded beyond racial perimeters, and most of Taconic's grants over the years have been to black-related causes. Those that have not been, have otherwise been to causes on the cutting edge of social problems. Taconic gives no grants to building and endowment programs, to higher education, health, or to programs of a purely cultural nature. The Curriers predeceased Ailsa, who might have left some of her money to Taconic Foundation, but she didn't.

Audrey's Cousin Timothy, Paul's son, has established his Sachem Fund with similar orientation, but devoid of the civil rights preoccupation. Timmy's Sachem Fund looks to be relatively modest with its mere $2 million in assets (14 per cent in Gulf), but Timmy throws in money when he sees a deserving project. The introduction to Sachem's first cumulative report says that Sachem's "primary objective is to help create sufficient impetus, through the support of innovative planning and programming, to effect changes in basic institutional response patterns, and by so doing to facilitate the development of a climate more receptive to change within society." One more reading of the sentence brings home that Sachem seeks to change "the system"—the system of Judge Thomas Mellon, A. W. Mellon, General Richard King Mellon, and yes even of Paul Mellon. Again from its first cumulative report, Sachem does not view itself in "the role of philanthropist, but rather that of an active participant in the change process—and in some instances, as antagonist." Among Sachem's many enlightened grants over the years have been contributions in support of patients' rights, prisoners' rights, Puerto Rican rights, elderly rights, adolescents' rights, Indian rights, and women's rights; but it has also given money to an occasional old-fashioned cause like the N.A.A.C.P. Legal Defense Fund (black rights). Its board consists, essentially, of Timmy and his wife, Susan. A third director, Nathan Pearson, can be assumed to support Timmy's decisions even if it kills him, as it sometimes may. Until recently Sachem had an executive director, Ernest L. Osborne, but Osborne left early in 1977 to accept a federal position, and Timmy himself is now the foundation's chief cook and bottle washer.

Sachem's second cumulative report, released in 1977, announced that thenceforth Sachem would not accept grant proposals but would be initiating projects itself in the areas of transportation and land-use management. Timmy, who studied city planning at Yale, is greatly interested in problems of developing and promoting mass transportation, and in ways of alleviating highway congestion. Paul is a more philosophical sort than Ailsa was; perhaps he will leave a couple of peppercorns to Sachem.

The foundations associated with the four children of the General—Landfall (Richard P.), Rachelwood (Connie B.), Loyalhanna (Pross), and the Cassandra Mellon Henderson Foundation—share roughly the same administrative personnel and substantially similar portfolios. None of them own any stock in any of the Mellon companies. Their combined assets as of January 1, 1977, totaled a mere $3.5 million. The choice of charities for each varies according to the whims of the separate donors. All except the Cassandra Mellon Henderson Foundation seem to be contributing to the kinds of charities that private charitable foundations should be supporting. In 1975, the year for which the author studied their contributions, the Henderson Foundation made all of its grants to the college that Cassandra's husband attended and to four private schools, all apparently institutions with which Cassandra's immediate family had personal ties. The other three foundations were contributing to conservation efforts, civic and cultural projects and social services, and made educational grants other than for the operating expenses of their own schools.

The three private foundations associated with the children of W. L., with total assets of $2.5 million, are similarly personal in their orientations. They give to rather routine charities. Over the years each of them has made occasional but irregular contributions to their brother Dr. Larry Mellon's hospital in Haiti. All are disproportionately invested in Gulf, but given their relatively small size, it does not much matter.

Insofar as philanthropy is concerned, it is still true or nearly true that

"Nothing moves in Pittsburgh without the Mellons." In 1970 the Pittsburgh *Post-Gazette* estimated that 43 per cent of the total foundation monies in the greater-Pittsburgh area (which excludes the Andrew W. Mellon Foundation, a New York corporation) were in Mellon family foundations. Given the fact that the Richard King Mellon Foundation, the Sarah Scaife Foundation, and the A. W. Mellon Educational and Charitable Trust concentrate their benefactions on greater-Pittsburgh causes, and that the Andrew W. Mellon Foundation occasionally helps out as well, the significance of Mellon family foundations in Pittsburgh philanthropy looms even larger than the 43 per cent figure would indicate.

The concentration of so much of the family benefactions in western Pennsylvania is largely attributable to the General's influence, but the Mellons have been spectacular donors in Pittsburgh at least since 1921. That year A. W. and R. B. presented the University of Pittsburgh with a fourteen-acre chunk of the Frick estate, then valued at $2.5 million, for the new skyscraper university envisioned by Chancellor Bowman, formally known as the "Cathedral of Learning," informally as "Bowman's Erection." Since then the family philanthropies have been essential to the well-being of the city and its major institutions. W. L. spent himself out (well, not quite) by building and endowing a school of industrial management for Carnegie Tech. In 1948 the A. W. Mellon Educational and Charitable Trust bought the University of Pittsburgh a $13.6 million Graduate School of Public Health. In 1963 Paul Mellon, who keeps out of Pittsburgh whenever possible, personally gave the Pittsburgh Symphony half a million dollars, in addition to the half-million given by the A. W. Mellon E and C T, to help establish the symphony's endowment. In 1974 the Richard King Mellon Foundation earmarked $10 million for the Carnegie Institute. The Sarah Scaife Gallery has been discussed above. Family grants to the city's medical facilities are commemorated in the names of such structures as the attractive contemporary Mellon Pavilion at West Penn Hospital, and the Alan Scaife Building at the University of Pittsburgh Medical School. The participation of the combined Mellon foundations was essential to the success of the renaissance. If one wants to do something nice in Pittsburgh, the best place to start is on the thirty-ninth floor.

The Mellon foundations have been similarly vital in Westmoreland County philanthropy and particularly in brick-and-mortar projects, conservation, and environmental protection efforts in and around Ligonier.

The National Gallery has been dependent on the family ever since A. W. paid for its opening. Many other donors have given fabulous collections to it, but whenever the gallery has wanted to buy something for cash money it has usually looked to the Mellons singularly or collectively. During her lifetime Ailsa wrote many of the gallery's larger checks, as well as leaving it the more valuable items of her own collections. When the directors felt they had pestered Ailsa enough in any given season, they might look elsewhere. W. L. would occasionally help out, and he bought the gallery one of its finest American works, Winslow Homer's seascape "Breezing Up," featured on a United States commemorative postage stamp. One of its most engrossing modern canvases, Marsden Hartley's expressionist painting "Mount Katahdin" (1942), bears a tag identifying it as a gift of Mrs. Mellon Byers, the General's daughter Connie. A major addition to the gallery, under construction as of this writing, is being paid for principally by the Andrew W. Mellon Foundation, at a cost that will run into many millions.

None of the Mellon foundations were guilty of the kind of self-serving abuses that brought about the modest degree of taxation and the restrictions on foundation financial doings that were instituted with the Tax Reform Act of 1969. By the usual tests by which a foundation's "good citizenship" is measured, the Mellon foundations pass muster, if only marginally. Nielsen rated the civic strengths and weaknesses of the nation's biggest foundations in 1972 and found all of the three largest Mellon foundations weak on "significant innovative programming," on "degree of independence of donor family and company," and on "degree of board diversification." He passed Andrew W. but flunked Richard King and Sarah in "significant investment diversification" and passed the General but flunked Andy and Sarah for "development of defined programming." For the most part his characterizations would still be accurate today.

All of the Mellon foundations have been "conduit" foundations, as opposed to guiding foundations, but things could be worse. They could be unabashedly self-serving foundations, and none of them are. Being uninnovative may not be good, but then, being innovative may not be good either. "Conservative" readers may think it just as well that Audrey Bruce Currier's "liberal" Taconic Foundation is not more "innovative." "Liberal" readers can sleep securely knowing that Richard Mellon Scaife's Carthage Foundation is not likely to ever become innovative.

The main shortcomings of the Mellon foundations today would probably be in the areas of "investment diversification" and "independence of donor family and company." R. K.'s immediate family dominates the board of the Richard King Mellon Foundation, and all of the larger Mellon foundations are heavily overinvested in the Mellon companies. Eleven of the sixteen family foundations own stock in Gulf, totaling 5.6 per cent of Gulf's ownership. Gulf represents 40 per cent of the total assets of all sixteen foundations. Three Mellon foundations own almost 13 per cent of First Boston (mostly non-voting stock), three own a little more than 10 per cent of General Reinsurance, three own a little more than 5.3 per cent of Mellon National. Traditionally this kind of portfolio lineup would have been held to signify a family effort to preserve family control of its corporations against the ravages of death taxes. Such considerations may explain to some extent how the Mellon foundations came to own such large percentages of the Mellon businesses. Since the death of the General, however, no one in the family has had much interest in control. The continuance of the situation is probably more nearly explicable in terms of the practicalities of liquidation. It would be difficult for the Mellons to dispose of any significant block of Gulf without having adverse effect on the market price of Gulf stock, an effect probably more serious to Gulf's "little" stockholders than to the Mellons themselves. Little by little over the years they are reducing their foundations' holdings in the Mellon companies.

The Mellon foundations tend to show interest in the same investments and to acquire stock in the same companies. The big-three Mellon foundations now own a total of 3.8 per cent of Hanna Mining, and many of the foundations are heavily interested in Tampax, a corporation that historically has maintained a healthy flow of dividends. This situation indicates that they are all influenced by the same investment analysts at Mellon Bank, rather than an effort on their part to use tax-sheltered foundation money to take control of yet another corporation.

The cost of philanthropy to the United States Treasury is high indeed. All totaled, the sixteen Mellon foundations owned as of January 1, 1976, 12,602,326 shares of Gulf Oil. As the various Mellons gave those shares of stock to their foundations over the years they either avoided substantial death taxes or took income tax deductions, and equally important, they insulated the dividends from those shares from future income taxes. Until 1969 dividends from foundation-owned stocks were exempted from federal income taxes because they were devoted to "charitable purposes" which in the view of legislative policy makers ought to be encouraged. Since then foundations have paid an "excise tax," as it is called, of 4 per cent of their income from dividends and interest, but that rate is probably lower than the rate that the reader is currently paying the Internal Revenue Service. To the extent that those 12,602,326 shares of Gulf are insulated from taxes, to the extent that the combined billion-dollar Mellon foundation portfolios are insulated from taxes, to the extent that the untold billions of private foundation portfolios across the country are insulated from taxes, the tax burden of everyone else is increased correspondingly. Those Gulf dividends (or

Ford dividends in the case of the Ford Foundation, or Standard Oil dividends in the case of the Rockefeller Foundation) are devoted to charities or to civic endeavors, but they are endeavors favored by the Mellons, or by the trustees of the Ford or Rockefeller foundations. They are projects with which the reader may not be in sympathy. Does the reader approve of the tax-favored work of Audrey Bruce Currier's Taconic Foundation, or does the reader approve, instead, of the tax-favored work of Richard Mellon Scaife's Carthage Foundation. Many readers are likely to feel that the work of either the one or of the other should not be receiving tax favors. Both are.

Wright Patman got apoplectic about the situation, and in the 1960s a subcommittee of his House Banking and Commerce Committee undertook an eight-part series of studies, each titled *Tax-Exempt Foundations and Charitable Trusts: Their Impact on Our Economy*. The fourth installment of it, published in 1966, highlighted the matter of use of foundation money, curiously (or perhaps not so curiously) by reference to Paul's Bollingen Foundation, since absorbed into the Andrew W. Mellon Foundation:

> A good case can be made for the desirability of resisting philistinism through support of the arts and of esoteric research, but when such activities are carried out not only wholesale but with explosive abandon—and all, ultimately, forcing the American taxpayer to take part in the subsidy—the question naturally arises: cannot extremely wealthy corporations and extremely wealthy families afford to fight philistinism on their own, as a taxable effort, without dipping into the pocket of the already hard-pressed taxpayers? Or at least, cannot a stiffer judgment be made of such expenditures. For example, the Bollingen Foundation of New York City, which is supported with tax-free Andrew Mellon money, subsidizes research into such matters as "the works of Hugo von Hofmannsthal," and "the phenomenology of the Iranian religious consciousness," and "the origin and significance of the decorative types of medieval tombstones in Bosnia and Herzegovina"—all beneficial, perhaps, in some way; but on the other hand, perhaps very little of it is beneficial. In either event the typical American taxpayer, perhaps not quite so excited about the prospect of helping to support a revival of Hofmannsthalship, may soon begin to wonder if a better and more precise reckoning might not be demanded by the Treasury of the billions of dollars that flow out of the ordinary channels of taxation and into exotic "scholarship" each decade, while basic education shrivels for lack of money.

Patman himself covered much the same ground, but more colorfully, in a speech to Congress:

Congress certainly cannot complain if the entire Mellon banking family assembles in one of their Pittsburgh mansions each evening for a roundtable discussion of the decorative types of medieval tombstones in Bosnia and Herzegovina. If the Mellons are more interested in medieval tombstones than in Pittsburgh poverty and care to spend their money studying twelfth- and thirteenth-century church construction, that is the Mellons' affairs. However, there is nothing upon either Congress or the American citizens to give the Mellons tax-free dollars to finance their exotic interests.

In the 1960s, when private charitable foundations were growing in number, in individual size, and in total size, the situation began to parallel in a minor way the growth of the church in the Middle Ages: economic assets increasingly removed from the tax base for charitable purposes, thereby increasing the tax burdens of everyone else, while the economy at large was becoming increasingly concentrated in fewer and fewer hands. Patman led the crusade that led to the imposition in 1969 of the 4 per cent tax on foundation income, and statutory requirements that foundations pay out at least 6 per cent of the fair market value of their assets each year, and other requirements limiting the percentage of new interest that any single foundation might take in any particular corporation. Patman was dissatisfied that Congress had not gone far enough.

The contributions of the Mellon foundations are visible all around Pittsburgh and in Washington, and invisible but nonetheless real throughout the nation. So too are the contributions of Andrew Carnegie visible and felt in many sections of the United States and the British Isles, contributions made by the steel baron long before institution of the income tax or of federal death taxes. It may be that the motivation for Carnegie's philanthropy was no purer than the motivation for Howard Hughes's philanthropy, but at least Carnegie's philanthropy did not have the result of shifting tax burdens to poorer taxpayers. It seems reasonable to conclude that there would be less philanthropy and less charitable giving if the tax encouragements to philanthropy and charity were to be removed, but philanthropy would not disappear.

Still it may be that private foundations should be encouraged to some extent by favorable tax laws. They do make for a richer and more varied life in America, and do function as one of those factors in pluralistic America that help to maintain the United States as a free society. The nation is both richer and freer by having both Taconic and Carthage.

Because the efforts of the federally funded National Endowment for the Arts and National Endowment for the Humanities must satisfy the demands of a majority speaking through their congressmen, they are not likely to support, and have not significantly supported, either the cultural niceties of the past or the emerging artistic and scholastic movements of the future. President Jimmy Carter's appointment in 1977 of politico-cleric Joseph Duffey to be head of the National Endowment for the Humanities has been generally taken to signify an end to "elitist" tendencies within that publicly funded "foundation." That should be fine, so long as there are others—such as private foundations—in a position to support less "popular," less readily popularized aspects of the fine and the liberal arts. It may well be that what the United States needs at this juncture in its cultural history is not so much more "popular" arts and scholarship, but rather a revival of Hofmannsthal-ship, or an increased interest in medieval Bosnian-Herzegovinian tomb-stones. If so, then the world will come to regret that the Andrew W. Mellon Foundation, successor to Bollingen, no longer funds esoteric scholarship, and currently spends much of its monies on the kinds of projects to which the National Endowments gravitate.

The Mellons of today are a varied group, but when the large collection of them assembled for a 1970 reunion at Rolling Rock, the elders and the youngers made a sharp contrast. The elders clustered together to relive days in a world when fabulous wealth insured every conceivable convenience, service and luxury, and especially insured insulation from the concerns and worries of ordinary men and women, and from responsibility for those concerns and worries.

Meanwhile, some of the younger Mellons clustered too, to share a "toke" of the good marijuana freshly imported by one of the college-age cousins, and to talk about responsibilities. Many of the younger Mellons are neither insulated nor unconcerned, and feel that they should carry the responsibili-ties, as well as enjoy the benefits, of their wealth. The complex arrangements dictated by tax considerations and worked out by advisors to parents and grandparents have deprived most of the younger Mellons of control of both the principal and of the direction of their fortunes. In large measure, control of the wealth that the Judge's sons created has passed from his heirs to a cadre of anonymous professionals—from people such as A. W. or the General, presumably accountable (at least to themselves) because they were flesh-and-blood, to a mentality, invisible and unaccountable.

There is some resentment among younger Mellons that they have not had sufficient input into the way that the power that accompanies their wealth has been exercised by their money managers, and considerable feeling that they should attempt to take a more active—and more liberal—role in the operation of the Mellon enterprises. Two have playfully maintained a file of news clips detailing "Gulf Oil Atrocities." One who regards the older generation as having been "irresponsible" says that he wants the younger generation to "take responsibility so that our children won't have to clean up the bad karma that has been left behind." Most of the young Mellons —both "responsible" young Mellons and "old-guard" youths—accept Dr. Mellon of Haiti as the finest of their elders. (Paul Mellon, oddly, also rates very highly—"he's a very conscious man," says one of the more "left-oriented" relatives.)

To a greater or lesser extent, Mellons from the A. W., R. B., and W. L. lines of the family have had to adjust to the problems that accompany wealth. The Judge wrote that "happiness does not increase proportionately with wealth . . . wealth adds nothing to enjoyment. But if happiness does not increase proportionately with wealth, it is to be remembered that hardships and discomforts never fail to increase proportionately with poverty." The Mellons have been spared the unhappinesses related to poverty, but at the same time they have been faced with a greater degree of responsibility for their own life patterns than the majority of people, for whom financial considerations have had to be determinative. Their wealth has freed them to a greater extent than most to ponder the meaning and purposes of life and the manner in which they are each experiencing their own lives— considerations that may be unhappiness-producing exercises, and particularly so for those who may be living essentially unproductive lives.

If divorces be any indication of "life problems," then the Mellon record speaks loudly. Each of the principal characters in Book IV was either divorced or was on the giving or receiving end of a quick-change marriage. The same is true for most of the personalities in this section. Three of the four children of the General have been divorced, one of them three times. One of Paul's two children has been divorced. From W. L.'s line, three of Peggy Hitchcock's five children have been divorced; one of Matthew's two sons has never married and the other has been divorced three times. W. L. Junior's only child was a suicide. The incidence of divorce in the "poor" T. A. line of the family is very much lower. This may mean only that wealth frees the wealthy to change their domestic situations with greater ease than the rest of us, and that we would do it too if it were economically feasible. Or, it may mean that those freed from poverty-related unhappinesses have the leisure necessary to involve themselves in more personally related forms of unhappiness.

Young Mellons of the rich branches of the family have used the freedoms that come with wealth differently. Two who nicely highlight the differing possibilities that accompany a financially secure life would be Matthew's two sons, Karl and Jay (James Ross Mellon), born in 1937 and 1942.

One can meet aspects of Jay in his book *African Hunter,* roughly half of which was authored by Jay, the remainder of it contributed by other authorities on the subject of hunting in Africa. *African Hunter* is a profusely illustrated oversized coffee table book. Many of the fine photographs in it were taken by Jay, and some by his friend Peter Beard, the inspired photographer of life and death in Africa. The text consists of a series of separate adventure stories about the quest for specific species interspersed with articles of guidebook or handbook substance and semi-academic zoological discourse. There is a Fielding-like chapter on the ins and outs of arranging your safari (there are no Frommer safaris). An experienced hunter might try outfitting his own safari. Jay writes that "in the course of completing my African collection, I saved well over $100,000 by outfitting dozens of my own safaris," a creditable thrift for one then in his early thirties, worthy of a descendant of Judge Thomas Mellon. There is also some tax-planning advice:

> Any recognized American museum, no matter how small or obscure, is allowed to accept your money on a tax-deductible basis and then use it to send you on a safari to shoot game animals for its collections. If you should happen to bag a few good trophies for yourself on a license you paid for personally, no one could object to that, any more than if you had gone fishing in your spare time instead. Is there, perhaps, a little museum tucked away somewhere in your area? Better find out. An arrangement favorable to both you and the museum can often be worked out.

The Carnegie Institute's museum has used much of Jay's contributions to it to send him on tax-deductible hunts, though not one of his trophies was on display when the author read the name tags on the Carnegie's seemingly comprehensive collection in 1976.

African Hunter was published in 1975 by Harcourt Brace Jovanovich, but at $39.95, it probably graces few coffee tables other than this author's. *Book Review Digest* does not include any reviews of *African Hunter.*

Jay's preface says that *African Hunter* was inspired by Major H. C. Maydon's similar work of forty years earlier, *Big Game Shooting in Africa,* a book seemingly as vital in Jay's life as Benjamin Franklin's autobiography was in his great-great-grandfather's. "No book will ever again control my life so completely," he writes of Maydon's book. He invites hunters of decades hence to again produce a book in the Maydon mold, but as his own dust jacket suggests, *African Hunter* is "very probably the last book of its kind."

The book is dedicated to Prince Abdorreza Pahlavi, brother of the Shah of Iran, "for his superlative trophy collection and his invaluable contributions to wildlife conservation," and the prefatory pages talk a lot about conservation, the need for conservation, and the hunter's positive role in conservation efforts by thinning out herds that would otherwise perish entirely from overpopulation. In a contributed introduction to *African Hunter*, Prince Pahlavi points out that "wildlife must be harvested in order to be preserved for posterity." Once past the roman-numeraled pages and into the text, the reader is no longer lectured about conservation; the text for the most part evokes pictures of the Rudyard Kipling era when the sun never set on the British empire—days that one would have thought had long ago ended, days when rich men's sons hunted with Middle Eastern potentates totally unaware of and unconcerned about their own contributions to wildlife conservation.

Because it was written over a period of years and covers many different aspects of hunting, Jay's style is not uniform throughout the book, but all of it is well written and often engrossing. He makes nice use of adjectives and adverbs ("a faintly azure cupola"; "a preternaturally still forest"). Often the style is appealingly Edwardian. Occasionally he shows a touch of Olympian humor, as in a reference to environmental mismanagement in North Africa "practiced with boundless imagination and perseverance by the local Arabs." Most of the book deals with the excitement of the chase and the kill, and those portions of the book are written in the style of men's adventure magazines:

> Suddenly he was beside me, still hidden but making deep purring sounds. Kaunge's leathery hand tightened on my arm; the nails of his shriveled old fingers dug into me like talons. We froze like statues. Our eyes narrowed to slits. Our breathing stopped. The largest, most magnificent leopard either of us had ever seen was walking single-mindedly toward his meat.

At places the book seems almost a caricature of great-white-hunter literature, and Jay himself comes across as a hard-living adventurer.

Like so many Mellons, Jay has a powerful nostalgia for the good old days —in his case, days of long before his birth in 1942. In his book he mourns the passing of the huge European-owned estates in Kenya, with the passing of which "a whole world is coming to an end—the world of settler Kenya with its fabled eccentrics, its racing, steeplechases, club life, and the refreshingly libertine society of 'Happy Valley.' For some, settler Kenya was a real paradise; for others, merely 'a place in the sun for shady people.' But whatever it may have been, the last traces of it will vanish with the big estates." He especially enjoyed hunting in isolated sections of Tanzania, where "no one had seen a safari for several years and where local guides often asked no more for their work than the meat from my kills. This was a country where a hunter could still feel he was in Africa."

The Jay of *African Hunter* is a character out of settler Kenya—both in his robust and earthy living, and in his typically "colonial" attitudes. The book is spotted with an occasional "noble savage" (the African equivalent of Gunga Din), especially members of "unspoiled" tribes, but more often his references to black Africans are denigrating. ("The locals, ever greedy for monkey meat, had so persecuted their not-too-distant cousins . . .") The staff from an Ethiopian hunt for the Nile lechwe—a species of antelope—seems to have been typical of the Africans with whom he has dealt:

> Apart from the cook, a bright young Amhara girl, they are not likely to profit from instruction. Antonio, the half-breed truck driver, is a callous jack who treats machinery as if it had a life of its own, independent of maintenance and careful handling. The government-appointed inspector, a Shoan Galla named Hussein, is even-tempered but bone-idle and scared silly of the Anuaks. There is also a young Amhara named Haile who can always be found sitting, leaning or reclining. Of the two Anuaks, Oubour is the more useful—he at least has hunted before. The other, Oumut, has a mind that must be made up of square wheels or of teeth that don't fit into one another—when Thomas asks him a question, I can practically hear the horrid grating. So much for introductions. We're going to find the Nile lechwe in spite of these rogues.

At one point in the book he mentions himself thinking of himself in the third person as "bwana," and when he writes the word "boy" in referring to an adult male African it is without that embarrassment that would have required enclosure of the word within quote marks.

Jay has little sentimentality about either men or animals. When he has killed a rare and beautiful antelope he writes that he "dumped" it or "potted" it. Here is no Minoan ballet with the bull. Only for a moment while hunting chimpanzees did he have cause to consider the weepy aspects of hunting, but after a brief reflection on "the gorge-lifting sentimentality —most of it commercially inspired—that has come to surround chimpanzees . . . I blasted that ape with downright enthusiasm and have felt clean inside ever since." His attitude toward man is parallel. He reports on his visit to the ritualistically disfigured platter-lipped Ubangi women that "they were fifteen shriveled old hags with mouths like platypuses." When he questioned the tribesmen about their traditions, "one hag replied," only to be contradicted by "a second hag." He relates that on someone else's safari in pursuit of the Walia antelope, one of the bearers had fallen into a vast abyss and had been "turned into raspberry jam."

One interesting aspect of the book is the hints that it gives toward an understanding of "the hunt" as a sexual act. A number of passages have a decidedly sexual ring to them. Chasing his prey, Jay writes that "my excitement mounted to near insanity"; a giant eland bull is described as "the object of all my longings, the cause of my frustrations." After a tense, slow pull of the trigger, Jay writes that "I lay there gasping like a spent swimmer." Swimmer?

This author does not claim to understand the genre of the hunter, or to have any basic sympathy for it. Jay tells of it lyrically, but his series of exciting short stories cannot be stripped from the social, philosophical, and political implications that accompany them. In the totality, the story of the African hunter is based on exploitation of men and of animals, and the color, callousness, and relish with which Jay depicts the exploitive aspects of the hunt make one wonder what, precisely, constitutes the lure of it for him. The most commonly used word in the book is surely "trophy," "trophy," "trophy," used with such regularity as to drive the reader to the dictionary to be certain of the meaning of "trophy." What the trophies signify beyond a tangible memento of an experience is not clear, but it is clear that they do have some further significance for Jay. He reports on his shooting of an oryx (a variety of antelope) that after he pulled the trigger "a moment passed before I heard the delicious wunk that pays for the pain of all. My quarry had fallen—an undistinguished bull of 40 inches [length of the horns] and one I would never have shot except to prove a point."

After a close and critical reading of *African Hunter,* the author met Jay and was confounded to find a compelling young man of thirty-five, the exemplar of grace, refinement, and fashion, without a hint of the rampant machismo that pervades his book.

He is on the tall side of medium height, lean but firmly built and fine-boned. His complexion is dark—perhaps partly the result of one of his jungle illnesses—his eyes are lustrous, dark, and shiny. His hair is a glossy jet black but heavily streaked with premature white, parted but all brushed backward. It is slightly "too" long, but an appropriate length for Manhattan's Upper East Side. His features are delicate and sensuous, handsome-beautiful in a unique way not captured in the photographs in *African Hunter.* His fingers are long and thin. He was immaculately dressed in a checked suit, white shirt with buttoned-down collar, a nondescript tie, and with a maroon handkerchief stuffed partly into his jacket's breast pocket.

Jay is a flowing conversationalist, with rich and artful diction that is sometimes mystifying. ("India is a vast vegetable," he says.) He has a slightly clipped "colonial" accent. The range of his knowledge is amazing. Jay is an unregenerate Edwardian gentleman ("I'm a bit of a Bourbon"), one of the last and most appealing of the *Sonnenkinder.*

Jay was educated at St. Paul's and Yale, but he wasn't around much at Yale, and from his classbook he appears to have taken no part in campus life. Whenever possible he got out of New Haven and into Manhattan, where he had a lot of friends and enjoyed the social whirl. He passed up Yale's graduation exercises, and by the time that the diplomas were being handed out Jay was "home" on safari in Africa.

From his earliest days Jay was absorbed with guns and hunting. His father, Matthew, recalls that when Jay was about five, "I bought him a rubber gun, and he pointed it at the little German girl that we had living with us, and she ran away squealing; he told me recently that that was the time that he first realized the power in a gun." While still a child he learned to take apart and reassemble his father's old World War I pistol, and he began hunting rabbits, snakes, and birds. According to his book's dust jacket, at the age of eighteen he led a Carnegie Museum expedition to East Africa "which collected more than 3500 bird, mammal, and reptile specimens for scientific study." After Yale, Nairobi was his principal home during five years of hunting. "Hunting is an excuse that you hang a lot of things on in your twenties," he says. Now he says that he is "sated" on hunting, though he still enjoys bird shooting, especially hunting driven pheasants in Europe, and on a recent trip to India he shot a tiger, he says "for old times' sake."

At the time of our interview Jay was engrossed in putting together a very different kind of book than *African Hunter,* a book of Lincoln photographs interspersed with quotes from Lincoln's addresses and from the great biographies of him. He said that the book will incorporate "all the varied ways that you know a historical person," and then he discussed the varied ways. He is a passionate admirer of Lincoln, seemingly an unlikely hero for even a "reformed" big game hunter. His hallway is hung with a series of obscure but haunting photographs of the President. "I enjoy making books," he says, and is pleased that "if anything should happen to me, my book will be left behind."

His New York apartment is one flight over his mother's, and though he has "lived" there several years already, he hasn't quite gotten around to furnishing it. The only room that looks to be inhabited is his study. It is furnished comfortably but unostentatiously with the kind of furniture sold at W. & J. Sloane, the New York furniture store that caters to the upper middle class rather than to the very rich. The only taxidermy in evidence is a stuffed peacock with spread feathers that he purchased in India, a huge masterpiece of nature's art that dominates his vestibule, plus a couple of small stuffed birds and a small fox-sized creature in the study. He says that his big game heads would not fit in with the surroundings, and they wouldn't; they are in cold storage in Mount Vernon, just outside New York City. The neatness and order of the study seemed out of character for such a romantic.

Jay does not spend that much time in New York but likes the city in the summer, the season when most who can afford to flee it do so. In July he says that New York is free of its "usual grate—just before Christmas it's at its highest, the stores all crowded, the parties. Then it tapers off in ski season, and reaches its low point in the summer, and then picks up again." He says that the city's "grate" could be scientifically measured and charted by tests on his own metabolism.

He travels a lot. During the five years between 1971 and 1976 he visited India several times, and lived there for seven months at one stretch and perhaps for two years all totaled, busying himself with "partying, mountain climbing, and a little hunting." He speaks poetically about Indian fatalism, which he attributes to "the depth and antiquity of their poverty." At first the poverty and the "incredible futility" were disturbing to him, but he says that "your social conscience gets numb to it." India, he pointed out, is the last surviving ancient civilization, and then he discoursed on the ancient civilizations: how the Aztecs were destroyed by the Spaniards, the Greeks by the Romans, the Romans by the barbarians, and in more recent times how the civilization of ancient China was obliterated in one generation by the Chinese communists. He says that the only solution to India's vast wretchedness would probably be total communization, thereby spelling the end to the traditions of the last ancient civilization. He did not foreclose the possibility that the wretchedness ought to be ended, and the cultural price tag paid.

He goes to Pittsburgh occasionally to keep track of his financial affairs, which are handled for him by the trust department at Mellon National. He is not really interested in such matters, but forces himself to follow them on the theory that if the people at Mellon Bank think he does not care, they may stop caring too. Pittsburgh is not his kind of city. He says that Pittsburgh attitudes lag behind those of the rest of the world, that the values and orientations of the city's upper classes remain little removed from those of Judge Mellon and his sons and are still strongly dominated by their Scotch-Irish Calvinism. There is not a touch of that in Jay. He says with a little grin that "Calvinism is contagious rather than hereditary." He blames the work-success ethic for what he regards as a tremendous amount of drinking in Pittsburgh; the emotional part of living there is drowned in alcohol, and Rolling Rock is full of "half-burned-out livers."

He is interested in his family's history more out of curiosity than out of any sense of Mellonhood (*African Hunter* is by "James Mellon" not "James Ross Mellon"). He has read both *Thomas Mellon and His Times* and *Judge Mellon's Sons,* and says that "those old-timers were tight like tics." In New York he sees something of his first cousins the Hitchcocks, and when in Pittsburgh he sees his first cousins the Waltons and the Whetzels, and something of Pross Mellon, his second cousin once removed, born the same year as Jay. Otherwise he is out of touch with the scattered descendants of Judge Mellon. He never knew his first cousin William Larimer Mellon III, son of Dr. Mellon of Haiti, or his third cousin John Sellers, whose period at Yale overlapped with Jay's. Though Paul's son Timothy was in the same class with Jay at Yale, they were scarcely aware of each other's existence, a matter that Jay ascribes to temperamental differences. He characterizes Timothy as "very conscientious," whereas "I enjoy a good debauch."

He sees relatively little of his brother, Karl, but takes a fatherly interest in Karl's oldest son, Christopher, twenty as of this writing.

Jay has a great admiration for his uncle Dr. Mellon of Haiti, "a real success story of a man who's found happiness," but he realizes that that kind of life is not for him. He is an outgoing, very social sort, a combination of an archaistic learned romantic and an up-to-date playboy jet-setter, still looking for new outlets for his adventuresome spirit.

No two brothers could be less alike than Jay and his older brother, Karl, unless it were their father, Matthew, and Matthew's brother, Larry. Jay represents the traditions of yesterday's English upper class; Karl represents the tradition of Bohemian democracy of people like Walt Whitman and Allen Ginsberg.

Matthew had warned the author that Karl "dresses sloppy, sloppy," and the author's first view of Karl confirmed his father's description. We met at a general store/gas station on Alternate Route 1 midway between Bangor and Bar Harbor. The author was parked away on the side of the road when Karl drove his old blue van up to the gas pump, jumped out, and began putting five dollars' worth of gas into his van before the attendant could serve him. Karl does not like to be served. He was wearing a faded raspberry-colored corduroy jacket that had obviously seen better years, baggy pants, and dirty shoes. He had a full beard and wild long hair, both heavily specked with gray though still essentially black. His face is notable for its strong eyes and features, and though he was then a little heavy, it was easy to see that he was once the very handsome young man that the photographs of him in *Watermellons* show him to have been.

After Karl paid for his gas, the author followed him over a long dirt road to the semi-finished cottage where he, his wife, Bonnie, and her six or seven children from before their marriage were living. His van had a long whip antenna, indicating a CB radio (Karl's "handle" is "Night Train"), but the upper reaches of it had been bent over and tied down to the body of the van, signifying that the CB was not being used regularly.

The cottage was rustically but comfortably furnished. Though it was August, it was a cold day in Maine, and Karl turned on all the burners and the oven of the kitchen stove for heat. After many years in Maine he has acquired a Down Easter's twang and syntax. The picture was complete. This scion of privilege had become a bona fide Maine backwoodsman. But then the little signs came out. His diction was not always "gentlemanly," but his gestures were, and there was a "bred" tone to an occasional word. The sixteen-ounce Schlitz beers were poured into delicate tulip-shaped wine glasses. In the course of the long interview he quoted Shakespeare, alluded to Tennessee Williams, and discoursed on the cultural and symbolic significance of his father's 1928 trip down the Mississippi River as a Wagnerian Rhine journey (he used the German words for "Rhine journey").

Karl is a keen observer with an impressive intellect and a good eye for sham, and he speaks openly and bluntly. His formal schooling was limited, but he does not regret that; he is obviously "educated" and despite his trappings, cultured. There was a lesson to the visit. You can take the aristocrat out of his class, but you cannot take the class out of the aristocrat.

Karl was born in 1937, and by his own account was a rebellious boy from the start. He went to several private schools—he was tough to keep in school—and enjoys relating his experience at one. "My father had sent me to this third-rate prep school in Worcester, and told them that if they could keep me a year he'd buy them a swimming pool. When I learned about it, I bribed the chauffeur to come up and get me, and when he arrived, I walked into the headmaster's office, lit up a cigarette, told him, 'You ain't gettin' no swimmin' pool,' and walked out."*

His schooling was interrupted by his institutionalizations. He sounds like a sensitive civil libertarian when he describes the "rubber room," shock therapy, and the tendency of attendants at mental hospitals to interpret any comment from a patient as confirmation of the patient's "insanity," and he

*Matthew writes in *War Log* that at St. John's Military School, one notable hellion was known as "Horrible Horace." "Horace was always in trouble but it was common knowledge that he couldn't be fired because his father had given the school a new gymnasium together with a swimming pool."

recounts the many ways that his own experiences in asylums parallel those shown in *One Flew Over the Cuckoo's Nest* and other movies about life in the asylum. He was first institutionalized when he was about fourteen, when his mother, Gertrud, Matthew's first wife, took him for a visit—"just a visit, that's all"—to a Doctor So-and-So. Next he knew, he was locked into the top security ward. He escaped by passing himself off as the son of an older patient. Ultimately he was placed at the famed Menninger Institute, where, he says, "no one got better but no one got worse." Marriage was his exit from the Institute. In the dead of night, Karl and Ann eloped from the Menninger Institute and were wed.

It might appear at first blush that the marriage of two teenaged escapees from a mental asylum would not be particularly well starred, and it wasn't. They had two children, Christopher and Andrea, before their divorce. He married his second wife, Anne (he identifies them as Ann No. 1 and Anne No. 2), in 1962 in a widely reported "society" wedding. After two more children, they were divorced. Both Ann(e)s were from prosperous, socially prominent families. His third wife was "Bonnie", whose background as the daughter of a provincial Maine fisherman was very different, and whose prior life had not been easy.

Karl has been mostly separated from his four children, but Bonnie's children have grown up with him, and he has considerable paternal affection for them and speaks of them as "my kids." Karl says that life with Bonnie was exciting, and it surely was. In December 1975 David Norwood, a young Maine boy, satisfied himself that Bonnie should be freed from Karl, and stalked Karl with a high-powered deer rifle. While Karl was in his kitchen, Norwood approached the house and took aim at him through the window. Karl was unaware of the assailant's approach, but at the crucial moment turned aside and began moving outside the scope of Norwood's rifle. Norwood shot, but too late to do Karl serious injury. His bullet merely creased Karl's back and Karl was released from the hospital emergency room with a large Band-Aid on his back. With Norwood behind bars, Karl smiled broadly as he told of the incident, which he said was "in the great American tradition: being shot in the back is the next best thing to being crucified." At the time of our interview he compared Bonnie favorably with the pedigreed Annes. "Bonnie really cares for me—not just because she's supposed to care, because she's been brought up to care, but because she really cares." Shortly after our interview they separated.

Over the years Karl has been engaged in various businesses, mostly related to the sea, the love of which he has inherited from his father, Matthew, and his grandfather W. L. At the age of twenty-five Karl personally designed and built *Hilgendorf,* a magnificent barkentine of sixty-nine gross tons patterned after a nineteenth-century Dutch coastal schooner. The vessel was built on the lawn of his Greenwich, Connecticut, estate. Matthew reported the course of its brief life in *Watermellons:* "She had a grand run down to Maine, where she caught fire and burned, much to the distress of her owner and his friends, who were anticipating a cruise around the world." Thereafter he owned several other vessels described in *Watermellons,* some of impressive size, and he was active in commercial fishing and lobstering along the coasts of Maine and Canada. He left the business because of licensing problems with Canadian authorities and the adverse effects on the area's supply caused by the entrance of the Russian fishing fleet.

Karl has not read either *Thomas Mellon and His Times* or W. L.'s *Judge Mellon's Sons,* though he speaks with great affection of his grandfather W. L., one of his favorite people. He knows almost no one from any of the other branches of the family tree, and has had almost no contact even with the other descendants of W. L. He never knew his cousin W. L. III, and sees little of his Hitchcock cousins. ("If Billy Hitchcock and I had ever gotten together, the whole world would have gone up in a puff," he says.) He has not attended either of the two Mellon family reunions, and he lumps reunions with "funerals and things like that—tacky." He has not been to Pittsburgh in years, and is hostile to the city and its inhabitants. He is uncertain as to whether he has ever been to Ligonier, but if so, he has no recollection of it, and he is disapproving of what he calls the "minuet" life at Rolling Rock. He has relatively little contact with either of his parents, and regrettably little with his children. He scarcely knew his son Christopher until Christopher became a student at nearby Colby College in Waterville, Maine; since then, a fine relationship has developed between them as new friends, one older, one younger.

Most of Karl's attitudes are purely American. He takes real pride in his country's status as the world's leader. He describes Ray Kroc, "McDonald" of the hamburger chain, as "the Galileo of our era because he figured out how to feed us cheaper than we can feed ourselves." He is very proud of his clean driving record, which he attributes to the fact that "I obey the traffic laws"—except, of course, the fifty-five-mile-per-hour speed limit— "but I'm careful." He looks forward to the complete assimilation of the American Negro, and regrets that there are not more American orientals to be assimilated too. "The mongrel is the strongest dog," he says. His presidential preference in 1976 was the same as it has been for as far back as he can recall. Neither. He is not optimistic about the future and says that

the end must now come to "the country's romance with alcohol and autos
. . . for two hundred years there was a big party and now someone has to
pay for that party." He sees petroleum "going the way of whale oil" (a
matter that his father disputes), and views the next fifteen years as crucial
for mankind. He is not sympathetic to hunting. "I tell my kids, 'Don't
murder a fish unless you're gonna eat it.' "

Karl has a powerful interest in, identification with, and empathy for "the
people," or, as he calls them, "the rednecks," which, as he uses it, is a term
of affection and admiration. "Rednecks are great. Without rednecks we
wouldn't have a country!" As a child he was closest to a "redneck" domestic
servant, and he describes the situation of the common man feelingly:

> The world explodes so fast on him. First the guy's in high school, the next thing
> you know he's married with kids and responsibilities and a mortgage, and he
> feels guilty if he gets a car with one more piece of chrome than necessary, or
> that doesn't get forty miles per gallon, and he's guilty if he drinks too much
> and he's guilty if he looks at another woman. He's got all this guilt on him.
> And the woman's got it much worse. She's got all that plus the isolation.

> The farm belt folk have it even worse, because they were told they were the
> backbone of the country, and of course they were getting shit for their work,
> not what they should have been getting for their crops or their work, and it
> was drummed into them in school to be good, not to do this or that, and they
> lived like they were supposed to, got married, and lived by the home code, and
> then suddenly whammo, they find out that nobody else is paying attention to
> those values any more.

Karl has experienced their existence. He once ran up $80,000 in unneces-
sary bills, he says, because he wanted to taste the plight of the common
debt-ridden American citizen. Over the years he has held many blue-collar
jobs, most recently as a long-haul truck driver. He was a hard driver,
driving long hauls without stopping for sleep, and averaging 2000 to 2500
miles a week. He is proud to say that he became the "best" truck driver with
the company, which he explains means that he generated the most income
for the corporation. He is equally proud that during his periods of hardest
work he was earning more money from driving truck than he was getting
from his trust funds. Trucking, he says, is a hard life. "The boss is buying
your health—paying you to exhaust yourself." If he had to live that life
permanently, he is sure that he would be as narrow-minded as the least
enlightened teamster. He keeps his trucking money separate from his trust
income, and says that he is much more tight-fisted with the money that he
"earned." He says that the masses are composed of people "paying the taxes
twice, buying the Budweiser beer, supporting that, and paying their own

taxes, and dying quietly, and since they do that for us, we shouldn't get in their way too much and ought to let them alone." He enjoys his privileged existence and says that he would not want to lose it, but that he could not argue if the proletariat (not his word) were to rise up and tell him, "You did not earn that money and we're going to take it." He listens to and enjoys the redneck music that he hears on the radio, and feels an uncanny ability to predict whether any particular new record will be a hit. His favorite at the time of our interview was "Rhinestone Cowboy," a country-and-western song that Karl says is the story of the American ethic and the American tragedy. He knew the lyrics to it and recited snatches of them: ". . . there's been a lot of compromisin' on the way to my horizon."

Money and familial background have been a mixed blessing for Karl. He has not enjoyed the "comforts" that money brings—Karl was never much into "comforts"—but he has enjoyed the security of money and even the possibilities of extravagance. On the other hand, there has been a price to pay for the "advantages," which Karl has bitterly resented having to pay. He recalls that at an early boarding school the headmaster shook hands with every student each night at bedtime, addressing each boy by his last name. When he came to Karl, the headmaster took liberties with Karl's name. "Good night, Millions," he said playfully. He says that "people make a moral judgment and a moral assessment of you on the basis of the name." When he was trucking, people asked him, "Why are you working this job with all your money, taking bread out of someone else's mouth?" Such accomplishments as he has attained have been attributed by others to familial advantage. Everything about him has been gauged in the context of his status as a Mellon. As he spoke, the author felt a tinge of guilt for having thought at the outset, "This hippie is a *Mellon?*"

Over his lifetime Karl has pondered much about why he has "deserved" both the benefits and burdens of Mellonhood. He often sounds like his uncle Dr. Mellon of Haiti (whom he scarcely knows) in discussing the milieu against which his own lifestyle constitutes a rebellion, a milieu in which "people live a great lie in which the greatest sin is to lie." He has had several run-ins with the summer colony of Mount Desert Island, Maine. Ultimately he admits that he takes some delight in the way that his long hair "fakes out everyone." He insists that his old "insanity" turned on his rebellion against a world that had ended with World War I, and an unwillingness to be forced into the mold and accept the values of a "gentleman" of times gone by. He views his institutionalizations as the modern equivalent of the practice of French nobles of the Louis XIV–XVI period of having rebellious or overly independent sons placed in "protective" custody. He insists that he was never "crazy," never crazier than he is right now, and though Karl at forty-one is clearly an eccentric, any inference of lack of "sanity" in him would have to be based on his seemingly cosmic senses of reality, irony, and absurdity, and his occasional flashes of Zeus-like strength.

The women of the wealthiest A. W. and R. B. branches of the family tree remain largely a cloistered lot. Only one of them, the General's daughter Cassandra, has any ongoing contact with Pittsburgh. Like most Mellon women, she was extremely shy as a girl. She went to Miss Porter's School, was the honoree at appropriate debutante rites in 1958 (1000 attended the principal affair), and married George Henderson in 1961. Since their marriage Henderson has brought her out of her shell somewhat. Henderson, sixteen years older than Cassandra, is of humble origins. His father was a mailman in Sharon, Pennsylvania. He went to Sharon High, '42, fought in World War II, and then went to Allegheny College, '50. He is nominally a stockbroker in Pittsburgh, but he is obviously in a position to make his own hours and he does. The Hendersons spend a lot of time out at their own eighty-nine-acre chunk of Rolling Rock, on Mrs. Burrell's yacht cruising out of Cape Cod or Florida ports, or in southern France. Politically, Henderson says, "I am very conservative," a matter which he attributes to having grown up in the depression. He has not broken off from his childhood friends, and the Hendersons' social life includes people from a wide variety of socio-economic backgrounds. Their lack of "snobbery" has made them well liked by Pittsburghers from a much wider circle than any of Cassandra's siblings. She is the only one of the General's four children who has not been divorced; one family member says the only one that turned out "all right."

Other reticent rich Mellon ladies have been known principally by their dynamic husbands, who might seem to have "used" the women, some for good purposes, some for less good.

Paul's daughter Cathy is one of the quietest of the girls. She went to Foxcroft, '54, debuted without publicity at Oak Spring in 1955, and studied at Mount Vernon Junior College. While a freshman there in 1956, she met John Warner. Warner was the son of a prominent but not wealthy Washington physician. He was bright, aggressive, tall and ruggedly handsome. He had a checkered academic career, was in and out of schools and in and out of World War II and the Korean War, but finally settled down to law school at the University of Virginia, from which he graduated in 1956. He clerked briefly for the highly regarded Washington judge E. Barrett Prettyman, and practiced for a short time privately before becoming a "government lawyer" as an assistant U.S. attorney in Washington in 1957. That summer he and Cathy married.

In 1960 Warner left the government to work in the presidential campaign of then Vice President Richard M. Nixon. After Nixon lost to John F. Kennedy, Warner entered the Washington firm of Hogan & Hartson, the firm that had defended A. W. in his tax trial of decades before. When Nixon rose from the dead in 1968, Warner again joined up as director of National Citizens for Nixon and Agnew, and after their victory he let it be known that he was available for the post of Secretary of the Navy. Still a little too young for such a vital position during the heat of the Vietnam war, he was started as an undersecretary and ultimately promoted to Secretary of the Navy in 1972. For one reason or another, two years later he was shunted to the position of director of the American Revolution Bicentennial Administration, a ceremonial function in the truest possible sense. Warner, currently untitled, prefers to be identified as the former Secretary of the Navy.

By the time of the Bicentennial, the Warners had divorced. After sixteen years and three children, they received an Idaho divorce in August of 1973. Their incompatibility revolved around Warner's political interests. He told *Esquire*'s Aaron Latham, "My first marriage broke up over politics. . . . When I was Secretary of the Navy, my wife had to be involved in all kinds of political functions, but she was very shy and couldn't stand it." There were also differences in their policy orientations so deep as to be painful: "We disagreed on Vietnam. I was in the administration and thought we had to finish something we had started. My wife was almost a student radical."

It was an amicable divorce. Cathy bought a fine Washington townhouse adjacent to the home in which he continued to reside, and the two share custody of their children, who live mostly with their father. After sixteen years as a Mellon in-law, Warner emerged a very wealthy man indeed.

Warner is now remarried, to the former Elizabeth Taylor of Los Angeles and many other places, and lives with his new wife on the 2000-acre estate in Virginia's hunt country that he did not own before he knew the Mellons. His new wife, a woman of some experience, has described Warner as "the best lover I've ever had." He is currently gearing for a race for the United States Senate in 1978, and he and Liz, as his second wife is known, are almost continually on the hustings, making the rounds of political rallies, fairs, parades, sporting events, and church functions (though Liz identifies herself as "Jewish"). He is a Republican. "I lean a little to the right," says Warner.

In a nationally televised interview with Barbara Walters, Warner reflected all the humble and sincere down-home values of early Nixon. After sixteen years of being known as his father-in-law's son-in-law he is not at all uncomfortable about now being known as his wife's husband. He appreciates that it has real value for him in the political world, and is not backward about running as *Mr.* Elizabeth Taylor. On Barbara Walters's show he referred to the possible candidate as "we" and said that the question for the voters would be whether they want "us." Liz, looking and sounding like the prettier twin sister of Bella Abzug, seems to feel right at home in the political world. In the Walters interview Warner appeared a superficial and sanctimonious person, a striver from his mentor's mold, but in a conservative state like Virginia, where the voters appreciate their "betters," it is not unlikely that he will be able to turn Miss Mellon's money and Miss Taylor's crowd-drawing appeal into a seat in the United States Senate.

Cathy has also remarried, but to a very different man than Warner. Her new husband, Ashley Carrithers, of Cleveland, Ohio, is so reticent that he does not appear in the Cleveland "Blue Book" or in the City Directory, and there is no trace of him in the New York *Times*'s data bank computer.

Cathy's cousin Audrey Bruce Currier, daughter of Ailsa and David Bruce, was born in 1933 and was in her early teens when her parents separated. She was close to her father but after the divorce he started a second family and their direct contact became more limited. She went to Foxcroft and debuted first in Baltimore's "little season" in June of 1952 and later in New York. She went to college at Radcliffe. Classmates and Harvard people who knew her at school describe her as very quiet and very shy, someone that no one seemed to know at all. One who was close to her husband told the author that "she lived completely in the shadows." Her Uncle Paul described her in 1970 as

> extremely shy and introspective—a true introvert . . . Although today clamor and protest and immediacy and violence seem most fashionable and all-pervading, Audrey's most praiseworthy and notable characteristics were, in total contrast, quietness, modesty, patience, thoughtfulness, and sincerity. She was a lovable person and in her shy way she loved all men and women, all children, all animals.

Perhaps she needed a companion who was more outgoing. Such a one was Stephen Currier.

Currier was the son of an Arizona artist. His parents separated somewhere along the line and his mother then married the New York banker

Edward M. Warburg, well known in Jewish philanthropic circles. Currier went to Harvard at about the same time as Audrey was at Radcliffe and was working as an assistant at a Boston art gallery when the two were secretly married by a justice of the peace in November of 1955. "Society" does not take well to elopements. The disclosure of the marriage in April of 1956 led to her being dropped from the Social Register.

Whether the family at large disliked Currier from the start or grew to dislike him is uncertain. One family member with whom the author spoke said that too often people who marry into the family show a contempt for money while enjoying its benefits, and spoke with apparent disgust of Stephen Currier's subsequent trips to Pittsburgh for "satchels full of money." According to that source, the marriage was "a terrible blow for Ailsa."

The Curriers settled in New York City, where Stephen became deeply involved in the civil rights movement of the late 1950s and '60s. They established the Taconic Foundation, which became important in the writing of civil rights legislation of the 1960s and in most of the direct and indirect concerns of the black minority. Currier became the president of Urban America, Inc., a group dedicated to creating more low-income housing and to enlightened city planning. He never gave a sign of any interest in seeking public office but he gave financial backing to many liberal and progressive candidates and he enjoyed the easy familiarity with big-name political leaders of New York City and State that came with his importance as a key financier of the civil rights movement. By the late 1960s white liberals like himself were beginning to be shuffled out, or to drop out of the civil rights movement, but Currier's dedication to cause showed no sign of waning.

Meanwhile the Curriers enjoyed substantially the same lifestyle as the General's children were enjoying at Rolling Rock. In 1961 they bought Kinloch, a twenty-three-*bath*room castle on 1600 acres at The Plains (that is the name of the town), Virginia, in the hunt country not far from Uncle Paul's Oak Spring and John Warner's estate. Audrey largely retreated there. According to one family friend, Audrey "was never really happy until they got Kinloch." The Curriers employed 110 people year round at Kinloch, and more in the summer. The local Episcopal minister has said that at Kinloch

> There was always work for anyone who needed a job, particularly the area's young boys in the summers. . . . It was "make work." He kept eight or ten people busy just building fences. He'd have them build a fence all the way

around the place, and by the time they got through it was time to start mending.

The Reverend pointed to innumerable private good works that the Curriers had performed in the community, all circuitously channeled so that the benefactor would be anonymous, all handled, as much as possible, in a manner to preserve the dignity of the recipient. In short, the Curriers lived up to the very highest standards and fulfilled the most rigorous of the self-imposed responsibilities of the most honorable segments of the English gentry, just as, without doubt, Audrey's relatively conservative Uncle Paul does in Upperville. Almost nobody in the small and provincial Virginia town was aware that the Curriers were leading civil rights radicals up north.

In 1967 the Curriers, he thirty-six and she thirty-three, were reported missing when a chartered private plane disappeared on the short flight between Puerto Rico and the Virgin Islands. Coast Guard spokesmen speculated that the pilot, a professional with many years' experience, had suffered a heart attack on the flight. No traces were ever discovered. Currier was identified in obituaries as the "internationally known philanthropist," Audrey as the daughter of Ambassador David K. E. Bruce. A memorial service in their honor was attended by the wife of the United States President, Mrs. Lyndon B. Johnson, New York governor Nelson Rockefeller, United States senator Robert F. Kennedy, and New York mayor John Lindsay. Lloyd K. Garrison, president of the New York City Board of Education and Currier's older friend and associate in progressive causes, delivered the eulogy.

Audrey shared Stephen's concern for the rights of black citizens, but she was a far cry from being an activist. Paul has said that "to be a good mother was uppermost in her mind." With Stephen's encouragement she was beginning to come out of her shell at the time of her death. Even Ailsa, removed from civil rights concerns in her sepulcher, was beginning to mellow on Taconic's work at the time of Audrey's passing. Instead, however, of leaving some of her own vast estate to Taconic, Ailsa memorialized Audrey by funding Currier House, a $5.4 million residential unit at Radcliffe, which opened in 1970 after Ailsa's own passing.

At the time of the disappearance the Curriers had three children, daughters ten and eleven and a boy of six, who have been raised mostly by their guardian, Yale Law School professor John Simon, who also heads the Taconic Foundation. The girls were sent to progressive private schools that the Curriers would have favored and to respectable colleges. Now young adults, they gravitate to Kinloch and ride a lot. Insofar as they are politically attuned, they are "liberals" of their period, oriented to the ecological and environmental causes that succeeded civil rights as the major concern for decent-thinking young people. The boy, fourteen as of this writing, is also at a progressive boarding school. They see something of Uncle Paul's family, but otherwise do not have significant family contact.

Audrey had a mere $30 million in her name at the time of her demise, some of which was left to Taconic, some to her children. If Ailsa had good counseling, she probably provided for Audrey with "generation-skipping trusts," trusts that paid only income to Audrey and left the real assets to Audrey's children. If so, then the Currier children will always be comfortable.

One of the most interesting stories in this book is that of Cordelia Scaife May, daughter of Sarah Mellon Scaife, granddaughter of R. B., and as such, probably the wealthiest Mellon woman living. "Cordie," as she is known in the family, was born in 1928 and educated at Foxcroft, after which she studied at Carnegie Tech and the University of Pittsburgh. In 1949 she married Herbert A. May Jr., son of the highest-ranking courtier to Sarah's brother "the King." Herb Jr. showed promise of following in his father's footsteps. He was tall, handsome, gentlemanly, and devoted to the Rolling Rock ethos. He started to ride at the age of four, "hunted" with the Rolling Rock hounds by the time he was twelve. He went to Choate and to the University of Virginia (a very "social" college) and fought in World War II as a lieutenant commander in the Navy. He was awarded the Bronze Star. The pinup over his Navy berth was of Cake Dish, his favorite steeplechase horse. At the time of his marriage to Cordie in 1949, Herb Jr. was already secretary of the Rolling Rock Hunt; his future in the social world was certain. J. Blan van Urk's *Story of Rolling Rock* is chock full of references to the Herbs, father and son.

Carpenters and decorators worked two weeks preparing the Scaifes' Penguin Court for the Scaife-May wedding, and it was worth it. The Pittsburgh *Press* cited "decorators" for the assertion that the reception layout "far outshone" the one at a recent King Ranch wedding in Texas. A thousand guests danced to the music of Emil Coleman's orchestra, which took the night off from its usual assignment at the Waldorf-Astoria in order to play in Ligonier.

How long the marriage lasted has never been revealed. Perhaps it was a matter of a couple of days, at the most a matter of a couple of months. Within six months the marriage had been legally dissolved. May remarried a couple of years later, outlived his second wife, then married again, and died at the early age of forty-nine of unreported causes in 1969. At the time he was still active in hunt circles.

After her separation from May, Cordie went into seclusion and never quite came out of it. Her separation was never "announced," she continued to use the name Cordelia Scaife May, and the public had no hint of her marital discord until May's remarriage was made known two years later. With one spectacular exception, Cordie has stayed out of the press. The exception concerned her involvement with her childhood friend Robert W. Duggan.

Of Irish Catholic background, Duggan's father was the head of an important ice business in Pittsburgh, and he bought a fifty-seven-acre farm in Ligonier when prices were still low. Over the years the Duggan estate grew to a respectable 240 acres. Duggan grew up principally in Ligonier, and was welcomed into the Rolling Rock circle. He became close to Cordie and her brother, Richard, and as a lawyer was "cut in" for a portion of the $300,000 attorneys' fees for processing the estate of their mother when Sarah passed away in 1965. He entered Republican politics and in 1964 was elected district attorney for Allegheny County. The Scaifes were his principal financial backers in politics, and about the only private clients that he represented.

As district attorney, Duggan quickly won acclaim for his fearless war against mobsters, and for his campaigns against pornographers. In 1970 conservative Pennsylvania Republicans spoke of him seriously as a gubernatorial prospect, though Duggan required a little more seasoning before he was ready for a run of such magnitude. The following year Richard Scaife served as treasurer of Duggan's successful re-election campaign. Here was respectability personified.

At the same time there was another side to Duggan, commonly known in the city's under class but unknown and unbelievable to all but a handful of his upper-crust backers. He was a flamboyant fellow who lived a fast, flashy life. Stylistically he was a prohibition-era figure, aspects of him reminiscent of the incorruptible F.B.I. men of the 1920s, other aspects of him disconcertingly paralleling those of their prey. He seemed to have more money than added up. He acquired important holdings in Florida real estate, lived a jet-setter's life, and was somehow able to keep up with the Rolling Rock gentry although he was really not of their financial standing. State drug enforcement officials grumbled about lack of cooperation from his office. He had an odd rapport with Pittsburgh's street people, who knew him as "Dixie" Duggan, and thought of him as one of their own. Quiet rumor named him as the silent backer of one of Pittsburgh's better-known gay clubs. In 1973 Naples, Florida, police claimed to have clocked his sports car at over 110 miles per hour; Dixie claimed that he had only been going 85. Images of their D.A. racing through the Everglades at high speeds excited the imaginations of Pittsburgh's commoners, while giving the stodgier elements cause for reflection. His Jekyll-Hyde existence was beginning to come to light. Dixie was one of Cordie's few friends, and sometimes he escorted her to functions.

In 1973 Dixie's world began to fall apart. The chief detective in his office, Sam Ferraro, was indicted and convicted of having sold "protection" to racketeers in the numbers game. What about Dixie? A grand jury looked into the matter and subpoenaed Ferraro, but the detective knew what loyalty was all about. He wouldn't talk and was jailed for contempt. State investigators began looking into Duggan's campaign financing. In 1971 he had passed on to Richard Scaife cash contributions totaling almost $10,000, all in large bills. At Richard's request, Duggan had provided him with a list of names of the contributors for reporting purposes but the state investigators discovered that the names were phony. Duggan had involved Richard in a campaign fraud. Richard soured on him badly, but Cordie remained a loyal friend. Federal investigators began looking into Dixie's tax returns and finally subpoenaed Cordelia Scaife May and her records; perhaps they held a clue to irregularities in Duggan's returns. The ink was hardly dry on the subpoena when Duggan, a bachelor of forty-seven years, and Cordie, a divorcee, aged forty-five, disappeared to Zephyr Cove on the south shore of Lake Tahoe, where on August 29, 1973, they were married. The "marrying Sam" told reporters for the Pittsburgh *Press* that he performed about 500 weddings a year in his knotty-pine-covered "marrying-room" overlooking Nevada's Route 50. A wife cannot be forced to testify against her husband.

It didn't matter. Sam Ferraro finally decided that he had better "talk," and while he was talking, on March 4, 1974, a single blast from a double-barreled twelve-gauge shotgun pierced Dixie Duggan's chest. He died instantly on his Ligonier estate. St. Paul's Cathedral in Oakland was jammed with the almost two thousand mourners; Cordie walked behind the coffin of her husband of six months, kept herself erect, and blinked back her tears.

Although the coroner's repeated attempts to simulate what had happened established the unlikelihood of either foul play or accident, thousands of people in Pittsburgh still believe that the wound was not self-inflicted, or at least not intentionally, and refuse to accept the coroner's all but inevitable conclusion. Dixie has gone on to legendhood in Pittsburgh that in some circles equals that of Carnegie and Frick (A. W. was not of the meat for legend), while Cordie, Cordelia Scaife May as she now identifies herself, has faded back, far back into the background, where she always felt most comfortable.

The last and youngest of the richest Mellon women, the only one to live a life in the social whirl, is the General's daughter Connie. Born in 1941, Connie went to Miss Porter's, Briarcliffe College, and studied at the National Academy of Fine Arts. Her debut at Huntland Downs in June of 1959 featured dancing to the music of Emil Coleman, or, for those that preferred, ice skating on a rink constructed especially for the occasion. In 1962 she married William R. G. Byers, of Old Westbury, Long Island, himself descended from an old Pittsburgh industrial family. They moved to Washington, where he became an officer at the Department of Health, Education and Welfare. The Byerses divorced, remarried each other, and divorced again. In 1971 Connie married J. Carter Brown, director of the National Gallery, but that marriage terminated after three years in 1974. Brown remarried in 1976. Connie is currently single and goes by the name Mrs. Constance B. Mellon. She has remained active over the years in Washington affairs, serving on boards and committees of the National Ballet, CARE-Medico, the John F. Kennedy Center for the Performing Arts, Miss Porter's School, and the Committee to Save Canterbury Cathedral. A 1970 New York *Times* report of a National Gallery dinner hosted by Paul reported that Connie attended in a long black Givenchy dress studded with gold nailheads, and quoted her as saying, "I told my hairdresser that with my black hair and this black dress I was afraid my pale face would look like a slice of Camembert cheese."

As a group, the women of the "poorer" branches have probably lived more interesting lives. One, Mary Wise Peeples, great-great-granddaughter of the Judge from the line of his eldest son, T. A., and granddaughter of Edward P. the architect, spent a lot of time in Africa and served as secretary to Lowell Thomas and then to Condé Nast before settling down in Memphis, Tennessee. Others, such as Peggy Hitchcock's younger daughter, also named Peggy (Margaret), have chosen alternate lifestyles. The younger Peggy, born in 1933, attended Miss Porter's, Bryn Mawr, and Barnard, debuted in 1951, and in 1965 married Dr. Louis Scarrone Jr., a Yale Medical School graduate. Then she became interested in astrology and the occult, separated from Scarrone, and subsequently married Walter H. Bowart, who shares her interests.

Bowart, a decent, bright, and friendly man, published an alternate-alternate paper in New York City, *The East Village Other,* and organized an "underground press" syndicate before their marriage. Now the Bowarts live in Tucson, Arizona, where Walter published the short-lived *Omen,* a journal of the occult. Currently he is working on a book about the Central Intelligence Agency. He has been badly received by most of the family's stodgier members. Mothering their two children keeps Peggy pretty busy, but she manages to make time for a daily yoga session. Though Walter is an outgoing sort, after seven years in Tucson the Bowarts are still not listed in the city directory, let alone the phone book, and they are little known even in the city's fringe world. They share the low profile of the rest of the Mellon family.

At least one of the Judge's "daughters" is living with her lover in a cold-water structure in upper New York State, where they are raising their "love child."

Other daughters of the Judge are active and valuable proponents for change within the mainstream. One such is Helen Claire, from the "poor" T. A. line. On the day of our interview, Helen was suffering from what must have been one of the most aggravated head colds in medical history; she sounded awful and was quite obviously not looking her best. Even sick, her face is "pretty" enough, though it is not a face that anyone could call glamorous. Her form is perhaps a bit *too* lean, and on the day of our visit, the cast of her complexion was determined by her horrid cold. Under these very worst of circumstances, Helen Claire's irrepressible personality came through vibrantly. She is warm, generous, feeling, vivacious, fresh, alive. Her exposures to art, literature, and the dance have been extensive to the point of esoterica, but she wears her culture nicely, and the prominent hallmark of it is her receptivity to aesthetic and humane feeling.

Helen's mother, also named Helen but known as "Patsy," last of T. A. Junior's children, was born in 1914. Of all the publicity-hating Mellons, Helen Senior has been as reticent as any. She attended Sarah Lawrence, developed an interest in ornithology, and in 1936, at the age of twenty-two, married Adolph W. Schmidt in a "society wedding" attended by every Mellon extant.

Schmidt, father of Helen Claire, is well known in Pittsburgh from having been the front man for many Mellon family civic and philanthropic concerns as an employee of the wealthier branches of the family. He was an official of the Allegheny Conference and personally important in the Pittsburgh renaissance, a "governor" of T. Mellon & Sons, and president of the A. W. Mellon Educational and Charitable Trust. He was the family agent who most often came in contact with Pittsburgh's intelligentsia, who knew him as the man in the Mellon empire that could read. The Litchfield

Document, a liberally oriented analysis of problems at University of Pittsburgh during Chancellor Litchfield's period, described him thus:

> Within the Mellon clan, the dark, intent, courteous Adolph Schmidt is probably the person with the most intelligent concern and understanding of educational needs and social problems. He works enthusiastically with the professionals on the 39th floor and is more at ease with ex–college professors on his staff, than the Mellon-dominated Rolling Rock Hunt Club congerie.

Schmidt became well regarded in high-level Republican circles as an expert on, and sometime participant in, NATO affairs during the administration of President Eisenhower. In 1969 he was appointed United States ambassador to Canada, a position that he held for almost five years until retiring in January 1974. From his many speeches he seems a unique mixture of liberal and conservative.

The Schmidts' daughter grew up in Pittsburgh and Ligonier, and traveled in the world of her wealthier distant cousins. The Schmidts, of course, lived in a smaller house than wealthier Mellons lived in, but Helen Claire was never aware of any difference between them on the basis of wealth. "Mommy had grown up in a big, big house and didn't like it, and I thought that's why we lived in a littler house." She went to Westover School and was honored at a huge and lavish debutante party. The next day she read in the newspapers that U.S. Steel employees had gone on strike, and she felt uncomfortable about the juxtaposition of the foolishnesses of the night before with the hardships ahead for so many of Pittsburgh's blue-collar people. She could understand the "fury" (her word) that would have been directed against her and her world if "they" had only known. She is proud of her third cousin once removed Rachel Walton Whetzel, who reached debutante age in the early 1970s but refused to participate in the rites.

Before going on to college, Helen went to Paris, where she studied art and piano and became entranced with the ballet. At an old age at which to begin such pursuits, she started to study ballet. She returned to the United States and entered Sarah Lawrence College, but spent more of her time in intensive ballet studies in New York City. To overcome the disadvantage of her late start in the dance, she pushed herself to and past the point of exhaustion, until one day a shampoo bottle fell and shattered on the shower floor, causing lacerations to her foot that ended her career as a ballerina before it had had a chance to begin.

After college Helen married James Truman Bidwell Jr. Bidwell was the son of the chairman of the board of governors of the New York Stock Exchange, had been educated at St. Paul's, Yale, and Harvard Law School, and was affiliated with a prestigious New York firm. They settled in Manhattan, where Helen studied art and art history at New York University's Institute of Fine Arts. She received a master's degree there in 1956. Her parents were never enthusiastic about her interest in the dance or in art, but Gertrud Mellon, Matthew's first wife, became her close friend while Helen was in college, encouraged her, and opened new worlds for her in art appreciation.

Helen worked for a while as a research assistant for the Arab League at the United Nations and published articles on the Alhambra and on Islamic pottery in their magazine, *Arab World*. She held a job as an assistant to an art restorer. But her marriage did not work out; the Bidwells separated and Helen relocated to Washington.

In Washington Helen fell into an interim position as an instructor in art history at George Washington University, worked on a Treasury Department catalogue of the art and architectural details of the Treasury Building, held a position working on grants with the National Endowment for the Arts, and ended up at the Washington office of the State University of New York. There she met her present husband, William F. Claire, director of the university's Washington office and a poet whose tastes and instincts are in tune with Helen's. Claire published *Voyages,* a literary magazine, with the assistance of his older friend Mark van Doren for seven years, but abandoned the periodical after Van Doren's death. The Claires' son, Mark, is named for Van Doren.

Helen has had some contact with other Mellons in New York, Washington, and Pittsburgh, not so much as relatives but as other people who travel in similar circles. She read *Thomas Mellon and His Times* more for the light that it sheds on what she calls "the development of the national mentality" than for its value as a family history. Though she grew up in Pittsburgh, she feels the alienation from it that most of the Mellons who have left feel. Pittsburgh, she says, is the world of "the preservers." "It's hard to go back to Pittsburgh, it's like going back in the cocoon."

Several years ago, Claire took Helen to a National Press Club meeting at which the guest speaker was Gloria Steinem. The meeting was Helen's first exposure to the women's movement, and Steinem's stories of women passed over, their "worth" as human beings denigrated, made Helen cry. "I was quite embarrassed; people don't cry in public." Reflecting on her own past, she began to understand disappointments in her own employment history. She began to appreciate the parallels between the situation of so many women and that of so many blacks, and she says that her involvement in the women's movement increased her awareness of and sympathy for the blacks of America. She became, she says, "radicalized." She became involved in Women's Ordination Now (WON), a group that supported the "radical" elements in the Episcopal Church pushing for full equality of women in the church, and she was active in ecclesiastical defense efforts for heretical clergymen that permitted women to preach in their churches. She worked closely with NOW, National Organization of Women, though she is uncertain as to whether she was ever formally a member. Helen skirted the question whether other young Mellon women shared her interest, but it seemed clear from her discussion of "old" family attitudes and of Pittsburgh today, that she stands pretty much alone in her dedication to women's rights.

WON won its battle in the fall of 1976, when the Episcopal Church altered its policy dating back to Henry VIII and formally began admitting women to its priesthood. At about that time Helen realized that, for all of her liberation, in the most important of ways she was emulating the life pattern of the most old-fashioned Pittsburgh matron. Her infant son was being raised not by herself but by a governess. The governess was fired. Helen curtailed her outside interests. Despite powerful temptations, her principal place is now in the home, raising her child. It is a pleasant home, a largish house in one of the nicest sections of Washington, D.C., at the westerly end of Georgetown. It is decorated with things that she and her husband have picked up on their travels, an eclectic assortment—a few Indian miniatures, a Chinese screen, a dada collage done by a six-year-old who was to become known as e. e. cummings, some oriental rugs. Her surroundings are entirely pleasant, though Helen feels something lacking. She recently filled out a form that had a blank for "occupation." "Housewife," she wrote, gritting her teeth.

The reader has already met most of the richer young Mellon gentlemen: Pross and Richard from the General's line; Sarah's son, Dickie Scaife; Matthew's sons, Karl and Jay. Also fairly well off would be Paul's son, Timmy, and the Hitchcock twins, Billy and his brother, Tommy Hitchcock III.

Possibly the ablest of all living Mellons is Paul's unknown son Timmy. At the bank, Tim is thought of as the only young Mellon of real ability. Tim has little in common with his family other than the similarity of his looks to his father's, the way that he protects his privacy, and his shyness or reserve, whichever it be. Thirty-five as of this writing, he has passed out of a rather left-wing period, but he retains the concern and dedication of the progressive and he continues to be attracted to the causes of today. He is not an obtrusive activist and only once has he made any extensive public comment on any issue. In 1970 the distinguished professor Milton Friedman wrote an article in *The New York Times Magazine* the thrust of which was that the only social responsibility of business was to increase profits. Tim took a different view in a letter to the editor of the *Times* magazine:

> I speak not only as an investor in American corporations but also as a "stockholder" in other institutions: my Government, my community, my family, my society. As multiple stockholders we all make complex and sometimes conflicting demands upon these institutions. When we demand that automobiles be designed so as not to foul the air, we are weighing a 1% reduction in corporate profits against a 10% increase in the cost of remaining healthy. When we applaud efforts to hire the "hard-core unemployed," we are mindful as much of the staggering economic and social costs of welfare and urban renewal as we are of the horrifying plight of many of these individuals. Stockholders seek not to incapacitate the corporate mechanism, but to maximize our over-all economic and social portfolio.

Tim is neither sanctimonious nor self-righteous and he does not personally proselytize. Though there is something of a gap between himself and his father in terms of values, orientation, and lifestyles, they maintain the kind of relationship that Paul maintained with his own very different father. When Paul comes to Yale he generally stays at Tim's two-bedroom house in nearby Guilford. On such occasions one can see Paul's gas-guzzling Mercedes parked next to Timmy's ecologically respectable Volkswagen Rabbit.

Tim was born in 1942, attended Milton Academy in Milton, Massachusetts, worked a summer at Mellon Bank, and went to Yale ('64). At Yale he sometimes ranked close to the top of his class academically and was accepted into Yale's Scholar of the House program, which is reserved for the most promising students. His Scholar of the House thesis, *The Peronist Movement in Argentine Politics,* is a very impressive work, a lengthy and competently written piece that would compare favorably with most doctoral theses. As a senior he affiliated with Paul's senior society, Scroll and Key.

Between his junior and senior years, just short of his twenty-first birthday, Tim married Susan Crawford Tracy, a Bryn Mawr College graduate a couple of years older than himself. Susan, as progressive as her husband, is perhaps a little more widely known than he is in activist circles. Some regard her as the more forceful of the two, and the one more nearly responsible for their joint views on matters of public policy. When Tim and Susan contributed $60,000 to help rebuild an American-bombed hospital in North

Vietnam, Tim attributed his interest in the charity to righting what he called a "senseless accident," while Susan spoke in more highly politicized terms in labeling their donation "a very personal expression of horror and grief at the destruction carried on in the name of America." For whatever it may mean, however, he is registered as a Democrat (possibly the only "rich" Mellon Democrat) while she is listed as a Republican. Tim's "cousin" and classmate at Yale, Jay, describes Susan as he describes Tim: "very conscientious, terribly committed." Tim and Susan do not have children.

After Yale Tim took a graduate degree in city planning at Yale's Art and Architecture School in 1966, then worked for a while at the Yale Computer Center attempting to apply computer techniques to problems of city planning. Though he is currently "unemployed," he takes a semi-active interest in a couple of small businesses in southern Connecticut, one involved in distribution of computer materials and the other in promoting and installing solar heating systems.

In 1969 Tim founded his progressively oriented Sachem Fund. Since then he has channeled over $4 million of his contributions through it and goes into its New Haven offices about once a week. He also serves on the board of governors of New Haven University, a community school that educates a less-advantaged student body than Tim's nearby alma mater. Though he seems to have isolated himself from most of the Yale community, he shows up frequently at the New Haven University campus.

Since college days Tim has gravitated to the town of Guilford, an early American settlement on Long Island Sound about twenty minutes east of New Haven. During college he dated a Guilford girl. After his marriage he and Susan rented in Guilford until they built their own home there in 1969. Their lot is a half-acre piece right on the sound and it cost $65,000 when Tim bought it just after college in 1964. In 1969–70 they built a contemporary home on it of unimpressive size (2300 square feet), five rooms, two bedrooms, finished in stucco. It is a U-shaped building with a patio in the center, the open end of the U blocked off by a garage that faces the street. Only the garage is visible from the street, and no windows are visible from oceanside. It must have some nice features, as it cost about $175,000 to build in 1970, or about seventy-five dollars a square foot at a time when developers were making middle-class castles to sell at twenty dollars a square foot. Since then Timmy has added solar heat to the home.

To get to Timmy's house in the prestigious Sachem's Head section of Guilford, one passes at least two signs entreating the curious to turn around. Tim's house is at the most out-of-the-way corner of Sachem's Head. Most of the mailboxes, at least, have names on them, except for one bearing only the initials "T.M." Sachem's Head is very private, and Tim, in all respects a very private person, is into privacy. Sachem's Head is also very exclusive. Tim is not into exclusivity. In 1977 Steven Leninski, a Ukrainian immigrant who made himself a millionaire in the building trades in Guilford, bought at Sachem's Head and traumatized the community by posting a large sign inviting the general public to use his portion of the beach. Leninski told the press, "I believe every successful immigrant should give something back to the country. Everyone should put back a tree or a bush. I am putting back the beach." Many at Sachem's Head clustered in their lawyers' offices and others went into quiet mourning, while Timmy Mellon bicycled over to the nonconformist's house to introduce himself and to wish Leninski well. For the balance of the summer Tim and Susan frequently bicycled past Leninski's, never failing to give him a friendly wave.

After forty years in Upperville, Paul is virtually unknown even to other hunt-country aristocrats. Timmy, on the other hand, mixes quietly in Guilford. He tools around town in a pickup truck, usually garbed in a turtle neck sweater and simple trousers. No one with whom the author spoke could recall ever seeing him wearing a necktie or a sports jacket, let alone a suit. He is well liked. Most townspeople describe him as quiet and courteous. "A nice boy," an older Sachem's Head lady said. Many people in Guilford know him, though few of those who would want to know him do.

Billy Hitchcock, William Mellon Hitchcock, is the "black sheep" of the Mellon family. The Judge would have been dismayed by Billy's history, but not surprised, and would have pointed to Billy as confirmation of his theory that "Where a family has enjoyed their career of wealth and prosperity for a generation or so, we may expect 'degenerate sons'; not invariably, but more frequently than otherwise."

Born to great wealth on his father's side, as well as his mother's, Billy Hitchcock never had a worry. With perhaps a touch of exaggeration in the early 1970s he estimated his trust funds at about $160 million, producing an annual income to him of several million dollars. But Billy, as nearly everyone knows him, was never cut out to be an "idle rich." He is an imaginative, energetic, competent fellow, with instinctive organizational ability coupled with tremendous charm that makes him a natural leader. He is also clever and exploitive, with a hunger for adventure. Illegality heightens any adventure. It was almost destined that Billy Hitchcock would become, as the *Village Voice* described him, the man who transformed the manufacture of LSD "from a decentralized cottage industry to big business."

Billy was five when his father was killed. He went to St. Paul's, his father's school, but was expelled for misbehavior. He studied a while at the University of Texas and worked as a roughneck on a Texas oil rig. His first brush with the law came in 1957, when at the age of eighteen he became the central figure in a bizarre false complaint to the police. According to the Pittsburgh *Press* account of it, Billy told the police that on June 13, 1957, someone had shot at him and had tried to run his vehicle off the road. The next day two men had stopped him on New York's Park Avenue and had demanded that $100,000 be delivered to them on June 17 at the Westbury High School on Long Island. On the given date, a mob of disguised policemen filtered around the fringes of the schoolyard to nab the extortionists. Nobody showed. There were no extortionists. A month later the police came back to the Hitchcock mansion with a warrant to arrest Billy for having hoaxed them. It was a prank, but an alarming and inexplicable one —inexplicable except perhaps in terms of the delight that Billy has taken in "playing" the establishment.

He seemed to settle down in the 1960s. He became associated, at least in name, as a stockbroker with his father's old firm, Lehman Brothers; he married well and had two children. Underneath, Billy was still playing the establishment. In 1969 the establishment began winning the game. That year one of the coterie of lawyers that had been associated with Billy was passing through Los Angeles customs with a wad of a bankroll too large to escape the attention of customs officers. How much was it? $100,000. Where did it come from? Switzerland. Whose was it? Hitchcock's. Internal Revenue Service was notified. Billy's Swiss banker, Johan F. "Freddy" Paravicini, quickly came up with a letter for Billy to give to I.R.S. saying that the money was a loan to Billy from Paravicini Bank Ltd., but Paravicini's own credibility was suspect with federal investigators. Billy's wife made the situation worse by filing for divorce, and including among the court papers an affidavit stating that Billy had a Swiss bank account in which he placed the profits that he was making from the illegal manufacture of drugs. On the advice of lawyers and accountants, it was decided that Billy had better file amended tax returns and pay another half-million in income taxes, so he did, but it was too late to call it all off.

It took almost four years for the government to piece together its full file, but in 1973 Billy was indicted for income tax evasion. The government charge was that he had evaded $543,000 in income taxes between 1966 and 1968. In the course of the government's investigation it was determined that he had also been buying American stocks through Paravicini's bank—a total of $40 million in stock—entirely on credit, in violation of S.E.C.

trading rules that set limits on the amount of "margin" that a buyer can use. Billy was indicted for that as well. The S.E.C. violation was a minor matter carrying a maximum of two years in prison, which as felonies go, is not a very serious matter. The income tax charges were more alarming and threatened Billy with up to twenty-four years in the federal penitentiary. Any "deal" that might be made with the prosecutors would require that Billy give full cooperation to federal investigators. He called his closest friend in the drug trade, Robert "Tim" Scully, six years younger than himself, a lean, intensive self-taught scientist whose IQ exceeds the scales. Billy explained the situation. He would have to "talk," to go "state's evidence." Would Scully go with him, and possibly save his own neck too? The answer was no. With Billy's cooperation, the police proceeded to arrest Scully and the other principal operatives in California's most important "acid" manufacturing enterprise. Billy contributed some $10,000 for Scully's attorneys' fees, but testified against him. Most of the details of Billy's involvement in the drug trade came out in the five-month trial at San Francisco of Scully; Dr. Lester Friedman, the Case Western Reserve professor who simplified the process for making LSD; and a third principal.

Billy first became seriously involved in the psychedelic world in 1963, when he befriended Dr. Timothy Leary, just ousted from his Harvard position in the controversy that brought "acid" to the attention of the American public. Billy rented Leary his fifty-five-room mansion at Millbrook, New York, for a nominal sum. Leary used it for several years for what the *Village Voice* described as "a monster party which often filled the mansion with 50 or 60 hippies at a time, their eyeballs full of the latest batch of LSD." Billy was there much of the time. The situation got so wild that the prosecutor for Dutchess County, New York, an unknown named G. Gordon Liddy, had Billy arrested for maintaining a nuisance. Nothing came of that arrest.

Meanwhile, Billy developed his contacts in the world of illicit chemistry, and according to the *Voice*'s hostile account, put together and bankrolled a combination of people that included Swiss and Bahamian funny-money bankers, high-powered and low-powered lawyers, spaced-out geniuses, and motorcycle thugs to form the world's leading manufacturer and distributor of "Orange Sunshine." In the tradition of the sons of Judge Mellon, it was a fully integrated operation. Billy insisted both at the trial of his associates and to the *Voice*'s reporter that he had never imagined that what his associates were up to was in any way illegal.

Billy was the principal government witness at the San Francisco trial. He was not a particularly strong witness. He admitted that he had perjured himself four times during Internal Revenue and S.E.C. investigations and before a federal grand jury. He admitted that his own drug usage had been extensive. After a lengthy listing of substances with which he had experimented, the prosecutor asked casually, "Omitted anything?" Billy responded quietly, "Yes, heroin." He acknowledged that he was awaiting sentencing on his guilty pleas to income tax evasion and to S.E.C. violations, and that the government had promised to recommend leniency in exchange for his testimony. He was not a strong witness, but he was strong enough. Scully was sentenced to twenty years in prison, the others to lesser terms. Billy was not prosecuted on any drug charge, but got five years suspended and $20,000 in fines for his "white collar" crimes.

Today Billy is remarried, living with his new wife in the same apartment building as his mother on the Upper East Side of Manhattan. He busies himself making and planning movies and TV documentaries, such as an exposé of the situation at Manhattan's Bellevue Hospital. He is still matching wits with the establishment, but no longer in a self-destructive fashion. Indeed, his current endeavors are probably socially desirable.

There is something irrepressible about Billy that makes him tremendously likable notwithstanding his violations of both the code of state and the code of silence. He is spontaneous and creative, with an ability to tune into the wavelengths of almost everyone with whom he comes in contact. He is not unenlightened on matters of public policy. He is informal. He came to an interview with the *Voice*'s reporter in dungarees, cowboy boots, and a plaid western shirt, and he was wearing Indian jewelry. It was a costume which he might reasonably have thought would appeal to a reporter from the *Village Voice*. While the particular journalist was disimpressed, she did describe Billy as "tall, handsome, charming and intelligent," and reported that "most everyone rather likes the lean 34-year-old from the maids who call him 'Mr. Billy' to the narcs and government lawyers whose job it was to prosecute him." Billy declined to see this author in the most reasonable and charming of the many rebuffs received during the writing of this book.

Billy's twin brother, Thomas Hitchcock III, showed early signs of pursuing a similarly adventurous lifestyle. In 1963 the New York *Daily News* reported that Tommy III, "daredevil son of a daredevil father," had escaped death when his Ferrari crashed at over 100 miles an hour in a 300-mile sports car race. Tommy's principal injury in the crash was a fracture to a small spinal bone, and he emerged from his hospitalization as unafraid as ever. Two years later the New York *Herald Tribune* carried a similar report. That time Tommy's car was identified as a Brabham, the speed as ninety. The crash, in a Formula Three race at Silverstone, England, was described as "spectacular." Since then Tommy III seems to have taken a more serious tack. He went to Harvard, worked a while at Mellon Bank, and most recently was attending law school in Ohio. He has gone "straight." One family source told the author that Tommy III avoids his unconventional siblings as much as possible.

The young men of the T. A. branch, the "poor" branch of the family, have never been in a position to enjoy a life of leisure and luxury, and perhaps because of their relative poverty (and it is only a relative poverty; none of the Judge's descendants have been "poor") they have developed themselves more fully than have the young men of the wealthier branches of the family. Tom Schmidt, Helen's younger brother, born in 1940, went to Groton, Princeton, and Harvard Law School. He practiced law in a private firm in Pittsburgh for a while, and for the past several years has done "public interest" legal work more to his liking at the Western Pennsylvania Conservancy headed by Joshua Whetzel, spouse of his third cousin. A creative and talented young man, while a Princeton student he converted a vacant building into an art studio and spent a lot of his time painting. His second cousins, Edward Mellon Leonard and Craig Leonard Jr., both grandsons of Edward P. the architect, are also lawyers, one in San Francisco and the other in New York. Edward Mellon Leonard received heroic decoration for his service as a Navy pilot in the Vietnam war. The Leonards' cousin Henry A. Wise III is a banker in Wilmington. Wise wears his Mellonhood so softly that not even close business associates are aware that he is, after all, a great-grandnephew of the greatest Secretary of the Treasury since Alexander Hamilton. The author interviewed two of the "poor" young men, Charles Abernethy and Thomas Mellon.

Charles N. Abernethy III, a great-great-grandson of the Judge by way of Mary McClung, was born in 1943. His father was a high-ranking civil servant with the Veterans Administration in Pittsburgh, very comfortable but never "rich" by Mellon standards. Abernethy himself went to Shadyside, and then took an engineering degree at Carnegie Tech. He worked for a while as a technical writer and then went for his doctorate to Penn State, where he got his Ph.D. in 1970. The abstract in *Dissertation Abstracts* of his thesis, *Individual Styles of Attention Allocation Under Normal and Stressful Conditions,* is so dense that this author did not attempt to delve deeper into the subject.

At the time of our interview, Abernethy was employed in Cambridge, Massachusetts, at the Transportation Systems Center, an adjunct but not an integral part of the United States Department of Transportation. As an example of his work he cited a project that he had been working on designing new taxicabs that would be accessible to people confined to wheelchairs. He is otherwise interested in ways of making public transportation and mass transportation more accessible and practical for the handicapped. He has spent a lot of time in wheelchairs himself, better to appreciate the practical aspects of the problem. Though he has been interested and engrossed in his work, he is disturbed by an inordinate inefficiency and sometime incompetence in the federal bureaucracy, and admits that the thought of returning to the academic community appeals to him.

Abernethy's apartment is some thirty miles west of Cambridge, and he proves his dedication to mass transportation. Instead of driving to work, he takes a bus to Boston and then the BMT over to Cambridge. Outside of his apartment sits a small blue Opel, a practical car that is conservationally and environmentally acceptable.

Abernethy is more socially and politically attuned than most engineers, which explains why he is in "public-service" engineering. He says that he was part of a generation moved by what he describes as "Kennedy motivations." He has voted Democratic in the past several elections, but is reluctant to call himself a liberal and cites, as an example of his deviation from usual liberal lines, his lack of sympathy for most aspects of the existing public welfare system, which he believes has led to monstrous situations in New York City and other urban communities.

He wears wire-rimmed glasses, and his nearly full beard is neatly trimmed. He is thin and wiry and obviously in top physical condition. Many years ago he damaged a lung while mountain climbing in the Canadian Rockies, and he began running as a form of physiotherapy for his lungs. He still runs every day. His dress is "modish" but not hip. When the author saw him he was wearing an ocher Viyella-like shirt, crisply pressed checkered pants, and Frye "harness" boots—the glossy mahogany-colored ones with the square toes and the shiny ornamental brass rings strapped, ostensibly for protection, at about the spot where the ankles will settle. He is well spoken in precise engineer's language, and is obviously a very bright guy.

His apartment is simply but tastefully furnished. There is a guitar in the corner that he used to plunk in his college days. His record collection indicates diverse up-to-date tastes, including, among others, albums by the British rock and roll group Herman's Hermits, Sinatra, pop folk singers Bob Dylan and Judy Collins, together with a modest sampling of classical music. At the time of our interview he was living alone; a girl that he has lived with "off and on" for several years was away completing her own education.

His Mellon background plays no part in his existence or self-concept. He is not steeped in family lore, has read portions of *Thomas Mellon and His Times* but none of *Judge Mellon's Sons,* and he was unaware of (and not much interested in) James Ross Mellon's published *Letters.* He has some contact with his immediate cousins, the other offspring of Mary McClung, but none with any of the other members of the extended family. He was at Shadyside with his second cousin once removed, Pross Mellon, one year older than himself, and knew him there slightly, but only as any other schoolmate and not as a distant relative. He follows one Mellon business, Gulf Oil, in which he owns a modest interest given to him as a child. Gulf is in bad shape, he says, and has been ever since the death of his first cousin twice removed, Richard King Mellon. He is critical of "the oil companies" as a group, including Gulf. He is neutral about Pittsburgh, and can see himself returning to it. When the author commented that Abernethy was the first Mellon he had met who had left Pittsburgh but could see himself returning to it, Abernethy responded, without any touch of either embarrassment or moral rank pulling, "I'm not a cosmopolitan person." He did not go to the family reunion in Ireland in 1968, but he almost went to the family reunion at Ligonier in 1970. He went out to Ligonier that day, but never made it to the reunion. He spent the day not far from Rolling Rock visiting and studying a house that had been designed by Frank Lloyd Wright.

Thomas Alexander Mellon IV, known as Alec, is Abernethy's second cousin (they have never met). Alec attended the family reunion in Ireland in 1968, and says that he has read "parts" of *Thomas Mellon and His Times,* but he has had almost no contact with Mellons beyond his immediate family. He is clearly proud to be a Mellon, though the matter of his background has had no more than sentimental significance for him, and no practical beneficial effects.

Alec is the son of Ned of the Mellon-Stuart construction enterprise and Ned's second wife. He was born in temporary Army quarters in 1946, and suffered serious illnesses in infancy and early childhood. He was never much of a student, and is still a poor reader though a competent writer. He went to a number of prep schools, where he did little beside play soccer, then to a Florida junior college. He entered and dropped out of Stetson University in De Land, Florida, and then returned there to become absorbed in the study of art history and in the potentials of photography as an art form. After college he began work as a photographer with the guidance and encouragement of F. Victor Rachner, a photographer of considerable regional distinction. Since then he has worked principally as a photographer, with time out for commercial fishing for fresh-water catfish on the St. Johns River in Florida. He owns an impressive array of studio equipment, but prefers to work in the more flexible 2¼ x 2¼ format. While the author was visiting at Alec's Mellon Studio in St. Augustine, Florida, a young actor came in for promotional photos. Instead of a formal studio setting, Alec took him outside and sat the actor on the sea wall in front of his studio for less stilted photographs. From the conversation between Alec and the actor it appeared that Alec was the usual photographer for St. Augustine's "artsy" set. At lunch Alec was well known in the local restaurant by people whose clothing indicated diverse economic and social stations. Since the author's visit to him, Alec has relocated to nearby Jacksonville, Florida, where he works with a group of commercial photographers, but he still works regularly for the St. Augustine *Traveler,* the town's semi-alternate weekly, and he keeps in close touch with his family in Summer Haven, where Ned's house contains an apartment available to Alec when he wants it. As of this writing, Alec is unmarried and seems to like it that way.

Alec occasionally displays his portfolio of creative photography at area art shows and craft exhibitions. It includes haunting landscapes, an artistically composed photograph of a marijuana plant ("No, I didn't grow it, but I know who did," he says with a grin), and what must rank among the best soft-porn photographs ever taken of the photogenic Mick Jagger. When we met, Alec was thirty and had already been designated a *National Geographic* area photographer. It seems only a matter of time before he is a "known" photographer, though he started out far behind many of his more advantaged cousins.

Two of the most promising of the Judge's descendants, both his great-great-grandsons, took their own lives. John Sellers was the son of Elizabeth Mellon Sellers, a daughter of T. A. II (and sister of Ned and of Helen Schmidt), and from the accounts of family members, a very wonderful woman. She was the only member of the family praised by all of the Mellons with whom the author spoke. "E," as she was known, married a difficult man from an old Pittsburgh family, who ended up as one of the lesser vice presidents of Koppers Company. Their only child, John, was born in 1944, and went to Yale. He was a very nice-looking boy, who stood well in his class and who had a sense of dedication. He gave part of his time to tutoring disadvantaged youngsters in New York City. One day in 1967 he threw himself in front of a New York City subway. "E" lived on another six years and died a draining and difficult death at the age of sixty-nine in 1973.

John's third cousin, William Larimer Mellon III, the only child of Dr. Mellon of Haiti, was born in 1932 and lived to establish himself more fully than did John. After his parents were divorced, he lived with his mother in Los Angeles, but spent summers on his father's ranch in Arizona. Occasionally the father would drive the long distance from the ranch to California to visit his little boy, but the father's appearance in his dusty ranch hand's outfit would embarrass the young son. He went to school in Los Angeles and then to St. Paul's, where he played football and soccer and sang in the glee club. From there he went on to Princeton. There he became active on the *Princeton Tiger,* the magazine published by Princeton undergrads, rising in his senior year to be its editor. His many articles in it, and an occasional piece in the *Nassau Literary Magazine,* indicate considerable basic ability marred by a sophomoric attachment to Hemingwayese that he would surely have outgrown with time. After college he served two years in the Air Force, married LeGrande Council, continued his writing, and began making films. According to his obituary in the *Princeton Alumni Magazine,* his non-fiction appeared in the international edition of *Life* and his fiction was published in the *Quarterly Review of Literature of California,* a journal so obscure that it is not available at either Yale's library or the Library of Congress.

Over his four years at Princeton, W. L. III began to gravitate more closely toward his father. When he entered Princeton, he gave his address as Beverly Hills, his mother's home; by the time of his graduation he listed it as New Orleans, where his father was completing his medical education at Tulane. He became involved in his father's work, made a "fund-raising" movie about his father's efforts in Haiti, and worked at the Hôpital Albert Schweitzer himself. Those who worked with him remember him as quiet, smart, and capable. Finally he decided to follow completely in his father's footsteps, and he entered Boston University as an undergraduate pre-med student. His father looked forward to the time when his son would replace him. In 1963, at the age of thirty, while pursuing his pre-med studies, he was reported missing. Two days later he was found on a backwoods Cape Cod road not far from his home slumped over in his car, dead from an overdose of barbituates. His widow now runs a dance band.

At the time of W. L.'s *Judge Mellon's Sons,* W. L. III was too young to have warranted much attention in his own right, and his grandfather lumped him in a paragraph with his cousin James Mellon Walton:

James Walton is doing very well at St. Paul's and William Larimer Mellon III is also doing well in a school in Los Angeles. In William's marked tendency to persevere in anything he tackles I see a reflection of qualities that counted heavily in our past. Although these two boys were too young for the war, it is by no means certain that they will not be caught in its backwash and still have to serve in the Army and Navy before they can begin their careers. That will be important service and I do not discount it. Nevertheless, it is my hope that none of my grandchildren shall ever allow themselves to lose sight of the fact that their talents are greatly needed in this world.

No one appears at the moment to be in a position to coordinate the vast interests of the Mellon family as a family.

Paul would probably disapprove of efforts at coordination, and he personally abdicated such responsibilities when A. W. died. His son Timmy's orientations would cut against him exercising or wanting to exercise any empirical role, and Dickie Scaife has shown no interest. The daughters of the wealthier branches have had any executive ability trained out of them. Of the wealthiest Mellons, only the General's son Pross has shown any real interest in a traditional executive role, and he has yet to show any sign of tremendous ability. At the time of the General's death in 1970, Frank Denton said of the General's two sons, then thirty-one and twenty-eight, "These are good kids but the two sons are both too young to be effective at this point." The following year a major New York *Times* spread on the family headed "Young Mellons Have Yet to Assume Control" attributed to "Pittsburgh sources" the thought that the General's sons, "both young and without distinguishing records either in school or in business, will have to earn family leadership roles." The *Times* source viewed the General's widow as exceeding either in terms of "intellect and the instinct for power." A family member with whom the author spoke in 1976 indicated that the situation had not changed in the five years since, and shared the still general impression that neither Pross nor his brother Richard had yet shown mettle, and that their mother, Mrs. Burrell, chairman of Richard K. Mellon & Sons, was the ablest of the lot and still the "strong man" of the General's branch of the family. As late as March of 1976, the Pittsburgh *Post-Gazette* reported that "Though nominally in charge of the financial end of the business, Prosser Mellon is generally regarded as a figurehead." At the bank he is not yet highly regarded. Pross, however, goes through the motions and is about the only one left from the rich branches of the family who seems to feel any internal compulsion to carry on the traditions of the Judge and the General. He was adopted into the traditions, not born into them, which may hold some clue to his greater dedication to them than has been shown by most of the Judge's other descendants.

Who, if anyone, is to coordinate the family's interests is an important question when one considers the vast potential power of the Mellon wealth.

When that power is computed out into dollars, it becomes awe-inspiring. The visible portion of their wealth would tabulate as follows:

	PERCENTAGE OF OWNERSHIP	VALUE AS OF JANUARY 1, 1978
Gulf	18%	$ 938,270,000
Alcoa	21%	336,122,200
Mellon National	38%	187,111,900
General Reinsurance	20%	185,300,000
Koppers	20%	113,109,500
Final interest in Carborundum	20%	107,793,100
First Boston	20%	8,151,400
Total Holdings in Mellon Companies		1,875,858,100
Holdings of family foundations in other *than Mellon Companies (as of January 1, 1977)*		512,000,000
Total visible and readily computable assets of Mellon empire		$2,362,090,300

The above table includes nothing for preferred stock that the family almost certainly still owns in Alcoa and Koppers, nothing for the vast acreage and installations at Rolling Rock and Upperville, nothing for the choice real estate that the family owns in Hawaii, Arizona, Florida, Colorado, or any of Paul Mellon's other homes, nothing for Paul's remaining collections (including his collection of impressionist paintings) or for whatever less-publicized collections may be owned by the rest of the family. Most important, it puts no value on whatever investments were made with the proceeds of the 52 per cent of Gulf that the family owned but has sold off, an interest which at today's market would be valued at $2,710,557,600. It places no value on whatever investments might have been made with the 35.22 per cent of Alcoa's Canadian affiliate, Alcan Aluminium, that the family once owned but sold, an interest that today would be worth $374,124,700, nor does it place a value on the 14.22 per cent of Alcoa that the family has sold, today worth $227,602,720, or on the half of Carborundum long ago sold by the family, today worth $269,482,750. It places no value on whatever might have been done with the vast real estate holdings once owned jointly by A. W. and R. B.—R. B.'s half of which was valued at almost $200 million in the depths of the Great Depression when R. B. died. It places no value on whatever investments might have been made with those dividends, rents, and interest payments received by the family that were not eaten up by income taxes, living expenses, and charitable grants.

It is possible to speculate on the current value of the entire iceberg only if one proceeds on a set of assumptions: 1) Assume that about 20 per cent of the monies from the sale of Gulf, Alcan, Alcoa, and Carborundum were taken by capital gains taxes; 2) assume that the rest of those monies were invested in other securities, in real estate, or in chattels that have done about as well over time as Gulf, Alcan, Alcoa, and Carborundum; 3) assume that all of the dividends were eaten up by taxes, living expenses, or charitable contributions; 4) assume that all of the collections and all of the real estate other than the traditional family homesteads at Upperville and Rolling Rock were acquired with part of the proceeds of the sales; 5) assume that the non-Mellon aspects of the foundation portfolios were acquired with part of the proceeds of the sales; 6) assume that the Alcoa and Koppers preferred stock is worthless, that the funds once invested in the real estate owned jointly by A. W. and R. B. have been squandered, and that nothing else that any of the Mellons might own is worth anything at all. Proceeding on such assumptions, one can arrive at a conservative estimate of the combined Mellon worth as of January 1, 1978, as follows:

Total holdings in Mellon companies	$1,875,858,100
Value of whatever was acquired by sale of Gulf (80% of $2,710,557,600)	2,168,446,000
Value of whatever was acquired by sale of Alcan (80% of $374,124,700)	299,299,760
Value of whatever was acquired by sale of Alcoa (80% of $227,602,720)	182,082,170
Value of whatever was acquired by sale of Carborundum prior to the Kennecott offer (80% of $269,482,750)	215,586,200
Value of the Oak Spring-Rokeby installations at Upperville	0
Value of the Rolling Rock estates	0
Value of the Manhattan, Hawaii, Arizona, Florida, Colorado, Aruba, and Cape Cod properties owned by various family members	0
Value of Alcoa and Koppers preferred stock owned by the family	0
Value of whatever might have been acquired with the proceeds of Mellon-owned real estate	0
Value of any and all collections	0
Value of anything else any Mellon might own	0
Conservative estimate of total Mellon family assets	$4,741,272,230

At $4.7 billion, the Mellons far outstrip any other American family, including the new-monied oil families of Getty and Hunt, or that of shipping magnate Daniel Ludwig. The old-monied families of Rockefeller, Du

Pont, and Ford are all relative paupers. Inasmuch as the $4.7 billion computation is arrived at by resolving most possibilities in favor of the "poverty" of the Mellons, it does not seem unreasonable to estimate their combined net worth (including the billion dollars in Mellon family foundations) at something well in excess of $5 billion.

Money is symbolic power, but power nonetheless. Mellon money controls Gulf, with direct power over the destinies of thousands across the world and, because of its importance in the petroleum industry, indirect power over all of us. Almost as significant, Mellon money controls Mellon National, which in turn controls a varying $8 to $10 billion in trust assets that could be used to control several dozens of other major corporate entities. It controls the world's largest producer of aluminum, today a vital substance. Its influence reaches very much further still.

All of this power is centralized on the thirty-ninth floor, where the offices of the wealthy branches of the family are located. P. O. Box 1138 serves as a good address for any of them; it receives the mail for such diverse entities as the Grant Foundation that supports Dr. Mellon's Haitian hospital, and Paul's man Nathan Pearson. The thirty-ninth floor represents an unseen but powerful gravitational force.

If this situation is in any way upsetting to the reader, the reader is not alone—it is equally upsetting to the Mellons. They do not want to read their names linked with Gulf scandals. The wealthier, older Mellons do not want the responsibilities that accompany power and control; younger Mellons enjoy the benefits but have neither the power nor the control. Since the time of the General, the family has tried to avoid the appearance that the interests of the Mellon companies were intermeshed, but the existence of T. Mellon & Sons, the family's formal round table, perpetuated the rough intermeshing of the family's overall interests. Paul, sensitive to the family's potential as a political target, was never enthusiastic about T. Mellon & Sons, and he caused it to disband immediately after the death of the General.

For years the family has been steadily, gradually reducing its interest in the Mellon companies. Many times annually their names appear in the S.E.C. filings reported in the *Commercial & Financial Chronicle* as selling off small pieces of one or another of the historic elements of their empire. They are diversifying their holdings partly in response to safety considerations, partly to reduce their degree of ongoing responsibility for corporate doings.

The author made a separate index card for the name of each living Mellon and for the name of each director of each Mellon company and foundation.

Relatively few names cropped up more than once or twice. There is surprisingly little cross-fertilization between the various Mellon interests, probably less than would occur quite innocently, and the degree of what cross-fertilization there is seems to be decreasing rather than increasing. Many of the names do hook up elsewhere. For an example, the board of the important Chemical Bank of New York City includes a former Carborundum director and also the treasurer of Cordelia Scaife May's Laurel Fund. It is possible that the two gentlemen are entirely unaware of their mutual involvement in a "Mellon web," and in any case their contact at Chemical Bank does not seem particularly alarming. The author looked up all of the names on the index cards on the stockholder lists of Koppers and Mellon National Bank, and though many of the people may hold stock in the names of nominees, the general absence of the names of Mellon affiliates on the stockholder lists of these two Mellon companies further confirms the impression that people involved in one Mellon concern do not take an interest in the affairs of other Mellon entities.

It seems likely that the people on the thirty-ninth floor do talk to one another, but at least formalistically they are going their own ways. It is probably not just a formalistic matter either. Jerry McAfee, Dorsey's successor as chief executive officer at Gulf told *Time* that "Gulf is a lot different than it was in the 1950s, when Richard King Mellon was active. The General spoke with authority and had a lot of influence. But there is no overriding Mellon influence today."

Older people in Pittsburgh still cite and many believe the old saw, "Nothing moves in Pittsburgh without the Mellons." If "the Mellons" be taken as a reference to the Mellons as institutions—as a reference to Mellon Bank and the Mellon foundations—then "nothing moves" still has substantial truth to it. In the sense that it is usually spoken, however, "the Mellons" refers to people, individual Mellons acting either individually or collectively —anthropomorphic Mellons. In that sense the myth has validity only insofar as it constitutes a self-fulfilling prophecy.

Those who believe that "nothing moves in Pittsburgh without the Mellons" are likely to proceed on the assumption that nothing moves in Pittsburgh without the Mellons; they are likely to proceed with caution and deference in areas sensitive to the Mellons or to their interests. One of the clerks at "Orphans' Court," in explaining why he could not show A. W.'s papers to the author (the documents of his estate and trusts, unlike the revelations about humbler men, are sealed from prying eyes and kept in a locked vault), looked around carefully to be certain that he was not being overheard before whispering, "Let me give you a tip. The Mellons own this town." It was obvious that he disapproved of the situation, and also that he believed in the powers from on high. Many older Pittsburghers seem to proceed on a kind of local version of Pascal's wager: Work on the assumption that the Mellons "run this town," and if they do, then you have proceeded on the correct assumption; if they don't, what have you lost? In terms of significant power exercised directly by individual Mellons to affect specific situations, however, Pittsburgh has long ceased to be the "Mellon patch."

The individual Mellons, of course, could exercise considerable influence on the bank, and determinative influence on the various foundations that they have established. That influence, however, would be indirect rather than direct, an important distinction in analyzing the substance of the myth of anthropomorphic Mellon power today. At the bank, no Mellon would presume to second-guess the career bankers who now serve in all of the bank's major leadership positions; and even in their own foundations their individual or collective instincts are largely molded by the influence of professional staffs of varying degrees of sophistication.

It is a virtual certainty that what coordination (and what control and accountability) there is of Mellon influence in the Mellon empire will continue to diminish. As the family becomes more and more spread out, it seems likely that the decisions of the Mellon entities will become even more "professionalized." Despite the champing of some younger Mellons, more and more decisions will be made by upper-middle management people, causing further decline in anthrophomorphic Mellon power. The wealth—the symbolic power—becomes sliced into smaller and smaller pieces of pie. The General's wealth, divided among four children, a wife, and a major foundation, gives each of the individuals something less than a quarter of the symbolic power that the General wielded, and R. K. wielded probably no more than half of the symbolic power that R. B. could exercise. Already Henry Clay Frick's stock in what is today's Mellon National is owned by over sixty different entities, and in sufficient time the same will surely be true of what was once the General's or Paul's or Ailsa's holdings in the bank. Important changes in the federal gift and death tax scheme enacted in 1976 also promise to hasten the diminution of individual Mellon power. Until 1976 wealthy people could give their money to children and grandchildren while living, paying only the relatively modest gift tax, rather than the much hungrier estate tax. In 1976 the differential in gift and estate tax rates was eliminated. This change will make it impossible for wealthy people to channel off their fortunes relatively unscathed by taxes, as the General, Ailsa, and Sarah did, and as Paul has probably provided for. Henceforth when Mellon wealth gets passed on, the greater portion of it will be passed on to the Internal Revenue Service.

The prospects for combination of Mellon power become increasingly improbable as the closeness of the family continues to diminish. Matthew wrote in *Watermellons* that in former times "there was a closeness and loyalty in our family that has nearly disappeared." It was the closeness and loyalty of all immigrant families, and it was founded on the fears and insecurity of the Judge's youth. The lessons of struggle in the new world and of life in the depression of 1819 instilled in the Judge, and he passed on to his sons, the sense of familial loyalty. Memories of the depression of 1819 faded and then were lost, and the closeness and loyalty of the family was lost with the memories.

The deaths of J. R., R. B., and A. W. between 1933 and 1937 spelled the beginning of the end of the closeness. It survived throughout the next several decades but to a much diminished extent, marred by a panoply of intra-family jealousies, many of which revolved around the General and his role in the family. When Maxim Armbruster compiled the first family tree of the descendants of Judge Thomas Mellon in the late 1950s, he was surprised at the lack of contact between members of the family, manifested by ignorance of such things as the names of spouses of cousins. In the late 1960s the rich cousins Ailsa and Sarah both died, to be followed in 1970 by the General, the last cohesive force in the family. Today "the Mellons" are a large, amorphous group of people whose relationships range down to fourth cousin, with all of the exotic varieties of relationships in between. For the most part they scarcely know one another and have no contact and virtually no sense of "Mellonhood." In many cases their interests and orientations are so widely different as to make it unlikely that they would be "friends" if they did know one another. It seems a remote possibility, to take the most exaggerated example, that Paul's left-oriented son, Timmy, and Tim's second cousin, Sarah's right-oriented son, Richard M. Scaife, will ever coordinate their interests.

Young Mellons also have a lot of other names than Mellon—Scaife, Currier, Henderson, Hitchcock, Bowart, from the wealthier branches of the family—and that too is important in shaping the attitude of these people toward themselves as part of a Mellon family.

The Judge appreciated the significance of a man's family name. He wrote that "every one entertains a natural love and affection for his name. It is so closely related as to seem part of himself." One's identification with a family is likely to turn on his surname. Thus Richard Mellon Scaife is likely to think of himself as a Scaife rather than as a Mellon. When he writes his signature, the "Richard" and the "M." are grouped together as one unit of letters, or sometimes separated by a relatively small space, followed by a remarkable space before the next group of letters forming "Scaife." He is telling us that his name is Scaife, not Mellon-Scaife. In 1974 he changed the name of the Sarah Mellon Scaife Foundation to the Sarah Scaife Foundation, and its Sarah Scaife Gallery is named just that. He has named his children Jennie King Scaife, thereby commemorating the maiden name of his grandmother, and David Negley Scaife, honoring his great-grandmother's maiden name, instead of commemorating his mother's maiden name, the most clearly distinguished name in his background, the name for that cluster of his ancestors to whom he, Jennie King, and David Negley owe their advantages. It does not seem likely that these children will ever view themselves as a real part of any family named Mellon. It is even less likely that someone named Huysman, whose mother's name was Stone, whose grandmother's name was Stone, whose great-grandmother's name was McClung, but whose great-great-grandfather happened to have been named Mellon, will have much of an interest in the Mellon family, let alone aspire to Mellon family leadership. If another General is to emerge from the next generation, it will almost certainly be a boy named Mellon. The girls, even if they should be socialized in a manner less sex-role stereotyped than their mothers and aunts, are likely to assume other names and familial identifications.

The name "Mellon," the Judge tells us, "originated among the Greeks, where, in the Theban dialect, it meant 'future hope.' . . . therefore, in the language where it originated, every young Mellon may be truthfully regarded as a 'young hopeful.' " The possible "future hopes"—the family's male children named Mellon—are very few in number. From the A. W. line there are none; Paul's grandchildren are named Warner and Ailsa's are named Currier. There are no male children named "Mellon" in the T. A. line. The death of the name "Mellon" in those branches of the family is foreseeable. From the R. B. branch there are only the two sons of the General's son Richard: Richard Adams Mellon, born in 1963, and Armour Negley Mellon, born in 1965. In the J. R.-W. L. line there are only Karl's three sons: Christopher Karl Mellon, born 1957, Matthew Taylor Mellon II, 1964, and Henry Cox Stokes Mellon, 1966. Of these five, the author interviewed the eldest of tomorrow's Mellons, Karl's son Christopher.

As much as looks can tell the story, Christopher is a $\mu\epsilon\lambda\lambda o\nu$—a future hope. He looks like an idealized ancient Greek marble of "Youth," six feet one, lean and sinewy built, all muscle yet naturally graceful. His face is pleasing and his profile handsome.

Chris went to Loomis, a well-regarded prep school in Windsor, Connecticut, and then to Colby College in Waterville, Maine, where the author saw him at the end of Chris's sophomore year. He was living at the KDR fraternity house in rather typical college-boy surroundings, the walls covered with posters and photographs, a rather worn Afghan Bokhara rug on the floor. His collection of phonograph records was representative of what a with-it college boy listens to, heavy on folk and rock (Jimi Hendrix's "first," according to Chris, was Hendrix's "greatest"). He described his college roommate, a studious pre-dental lad, as "just great."

Chris is a 1960s college boy at a 1950s college. He was the only longhair that the author saw on the campus, his long brown hair gathered into a ponytail. Most of Colby's students, he says, are very, very "straight." Though the dorms at Colby are largely co-ed, Chris says that Colby will be the last place to be hit by the sexual revolution. If Chris feels out of place with most of the Colby student body, most of the Colby student body do not feel out of place with him. As we strolled about Waterville, Colby girls crossed the street so as to be able to strike up conversations with him ("What are you doing for lunch, Chris?") and at the sandwich shop virtually everyone knew him and came over to our table to give him a " 'lo Chris." He said that nobody asks him whether he is one of *the* Mellons because few Colby students are aware that there are such people as *the* Mellons.

Chris has little sense of Mellonhood. He has never met his grandfather Matthew's sister Rachel or Matthew's brother, Dr. Mellon of Haiti, though he knows Peggy Hitchcock's people, and he met Pross Mellon when his Uncle Jay took him hunting at Rolling Rock. The name "Scaife" did not ring a bell with him. He gets along well with the people at Mellon Bank who administer a small trust that Matthew established for him, though when he asked them if he could have a car his request was answered not by the bankers but by a stern letter from his Uncle Jay about extravagance. He has not read any of the family writings other than Matthew's books and Jay's *African Hunter.* He occasionally glances at the market quotations for Gulf Oil. Gulf, he says quite correctly, "is a good dividend payer."

It is obvious from a visit with Chris that his father, Karl, is correct when he says that Chris "has a few smarts." Chris showed the author one of his recent pieces done for a creative writing course, a short writing titled "Bean Soup" describing the drinking of soup in designedly sensuous terms. It was nicely done and promising. It is also apparent from a visit that grandfather Matthew is correct when he says that academically Chris is "a little lazy." At the time of our interview, Chris was about to drop out of Colby. He was remaining there only because he had accepted the responsibility of coaching a squad of Waterville "little kids" in soccer a couple of hours each day for a term that coincided with the Colby school year, and he felt that he owed a responsibility to them to see the job through. Anyway, he was getting paid for it: $2.50 an hour. He was uncertain as to his future plans, but he was certain that they would not include the U.S. Army. Just that day he had been summarily rejected for Army enlistment as the result of his answer to the question "Have you used marijuana in the past six months?" Chris does not seem inclined to build or maintain an empire. It seems quite certain that he will not be founding the Gulf Oil of the twenty-first century, and reasonably certain that he will not become a significant Secretary of the United States Treasury. By the dollar-ticked standards of Judge Mellon and his sons, Christopher Mellon will probably be a failure.

The author enjoyed a long interview with Chris. He has obviously done a lot more living than most people twice his age, and he can handle his personal relationships as a fully mature person. Still, he preserves the exuberance of youth and the young person's freedom from reaction on the basis of stereotype. He is a young man completely without artifice, neither consciously *in* fashion nor consciously *out* of fashion in his lifestyle or opinions. Chris seems, at his relatively young age, to have sorted out what is important to him, and that seems to be people. He likes people, is considerate of people, and he wants to know and to be with people. He is a success as a human being at the remarkable age of twenty. Chris may or may not be typical of the Mellons now embarking on adulthood; he is typical of the best in America's young people today.

The dollar-ticked standards, however, survive both in the Mellon family and in the culture of which it is a part. In explaining why he did not write this book, Matthew Mellon, an able writer and a student of his family's lore says matter-of-factly, "After all . . . the great days of the family are over."

THOUGHTS IN A MELLON PATCH

A POEM BY PAUL MELLON
WRITTEN AS A SOUVENIR OF THE MELLON FAMILY REUNION
ROLLING ROCK, LIGONIER, PENNSYLVANIA

SEPTEMBER 1, 1970

If Grandpa Thomas with his plough
Could only see us Mellons now
(Especially those who misbehave!)
He'd turn abruptly in his grave.

A Puritan who had the gift
Of soberness and work and thrift,
He'd scarce believe we'd be such fools
To sun ourselves at swimming pools

And ride around in fancy cars,
Smoke cigarettes and big cigars,
Drink alcohol like mothers' milk,
And dress ourselves in brightest silk.

And he might think our clothes outrageous,
Our mini-skirts, like mumps, contagious,
Our rock and roll too loud to bear,
Too wild our boys with maxi-hair.

But other days bring other ways,
And while each child and grandchild pays
The Piper, (each great-grandchild too)
Such revolutions are not new.

Each generation has its rules,
And Mellons never have been fools.
Some have thrived, a few have failed,
But hardly *any* have been jailed.

Though some of us are fond of horses,
And some have scandals and divorces,
And some like fishing, some like art,
Our paths are never far apart.

We mind our business, love our friends,
Grow old, collect our dividends,
Nor do we shrink from healthy toil,
(Though sometimes it is eased with oil!)

Each generation has to face
Its triumphs or its faults with grace.
Each, as it labors or relaxes,
Itself is faced with Death and Taxes.

So, though he was a stern old Judge,
I'm sure he wouldn't now begrudge
Our foibles and extravaganzas,
(Or even these poor foolish stanzas!)

Perhaps he'd smile from up above
With ancient grand-paternal love
To see us dance and dine and wine,
All Mellons on his fruitful vine.

Bibliography

Of America's "rich" families, the Mellons have been about the most neglected by writers. The Mellons like it that way. The only sources by "outsiders" that purport to be accounts of the family as a family are a published speech by Frank Denton given at a Newcomen Society function, "The Mellons of Pittsburgh," which makes clear how little the founding Mellons revealed themselves even to this closest of associates, and an excellent three-part series, also entitled "The Mellons of Pittsburgh," by Charles J. V. Murphy in *Fortune,* October, November, and December 1967. Of the three commercial books on individual Mellons, neither Philip H. Love's *Andrew W. Mellon: The Man and His Work* nor William S. Hoffman's *Paul Mellon: Portrait of an Oil Baron* is worth bothering with. Harvey O'Connor's *Mellon's Millions,* principally a biography of A. W. but containing much of value about the family, discussed on page 308 of the text, provided a lot of the basic spade work for this author, as it will for all future biographers of A. W. or family historians, and despite O'Connor's pervading crusading, it remains the best readily available source on A. W. Professor Lawrence L. Murray's fine doctoral thesis, *Andrew W. Mellon, Secretary of the Treasury, 1921–1931: A Study in Policy,* available through University Microfilms, Ann Arbor, Michigan, presents a more balanced approach to its subject. A biography of A. W. by the distinguished biographer Burton J. Hendrick was commissioned by the family in the 1940s, but they decided against publication of his finished manuscript. Copies of it are in the possession of A. W.'s son, Paul, and of Hendrick's granddaughter, Mrs. Robert J. Rusnak of Elmhurst, Illinois. The author suspects that the celebrated historian Allan Nevins had access to the Hendrick manuscript for his sensitive *Dictionary of American Biography* sketch of A. W.; Nevins includes data in it that would be without authority unless the authority were to have been Hendrick's manuscript.

Magazine sketches may be picked out of the *Reader's Guide to Periodical*

Literature. Many of those published during A. W.'s period as Secretary of the Treasury are critiqued in the bibliography to Professor Murray's thesis.

Newspaper accounts and critiques other than those listed in the New York *Times* index, or locatable by use of the little-available New York *Times* data-bank computer or the Bell and Howell index to the Washington *Post* are hard to get hold of. The public clipping collections maintained by the Carnegie Institute and the Western Pennsylvania Historical Society, both in Pittsburgh, contain many local clips about varied Mellons and associates. For the period when A. W. was Secretary, the indexed scrapbooks of Charles Hamlin at the Library of Congress Manuscript Division include many insightful New York *World* editorials and articles, some of which, though unsigned, are attributed by Yale's Lippmanniana archives to Walter Lippmann. Harvey O'Connor's clipping collection, along with his papers, is available at the Walter Reuther Library at Wayne State University in Detroit. Both were helpful.

Family writings, all privately printed and mostly obscure, have been more useful to this author in providing both the basic sketch and insights than any of the "outsiders' " pieces. Most notable of the family works would be the Judge's memoirs, *Thomas Mellon and His Times,* critiqued on pages 51–52, and W. L.'s *Judge Mellon's Sons,* pages 32, 351. Also very useful have been James Ross Mellon's *Letters* and Matthew T. Mellon's three volumes, *The Grand Tour; War Log, 1917–18;* and especially *Watermellons,* which sometimes reaches heights of fine literature. All three should now be available at the Library of Congress. Mary McClung, a highly literate and spirited lady from the "poor" branch of the family, wrote an unpublished family history the manuscript of which is in the possession of her son, Samuel A. McClung III, in Pittsburgh. Other family writings are mentioned in the text and all are listed below for the consideration of those who might, for some bizarre reason, care to read "everything" by any Mellon.

Public manuscript collections are of little use either for A. W.'s biographers or for family historians. Most helpful (and they only for A. W. material) are the Treasury Department's papers for the 1920s, Record Group 56 at the National Archives, the State Department's files for the period also at the National Archives, the papers of the British Foreign Office at the Portugal Street branch of the Public Record Office in London, the diaries of Charles Hamlin at the Library of Congress Manuscript Division, the Henry Stimson diaries at Yale, and the Henry Morgenthau diaries at the Roosevelt Library, Hyde Park, New York. The papers of Presidents Harding, Coolidge, and Hoover are all surprisingly weak on A. W. material.

A. W.'s own papers are in Paul Mellon's possession, held so tightly to the bosom that since Hendrick wrote, Paul has refused all requests for access to them, including that of Professor Murray, the legitimacy of whose purpose was above question.

The author regrets that there are no source notes to this book. The reason is cost. Full documentation of this book would require a significant increase in its retail price to provide material that would interest virtually nobody.

The following bibliography includes most but not all of the books that would have appeared in the source notes had there been any, plus an occasional work that was just good background reading. Most of the magazine articles that the author consulted have been omitted, though a few particularly useful or insightful ones are included, listed under the name of the author of the article. Most newspaper pieces have also been omitted from this bibliography, but the most useful, interesting, curious, controversial, or obscure newspaper pieces have been included. For the most part, newspaper pieces that might be located through the New York *Times* or Washington *Post* indexes have been omitted. With a couples of exceptions, newspapers have been alphabetized under the name of the city in which they are published, thus, the *Sun* will be found under "B" for Baltimore. Manuscript collections have been omitted.

Acheson, Edward Goodrich. *A Pathfinder.* New York: The Press Scrap Book, 1910.

Adams, Samuel Hopkins. *Incredible Era: The Life and Times of Warren Gamaliel Harding.* Boston: Houghton Mifflin Company, 1939.

Ailsa Mellon Bruce Collection in Carnegie Museum of Art. Pittsburgh: Art and Nature Shop of Carnegie Institute, undated.

Alberts, Robert C. *The Good Provider: H. J. Heinz and His 57 Varieties.* Boston: Houghton Mifflin Company, 1973.

Armbruster, Maxim Ethan, compiler. "Mellon Family Chart." Undated manuscript at Carnegie Institute, Pittsburgh.

Astorino, Samuel J. "The Contested Senate Election of William Scott Vare." *Pennsylvania History,* Vol. 28 (April 1961), pp. 187–201.

———. *The Decline of the Republican Dynasty in Pennsylvania, 1929–1934.* Ph.D. thesis, University of Pittsburgh, 1962.

Baltimore Sun. May 19, June 4, 1911, and May 26, 1912 (all on A. W.'s divorce). September 1, 1913 (A. W. and Nora to remarry?). September 19, 1921 (early sketch of Ailsa). December 25, 1921 (early sketch on David Bruce). October 25, 1922 (Ailsa to marry Gilbert?). August 24, 1923 (Bruce's candidacy). January 17, 19, 1925 (Bruce to marry

Regina Mellon). January 18, 1926 (Pinchot attacks W. L.). May 23, 1926 (Ailsa to lead Baltimore society). May 29, 30, 1926 (Ailsa's wedding). September 30, 1928 (Bruce works for Smith for President). July 9, 1930 (Paul's plans). April 29, 1931 (A. W. to buy Rokeby). January 8, 1932 (laughs at Patman's effort to impeach A. W.). February 2, 1935 (Paul's marriage). March 23, 1935 (A. W. philosophical about depression). May 27, 1935 (on the Mellons' destitute cousin). April 2, 1937 (the Rolling Rock labor dispute). August 27, 1937 (Bruce on A. W.'s passing). September 24, 1937 (R. K. sketch). January 17, 1938 (W. L. Jr's. divorce). July 8, 1941 (Paul enlists). September 11, 1941 (Paul in Army). April 20, 1945 (Bruces' divorce). April 23, 1956 (marriage of the Curriers announced). August 29, 1963 (let there be sand dunes at Paul's Cape Cod home).

Barnard, Harry. *Independent Man: The Life of Senator James Couzens.* New York: Charles Scribner's Sons, 1958.

Barnes, John K. "What Manner of Man Is Mellon?" *World's Work,* March 1924, p. 541.

Barron, Clarence W. *They Told Barron.* Edited by Arthur Pound and Samuel Taylor Moore. New York: Harper & Brothers, 1930.

Beazell, William Preston. "My Brother and I." *World's Work,* March and April 1932.

Beebe, Lucius. *The Big Spenders.* Garden City, N. Y.: Doubleday & Company, Inc., 1966.

———. "Mellon—Croesus and Corinthian." *Outlook and Independent,* February 4, 1931, p. 176.

Behrman, S. N. *Duveen.* New York: Random House, 1952.

Bent, Silas. *Strange Bedfellows.* New York: Horace Liveright, 1928.

Bernstein, Irving. *The Lean Years: A History of the American Worker, 1920–1933.* Boston: Houghton Mifflin Company, 1960.

Birmingham News (Birmingham, Alabama). December 19, 1926 (Wm. H. Crawford's first impression of A. W.).

Blakey, Roy G. and Gladys C. *The Federal Income Tax.* New York: Longmans, Green and Co., 1940.

Boston Transcript. November 2, 1922 (early society note on Ailsa).

Bowden, Robert Douglas. *Boies Penrose.* New York: Greenberg, 1937

Bradford, Gamaliel. *The Quick and the Dead.* Boston: Houghton Mifflin Company, 1931.

Bulletin-Index (Pittsburgh). March 8, 1934 (Matthew on religion and the Nazis).

Butler, Nicholas Murray. *Across the Busy Years,* 2 vols. New York: Charles Scribner's Sons, 1939.

Butterfield, Roger. "The Millionaire's Best Friend." *Saturday Evening Post,* March 8, 1947 (on David Finley).

Cantwell, Robert. "They Led the Life of Riley." *Sports Illustrated,* November 19, 1973 (on Paul's military career).

Carr, Charles C. *Alcoa: An American Enterprise.* New York: Rinehart & Company, Inc., 1952.

Chandler, Lester V. *Benjamin Strong, Central Banker.* Washington: The Brookings Institution, 1958.

Chisholm, Archibald H. T. *The First Kuwait Oil Concession Agreement: A Record of Negotiations, 1911–1934.* London: Frank Cass, 1975.

Claire, Helen. Articles in *Arab World,* April 1966 and July 1966.

Clark, James A. and Halbouty, Michael T., *Spindletop.* New York: Random House, 1952.

Clark, John P. *The Donora Story.* Donora, Pennsylvania: 1976.

Cortissoz, Royal. *An Introduction to the Mellon Collection.* Boston: The Merrymount Press, 1937.

Country Life. "Full Length Portrait of a Country Gentleman." May 1934.

Cowles, Alfred. *The True Story of Aluminum.* Chicago: Henry Regnery Company, 1958.

Crile, George III. "The Mellons, the Mafia, and a Colonial County." *Washington Monthly,* June 1975.

Daugherty, Harry M., and Dixon, Thomas. *The Inside Story of the Harding Tragedy.* New York: The Churchill Company, 1932.

Davenport, Walter. "A Day with Andrew Mellon." *Colliers,* March 29, 1930, p. 13.

———. *The Power and the Glory: The Life of Boies Penrose.* New York: Putnam's Sons, 1931.

Davis, Mac. *100 Greatest Sports Heroes.* New York: Grosset & Dunlap, Inc., 1954, rev. ed. 1958 (on Tommy Hitchock).

Dawes, Charles G. *The First Year of the Budget of the United States.* New York: Harper & Brothers, 1923.

———. *Notes as Vice President, 1928–1929.* Boston: Little, Brown and Company, 1935.

Denton, Frank. *The Mellons of Pittsburgh.* New York: The Newcomen Society of England, 1948.

Detroit News. April 24, 1925 (gridiron skit about A. W. and Couzens).

Documents on British Foreign Policy, 1919–1939, Series IA, Vol. II. Edited by W. N. Medlicott et al. London: Her Majesty's Stationery Office, 1968.

Documents on British Foreign Policy, 1919–1939, Second Series, Vol. II, 1931. Edited by E. L. Woodward and Rohan Butler. London: His Majesty's Stationery Office, 1947.

Edwards, Junius. *The Immortal Woodshed.* New York: Dodd, Mead & Company, 1955.

Faust, George H. *Economic Relations of the United States and Colombia, 1920–1940.* Ph.D. thesis, University of Chicago, 1946.

"Final Report: The Pittsburgh Renaissance Project: The Stanton Balfour Oral History Collection." September 1974. Oral histories on the renaissance, available at Pennsylvania Division of the Carnegie Library, Pittsburgh.

Finley, David Edward. *A Standard of Excellence: Andrew W. Mellon Founds the National Gallery of Art at Washington, D. C.* Washington: Smithsonian Institution Press, 1973.

Fite, Gilbert C. *George N. Peek and the Fight for Farm Parity.* Norman, Oklahoma: University of Oklahoma Press, 1954.

French Paintings from the Collections of Mr. and Mrs. Paul Mellon and Mrs. Mellon Bruce. Washington: National Gallery of Art, 1966.

Fuess, Claude M. *Calvin Coolidge: The Man from Vermont.* Hamden, Connecticut: Archon Books, 1965.

Galbraith, John Kenneth. *The Great Crash, 1929.* Boston: Houghton Mifflin Company, 1955.

Gerhart, Eugene C. *America's Advocate: Robert H. Jackson.* Indianapolis: The Bobbs-Merrill Company, Inc., 1958.

Gilbert, Clinton W. "Andrew W. Mellon, Secretary of the Treasury." *Current History,* July 1931, p. 521.

Gordon, Ernest. *The Wrecking of the Eighteenth Amendment.* Francestown, New Hampshire: The Alcohol Information Press, 1943.

Greensburg (Pa.) *Tribune-Review.* March 6, 7, 1974 (death of Dixie). May 14, 1974 (editorial against Nixon).

Guffey, Joseph F. *Seventy Years on the Red Fire Wagon.* Privately printed, 1948.

Gunther, John. *Inside U. S. A.* New York: Harper & Brothers, 1947.

Harned, Joseph and Goodwin, Neil, eds. *Art and the Craftsman: The Best of the Yale Literary Magazine, 1836–1961.* New Haven: The Yale Literary Magazine, 1961.

Harper, Frank C. *Pittsburgh: Forge of the Universe.* New York: Comet Press Books, 1957.

Harvey, George. *Henry Clay Frick: The Man.* New York: Charles Scribner's Sons, 1928.

Hays, Will H. *The Memoirs of Will H. Hays*. Garden City, New York: Doubleday & Company, Inc., 1955.

Henriques, Robert. *Bearsted: A Biography of Marcus Samuel*. New York: The Viking Press, 1960.

Hicks, John D. *Republican Ascendancy: 1921–1933*. New York: Harper & Brothers, 1960.

Hirsch, Abby. "Where Is Elizabeth, Where Is Catherine?" *New York Sunday News Magazine*. June 20, 1976 (on Karen Boyd Mellon and the "kidnapping").

Hoffman, William S. *Paul Mellon: Portrait of an Oil Baron*. Chicago: Follett Publishing Company, 1974.

Holbrook, Stewart H. *The Age of the Moguls*. Garden City, New York: Doubleday & Company, Inc., 1953.

Hoover, Herbert. *The Memoirs of Herbert Hoover*, Vol. II: *The Cabinet and the Presidency, 1920–1933*. New York: The Macmillan Company, 1952.

———. *The Memoirs of Herbert Hoover*, Vol. III: *The Great Depression, 1929–1941*. New York: The Macmillan Company, 1952.

Hoover, Irwin Hood (Ike). *Forty-Two Years in the White House*. Boston: Houghton Mifflin Company, 1934.

Hunt, Roy A. *The Aluminum Pioneers*. New York: The Newcomen Society in North America, 1951.

Hutton, Ann Hawkes. *The Pennsylvanian: Joseph R. Grundy*. Philadelphia: Dorrance & Company, 1962.

Irey, Elmer L., as told to William J. Slocum. *The Tax Dodgers*. New York: Greenberg, 1948.

James, Marquis. *Mr. Garner of Texas*. Indianapolis: The Bobbs-Merrill Company, 1939.

Johnson, Lady Bird. *A White House Diary*. New York: Holt, Rinehart and Winston, 1970.

Josephson, Matthew. *The Robber Barons: The Great American Capitalists, 1861–1901*. New York: Harcourt, Brace and Company, 1934.

Journal of Commerce (New York). December 11, 1925 (A. W. warns against real estate speculations and buying "on time").

Kent, Frank. "Andrew Mellon." *New Republic*, March 24, 1926, p. 135.

———. Columns in *Baltimore Sun*, April 16, 17, 1926, and *Pittsburgh Press*, November 29, 1931.

Kiplinger, Willard M. *Washington Is Like That*. New York: Harper & Brothers, Publishers, 1942.

Krock, Arthur. *The Consent of the Governed and Other Deceits.* Boston: Little, Brown and Company, 1971.

———. *Memoirs: Sixty Years on the Firing Line.* New York: Funk & Wagnalls, 1968.

La Follette, Belle Case, and La Follette, Fola. *Robert M. La Follette.* Two volumes. New York: The Macmillan Company, 1953.

Laidler, Harry W. *Concentration of Control in American Industry.* New York: Thomas Y. Crowell Company, 1931.

Latham, Aaron. "National Velveeta." *Esquire,* November 1977 (on Liz and Warner).

Latrobe, Ferdinand. *Iron Men and Their Dogs.* Baltimore: Ivan R. Drechsler, 1941.

Levine, Faye. *The Culture Barons.* New York: Thomas Y. Crowell Company, 1976.

Lief, Alfred. *Democracy's Norris.* New York: Stackpole Sons, 1939.

Ligonier: The Town and the Valley. Ligonier, Pennsylvania: Joseph C. Duval, 1976 and 1977.

Lippmann, Walter. *Interpretations: 1933–1935.* Selected and edited by Allan Nevins. New York: The Macmillan Company, 1936.

———. *Men of Destiny.* New York: The Macmillan Company, 1927.

"Litchfield Document." *The Pittsburgh Forum,* February 18, 1972 (on problems of the University of Pittsburgh and the Mellon role therein).

Long, Haniel. *Pittsburgh Memoranda.* Santa Fe, New Mexico: Writers' Editions, 1935.

Lorant, Stefan. *Pittsburgh: The Story of an American City.* Garden City, New York: Doubleday & Company, Inc., 1964.

Lord, Russell. *The Wallaces of Iowa.* Boston: Houghton Mifflin Company, 1947.

Love, Philip H. *Andrew W. Mellon: The Man and His Work.* Baltimore: F. H. Coggins & Co., 1929.

Lowe, Herman A. "Pennsylvania: Bossed Cornucopia." In *Our Sovereign State,* edited by Robert S. Allen. New York: The Vanguard Press, 1949.

Lowitt, Richard. *George W. Norris: The Persistence of a Progressive, 1913–1933.* Urbana, Illinois: University of Illinois Press, 1971.

Lowry, Edward G. *Washington Close-Ups.* Boston: Houghton Mifflin Company, 1921.

Lubove, Roy. *Twentieth-Century Pittsburgh: Government, Business, and Environmental Change.* New York: John Wiley & Sons, Inc., 1969.

Lundberg, Ferdinand. *America's 60 Families.* New York: The Vanguard Press, 1937.

Manchester, William. *The Death of a President.* New York: Harper & Row, 1967.

McClung, Mary Mellon. *Sheepshead Point.* Philadelphia: Dorrance & Company, 1946.

McCoy, Donald R. *Calvin Coolidge: The Quiet President.* New York: The Macmillan Company, 1967.

McGeary, M. Nelson. *Gifford Pinchot: Forester-Politician.* Princeton, New Jersey: Princeton University Press, 1960.

MacKay, Kenneth Campbell. *The Progressive Movement of 1924.* New York: Columbia University Press, 1947.

Mellon, A. W. *Taxation: The People's Business.* New York: The Macmillan Co., 1924.

Mellon, James. *African Hunter.* New York: Harcourt Brace Jovanovich, 1975.

Mellon, James Ross. *Letters.* Pittsburgh: privately printed, 1935.

Mellon, Matthew T. *Early American Views on Negro Slavery.* New York: Bergman Publishers, 1969.

———. *The Grand Tour: 1914.* No publication data available.

———. *War Log: 1917–18.* Privately printed, 1975.

———. *Watermellons.* Privately printed, 1974.

———. *Zwei Vortäge.* Kitzbühel, Austria: Ritzerdruck, no date.

Mellon, Paul. Pieces in *Yale Literary Magazine,* November 1925, December 1927, November 1928, December 1928, January 1929, March 1929, and June 1929. Speeches: when presenting farm to Virginia Polytechnic Institute, 1949, in *Congressional Record,* Vol. 95, page A5156; on A. W. Mellon commemorative stamp, 1956, *Congressional Record,* Vol. 101 p. 752; at Cape Hatteras National Seashore, 1958, *Congressional Record* of April 29, 1958; at Virginia Museum of Fine Arts, 1963, privately printed; at Foxcroft commencement, 1964, in *Congressional Record* of June 18, 1964; and at the dedication of Currier House, 1970, privately printed. Poem "Thoughts in a Mellon Patch," privately printed, 1970.

Mellon, Rachel Hughey Larimer. *The Larimer, McMasters and Allied Families.* Philadelphia: Lippincott, 1903.

———. *William Penn: A Short Account of His Life and Views.* Revised and edited by her grandson Matthew Mellon. Privately printed, 1972.

Mellon, Thomas. *Thomas Mellon and His Times.* Pittsburgh: privately printed, 1885. Reprint: New York: Kraus Reprint Co., 1969. Abridged edition, edited by Matthew T. Mellon; Belfast: privately printed, no date.

————. "Reminiscences of Hon. James Ross" (written 1896) in *Western Pennsylvania Historical Magazine,* Vol. 3, pp. 103–108.

Mellon, Thomas Jr. [II]. *Army "Y" Diary.* Pittsburgh: The Crescent Press, 1920.

Mellon, Thomas Alexander IV. "Rolling Stoned." *Traveler* (St. Augustine, Florida), August 29, 1975.

Mellon, William Larimer, with Boyden Sparkes. *Judge Mellon's Sons.* Privately printed, 1948.

Mellon, William Larimer III. Articles in *The Princeton Tiger,* November 13, 1953; March 4, 1954 (two pieces); April 1, 1954; November 18, 1954; December 9, 1954; and an article in *The Nassau Literary Magazine,* April 1953.

Mellon National Bank: A Brief Historical Sketch of the Bank, Beginning with its Founding by Thomas Mellon in 1869. Pittsburgh: privately printed, 1944.

Mencken, H. L. *Prejudices: Sixth Series.* New York: Alfred A. Knopf, 1927.

Michelmore, Peter. *Dr. Mellon of Haiti.* New York: Dodd, Mead & Company, 1964.

Morell, Parker. *Diamond Jim: The Life and Times of James Buchanan Brady.* Garden City, New York: Garden City Publishing Company, Inc., 1934.

Morris, Joe Alex. "Doctors vs. Witchcraft." *Saturday Evening Post,* September 16, 1961 (Dr. Mellon of Haiti).

Murphy, Charles J. V. "The Mellons of Pittsburgh." *Fortune,* October, November, and December 1967.

Murray, Lawrence Leo, III. *Andrew W. Mellon, Secretary of the Treasury, 1921–1932: A Study in Policy.* Ph.D. thesis, Michigan State University, 1970.

————. "Andrew W. Mellon, the Reluctant Candidate." *The Pennsylvania Magazine of History and Biography,* Vol. XCVII, No. 4, October 1973.

Murray, Robert K. *The Harding Era: Warren G. Harding and His Administration.* Minneapolis: University of Minnesota Press, 1969.

Myers, Gustavus. *History of the Great American Fortunes.* New York: The Modern Library, 1936.

Nash, Gerald D. "Herbert Hoover and the Origins of the Reconstruction Finance Corporation." *Mississippi Valley Historical Review,* XLVI, December 1959, pp. 455–68.

National Enquirer. April 13, 1976 (on Pross, Karen, and the "kidnapping").

National Observer. June 9, 1969 (Dr. Mellon of Haiti).

Neuberger, Richard L., and Kahn, Stephen B. *Integrity: The Life of George W. Norris*. New York: The Vanguard Press, 1937.
Nevins, Allan. "Calvin Coolidge." *Dictionary of American Biography.*
———. "Andrew W. Mellon." *Dictionary of American Biography.*
New Haven Advocate. August 10, 1977 (the beach at Sachem's Head).
New Haven Register. January 15, 1973 (Tim gives $60,000 to rebuild Hanoi hospital).
New York American. May 4, 1945 (the Bruces' divorce). May 8, 1952 (Audrey Bruce's debut schedule).
New York Herald Tribune. March 1, 1923 (Nora to wed Lee). April 16, 1930 (R. B. and the East Liberty Presbyterian Church). July 9, 1930 (Paul's plans). April 10, 1932 (A. W. to keep "wet" embassy in London). December 27, 1933 (Paul wins race to Central Park Casino). May 11, 1934 (Lippmann on the "indictment" of A. W.). April 23, 1937 (Lippmann doubts bona fides of motives of institution of Alcoa antitrust case). May 6, 1944 (Tommy Hitchcock's will). May 2, 1948 (Paul and "Bunny" wed). July 11, 1965 (Tommy Hitchcock III's second major crash).
New York Sunday Mirror. June 3, 1945 (background of the Bruce divorce, in magazine section).
New York Daily News. April 21, 1945 (the Bruces' divorce). August 25, 1963 (Tommy Hitchcock III's first major crash). March 21, 1976 (on the "kidnapping").
New York Telegram. December 29, 1930 (useful sketch of Tommy Hitchcock).
New York Times. May 26, June 3, 4, 13, 16, 17, 18, 28, July 9, 13, 14, 15, 23, August 2, December 8, 1911, March 17, May 12, July 4, 1912 (all on the A. W. divorce). January 20, 1915 (obituary of Alexander Grange). May 2, 1971 (major sketch of family).
New York World. February 8, 1921 (editorial on A. W.'s "qualifications" for office). September 26, October 2, 6, 8, 9, 1924 (on A. W.'s interests in Alcoa). May 4, 1926 (explanation of Bruce engagement to "Regina Mellon"). June 15, 1926 (editorial on 1926 Pennsylvania primary). June 16, 17, 1926 (on A. W. and the Haugen bill). July 14, 1926 (A. W.'s settlements of foreign war debts). July 9, 1930 (Paul's plans).
New York World-Telegram. February 4, 1932 (A. W.'s resignation). March 8, 1948 ("Bunny" and Lloyd).
The New Yorker. October 5, 1963 (Paul).
Nielsen, Waldemar A. *The Big Foundations*. New York: Columbia University Press, 1972.

Norris, George W. *Fighting Liberal.* New York: The Macmillan Company, 1945.

North American (Philadelphia). May 7, 8, 26, June 4, 8, 10, 11, 13, 14, 16, 17, 24, 28, August 1, November 15, 1911, and May 26, 1912 (fullest coverage of A. W.'s divorce).

O'Connor, Harvey. *How Mellon Got Rich.* New York: International Pamphlets, 1933.

———. *Mellon's Millions.* New York: Blue Ribbon Books, 1933.

O'Connor, Richard. *The Oil Barons.* Boston: Little, Brown and Company, 1971.

One Hundred Years of Banking: The History of Mellon National Bank and Trust Company. Pittsburgh: privately printed, no date.

O'Reilly, Tom. "Happy Birthday, Dear Richard." *Town and Country,* June 1951 (on R. K.).

Patman, Wright. *Bankerteering, Bonuseering, Melloneering.* Paris, Texas: Peerless Printing Company, 1934.

Pearson, Drew, and Allen, Robert. *Washington Merry-Go-Round.* New York: Blue Ribbon Books, Inc., 1931.

People. February 14, 1977 (Warner and Liz).

Pepper, George Wharton. *Family Quarrels: The President, the Senate, the House.* New York: Baker, Voorhis & Company, 1931.

———. *Philadelphia Lawyer.* Philadelphia: J. P. Lippincott Company, 1944.

Philadelphia Daily News. February 25, 1950 (fate of *Big Vag*).

Philadelphia Evening Bulletin. March 5, 1935 (on Paul and Ailsa). October 5, 1956 (jury awards $105,000 against Richard M. Scaife).

Philadelphia Inquirer. June 6, 1924 (W. L. to be Republican national treasurer). June 6, 1926 (Ailsa and Bruce, in magazine section). June 13, 1926 (death of Alexander Laughlin). November 17, 1927 (Sarah marries Alan Scaife). December 2, 9, 1933 (R. B.'s death). November 8, 1940 (R. B.'s mansion to be demolished). July 14, 1943 (R. K. in the Army). February 27, 1948 ("Bunny" and Lloyd divorced). March 31, 1952 (remembrances of Tommy Hitchcock). April 11, 1953 (obituary of Edward P., the architect). February 18, 1962 (R. K. to be compromise gubernatorial nominee?). March 5, 1967 (effect of the death of the Curriers on The Plains, Va.). January 25, 1968 (Adolph Schmidt on family planning, disputes claim it is anti-Negro). March 12, 1968 (obituary of Alexandra Mellon Grange Holloway). March 26, 1972 ("Suzy" describes Bunny's Paris flat). October 26, 1972 (Scaife describes self). February 1, 1973 (Mellon contributions in 1972 congres-

sional elections). March 3, 1973 (Billy Hitchcock's income tax problems). October 29, 1973 (shake-up at the *Tribune-Review*). November
25, 1973 (Scaife's influence at Carnegie-Mellon). March 5, 6, 1974
(death of Dixie). October 11, 1974 (Shapp critical of Mellon Bank).

Philadelphia Leader. April 11, 1926 (W. L. to lead Pepper forces in '26
primary).

Philadelphia Record. January 3, 1927 (W. L.'s political interests). May 4,
1928 (Mellon dominance of Republican party in Pennsylvania). November 19, 1930 (W. L. Jr. secretly married). April 4, 1937 (the Rolling
Rock labor dispute). November 24, 1937 (W. L. Jr. buys ranch). September 29, 1940 (R. K.s hunting). December 31, 1942 (the R. K.s
social lions in D.C.).

Pittsburgh Commercial Gazette. April 19, 1887 (death notice on George).
November 17, 1897 (wedding of R. B. and Jennie). January 24, 1899
(obituary of T. A.).

Pittsburgh Dispatch. June 20, 1909 (obituary of Sarah Jane).

Pittsburgher. October 1977 (Tony Grosso recalls Paul).

Pittsburgh Gazette. January 11, 1912 (obituary of Mrs. T. A.).

Pittsburgh Gazette-Times. February 4, 1908 (obituary of the Judge). September 4, 1922 (Matthew scales the Matterhorn).

Pittsburgh Post-Gazette. August 22, 1933 (Carnegie librarian "denounces"
O'Connor's *Mellon's Millions*). December 2, 8, 1933 (R. B.'s death).
November 16, 18, 1938 (Jennie's death). August 19, 1946 (obituary of
T. M. II). April 16, 1948 (obituary of T. A. Jr.). November 20, 1958
(interview with Mrs. R. K.). December 29, 1965 (Sarah Scaife's obitu-
ary). October 30, 1967 (biographical sketch of Ned). June 5, 1970
(Denton on the significance of R. K.'s death). November 13, 1972
(Ned's retirement). November 9, 10, 1973 (Cordie and Dixie wed).
March 1, 1974 (death of Dixie). November 14, 1974 (obituary of John
Walton).

Pittsburgh Press. May 23, 1926 (Ailsa's wedding). May 24, 1926 (sketch of
Ailsa). May 30, 1926 (Ailsa's wedding). December 16, 1926 (marriage
of Peggy to Tommy Hitchcock). January 20, 1930 (A. W. declines to
give personal opinion of prohibition). June 21, 1930 (W. L. Jr. to wed
Miss Rowley). November 18, 1930 (W. L. Jr's. prior marriage announced). August 9, 1931 (W. L. Jr. gets traffic ticket). February 5,
1932 (A. W. appointed ambassador). March 25, 1933 (A. W. comes
"home"). May 5, 6, 1933 (W. L. Jr.'s "disorderly conduct" arrest).
June 26, 1933 (debut of Alexandra Mellon Grange). December 1, 1933
(R. B.'s obituary). December 9, 1933 (R. B.'s will). April 15, 1934

(A. W. and John D. Rockefeller spoofed at Gridiron dinner). February 10, 1935 (Mellon role in Pittsburgh society). March 25, 1935 (the Mellon houses then and now). May 31, 1935 (inventory of R. B.'s estate). August 24, 1935 (Paul to discuss relative merits of British and American steeplechase racing on radio). June 28, 1936 (Mellon-Schmidt wedding). August 13, 1936 (Paul catches fever fishing with Hemingway). August 27, 1937 (on A. W.'s appearance). September 20, 1937 (full text of A. W.'s will). January 15, 19, 1938 (W. L. Jr.'s divorce). February 5, 6, 1938 (W. L. Jr's wife remarries). November 15, 1938 (death of Jennie). August 25, 1940 (Mrs. W. L. Jr. divorces second husband). July 20, 1941 (Paul's experiences in the Army). July 28, 1941 (horse falls on Dickie Scaife). February 2, 1942 (Mrs. Paul Mellon backing New York luxury restaurant). August 19, 1946 (sketch of T. M. II). August 28, 1946 (will of T. M. II). October 1, 1946 (sketch of Herb May, Jr.). October 12, 1946 (obituary of Paul's first wife). January 11, 1947 (T. M. II's collections). April 16, 1948 (obituary of T. A. Jr.). June 30, July 1, 1949 (Cordie and Herb marry). April 22, 1951 (Rachelwood). July 6, 1954 (W. L.'s estate). February 27, 1955 (Dr. Mellon of Haiti). July 14, 1957 (Billy Hitchcock's first arrest). September 8, 1957 (big article on the Scaifes). June 22, 1958 (debut schedule for Cassandra). July 24, 1958 (Alan Scaife obituary). June 21, 1959 (Connie's debut). August 28, 1960 (Mrs. Richard Scaife). June 21, 1961 (Stacy Lloyd's coming out party). September 18, 1964 (useful sketch of R. K.). September 15, 1965 (Paul's New York apartment). July 10, 1966 (Church in Wilderness to be demolished). August 17, 1966 (account of a Mellon party in honor of "Dearest Jackie"). February 1, 1967 (Currier estates and wills). April 16, 1967 (on the Curriers in The Plains). February 5, 1968 (James M. Walton and the Carnegie Institute). June 22, 1969 (Joshua Whetzel and the Western Pennsylvania Conservancy). January 9, 1972 (Dickie Scaife in politics). May 13, 1973 (the Judge's first home, in "roto" section). July 29, 1973 (on Dixie Duggan's lifestyle). November 6, 1973 (Cordie and Dixie marry). March 13, 1974 (coroner on Dixie's death). December 16, 1974 (sketch of Denton). July 26, 29, 1975 (sketch of Walter Curley).

Pittsburgh Sun-Telegraph. February 5, 1933 (A. W. appointed ambassador). January 26, 1934 (Alan Scaife heads Pittsburgh Coal). May 7, 1937 (A. W.'s last public speech). August 29, 1937 (the Mellons' destitute cousin gives remembrances of A. W. as a boy). March 19, 1942 (obituary on Mrs. W. L.). June 1, 1942 (the R. B.s to be moved to East Liberty Presbyterian Church).

Princeton Alumni Weekly. December 3, 1963 (obituary of W. L. III).

Ratner, Sidney. *American Taxation: Its History as a Social Force in Democracy.* New York: W. W. Norton & Company, Inc., 1942.

Roosevelt, Mrs. Theodore Jr. *Day Before Yesterday.* Garden City, New York: Doubleday & Company, Inc., 1959.

Ross, Ishbel. *Grace Coolidge and Her Era.* New York: Dodd, Mead & Company, 1962.

Rothbard, Murray N. *America's Great Depression.* Princeton, New Jersey: D. Van Nostrand Company, Inc., 1963.

Ryan, Pat. "A Man of Arts and Letters." *Sports Illustrated,* March 16, 1970 (Paul).

Sampson, Anthony. *The Seven Sisters: The Great Oil Companies and the World They Made.* New York: The Viking Press, 1975.

San Francisco Chronicle. November 20, 1973 (Billy Hitchcock's testimony in drug trial).

Scaife, Alan Magee. *Scaife Company, 1802–1952.* New York: Newcomen Society in North America, 1952.

Scaife, Sarah and Scaife, Alan. *Arabian Interlude: Notes of a Brief Trip in the Interior of Little Known Southern Arabia, February, 1951.* Pittsburgh: 1951.

―――. *Travelog: Notes of a Trip through Africa, the Middle East, the Mediterranean and Europe, January–April, 1950.* Pittsburgh: 1950.

Schoyer, Will and Schoyer, Maxine. *Scaife Company and the Scaife Family, 1802–1852.* Pittsburgh: 1952.

Schriftgiesser, Karl. *This Was Normalcy.* Boston: Little, Brown and Company, 1948.

Seldes, George. *Freedom of the Press.* Indianapolis: The Bobbs-Merrill Company, 1935.

―――. *Tell The Truth and Run.* New York: Greenberg, 1953.

Sinclair, Andrew. *Prohibition: The Era of Excess.* Boston: Little, Brown and Company, 1962.

Smith, Dixey, and Beasley, Norman. *Carter Glass.* New York: Longmans, Green and Co., 1939.

Soule, George. *Prosperity Decade.* New York: Rinehart & Company, Inc., 1947.

Stackpole, E. J. *Behind the Scenes with a Newspaper Man.* Philadelphia: J. B. Lippincott Company, 1927.

Starling, Edmund W. *Starling of the White House.* New York: Simon and Schuster, 1946.

Stave, Bruce M. *The New Deal and the Last Hurrah: Pittsburgh Machine Politics.* Pittsburgh: University of Pittsburgh Press, 1970.

Stokes, Thomas L. *Chip off My Shoulder.* Princeton: Princeton University Press, 1940.

Swetnam, George. *Pittsylvania Country.* New York: Duell, Sloan & Pearce, 1951.

Tebbel, John. *The Inheritors: A Study of America's Great Fortunes and What Happened to Them.* New York: G. P. Putnam's Sons, 1962.

Thompson, Craig. *Since Spindletop: A Human Story of Gulf's First Half-Century.* Pittsburgh: Gulf Oil Co., 1951.

Time. April 12, 1937 (R. K. and the Rolling Rock labor dispute of 1937).

Timmons, Bascom N. *Garner of Texas.* New York: Harper & Brothers, 1948.

Two Hundred Years in Ligonier Valley, 1758–1958. Ligonier, Pa: The Ligonier Bicentennial Association, Inc., 1958.

United States Congress. House of Representatives. *Commercial Banks and Their Trust Activities: Emerging Influence on the American Economy.* Two volumes. Staff report for the Subcommittee on Domestic Finance, Committee on Banking and Currency, Ninetieth Congress, Second session.

United States Congress. House of Representatives. *Hearings Before the Committee on the Judiciary on Charges of Hon. Wright Patman Against the Secretary of the Treasury.* Seventy-second Congress, First session.

United States Congress. House of Representatives. *Tax-Exempt Foundations and Charitable Trusts: Their Impact on Our Economy.* Subcommittee on Domestic Finance of the Committee on Banking and Currency. Eight installments; Eighty-seventh through Ninety-second Congress.

United States Senate. *Hearings Before the Committee on Interstate Commerce Pursuant to S. Res. 105.* Seventieth Congress, First Session.

United States Senate. *Hearings Before the Select Committee on Investigation of the Bureau of Internal Revenue Pursuant to S. Res. 168.* Eight volumes. Sixty-eighth Congress.

United States Senate. *Hearings Before the Committee on Public Lands and Surveys Pursuant to S. Res. 101.* Seventieth Congress, First Session.

United States Senate. *Hearings Before A Special Committee Investigating Expenditures in Senatorial Primary and General Elections Pursuant to S. Res. 195.* Sixty-ninth Congress, First Session.

Van Trump, James P. *September Solstice, 1966.* Pittsburgh: The Pittsburgh Bibliophiles, 1967.

Van Urk, J. Blan. *The Story of Rolling Rock.* New York: Charles Scribner's Sons, 1950.

Waldman, Louis. *The Good Fight: A Quest for Social Progress.* Philadelphia: Dorrance & Company, 1975.

Walker, John. *Self-Portrait with Donors.* Boston: Little, Brown and Company, 1969.

Wall, Joseph Frazier. *Andrew Carnegie.* New York: Oxford University Press, 1970.

Wall Street Journal. December 4, 1975; January 13, 1976 (Mellon role in Gulf Oil scandal).

Washington Daily News. January 30, 1924 (effect of "Mellon Plan" on Mellon pocketbook).

Washington Post. March 13, 1912 (R. B. goes to President Taft's). April 24, 1977 (sketch of Paul).

Washington Evening Star. March 24, 1929 (how A. W. buys a painting).

Wendel, William H. *The Scratch Heard 'Round the World: The Story of the Carborundum Company.* New York: The Newcomen Society in North America, 1965.

Werner, M. R. *Privileged Characters.* New York: Robert M. McBride & Company, 1935.

Werner, M. R., and Starr, John. *Teapot Dome.* New York: The Viking Press, 1959.

White, Edward. *A Century of Banking in Pittsburgh.* Pittsburgh: The Index Company, 1903.

The White House Gardens. New York: Great American Editions Ltd., 1973.

White, William Allen. *A Puritan in Babylon.* New York: The Macmillan Company, 1938.

Woolf, S. J. *Drawn from Life.* New York: Whittlesey House, 1932.

Worth, Mary Jo. "The Story of the Acid Profiteers." *Village Voice,* August 22, 1974 (on Billy Hitchcock).

Acknowledgments

It is impossible to write a book such as this without assistance from libraries and librarians. I am pleased to acknowledge the help rendered me by the staffs of the Hartford Public Library, the Yale Library, the Foundation Center Library in New York City, the Hillman Library at the University of Pittsburgh, the Carnegie Library of Pittsburgh, and the Tyrell Historical Library in Beaumont, Texas; and by the archivists at the National Archives, the Western Pennsylvania Historical Society, Pittsburgh, and the Franklin D. Roosevelt Library at Hyde Park, New York.

A number of people assisted me in researching the project: Mrs. Atwood Dennis of West Branch, Iowa, who perused the Hoover Library collections on my behalf; Kenneth G. Raffield of Old Coulsdon, Surrey, who performed like services at the Public Record Office in London and who did other imaginative sleuthing for me in England; Leonard Reed of Dallas, Texas; and Naomi Nomizu of Providence, Rhode Island, who performed the most tedious of research assignments for me at the Yale Library. I am grateful to and impressed by the efficient and courteous staff of the office of Rita Wilson Kane, Clerk of the Orphans' Court in Pittsburgh. I have profited from the insights and advice of Dr. Yale David Koskoff of Pittsburgh, Felix Klein of New York City, John P. Clark of Donora, Pennsylvania, Dr. Leonard Zamore of New Haven, Connecticut, the Reverend Rufus S. Lusk of The Pelhams, New York, and Hugh Rawson, my editor at Thomas Y. Crowell Company. My wife, Charlotte, assisted in many aspects of the project.

I interviewed twelve of the Judge's descendants and a number of other people who have been associated either with the family or with members of it over the years. With only a few exceptions, I have not attempted to mask the identities of those with whom I spoke, but as it is possible that a separate rostering of them might cause one or more of them embarrassment, I forbear doing so. I am, nonetheless, grateful to them all.

I am indebted to my secretary, Carol D'Agostino, for keeping me sane throughout the project and to my present and past associates in the practice of law, Stewart M. Schimelman and Bruce Morris, for carrying the load. The manuscript was typed by Carol Terry.

Writing this book has been a gratifying experience in large part because of the satisfaction of working with all of these people.

DAVID E. KOSKOFF

Plainville, Connecticut
January 3, 1978

Photo credits in alphabetical order

ALUMINUM COMPANY OF AMERICA, p. 204, middle left and right; p. 205, top

CARBORUNDUM COMPANY, p. 204, bottom left

CARNEGIE LIBRARY, p. 200, left; p. 204, top left and right; p. 205, bottom; p. 208, bottom; p. 214, top left; p. 218, top right; p. 220, left

GRANT FOUNDATION, p. 219, bottom

HISTORICAL SOCIETY OF PENNSYLVANIA, p. 201, bottom; p. 202, top right; p. 210, top left and right

KOPPERS COMPANY, p. 204, bottom right

DAVID KOSKOFF, p. 217, inset; p. 218, bottom; p. 223, top; p. 225, top left and right; p. 227, bottom; p. 228

LIBRARY OF CONGRESS, p. 200, top right; p. 201, top; p. 202, top left; p. 208, top right; p. 212; p. 214, top right; p. 215

CHRISTOPHER MELLON, p. 224, top

FROM JAMES ROSS MELLON, *Letters* (1935), p. 197, top and bottom left; p. 199, bottom; p. 206, top left

COLLECTION OF DR. MATTHEW T. MELLON, p. 218, top left

FROM THOMAS MELLON, *Thomas Mellon and His Times* (1885), p. 197, top right

FROM THOMAS MELLON, JR., *Army "Y" Diary* (1920), p. 207, top

THOMAS ALEXANDER MELLON IV, p. 217, main photo; collection of Thomas Alexander Mellon IV, p. 226, right

FROM RACHEL HUGHEY LARIMER MELLON, *The Larimers, McMasters and Allied Families* (1903), p. 198, top

FROM WILLIAM LARIMER MELLON AND BOYDEN SPARKES, *Judge Mellon's Sons* (1948), p. 197, bottom right; p. 206, top right and bottom

NORTH AMERICAN (1912), p. 203, right

PITTSBURGH POST-GAZETTE p. 209, top and bottom right; p. 210, bottom; p. 213, top; p. 219, top; p. 220, right; p. 221, top and bottom left; p. 222, top; p. 223, bottom; p. 224, bottom; p. 226, top left; p. 227, top left

PITTSBURGH PRESS, p. 209, bottom left; p. 222, bottom; p. 227, top right

UNITED PRESS INTERNATIONAL, p. 209, top left; p. 211, bottom

UNITED STATES INFORMATION AGENCY, p. 200, second, third, fourth right; p. 202, bottom; p. 203, left; p. 214, bottom

UNITED STATES OFFICE OF WAR INFORMATION, p. 208, top left

WESTERN PENNSYLVANIA HISTORICAL SOCIETY (Thomas Mellon Galey), p. 198, bottom; p. 199, top; p. 207, bottom

WIDE WORLD, p. 211, top; p. 213, bottom; p. 216; p. 221, bottom right; p. 225, bottom; p. 226, bottom left

Index